A. P. Robinson.
University
of.
Newcastle.

Computer Methods in Civil Engineering

UNIVERSITY SERIES IN CIVIL ENGINEERING

Computer Methods for Civil Engineers

R.J.Cope
Senior Lecturer

F.Sawko
Professor

R.G.Tickell
Lecturer

Department of Civil Engineering, Liverpool University

McGRAW-HILL Book Company (U.K.) Limited

London · New York · St Louis · San Francisco · Auckland · Bogotá · Guatemala
Hamburg · Johannesburg · Lisbon · Madrid · Mexico · Montreal · New Delhi
Panama · Paris · San Juan · São Paulo · Singapore · Sydney · Tokyo · Toronto

Published by
McGRAW-HILL Book Company (UK) Limited
MAIDENHEAD · BERKSHIRE · ENGLAND

British Library Cataloguing in Publication Data

Cope, R. J.
Computer methods for civil engineers.
1. Civil engineering – Data processing
I. Title II. Sawko, F. III. Tickell, R. G.
624'.028'54 TA153

ISBN 0-07-084129-2

Library of Congress Cataloging in Publication Data

Cope, R. J. (Robert J.)
Computer methods for civil engineers.

(University series civil engineering)
Includes bibliographies and indexes.
1. Civil engineering – Data processing.
I. Sawko, F. II. Tickell, R. G. (R. Geoff)
III. Title. IV. Series: University series in civil engineering.
TA345.C66 624'.028'54 82-93
ISBN 0-07-084129-2 AACR2

2345 AP 8543

Printed in Great Britain at the Alden Press
Oxford London and Northampton

CONTENTS

CONSULTING EDITORS' FOREWORD

McGraw-Hill's *University Series in Civil Engineering* has been planned to make available to students and lecturers a number of useful textbooks that reflect the philosophy of the Consulting Editors and the Company, namely that the emphasis of engineering degree courses should be on the fundamental principles. Therefore the primary aim of the books in the Series is to develop a sound understanding of the subject matters and an ability to apply the relevant scientific principles to the solution of practical problems. Where familiarity with an empirical method is desirable, the technical background is explained, so that the student understands the *why* as well as the *what* and the *how* of the subject.

Four books have been published in the series to date:

Atkinson, J. H. and Bransby, P. *The Mechanics of Soils An introduction to critical state soil mechanics*

Atkinson, J. H. *Foundations and Slopes An introduction to applications of critical state soil mechanics*

Thompson, P. *Organization and Economics of Construction*

and this latest work,

Cope, R. J., Sawko, F. and Tickell, R. G. *Computer Methods for Civil Engineers*

Computer Methods for Civil Engineers shows the reader, with examples and computer listings, how to use the computer to solve problems in various branches of civil engineering: structures, soil mechanics, fluid mechanics, management, highway and traffic engineering. It begins by explaining the basic principles of communicating with the computer, and of numerical methods needed to translate the engineering problem into a form suitable for computer processing. FORTRAN has been used as the language most widely employed and most convenient for engineering applications throughout the world. Mastery of FORTRAN makes it relatively easy to use BASIC if the need arises; the principal differences between the two are outlined in the Appendix.

The Consulting Editors wish to thank their colleagues in the universities and industry for their valuable advice concerning the development of the Series; the initiative and foresight of McGraw-Hill's former Editor, Ian Pringle, have contributed much to its successful launching. In particular, they wish to record the exemplary care and attention devoted to the Series by McGraw-Hill's Editor, John M. W. Smith.

F. K. KONG and R. H. EVANS

PREFACE

To an engineer, a computer is a tool – an extremely useful one. To use a tool properly it has to be understood and mastered. Within the civil engineering industry computer usage is rather variable, ranging from very intensive to none even within one office. As one senior engineer lightheartedly remarked: 'I have two types of engineers in my office; those who spend months doing by hand what a computer could do in a few seconds, and those who spend months preparing for a computer calculations that could be done by hand in a few minutes.'

There is little doubt that proper use of computers brings substantial benefits in the form of speeding up the design process and eliminating arithmetical errors, together with the possibility of trying different schemes and thus improving the chance of a better final solution. Successful use can only be achieved after a process of learning and practice. This book explains the basic principles of communicating with the computer and of numerical methods needed to translate the engineering problem into a form suitable for computer processing.

First the language. Methods of communicating with the machine have undergone considerable change as a result of development of input–output devices and of sophisticated compilers. In this text FORTRAN has been used as the language currently most widely employed and most convenient for engineering applications throughout the world. Mastery of FORTRAN makes it relatively easy to use BASIC, which is currently favoured for desk top microcomputers. The principal differences between the two have been outlined in the Appendix.

Second the numerical techniques. An engineering problem is seldom, if ever, in a form suitable for direct computer processing. It has to be converted to a numerical model using one of the many techniques described here. Many of these techniques, such as equation solving procedures or curve fitting, have existed for a long time, while others, such as finite element methods, have developed alongside computers and cannot be used without them.

The book has been designed for students of engineering and practising engineers. The first three chapters covering the language and numerical techniques should be studied by everyone irrespective of his speciality, since it is important to be aware of the various numerical techniques currently available. The specialist chapters give some examples of applications in specific subject areas. They are not intended to be comprehensive, and suggestions for further reading are included.

The preparation of this text has not been easy because of its breadth of coverage. It was my editorial responsibility to ensure the right balance between sections, and if there is to be criticism of subject matter then I have to accept the blame. All the contributors are members of staff at the Department of Civil Engineering at Liverpool University. I would like to thank all those of my colleagues who have readily given their views and opinions without becoming authors, to John Wilkinson for his help with development of computer programs, to Barbara Cotgreave for preparation of figures and diagrams, and to Christine Cope, Frances Zimmermann, and Donna Girling for typing the text.

F. Sawko
Editor

CHAPTER
ONE

INTRODUCTION TO COMPUTERS

1.1 DEVELOPMENT OF COMPUTERS

The concept of numbers is thought to date from about 100 000 BC, but the earliest evidence of number representation comes from the early Egyptian civilizations. The pace of development of calculating aids since then has grown exponentially. Counting boards which developed into the abacus are thought to have been in use in the first century BC, yet even in the seventeenth century arithmetic had not become part of the general knowledge of the educated man. Of course, those engaged in science and commerce were capable of considerable mathematical sophistication and the seventeenth century witnessed the pioneering work of such giants as Pascal, Leibnitz, and Newton. Among their other achievements, Pascal and Leibnitz are credited with inventing the first mechanical calculating machines.

Mechanical calculators gradually increased in quality and importance but the next major conceptual advance did not come until the nineteenth century when Babbage designed the first computer. The mechanical device he envisaged would have been capable of storing intermediate results and of entering data and sequences of instructions to be performed on the data from sets of perforated cards. It was not built, and there is doubt as to whether the design could have been realized with the mechanical technology then available.

It was not until nearly the middle of the twentieth century that computers embodying Babbage's concept were produced. Developments took place at a number of centres around the world and at first concentrated on electromagnetic devices using electromechanical switches. In 1944 the Harvard Mark I computer was completed and in England the Colossus computer was produced for the purpose of cryptanalysis, to assist with deciphering coded messages. As with many ultimately beneficial developments, pressures brought about by war accelerated progress in automatic computation.

These electromechanical marvels were soon superseded by electronic computers and speed and reliability were no longer limited by mechanical switches. The earliest of the electronic computers, the ENIAC (Electronic Numerical Integrator and Calculator), started operations in the USA in 1946. Physically it was a large machine, being over 100 feet long, weighing about 30 tons, and consuming 140 kilowatts of power.

Computer technology took two steps forward almost immediately with the conversion of internal arithmetic from decimal to binary form and with the introduction of the capability to store a 'program' internally in coded form. (The word 'program' is used throughout this text to denote a set of detailed, sequenced instructions.) The first general purpose electronic digital computer in England, the EDSAC (Electronic Delay Storage Automatic Calculator) executed its first program in 1949 at the University of Cambridge. The first commercial computer, the UNIVAC (Universal Automatic Computer), was operational in 1951 in America.

After the early 'fifties improvements followed in quick succession. Valves which had replaced mechanical switches were themselves replaced by semiconductors or solid state transistor switches. The rapid improvements in semiconductor and integrated circuitry technologies enabled dramatic reductions to be made in size, cost, and power requirement, and led to the development of minicomputers in the 'sixties and to microcomputers in the late 'seventies. Minicomputers occupy only a few cubic feet and can be operated in a normal office environment.

Once it became possible to fabricate a single semiconductor device to contain the thousands of circuit elements necessary to perform all the arithmetic and logical functions of a computer, the age of the microprocessor began. Microprocessors are manufactured as monolithic 'chips', each occupying a fraction of a cubic inch, and they have led to the latest type of computer, the 'microcomputer'. Modern microcomputer systems have more power than the early mammoths of the 'fifties and they are rapidly becoming standard design office equipment.

1.2 DEVELOPMENT OF COMPUTER USAGE

Engineers avail themselves of aids to calculation to improve their productivity. Before the mid 'sixties, such aids were limited to tables of commonly used functions such as sines, tangents, and logarithms, and to mechanical devices such as adding machines and slide rules. In the early 'sixties the professional civil engineer made little use of computers, although university research workers were developing many of the techniques now in general use. Today, electronic calculators and computers capable of storing programs of instructions are commonplace in design offices. Indeed, few of the more complex engineering calculations are undertaken without some computer involvement.

As computing capacity increased and costs decreased, more attention was paid to making their use easier. The earliest computers could only be operated in a protected environment and their use was restricted to specialists, as programs had to be written in terms of the simplest computer operations. Program instructions at the most fundamental level are called 'machine language instructions', and consist of strings of numbers. Each instruction is basic and cannot be subdivided by a programmer. To make program writing easier, symbolic 'assembly' languages were developed. While these are a step forward, they retain the disadvantages of being unique to a particular computer type and of referring directly to machine operations. There is a one-to-one correspondence between an assembly language instruction and a machine language instruction.

In 1957 a programming language called FORTRAN (Formula Translation) was produced by IBM (International Business Machines Limited). This enabled scientific calculations to be programmed using symbols and instructions that could be readily appreciated by engineers and scientists. A FORTRAN instruction is translated by a program provided by the manufacturer and known as a 'compiler' into equivalent machine code instructions. With a higher-level language such as FORTRAN a programmer is freed from having to specify precisely how data is to be stored within a computer, and from having to specify detailed computer operations. In 1958 FORTRAN II was produced and a multiplicity of FORTRAN systems followed. To enable exchange of programs between users, and a particular program to be usable on a number of different computers, standardization was desirable. In 1966 the American National Standards Institute codified a language that has become known as FORTRAN IV. FORTRAN IV is the most widely used language for engineering programs. Since its introduction there has been a tremendous increase in computer usage by engineers and a massive effort to produce programmed solutions to engineering problems. This investment will ensure the dominance of FORTRAN IV for the foreseeable future. Chapter 2 of this text described the main features of programming in FORTRAN IV, as a knowledge of the language is a vital tool in the modern engineer's kitbag.

Certain types of problem calculations occur so frequently that it is worth while to have a special language for them. These languages adopt specific phrases and key words of prospective users which are formed into a Problem-Oriented Programming Language. One of the earliest of these, STRESS (Structural Engineering Systems Solver), was produced in the USA as early as 1963. In the UK, the most widely used Problem-Oriented Programming Language is GENESYS (General Engineering System) and this, like its earlier American counterpart, ICES (Integrated Civil Engineering System), has program modules written in a dialect of FORTRAN IV. These languages are known as GENTRAN and ICETRAN, respectively. To analyse a structure using one of these systems, statements can be written specifying its nature and size, the loads acting on it and the results desired in the terminology of everyday use. With such systems, computer usage has been extended to those with almost no programming knowledge. However, to take maximum advantage of them an engineer needs a knowledge of FORTRAN, so that he can add additional programming modules to perform particular tasks and to use all of the facilities of the command statements available in the problem oriented language.

A comparison of typical instructions in a machine code, a symbolic assembly language, FORTRAN, and a problem-oriented language is shown in Fig. 1.1.

1.3 COMPUTER SYSTEMS

It is not necessary to know in detail how computers work in order to use them. To write efficient programs, however, and to decide which facilities to use, it is necessary to understand a little about the main components of a computer system and how they are organized. In the jargon of the computer world, the physical machinery is known as 'hardware' and the programs that control operations are called 'software'.

1.3.1 Hardware

The components of a computer's hardware are shown schematically in Fig. 1.2. There are four basic parts, a central processing unit (cpu), a means of 'input' to get data into the system, a means of 'output' to get data out of the system, and secondary storage facilities.

1100110011110011 0011111100101111	Binary Coding (16 bit words)

SUBO 1,1
SKPDN TTI
JMP .-1
DIAS 0,TTI
ADDL 1,1
	Symbolic Assembly Language

J=1 A=A*C+SIN(X+Y/100.) IF (A.EQ.STRESS) GOTO 6	FORTRAN Statements
STRUCTURE IS A PLANEFRAME USE MEMBERS 'GROUP-1' USE SUPPORTS 'BASES' APPLY 'CASE-1' PRINT FORCES FOR LOAD 'CASE-1' PLOT STRUCTURE 'PORTAL' AT SCALE 1/100	Problem Oriented Language (GENESYS)

Figure 1.1 Programming languages

The central processor unit is the heart of a computer system and it consists of three basic parts, a control unit, an arithmetic/logic or calculating unit, and the primary storage. Operations within a computer are coordinated by the control unit under the direction of instructions from a program or software. It directs all units of the system and controls the flow of data between them during processing of a problem. As components of the hardware operate at different speeds, the control unit activates them and then turns to other instructions while waiting for an action to be completed. In this way, several peripheral devices can be kept operating simultaneously with computing and the activities of several programs that make differently timed demands can be interleaved to optimize usage of facilities.

The arithmetic/logic unit is where the operations of adding, subtracting, multiplying, dividing, and logic are performed. On some advanced computers there may be two or more interconnected processors, each with its own arithmetic/logic unit. With these 'multi-processing' computers, different instructions of the same, or of different programs can be executed simultaneously.

The third part of the central processor unit is the fast access, or primary store, that a computer uses for data being manipulated. All data entering a computer are converted into strings of binary numbers and stored. The unit of storage is called a 'word' and a 'wordlength' is the number of binary digits or 'bits' used to define a single entity of storage. Sometimes a wordlength is quoted in 'bytes', where a byte is equivalent to 8 bits. On a large computer the primary storage or memory can be of the order of half-a-million 24-bit words. The speed of operation can be gauged by considering an arithmetic process. On a fast modern computer two numbers can be transferred from their locations in the primary storage, added, and the result sent to a location in the primary store in about one ten-millionth of a second.

There are various ways of feeding information into a computer. One of the most common methods is to record data, including user programs, by punching a sequence of holes in a 'deck' of cards or in a continuous paper tape. Machines with a keyboard like a typewriter's are used and a speed of about 2 characters per second

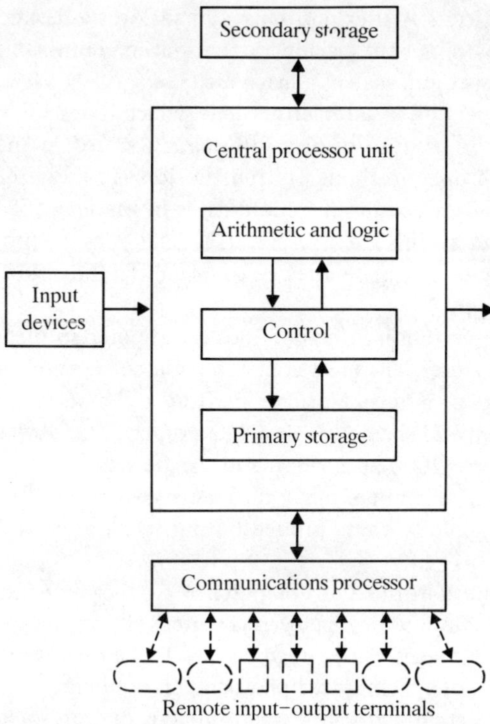

Figure 1.2 Schematic view of computer hardware

can be achieved. With a paper tape, one row of holes across the width of the tape represents a character; with punched cards, a column of holes represents a character. The information on a deck of cards or on a paper tape is read into a computer by devices that illuminate a line of holes at a time and detect the patterns by means of photoelectric cells. Typical reading speeds range from 500 to 2000 characters per second for both paper tape and cards.

On many computer systems it is possible to feed data directly from a remote keyboard resembling a typewriter.

When a lot of data from remote automatic recording devices is to be input, magnetic tape reels or cassettes can be used. A full reel of tape can contain information equivalent to about 400 000 fully punched cards.

Some large computing systems have devices that can read information from specially prepared documents. A 'MICR' (Magnetic Ink Character Recognition) device can read letters and numbers printed by special typewriters. An 'OCR' (Optical Character Recognition) device can read a variety of marks and characters printed on paper. At present the printing must conform to strict standards to be read reliably. 'Optical mark' and 'mark-sense' readers detect the presence or absence of pencil marks in specified positions on a form. Many areas of data collection can be simplified by using preprinted forms that require a user to mark appropriate boxes with a pencil.

Of particular interest to engineers are facilities to record data from graphical information such as drawings. A device to input the coordinates of points on drawings or graphs is called a 'digitizer'. A user positions a cursor over a desired point and by depressing a control key causes the machine to transmit its coordinates to a computer or to an intermediate medium such as a magnetic tape.

With some computer systems operated in interactive mode, which is described in Sec. 1.3.3, a cathode ray tube is used to display information stored in the computer, graphically. Provided with many cathode ray tube devices is a means of pointing at displayed information and of causing the coordinates of the identified point to be transmitted to the computer. This is a very powerful facility, as the program responsible for displaying the picture can be directed to take different actions according to the coordinates sent.

Just as there are many ways of getting information into a computer so there are many ways of returning data to a user. The most common requirements are for printed documents and for drawings or graphs. Most results from a computer are printed as pages of alphabetic and numeric characters via a 'line printer'. This device prints a whole line at a time and up to 2000 lines per minute can be achieved with up to 160 character positions per line. There are many different types of printing machines available, and it is also possible to route printed output to the keyboard machines used for data input.

Automatic 'X–Y plotters' can be controlled by computer to produce drawings or graphs. Results in graphical form can also be displayed for direct viewing on the screen of a cathode ray tube. Screen images can be recorded, and when necessary moving pictures can be created by use of synchronized photographic equipment.

The amount of data stored by a computer can run into billions of words and access is at rates much faster than those for data input or output. Primary storage is relatively expensive, so secondary storage devices hold most of the data. Most computers hold information on magnetic tapes or magnetic disks. A typical magnetic tape can store twenty million characters and information can be transferred to and from the primary memory at rates of between 20 000 and 160 000 characters per second. Magnetic tapes have the disadvantage that information has to be accessed serially. This means that all records preceding a wanted file have to be read in series until the desired record is reached. Several minutes can be absorbed by this operation and for many purposes it is more efficient to use a 'random-access' or 'direct-access' device such as a magnetic disk. Typically, it takes two hundred milliseconds to locate and read a record on a disk, and a disk may hold one hundred million characters. To put these approximate figures into some perspective, a computer using magnetic disks could store the equivalent of several hundred Christian Bibles, and any verse in any one of them could be found and read in a fraction of a second.

For many tasks a user need not consider storage allocation in any detail as many computer systems present a large 'virtual memory'. Although this can be considerably bigger than the primary storage area, it is treated by a user as though it were part of the central processor.

1.3.2 Software

From the above description of a modern computer system it is clear that its effectiveness depends on the skill of programmers and users. A computer has no brain

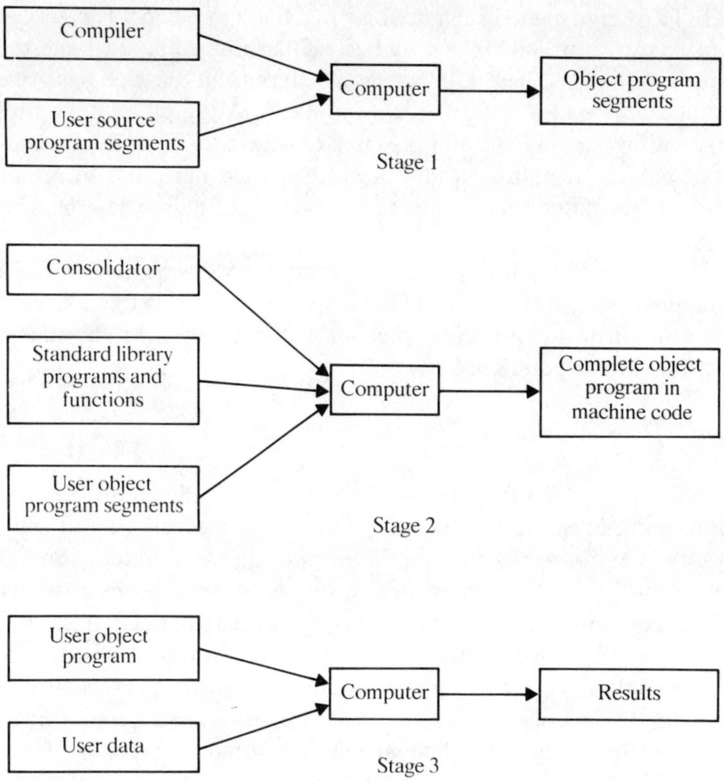

Figure 1.3 Producing and executing a program

capable of independent action and can neither assist nor hinder activities wilfully. Its versatility derives from the non-specific nature of its controls. A computer's actions are dictated by programs or 'software' and the same computer system can be used for such diverse tasks as bridge design, traffic control, and the production of engineering drawings.

A computer is enabled to perform a particular task by placing a program of instructions in its store. Programs that control computer hardware are termed the 'system software' or 'operating system'. An operating system is an integrated set of control and processing programs designed to ensure efficient use of the computer and to simplify user access. It controls input and output peripherals, allocates system resources according to specified priorities, and interprets user control instructions. It contains a library of standard routines to simplify program writing and programs to enable a user to amend files and to convert a program to machine code ready to be executed.

The program to translate a user's 'source' program from FORTRAN is called a 'compiler' and the program that combines this with standard library routines is sometimes called a 'consolidator'. The final program of machine code instructions is called the 'object' program. Only a grammatically correct source program can be converted into an object program for execution and most compilers and consolidators are designed to detect and report any syntax errors present. The main stages undergone by a correct FORTRAN program are illustrated in Fig. 1.3.

When a FORTRAN program is submitted to a computer system it is preceded by a number of control instructions that dictate the facilities to be used and the processes to be undertaken. These commands are dependent on the operating system in use, but are devised to minimize user problems. A typical set of control instructions may tell a computer to edit a FORTRAN text, to compile and consolidate the resulting program, to execute it with specified data, and to return results via particular output devices. Such instructions take only a few lines or punched cards.

By virtue of simple control instructions to the system software, and use of a high-level programming language such as FORTRAN, an engineer is freed to concentrate on the solution to his particular problem without having to give undue thought to the details of computer operations.

1.3.3 Modes of usage

An engineer can use computing facilities from a design office. Some offices have their own computer facilities, others have access to remote machines. Small computers tend to service programs in sequence, larger ones appear to execute several programs simultaneously using a 'time-sharing' operating system. When a central processor has sufficient power to handle many programs stored in primary memory, it is advantageous to utilize that capacity by ordering operations so that a processor is continually active. Time-sharing systems are made possible because of the variations in lengths of time needed for different operations, and because operations of a particular type rarely occur simultaneously in different programs. 'Time-sharing' systems are popular with engineers because they enable them to share computing facilities with others and to pay only for computing time actually used.

Modes of computer usage are usually categorized as 'on-line' or 'off-line'. In the off-line mode, data, which may include a program and input or output files, are handled without a user having direct access to the central processor unit. In this mode 'jobs' are accepted by the computer and stored in a queue for future processing. This procedure is called 'batch' processing. In this mode, decks of cards can be read by a card reader situated in a design office and the information transmitted electronically to a remote computer or they can be physically delivered to a computer centre. Alternatively, sets of instructions can be typed on a keyboard and transmitted to a file in the secondary storage. Similarly, results can be produced on a local or a remote line printer, X–Y plotter or other output device.

In some instances it can be more convenient to use a computer 'on line'. In this mode of operation a user can attract the attention of the central processor. Messages can be sent from a keyboard, with the information displayed on a paper roll or a cathode ray tube. For economy, this type of usage is usually restricted to computers operated under a time-sharing system and for tasks needing limited use of the central processor. It is commonly used for giving a short list of instructions to initiate operations on information previously input to the computer in off-line mode. Typical actions might include amending a file, ordering compilation and consolidation of a source program into an object program, and initiating 'loading' of a program for subsequent execution.

On-line computing is sometimes called 'interactive' processing, since a user monitors and controls operations while a program is actually being executed. When amending a file, for instance, the editing program issues prompts to the user and it has then to receive further data from the user before it can perform, or even know the nature of, its next instruction. Editing programs are not intelligent, but are designed so that the sequence of operations to be performed is dictated by parameters whose values are set while the program is running.

In recent years, interactive techniques have been incorporated into programs to solve engineering problems. Design does not follow a fixed route, as parameters are set and amended according to the behaviour of trial solutions. Interactive computing is ideally suited to this process and is greatly enhanced by the use of graphical terminals, since much complex data can be displayed on a very small picture. This mode of computing is relatively expensive, as rapid response is needed by the engineer and large portions of programs and data files have to be resident in the central processor while the decision to determine the next instruction is being taken. This mode of computing has only become possible by virtue of the dramatic fall in costs during the 'seventies but as yet few efficient systems have been developed.

1.4 PROGRAMMING

Engineering problems rarely occur in a form suitable for exact solution. Complexities are first reduced and a mathematical model of a system is sought to

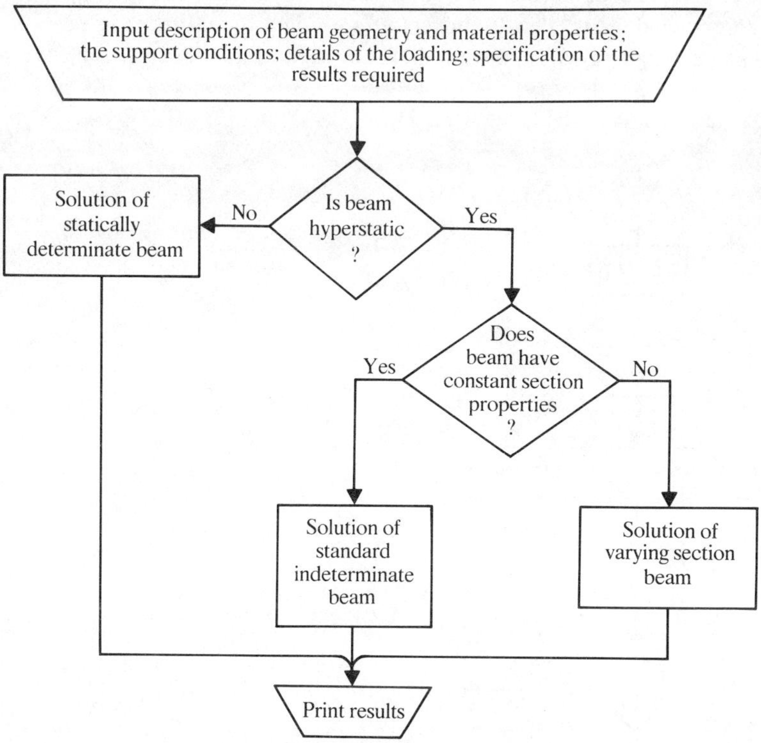

Figure 1.4 Flowchart of an overall solution process

predict the main aspects of its behaviour. To obtain information from this model it is often necessary to solve algebraic or differential equations. As computers deal with numerical quantities, the solution procedure has to be broken down into a sequence of steps dealing with numbers. This stage of numerical analysis often introduces additional approximations. Some of the more common numerical methods used by civil engineers are described in Chapter 3 and applications of them are given in subsequent chapters.

A series of instructions for the step-by-step solution of a problem is called an 'algorithm' and a convenient way of constructing one is to form a flowchart. This is made up of a set of boxes, the shapes of which indicate the nature of the operations to be performed, and connecting arrowed lines that show the flow of operations. In this text, only four shapes of box are used: a rectangle indicates any processing operation that is not a decision; a diamond indicates a decision; a trapezium indicates a data transfer, and a small circle indicates a connection to a part of the flowchart not shown.

Before any solution process is coded into FORTRAN, a hierarchy of algorithms is produced. These are used firstly to isolate the main stages in a solution, and then to define solution steps in progressively greater detail. For example, the main stages in a program to predict response of a beam to loading might be as described in Fig. 1.4, while part of a detailed description of one of the stages might be as shown in Fig. 1.5. Producing algorithms is one of the most creative aspects of programming and calls for considerable concentration and ingenuity. It is not a straightforward procedure but is cyclic in nature and continually generates the need to review previously constructed parts. Pencil and eraser are called for rather than pen and ink. Only when a programmer is convinced that an algorithm is correct, and covers

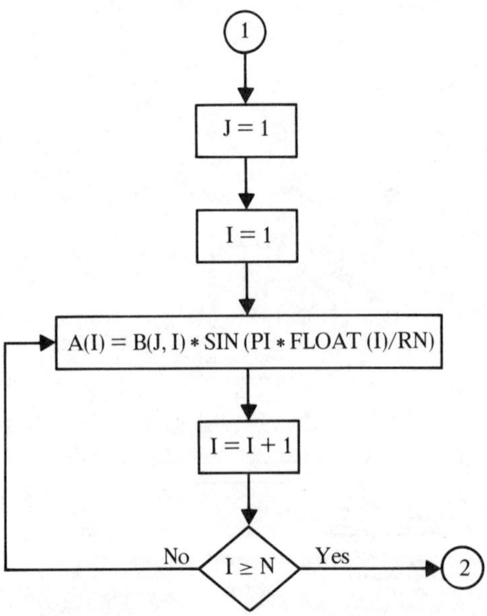

Figure 1.5 Flowchart of a detailed process

all possibilities that could be encountered during execution, should a solution be coded into FORTRAN.

As with all languages, FORTRAN is constructed to a set of rules. However, unlike most languages, FORTRAN text is submitted to a machine. In human communication, imagination can be used to interpret inaccurate use of language, but a computer has no such facility and the utmost care must be taken. The syntax is not extensive and most of it is described and illustrated in Chapter 2.

Before describing the language, it is pertinent to consider the last piece of computer jargon of this chapter – 'gigo'. This is an acronym for 'garbage in, garbage out' and is to remind us that the results produced from unreliable data, or by unreliable programs, are equally unreliable. Programming and use of computers generally are activities that require great care and thought.

SUGGESTIONS FOR FURTHER READING

1. Ralston, A., *Introduction to Programming and Computer Science*, McGraw-Hill, New York, 1971.
2. Laver, M., *Introducing Computers*, HMSO, London, 1979.
3. Bowden, B. V., *Faster than Thought*, Pitman, London, 1953.

CHAPTER

TWO

PROGRAMMING WITH FORTRAN

Once a detailed set of instructions for the solution of a particular problem has been produced, the next step is to code it into a language acceptable to a computer. In this chapter programming in Standard FORTRAN IV is explained. The syntax of this language is defined by the American National Standards Institute (ANSI) and most modern computers have facilities to deal with it. A knowledge of FORTRAN is useful to engineers who do not themselves code programs, as well as to those who do, as there is an ever-growing body of literature containing texts of FORTRAN programs for solving engineering problems.

2.1 CHARACTER SET

The characters available in standard FORTRAN are:

letters of the alphabet A–Z

decimal digits 0–9

special characters + – * / ( ) . , space or blank, $

In this text, when it is necessary to indicate a space the symbol ∧ will be used. When it is not obvious whether zero or the letter 'O' is intended, Ø will be used for zero.

2.2 LINES

A program consists of a list of lines. Each line can contain up to seventy-two characters and certain positioning rules must be followed. The positions of characters on a line are referred to as columns, by analogy with positioning on a punched card.

There are four types of FORTRAN line: 'initial' line, 'continuation' line, 'comment' line, and 'END' line.

2.2.1 Initial line

Most lines of a program are initial lines. An initial line forms the first line of a statement. Columns 1–5 may contain an unsigned integer that labels the statement for reference from other statements. Columns 7–72 contain characters arranged to form a FORTRAN statement. Spaces within a statement are not significant and can be used to improve appearance for easy comprehension.

2.2.2 Continuation line

When it is impossible to complete a statement on a single line, it can be continued on to subsequent lines. To indicate that the characters are to be treated as part of the statement on the previous line, a character, other than Ø or ∧, is inserted in column 6. This character is not treated as part of the statement. Up to 19 successive continuation lines may be used. Columns 1–5 and columns beyond the 72nd should be left blank.

2.2.3 END line

An END line consists of blanks and the word END positioned in columns 7–72. It is not strictly a FORTRAN statement, but is used to indicate to the compiler, the program in the software that translates user source programs, that the end of a program segment has been reached. Every program unit must finish with an END line. Initially, we shall consider programs consisting of one segment, but later, in Sec. 2.13, we shall consider the use of a main program with a number of sub-programs, each of which must finish with an END line.

2.2.4 Comment line

A comment line has the character C in the first column and any other characters in columns 2–80. Comment lines do not affect a program in any way. They are used to insert explanatory text to assist comprehension. They can be placed anywhere, except immediately prior to a continuation line.

2.2.5 Data lines

Data for a FORTRAN program is submitted in lines, and the full 80 character positions of a card are used.

2.3 EXAMPLE – SOLUTION OF QUADRATIC EQUATION

Now that characters and lines have been defined, it is instructive to try and understand a FORTRAN program for solution to a well known problem. The program is to find the roots of n equations of the type $ax^2 + bx + c = 0$. The algorithm is set out in the flowchart shown in Fig. 2.1. Note that the programmer has anticipated all eventualities: $a = 0$; complex roots; and equal roots. The numbers that appear by statement boxes of the flowchart are the same as those used for labels of corresponding instructions in the program given in Fig. 2.2.

Do not worry if you cannot follow all of the steps in detail. They will become clear as the text proceeds. Note that the program is composed from the allowable character set and, as lower-case letters are not allowed, the programmer has used upper-case throughout. Note, too, the use of comment lines for explanatory text, the use of a continuation line for the statement labelled 601, and the final END line.

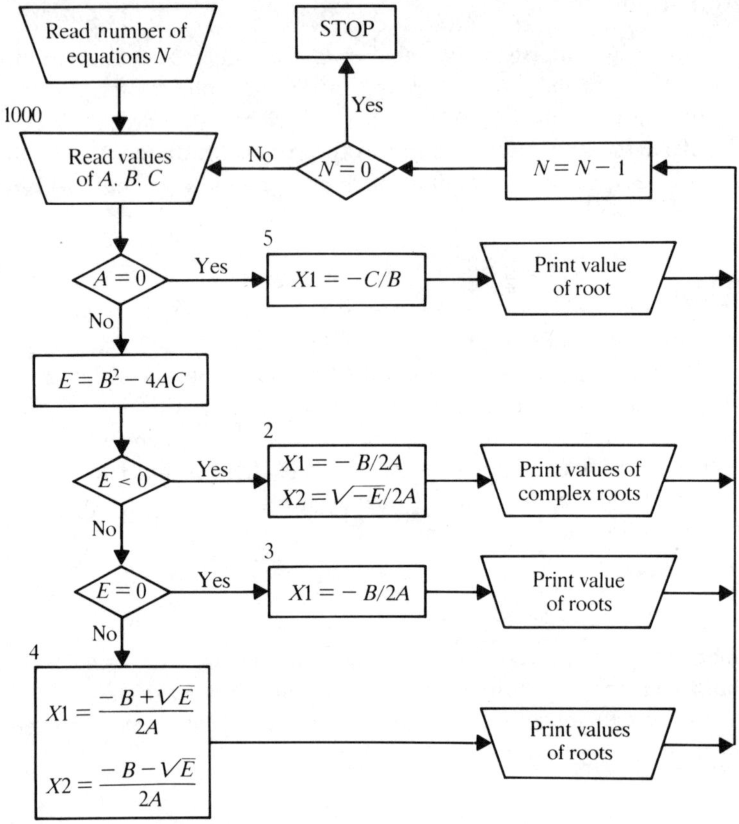

Figure 2.1 Flowchart for quadratic equations

```
C INPUT NO. OF EQUATIONS N
      READ(5,501)N
C INPUT EQUATION COEFFICIENTS
 1000 READ(5,502)A,B,C
C PRINT VALUES READ IN
      WRITE(6,601)A,B,C
C IF A LINEAR EQUATION DO STATEMENT WITH LABEL 5 NEXT
      IF(A.EQ.0.0)GOTO 5
C CALCULATE VALUE OF EXPRESSION TO BE SQUARE ROOTED
      E=B*B-4.0*A*C
C IF NEGATIVE DO STATEMENT WITH LABEL 2 NEXT
C IF ZERO DO STATEMENT WITH LABEL 3 NEXT
C IF POSITIVE DO STATEMENT WITH LABEL 4 NEXT
      IF(E)2,3,4
C COMPLEX ROOTS
 2    WRITE(6,602)
      X1=-B/(2.0*A)
      X2=SQRT(-E)/(2.0*A)
```

Figure 2.2 Program to solve quadratic equations

```
C PRINT REAL PART OF COMPLEX NUMBER X1 FOLLOWED
C BY IMAGINARY PART X2
      WRITE(6,603)X1,X2
      X2=-X2
      WRITE(6,603)X1,X2
C DO STATEMENT WITH LABEL 100 NEXT
      GOTO 100
C EQUAL ROOTS
 3    WRITE(6,604)
      X1=-B/(2.0*A)
      WRITE(6,605)X1,X1
C DO STATEMENT WITH LABEL 100 NEXT
      GOTO 100
C TWO REAL ROOTS
 4    WRITE(6,606)
      X1=(-B+SQRT(E))/(2.0*A)
      X2=(-B-SQRT(E))/(2.0*A)
      WRITE(6,605)X1,X2
C DO STATEMENT WITH LABEL 100 NEXT
      GOTO 100
C LINEAR EQUATION
 5    WRITE(6,607)
      X1=-C/B
      WRITE(6,608)X1
C REDUCE THE VALUE OF N BY 1
 100  N=N-1
C WHEN N=0 ALL EQUATIONS HAVE BEEN SOLVED
      IF(N.EQ.0)STOP
C IF N IS NOT ZERO DO THE STATEMENT WITH LABEL
C 1000 NEXT TO INPUT COEFFICIENTS OF THE NEXT EQUATION
      GOTO 1000
C INPUT AND OUTPUT LAYOUT IS GIVEN BY FORMAT STATEMENTS
C THE SECOND NUMBER IN READ AND WRITE STATEMENTS IS THE
C LABEL OF THE FORMAT STATEMENT TO BE USED
 501  FORMAT(I2)
 502  FORMAT(3E15.8)
 601  FORMAT(1H‸,15HSOLUTION‸OF‸:-‸,E15.8,7H‸X**2‸+,E15.8,
     14H‸X‸+,E15.8,6H‸=‸0.0)
 602  FORMAT(18H‸ROOTS‸ARE‸COMPLEX)
 603  FORMAT(11H‸REAL‸PART‸,E15.8,12H‸‸IMAG‸PART‸,E15.8)
 604  FORMAT(16H‸ROOTS‸ARE‸EQUAL)
 605  FORMAT(7H‸ROOT‸1,E15.8,8H‸‸ROOT‸2,E15.8)
 606  FORMAT(27H‸ROOTS‸ARE‸UNEQUAL‸AND‸REAL)
 607  FORMAT(14H‸NOT‸QUADRATIC)
 608  FORMAT(15H‸VALUE‸OF‸X‸:-‸,E15.8)
      END
```

Figure 2.2 (*continued*)

2.4 CONSTANTS

A constant is a known numerical quantity that cannot be altered during program execution. For example, in the statement

```
AREA=3.141593*R*R
```

the number is a constant, but R and AREA are names of variables and can be set to different values by statements in the program.

2.4.1 INTEGER constants

An INTEGER constant is a whole number. It consists of a string of digits and may be preceded by a sign. Examples of three INTEGER constants are: 0, 9826, and −20. Note that commas cannot be used to group digits and no decimal point is allowed. The representation of an INTEGER quantity inside a computer is exact and their use is mainly confined to special circumstances. An INTEGER constant in a computer that uses 16-bit words could lie in the range ± 32 767 and the range on a computer that uses 24-bit words could be ± 8 388 607.

2.4.2 REAL constants

A REAL constant contains either a decimal point or an exponent or both. Examples of REAL constants are

0.00123	.00123	1.23E − 3	123E − 5
345.0	345.	345E0	34.5E1

Note that commas cannot be used to group digits. With the exponent form, a number is followed by the letter E and then by an INTEGER which together signify that the number is multiplied by 10 raised to the power stated by the INTEGER.

REAL quantities are stored in floating-point form with values covering a much larger range then INTEGER quantities. More than one computer word may be allocated to store a REAL quantity and the range of a value depends upon how the storage is apportioned between mantissa and exponent. Typically, for computers that use 16-bit words the mantissa is accurate to 7 or 8 decimal digits and the range of values is $\pm 10^{\pm 18}$, while for computers that use 24-bit words, the mantissa is accurate to 11 decimal digits and the range of values is $\pm 10^{\pm 76}$.

2.4.3 DOUBLE PRECISION constants

Although the range of REAL quantities is more than adequate for most purposes, there are occasions when a programmer needs values to be stored to greater accuracy. To increase the number of significant decimal digits in the mantissa, DOUBLE PRECISION quantities are used. A DOUBLE PRECISION constant is written as the exponential form of a REAL constant but with the E replaced by D. An example of a DOUBLE PRECISION constant is:

```
3.14159265358979324DO
```

On a 16-bit word computer, 15 decimal digits can be used and on a 24-bit word computer, use of 20 decimal digits is typical. Operations using DOUBLE PRECISION quantities proceed more slowly than those using REAL quantities and they should be used only when absolutely essential.

2.4.4 COMPLEX constants

COMPLEX constants are used to represent complex numbers such as $X+\sqrt{-1}\,Y$. They take the form (X, Y) where X and Y are REAL constants. Examples of COMPLEX constants are (6.12, −12.2) and (.612E1, −.122E2). The brackets and commas are part of the representation and must be used.

2.4.5 LOGICAL constants

There are two LOGICAL constants. They are .TRUE. and .FALSE. . The full stops are part of the constants and must be used.

2.5 VARIABLES

In FORTRAN, variables are identified by symbolic names. A name is made up of from one to six letters and digits, but the first character must be a letter. Programmers usually choose names that are associated with the items they represent. Possible names for variables are:

```
A, X, STRESS, A1, X123, LOAD
```

Five types of variables are permitted: INTEGER, REAL, DOUBLE PRECISION, COMPLEX, and LOGICAL. The possible ranges of values of these types are the same as those for the corresponding constants. The types of variables can be set in declaration statements at the head of a program. Typical declaration statements are:

```
INTEGER A1, B, Z, COUNT
REAL LOAD, LOADA
DOUBLE PRECISION X, Y
COMPLEX IA, BR
LOGICAL TEST, CHECK
```

Declaration statements consist of the 'type' name followed by a list of variable names. Commas are used to separate variable names and there is no terminating symbol to a list. Each declaration type must be on an initial line, but lists can use continuation lines. A declaration statement sets the type of a variable for the particular program segment it heads. Variables passed between different segments should have their types defined in each of the segments in which they appear.

To save effort, all variable names having their first character in the range I to N are assumed to be of INTEGER type and all others to be of REAL type unless specified otherwise in a declaration statement. It is thus possible, and indeed not unusual, to have a program without a declaration statement. In the program illustrated in Fig. 2.2, variables *A, B, C, E, X*1, *X*2 are by default of type REAL and *N* is of type INTEGER.

2.6 ARRAYS

An array is an ordered set of values referred to by a single variable name. To enable an element of an array to be accessed, the variable name is 'subscripted'. A subscripted variable in FORTRAN can have from 1 to 3 dimensions. A subscripted variable can store values of any one of the types described for variables. Declaration of subscripted variables can be made using one of the five type declaration statements or by a DIMENSION statement. Typical declaration statements are:

```
REAL STRESS(40), INT(10, 100), LOAD
INTEGER FORCES(5, 20), A1, B1
DIMENSION XY(100, 2), N(50)
```

The variable STRESS is a one-dimensional array of 40 REAL elements, INT is a two-dimensional array, or matrix, of REAL elements, with 10 rows and 100 columns. Subscripts in declaration statements of main programs must be INTEGER constants.

An individual element of any array is referenced by use of subscripts. Thus STRESS(5) refers to the fifth element of STRESS and *XY*(*I*, 1) refers to the element in the *I*-th row and first column of *XY*. Subscripts must be of INTEGER type. In standard FORTRAN IV array element subscripts can be simple arithmetic expressions. These are limited to the form *IC***IV*+*IK*. *IV* is an INTEGER variable name, *IC* and *IK* are INTEGER constants. The permissible range is given by the two conditions $IC \nless 0$, and $IK > 0$ when $IC = 0$.

2.7 ARITHMETIC

2.7.1 Arithmetic expressions

An arithmetic expression is a sequence of arithmetic operators, constants, variables, array elements, or FUNCTIONs. FUNCTIONs are discussed in Secs 2.9 and 2.13. When one appears in an arithmetic expression, it is treated as a variable whose value is first evaluated in a sub-program.

2.7.2 Arithmetic operators

FORTRAN arithmetic expressions are similar to the algebraic expressions they represent and the following characters are used as arithmetic operators:

+ for addition

— for subtraction

* for multiplication

/ for division

** for exponentiation

Parentheses, or round brackets, can also be included in arithmetic expressions to order the sequence of operations to be performed.

Examples of arithmetic expressions are:

1. W*A*B**2/S**2 for $\dfrac{WAB^2}{S^2}$

2. P*A*B*(A+2.0*B)/(2.0*S**2) for $\dfrac{PAB(A+2B)}{2S^2}$

3. (A+B)/(C+D/(F+G)) for $\dfrac{A+B}{C+\dfrac{D}{F+G}}$

To ensure that expressions are unambiguous there are a few simple rules governing their construction:

No two arithmetic operators may be adjacent, but an operator can be next to a bracket. Thus −A+B*(−C) is valid, while −A+B*−C, B*(−C)+−A and −A+B(−C) are invalid.

Parentheses can be nested and values are determined working outwards from the innermost pair of brackets.

The order of evaluation usually proceeds from left to right, although this cannot be relied upon except for INTEGER division, which is specified as part of the Standard. When in doubt use parentheses. The priority of operation is

1. innermost brackets;
2. exponentiation;
3. multiplication and division;
4. addition and subtraction.

Special care should be taken with exponentiation. A**B**C is ambiguous and should be written as either A**(B**C) or (A**B)**C according to which is intended.

2.7.3 Arithmetic assignment

An arithmetic assignment statement has the form

$$V = AE$$

where V is a variable name and AE is an arithmetic expression, constant, variable name, array element, or FUNCTION. Execution of the statement causes AE to be evaluated and the numerical result assigned to V. The following are examples of arithmetic assignment statements:

```
X=1.0
```

```
Y=A+B/C**2+SIN(X)

Z=Z+10.0
```

The latter is a powerful construction and should be read '*Z* is assigned the current value of *Z* plus 10.0'. The '=' character does not indicate equality, but is dynamic, and implies 'is set equal to'.

2.8 EVALUATION OF ARITHMETIC EXPRESSIONS

Variables and constants of different types can be used in arithmetic expressions. The full range of permitted combinations and types of results are set out in Tables 2.1 and 2.2.

Table 2.1 Type of result of *A*/*B*, *A*B*, *A*+*B*, *A*−B**

Type of *A* \ Type of *B*	INTEGER	REAL	DOUBLE P.	COMPLEX
INTEGER	INTEGER	Invalid	Invalid	Invalid
REAL	Invalid	REAL	DOUBLE P.	COMPLEX
DOUBLE P.	Invalid	DOUBLE P.	DOUBLE P.	Invalid
COMPLEX	Invalid	COMPLEX	Invalid	COMPLEX

Table 2.2 Type of result of *A**B***

Type of *A* \ Type of *B*	INTEGER	REAL	DOUBLE P.	COMPLEX
INTEGER	INTEGER	Invalid	Invalid	Invalid
REAL	REAL	REAL	DOUBLE P.	Invalid
DOUBLE P.	DOUBLE P.	DOUBLE P.	DOUBLE P.	Invalid
COMPLEX	COMPLEX	Invalid	Invalid	Invalid

2.8.1 Floating-point arithmetic

Most calculations are performed using floating-point arithmetic with REAL quantities. INTEGER quantities may not appear in expressions involving floating-point quantities, except as exponents. It is more efficient to raise a quantity to an INTEGER power than to a REAL power. A negative quantity may not be raised to a REAL power.

Arithmetic operations on floating-point quantities introduce roundoff errors. The result of an operation is calculated within a computer to more significant digits than are used for its subsequent stored form and then rounded. Most values thus contain errors, although they are usually acceptably small.

A major source of error can arise from subtracting nearly equal numbers. Suppose $A-B$ is to be evaluated with $A = 222\,222\,200\,000$ and $B = 222\,221\,100\,000$. If the operation is performed on a computer that stores values to 6 digits,

```
A-B=(222222.E6-222221.E6)=1.00000E6
```

whereas the required result is 1 100 000. The percentage error in the stored value of the result is several orders of magnitude greater than the errors in the stored values of *A* and *B*.

Table 2.3 Result of arithmetic assignment $V = AE$ (arithmetic expression)

Type of V \ Type of AE	INTEGER	REAL	DOUBLE P.	COMPLEX
INTEGER	Assign	Truncate¶	Truncate¶	Invalid
REAL	Assign†	Assign	Assign‡	Invalid
DOUBLE P.	Assign	Assign§	Assign	Invalid
COMPLEX	Invalid	Invalid	Invalid	Assign

† It may not always be possible to retain all digits.
‡ Some digits lost.
§ Some computer systems produce a value of greater accuracy than that which would be given by straightforward REAL arithmetic.
¶ Truncate – Truncate and assign, (decimal component ignored).

Sometimes parentheses can be used to reduce the effects of roundoff errors. Suppose $A+C-B$ is to be evaluated and it is known that the values of A and B are of similar magnitude and are very much greater than the value of C. In such cases it is preferable to order the operations $(A-B)+C$ by using parentheses. For example, if A and B have the values of the previous example and $C = 485\,888$ then the value given is 1.48589E6, in comparison with the required value of 1 585 888, but any other ordering of operations gives 1.00000E6.

Care should be taken to ensure that unacceptable errors are not created, and, when necessary, DOUBLE PRECISION quantities should be used.

The order of operations can lead not only to loss of significance but also to 'overflow'. The magnitude of values is limited, and an attempt to create a value larger than the allowable limit causes an 'overflow' failure that stops execution of a program. Suppose A*B/C is to be evaluated and values of A, B, and C are all in the neighbourhood of 10^{40}. If the multiplication is done first then a number greater than the computer can store is created and failure results. The problem is overcome by using parentheses to ensure that the division is performed first: A*(B/C).

2.8.2 Arithmetic with INTEGERs

Arithmetic using INTEGER quantities is used in special circumstances. An INTEGER is represented exactly and, when division is performed, the result is truncated. Thus, for example, if I=6 and J=5, then I/J yields 1 and J/I yields 0.

When the result of evaluating an arithmetic expression involving floating-point quantities is assigned to an INTEGER variable it is truncated. The full range of possibilities of arithmetic assignment actions is illustrated in Table 2.3.

One of the uses of arithmetic with INTEGERs is to check for factors. For example M/N*N, which is evaluated from left to right, is only equal to M when N is a factor of M. In particular, an even number can be detected by comparing the value of M/2*2 with M. They are equal only when M is even. An example of the use of this type of construction can be seen in the program of Fig. 2.8.

2.8.3 Conversion of type

To enable a quantity of different type to be included in an arithmetic expression, a standard FUNCTION can be used to change the type of its value for use in the expression. FUNCTIONs in general are discussed in Sec. 2.9. For our purposes, it is sufficient to note that *IFIX(RE)* converts the value of the REAL arithmetic expression *RE* to INTEGER form and *FLOAT(IE)* converts the value of the INTEGER arithmetic expression *IE* to REAL form.

2.8.4 Illustrative examples

Two further examples of uses of INTEGER arithmetic will clarify the features described.

If *ANGLE* is the name of a REAL variable that holds the value of an angle in radians and *DEG, MIN, SEC* are names of INTEGER variables, then the value of the angle in degrees, minutes and seconds can be obtained using:

```
ANG=ANGLE*57.29578

DEG=ANG

MIN=(ANG-FLOAT(DEG))*60.0

SEC=((ANG-FLOAT(DEG))*60.0-FLOAT(MIN))*60.0+0.5
```

This type of construction can be used for conversion between any two sets of units.

For the second example, a statement to add the whole number part of REAL variable *B* to the value of REAL variable *A* is given:

```
A=A+FLOAT(IFIX(B))
```

2.9 STANDARD FUNCTIONS

A FUNCTION reference may appear in an arithmetic expression or logical expression; see Sec. 2.10.4.1. It has the form $F(A_1, A_2, \ldots, A_n)$. F is the FUNCTION name, A_1 to A_n are actual arguments that can be variable names, constants, expressions, and FUNCTION references. A FUNCTION name returns a value to the expression where the FUNCTION reference occurs. The type of the value is determined either by the first letter of the name, or by inclusion of the name in a declaration statement.

Evaluation of the square root, logarithm, or sine of a quantity is done so frequently that FORTRAN compilers supply a library of Standard FUNCTIONs for these and other commonly occurring mathematical functions. A particular compiler can have an extensive range of 'Standard' FUNCTIONs and a user should consult a manual to see what is available. All compilers must provide the minimum list of the ANSI Standard and to ensure that a program will work on any computer only FUNCTIONs in that list should be used.

2.9.1 Intrinsic FUNCTIONs

The most commonly used Intrinsic FUNCTIONs are for:

1. determining the absolute value of an argument (For each of these FUNCTIONs the type of value returned is the same as that of the argument.):

ABS(RE)	returns the absolute value of the REAL arithmetic expression *RE*
IABS(IE)	returns the absolute value of the INTEGER arithmetic expression *IE*
DABS(DPE)	returns the absolute value of the DOUBLE PRECISION arithmetic expression *DPE*

2. changing the type of the value of an expression:

FLOAT(IE)	returns the REAL equivalent of the INTEGER arithmetic expression *IE*
IFIX(RE)	returns the INTEGER equivalent of the REAL arithmetic expression *RE*
SNGL(DPE)	returns the REAL equivalent of the DOUBLE PRECISION expression *DPE*
DBLE(RE)	returns the DOUBLE PRECISION equivalent of the REAL expression *RE*

3. transferring the sign of an expression:

$SIGN(RE_1, RE_2)$ $ISIGN(IE_1, IE_2)$ $DSIGN(DPE_1, DPE_2)$	return the sign of the second argument multiplied by the absolute value of the first argument

2.9.2 Basic external FUNCTIONs

The main difference between intrinsic and external FUNCTIONs is that external FUNCTIONs can be used in EXTERNAL statements (see Sec. 2.13.4) and their names can, therefore, be used as arguments to user-supplied FUNCTION and SUBROUTINE sub-programs. The most commonly used external FUNCTIONS are for:

1. determining the square root of an expression:

SQRT(RE) DSQRT(DPE) CSQRT(CE)	return the square root of the expressions; (*CE* is an arithmetic expression of COMPLEX quantities)

2. determining the exponential of an expression:

EXP(RE) DEXP (DPE) CEXP(CE)	return e raised to the power given by the values of the expressions

3. determining the natural logarithm of an expression:

ALOG(RE) DLOG(DPE) CLOG(CE)	return the natural logarithm of the expressions

4. determining the common logarithm of an expression:

ALOG10(RE) DLOG10(DPE)	return the logarithm to the base 10 of the expressions

5. determining trigonometric values:

SIN(RE) DSIN(DPE) CSIN(CE)	return the sine of the expressions which must be in radians

COS(AE) DCOS(DPE) CCOS(CE)	return the cosine of the expressions which must be in radians
ATAN(AE) DATAN(DPE)	return the inverse tangent of the expressions in the range $-\pi/2$ to $\pi/2$ radians
ATAN2(AE_1, AE_2) DATAN2(DPE_1, DPE_2)	return the inverse tangent of the first argument divided by the second argument. The result is in the range $-\pi$ to π radians

6. determining hyperbolic values

TANH(AE)	returns the hyperbolic tangent of the REAL arithmetic expression

The types of the values returned by all the above external FUNCTIONs are the same as those of their arguments.

The FUNCTION *SQRT* is used in the program for quadratic equation solution in Fig. 2.2 and further examples are now given in program statements for coordinate transformations. Let *R, X, Y, Z, PHI,* and *THETA* be the names of REAL variables holding values of Cartesian and polar coordinates in accordance with Fig. 2.3. Program statements to effect the coordinate transformation from Cartesian (*X, Y, Z*) to polar (*R, THETA, PHI*) are

```
R=SQRT(X**2+Y**2+Z**2)
THETA=ATAN2(Y, X)
PHI=ATAN2(SQRT(X**2+Y**2),Z)
```

and from polar to Cartesian are

```
Z=R*COS(PHI)
X=R*SIN(PHI)*COS(THETA)
Y=R*SIN(PHI)*SIN(THETA)
```

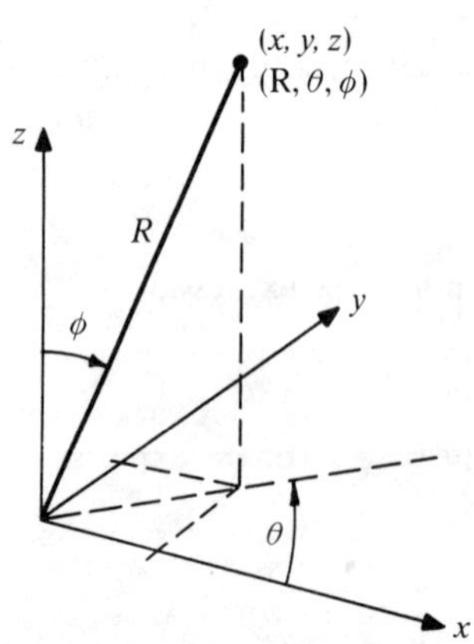

Figure 2.3 Transformation of coordinates

2.10 CONTROL STATEMENTS

Normally FORTRAN statements are executed sequentially, but very few processes can be described without the need for conditional statements, and the ability to transfer control to a statement other than the next in line. The following control statements are available in FORTRAN: unconditional GOTO, computed GOTO, arithmetic IF, logical IF, DO, PAUSE, STOP, CALL, RETURN. Labels are used to specify statements to which control is to be transferred. A label is an unsigned INTEGER positioned in columns 1 to 5 of an initial line (see Sec. 2.2.1).

2.10.1 Unconditional GOTO

To direct a computer to execute a particular labelled statement next, the GOTO statement is used. Its general form is

```
GOTO IC
```

where *IC* is an unsigned INTEGER constant of up to 5 digits which corresponds to the label of the statement to be executed. The labelled statement must be in the same program segment as the GOTO statement. Examples of usage can be seen in the program for solution of quadratic equations in Fig. 2.2.

2.10.2 Computed GOTO

A computed GOTO statement is used to transfer control to one of a number of labelled statements. The general form is

GOTO (label 1, label 2, . . . , label *i*, . . . , label *n*), IV

where 'label *i*' is the label of a statement in the same program segment and *IV* is the name of an INTEGER variable. The value of *IV* must lie in the range 1 to *n*, the number of labels in the list. Control is transferred to the *IV*-th label. The labels can be put in any desired order and a label can appear more than once in the list. An example of a computed GOTO statement is

```
GOTO(99, 1, 10, 110, 1, 20), KEY
```

When *KEY*=1 control is transferred to the statement labelled 99, when *KEY*=3 control is transferred to the statment labelled 10, etc.

2.10.3 Arithmetic IF

The arithmetic IF statement is used to transfer control to one of three labels according to whether the value of an arithmetic expression is negative, zero, or positive. It has the form

IF(AE) label 1, label 2, label 3

The arithmetic expression *AE* can be of type INTEGER, REAL, or DOUBLE PRECISION. The labels must refer to statements in the same program segment and any two of them can be the same. When the value of *AE* is negative control is transferred to the statement with label 1, when zero to the statement with label 2, and when positive to the statement with label 3.

An example of usage can be found in the program to solve quadratic equations in Fig. 2.2. In that example, note how unconditional GOTO statements are used in conjunction with the arithmetic IF statement to isolate blocks of program.

2.10.4 Logical IF

This statement tests a logical expression and when it is true executes the statement on the same line. Its general form is

IF (logical expression) executable statement

The executable statement may not be another logical IF nor a DO statement.

2.10.4.1. Logical expression

A logical expression can be a variable of LOGICAL type, a sequence of LOGICAL type variable names and operators, or it can be a relational expression. It can only have the values true or false.

2.10.4.2 Logical variables

Variables can be set to LOGICAL type in a declaration statement at the head of a program segment (see Sec. 2.5), and assigned values by logical assignment statements. A logical assignment has the form

$$LV = \text{logical expression}$$

where LV is the name of a variable or array element of LOGICAL type. Examples of assignment statements are

```
A=.TRUE.
TEST(6)=.FALSE.
```

2.10.4.3 Logical operators

FORTRAN has three logical operators:

```
.AND.
.OR.
.NOT.
```

These are the Boolean operators 'and', 'or', and 'not'. Examples of logical expressions incorporating logical operators are

X.AND.Y	this is true when both X and Y are true
X.OR.Y	this is true when either X or Y is true
.NOT.X	this returns the opposite of X

2.10.4.4 *Relational expressions*

Relational expressions have the general form

$$AE_1 \text{ relational operator } AE_2$$

where AE_1 and AE_2 are arithmetic expressions of the same type. COMPLEX types are not permitted.

2.10.4.5 *Relational operators*

The relational operators are

.EQ. equals	.GT. greater than	.LT. less than
.NE. not equal to	.GE. greater than or equal to	.LE. less than or equal to

2.10.4.6 *Examples and comments*

Examples of statements using logical expressions are

1. `X=Y.AND.C.GT.100.0`
   Here *X* and *Y* are LOGICAL variables and *C* is a REAL variable. *X* is assigned the value .TRUE. when *Y* is true and $C > 100.0$ otherwise it is assigned the value .FALSE..
2. `IF(X.OR.Y)C=10.0`
   When either of the LOGICAL variables *X* or *Y* is true, the REAL variable *C* is assigned the value 10.0.
3. `IF(0.0.LT.C.AND.C.LT.10.0) GOTO 100`
   Control is transferred to the statement labelled 100 when the value of the REAL variable *C* lies between 0 and 10.
4. `IF(X.AND. .NOT.Y) GOTO 10`
   Control is transferred to the statement labelled 10 when *X* is true and *Y* is false.

The order of processing logical expressions is innermost parentheses and FUNCTION references; arithmetic expressions; relational operators, .NOT., .AND., and finally .OR.. The order of precedence of all operators is given in Table 2.4.

Parentheses should be used to ensure there is no ambiguity in logical expressions.

When using relational operators, especially .EQ., remember that floating point quantities are represented approximately, and particular care should, therefore, be taken with REAL and DOUBLE-PRECISION items.

Table 2.4 Hierarchy of operators

1.	**
2.	*/
3.	+ − at the beginning of an expression
4.	+ − within an expression
5.	.LT. .LE. .GT. .GE. .EQ. .NE.
6.	.NOT.
7.	.AND.
8.	.OR.

2.10.5 DO statement

Sequences of statements for repeated execution are so common a feature of programs that FORTRAN provides a standard construction. It has the general form

DO 'label' IV=ISTART, IFIN, ISTEP

Here 'label' is a statement label which must occur later in the program segment. *IV* is the name of an INTEGER variable. *ISTART, IFIN, ISTEP* are INTEGER variable names or constants. The action of a DO statement is to assign the value of *ISTART* to *IV* and then to execute the statements up to and including the labelled statement referenced. *IV* is then incremented by the value of *ISTEP* and, if the result is not greater than the value of *IFIN*, the process is repeated. When *IV* becomes greater than *IFIN*, control is transferred to the statement immediately following the labelled statement defining the extent of the DO statements influence.

To illustrate use of a DO statement, consider program statements to determine e^x to a specified number of terms $(n + 1)$. Let the calculated value of e^x be stored in *EX* and the value of the last term calculated be stored in *TM*. The series for evaluation is

$$e^x \simeq 1 + \sum_{i=1}^{n} \frac{x^i}{i!}$$

and corresponding program statements are

```
      EX=1.0
      TM=1.0
      DO 10 I=1, N, 1
      TM=TM*X/FLOAT(I)
10    EX=EX+TM
```

2.10.5.1 Restrictions on DO statements

1. At the time of execution of a DO statement the values of *ISTART, IFIN,* and *ISTEP* must be greater than zero. *ISTEP* can be omitted when the increment is unity and the first line of a DO loop then has the form

   DO 'label' IV=ISTART, IFIN

2. The variables *IV, ISTART, IFIN, ISTEP* may be used in a DO loop, but their values must not be changed.
3. A DO loop may only be entered via a DO statement. Do not attempt to transfer control from outside a DO loop to a labelled statement in its range.
4. The terminal statement of a DO loop must not be another DO, arithmetic IF, RETURN, STOP, PAUSE, CALL, or FORMAT statement, nor a logical IF statement containing one of the prohibited statements. The problems caused by this restriction are resolved by using a CONTINUE statement (see Sec. 2.10.6).
5. The value of *IV* is not defined when a DO statement terminates naturally and should not be assumed to be equal to the value of *IFIN*. When execution is transferred to a statement outside the range of the DO statement before normal termination, its value is retained.

2.10.5.2 Nesting of DO statements

When the range of a DO statement contains another DO statement the DOs are said to be 'nested'. The range of an inner DO loop must be completely contained within the range of outer loops. Nested DO statements may, however, share the same terminal statement. In this case the control variable *IV* of a particular loop is incremented and tested only after all of the inner loops have terminated. When a terminal statement is shared, control may only be transferred to it from within the innermost DO loop.

2.10.5.3 Use with subscripted variables

When using subscripted variables with nested DO loops to control the variation of subscripts, it is more efficient to vary the leftmost subscript most rapidly. This is because arrays are stored in successive storage addresses by columns and this ordering causes the minimum number of internal computations to locate array elements. For example the array $A(3, 3)$ has its elements stored in the sequence $A(1, 1)$, $A(2, 1)$, $A(3, 1)$, $A(1, 2)$, $A(2, 2)$, $A(3, 2)$, $A(1, 3)$, $A(2, 3)$, $A(3, 3)$. To set all of the elements of A to zero one would use

```
      DO 10 I=1, 3
      DO 10 J=1, 3
10    A(J, I)=0.0
```

to cause the elements to be accessed in the above sequence.

2.10.5.4 Illustrative examples

1. Select the largest value from a one-dimensional array PRESS having N positive elements:

```
      VAL=0.0
      DO 12 I=1, N
12    IF(PRESS(I).GT.VAL)VAL=PRESS(I)
```

2. Order the elements of PRESS from largest to smallest. A flowchart of operations is given in Fig. 2.4, and the coding is shown in Fig. 2.5. Each element of PRESS is considered in turn in the DO loop using control variable J. The elements in rows below and including the J-th are examined in the DO loop using the control variable I. The largest of them is extracted and later interchanged with the J-th element.
3. Given matrices A and B of order $N \times M$, form their sum when variable $KEY=5$, their difference if $KEY=8$, and store the result in array C. Otherwise, set all elements of C to zero. Suitable coding is shown in Fig. 2.6.

2.10.6 CONTINUE statement

This is a labelled dummy statement and causes no action. Its main use is to provide a terminal statement to a DO loop when the final executable statement in the range

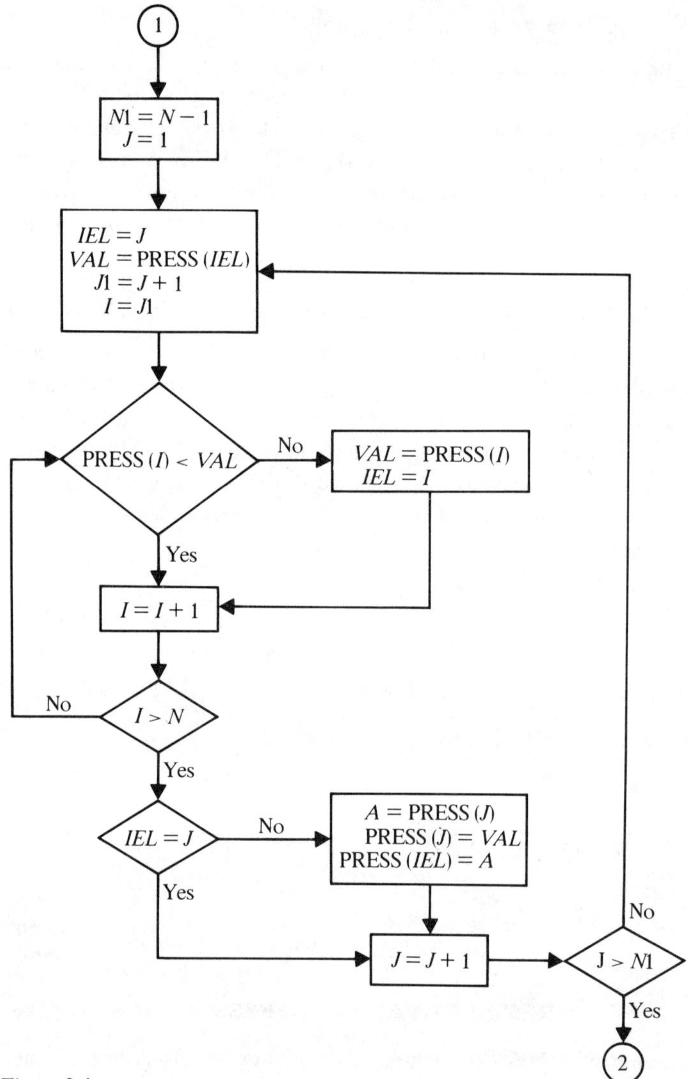

Figure 2.4

is of a prohibited type, or when control is to be transferred to the DO statement without further action being taken. It has the general form

label CONTINUE

2.10.7 PAUSE statement

A PAUSE statement has one of two forms:

PAUSE

and

PAUSE *n*

where n is a string of up to five number characters, each in the range 0 to 7. When a PAUSE instruction is executed, computer operations are suspended until a user depresses a control key on a computer console. Use of 'PAUSE n' also causes the value of n to be transmitted to the console for identification. When the control key is activated, the program restarts at the next instruction. PAUSE is rarely used with batch processing and is most useful with interactive computing, when a user needs to assimilate information before further action can be taken.

```
      N1=N-1
      DO 13 J=1,N1
      IEL=J
      VAL=PRESS(J)
      J1=J+1
      DO 20 I=J1,N
      IF(PRESS(I).LT.VAL) GOTO 20
      VAL=PRESS(I)
      IEL=I
20    CONTINUE
      IF(IEL.EQ.J) GOTO 13
      A=PRESS(J)
      PRESS(J)=VAL
      PRESS(IEL)=A
13    CONTINUE
```

Figure 2.5

```
      I=3
      IF(KEY.EQ.5)I=1
      IF(KEY.EQ.8)I=2
      GOTO(12,9,14),I
14    DO 1 J1=1,M
      DO 1 J2=1,N
1     C(J2,J1)=0.0
      GOTO 100
12    DO 2 J1=1,M
      DO 2 J2=1,N
2     C(J2,J1)=A(J2,J1)+B(J2,J1)
      GOTO 100
9     DO 3 J1=1,M
      DO 3 J2=1,N
3     C(J2,J1)=A(J2,J1)-B(J2,J1)
100   CONTINUE
```

Figure 2.6

2.10.8 STOP statement

A STOP statement has one of two forms:

STOP

and

STOP n

When it is executed, operations are terminated and the program is deleted from the primary store. A program must contain at least one STOP statement. The parameter n has the same effect, and is subject to the same restrictions, as the corresponding parameter in the PAUSE statement.

2.10.9 CALL and RETURN statements

A CALL statement transfers control to a named SUBROUTINE sub-program (see Sec. 2.13.2). The statements of the sub-program are executed until a RETURN statement is executed. This has the effect of transferring control back to the program segment containing the CALL statement and to the statement immediately following it. CALL statements have one of two general forms:

CALL name $(A_1, A_2, \ldots, A_i, \ldots, A_n)$

and

CALL name

The arguments A_1 to A_n are substituted for the dummy arguments when the SUBROUTINE is executed (see Sec. 2.13.2). They are usually constants, the names of variables, array elements, or arrays. The SUBROUTINE 'name' must be a valid FORTRAN variable name and must be used in no other context in a program.

A RETURN statement consists simply of the characters RETURN. All SUBROUTINE and user-supplied FUNCTION sub-programs, see Sec. 2.13.1, must contain at least one RETURN statement.

2.11 DATA TRANSMISSION

With the facilities described above it is possible to construct programs to perform complex calculations, and attention is now turned to problems of transmitting information between program variables and peripheral devices such as a card reader, a line printer, and secondary storage devices such as disks and magnetic tapes.

2.11.1 Records

Information is input and output in the form of 'records'. A record is a string of characters that are to be read or written in one operation. In FORTRAN, READ and WRITE statements are used to perform the operations.

Two varieties of record are available: unformatted and formatted. An unformatted record contains information in machine code and is not normally intended for human examination. Its main use is for transmitting information between variables and the secondary storage devices. A formatted record is in normal alpha-numeric form and is divided into fields. Each field represents the value of a variable or a string of text data presented in a specified form via a FORMAT statement (see Sec. 2.11.4).

Although someone new to programming tends to concentrate on the data processing aspects, later on problems of data transmission will grow in importance. Data preparation can be tedious and in consequence errors are made. To minimize problems and to facilitate checking, data should be arranged neatly. Tabulate whenever possible, and to aid checking always print out values read in. Information output to a user should be arranged in a manner that is pleasing and easy to understand. Tabulate when possible and incorporate strings of text to explain the nature of results and the units in which they are expressed.

2.11.2 READ and WRITE statements

READ and WRITE statements have two basic forms:

```
READ(IDVN, label) list
WRITE(ODVN, label) list
```

and

```
READ(IDVN) list
WRITE(ODVN) list
```

The first two statements are used with formatted records and the last two statements with unformatted records. Examples of READ and WRITE statements can be seen in Fig. 2.2.

IDVN is an INTEGER constant or variable that is associated with a particular input device in a control statement that preceeds the FORTRAN program. In this text, *IDVN* is 5 for a card reader. *ODVN* is similarly associated with an output device and, in this text, is 6 for a line printer. 'label' is an INTEGER constant corresponding to the label of the FORMAT statement used to specify layout. Input and output lists are optional.

2.11.3 Input and output lists

Input and output lists are of the form

$$V_1, V_2, \ldots, V_i, \ldots, V_n$$

where each V_i can be a variable or array name, an array element, or an implied DO loop (see Sec. 2.11.3.1). The appearance of a variable or array element in the list specifies that its current value is to be transmitted. An array name without subscripts causes all the elements of the array to be transmitted by column in the order described in Sec. 2.10.5.3.

For example, if *POINT, EX, EY, EXY* are variable names, *X* is a one-dimensional array of 20 elements and *Y* is a two-dimensional array having 100 rows and 3 columns, execution of

1. `READ(5,50)POINT, EX, EY, EXY`
   causes four values to be input from a formatted record and the variables in the list set to their values in turn.
2. `READ(5,501)X`
   causes twenty values to be input from a formatted record and the elements of *X* to be assigned in turn to those values.

3. WRITE(6, 600)X(1),X(5), POINT
   causes the current values of the array elements and the variable *POINT* to be printed.
4. WRITE(6, 601)Y
   causes all of the values in array Y to be printed in the order $Y(1, 1)$, $Y(2,1)$ to $Y(100, 1)$; $Y(1, 2)$, $Y(2, 2)$ to $Y(100, 2)$; $Y(1, 3)$, $Y(2, 3)$ to $Y(100, 3)$.

2.11.3.1 *Implied DO statement*

An implied DO statement has the general form

$(V_1, V_2, \ldots, V_i, \ldots, V_n,$ IV=ISTART, IFIN, ISTEP)

Its action is similar to that of a DO statement and it is subject to similar restrictions (see Sec. 2.10.5.1, items (1), (2), and (5)). Each of the V_i can be a variable or array name, an array element, or an implied DO statement.

For example, to read values into the first 10 elements of the array X of the previous section one could use

```
READ(5,51)(X(I), I=1, 10)
```

To print the values of Y in 100 rows of 3 columns one could use

```
WRITE(6,61)((Y(I, J), J=1, 3), I=1, 100)
```

Further examples are given after we have considered how records are arranged.

2.11.4 FORMAT statement

This is a non-executable statement and has the form

label FORMAT (specification)

A FORMAT statement must be labelled. The 'specification' describes the layout of data to be transmitted and consists of 'field-descriptors' and 'field separators'. When the series of fields has been exhausted and more variables remain in the list for transfer, a new record is begun. This can be the next line or card image, and the series of field descriptors in the FORMAT statement is scanned again. FORMAT statements can be placed anywhere in a program segment and it is usually convenient to group all of them together near the end (see for example Fig. 2.2).

2.11.5 Field descriptors

Only the most commonly used descriptors are discussed here. For the full range of facilities a more advanced text should be consulted.

2.11.5.1 I *descriptor for INTEGER variables*

To transmit an INTEGER quantity the I descriptor is used. This has the form Iw, where w is the total width of the character field. On input, it causes the next w characters of the external record to be read, converted to INTEGER form, and assigned to the corresponding variable in the input list. The characters of the external field must form an INTEGER number, with or without a sign. Leading blanks or spaces are ignored but others within the field are treated as zeros. When used for output, the I descriptor causes the value of the corresponding variable in the output list to be written as an INTEGER number. It is right-justified, occupies *w* character positions, and has leading spaces to fill the field if necessary.

For example, if values for *I, J, K* are to be read from a card with 5 columns allocated for each value and then printed in a single column on a line printer, the following statement could be used:

```
      READ(5,53)I, J, K
      WRITE(6,64)I, J, K
53    FORMAT(I5, I5, I5)
64    FORMAT(1H∧, I5)
```

The characters 1H∧ are used for carriage control, as explained in Sec. 2.11.7. When a particular field descriptor is repeated, a condensed form is available, which uses a repetition number in front of the descriptor letter. Thus, in the example, the FORMAT statement with label 53 could be replaced by

```
53    FORMAT(3I5)
```

If the values of *I, J, K* are 1, −20, 1000 the data could be:

```
∧∧∧∧1∧∧−20∧1
```

and the line printer would write

```
∧∧∧∧1
∧∧−20
∧1000
```

(∧ indicates a blank or space character).

As a second example, consider a two-dimensional array NODES having *N* rows and 8 columns which is to be filled with INTEGER values. The value of *N* must be assigned before the READ statement is executed, otherwise it is meaningless. One record is used for each row of NODES and gives first the number of the row and then its 8 values. This is a relatively safe way of transmitting a table of information and does not rely upon data cards being submitted in a particular order. For convenience all values are transmitted from a field width of 5 columns since most cards have vertical lines printed on them at 5 or 10 column spacings. Suitable statements are

```
      READ(5,5000)(I,(NODES(I, J),J=1,8),K=1, N)
5000  FORMAT(9I5)
```

Note that, as explained in Sec. 2.11.4, when the series of field descriptors, in this case 9I5, is exhausted and more variables remain in the list for transfer, a new record is begun and the series of field descriptors is scanned again. In this example, *N* new records are begun.

2.11.5.2 F, E, D *descriptors for floating-point variables*

To transmit floating-point quantities, the F, E, and D descriptors are used. These have the forms F*wd*, E*wd* and D*wd*, where w is the total width of the character field and d is the number of digits in the mantissa following the decimal point.

On input, all three descriptors cause the next w characters of the external record to be read, converted to floating-point form, and assigned to the corresponding variable of the input list. The D descriptor is used solely for DOUBLE PRECISION quantities. The characters of the external field can consist of: an optional sign, a string of digits with or without a decimal point, and an optional exponent. The exponent part has a maximum width of 4 characters and has the form E$\pm nn$ or D$\pm nn$, where n is a number character. Short forms are permitted. The sign may be left out if positive and the exponent can be a single digit. The exponent should, however, be right justified.

If the characters in the external field contain a decimal point, it overrides the position specified by d in the field descriptor.

For example, if values are to be read and assigned to variables A, B, C, and D then one could use:

```
      READ(5, 52)A, B, C, D
52    FORMAT(4F15.5)
```

or

```
      READ(5, 53)A, B, C, D
53    FORMAT(4E15.5)
```

In either case, a suitable record to set A, B, C, and D to 0.121 21 is

```
∧∧∧∧∧∧∧∧∧.12121∧∧∧.12121∧∧∧∧∧∧∧∧∧∧∧∧1.2121E−1∧∧∧∧∧∧∧∧∧∧12121
```

On output, the F descriptor causes the value of the corresponding variable in the output list to be printed as a decimal number with d digits after the decimal point. w should be greater than d by at least 2 to allow for the decimal point and a possible sign. The number is right justified in the field. The E descriptor outputs the value as a decimal fraction less than unity with an exponent. w should be greater than $d + 6$ to allow for the general form of $\overline{\wedge}$0.*nnnnn*E$\overline{\wedge}$*nn*, where $\overline{\wedge}$ indicates a space for a positive value and − for a negative value.

For example, if values of a two-dimensional REAL array XY having 20 rows and 5 columns are to be printed in a table, the following statements could be used:

```
      WRITE(6, 600)((XY(I, J),J=1, 5),I=1, 20)
600   FORMAT(1H∧,5F12.4)
```

The decimal points will be in vertical alignment and spaces will be printed in positions not required for characters. If the size of the elements of XY vary considerably, or if their range cannot be predicted in advance, it is better to use the more versatile E descriptor and the FORMAT statement could then be replaced by:

```
600   FORMAT(1H∧,5E12.5)
```

The decimal points and exponent symbols will be in vertical alignment and all values are printed to the same relative accuracy.

2.11.5.3 F *and* E *descriptors for COMPLEX variables*

Values of COMPLEX variables can be transmitted using E and F descriptors. On input, the next *two* fields are read and assigned to the real and imaginary parts of the variable in turn. On output, the real and imaginary parts of a variable also require their own field descriptors. For example the statements

```
      READ(5,50)Z
      WRITE(6, 62)Z
50    FORMAT(2F10.5)
62    FORMAT(1H∧,E12.5, F10.5)
```

cause the next two fields to be read to form the internal representation of the value of the complex variable Z, and the real part to be printed in E form with the imaginary part in F form.

2.11.5.4 L *descriptor for LOGICAL variables*

To transmit a LOGICAL value the L descriptor is used. It has the form Lw, where w is the total width of the field. On input, it causes the next w characters to be read and converted to the internal representation of .TRUE. or .FALSE.. The characters of the external field consist of optional spaces followed by one of the characters T or F, followed by any optional sequence of characters. On output, the L descriptor causes a field of $(w - 1)$ spaces followed by either T or F, according to the value of the variable, to be printed.

2.11.5.5 A *descriptor for characters*

The A descriptor has the form Aw, where w is the total width of the character field. It is used to transmit characters which are to be processed. The action is not independent of the computer to be used and is related to the number of characters that are associated with a variable type. Problems of interchangeability of programs between computers are minimized if w is kept small, as difficulties are most usually encountered when w is greater than 4.

On input, the A descriptor causes the next w characters of the external record to be read and assigned to the corresponding list element. If N is the number of characters held in a storage location of a particular machine, then, when $w < N$, the characters are stored in the w left most positions and space characters are inserted to follow them, and when $w > N$, the right most N characters are stored. When used for output, the A descriptor causes the w left most characters in the storage unit whose name appears in the output list to be transmitted when $w \leqslant N$, otherwise $(w - N)$ spaces are prefixed to the N characters and transmitted with them.

For example, if a computer manual states that a REAL variable holds eight characters, statements to read *NC* cards of text and to print them as a heading to an output listing are:

```
          DIMENSION TITLE(10)
          READ(5,51)NC
          DO 2 I=1, NC
          READ(5,52) TITLE
  2       WRITE(6,61) TITLE
 51       FORMAT(12)
 52       FORMAT(10A8)
 61       FORMAT(1H∧,10A8)
```

2.11.5.6 H *or Hollerith descriptor*

The H descriptor has the form *w*H*ccccc* where *w* is the total number of characters '*c*', *including spaces*, which follow the H character. It is used for the input and output of characters, which are not to be manipulated. No list element is associated with the H descriptor.

When used for input it causes the next *w* characters to be read and stored, overwriting the characters in the Hollerith field. For example, the statements

```
          READ(5,50)
          WRITE(6,50)
 50       FORMAT(25H∧∧∧∧∧∧∧∧∧∧∧∧∧∧∧∧∧∧∧∧∧∧∧∧∧)
```

have the effect of reading from a record the first 25 characters, storing them as characters in the FORMAT field and printing the last 24 characters. The first character is used for carriage control (see Sec. 2.11.7).

When used for output, the H descriptor causes the *w* characters of the Hollerith field to be transmitted. If the first character transmitted is the first character of a record, it is used for carriage control (see Sec. 2.11.7). For example

```
          WRITE(6,61)X, A
 61       FORMAT(3H∧X=, F10.5, 5H∧∧∧A=, F10.5)
```

causes the characters '*X*=', then the value of *X*, then 3 spaces followed by '*A*=', and finally the value of *A* to be printed on a line.

The H descriptor can also be used in a DATA specification (see Sec. 2.12).

2.11.5.7 X *descriptor*

The X descriptor has the form *w*X where *w* is the total width of the field. No list element is associated with it. On input the effect of the X descriptor is to cause the next *w* characters of the input record to be ignored. When used in an output statement it causes *w* spaces to be transmitted.

2.11.6 Field separators

Field descriptors must be separated by either a comma or a solidus. The solidus has the effect of causing a new record to be read or written as well as acting as a separator. As a result, the next character to be output following a solidus is always used for carriage control.

2.11.7 Carriage control

The first character of each record output under FORMAT control is used to specify line spacing. These first characters should be one of the following:

∧ (space)	starts a new line
Ø (zero)	skips a line and starts a new line
1	starts a new page
+	no new line

2.11.8 FORMAT control

For formatted data transmission, each field descriptor is examined in turn and values transmitted accordingly. Descriptors may be enclosed in parentheses and preceded by a repeat count, but a maximum of only two levels of internal parentheses are permitted.

The number of records transmitted is determined by FORMAT control, and by interaction between the READ or WRITE statement and the FORMAT specification. When a solidus is encountered on input, a new record is started and any remaining values of the previous record are ignored. When a solidus is encountered during output, a new record is started and a carriage control character is required. If, on reaching the closing bracket of a FORMAT statement, there are still elements in the input/output list with values for transmission, then a new record is started. In this case there are two possibilities. When the FORMAT statement contains no internal parentheses, the next descriptor taken is the first in the list. When there are internal parentheses, control resumes at the right most complete group of field descriptors.

At first, formatted data transmission may appear more complicated than it in fact is. To clarify some of the rules, a few illustrative examples are given and they should be studied in conjunction with the above sections.

2.11.9 Illustrative examples

1. To print a heading to a page of output

```
      WRITE(6, 60)
      WRITE(6, 61)
60    FORMAT(1H1, 13HBEAM∧ANALYSIS/1H∧, 13(1H–)///7X, 6HFORCES)
```

```
61      FORMAT(4X, 2HFX, 4X, 8HFYΛΛΛΛFZ)
```

would result in

```
                    BEAM ANALYSIS
                    -------------

                        FORCES

                    FX      FY      FZ
```

The first record of the format labelled 60 consists of the character 1 that acts as a carriage control to direct the printer to start at the head of a new page, and 13 characters of text. The first solidus terminates this record and causes it to be printed. The second record consists of a space character that acts as a carriage control to start a new line and 13 minus characters, which serve to underline the previously printed text. The first of the three slashes which follow causes this record to be printed. The next two slashes cause empty records to be transmitted, as there are no field descriptors preceding them. The effect is to leave two blank lines. The final record consists of 7 spaces followed by 6 alphabetic characters. The first of these spaces acts as a carriage control and the remaining 12 characters are printed when the closing bracket of the FORMAT statement is reached.

2. To input a card containing an INTEGER and a REAL value, followed by a number of cards with each holding an INTEGER and 3 REAL variables,

```
        READ(5, 500)N, F, (J, (XYZ(J, K), K=1, 3), I=1,N)
500     FORMAT(I5, E15.6/(I5, 3E15.6))
```

The opening bracket of the FORMAT statement causes a new record, in this case a card, to be read. There are two descriptors in the record and values are taken and assigned to the variables N and F in turn. The solidus causes a new record to be read, and the parentheses indicate that four values are to be transmitted from it. The closing bracket of the FORMAT statement is then reached, and, as there are elements still in the input list, FORMAT control of operations is retained and a new record is read. As the FORMAT statement contains inner parentheses, the field descriptors in those parentheses are used again and four values are transferred. The closing bracket is reached and so the process continues until the list of elements in the READ statement is exhausted. Altogether $(N + 1)$ cards are read.

3. To print values of an array having 12 rows and 12 columns in a headed table,

```
        WRITE(6, 601)((S(I, J), J=1, 12), I=1, 12)
601     FORMAT(1HΛ, 10X, 12HSTIF.ΛMATRIX, (/6X, 12 (F6.4, 2X)))
```

These statements cause the 12 rows and columns of S to be printed in a table with 2 spaces between each column and a blank row between each row of values. The first record is terminated by the solidus which causes the heading to be printed. The next record consists of 6 spaces, the first of which is used for carriage control, followed by 12 sets of floating point numbers and 2 spaces. The closing bracket of the FORMAT statement causes this record to be printed. As the variable list is not exhausted control passes to the outermost of the inner parentheses. The solidus causes a blank record to be output and the closing bracket of the FORMAT statement then causes the next line of values to be printed. The process continues until the output list of the WRITE statement is exhausted.

Table 2.5

Tensile strength, N mm^{-2}	Relative frequency
1.45–1.54	0.02
1.55–1.64	0.04
1.65–1.74	0.09
1.75–1.84	0.15
1.85–1.94	0.11
1.95–2.04	0.23
2.05–2.14	0.06
2.15–2.24	0.12
2.25–2.34	0.07
2.35–2.44	0.06
2.45–2.54	0.03
2.55–2.64	0.01
2.65–2.74	0.01

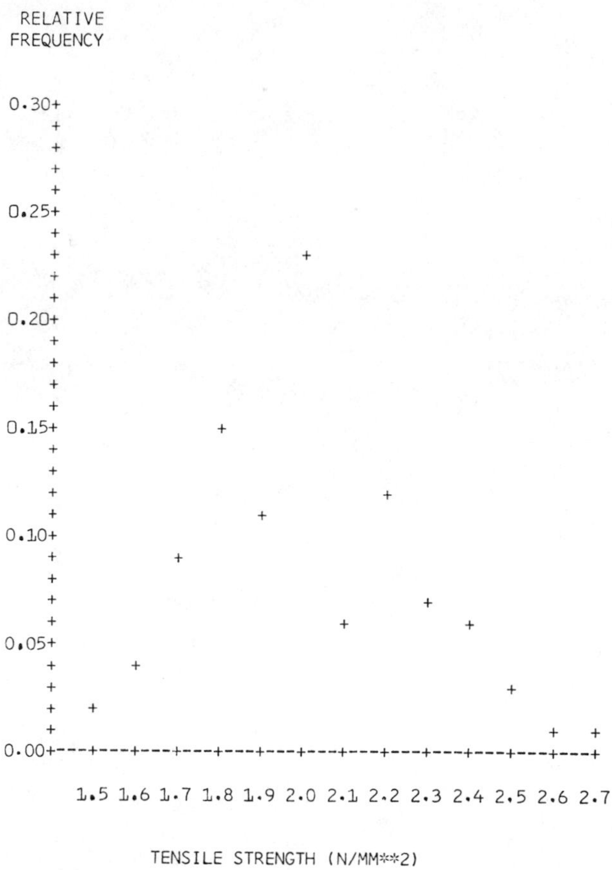

Figure 2.7 Histogram plot

4. FORMAT statements can be used to plot schematic graphs and histograms on a line printer. In this example, a histogram showing the relative frequencies of tensile strengths for concrete specimens is plotted. A relative frequency is defined here to be the number of results falling in a particular range divided by the total number of results. For the values given in Table 2.5, the histogram shown in Fig. 2.7 is produced. The program and data cards are shown in Fig. 2.8 and should be studied with the following explanatory notes:
   (a) Values of tensile strength to be printed along the ordinate axis are determined and stored in array *TS*.

```
      INTEGER PLUS,SPACE,CHARS(53)
      REAL TS(13),FD(13)
      DO 1 I=1,13
1     TS(I)=1.4+FLOAT(I)/10.0
      READ(5,50)(FD(I),I=1,13)
      READ(5, 51)PLUS,SPACE
      WRITE(6, 60)
      DO 10 I=1,30
      I30=31-I
      DO 11 J=2,53
11    CHARS(J)=SPACE
      CHARS(1)=PLUS
      IF(I30/5*5.NE.I30)GOTO 12
      ORD=FLOAT(I30)/100.0
      WRITE(6, 61)ORD
      GOTO 13
12    WRITE(6, 62)
13    DO 14 J=1,13
      IFD=FD(J)*100.001
      IF(IFD.NE.I30)GOTO 14
      IX=4*J+1
      CHARS(IX)=PLUS
14    CONTINUE
10    WRITE(6, 63)(CHARS(J),J=1,53)
      WRITE(6, 64)(TS(I),I=1,13)
50    FORMAT(13F3.2)
51    FORMAT(2A1)
60    FORMAT(1H1,9H^RELATIVE/10H^FREQUENCY//)
61    FORMAT(1H^,F4.2)
62    FORMAT(1H^)
63    FORMAT(1H+,4X,53A1)
64    FORMAT(1H^,5H0.00+,13(4H---+)//
     17X,13F4.1///14X,27H^TENSILE^STRENGTH^(N/MM**2))
      STOP
      END
```

Data Cards

```
.02.04.09.15.11.23.06.12.07.06.03.01.01
+^
```

Figure 2.8 Histogram program

(b) Values of relative frequency for a particular test are input and stored in array *FD*. Characters to be used for plotting are input and stored in variables SPACE and PLUS.

(c) The title of the vertical axis is printed.

(d) The DO statement with terminating label 10 is started. Each run through the statements within its control sets up and prints the characters forming a line of the histogram. The first character of each line is set to + and the next 52 characters are initially assigned the space character. The characters used for a line are stored in array CHARS.

On every fifth line the appropriate value of relative frequency is to be printed alongside the vertical axis. The program checks whether it is dealing with such a line and prints either a value or a blank record.

(e) The program then starts the DO statement with terminating label 14. This loop is executed 13 times, once for each of the ranges of tensile strength. The values of relative frequencies input are compared in turn against the value corresponding to the vertical axis value of the line to be output. When there is agreement the character stored in PLUS replaces the space character in CHARS which occupies the position corresponding to that particular tensile strength.

(f) The statement with the terminating label 10 of the outer DO statement causes the characters stored in CHARS to be printed. The carriage control character in the corresponding FORMAT is a +, and therefore no new line is taken.

(g) When the histogram has been plotted, a WRITE statement causes the text and the values from array *TS*, to be printed at the foot of the figure.

5. To input four values from each of a deck of N cards with columns 1–10, 21–30, 41–50, 61–70 reserved for comments,

```
      READ(5,58)N, (POINT(I), (STRAIN(I, J), J=1, 3), I=1, N)
58    FORMAT(I5/4(10X, E10.4))
```

From the first card, the value of *N*, right justified in the first five columns, is transmitted. From each of the following *N* cards, floating-point numbers in columns 11–20, 31–40, 51–60, 71–80 are transmitted. A typical data card following the first one could be

```
POINT∧∧∧∧∧∧∧∧∧∧10.E1∧STRAIN∧A=∧∧1.234E−5∧STRAIN∧B=∧∧3.412E−6
∧STRAIN∧C=∧−1.289E−5
```

2.11.10 FORMAT specification during execution

For programs that use a variety of data, it can be convenient to define a FORMAT specification as part of the data. This is done by replacing the FORMAT label in the corresponding READ and WRITE statements by an array name. The appropriate FORMAT specification, which must consist of all of the field descriptors, separators and parentheses necessary, cannot include the H descriptor.

For example, to transmit information punched on *N* cards with the layout of values specified on the first data card, one could use

```
      REAL FOT(9), DATA(1000)
      READ(5, 52)N, FOT
      READ(5, FOT)(DATA(I), I=1, N)
52    FORMAT(I5, 9A4)
```

The first data card for 30 values punched 8 to a card could be

```
∧∧∧30∧∧(8E10.4)
```

2.11.11 Secondary storage control statements

When a program transmits information to and from magnetic tapes and disks, the positioning of the read/write head can be manipulated to access a particular record. A set of records on a secondary storage unit is called a 'file' and each file is associated with an INTEGER number by a control statement that precedes the FORTRAN program statements. Definitions of such statements are given in manuals for particular operating systems.

Records can be formatted using the techniques described above, but it is more usual to use unformatted records that hold a copy of the binary patterns of values stored in a computer.

READ and WRITE statements without a FORMAT label are used to transmit information in the next record. When there is no input list, the reading head is moved to the start of the next record. Thus, the READ statement can be used to move the head forward to reach a desired record.

There are two statements for moving the read/write head back towards the start of a file:

BACKSPACE *n*

REWIND *n*

A BACKSPACE statement positions the read/write head at the start of the record which was last transmitted. A REWIND statement positions the read/write head at the start of a file. *n* is the INTEGER constant or variable associated with the particular magnetic tape transport or disk file. It should be mentioned that many computer systems have their own idiosyncrasies when handling secondary storage, and local manuals should always be consulted.

In Standard FORTRAN, there is no means of altering data in a record and retaining the following records. To amend a file, it is necessary to copy it to a second file and to make the alterations while the new file is being set up.

To illustrate control of secondary storage, a number of examples are given.

1. To transmit the contents of two-dimensional array *D* having 30 rows and 50 columns to a magnetic disk file associated with the number 20 in such a manner as to have a distinct record for each row:

```
         REWIND 20
         DO 10 I=1, 30
   10    WRITE(20)(D(I, J), J=1, 50)
```

2. To transmit the contents of the disk file to array *A* so that the rows of *A* are in reverse order to those of *D*. The first row of *A* is the same as the last row of *D* and so on:

```
         DO 11 I=1, 30
         BACKSPACE 20
         READ(20)(A(I, J), J=1, 50)
         BACKSPACE 20
   11    CONTINUE
```

3. To transmit the values of every second record of the file, starting at the beginning, into rows of array *C*:

```
         REWIND 20
         DO 12 I=1, 15
         READ(20)
         READ(20)(C(I, J), J=1, 50)
   12    CONTINUE
```

4. To form a new file composed of the first 20 rows, and the last 5 rows of *D*, with the first five rows of *A* replacing the 21st–25th rows of *D*. Suppose that the contents of *D* are no longer available in the primary store.

```
         REWIND 20
         REWIND 21
         DO 5 I=1, 20
         READ(20)(X(J), J=1, 50)
    5    WRITE(21)(X(J), J=1, 50)
         DO 6 I=21, 25
         READ(20)
    6    WRITE(21)(A(I-20, J), J=1, 50)
         DO 7 I=26, 30
         READ(20)(X(J), J=1, 50)
    7    WRITE(21)(X(J), J=1, 50)
```

2.12 DATA STATEMENT

A DATA statement sets values to variable names before a program is executed. It is thus a non-executable statement and takes the form

```
DATA V/D/
```

or

```
DATA V1/D1/, V2/D2/, . . . , Vi/Di/, . . . , Vn/Dn/
```

where V_i is the list of variable names or array elements with commas as separators, and D_i is a list of corresponding initial values for those variables. Any of the constants in a D_i list may be preceded by $IC*$, where IC is an INTEGER constant. This has the same effect as repeating that constant IC times.

For example, to set $A = 6.0, B = 12.0$, and $C(1, 3) = 1.E6$, either of the statements

```
DATA A/6.0/, B/12.0/, C(1, 3)/1.E6/
```

or

```
DATA A, B, C(1, 3)/6.0, 12.0, 1.E6/
```

could be used.

To set text data, Hollerith descriptors are used. For example, to set PLUS to + and SPACE to ∧,

```
DATA PLUS, SPACE/1H+, 1H∧/
```

could be used.

Items listed in a COMMON statement (see Sec. 2.14.2) can be initialized only by a DATA statement in a BLOCK DATA sub-program (Sec. 2.14.3).

2.13 SUB-PROGRAMS

Programs often require the same sequence of operations to be incorporated into different places. For example, matrix multiplication or solution of linear simultaneous equations may be needed at different stages in a solution. Program writing and comprehension is made much easier when such routines appear once only and are referred to when needed. FORTRAN allows them to be coded as SUBROUTINE and FUNCTION sub-programs. A complete program can thus consist of a main segment and a number of sub-programs.

2.13.1 FUNCTION sub-program

Standard supplied FUNCTIONs have already been described (see Sec. 2.9). All FUNCTIONs are referenced in the same way, by including a FUNCTION reference in an arithmetic or logical expression. Standard FUNCTIONs and statement FUNCTIONs (see Sec. 2.13.3) return single values, by means of the FUNCTION name, to the expressions in which they are referenced. FUNCTION sub-programs can also amend values of the actual arguments and of items in COMMON blocks (see Sec. 2.14).

A FUNCTION sub-program consists of a FUNCTION statement, followed by statements to give its name a value, at least one RETURN statement, and an END line. A FUNCTION statement has the form

$$\text{T FUNCTION F}(A_1, A_2, \ldots, A_i, \ldots, A_n)$$

T is an optional type declaration (see Sec. 2.5) for the FUNCTION name F, which should be unique. Each A_i is a 'dummy' argument, of which there must be at least one.

To avoid complication, each dummy argument should be restricted to a variable or array name. The dummy arguments correspond to names used in the body of the sub-program. The 'actual' arguments in the FUNCTION reference replace the dummy arguments and should correspond in number and type with them. However, actual arguments can also be expressions.

For example, a FUNCTION sub-program to calculate sinh (x) from $(e^x - e^{-x})/2$ is

```
FUNCTION SINH(X)
X1=EXP(X)
X11=1.0/X1
SINH=(X 1-X11)*0.5
RETURN
END
```

and typical calling sequences referencing the FUNCTION are

```
D=A+B*SINH(E)
H=C*B/SINH(Q(I)*D)
Z=SINH(6.0)
```

Note that a value must be assigned to the name of the FUNCTION. The values of actual arguments can be changed in a sub-program, as can values in a COMMON block (see Sec. 2.14). Variable and array names not included in the list of dummy arguments, nor in a COMMON block, have no association with variables having the same name in other program segments. Labels in a program segment are only relevant in that segment. For simplicity, a variable name in a COMMON or EQUIVALENCE statement should not be used in an argument list. Also for simplicity, arrays in a sub-program should contain the same number of elements as corresponding arrays in the program units in which they are referenced.

As a further example, consider a calling statement and FUNCTION subprogram to assign the square root of the modulus of the sum of elements I to J of array Q to S, and to transfer control to statement labelled 10 if the sum is < 0, to 11 if it equals 0 and to 7 when it is > 0.

```
REAL FUNCTION SUM(A, N, M, S)
DIMENSION A(M)
SUM=0.0
DO 10 I=N, M
```

```
10      SUM=SUM+A(I)
        S=SQRT(ABS(SUM))
        RETURN
        END
```

A suitable statement is

```
IF(SUM(Q, I, J, S)) 10, 11, 7
```

In this example, only the value of argument S is changed in the program segment containing the calling statement. There must be statements labelled 10, 11, and 7 in the calling segment and the statement labelled 10 has no connection with the one labelled 10 in the FUNCTION sub-program.

2.13.2 SUBROUTINE sub-program

A SUBROUTINE sub-program is referenced by a CALL statement (see Sec. 2.10.9) in another program segment. No value is associated with a SUBROUTINE name, which, therefore, has no type, and values are returned to the calling unit by assigning new values to actual arguments or to items in COMMON blocks.

A CALL statement transfers control to the first executable statement in the named SUBROUTINE. When a RETURN statement is executed in that SUBROUTINE, control is transferred to the statement immediately following the CALL statement in the calling program segment.

A SUBROUTINE statement has one of the general forms

$$\text{SUBROUTINE S}(A_1, A_2, \ldots, A_i, \ldots, A_n)$$

or $\quad$ SUBROUTINE S

where S is the SUBROUTINE name, which must be a unique and valid FORTRAN name, and each A_i is a dummy argument. Following the SUBROUTINE statements are any type statements, executable and non-executable statements, including at least one RETURN statement, and finally an END line.

An example of a SUBROUTINE to print error messages is

```
        SUBROUTINE ERMES(IER)
        WRITE(6, 50)IER
        STOP
        RETURN
50      FORMAT(13H∧ERROR∧NUMBER, I4)
        END
```

Note that a RETURN statement must be included, even when it can never be executed. Possible calling statements are

```
        CALL ERMES(10)
and     IF(E.GT.0.0) CALL ERMES (99)
```

2.13.3 Statement FUNCTION

When a FUNCTION can be written as a single statement, it may be written as a statement FUNCTION rather than as a FUNCTION sub-program. Statement FUNCTIONs must appear immediately before the executable statements of a program segment and are only available in that program unit. A statement FUNCTION has the general form

$$F(A_1, A_2, \ldots, A_i, \ldots, A_n)=E$$

where F is the FUNCTION name, each A_i is a dummy argument, and E is an arithmetic or logical expression. F must be a valid, unique FORTRAN name. Its type is fixed by the first letter of that name, unless the name appears in an earlier type declaration statement (see Sec. 2.5). The expression E should not refer to array names, nor to array elements.

An example of a statement FUNCTION follows. The program statements input the densities and radii of a number of circular sections and output their weights per unit length.

```
      REAL AREA, PI
      DATA PI/3.1415926536/
C     STATEMENT FUNCTION DEFINITION FOLLOWS
      AREA(R)=PI*R**2
      DO 10 I=1, 100
      READ(5, 50) DENS, RADIUS
      WT=DENS*AREA(RADIUS)
10    WRITE(6, 61)DENS, RADIUS, WT
```

2.13.4 EXTERNAL statement

When a sub-program name appears as an actual argument of another sub-program, it must be identified as such in an EXTERNAL statement at the head of the program segment in which the calling statement appears. The form of an EXTERNAL statement is

$$\text{EXTERNAL } F_1, F_2, \ldots, F_i, \ldots, F_n$$

where each F_i is the name of a sub-program which is used as the actual argument of another sub-program. Neither a statement FUNCTION name, nor an intrinsic FUNCTION name (see Sec. 2.9.1), may be used as an argument and neither may, therefore, appear in an EXTERNAL statement.

For illustration, consider the following segments of a program:

```
      EXTERNAL SIN, COS, TAN

      READ(5, 51)A
```

```
CALL TRIG(SIN, A, B)
CALL TRIG(COS, A, C)
CALL TRIG(TAN, A, D)
WRITE(6, 61)A, B, C, D
-
-
END

SUBROUTINE TRIG(F, A, B)
B=F(A)
RETURN
END

FUNCTION TAN(X)
TAN=SIN(X)/COS(X)
RETURN
END
```

SIN and COS are names of basic external FUNCTIONs and, when they appear in the argument list of another sub-program, must be defined in an EXTERNAL statement. TAN is the name of a FUNCTION supplied by the programmer and, as it appears in an argument list, it too must appear in the EXTERNAL statement. The use of SIN and COS in TAN are for reassurance that FUNCTION names do not have to appear as arguments.

2.13.5 Programming efficiency

SUBROUTINEs and FUNCTIONs are true sub-programs. Their local variables are independent of those having the same names in other program segments and they can be compiled as independent programs. These factors have important consequences for programming efficiency. By splitting complex programs into segments, each part can be written and checked separately. Since many programs require sub-programs to accomplish commonplace tasks, such as solution of linear simultaneous equations, such sub-programs should be written with ease of usage in mind. A user, or group of users, should aim to collect a library of efficient sub-programs.

To ensure maximum versatility when arrays are involved, FORTRAN permits INTEGER variables to be used in place of constants in a DIMENSION statement of a sub-program. In this case both the array name and the variables must appear as dummy arguments. For example,

```
SUBROUTINE TR(A, N, M)
DIMENSION A(N, M)
```

The actual arguments in a CALL statement corresponding to N and M should be INTEGER expressions whose values correspond to the numbers of rows and columns of the array whose name is paired with A in the CALL statement.

This facility is not intended as a means of changing an array size during execution of a program, but to enable sub-programs to be transferable between programs which use arrays of different size. 'A' should be paired only with arrays of the same size in any particular program.

2.14 CONTROL OF PRIMARY STORAGE

A programmer can control the storage of variables using COMMON and EQUIVALENCE statements. When used, they are placed amongst other non-executable statements at the head of program segments.

2.14.1 COMMON statement

COMMON statements enable a programmer to specify that certain areas of storage are reserved for particular variables in different program segments. Thus, values obtained in one segment can be used in another, without them being referred to in an argument list.

Unlabelled, or blank, COMMON statements take the form

$$\text{COMMON } V_1, V_2, \ldots, V_i, \ldots, V_n$$

where each V_i is a variable or array name. Arrays can have their dimensions set in a COMMON statement provided they are not set in any other type or DIMENSION statement. The storage required for the items listed in a COMMON statement is referred to as a 'COMMON block'.

For example, if the COMMON statements of a main program and a sub-program were

```
C     IN MAIN PROGRAM SEGMENT
      COMMON I, J, X(100)
```

and

```
C     IN A SUB-PROGRAM
      COMMON K, L, Y(100)
```

the variables I and K refer to the same value; J and L refer to the same value and there is a one-to-one correspondence between the elements of X and Y such that $X(M) = Y(M)$, for $M = 1$ to 100.

Items in COMMON statements need not be of identical form and blank COMMON blocks need not be of the same length. For example,

```
C     IN MAIN PROGRAM SEGMENT
      COMMON I, J, X(100)
```

and

```
C       IN A SUB-PROGRAM
        COMMON M(2), A(50), B(10), C
```

produces the following correspondence between variables:

main program	sub-program
I	M(1)
J	M(2)
X(1)	A(1)
X(2)	A(2)
.	.
.	.
.	.
X(50)	A(50)
X(51)	B(1)
X(52)	B(2)
.	.
.	.
.	.
X(60)	B(10)
X(61)	C
.	
.	
.	
X(100)	

As representations of variables of different type may occupy different numbers of computer words, it is safest to pair only variables of the same type in COMMON statements.

The elements of two- and three-dimensional arrays are stored in the orders described in Sec. 2.10.5.3. Since operations on an array of one-dimension are performed more efficiently than on a multi-dimensional array, the following can be a useful construction:

```
C       IN MAIN PROGRAM SEGMENT
        COMMON X, A, B(3, 2)
```

and

```
C       IN A SUB PROGRAM
        COMMON X, C, D(6)
```

This produces the following correspondence:

main program	sub-program
X	X
A	C
B(1, 1)	D(1)
B(2, 1)	D(2)
B(3, 1)	D(3)
B(1, 2)	D(4)
B(2, 2)	D(5)
B(3, 2)	D(6)

Often, variables are needed temporarily, to hold intermediate data. By associating such variables in different segments with the same storage space, a saving can be achieved. It is good practice to use unlabelled COMMON as a 'scratch pad' in this way. For example,

```
C     IN MAIN PROGRAM SEGMENT
         COMMON SPAD(1000)
C     IN A SUB PROGRAM
         COMMON A(50), B(100, 2), C(250)
C     IN ANOTHER SUB PROGRAM
         COMMON A, Z(20, 20), I, J, L(5, 10, 10)
```

Pairing variables of the same type is less important in this situation, as the aim is to conserve memory and not to pass values between program segments.

2.14.2 Labelled COMMON blocks

A COMMON statement can also take the form

$$\text{COMMON}/N_1/V_1$$

$$\text{COMMON}/N_1/V_1/N_2/V_2 \cdots /N_i/V_i \cdots /N_n/V_n$$

where each N_i is a valid FORTRAN name that should not be used for any other purpose. It has no value or type associated with it. Each V_i is a list of variable and array names separated by commas.

Labelled COMMON blocks are used almost exclusively for transferring values between program segments. The length (number of words) of a labelled COMMON block must be the same in each program segment in which it appears.

2.14.3 BLOCK DATA sub-program

A BLOCK DATA statement heads a BLOCK DATA sub-program, and this is used only to give initial values to items in labelled COMMON blocks. Items in unlabelled or blank COMMON blocks cannot be initialized. A BLOCK DATA sub-program may contain only type declaration, DIMENSION, COMMON, EQUIVALENCE, and DATA statements, and an END line. All of the variables in a labelled COMMON block must appear in the list even when only some of them are to be given initial values. An example of a BLOCK DATA sub-program is

```
BLOCKDATA
COMMON/CONST/PI, GAUSS, SYMB(3), FLAG
REAL GAUSS(2)
LOGICAL FLAG
DATA PI, GAUSS(1), FLAG/3.141592654, – .5773502692, .TRUE./
DATA SYMB(1)/1H+/, SYMB(2)/1H–/, SYMB(3)/1H*/
END
```

The DATA statements must follow the type declaration and COMMON statements.

2.14.4 EQUIVALENCE statement

An EQUIVALENCE statement is a non-executable statement that has the general form

$$\text{EQUIVALENCE}\,(V_1),\ (V_2),\ \ldots\ (V_i),\ \ldots\ (V_n)$$

where each V_i is a list of variable names and array elements that are to share the same storage location. A dummy argument may not appear in an EQUIVALENCE list and an element in a two- or three-dimensional array may be referred to by a single subscript. For example, the statements

```
DIMENSION XY(100, 2), A(140), Z(20, 3)
EQUIVALENCE(XY(1, 1), A(1), Z(1))
```

cause the first elements of all the arrays to occupy the same storage location. As array elements are stored sequentially, the following correspondence between array elements is also ensured:

```
XY(1, 1)     A(1)      Z(1, 1)
XY(2, 1)     A(2)      Z(2, 1)
   .          .           .
   .          .           .
XY(20, 1)    A(20)     Z(20, 1)
XY(21, 1)    A(21)     Z(1, 2)
```

```
XY(22, 1)      A(22)      Z(2, 2)
    .            .          .
    .            .          .
XY(60, 1)      A(60)      Z(20, 3)
    .            .
    .            .
XY(40, 2)      A(140)
```

Thus, for example, whenever $XY(21, 1)$ or $A(21)$ or $Z(1, 2)$ is assigned a new value, they all take the new value.

The EQUIVALENCE statement is used to save space in a particular program segment when information needed in one part is not needed by later statements. It is useful when it is convenient to store data in a different way for further processing. This usually entails putting data assembled in a two-dimensional array into a one-dimensional array. A further use of the EQUIVALENCE statement is to knit together parts of a program written by different people. It is often easier to retain different variable names referring to a single quantity than to change one of them throughout a part of a program.

Programmers attempting great sophistication by producing intricate interrelationships between variables listed in EQUIVALENCE and COMMON statements can create considerable trouble for themselves. For the vast majority of applications, variables in COMMON and EQUIVALENCE statements can be kept separate. Aim always for simplicity and ease of comprehension. For the same reasons, avoid pairing variables of different types in EQUIVALENCE and COMMON lists. When it is absolutely necessary to go counter to these guidelines, consult a FORTRAN reference manual and check results thoroughly.

2.15 ORDERING OF SPECIFICATION STATEMENTS

For all program segments, except BLOCK DATA sub-programs (Sec. 2.14.3), there are no rules for the order of specification statements. However, many compilers are restrictive and the following sequence is generally acceptable.

1. Type declaration (REAL, INTEGER, LOGICAL, DOUBLE PRECISION, COMPLEX – in any order).
2. Subscript declaration (DIMENSION).
3. Storage control (COMMON, Labelled COMMON, EQUIVALENCE).
4. Functions used as arguments (EXTERNAL).
5. Preset values (DATA).
6. Statement FUNCTIONs.

2.16 LITTLE-USED FACILITIES

In this section, brief mention is given to statements allowable in Standard FORTRAN which, in the authors' experiences, are little used.

2.16.1 ASSIGN statement

This sets a value to the variable of an assigned GOTO statement. It has the general form

ASSIGN label TO IV

where label is a statement label in an assigned GOTO statement and *IV* is the name of an INTEGER variable in the same statement. For example,

ASSIGN 10 TO IJK

2.16.2 Assigned GOTO statement

This has the form

GOTO IV, (label 1, label 2, . . . , label *i*, . . . , label *n*)

where *IV* is an INTEGER variable which has been given a value in an ASSIGN statement prior to execution of the assigned GOTO statement. Each label *i* corresponds to a statement label in the same program segment. *IV* must be equal to one of the label *i* values, and control is transferred to the statement with that label.

2.16.3 ENDFILE statement

This has the general form

ENDFILE *n*

where *n* is the INTEGER constant or variable associated with a magnetic tape transport or disk file. ENDFILE statements exist in FORTRAN as a hangover from the past, when it was necessary to mark magnetic tapes for convenience of off-line printing. They should not be used with secondary storage media that is read under program control as there is no way in Standard FORTRAN of reading an ENDFILE record.

2.16.4 COMPLEX FUNCTIONs

In the authors' experiences, programs dealing with solution to civil engineering problems rarely need to use COMPLEX quantities. Calculations involving COMPLEX items have not been dealt with in any detail and an interested reader should consult a more advanced text. To assist users, FORTRAN supplies Basic External FUNCTION CABS, and Intrinsic FUNCTIONs REAL, AIMAG, CMPLX, CONJG in addition to those described in Sec. 2.9.

1. CABS has a COMPLEX expression as argument and returns its modulus as a REAL value.
2. REAL has a COMPLEX expression as argument and returns its real part as a REAL value.
3. AIMAG has a COMPLEX expression as argument and returns its imaginary part as a REAL value.

4. CMPLX has two REAL expressions as arguments and returns a COMPLEX value with the value of the first expression as its real part and the value of the second expression as its imaginary part.
5. CONJG has a COMPLEX expression as argument and returns its conjugate as a COMPLEX value.

2.17. EXAMPLE PROGRAMS

To illustrate use of many of the facilities described, two complete programs are explained. The first, to determine bending moments over a plate, involves mainly calculations with floating-point quantities. The second, to print a calendar for a specified year, involves sorting character strings for printing in a particular order and with manipulations performed using INTEGER arithmetic. Flowcharts are not provided and should be constructed by the reader from the FORTRAN texts.

2.17.1 Plate bending moments

The text of a program to determine values of bending moments M_x, M_y, M_{xy} at a grid of stations over a uniformly loaded, rectangular, simply supported plate, is given in Fig. 2.9. The stations are uniformly spaced on NXS lines parallel to the y axis and on NYS lines parallel to x, as shown on Fig. 2.10.

Moments are evaluated from the series

$$M_x = q\pi^2 a^2 \sum_{m=1,3}^{\infty} \left[\frac{4}{m^3 \pi^5} + m^2 A_m (1-\nu) \cosh \frac{m\pi y}{a} + m^2 B_m \left((1-\nu) \frac{m\pi y}{a} \sinh \frac{m\pi y}{a} - 2\nu \cosh \frac{m\pi y}{a} \right) \right] \sin \frac{m\pi x}{a}$$

$$M_y = q\pi^2 a^2 \sum_{m=1,3}^{\infty} \left[\frac{4\nu}{m^3 \pi^5} + m^2 A_m (\nu-1) \cosh \frac{m\pi y}{a} + m^2 B_m \left((\nu-1) \frac{m\pi y}{a} \sinh \frac{m\pi y}{a} - 2\cosh \frac{m\pi y}{a} \right) \right] \sin \frac{m\pi x}{a}$$

$$M_{xy} = (1-\nu) q a^2 \pi^2 \sum_{m=1,3}^{\infty} \left[m^2 A_m \sinh \frac{m\pi y}{a} + m^2 B_m \left(\sinh \frac{m\pi y}{a} + \frac{m\pi y}{a} \cosh \frac{m\pi y}{a} \right) \right] \cos \frac{m\pi x}{a}$$

where

$$B_m = \frac{2.0}{\pi^5 m^5 \cosh \alpha_m}$$

$$A_m = -B_m (\alpha_m \tanh \alpha_m + 2)$$

$$\alpha_m = \frac{m\pi b}{2a}$$

```
DIMENSION BMX(20,20),BMY(20,20),BMXY(20,20),MOM(3)
REAL NU,NU1,MXT,MYT,MXYT,MX,MY,MXY
LOGICAL XM,YM,XYM
COMMON/TITLE/MOM
DATA PI/3.141592654/
C BMX,BMY,BMXY STORE VALUES OF BENDING MOMENT ON A GRID
C OF NXS*NYS STATIONS IN THE X AND Y DIRECTIONS RESP
C MX,MY,MXY STORE VALUES OF MOMENTS DURING CALCULATIONS
C MXT,MYT,MXYT STORE THE LAST TERM CALCULATED
C NU STORES POISSONS RATIO, Q THE LOAD INTENSITY, A AND B
C SIDE LENGTHS,MAX STORES THE MAXIMUM NUMBER OF TERMS
C TO BE SUMMED,AND TOL STORES THE TOLERANCE TO LIMIT THE
C NUMBER OF TERMS ACCORDING TO THE DESIRED ACCURACY
      READ(5,50)Q,A,B,NU,NXS,NYS,MAX,TOL
      WRITE(6,60)Q,A,B,NU,NXS,NYS,MAX,TOL
C BMX,BMY,BMXY SET WITH UNLIKELY VALUES TO INDICATE
C WHEN CONVERGENCE NOT ATTAINED
      DO 200 I=1,NXS
      DO 200 J=1,NYS
      BMX(J,I)=1.E40
      BMY(J,I)=1.E40
  200 BMXY(J,I)=1.E40
C SET CONSTANTS
      QAP=Q*PI**2*A**2
      P4=4.0/PI**5
      NU1=1.0-NU
      PA=PI/A
      PBA=PI*B/(2.0*A)
      X=0.0
C DO STATEMENTS CONTROL STATION SELECTION, X AND
C Y ARE STATION CO-ORDINATES
      DO 100 I=1,NXS
      Y=-B/2.0
      X=X+A/(1.0+FLOAT(NXS))
      PXA=PA*X
      DO 100 J=1,NYS
      Y=Y+B/(1.0+FLOAT(NYS))
      PYA=PA*Y
      KX=0
      KY=0
      KXY=0
      MX=0.0
      MY=0.0
      MXY=0.0
      XM=.FALSE.
      YM=.FALSE.
      XYM=.FALSE.
C SUMMATION OF SERIES
      DO 30 M=1,MAX,2
```

Figure 2.9 Program for the plate bending moment

```
C CHECK IF ALL 3 SERIES CONVERGED
      IF(XM .AND. YM .AND. XYM) GOTO 100
      RM=FLOAT(M)
      PYAM=RM*PYA
      IC1=(IT-1)*6+1
      IC2=IC1+5
      PXAM=RM*PXA
      PM=PA/RM**3
      ALFM=RM*PBA
      BM=PM/2.0
      AM=-BM*(ALFM*TANH(ALFM)+2.0)
      SY=E1(PYAM, ALFM,-1.0)
      CY=E1(PYAM, ALFM, 1.0)
      SX=SIN(PXAM)
      CX=COS(PXAM)
      IF(XM) GOTO 10
      MXT=QAP*(PM+AM*NU1*CY+BM*(NU1*PYAM*SY-2.0*NU*CY))*SX
      CALL CONV(MXT,MX,KX,BMX(J,I),TOL,XM)
 10   IF(YM) GOTO 20
      MYT=QAP*(PM*NU-AM*NU1*CY-BM*(NU1*PYAM*SY+2.0*CY))*SX
      CALL CONV(MYT,MY,KY,BMY(J,I),TOL,YM)
 20   IF(XYM) GOTO 30
      MXYT=QAP*NU1*(AM*SY+BM*(SY+PYAM*CY))*CX
      CALL CONV(MXYT,MXY,KXY,BMXY(J,I),TOL,XYM)
 30   CONTINUE
C IF DO STATEMENT WITH TERMINATING LABEL 30 IS COMPLETED
C CONVERGENCE OF AT LEAST ONE OF THE SERIES NOT ATTAINED
      WRITE(6,61)X,Y,MX,XM,MY,YM,MXY,XYM
 100  CONTINUE
C PRINT RESULTS
      WRITE(6,62)
      CALL RES(BMX,NXS,NYS,1,A,B)
      CALL RES(BMY,NXS,NYS,2,A,B)
      CALL RES(BMXY,NXS,NYS,3,A,B)
 50   FORMAT(3E13.6,F3.2,3I2,E11.4)

 60   FORMAT(1H1,17HLOAD^INTENSITY^Q=,E13.6/
     13H^A=,E13.6,5X, 2HB=,E13.6,5X,15HPOISSONS^RATIO=,F4.2/
     25H^NXS=,I2,4HNYS=,I2,5X,18HMAX.^NO.^OF^TERMS=,I2/
     35H^TOL=,E11.4)

 61   FORMAT(1H^,20HSERIES^NOT^CONVERGED/3H^X=,E13.6,2HY=,E13.6/
     14H^MX=,E13.6,7HSTATUS=,L2/
     24H^MY=,E13.6,7HSTATUS=,L2/
     35H^MXY=,E13.6,7HSTATUS=,L2)
 62   FORMAT(//16H^BENDING^MOMENTS/1H^,15(1H*)/)

      STOP
      END
```

Figure 2.9 (*continued*)

```
      SUBROUTINE RES(BMOM,NXS,NYS,I,A,B)
      DIMENSION BMOM(20,20),MOM(3),X(6)
      COMMON/TITLE/MOM
C TABLES PRINTED FOR 6 VALUES OF X,NT=NO. OF TABLES
      NT=(NXS-1)/6+1
      DO 600 IT=1,NT
      WRITE(6,60)MOM(I)
      IF(IC2 .GT. NXS)IC2=NXS
      J=0
      DO 601 IC=IC1,IC2
      J=J+1
601   X(J)=A/(FLOAT(NXS)+1.0)*FLOAT(IC)
      WRITE(6,61)(X(IX),IX=1,J)
      Y=-B/2.0
      DO 602 IR=1,NYS
      Y=Y+B/(1.0+FLOAT(NYS))
602   WRITE(6,62)Y,(BMOM(IR,IC),IC=IC1,IC2)
600   WRITE(6,63)
      RETURN
60    FORMAT(1H^,50X,A3/1H^,50X,3H---/)
61    FORMAT(//1H^,105(1H*)/1H^,15H^^^^^Y^^^^/X=^^,
     C6E15.6/1H^,105(1H*))
62    FORMAT(1H^,7E15.6)
63    FORMAT(1H^,105(1H*)///)
      END
      BLOCK DATA
      COMMON/TITLE/MOM(3)
      DATA MOM(1),MOM(2),MOM(3)/3HBMX,3HBMY,3HMXY/
      END
      FUNCTION E1(PYAM, ALFM, S)
      E1=EXP(PYAM-ALFM)
      E2=EXP(-PYAM-ALFM)
      E3=EXP(-2.0*ALFM)
      E1=(E1+S*E2)/(1.0+E3)
      RETURN
      END
      SUBROUTINE CONV(MT,M,K,BMOM,TOL,L)
      REAL MT,M
      LOGICAL L
      M=M+MT
      IF(ABS(M).LT. 1.E-30) GOTO 13
      IF(ABS(MT/M).GT.TOL) GOTO 12
13    K=K+1
      IF(K.NE.3) RETURN
      BMOM=M
      L=.TRUE.
12    K=0
      RETURN
      END
```

Figure 2.9 (*continued*)

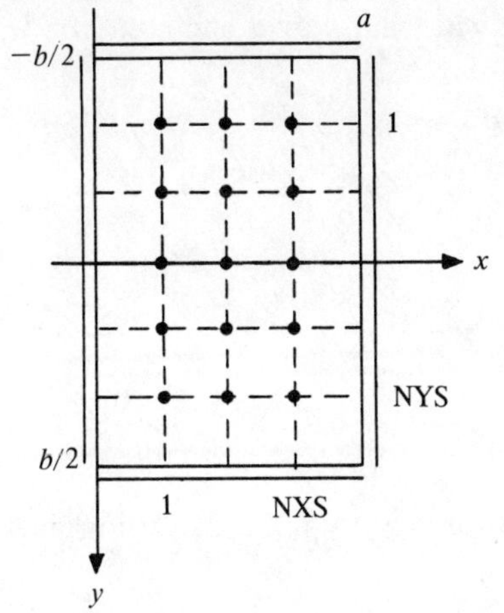

Figure 2.10

Parameters for a particular problem are first read in and printed. The variable *MAX* stores the economic upper limit for summation. A value of 99 is reasonable. The value of variable *TOL* is compared with the last term calculated divided by the sum of the terms calculated. When the value of *TOL* is greater than this ratio for three successive terms the program assumes that sufficient terms have been taken for the specified accuracy. For three-digit accuracy a value of 0.0001 is reasonable.

Logical variables *XM, YM, XYM* are true when the series for M_x, M_y, M_{xy} have converged. The operations to set them are similar for each series and are performed by SUBROUTINE CONV. The moments are stored in arrays *BMX, BMY, BMXY* when convergence is attained. To aid detection of stations at which the specified convergence tolerance was not satisfied, moment values of 1.E40 are printed. It is reasonable to suppose that this value could not be given by any other means, but, for safety, values of unconverged series are printed using the FORMAT with label 61.

The calculations are performed in nested DO loops. *I* controls the count through the stations in the *x* direction and *J* the count through the stations in the *y* direction, using the same terminating statement with label 100. To reduce the number of calculations, values are determined in the outermost loop possible. The DO loop controlled by *M* and with terminating statement labelled 30 contains the operations to sum the series for each station.

Results are printed using the SUBROUTINE RES and values from a typical analysis are shown in Fig. 2.11.

The program does not determine values from the given formulae in a straightforward manner. If it did so it would have to evaluate $e^{m\pi y/a}$ and $e^{m\pi b/2a}$ for increasing values of m and there is a possibility that values of too great a magnitude to be represented in a computer would be needed. This problem is overcome by combining $\cosh \alpha_m$ in the expression for B_m with $\sinh m\pi y/a$ and $\cosh m\pi y/a$, thus:

$$\frac{\sinh \dfrac{m\pi y}{a}}{\cosh \alpha_m} \equiv \frac{e^{m\pi/a(y-b/2)} - e^{-m\pi/a(y+b/2)}}{1 + e^{-m\pi b/a}}$$

and

$$\frac{\cosh \dfrac{m\pi y}{a}}{\cosh \alpha_m} \equiv \frac{e^{m\pi/a(y-b/2)} + e^{-m\pi/a(y+b/2)}}{1 + e^{-m\pi b/a}}$$

As $(y - b/2)$ and $-(y + b/2)$ are both negative for $-b/2 < y < b/2$ overflow does not occur.

```
LØAD INTENSITY Q= 0,250000E 00
A= 0,200000E 01        B= 0,240000E 01        PØISSØNS RATIØ=0,30
NXS= 4NYS= 4           MAX, NØ, ØF TERMS=99
TØL= 0,1000E-03

BENDING MØMENTS
***************

                                        BMX
                                        ---

**********************************************************************************
     Y     /X=      0,400000E 00   0,800000E 00   0,120000E 01   0,160000E 01
  -0,720000E 00     0,287582E-01   0,389821E-01   0,389821E-01   0,287582E-01
  -0,240000E 00     0,416778E-01   0,583109E-01   0,583109E-01   0,416778E-01
   0,240000E 00     0,416778E-01   0,583109E-01   0,583109E-01   0,416778E-01
   0,720000E 00     0,287582E-01   0,389821E-01   0,389821E-01   0,287582E-01
**********************************************************************************

                                        BMY
                                        ---

**********************************************************************************
     Y     /X=      0,400000E 00   0,800000E 00   0,120000E 01   0,160000E 01
  -0,720000E 00     0,245702E-01   0,364078E-01   0,364078E-01   0,245702E-01
  -0,240000E 00     0,308909E-01   0,469815E-01   0,469815E-01   0,308909E-01
   0,240000E 00     0,308909E-01   0,469815E-01   0,469815E-01   0,308909E-01
   0,720000E 00     0,245702E-01   0,364078E-01   0,364078E-01   0,245702E-01
**********************************************************************************

                                        MXY
                                        ---

**********************************************************************************
     Y     /X=      0,400000E 00   0,800000E 00   0,120000E 01   0,160000E 01
  -0,720000E 00     0,209452E-01   0,766115E-02  -0,766115E-02  -0,209452E-01
  -0,240000E 00     0,730886E-02   0,273483E-02  -0,273483E-02  -0,730886E-02
   0,240000E 00    -0,730886E-02  -0,273483E-02   0,273483E-02   0,730886E-02
   0,720000E 00    -0,209452E-01  -0,766115E-02   0,766115E-02   0,209452E-01
**********************************************************************************
```

Figure 2.11 Bending moments

2.17.2 Calendar

The text of a program to produce a calendar is given in Fig. 2.12 and a typical result is shown in Fig. 2.13. Calculations are performed using INTEGER arithmetic, and results are printed by transmitting characters rather than numerical values.

Data initialization statements set: array DM elements to the number of days in the months; the elements of array NM to abbreviations of the names of the months; the elements of array DS to abbreviations of the names of days of the week; and the elements of array ND to Hollerith representations of dates.

The year for which a calender is required is read in and the day on which 1 January of that year falls is determined. The days are given values 1 to 7, starting with Monday, and the calculation is based on the fact that 1 January in 1982 was a Friday. FUNCTION LEAP is used to take account of the effects of leap years. When the statement labelled 20 is reached, variable DAY holds the required value.

```
      INTEGER WEEK,DAY,YEAR,COUNT,DATES(12,6,7),DM(12)

C DATES STORES CALENDAR FOR EACH OF 12 MONTHS
C DM STORES NO. OF DAYS IN THE MONTHS
      DIMENSION NM(12),ND(32),DS(7),LINE(4,7)
C NM STORES NAMES OF MONTHS, ND STORES NUMBERS OF DAYS IN EACH MONTH,
C DS DAY NAMES, LINE HOLDS A LINE OF CHARACTERS FOR PRINTING
      LOGICAL LEAP
C LEAP IS A LOGICAL FUNCTION THAT IS TRUE FOR A LEAP YEAR

      DATA DM(1),DM(2),DM(3),DM(4),DM(5),DM(6),DM(7),DM(8),DM(9),
     1DM(10),DM(11),DM(12)/31,28,31,30,31,30,31,31,30,31,30,31/,
     2NM(1),NM(2),NM(3),NM(4),NM(5),NM(6),NM(7),NM(8),NM(9),NM(10),
     3NM(11),NM(12)/3HJAN,3HFEB,3HMAR,3HAPR,3HMAY,3HJUN,
     43HJUL,3HAUG,3HSEP,3HOCT,3HNOV,3HDEC/
      DATA ND(1),ND(2),ND(3),ND(4),ND(5),ND(6),ND(7),ND(8),ND(9),
     1ND(10),ND(11),ND(12),ND(13),ND(14),ND(15),ND(16),ND(17),ND(18),
     2ND(19),ND(20),ND(21),ND(22),ND(23),ND(24),ND(25),ND(26),ND(27),
     3ND(28),ND(29),ND(30),ND(31),ND(32)/
     43H^^^,3H^^1,3H^^2,3H^^3,3H^^4,3H^^5,3H^^6,3H^^7,3H^^8,
     53H^^9,3H^10,3H^11,3H^12,3H^13,3H^14,3H^15,3H^16,3H^17,
     63H^18,3H^19,3H^20,3H^21,3H^22,3H^23,3H^24,3H^25,3H^26,
     73H^27,3H^28,3H^29,3H^30,3H^31/
      DATA DS(1),DS(2),DS(3),DS(4),DS(5),DS(6),DS(7)/
     13HMON,3HTUE,3HWED,3HTHU,3HFRI,3HSAT,3HSUN/
C INPUT YEAR FOR WHICH CALENDAR REQUIRED
      READ(5,50)YEAR
      IF(YEAR.LT.1753) GOTO 999
C SET DAY FOR YEAR USING 1982 AS BASE LINE, DAY = DAY OF JAN 1
```

Figure 2.12 Program to print a calendar

```
C IN 1982 JAN 1 WAS A FRI
      DAY=5
      I=1982
 70   IF(I-YEAR)10,20,30
 30   I=I-1
      DAY=DAY-1
      IF(LEAP(I))DAY=DAY-1
      IF(DAY.LT.1)DAY=DAY+7
      GOTO 70
 10   DAY=DAY+1
      IF(LEAP(I))DAY=DAY+1
      I=I+1
      IF(DAY.GT.7)DAY=DAY-7
      GOTO 70
 20   CONTINUE
C SET NO. OF DAYS IN FEB.
      IF(LEAP(YEAR))DM(2)=29
COMPILE CALENDAR FOR PRINTING
      DO 3 K=1,7
      DO 3 J=1,6
      DO 3 I=1,12
 3    DATES(I,J,K)=0
      DO 4 I=1,12
      COUNT=1
      WEEK= 1
 6    DATES(I,WEEK,DAY)=COUNT
      DAY=DAY+1
      IF(DAY.LE.7)GOTO 5
      DAY=DAY-7
      WEEK=WEEK+1
 5    COUNT=COUNT+1
      IF(COUNT.LE.DM(I))GOTO 6
 4    CONTINUE
C PRINT CALENDAR
      WRITE(6,61)YEAR
      DO 8 I=1,9,4
      I3=I+3
      WRITE(6,62)(NM(J),J=I,I3),((DS(J),J=1,7),K=1,4)
      DO 8 WEEK=1,6
      DO 9 M=1,4
      IM1=I+M-1
      DO 9 DAY=1,7
      ID=DATES(IM1,WEEK,DAY)+1
C SET CHARACTERS FOR A LINE OF THE CALENDAR
 9    LINE(M,DAY)=ND(ID)
      WRITE(6,63)((LINE(J,K),K=1,7),J=1,4)
```

Figure 2.12 *(continued)*

```
8     CONTINUE
      STOP
999   WRITE(6,6999)
      STOP
6999 FORMAT(1H^,41HGREGORIAN^CALENDAR^NOT^IN^USE^BEFORE^1753)
50    FORMAT(I4)
61    FORMAT(1H1,10X,I4/11X,4H----)
62    FORMAT(///13X,A3,3(28X,A3)//1H^,4(7A4,3X))
63    FORMAT(4(7(1X,A3),3X))
      END

      LOGICAL FUNCTION LEAP(YEAR)
      INTEGER YEAR
      LEAP=.FALSE.
C YEARS NOT DIVISIBLE BY 4 ARE NOT LEAP YEARS
      IF(YEAR/4*4.NE.YEAR) RETURN
C YEARS DIVISIBLE BY 4 AND NOT BY 100 ARE LEAP YEARS
      IF(YEAR/100*100.NE.YEAR)GOTO 1
C YEARS DIVISIBLE BY 400 ARE LEAP YEARS
      IF(YEAR/400*400.NE.YEAR) RETURN
 1    LEAP=.TRUE.
      RETURN
      END
```

Figure 2.12 *(continued)*

The DO loop controlled by *I* and with terminating label 4 sets values of dates into DATES. The first subscript controls the month, the second subscript the week, and the third subscript the day. A month can contain days in up to 6 weeks and allowance is made for this. The values stored in DATES are not transmitted to the printer but are used to control which of the character sets stored in DS are to be sent.

The main body of output is transmitted in the DO loop controlled by *I* and terminating with the statement labelled 8. Variable *I* counts the three broad bands of output. Each band has a heading dictated by the FORMAT statement with label 62. Each line of output is assembled in array LINE from the character strings stored in array ND using subscripts determined from the values put in DATES. Within each of the bands, 6 lines are printed for the 6 possible weeks in any month. Note that when the value of an element of DATES is zero the first element of ND, which is three spaces, is printed.

```
  1982
  ----

              JAN                             FEB                             MAR                             APR
MØN TUE WED THU FRI SAT SUN    MØN TUE WED THU FRI SAT SUN    MØN TUE WED THU FRI SAT SUN    MØN TUE WED THU FRI SAT SUN
                  1   2   3      1   2   3   4   5   6   7      1   2   3   4   5   6   7                  1   2   3   4
  4   5   6   7   8   9  10      8   9  10  11  12  13  14      8   9  10  11  12  13  14      5   6   7   8   9  10  11
 11  12  13  14  15  16  17     15  16  17  18  19  20  21     15  16  17  18  19  20  21     12  13  14  15  16  17  18
 18  19  20  21  22  23  24     22  23  24  25  26  27  28     22  23  24  25  26  27  28     19  20  21  22  23  24  25
 25  26  27  28  29  30  31                                    29  30  31                     26  27  28  29  30

              MAY                             JUN                             JUL                             AUG
MØN TUE WED THU FRI SAT SUN    MØN TUE WED THU FRI SAT SUN    MØN TUE WED THU FRI SAT SUN    MØN TUE WED THU FRI SAT SUN
                      1   2          1   2   3   4   5   6                  1   2   3   4                              1
  3   4   5   6   7   8   9      7   8   9  10  11  12  13      5   6   7   8   9  10  11      2   3   4   5   6   7   8
 10  11  12  13  14  15  16     14  15  16  17  18  19  20     12  13  14  15  16  17  18      9  10  11  12  13  14  15
 17  18  19  20  21  22  23     21  22  23  24  25  26  27     19  20  21  22  23  24  25     16  17  18  19  20  21  22
 24  25  26  27  28  29  30     28  29  30                     26  27  28  29  30  31         23  24  25  26  27  28  29
 31                                                                                           30  31

              SEP                             ØCT                             NØV                             DEC
MØN TUE WED THU FRI SAT SUN    MØN TUE WED THU FRI SAT SUN    MØN TUE WED THU FRI SAT SUN    MØN TUE WED THU FRI SAT SUN
          1   2   3   4   5                      1   2   3      1   2   3   4   5   6   7              1   2   3   4   5
  6   7   8   9  10  11  12      4   5   6   7   8   9  10      8   9  10  11  12  13  14      6   7   8   9  10  11  12
 13  14  15  16  17  18  19     11  12  13  14  15  16  17     15  16  17  18  19  20  21     13  14  15  16  17  18  19
 20  21  22  23  24  25  26     18  19  20  21  22  23  24     22  23  24  25  26  27  28     20  21  22  23  24  25  26
 27  28  29  30                 25  26  27  28  29  30  31     29  30                         27  28  29  30  31
```

Figure 2.13 Calendar

2.18 CONCLUDING REMARKS

Writing computer programs in FORTRAN IV is not difficult provided a clearly constructed algorithm or flow chart has been produced first. A program can always be improved or written differently. Aim for simplicity and avoid complex constructions. Always bear in mind that a computer program is a means to an end, and not an end in itself. It should be written with a user's requirements in mind, and should, therefore, be easy and economical to use.

Dividing long programs into segments is vital. It makes checking easier and, as sub-programs can be developed in parallel, time is saved. A segmented program is also easier to amend to meet new circumstances.

To avoid needless computations within a program, check to ensure that within nested loops only calculations that provide new values are performed; other operations can be put in outer loops. For the same reason, only use relatively expensive operations, such as evaluation of a mathematical function, when necessary. Assign values of repeated, intermediate calculations to variables to avoid unnecessary operations.

A well written program makes efficient use of storage. Primary storage usually costs considerably more than secondary storage, and transmission of data between them is relatively inexpensive. Use labelled COMMON to transmit information between program segments and use an unlabelled COMMON or EQUIVALENCE statement to produce a scratch-pad for intermediate calculations.

Producing programs to perform calculations efficiently is only one aim of a good computer programmer. Considerable attention should also be given to the problems of the user who has to prepare the data and process the results. Data should be demanded in a logical order, and in an easily understandable form. Whenever possible, data should be in the form in which it is normally handled by a user. Results that are well spaced and annotated are more pleasing and less likely to lead to error than a list of numbers. When appropriate, tabulate or plot results. Always print the values of data actually read into a program to aid checking and identification. If necessary, make provision for data and results to be transmitted in a variety of ways.

Beginners often assume that their programs will work correctly first time. An experienced programmer rarely has this illusion. Do not despair if at first your programs do not work. Try not to blame the computer; the fault is almost certainly yours and can be quickly detected if you are prepared to examine the program objectively. Treat the program as though it had been written by someone else. Check the values of data printed to see if they correspond with those expected. Study each statement expecting to find at least one error. Check the program against the flowchart in the frame of mind that an error is to be expected. Check the algorithm itself.

If that process does not reveal the source of error insert WRITE statements to print intermediate results. Such statements can be controlled by Logical IF statements, using values of controlling variables input with the data to be processed, and can thus be used as often as required. Do not be fooled into believing that a program works until every possible route through it has been checked.

When a program or sub-program has been thoroughly tested, one or more working card decks should be stored in a safe place. Cards deteriorate through handling and a master copy will be found useful. Programs should be documented for future reference. Even program originators forget details of operations and data layout. A program specification should include a description of:

1. the purpose of the program;
2. the method used for the solution;
3. an algorithm or flowchart;
4. the program text;
5. the data layout;
6. the layout of results;
7. a sample of data and results.

Finally, be kind to users. Failure of a program during execution is often caused by faulty data. Whenever possible, insert statements to check the validity of data and to terminate execution with a helpful error message when a mistake is detected. Data input should take place before much processing is done to avoid excessive expense from an abortive run.

SUGGESTIONS FOR FURTHER READING

1. *Standard Fortran Programming Manual*, National Computer Centre, Manchester, 1972.
2. McCracken, D. D., *A Guide to Fortran IV Programming*, Wiley, New York, 1968.

2.19 INDEX

CHAPTER

THREE

NUMERICAL TECHNIQUES

3.1 MATRIX ALGEBRA

The solution to many engineering problems can be expressed as a set of linear simultaneous equations. To enable sets of equations to be manipulated, a shorthand form of notation is desirable. For example, the equations

$$\begin{aligned} Y_1 &= A_{11}X_1 + A_{12}X_2 + \cdots + A_{1m}X_m \\ Y_2 &= A_{21}X_1 + A_{22}X_2 + \cdots + A_{2m}X_m \\ &\cdots\cdots\cdots\cdots\cdots\cdots \\ Y_n &= A_{n1}X_1 + A_{n2}X_2 + \cdots + A_{nm}X_m \end{aligned}$$

can be written in matrix notation as

$$\begin{bmatrix} Y_1 \\ Y_2 \\ \cdot \\ Y_n \end{bmatrix} = \begin{bmatrix} A_{11} & A_{12} & \cdots A_{1m} \\ A_{21} & A_{22} & \cdots A_{2m} \\ \cdots & \cdots & \cdots \\ A_{n1} & A_{n2} & \cdots A_{nm} \end{bmatrix} \begin{bmatrix} X_1 \\ X_2 \\ \cdot \\ X_m \end{bmatrix}$$

or in a more condensed form as

$$\mathbf{Y} = \mathbf{A} \cdot \mathbf{X}$$

A two-dimensional matrix consists of rows and columns of coefficients. Each coefficient can be a numerical value, an algebraic expression or even a matrix. Matrix **A** in the example has n rows and m columns and the coefficient on the ith row and jth column is referenced by use of subscripts as A_{ij}. Matrix **Y** has n rows and one column and matrix **X** has m rows and one column. Matrices having a single column of coefficients are commonly referred to as vectors, since a vector quantity, such as a force at a point, can be represented by a list of components.

3.1.1 Vectors

Quantities needing both magnitude and direction for their description are called vectors. Forces and displacements are thus vectors while energy, which has no directional component, is a scalar. A vector is described with respect to a specified coordinate system, and the same physical quantity can be referred to an infinite number of axis systems.

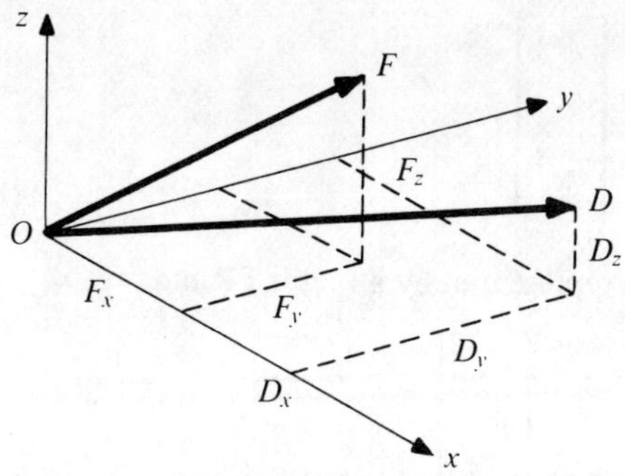

Figure 3.1 Force and displacement vectors

Vectors of up to three dimensions are amenable to geometric interpretation since their directions can be related to spatial axes. Although visualization of the direction of a vector can be useful, the algebraic rules for their manipulation are equally valid for vectors in 1, 2, 3, and N-dimensional spaces.

For example, a force acting at a point on a body is a vector quantity and it can be represented by its projections on three orthogonal axes. The force represented by **OF** in Fig. 3.1 can be defined by its components in the coordinate directions and it can be described in matrix form by

$$\mathbf{OF} = \begin{bmatrix} F_x \\ F_y \\ F_z \end{bmatrix}$$

In a similar manner the whole system of forces acting on N nodal points of a body can be regarded as a vector in N-dimensional space and described in matrix form by

$$\mathbf{F} = \begin{bmatrix} F_1 \\ F_2 \\ \cdot \\ \cdot \\ \cdot \\ F_N \end{bmatrix}$$

In this case each coefficient of the vector **F** is itself a three-dimensional vector having three components.

The coefficients of a vector need not refer to quantities of a similar type. Thus if a force **OF** and a couple **OM** act at a point, a single vector can be used to describe the loading at that point. In Fig. 3.2 the vectors representing the force **OF** and the couple **OM** are given a geometric interpretation. The couple is represented by a line drawn along its axis of rotation and having a length equal to its magnitude. Its positive direction is defined by the sign convention for the direction of rotation. In the figure an anticlockwise couple is taken to be positive. The vector **OM** can be defined by its components in the coordinate directions, thus

$$\mathbf{OM} = \begin{bmatrix} M_x \\ M_y \\ M_z \end{bmatrix}$$

The total force system at the point can be represented by a vector **FP** and

$$\mathbf{FP} = \begin{bmatrix} \mathbf{OF} \\ \mathbf{OM} \end{bmatrix} = \begin{bmatrix} F_x \\ F_y \\ F_z \\ M_x \\ M_y \\ M_z \end{bmatrix}$$

In FORTRAN programs a vector can be represented by a one-dimensional subscripted variable. For a structure with forces and displacements specified at N nodes, the forces could be stored in variable F and the displacements in variable D. Thus F and D would store ordered lists of force and displacement components

$$F = \begin{bmatrix} FX1 \\ FY1 \\ FZ1 \\ MX1 \\ MY1 \\ MZ1 \\ FX2 \\ FY2 \\ \cdot \\ \cdot \\ \cdot \\ MZN \end{bmatrix} \qquad D = \begin{bmatrix} DX1 \\ DY1 \\ DZ1 \\ TX1 \\ TY1 \\ TZ1 \\ DX2 \\ DY2 \\ \cdot \\ \cdot \\ \cdot \\ TZN \end{bmatrix} \begin{matrix} \left.\begin{matrix} \\ \\ \\ \\ \\ \\ \end{matrix}\right\} \text{components at node 1} \\ \left.\begin{matrix} \\ \\ \\ \\ \end{matrix}\right\} \text{components at node 2} \\ \\ \\ \end{matrix}$$

where, typically, $DX1$ is the translation of node 1 in the X direction and $TX1$ is the rotation of node 1 about an axis parallel to the X direction.

The following FORTRAN statements can be used to extract the forces at a particular node i:

```
I6=6*I
FX=F(I6-5)
```

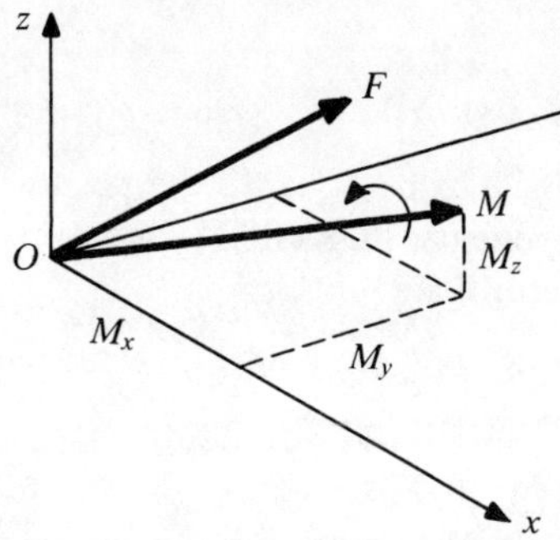

Figure 3.2 Moment and force vectors

```
      FY=F(I6-4)
      FZ=F(I6-3)
```

3.1.1.1 Properties of vectors

1. Two vectors are equal when all of their corresponding components are equal.

2. The sum of two vectors is formed by adding their corresponding components. For example, if in a computer program one set of *N* nodal displacements is stored in subscripted variable *D* and another set in *DD*, then the total displacements can be stored in variable *TD* using a *DO* loop construction (see Sec. 2.10.5):

```
      DO 1 I=1,N
    1 TD(I)=D(I)+DD(I)
```

3. The transpose of a vector is a matrix having a single row of coefficients. The operation of transposing is represented by the superscript T.

For example, if

$$\mathbf{A} = \begin{bmatrix} A_1 \\ A_2 \\ \cdot \\ \cdot \\ \cdot \\ A_N \end{bmatrix} \quad \text{and} \quad \mathbf{B} = \mathbf{A}^T \quad \text{then} \quad \mathbf{B} = [A_1, A_2, \ldots, A_N]$$

For convenience, a vector is often referred to either as a row vector of a column vector. The transpose of a column vector is a row vector and vice versa.

4. Multiplication of a vector by a scalar, or number, is performed by multiplying each component of the vector by that scalar. For example, if the total load caused by 10 times the load defined by **F** and 5 times the load defined by **FF** is to be represented by **TF** then $\mathbf{TF} = 10 \times \mathbf{F} + 5 \times \mathbf{FF}$ and each component is given by $TF_i = 10 \times F_i + 5 \times FF_i$. FORTRAN statements to perform the operation are:

```
        DO 100 I=1,N
100     TF(I)=10.0*F(I)+5.0*FF(I)
```

5. The length or modulus of a vector is defined to be equal to the positive square root of the sum of the squares of its components. FORTRAN statements to calculate the length *RLF* of an *N*-dimensional vector **F** are

```
        RLF=0.0
        DO 2 I=1,N
2       RLF=RLF+F(I)**2
        RLF=SQRT(RLF)
```

6. A unit vector is one having unit length. The components of the unit vector **UF** in the same direction as **F** can be obtained by dividing each component of **F** by its length. FORTRAN statements to do this are

```
        DO 3 I=1,N
3       UF(I)=F(I)/RLF
```

7. The components of a unit vector are called 'direction cosines', and they are used to specify the direction of an axis or vector with respect to a coordinate system. For example, a unit vector **UF** in the same direction as the vector **OF** is shown in Fig. 3.3 and it can be seen that the components of the unit vector are equal to the cosines of the angles between **OF** or **UF** and the coordinate axes. Direction cosines uniquely define the direction of a vector with respect to a particular set of axes. The unit vector **UF** is given by

$$\mathbf{UF}^{\mathrm{T}} = [\cos\alpha, \cos\beta, \cos\gamma]$$

8. The scalar or dot product of two vectors is defined to be equal to the sum of the products of corresponding coefficients. Only vectors with an equal number of coefficients can have a scalar product.

For example, the work done *WD* by forces **F** moving through corresponding displacements **D** is given by

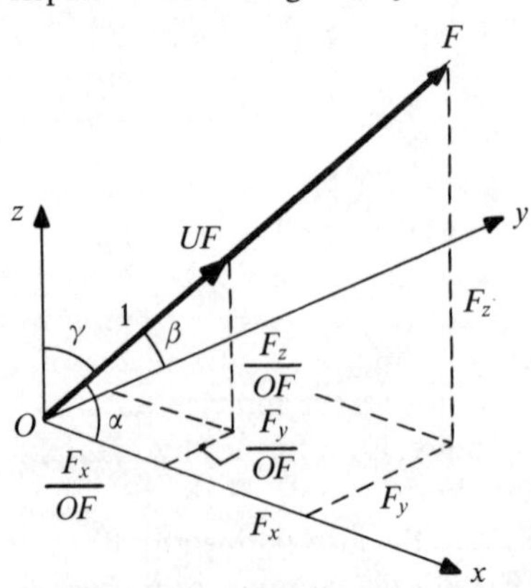

Figure 3.3 Unit vector

$$WD = \mathbf{F}^\mathrm{T} \cdot \mathbf{D} = \mathbf{D}^\mathrm{T} \cdot \mathbf{F} \qquad \text{or} \qquad WD = \sum_{i=1}^{n} F_i D_i$$

FORTRAN statements to calculate this scalar product are:

```
      WD=0.0
      DO 10 I=1,N
10    WD=WD+F(I)*D(I)
```

9. Two vectors whose scalar product is zero are said to be orthogonal.

3.1.2 Matrices

Matrices can be used in many roles. For example, a matrix is the means by which one vector can be expressed as a linear function of another vector. When used to represent simultaneous equations in the form $\mathbf{Y} = \mathbf{A} \cdot \mathbf{X}$, $\mathbf{A}$ expresses the relationship between vectors $\mathbf{X}$ and $\mathbf{Y}$. If the coefficients of each row of $\mathbf{A}$ are considered to be the components of a vector, then each component of $\mathbf{Y}$ is equal to the scalar product of the corresponding row vector and $\mathbf{X}$, thus:

$$Y_i = \sum_{j=1}^{m} A_{ij} X_j$$

An example of this use of matrices is the stiffness matrix of a beam which is formed from the slope deflection equations. With reference to Fig. 3.4,

$$\begin{bmatrix} M_1 \\ F_1 \\ M_2 \\ F_2 \end{bmatrix} = \begin{bmatrix} \frac{4EI}{L} & \frac{6EI}{L^2} & \frac{2EI}{L} & -\frac{6EI}{L^2} \\ \frac{6EI}{L^2} & \frac{12EI}{L^3} & \frac{6EI}{L^2} & -\frac{12EI}{L^3} \\ \frac{2EI}{L} & \frac{6EI}{L^2} & \frac{4EI}{L} & -\frac{6EI}{L^2} \\ -\frac{6EI}{L^2} & -\frac{12EI}{L^3} & -\frac{6EI}{L^2} & \frac{12EI}{L^3} \end{bmatrix} \begin{bmatrix} \theta_1 \\ V_1 \\ \theta_2 \\ V_2 \end{bmatrix}$$

or

$$\mathbf{F} = \mathbf{S} \cdot \mathbf{D}$$

Examples of the use and advantages of this notation can be found in Chapter 4.

A matrix can be used as a means of relating two vectors which describe the same physical vector quantity with respect to different axis systems.

For example, the force OF shown in Fig. 3.5 can be described by reference to the (x, y) or the (p, q) axes, thus

$$\mathbf{OF} = \begin{bmatrix} F_x \\ F_y \end{bmatrix} \qquad \text{with respect to } (x, y)$$

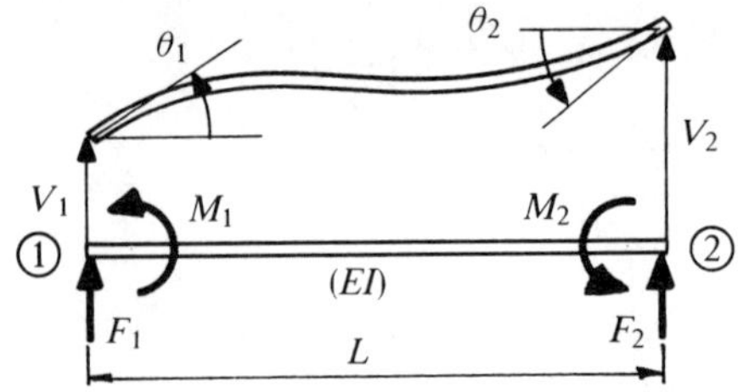

Figure 3.4 Beam flexure

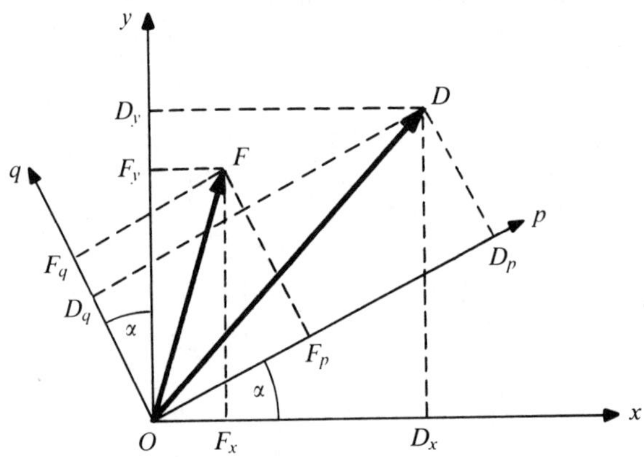

Figure 3.5 Vector components

and

$$\mathbf{OF} = \begin{bmatrix} F_p \\ F_q \end{bmatrix} \qquad \text{with respect to } (p, q)$$

From equilibrium,

$$F_p = F_x \cos\alpha + F_y \sin\alpha$$

$$F_q = -F_x \sin\alpha + F_y \cos\alpha$$

and in matrix form,

$$\begin{bmatrix} F_p \\ F_q \end{bmatrix} = \begin{bmatrix} \cos\alpha & \sin\alpha \\ -\sin\alpha & \cos\alpha \end{bmatrix} \begin{bmatrix} F_x \\ F_y \end{bmatrix} \qquad \text{or} \qquad \mathbf{F}_{pq} = \mathbf{T} \cdot \mathbf{F}_{xy}$$

This matrix equation effects a linear transformation from one axis system to another. This way of looking at a matrix equation is particularly important for stiffness analysis of structures, and for buckling and vibration problems when the transformation to principal axes is required. It is interesting to note that the sets of vectors formed by rows or columns of the transformation or rotation matrix **T** are orthogonal unit vectors. In fact, the first row of **T** holds the components of a unit vector in the p-direction specified with respect to the (x, y) axis system and the second row holds the components of a unit vector in the q-direction specified with respect to the (x, y) directions. Thus $F_p = \mathbf{U}_p \cdot \mathbf{F}_{xy}$ and $F_q = \mathbf{U}_q \cdot \mathbf{F}_{xy}$, where $\mathbf{U}_p$ and $\mathbf{U}_q$ are unit vectors in the p- and q-directions, respectively.

In a FORTRAN program a matrix is represented by a subscripted variable with two subscripts. The first subscript denotes the row number of a coefficient and the second subscript denotes its column number.

3.1.2.1 Terminology, properties, and manipulation of matrices

1. Two matrices are equal when all of their corresponding coefficients are equal. Thus when $\mathbf{A} = \mathbf{B}$, $A_{ij} = B_{ij}$, for all i and all j. Equality of two matrices only has meaning when they have the same number of rows and the same number of columns.

2. The sum of two matrices is formed by adding their corresponding coefficients. Thus if $\mathbf{C} = \mathbf{A} + \mathbf{B}$ then $C_{ij} = A_{ij} + B_{ij}$ for all i and all j. Matrices can only be summed when they have the same number of rows and the same number of columns. The result is a matrix having the same dimensions as its component matrices.

A FORTRAN SUBROUTINE to add or subtract matrices **A**, **B** and to store the result in **C** is described in Sec. 2.10.5.4.

3. Every matrix has associated with it another matrix called its 'transpose'. The rows of the transposed matrix correspond to the columns of the original matrix. Capital 'T' is used as a superscript to indicate transposition. For example, if $\mathbf{B} = \mathbf{A}^{\mathrm{T}}$ then $B_{ij} = A_{ji}$, for all i and all j.

A FORTRAN SUBROUTINE to store the transpose of **A** in **B** is

```
      SUBROUTINE TAB(A,B,N,M)
      DIMENSION A(M,N),B(N,M)
      DO1 J=1,M
      DO 1 I=1,N
    1 B(I,J)=A(J,I)
      RETURN
      END
```

4. A square matrix has the same number of rows and columns.

A FORTRAN SUBROUTINE to replace a square matrix by its transpose is

```
      SUBROUTINE TA(A,N)
      DIMENSION A(N,N)
      DO1 J=1,N
      DO 1 I=J,N
      C=A(I,J)
      A(I,J)=A(J,I)
    1 A(J,I)=C
      RETURN
      END
```

5. A symmetric matrix is a square matrix which is equal to its transpose. If **A** is a symmetric matrix then $\mathbf{A} = \mathbf{A}^{\mathrm{T}}$, or $A_{ij} = A_{ji}$, for all i and all j.

6. The terms A_{ii} constitute the leading diagonal of matrix **A**. A diagonal matrix has all coefficients not on the leading diagonal equal to zero. If **A** is a diagonal matrix $A_{ij} = 0$ when $i \neq j$. A unit matrix is a square diagonal matrix with all terms

on the leading diagonal equal to unity. A unit matrix is denoted by the symbol **I**. A scalar matrix is a diagonal matrix with all coefficients on the leading diagonal equal.

7. A matrix consisting entirely of zero coefficients is called a null matrix and is denoted by **0**.

8. An upper triangular matrix has all coefficients below and to the left of the leading diagonal equal to zero. Thus, if **U** is an upper triangular matrix then $U_{ij} = 0$, for $i > j$.

9. A lower triangular matrix has all coefficients above and to the right of the leading diagonal equal to zero. Thus if **L** is a lower triangular matrix then $L_{ij} = 0$, for $i < j$.

10. Multiplication of a matrix by a scalar has the effect of multiplying each of its coefficients by that scalar. Thus if $\mathbf{A} = C \cdot \mathbf{B}$ then $A_{ij} = CB_{ij}$, for all i and all j.

11. Mulitplication of matrix **A** by matrix **B** is defined by considering the rows of **A** and the columns of **B** to consist of the coefficients of vectors. The product of **A** and **B** is a matrix having as many rows as **A** and as many columns as **B**. If $\mathbf{C} = \mathbf{A} \cdot \mathbf{B}$ then each coefficient C_{ij} is given by the scalar product of the vector represented by the ith row of **A** and the vector represented by the jth column of **B**. Thus $\mathbf{A} \cdot \mathbf{B}$ can only be performed when the number of columns of **A** equals the number of rows of **B**. It should be noted that $\mathbf{C} = \mathbf{A} \cdot \mathbf{B}$ does not imply that $\mathbf{C} = \mathbf{B} \cdot \mathbf{A}$ nor even that $\mathbf{B} \cdot \mathbf{A}$ has any meaning! To avoid the possibility of error, it is customary to say that **A** 'premultiplies' **B**, or that **A** is 'postmultiplied' by **B**.

Multiplication of a matrix **A** by a unit matrix produces a matrix equal to **A**. Multiplication of **A** by a scalar matrix produces a matrix with coefficients equal to the corresponding coefficients of **A** multiplied by the scalar. Premultiplying **A** by a diagonal matrix produces a matrix with coefficients of a row equal to the corresponding coefficients of **A** multiplied by the corresponding diagonal coefficient. Postmultiplying **A** by a diagonal matrix similarly produces a matrix with coefficients corresponding to scaled columns of **A**.

A FORTRAN SUBROUTINE to determine $\mathbf{A} \cdot \mathbf{B}$ and to store the result in **C** is

```
      SUBROUTINE MULT(A,B,C,L,M,N)
      DIMENSION A(L,M),B(M,N),C(L,N)
C FOR EACH COEFFICIENT OF C WORKING ALONG THE ROWS
C SET C=A*B
      DO 1 I=1,L
      DO 1 J=1,N
C FORM SCALAR PRODUCT USING COEFFS OF ITH ROW OF A
C AND THE JTH COLUMN OF B
      C1=0.
      DO 2 K=1,M
2     C1=C1+A(I,K)*B(K,J)
```

```
1     C(I,J)=C1
      RETURN
      END
```

12. Commutative and associative rules of matrix algebra can be illustrated by longhand manipulation. For our purposes the more important rules are given below and should be studied:

(a) $\mathbf{A} + \mathbf{B} = \mathbf{B} + \mathbf{A}$
(b) $\mathbf{A} + (\mathbf{B} + \mathbf{C}) = (\mathbf{A} + \mathbf{B}) + \mathbf{C}$
(c) $\mathbf{A} \cdot (\mathbf{B} \cdot \mathbf{C}) = (\mathbf{A} \cdot \mathbf{B}) \cdot \mathbf{C}$
(d) $\mathbf{A} \cdot (\mathbf{B} + \mathbf{C}) = \mathbf{A} \cdot \mathbf{B} + \mathbf{A} \cdot \mathbf{C}$
(e) $(\mathbf{A} + \mathbf{B})^{\mathrm{T}} = \mathbf{A}^{\mathrm{T}} + \mathbf{B}^{\mathrm{T}}$
(f) $(\mathbf{A} \cdot \mathbf{B})^{\mathrm{T}} = \mathbf{B}^{\mathrm{T}} \cdot \mathbf{A}^{\mathrm{T}}$
(g) $(\mathbf{A} \cdot \mathbf{B} \cdot \mathbf{C})^{\mathrm{T}} = (\mathbf{B} \cdot \mathbf{C})^{\mathrm{T}} \cdot \mathbf{A}^{\mathrm{T}} = \mathbf{C}^{\mathrm{T}} \cdot \mathbf{B}^{\mathrm{T}} \cdot \mathbf{A}^{\mathrm{T}}$
(h) $\mathbf{A} \cdot \mathbf{B}$ does not necessarily give any mean to $\mathbf{B} \cdot \mathbf{A}$
(i) $(\mathbf{A} + \mathbf{B})^2 = \mathbf{A} \cdot \mathbf{A} + \mathbf{A} \cdot \mathbf{B} + \mathbf{B} \cdot \mathbf{A} + \mathbf{B} \cdot \mathbf{B}$
(j) $\mathbf{I} \cdot \mathbf{A} = \mathbf{A} \cdot \mathbf{I} = \mathbf{A}$

3.1.2.2 Determinant of a matrix

1. Every square matrix has a scalar quantity associated with it and known as its determinant. The determinant of $\mathbf{A}$ is written symbolically as $|\mathbf{A}|$, det $\mathbf{A}$, or $\Delta\mathbf{A}$.

2. The determinant of a 2 x 2 matrix $\mathbf{A}$ is defined by the rule:

$$|\mathbf{A}| = \begin{vmatrix} A_{11} & A_{12} \\ A_{21} & A_{22} \end{vmatrix} = A_{11}A_{22} - A_{12}A_{21}$$

The determinant of a matrix with more than two rows is defined by successively developing the matrix using minors until only determinants having two rows are to be evaluated. The development of matrix $\mathbf{A}$ using coefficients of the first row is

$$|\mathbf{A}| = A_{11}(-1)^{1+1}|\mathbf{M}_{11}| + \cdots + A_{1j}(-1)^{1+j}|\mathbf{M}_{1j}| + \cdots + A_{1n}(-1)^{1+n}|\mathbf{M}|_{1n}$$

where $\mathbf{M}_{ij}$ is the minor of A_{ij} and is the matrix remaining when the i-th row and the j-th column have been removed from $\mathbf{A}$. The term $(-1)^{i+j}\mathbf{M}_{ij}$ is sometimes called the 'co-factor' of A_{ij}. Consider, for example, evaluation of the determinant of a 3 x 3 matrix:

$$\begin{vmatrix} 1 & 2 & 3 \\ 4 & 2 & 6 \\ 5 & 0 & 3 \end{vmatrix} = 1\begin{vmatrix} 2 & 6 \\ 0 & 3 \end{vmatrix} - 2\begin{vmatrix} 4 & 6 \\ 5 & 3 \end{vmatrix} + 3\begin{vmatrix} 4 & 2 \\ 5 & 0 \end{vmatrix}$$

$$= 1(2.3 - 6.0) - 2(4.3 - 6.5) + 3(4.0 - 2.5) = 12$$

A determinant can be developed using the coefficients of any row or column; thus, for example, using the coefficients of the second column;

$$\begin{vmatrix} 1 & 2 & 3 \\ 4 & 2 & 6 \\ 5 & 0 & 3 \end{vmatrix} = 2(-1)^{1+2} \begin{vmatrix} 4 & 6 \\ 5 & 3 \end{vmatrix} + 2(-1)^{2+2} \begin{vmatrix} 1 & 3 \\ 5 & 3 \end{vmatrix} + 0(-1)^{3+2} \begin{vmatrix} 1 & 3 \\ 4 & 6 \end{vmatrix}$$

$$= -2(4.3 - 6.5) + 2(1.3 - 3.5) = 12$$

3. The coefficients of a matrix can be processed to facilitate computation of its determinant. Some of the more useful properties that can be used are:

(a) The determinant of a matrix is equal to the determinant of its transpose. Thus corresponding rows and columns of a matrix can be interchanged without affecting the value of the determinant
(b) If all of the coefficients in a row or column are multiplied by a scalar the value of the determinant is multiplied by that scalar.
(c) If any two rows, or any two columns, of a matrix are interchanged, the value of the determinant is multiplied by -1.
(d) If any row (or column) of coefficients is multiplied by a scalar and then added to the coefficients of any other row (or column) respectively, the value of the determinant is unchanged.
(e) If the coefficients of any two rows or any two columns are in direct proportion, the value of the determinant is zero.
(f) The determinant of a diagonal or triangular matrix is given by the product of the terms on the leading diagonal.

For example, the determinant of the above matrix can be evaluated by first processing its coefficients to produce an upper triangular matrix having the same determinant:

$$\begin{vmatrix} 1 & 2 & 3 \\ 4 & 2 & 6 \\ 5 & 0 & 3 \end{vmatrix} = \begin{vmatrix} 1 & 2 & 3 \\ 3 & 0 & 3 \\ 5 & 0 & 3 \end{vmatrix}$$ (by subtracting the terms in row 1 from the corresponding terms in row 2)

$$= -\begin{vmatrix} 2 & 1 & 3 \\ 0 & 3 & 3 \\ 0 & 5 & 3 \end{vmatrix}$$ (by interchanging the first and second columns)

$$= -\begin{vmatrix} 2 & 1 & 3 \\ 0 & 3 & 3 \\ 0 & 0 & -2 \end{vmatrix}$$ (by adding $-\frac{5}{3}$ times the terms in the second row to corresponding terms in the third row)

$$= -2 \times 3 \times (-2) = 12$$

(determinant of upper triangular matrix equals product of diagonal coefficients)

4. An efficient automatic procedure for evaluating a determinant is called the 'method of Chio'. Developing a determinant with n rows by cofactors involves approximately factorial n multiplications. For example, to evaluate a determinant with only 20 rows over 2.4E18 multiplications are needed! This is not economic and a more efficient solution can be obtained by taking advantage of the 'rules of manipulation' described under (3) immediately above. These 'rules' are used to reduce progressively the order of the determinant to be evaluated and this is done by processing the coefficients of a matrix to produce an upper triangular matrix which has the same determinant.

Consider:

$$D = \begin{vmatrix} A_{11} & A_{12} \cdots A_{1n} \\ A_{21} & A_{22} \cdots A_{2n} \\ \cdots & \cdots \\ A_{n1} & A_{n2} \cdots A_{nn} \end{vmatrix}$$

Using rules (b) and (d), the coefficients of the first row are divided by A_{11}. This new row is then combined with all other rows in turn by subtracting from each term in each row R for $(R > 1)$ the product of the corresponding term in the new row 1 and the original first term in row R. In the matrix which results, terms in the first column, except the first, are zero. Thus:

$$D = A_{11} \left| \begin{array}{c|ccc} 1 & A_{12}/A_{11} & \cdots & A_{1n}/A_{11} \\ \hline 0 & A_{22} - \dfrac{A_{12}A_{21}}{A_{11}} & \cdots & A_{2n} - \dfrac{A_{1n}A_{21}}{A_{11}} \\ \cdot & \cdots & & \cdots \\ 0 & A_{n2} - \dfrac{A_{12}A_{n1}}{A_{11}} & \cdots & A_{nn} - \dfrac{A_{1n}A_{n1}}{A_{11}} \end{array} \right|$$

and hence, by expansion of the determinant with respect to the first column, the only non-zero part gives

$$D = A_{11} \begin{vmatrix} A'_{22} & A'_{23} \cdots A'_{2n} \\ A'_{32} & A'_{33} \cdots A'_{3n} \\ \cdots & \cdots \\ A'_{n2} & A'_{n3} \cdots A'_{nn} \end{vmatrix}$$

where $A'_{22} = A_{22} - (A_{12}A_{21}/A_{11})$, etc.

These operations are applied to the modified minor of each diagonal coefficient in turn, until only one term remains.

A FORTRAN SUBROUTINE to evaluate determinants using the method of Chio is shown in Fig. 3.6. In the program, the rows of each remaining submatrix

```
      SUBROUTINE DET(A,N,D,EPS)
      DIMENSION A(N,N)
C D-DETERMINANT OF MATRIX A
C EPS-MINIMUM VALUE OF BIGGEST TERM IN LEADING COLUMN
C BEFORE PROCESS PREMATURELY TERMINATED, D=0
C L SUBSCRIPT OF PIVOT
      L=1
      K=L+1
      D=1.0
C SELECT BIGGEST TERM IN LEADING COLUMN FOR PIVOT
C IMAX-ROW WITH PIVOTAL TERM BEFORE INTERCHANGE
 1    IMAX=L
      DO 2 I=K,N
 2    IF(ABS(A(I,L)).GT.ABS(A(IMAX,L)))IMAX=I
C IF ALL POSSIBLE PIVOTS SMALL D IS CLOSE TO ZERO
      IF(ABS(A(IMAX,L)).LE.EPS)GOTO 5
      GOTO 4
 5    WRITE(6,60)EPS
      D=0.0
      RETURN
 4    IF(IMAX.EQ.L)GOTO 6
C INTERCHANGE ROWS-COEFFICIENTS IN LOWER TRIANGLE IGNORED
      DO 3 J=L,N
      ATEMP=A(L,J)
      A(L,J)=A(IMAX,J)
 3    A(IMAX,J)=ATEMP
      D=-D
C CALCULATE TERMS IN NEW SUBMATRIX
 6    PIVOT=A(L,L)
      DO 7 J=K,N
      X=A(L,J)/PIVOT
      DO 7 I=K,N
 7    A(I,J)=A(I,J)-A(I,L)*X
C CHANGE SUBSCRIPT OF LEADING ROW, UPDATE VALUE OF D
      L=L+1
      K=K+1
      D=D*PIVOT
      IF(L.LT.N)GOTO 1
      D=D*A(N,N)
      RETURN
 60   FORMAT(1H^,11H^PIVOT^.LE.,E12.5,24H^DETERMINANT^SET^TO^ZERO)
      END
```

Figure 3.6 Evaluation of determinant

are automatically rearranged to make the term on the leading diagonal, called the pivot, the biggest term in its column before the processing described above commences. This is done to prevent division by zero being attempted, and to minimize roundoff errors by ensuring that the terms in the leading row are multiplied by a fraction before they are combined with terms in other rows. To achieve this, coefficients forming the row with the largest term in the relevant column are simply interchanged with corresponding terms in the leading row (the row containing the pivotal term). From rule (c) the effect of interchanging two rows is to change the sign of the determinant and this is taken into account by the program.

3.1.2.3 *Inverse of a matrix*

The equation $\mathbf{Y} = \mathbf{A} \cdot \mathbf{X}$, where $\mathbf{X}$ and $\mathbf{Y}$ are column vectors and $\mathbf{A}$ is a square matrix, suggests the existence of an inverse transformation $\mathbf{X} = \mathbf{B} \cdot \mathbf{Y}$. Matrix $\mathbf{B}$ is called the 'inverse' of $\mathbf{A}$ and is usually written as $\mathbf{A}^{-1}$, hence $\mathbf{X} = \mathbf{A}^{-1} \cdot \mathbf{Y}$. On combining the above equations it can be seen that $\mathbf{Y} = \mathbf{A} \cdot \mathbf{X} = \mathbf{A} \cdot \mathbf{A}^{-1} \cdot \mathbf{Y}$. Hence $\mathbf{A} \cdot \mathbf{A}^{-1} = \mathbf{I}$, the unit matrix, and, as $\mathbf{X} = \mathbf{A}^{-1} \cdot \mathbf{Y} = \mathbf{A}^{-1} \cdot \mathbf{A} \cdot \mathbf{X}$, $\mathbf{A}^{-1} \cdot \mathbf{A} = \mathbf{I} = \mathbf{A} \cdot \mathbf{A}^{-1}$.

The process of matrix inversion, or determination of the coefficients of $\mathbf{A}^{-1}$, will be postponed until after the solution of sets of linear simultaneous equations has been described. There are, however, a number of important properties of inversion that should be noted:

1. A square matrix whose determinant is zero has no inverse, and is said to be 'singular'.
2. The inverse of a symmetric matrix is itself symmetrical.
3. The inverse of a diagonal matrix is itself a diagonal matrix, and has coefficients equal to the reciprocals of the corresponding coefficients in the original matrix.
4. The inverse of an upper triangular matrix is an upper triangular matrix and the inverse of a lower triangular matrix is another lower triangular matrix.

Two useful rules of manipulation are:

1. $\mathbf{B}^{-1} \cdot \mathbf{A}^{-1} = (\mathbf{A} \cdot \mathbf{B})^{-1}$

but

2. $\mathbf{A}^{-1} + \mathbf{B}^{-1} \neq (\mathbf{A} + \mathbf{B})^{-1}$

3.1.3 Solution of linear simultaneous equations

If $\mathbf{Y} = \mathbf{A} \cdot \mathbf{X}$ represents a set of linear simultaneous equations, then their solution can be expressed using the inverse of matrix $\mathbf{A}$ as $\mathbf{X} = \mathbf{A}^{-1} \cdot \mathbf{Y}$. Determining a matrix inverse is, however, expensive and is not usually necessary.

The solution to a set of linear simultaneous equations can be expressed in terms of determinants by making use of Cramer's rule. This gives the solution of $\mathbf{Y} = \mathbf{A} \cdot \mathbf{X}$ as

$$X_i = \frac{|\mathbf{B}_i|}{|\mathbf{A}|}$$

$$\text{where } \mathbf{B}_i = \begin{bmatrix} A_{11} & A_{12} & \cdots Y_1 \cdots & A_{1n} \\ A_{21} & A_{22} & \cdots Y_2 \cdots & A_{2n} \\ \cdots & \cdots & \cdots & \cdots \\ A_{n1} & A_{n2} & \cdots Y_n \cdots & A_{nn} \end{bmatrix}$$

$\mathbf{B}_i$ is thus the matrix $\mathbf{A}$, but with its i-th column replaced by the vector $\mathbf{Y}$.

Solution of a set of equations by Cramer's rule requires the calculation of $(n + 1)$ determinants and the process is, therefore, too expensive for general use. Its value is rather to show the use of the determinant of $\mathbf{A}$ to indicate whether the equations have a solution, and, if so, whether roundoff errors are likely to be a problem during a solution process.

A number of useful deductions can be drawn by examining the form of Cramer's solution. When $\mathbf{Y}$ is a null vector, a non-trivial solution (a solution other than $X_1 = X_2 = \cdots = X_n = 0$) only exists when $|\mathbf{A}| = 0$. Equations of this type are called 'homogeneous' and their solution is discussed in Sec. 3.1.9.

For non-homogeneous equations ($\mathbf{Y}$ not a null vector) $|\mathbf{A}| = 0$ renders solution impossible. The most likely cause is that two rows of $\mathbf{A}$ are linearly dependent. As properly formulated equations to a physical problem should have a solution the operations leading to the formation of $\mathbf{A}$ should be re-examined. When $|\mathbf{A}|$ is close to zero numerical problems can be expected during solution of the equations.

3.1.3.1 Systematic Gaussian elimination

The first objective of Gaussian elimination is to produce an equation of the form $\mathbf{Y}^1 = \mathbf{U} \cdot \mathbf{X}$ from $\mathbf{Y} = \mathbf{A} \cdot \mathbf{X}$, where $\mathbf{U}$ is an upper triangular matrix. The process used to determine the coefficients of $\mathbf{U}$ is the same as that described for evaluation of the determinant of $\mathbf{A}$ using the method of Chio (see Sec. 3.1.2.2). The coefficients of $\mathbf{Y}^1$ are determined by treating $\mathbf{Y}$ as an additional column of $\mathbf{A}$. The procedure is most easily explained by means of a simple example.

$$\text{Let } \mathbf{Y} = \begin{bmatrix} 5 \\ 3 \\ -1.5 \end{bmatrix} \text{ and } \mathbf{A} = \begin{bmatrix} 2 & 3 & -1 \\ 4 & 4 & -3 \\ 3 & -4.5 & 1.5 \end{bmatrix}$$

To reduce numerical errors the rows of $\mathbf{A}$ and $\mathbf{Y}$ are rearranged to put the biggest coefficient in the first column on to the leading diagonal.

The rearranged matrices give

$$\begin{bmatrix} 3 \\ 5 \\ -1.5 \end{bmatrix} = \begin{bmatrix} 4 & 4 & -3 \\ 2 & 3 & -1 \\ 3 & -4.5 & 1.5 \end{bmatrix} \begin{bmatrix} X_1 \\ X_2 \\ X_3 \end{bmatrix}$$

X_1 is eliminated from the second and third equations by subtracting from them the first equation after it has been multiplied by their particular coefficient of X_1 and divided by its own coefficient of X_1.

Thus the modified second equation is determined from

$$\begin{array}{lcl} 5 & = & 2X_1 + 3X_2 - X_3 \\ \text{minus } 0.5 \times 3 & = & 0.5 \times 4X_1 + 0.5 \times 4X_2 - 0.5 \times 3X_3 \\ \text{to give } 3.5 & = & 0 + X_2 + 0.5X_3 \end{array}$$

and the modified third equation is determined from

$$\begin{array}{lcl} -1.5 & = & 3X_1 - 4.5X_2 + 1.5X_3 \\ \text{minus } 0.75 \times 3 & = & 0.75 \times 4X_1 + 0.75 \times 4X_2 - 0.75 \times 3X_3 \\ \text{to give } -3.75 & = & 0 - 7.5X_2 + 3.75X_3 \end{array}$$

The equations are then in the form

$$\begin{bmatrix} 3 \\ \hline 3.5 \\ -3.75 \end{bmatrix} = \left[\begin{array}{c|cc} 4 & 4 & -3 \\ \hline 0 & 1 & 0.5 \\ 0 & -7.5 & 3.75 \end{array}\right] \begin{bmatrix} X_1 \\ X_2 \\ X_3 \end{bmatrix}$$

Equations below the first are now rearranged to put the numerically biggest term in the second column on the leading diagonal.

$$\begin{bmatrix} 3 \\ \hline -3.75 \\ 3.5 \end{bmatrix} = \left[\begin{array}{c|cc} 4 & 4 & -3 \\ \hline 0 & -7.5 & 3.75 \\ 0 & 1 & 0.5 \end{array}\right] \begin{bmatrix} X_1 \\ X_2 \\ X_3 \end{bmatrix}$$

X_2 is eliminated from the third equation by subtracting from it the second equation after it has been multiplied by the third equation's coefficient of X_2 and divided by its own coefficient of X_2.

The equations become

$$\begin{bmatrix} 3 \\ -3.75 \\ \hline 3 \end{bmatrix} = \left[\begin{array}{cc|c} 4 & 4 & -3 \\ 0 & -7.5 & 3.75 \\ \hline 0 & 0 & 1 \end{array}\right] \begin{bmatrix} X_1 \\ X_2 \\ X_3 \end{bmatrix}$$

and they are now in the required form of $\mathbf{Y}^1 = \mathbf{U} \cdot \mathbf{X}$.

In general, the conversion of **A** to **U** is called 'triangular decomposition', and the coefficient on the leading diagonal of the row used to eliminate coefficients in the 'leading column' is called the 'pivot'. The operations described are readily extendable to sets of n equations and the mechanical nature of the computational steps is clearly evident in the example.

It can be seen from the example that the operations performed on the left-hand side vector **Y** are the same as those performed on each column of **A**. In a computer program it is convenient to take advantage of this and to use a single subscripted variable to store the coefficients of **A** and **Y**. If **A** is an $n \times n$ matrix, the $(n+1)$-th column of the corresponding subscripted variable is used to store the coefficients of **Y**.

As processing the coefficients of **A** is not affected by the **Y** vector, it is possible to solve equations with a number of **Y** vectors simultaneously. When there are m**Y** vectors, the $(n+1)$-th to the $(n+m)$-th columns of the subscripted variable are used to store the coefficients of the **Y** vectors, and the same operations are performed on each vector.

In the second phase of the solution, equations $\mathbf{Y}^1 = \mathbf{U} \cdot \mathbf{X}$ are solved to obtain the coefficients of **X**. They are obtained in reverse order, that is, starting with X_n and finishing with X_1. The process is known as 'back substitution' and is first illustrated on the example.

From the third equation $\quad X_3 = Y_3^1 / U_{33} = 3$

from the second equation
$$X_2 = \frac{Y_2^1 - U_{23}X_3}{U_{22}} = 2$$

and from the first equation
$$X_1 = \frac{Y_1^1 - U_{12}X_2 - U_{13}X_3}{U_{11}} = 1$$

The processing for back substitution can be performed on each $\mathbf{Y}^1$ vector as the coefficients of **U** remain unchanged. As the calculations reflect a simple pattern, automatic control of computation is relatively straightforward.

A SUBROUTINE to solve a set of n linear simultaneous equations using the above procedures is shown in Fig. 3.7. From the discussion of determinants in Sec. 3.1.2.2 it should be clear that the product of the diagonal coefficients of **U** is equal to plus or minus the determinant of **A**. As the value of the determinant is a useful indicator of the possibility of numerical errors in a solution it is calculated as part of the SUBROUTINE. A further quantity of use in assessing the accuracy of a solution is the product of the lengths of the vectors represented by the rows of **A**. This quantity is, therefore, also determined in the routine and its use is discussed in Sec. 3.1.3.4.

```
      SUBROUTINE GSOLVE(A,N,M,D,PRL,EPS)
      DIMENSION A(N,M)
C N-NO. OF EQUATIONS, (M-N)-NO. OF Y VECTORS
C D-DETERMINANT, PRL-PRODUCT OF LENGTH OF A ROWS
C EPS-SMALLEST ALLOWABLE PIVOT
```

```
C CALCULATE PRL
      PRL=1.0
      DO 31 I=1,N
      C=0.0
      DO 30 J=1,N
 30   C=C+A(I,J)**2
 31   PRL=PRL*SQRT(C)
C TRIANGULAR DECOMPOSITION
      D=1.0
      NP1=N+1
      NM1=N-1
      DO 3 IELIM=1,NM1
C IELIM-LEADING ROW
      I1=IELIM+1
C INTERCHANGE ROWS TO GIVE MAXIMUM PIVOT
      IP=IELIM
      DO 1 IROW=I1,N
  1   IF(ABS(A(IROW,IELIM)).GT.ABS(A(IP,IELIM)))IP=IROW
      IF(ABS(A(IP,IELIM)).LT.EPS)GOTO 90
      IF(IP.EQ.IELIM)GOTO 5
      D=-D
      DO 2 ICOL=IELIM,M
      ATEMP=A(IELIM,ICOL)
      A(IELIM,ICOL)=A(IP,ICOL)
  2   A(IP,ICOL)=ATEMP
  5   D=D*A(IELIM,IELIM)
      DO 3 IROW=I1,N
      C1=A(IROW,IELIM)/A(IELIM,IELIM)
      DO 3 ICOL=I1,M
  3   A(IROW,ICOL)=A(IROW,ICOL)-C1*A(IELIM,ICOL)
      D=D*A(N,N)
C END OF TRIANGULAR DECOMPOSITION, TERMS IN LOWER TRIANGLE IGNORED
C BACK SUBSTITUTION, REPLACE COEFFICIENTS OF Y WITH THOSE OF X
      DO 4 J=NP1,M
      A(N,J)=A(N,J)/A(N,N)
      DO 4 NT=1,NM1
      IROW=N-NT
      I1=IROW+1
      C1=A(IROW,J)
      DO 6 ICOL=I1,N
  6   C1=C1-A(IROW,ICOL)*A(ICOL,J)
  4   A(IROW,J)=C1/A(IROW,IROW)
      RETURN
 90   WRITE(6,60)
 60   FORMAT(1H^,28H^BADLY^CONDITIONED^EQUATIONS)
      STOP
      END
```

Figure 3.7 Gaussian elimination

3.1.3.2 Square root method for symmetric equations

Equations for many engineering solutions result in matrix **A** being symmetric, and advantage can be taken of this to reduce the amount of computation necessary to obtain a solution. A symmetric matrix **A** is first factorized into the product of an upper triangular matrix **T** and its transpose. Thus

$$\mathbf{A} = \mathbf{T}^{\mathrm{T}} \cdot \mathbf{T}$$

and the coefficients of **T** are determined using the rules of matrix algebra.

$$\begin{bmatrix} A_{11} & A_{12} \cdots A_{1n} \\ A_{12} & A_{22} \cdots A_{2n} \\ \cdots & \cdots \\ A_{1n} & A_{2n} \cdots A_{nn} \end{bmatrix} = \begin{bmatrix} T_{11} & 0 & \cdots 0 \\ T_{12} & T_{22} & \cdots 0 \\ \cdots & \cdots & \cdots \\ T_{1n} & T_{2n} & \cdots T_{nn} \end{bmatrix} \begin{bmatrix} T_{11} & T_{12} \cdots T_{1n} \\ 0 & T_{22} \cdots T_{2n} \\ \cdots & \cdots \\ 0 & 0 \quad \cdots T_{nn} \end{bmatrix}$$

By equating coefficients of the first row of **A**,

$$A_{11} = T_{11}^2 \qquad \text{hence } T_{11} = \sqrt{A_{11}}$$

$$A_{1j} = T_{1j}T_{11} \qquad \text{hence } T_{1j} = A_{1j}/T_{11} \qquad \text{for } j = 2 \rightarrow n$$

Then taking each subsequent row of **T** in turn;

$$T_{ii} = \sqrt{A_{ii} - \sum_{k=1}^{i-1} T_{ki}T_{ki}}$$

and

$$T_{ij} = \left(A_{ij} - \sum_{k=1}^{i-1} T_{ki}T_{kj}\right) \Big/ T_{ii}$$

since

$$\mathbf{Y} = \mathbf{A} \cdot \mathbf{X} \qquad \text{and} \qquad \mathbf{A} = \mathbf{T}^{\mathrm{T}} \cdot \mathbf{T}$$

$$\mathbf{Y} = \mathbf{T}^{\mathrm{T}} \cdot (\mathbf{T} \cdot \mathbf{X})$$

Let $\mathbf{B} = \mathbf{T} \cdot \mathbf{X}$; then $\mathbf{Y} = \mathbf{T}^{\mathrm{T}} \cdot \mathbf{B}$. **B** is a vector whose coefficients can be determined from those of **Y** and **T** by a process called 'forward substitution'. This is similar to the back substitution procedure described in Sec. 3.1.3.1, but terms are evaluated in the order $B_1, B_2, \ldots, B_n$.

Thus $B_1 = Y_1/T_1$, and each subsequent term $B_i = (Y_i - \Sigma_{k=1}^{i-1} T_{ki}B_k)/T_{ii}$. In a computer program the terms of **B** overwrite those of **Y** to save storage locations.

When the components of **B** have been determined, **X** is evaluated by use of a back substitution processing of

$$\mathbf{B} = \mathbf{T} \cdot \mathbf{X}$$

Thus $X_n = B_n/T_{nn}$, and $X_i = (B_i - \Sigma_{k=i+1}^{n} T_{ik} \cdot X_k)/T_{ii}$.

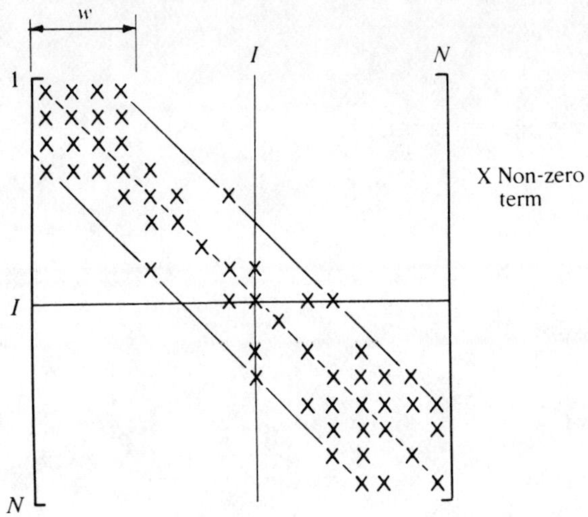

Figure 3.8 Banded matrix

3.1.3.3 Solution of symmetric equations of banded form

A matrix is said to be 'banded' when all of its coefficients beyond a certain offset from the leading diagonal are zero. The band width w of a symmetric matrix **A** is defined to be the largest number of coefficients in any one row of **A**, counting from the diagonal term to the rightmost non-zero term, as shown in Fig. 3.8. In general, the bandwidth is a function of the ordering of unknowns, and care should be taken to minimize w, as only coefficients within the bandwidth need to be stored in a computer program.

A SUBROUTINE to solve banded equations is given in Fig. 3.9. Coefficients of **A** and **Y** are stored in subscripted variable '*A*'. '*A*' has as many rows as **A** and $(w + nlc)$ columns, where nlc is the number of **Y** vectors for which solutions are required. Terms on the leading diagonal of **A** are stored in the first column of '*A*'. Each row of '*A*' corresponds to that part of the same row of **A** with terms from the leading diagonal to the rightmost limit of the bandwidth. Columns $(w + 1)$ to $(w + nlc)$ of '*A*' are used to store the **Y** vectors.

```
      SUBROUTINE BSOLV(A,N,W,WNLC,ES)
      DIMENSION A(N,WNLC)
      INTEGER W,WNLC,WP1,RR,R,WM1
      WM1=W-1
      NLC=WNLC-W
      WP1=W+1
      N1=N-1
      NP1W=N+1-W
C I,J-ROW AND COLUMN OF COEFFICIENT TO BE PROCESSED
      DO 200 I=1,N
C TRIANGULAR DECOMPOSITION****
      J=1
      I1=I-1
```

Figure 3.9 Solution of banded equations

```
 206  C=A(I,J)
      IF(J+I.GT.WP1)GOTO 201
      RR=1
      GOTO 202
 201  RR=J+I-W
C CHECK FOR FIRST ROW AND FOR COLUMN W IN OTHER ROWS
 202  IF(RR.GT.I1)GOTO 2030
C SUMMATION OF PRODUCTS
      DO 203 R=RR,I1
C IR,IRJ-COLUMN COUNTS
      IR=I+1-R
      IRJ=I+J-R
 203  C=C-A(R,IR)*A(R,IRJ)
 2030 IF(J.EQ.1)GOTO 204
C OFF DIAGONAL COEFFICIENT
      C=C/H
      GOTO 205
C COEFFICIENTS ON LEADING DIAGONAL
 204  IF(C-ES)99,99,2041
 2041 C=SQRT(C)
C H-DIAGONAL COEFFICIENT ON ROW I OF T
      H=C
C ALL COEFFICIENTS
 205  A(I,J)=C
C INCREMENT COLUMN COUNT FOR ROW I
      J=J+1
C CHECK IF ALL TERMS OF ROW PROCESSED
      IF(J.LT.WP1)GOTO 206
C FORWARD SUBSTITUTION****
C ROW I NOW HOLDS COEFFICIENTS OF T TRANSPOSE
C J-Y VECTOR COUNT
      J=WP1
      IF(I.GT.W)GOTO 207
      RR=1
      GOTO 208
 207  RR=I-WM1
 208  C=A(I,J)
C CHECK FOR FIRST ROW
      IF(RR.GT.I1)GOTO 2090
      DO 209 R=RR,I1
      IR=I+1-R
      C=C-A(R,IR)*A(R,J)
 209  CONTINUE
 2090 A(I,J)=C/H
      J=J+1
      IF(J.LE.WNLC)GOTO 208
 200  CONTINUE
C BACK SUBSTITUTION****
C ROW N
      DO 210 J=WP1,WNLC
 210  A(N,J)=A(N,J)/A(N,1)
```

Figure 3.9 (*continued*)

```
C ROWS N-1 TO ROW 1 IN TURN
      DO 213 II=1,N1
      I=N-II
      J=WP1
      H=A(I,1)
      IF((NP1W.GT.I)GOTO 215
      RR=N
      GOTO 216
  215 RR=I+WM1
  216 C=A(I,J)
      IP1=I+1
      DO 217 R=IP1,RR
      IR=R+1-I
  217 C=C-A(R,J)*A(I,IR)
      A(I,J)=C/H
      J=J+1
      IF(J.LE.WNLC)GOTO 216
  213 CONTINUE
      RETURN
   99 WRITE(6,999)
  999 FORMAT(1H^,37H^NEGATIVE^SQUARE^ROOT^MATRIX^SINGULAR)
      STOP
      END
```

Figure 3.9 *(continued)*

The SUBROUTINE for banded equations, BSOLV, comprises three main parts which are headed by COMMENT statements 'triangular decomposition', 'forward substitution', and 'back substitution'. The solution procedure is complicated by the housekeeping statements to keep track of the positions of coefficients. To assist comprehension, the limits for the positional counters are shown in Fig. 3.10.

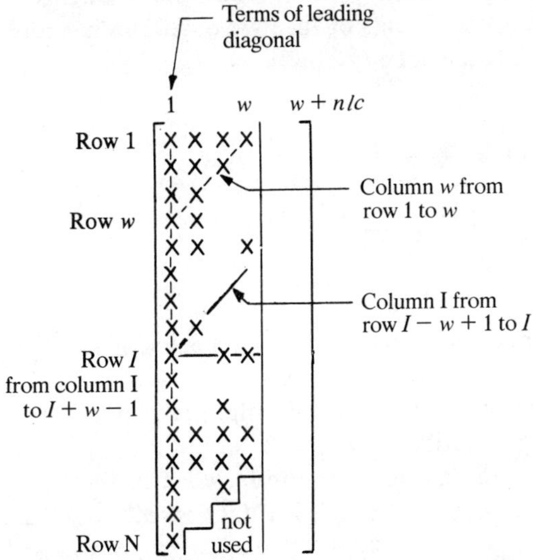

Figure 3.10 Stored form of banded matrix

3.1.3.4 Some comments on errors

Solution of any set of linear simultaneous equations by computer should be considered approximate. For equations resulting from an engineering problem, the coefficients of **A** and **Y** are subject to approximation, although with a stable system the solution is insensitive to small changes in their values. When small changes to the coefficients of **A** lead to large changes in the solution, the equations are said to be 'ill conditioned' and special care should be taken.

Numerical errors are introduced by roundoff during arithmetic operations. Row interchange in GSOLV helps to minimize this source of trouble by ensuring that terms are multiplied only by fractional quantities. This reduces the absolute magnitude of the roundoff errors induced. Roundoff errors can be reduced by processing the equations before solution to ensure that the diagonal terms of **A** are of the same order of magnitude. This can be done by dividing each equation by its coefficient on the leading diagonal of **A**.

One method of assessing the accuracy of a solution to $\mathbf{Y} = \mathbf{A} \cdot \mathbf{X}$ is to determine the vector of residuals **R**, where:

$$\mathbf{R} = \mathbf{Y} - \mathbf{A} \cdot \mathbf{X}$$

Ideally, each coefficient of **R** should be zero, and if they are all small the solution is probably reasonable. Clearly, this approach provides only a guide to the accuracy of a solution but it can detect gross errors. It is not an expensive check, as relatively few computer operations are needed, although an unprocessed copy of **A** has to be stored, and DOUBLE PRECISION may be needed to compute the coefficients of **R**.

Calculation of residuals does not necessarily provide a reliable check for ill conditioned equations. A useful indicator of ill conditioning is the determinant of **A**. When $|\mathbf{A}|$ is small the equations are ill conditioned and **A** is nearly singular. To produce a quantitative measure $|\mathbf{A}|$ is divided by the product of the lengths of the vectors whose components are the coefficients of the rows of **A**. This quantity is sometimes called the norm of the determinant and is given by

$$\text{Norm}\,|\mathbf{A}| = \frac{|\mathbf{A}|}{\prod_{i=1}^{n} \sqrt{\sum_{j=1}^{n} A_{ij}^2}}$$

A matrix is ill conditioned when the norm of the determinant is small in comparison with unity. For problems in which norm $|\mathbf{A}|$ is of the order 1.0E–K a change of the Kth significant digit of any of the coefficients of **A** can lead to changes in the order of 1.0EK in the solution.

Program statements to calculate the above terms are included in the SUBROUTINE GSOLV and similar coding can be added to BSOLV if desired. Note that for symmetrical equations, as

$$\mathbf{A} = \mathbf{T}^{\mathrm{T}} \cdot \mathbf{T}$$

it follows that

$$|\mathbf{A}| = |\mathbf{T}^{\mathrm{T}}| \cdot |\mathbf{T}|$$

and hence

$$|\mathbf{A}| = \prod_{i=1}^{n} T_{ii}^2$$

When ill conditioning is indicated or suspected, the coefficients of **A** can be amended within the tolerances used for their derivation and the new equations solved. Comparison of solutions gives a clear indication of whether **A** is in fact ill conditioned. Alternatively, as equations for engineering problems usually have variables with a physical significance, errors in their solution can often be detected by making use of physical laws. For example, when the equations are for a structural analysis the predicted reactions should be checked to ensure that they equilibrate the applied loading.

In situations when the accuracy of a solution is suspect, consideration should be given to carrying out calculations using DOUBLE PRECISION variables. Their use is relatively expensive but in some cases the cost can be justified. It is also possible to try and improve a solution by adopting an iterative procedure. If $\mathbf{X}_1$ is the approximate solution to $\mathbf{Y} = \mathbf{A} \cdot \mathbf{X}$, then a better solution is given by $\mathbf{Y} = \mathbf{A}(\mathbf{X}_1 + \Delta\mathbf{X}_1)$. As $\mathbf{R} = \mathbf{Y} - \mathbf{A} \cdot \mathbf{X}_1$, the equation $\mathbf{R} = \mathbf{A} \cdot \Delta\mathbf{X}_1$ provides a means of obtaining $\Delta\mathbf{X}_1$. The coefficients of $\Delta\mathbf{X}_1$ are determined by solving the equations, but as the matrix **A** is the same as that in the original equations, the triangularization of **A** need not be repeated. A better approximation to **X** is then given by $\mathbf{X}_i = \mathbf{X}_{i-1} + \Delta\mathbf{X}_{i-1}$ and the process is continued to a reasonable degree of accuracy.

3.1.4 Matrix inverse

Any one of the SUBROUTINES described for solution of linear simultaneous equations can be used to obtain the inverse of **A**. When **A** is an $n \times n$ matrix, n**Y** vectors are used, and together they form the $n \times n$ unit matrix **I**. If matrix **B** is compiled from columns corresponding to the solution vectors **X**, then

$$\mathbf{I} = \mathbf{A} \cdot \mathbf{B}$$

Since premultiplying both sides of this equation by $\mathbf{A}^{-1}$, the inverse of **A**, gives $\mathbf{A}^{-1} = (\mathbf{A}^{-1} \cdot \mathbf{A}) \cdot \mathbf{B} = \mathbf{I} \cdot \mathbf{B} = \mathbf{B}$, the solution of the n equations $\mathbf{I} = \mathbf{A} \cdot \mathbf{B}$ results in the inverse of **A** being computed and stored in **B**. This method is efficient, as the triangularization of **A** is done once only.

3.1.5 Quadratic form of a matrix

3.1.5.1 Bi-linear form

The bi-linear form of matrix **A** with respect to the vectors **X** and **Y** is denoted by $A(\mathbf{X}, \mathbf{Y})$. It is a scalar quantity and is defined by

$$A(\mathbf{X}, \mathbf{Y}) = \mathbf{X}^{\mathrm{T}} \cdot \mathbf{A} \cdot \mathbf{Y} = \sum_{i=1}^{m} \left(\sum_{j=1}^{n} A_{ij} X_i Y_j \right)$$

3.1.5.2 Quadratic form

The quadratic form of matrix **A** is a special case of the bilinear form, which is only applicable to square matrices. The quadratic form of a square matrix **A** with respect to the vector **X** is defined by:

$$A(\mathbf{X}, \mathbf{X}) = \mathbf{X}^{\mathrm{T}} \cdot \mathbf{A} \cdot \mathbf{X} = \sum_{i=1}^{n} \left(\sum_{j=1}^{n} A_{ij} X_i X_j \right)$$

3.1.5.3 Positive definite matrix

A square matrix, which has a positive quadratic form for any arbitrary non-zero vector **X**, is said to be 'positive definite'. Positive definite matrices possess many important properties, but as it is difficult to determine whether a particular matrix is in fact positive definite, the property is of limited use.

In some cases the quadratic form is associated with a physical quantity. For example, if the displacements **D** of a structure are related by the linear relationship $\mathbf{F} = \mathbf{S} \cdot \mathbf{D}$ to the external forces **F** which cause them, then the work done during application of those forces *WD* is given by

$$WD = 0.5\mathbf{D}^{\mathrm{T}} \cdot \mathbf{F} = 0.5\mathbf{D}^{\mathrm{T}} \cdot \mathbf{S} \cdot \mathbf{D}$$

Thus the quadratic form of a stiffness matrix **S** is proportional to the strain energy stored in a structure, and a positive definite stiffness matrix indicates that a structure is stable.

3.1.5.4 Matrix inequality

The statement $\mathbf{A} \leqslant \mathbf{B}$ implies that for any non-zero vector **X**
$\mathbf{X}^{\mathrm{T}} \cdot \mathbf{A} \cdot \mathbf{X} \leqslant \mathbf{X}^{\mathrm{T}} \cdot \mathbf{B} \cdot \mathbf{X}$.

3.1.6 Differentiation of matrix expressions

The rules for differentiation are derived by considering matrix expressions in their expanded forms. Derivatives of bilinear and quadratic forms are commonly required in finite-element analysis and will be illustrated.

1. If $\mathbf{Y} = \mathbf{A} \cdot \mathbf{X}$

$$\text{then } \frac{d\mathbf{Y}}{d\mathbf{X}} \text{ is defined to be } \begin{bmatrix} \dfrac{\partial \mathbf{Y}^T}{\partial X_1} \\ \dfrac{\partial \mathbf{Y}^T}{\partial X_2} \\ \vdots \\ \dfrac{\partial \mathbf{Y}^T}{\partial X_n} \end{bmatrix}$$

When $\mathbf{A}$ is independent of $\mathbf{Y}$ and $\mathbf{X}$, $d\mathbf{Y}/d\mathbf{X} = \mathbf{A}^T$.

This can be demonstrated by considering the two-dimensional case

$$\begin{bmatrix} Y_1 \\ Y_2 \end{bmatrix} = \begin{bmatrix} A_{11} A_{12} \\ A_{21} A_{22} \end{bmatrix} \begin{bmatrix} X_1 \\ X_2 \end{bmatrix} \quad \text{or} \quad \begin{aligned} Y_1 &= A_{11}X_1 + A_{12}X_2 \\ Y_2 &= A_{21}X_1 + A_{22}X_2 \end{aligned}$$

hence

$$\frac{\partial Y_1}{\partial X_1} = A_{11} \qquad \frac{\partial Y_2}{\partial X_1} = A_{21} \qquad \frac{\partial Y_1}{\partial X_2} = A_{12} \qquad \frac{\partial Y_2}{\partial X_2} = A_{22}$$

Thus

$$\frac{\partial \mathbf{Y}^T}{\partial X_1} = [A_{11}, A_{21}] \quad \text{and} \quad \frac{\partial \mathbf{Y}^T}{\partial X_2} = [A_{12}, A_{22}]$$

Using the above definition of $d\mathbf{Y}/d\mathbf{X}$ gives

$$\frac{d\mathbf{Y}}{d\mathbf{X}} = \begin{bmatrix} A_{11} \ A_{21} \\ A_{12} \ A_{22} \end{bmatrix} = \mathbf{A}^T$$

This result can be generalized to n dimensions by simply increasing the size of the matrices in the derivation.

2. If $Y = \mathbf{X}^T \cdot \mathbf{A} \cdot \mathbf{X}$ and $\mathbf{A}$ is a symmetric matrix independent of $\mathbf{X}$ then

$$\frac{dY}{d\mathbf{X}} = \frac{d}{d\mathbf{X}}(\mathbf{X}^T \cdot \mathbf{A} \cdot \mathbf{X}) = 2\mathbf{A} \cdot \mathbf{X}$$

This can be demonstrated by considering the two-dimensional case

$$Y = [X_1, X_2] \begin{bmatrix} A_{11} & A_{12} \\ A_{12} & A_{22} \end{bmatrix} \begin{bmatrix} X_1 \\ X_2 \end{bmatrix}$$

$$Y = A_{11}X_1^2 + 2A_{12}X_1X_2 + A_{22}X_2^2$$

$$\frac{\partial Y}{\partial X_1} = 2A_{11}X_1 + 2A_{12}X_2$$

$$\frac{\partial Y}{\partial X_2} = 2A_{12}X_1 + 2A_{22}X_2$$

Hence

$$\frac{dY}{d\mathbf{X}} = \begin{bmatrix} \dfrac{\partial Y}{\partial X_1} \\ \dfrac{\partial Y}{\partial X_2} \end{bmatrix} = 2\mathbf{A} \cdot \mathbf{X}$$

This result can be generalized to n dimensions by simply increasing the size of the matrices in the derivation.

3. If $Z = \mathbf{X}^T \cdot \mathbf{A} \cdot \mathbf{Y}$ and $\mathbf{A}$ is independent of $\mathbf{X}$ and $\mathbf{Y}$ then

$$\frac{\partial Z}{\partial \mathbf{X}} = \mathbf{A} \cdot \mathbf{Y} \qquad \text{and} \qquad \frac{\partial Z}{\partial \mathbf{Y}} = \mathbf{A}^T \cdot \mathbf{X}$$

This can be demonstrated by considering the two-dimensional case

$$Z = [X_1, X_2] \begin{bmatrix} A_{11} & A_{12} \\ A_{21} & A_{22} \end{bmatrix} \begin{bmatrix} Y_1 \\ Y_2 \end{bmatrix}$$

$$Z = A_{11}X_1Y_1 + A_{12}X_1Y_2 + A_{21}X_2Y_1 + A_{22}X_2Y_2$$

$$\frac{\partial Z}{\partial \mathbf{X}} = \begin{bmatrix} \dfrac{\partial Z}{\partial X_1} \\ \dfrac{\partial Z}{\partial X_2} \end{bmatrix} = \begin{bmatrix} A_{11}Y_1 + A_{12}Y_2 \\ A_{21}Y_1 + A_{22}Y_2 \end{bmatrix} = \mathbf{A} \cdot \mathbf{Y}$$

$$\frac{\partial Z}{\partial \mathbf{Y}} = \begin{bmatrix} \dfrac{\partial Z}{\partial Y_1} \\ \dfrac{\partial Z}{\partial Y_2} \end{bmatrix} = \begin{bmatrix} A_{11}X_1 + A_{21}X_2 \\ A_{12}X_1 + A_{22}X_2 \end{bmatrix} = \mathbf{A}^T \cdot \mathbf{X}$$

These results can be generalized to other dimensions by simply changing the size of the matrices in the derivation.

3.1.7. Orthogonal matrices

A square matrix is called an 'orthogonal matrix' when its rows represent a system of mutually orthogonal vectors, and its columns represent another system of mutually orthogonal vectors. Thus for an orthogonal matrix $\mathbf{A}$ having n rows and columns

$$\left.\begin{aligned} \sum_{j=1}^{n} A_{ij}A_{kj} &= 0 \qquad \text{for } i \neq k \\ \sum_{j=1}^{n} A_{ij}A_{kj} &= 1 \qquad \text{for } i = k \end{aligned}\right\} \text{ or } \mathbf{A} \cdot \mathbf{A}^T = \mathbf{I}$$

and

$$\left.\begin{array}{lll}\sum_{i=1}^{n} A_{ij}A_{ik} = 0 & \text{for } j \neq k \\ \sum_{i=1}^{n} A_{ij}A_{ik} = 1 & \text{for } j = k\end{array}\right\} \text{ or } \mathbf{A}^{\mathrm{T}} \cdot \mathbf{A} = \mathbf{I}$$

It follows that for an orthogonal matrix $\mathbf{A}^{\mathrm{T}} = \mathbf{A}^{-1}$, and that $\mathbf{A}^{\mathrm{T}} \cdot \mathbf{A} = \mathbf{A} \cdot \mathbf{A}^{\mathrm{T}} = \mathbf{A}^{-1} \cdot \mathbf{A} = \mathbf{A} \cdot \mathbf{A}^{-1}$.

The determinant of an orthogonal matrix is equal to ± 1 and for a positive definite orthogonal matrix it equals $+1$.

3.1.8 Transformation or rotation matrices

Matrices which effect a linear transformation from one coordinate system to another with the same origin are orthogonal. Rotation of axes by matrix transformations is a commonly required operation and will be considered in some detail.

3.1.8.1 Two-dimensional transformations

From Sec. 3.1.2 and with reference to Fig. 3.5, the relationship between the components of a force **OF** with respect to coordinate axes (x, y) and (p, q) is

$$\begin{bmatrix} F_p \\ F_q \end{bmatrix} = \begin{bmatrix} \cos\alpha & \sin\alpha \\ -\sin\alpha & \cos\alpha \end{bmatrix} \begin{bmatrix} F_x \\ F_y \end{bmatrix} \quad \text{or} \quad \mathbf{F}_{pq} = \mathbf{T} \cdot \mathbf{F}_{xy} \quad \text{and} \quad \mathbf{F}_{xy} = \mathbf{T}^{-1} \cdot \mathbf{F}_{pq}$$

T is a transformation or rotation matrix and inspection shows it to be an orthogonal matrix.

If the force **OF** acts on a planar structure and the displacements at its point of action are represented by **OD** as shown in Fig. 3.5, then

$$\begin{bmatrix} D_p \\ D_q \end{bmatrix} = \begin{bmatrix} \cos\alpha & \sin\alpha \\ -\sin\alpha & \cos\alpha \end{bmatrix} \begin{bmatrix} D_x \\ D_y \end{bmatrix} \quad \text{or} \quad \mathbf{D}_{pq} = \mathbf{T} \cdot \mathbf{D}_{xy}$$

where D_x and D_y are the components of **OD** in the x and y directions, and D_p and D_q are the components of **OD** in the p and q directions, respectively. If the forces and displacements specified with respect to the (p, q) coordinate system are related by stiffness matrix $\bar{\mathbf{S}}$ such that $\mathbf{F}_{pq} = \bar{\mathbf{S}} \cdot \mathbf{D}_{pq}$, then as $\mathbf{F}_{xy} = \mathbf{T}^{-1} \cdot \mathbf{F}_{pq}$ and $\mathbf{D}_{pq} = \mathbf{T} \cdot \mathbf{D}_{xy}$, $\mathbf{F}_{xy} = (\mathbf{T}^{-1} \cdot \bar{\mathbf{S}} \cdot \mathbf{T}) \cdot \mathbf{D}_{xy}$.

Using the property $\mathbf{T}^{-1} = \mathbf{T}^{\mathrm{T}}$ for an orthogonal matrix gives

$$\mathbf{F}_{xy} = \mathbf{T}^{\mathrm{T}} \cdot \bar{\mathbf{S}} \cdot \mathbf{T} \cdot \mathbf{D}_{xy} \quad \text{or} \quad \mathbf{F}_{xy} = \mathbf{S} \cdot \mathbf{D}_{xy}$$

The expression $\mathbf{T}^{\mathrm{T}} \cdot \bar{\mathbf{S}} \cdot \mathbf{T}$ is the stiffness matrix relating forces and displacements in the (x, y) coordinate system. Although it has been derived for a two-dimensional system, the form of this equation can be generalized in a straightforward manner.

Example Transformation for a plane framework member. A member of a plane framework is considered to transmit axial load, shear and bending couples as illustrated in Fig. 3.11. The transformation matrix for forces at an end of a member is

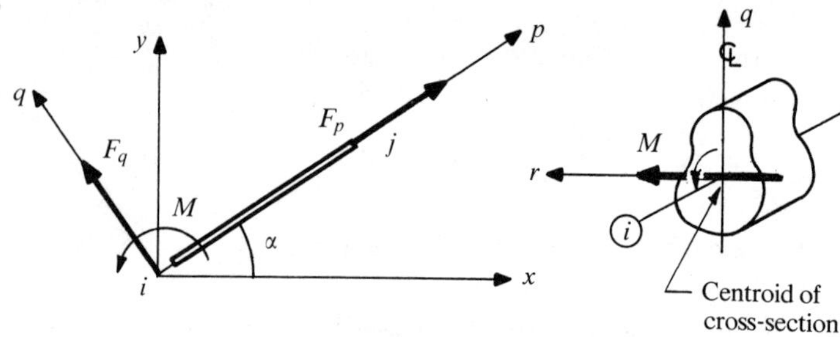

Figure 3.11 Plane framework member

$$\begin{bmatrix} F_x \\ F_y \\ M \end{bmatrix} = \begin{bmatrix} \cos\alpha & -\sin\alpha & 0 \\ \sin\alpha & \cos\alpha & 0 \\ 0 & 0 & 1 \end{bmatrix} \begin{bmatrix} F_p \\ F_q \\ M \end{bmatrix}$$

3.1.8.2 Three-dimensional transformations

If **OF** is a vector in three-dimensional space and $\mathbf{U}_x$, $\mathbf{U}_y$, $\mathbf{U}_z$ are unit vectors defining an orthogonal axis system, then **OF** can be represented by its projections in the (x, y, z) directions. Thus, with reference to Fig. 3.12

$$\mathbf{OF} \equiv \mathbf{F}_{xyz} = \begin{bmatrix} F_x \\ F_y \\ F_z \end{bmatrix}$$

$$\mathbf{U}_x = \begin{bmatrix} 1 \\ 0 \\ 0 \end{bmatrix} \qquad \mathbf{U}_y = \begin{bmatrix} 0 \\ 1 \\ 0 \end{bmatrix} \qquad \mathbf{U}_z = \begin{bmatrix} 0 \\ 0 \\ 1 \end{bmatrix}$$

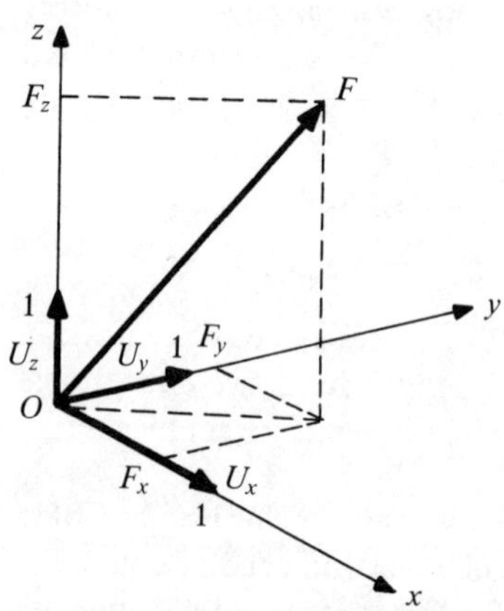

Figure 3.12 Three-dimensional vector

Note that $\mathbf{F}_{xyz}^{\mathrm{T}} \cdot \mathbf{U}_x = F_x$, $\mathbf{F}_{xyz}^{\mathrm{T}} \cdot \mathbf{U}_y = F_y$, and $\mathbf{F}_{xyz}^{\mathrm{T}} \cdot \mathbf{U}_z = F_z$. Thus the component of a vector in a particular direction is given by the scalar product of the vector and a unit vector in the required direction, when both are referred to a common axis system.

An alternative coordinate system with the same origin can be defined by an orthogonal set of unit vectors $\mathbf{U}_p$, $\mathbf{U}_q$, $\mathbf{U}_r$, as shown in Fig. 3.13. Using direction cosines as defined in Sec. 3.1.1.1, item 7, these axis directions are given by

$$\mathbf{U}_p^{\mathrm{T}} = [\cos\alpha_p,\ \cos\beta_p,\ \cos\gamma_p]$$

$$\mathbf{U}_q^{\mathrm{T}} = [\cos\alpha_q,\ \cos\beta_q,\ \cos\gamma_q]$$

$$\mathbf{U}_r^{\mathrm{T}} = [\cos\alpha_r,\ \cos\beta_r,\ \cos\gamma_r]$$

The vector **OF** can be represented by its components F_p, F_q, F_r in the directions of $\mathbf{U}_p, \mathbf{U}_q, \mathbf{U}_r$ by taking scalar products. Thus, for example,

$$F_p = \mathbf{F}_{xyz}^{\mathrm{T}} \cdot \mathbf{U}_p = \mathbf{U}_p^{\mathrm{T}} \cdot \mathbf{F}_{xyz} = [\cos\alpha_p,\ \cos\beta_p,\ \cos\gamma_p] \begin{bmatrix} F_x \\ F_y \\ F_z \end{bmatrix}$$

and hence

$$\begin{bmatrix} F_p \\ F_q \\ F_r \end{bmatrix} = \begin{bmatrix} \cos\alpha_p & \cos\beta_p & \cos\gamma_p \\ \cos\alpha_q & \cos\beta_q & \cos\gamma_q \\ \cos\alpha_r & \cos\beta_r & \cos\gamma_r \end{bmatrix} \begin{bmatrix} F_x \\ F_y \\ F_z \end{bmatrix}$$

or

$$\mathbf{F}_{pqr} = \mathbf{T} \cdot \mathbf{F}_{xyz}$$

If vector **OD** represents the displacements of point 0 caused by **OF**, and if $\mathbf{F}_{pqr} = \bar{\mathbf{S}} \cdot \mathbf{D}_{pqr}$, where $\bar{\mathbf{S}}$ is a 3 x 3 stiffness natrix relating force and displacement components in (p, q, r) directions, then $\mathbf{F}_{xyz} = \mathbf{T}^{\mathrm{T}} \cdot \bar{\mathbf{S}} \cdot \mathbf{T} \cdot \mathbf{D}_{xyz}$. The algebra

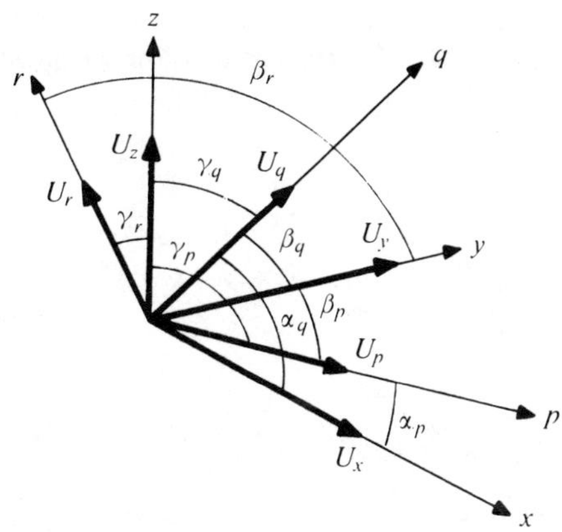

Figure 3.13 Unit vectors

necessary to establish this relationship is identical to that given above for the two-dimensional case.

The nine direction cosines are not independent, and relationships between them can be established by using the properties of an orthogonal matrix.

Thus

$$
\begin{aligned}
1 &= \cos^2 \alpha_p + \cos^2 \beta_p + \cos^2 \gamma_p \\
1 &= \cos^2 \alpha_q + \cos^2 \beta_q + \cos^2 \gamma_q \\
1 &= \cos^2 \alpha_r + \cos^2 \beta_r + \cos^2 \gamma_r \\
0 &= \cos \alpha_p \ \cos \alpha_q + \cos \beta_p \ \cos \beta_q + \cos \gamma_p \ \cos \gamma_q \\
0 &= \cos \alpha_p \ \cos \alpha_r + \cos \beta_p \ \cos \beta_r + \cos \gamma_p \ \cos \gamma_r \\
0 &= \cos \alpha_q \ \cos \alpha_r + \cos \beta_q \ \cos \beta_r + \cos \gamma_q \ \cos \gamma_r
\end{aligned}
$$

The above general formulation of transformation matrices for rotation of three-dimensional coordinate axes gives a useful illustration of matrix manipulation. It also provides a framework within which to discuss transformation matrices to rotate 'coordinate axes' for n-dimensional vectors and this is considered further in 3.1.9. It does not, however, result in a formulation that is readily usable for three-dimensional problems, and simpler formulations that take advantage of features of particular problems are usually derived.

Example Transformation matrix for a pin-ended space-framework member. Let (x, y, z) be a general spatial coordinate system and let (p, q, r) be an axis system related to a particular space frame member with p along the member and q parallel to the x–y plane as shown in Fig. 3.14. A pin-jointed member can only transmit axial forces, and if **F** is the vector representing the force on joint i, with components $[F_p, 0, 0]$ with respect to the (p, q, r) directions and $[F_x, F_y, F_z]$ with respect to the (x, y, z) directions, the transformation matrix **T** relating them can conveniently be determined in two stages.

First, let the (p, q, r) directions coincide with the basic coordinate directions (x, y, z) and then rotate (p, q, r) by an angle α about the r axis as shown in Fig. 3.15. If $[F_{p\alpha}, F_{q\alpha}, F_{r\alpha}]$ are the components of **F** with respect to these axes, the rotation matrix is

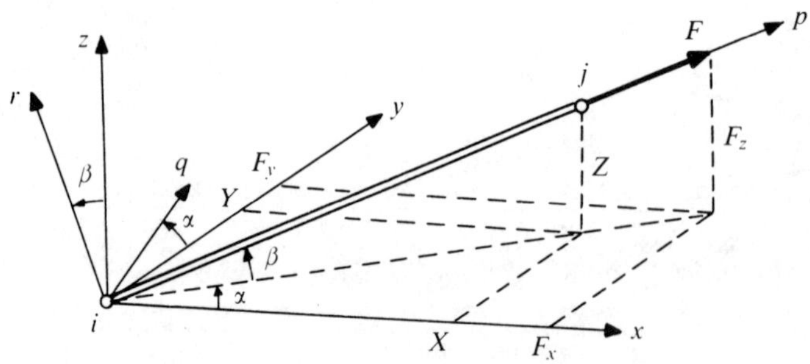

Figure 3.14 Pin-ended space framework member

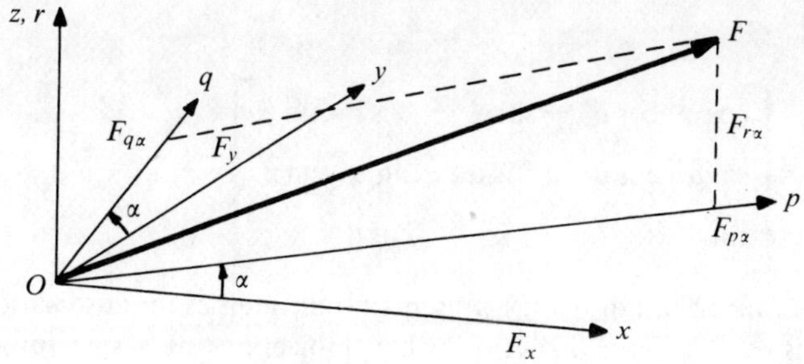

Figure 3.15 Rotation about *z*

$$\begin{bmatrix} F_x \\ F_y \\ F_z \end{bmatrix} = \begin{bmatrix} \cos\alpha & -\sin\alpha & 0 \\ \sin\alpha & \cos\alpha & 0 \\ 0 & 0 & 1 \end{bmatrix} \begin{bmatrix} F_{p\alpha} \\ F_{q\alpha} \\ F_{r\alpha} \end{bmatrix}$$

$$\mathbf{F}_{xyz} = \mathbf{R}_\alpha \cdot \mathbf{F}_{pqr\alpha}$$

The (p, q, r) axes are then rotated by an angle β about the q axis as shown in Fig. 3.16. If $[F_{p\beta}, F_{q\beta}, F_{r\beta}]$ are the components of $\mathbf{F}$ with respect to these axes, the rotation matrix is

$$\begin{bmatrix} F_{p\alpha} \\ F_{q\alpha} \\ F_{r\alpha} \end{bmatrix} = \begin{bmatrix} \cos\beta & 0 & -\sin\beta \\ 0 & 1 & 0 \\ \sin\beta & 0 & \cos\beta \end{bmatrix} \begin{bmatrix} F_{p\beta} \\ F_{q\beta} \\ F_{r\beta} \end{bmatrix}$$

$$\mathbf{F}_{pqr\alpha} = \mathbf{R}_\beta \cdot \mathbf{F}_{pqr\beta}$$

Combining the two stages gives $\mathbf{F}_{xyz} = \mathbf{R}_\alpha \cdot \mathbf{R}_\beta \cdot \mathbf{F}_{pqr\beta}$.

For this example, the (p, q, r) axes are now in the required directions, and therefore

$$\begin{bmatrix} F_{p\beta} \\ F_{q\beta} \\ F_{r\beta} \end{bmatrix} = \begin{bmatrix} F_p \\ F_q \\ F_r \end{bmatrix} = \begin{bmatrix} F_p \\ 0 \\ 0 \end{bmatrix} \quad \text{and} \quad \begin{bmatrix} F_x \\ F_y \\ F_z \end{bmatrix} = \mathbf{T}^{\mathrm{T}} \begin{bmatrix} F_p \\ 0 \\ 0 \end{bmatrix}$$

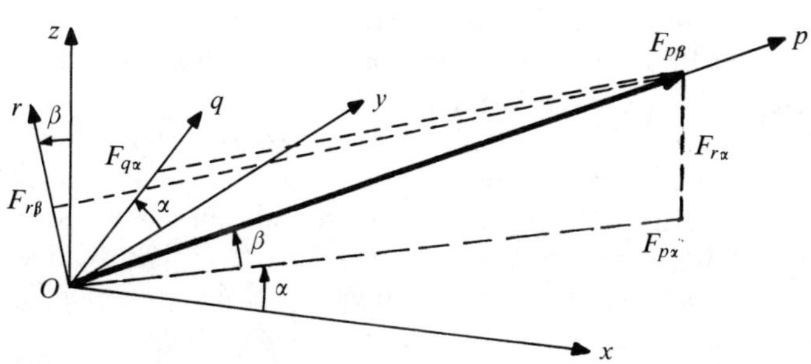

Figure 3.16 Rotation about *q*

where $\mathbf{T}^{\mathrm{T}}$ is given by $\mathbf{R}_\alpha \cdot \mathbf{R}_\beta$ to be

$$\mathbf{T}^{\mathrm{T}} = \begin{bmatrix} \cos\alpha\ \cos\beta & -\sin\alpha & -\cos\alpha\ \sin\beta \\ \sin\alpha\ \cos\beta & \cos\alpha & -\sin\alpha\ \sin\beta \\ \sin\beta & 0 & \cos\beta \end{bmatrix}$$

Evaluation of the transformation matrix presents no difficulties for automatic computation when it is in this form. However, when projections of a structural member are used to define the direction of the p axis a problem can arise with vertical members. With reference to Fig. 3.14,

$$\begin{aligned} \cos\alpha &= X/\sqrt{X^2+Y^2} = X/LXY \\ \sin\alpha &= Y/LXY \\ \cos\beta &= LXY/\sqrt{X^2+Y^2+Z^2} = LXY/L \\ \sin\beta &= Z/L \end{aligned}$$

hence

$$\mathbf{T}^{\mathrm{T}} = \begin{bmatrix} X/L & -Y/LXY & -XZ/(L\cdot LXY) \\ Y/L & X/LXY & -YZ/(L\cdot LXY) \\ Z/L & 0 & LXY/L \end{bmatrix}$$

For vertical members, as $X = Y = LXY = 0$, some of the coefficients of $\mathbf{T}$ are indeterminate. Inspection of Fig. 3.14 reveals that α can have any angle when a member is vertical and it is usually set to zero.

3.1.9 Eigenvalues and eigenvectors

Matrix transformations for vectors of n components play an important role in analysis. In general, the problem is to determine the particular transformation that produces a vector with components related to principal axes.

Consider two vector quantities and let the lists of their components, specified with respect to a particular coordinate system, be represented by $\mathbf{X}$ and $\mathbf{Y}$. Let a square matrix $\mathbf{A}$ exist such that $\mathbf{Y} = \mathbf{A}\cdot\mathbf{X}$. In the previous section, it was seen that the vector quantities can be specified with respect to another coordinate system by use of a rotation matrix $\mathbf{R}$. If the vector components with respect to the second coordinate system are stored in $\mathbf{X}'$ and $\mathbf{Y}'$, then $\mathbf{X}' = \mathbf{R}^{\mathrm{T}}\cdot\mathbf{X}$, $\mathbf{Y}' = \mathbf{R}^{\mathrm{T}}\cdot\mathbf{Y}$ and since $\mathbf{Y} = \mathbf{A}\cdot\mathbf{X}$, $\mathbf{Y}' = (\mathbf{R}^{\mathrm{T}}\cdot\mathbf{A}\cdot(\mathbf{R}^{\mathrm{T}})^{-1})\cdot\mathbf{X}'$, but, as $\mathbf{R}$ must be an orthogonal matrix, $(\mathbf{R}^{\mathrm{T}})^{-1} = \mathbf{R}$ and, therefore, $\mathbf{Y}' = (\mathbf{R}^{\mathrm{T}}\cdot\mathbf{A}\cdot\mathbf{R})\cdot\mathbf{X}'$ or $\mathbf{Y}' = \mathbf{A}'\cdot\mathbf{X}'$.

In the previous section, transformations of this kind were considered when $\mathbf{Y}$ represented a single force, $\mathbf{X}$ the corresponding displacement at its point of application, and $\mathbf{A}$ the stiffness matrix relating them in the original coordinate system. Similar equations can be written for general vectors in n dimensions. For example, $\mathbf{Y}$ could list the forces at each node defining a structure, $\mathbf{X}$ the corresponding displacements, and $\mathbf{A}$ the stiffness matrix for the whole structural system.

For some problems it is necessary to determine the particular rotation matrix to make $\mathbf{A}'$ a diagonal matrix. Thus

$$\mathbf{A}' = \begin{bmatrix} \lambda_1 & 0 & 0 & \cdots & 0 \\ 0 & \lambda_2 & 0 & \cdots & 0 \\ 0 & 0 & \lambda_3 & \cdots & 0 \\ \cdots & \cdots & \cdots & \cdots & \cdots \\ 0 & 0 & 0 & \cdots & \lambda_n \end{bmatrix}$$

For this case $\mathbf{A}'$ is called a 'spectral' matrix, which is usually denoted by **S**, and its diagonal coefficients are called 'eigenvalues'. The coordinate axes are called 'principal' axes, and the particular rotation matrix **R**, which by definition has coefficients equal to the direction cosines of the principal axes when referred to the original coordinate system, is called the 'normalized modal' matrix and is denoted by **N**. The coefficients of each column of **N** comprise the direction cosines of a principal axis, and the vectors represented by these columns are called 'eigenvectors'.

3.1.9.1 Homogeneous simultaneous equations

In Sec. 3.1.3 the concept of homogeneous equations of the form $\mathbf{A} \cdot \mathbf{X} = 0$ was introduced. Here we shall recast this equation in its more useful form $\mathbf{A} \cdot \mathbf{X} = \lambda \cdot \mathbf{X}$ for further consideration, and solution. Written in this way, it is readily appreciated that the equation is a special case of $\mathbf{A} \cdot \mathbf{X} = \mathbf{Y}$, in which the vectors **X** and **Y** are in the same direction. For an n-dimensional matrix **A** there are n possible values of λ and n corresponding directions of the vector **X**. There is insufficient information to enable the lengths of the **X** vectors to be determined.

The extended form of this equation is

$$\begin{bmatrix} (A_{11} - \lambda_i) & A_{12} & A_{13} & \cdots & A_{1n} \\ A_{21} & (A_{22} - \lambda_i) & A_{23} & \cdots & A_{2n} \\ \cdots & \cdots & \cdots & \cdots & \cdots \\ A_{n1} & A_{n2} & A_{n3} & \cdots & (A_{nn} - \lambda_i) \end{bmatrix} \begin{bmatrix} X_{1i} \\ X_{2i} \\ \cdot \\ X_{ni} \end{bmatrix} = \begin{bmatrix} 0 \\ 0 \\ \cdot \\ 0 \end{bmatrix}$$

For every matrix **A**, there is an $n \times n$ modal matrix, denoted by **M**, whose columns comprise the solution vectors **X**. The first column of **M** contains the coefficients of the first solution $\mathbf{X}_1$, and the i-th column the coefficients of the i-th solution $\mathbf{X}_i$.

To show that the **X** vectors are eigenvectors of **A** consider the product $\mathbf{A} \cdot \mathbf{M}$. This is a square n-dimensional matrix whose coefficients are given by

$$\begin{aligned} \mathbf{A} \cdot \mathbf{M} &= \mathbf{A} \cdot [\mathbf{X}_1, \mathbf{X}_2, \cdots, \mathbf{X}_i, \cdots, \mathbf{X}_n] \\ &= [\mathbf{A} \cdot \mathbf{X}_1, \mathbf{A} \cdot \mathbf{X}_2, \cdots, \mathbf{A} \cdot \mathbf{X}_i, \cdots, \mathbf{A} \cdot \mathbf{X}_n] \\ &= [\lambda_1 \cdot \mathbf{X}_1, \lambda_2 \cdot \mathbf{X}_2, \cdots, \lambda_3 \cdot \mathbf{X}_3, \cdots, \lambda_n \cdot \mathbf{X}_n] \end{aligned}$$

Hence

$$\mathbf{A} \cdot \mathbf{M} = \mathbf{M} \begin{bmatrix} \lambda_1 & 0 & 0 & \cdots & 0 \\ 0 & \lambda_2 & 0 & \cdots & 0 \\ 0 & 0 & \lambda_3 & \cdots & 0 \\ \cdots & \cdots & \cdots & \cdots & \cdots \\ 0 & & & & \lambda_n \end{bmatrix}$$

The diagonal matrix is the spectral matrix **S**, and $\mathbf{A} \cdot \mathbf{M} = \mathbf{M} \cdot \mathbf{S}$. Premultiplying both sides of the equation by $\mathbf{M}^{-1}$ gives $\mathbf{M}^{-1} \cdot \mathbf{A} \cdot \mathbf{M} = \mathbf{S}$. When the modal matrix **M** stores vectors of unit length in its columns it is denoted by **N** and repeating the above derivation gives $\mathbf{N}^{-1} \cdot \mathbf{A} \cdot \mathbf{N} = \mathbf{S}$.

Comparison of the above two sections shows that the normalized modal matrix **N** is a form of rotation matrix. Its columns give the directions of the principal axes for a system and are, therefore, eigenvectors. Use will be made of this analogy to solve homogeneous equations, but before proceeding to do that a two-dimensional example, which has a direct physical significance, will be studied to clarify some of the concepts introduced.

The state of stress at a point in a plane stress system can be described by three components. With respect to (x, y) axes these are the stress triad $(\sigma_x, \sigma_y, \tau_{xy})$ and with respect to a plane with normal at angle α to the x axis $(\sigma_n, \tau_{ns}, \alpha)$ as shown in Fig. 3.17. The relationships between these quantities can be determined by considering equilibrium of a small wedge-shaped piece of material and is described in standard strength of materials texts. Of interest here is determination of the value of $\alpha = \alpha_p$ such that there is no shear stress on the plane AB. Equilibrium of forces on the wedge OAB gives

$$\sigma_x \cos \alpha_p + \tau_{xy} \sin \alpha_p = \sigma_{np} \cos \alpha_p$$

$$\sigma_y \sin \alpha_p + \tau_{xy} \cos \alpha_p = \sigma_{np} \sin \alpha_p$$

Rearranging the equations, and putting them in matrix form, gives

$$\begin{bmatrix} (\sigma_x - \sigma_{np}) & \tau_{xy} \\ \tau_{xy} & (\sigma_y - \sigma_{np}) \end{bmatrix} \begin{bmatrix} \cos \alpha_p \\ \sin \alpha_p \end{bmatrix} = \begin{bmatrix} 0 \\ 0 \end{bmatrix}$$

The principal stresses σ_{np} on planes defined by α_p are thus eigenvalues of the matrix of stresses, and the solution vectors corresponding to **X** are seen to store the direction cosines of the normals to the principal planes, and are thus eigenvectors of the stress matrix.

For a non-trivial solution, the determinant of the matrix must be zero (see Sec. 3.1.3):

$$\begin{vmatrix} (\sigma_x - \sigma_{np}) & \tau_{xy} \\ \tau_{xy} & (\sigma_y - \sigma_{np}) \end{vmatrix} = 0$$

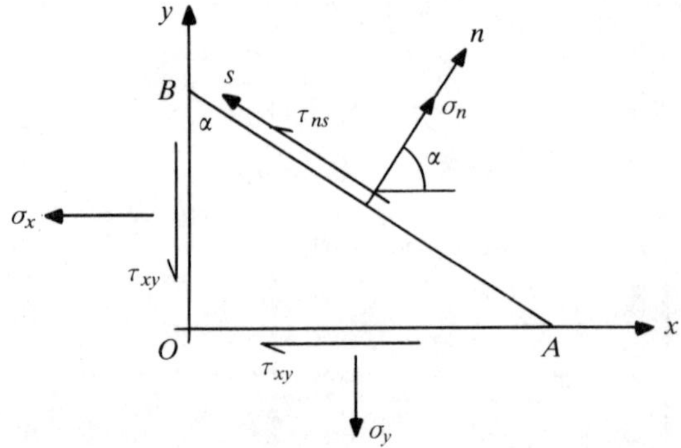

Figure 3.17 Principal stresses

hence

$$(\sigma_x - \sigma_{np})(\sigma_y - \sigma_{np}) - \tau_{xy}^2 = 0$$

and thus

$$\sigma_{np1,2} = \tfrac{1}{2}((\sigma_x + \sigma_y) \pm \sqrt{(\sigma_x - \sigma_y)^2 + 4\tau_{xy}^2})$$

The spectral matrix $\mathbf{S} = \begin{bmatrix} \sigma_{np1} & 0 \\ 0 & \sigma_{np2} \end{bmatrix}$.

The value of α corresponding to σ_{np1} is determined by back substitution. Thus, for example:

$$(\sigma_x - \sigma_{np1}) \cos \alpha_{p1} + \tau_{xy} \sin \alpha_{p1} = 0$$

and hence

$$\tan \alpha_{p1} = \frac{\sigma_{np1} - \sigma_x}{\tau_{xy}}$$

The normalized modal matrix $\mathbf{N}$ is given by

$$\mathbf{N} = \begin{bmatrix} \cos \alpha_{p1} & \cos \alpha_{p2} \\ \sin \alpha_{p1} & \sin \alpha_{p2} \end{bmatrix}$$

For a three-dimensional state of stress the eigenequation is

$$\begin{bmatrix} (\sigma_x - \sigma_p) & \tau_{xy} & \tau_{xz} \\ \tau_{xy} & (\sigma_y - \sigma_p) & \tau_{yz} \\ \tau_{xz} & \tau_{yz} & (\sigma_z - \sigma_p) \end{bmatrix} \begin{bmatrix} \cos \alpha_p \\ \cos \beta_p \\ \cos \gamma_p \end{bmatrix} = \begin{bmatrix} 0 \\ 0 \\ 0 \end{bmatrix}$$

where $\cos \alpha_p$, $\cos \beta_p$, $\cos \gamma_p$ are the direction cosines of the outward normal to a principal plane. Problems of three-dimensional stress states are solved in a manner similar to that outlined for a two-dimensional state of stress.

3.1.9.2 Properties of eigenvalues and eigenvectors

1. The sum of the eigenvalues of a matrix is called its trace and the trace of a matrix is also equal to the sum of the terms on its leading diagonal.
2. The product of the eigenvalues of a matrix is equal to its determinant.
3. The eigenvectors of a symmetric matrix are mutually orthogonal.
4. The eigenvectors of a positive definite symmetric matrix having no complex coefficients are real and positive.
5. The reciprocals of the eigenvalues of a matrix are equal to the eigenvalues of its inverse.
6. The eigenvectors of a matrix are also the eigenvectors of its inverse.

3.1.9.3 Determination of eigenvalues and eigenvectors and solution of homogeneous equations

Solution of homogeneous equations of two and three dimensions can be determined by hand calculation. The determinant of the matrix $(\mathbf{A} - \lambda \cdot \mathbf{I})$ is first expanded to obtain the characteristic polynomial $p(\lambda)$. This is then solved for the eigenvalues sought. The eigenvectors corresponding to each λ_i are then determined by back substitution to obtain $\mathbf{A} \cdot \mathbf{X}_i = \lambda_i \cdot \mathbf{X}_i$. One of the components of $\mathbf{X}_i$ is given an arbitrary value, usually 1, and its other components are determined by removing the corresponding equation and then solving the remaining $(n - 1)$ equations. Each $\mathbf{X}_i$ so determined is reduced to an eigenvector by dividing its components by the length of the vector. It should be recalled that only the direction of an eigenvector can be determined.

For problems involving vectors with more than three components, solutions using the characteristic polynomial are not usually attempted. Most computers have standard library programs to evaluate eigenvalues and the sophisticated techniques used are beyond the scope of this text. In many instances, however, an engineer requires only the largest eigenvalue of a positive definite matrix, and an iterative scheme to determine this is described. The method can be extended to allow calculation of a limited number of eigenvalues of decreasing size, but numerical errors limit this procedure to only a few values.

Consider solution to $\mathbf{A} \cdot \mathbf{X} = \lambda \cdot \mathbf{X}$.

Let $\mathbf{X}_i$ be an arbitrary vector with as many components as $\mathbf{X}$. For convenience the last component of $\mathbf{X}_i$ is usually set to 1 and the process converges most rapidly when $\mathbf{X}_i$ is a good estimate of $\mathbf{X}$. A better estimate of $\mathbf{X}$, $\mathbf{X}_{i+1}$ is given by

$$\mathbf{A} \cdot \mathbf{X}_i = \lambda \cdot \mathbf{X}_{i+1}$$

For convenience the last component of $\mathbf{X}_{i+1}$ is set to unity by dividing the right-hand side by the value of the component calculated. Again, it should be recalled that only the direction of $\mathbf{X}$ can be determined. After a number of iterations the process will converge to give the value of the largest eigenvalue and the direction of its corresponding eigenvector.

To clarify the operations involved in both methods, the largest eigenvalue and the direction cosines of the corresponding eigenvector are determined for the matrix

$$\mathbf{A} = \begin{bmatrix} 2 & 3 & -1 \\ 4 & 4 & -3 \\ 3 & -4.5 & 1.5 \end{bmatrix}$$

Example 1 Solution by means of the characteristic polynomial. The characteristic polynomial is given by expanding

$$\begin{vmatrix} 2-\lambda & 3 & -1 \\ 4 & 4-\lambda & -3 \\ 3 & -4.5 & 1.5-\lambda \end{vmatrix} = 0$$

Adding 3 times column 3 to column 2 gives

$$\begin{vmatrix} 2-\lambda & 0 & -1 \\ 4 & -5-\lambda & -3 \\ 3 & -3\lambda & 1.5-\lambda \end{vmatrix} = 0$$

Adding -3 times row 1 to row 2 gives

$$\begin{vmatrix} 2-\lambda & 0 & -1 \\ 3\lambda-2 & -5-\lambda & 0 \\ 3 & -3\lambda & 1.5-\lambda \end{vmatrix} = 0$$

Hence $(2-\lambda)\ (5+\lambda)\ (\lambda-1.5) - 3\lambda(2-3\lambda) - 3(5+\lambda) = 0$, which simplifies to $\lambda^3 - 7.5\lambda^2 - 5.5\lambda + 30 = 0$.

A root of this equation is determined, using the Newton–Raphson procedure as shown in 3.2.1.1, to be $\lambda_1 = 1.871$. The remaining roots are obtained by expanding $(\lambda-1.871)\ (\lambda-\lambda_2)\ (\lambda-\lambda_3) = 0$ and comparing coefficients with the characteristic equation to obtain

$$\begin{aligned} 30 &= -1.871\lambda_2\lambda_3 \\ 7.5 &= 1.871 + \lambda_2 + \lambda_3 \end{aligned}$$

The solution to these equations is $\lambda_2 = 7.709$ and $\lambda_3 = -2.0798$. The largest eigenvalue is, therefore, $\lambda_2 = 7.709$ and the corresponding eigenvector is determined by back substitution. Thus

$$\begin{bmatrix} (2\text{–}7.709) & 3 & -1 \\ 4 & (4\text{–}7.709) & -3 \\ 3 & -4.5 & (1.5\text{–}7.709) \end{bmatrix} \begin{bmatrix} X_1 \\ X_2 \\ 1 \end{bmatrix} = \begin{bmatrix} 0 \\ 0 \\ 0 \end{bmatrix}$$

Taking the first 2 equations,

$$\begin{aligned} -5.709X_1 + 3X_2 &= 1 \\ 4X_1 - 3.709X_2 &= 3 \end{aligned}$$

and their solution is

$$X_1 = -1.3853 \qquad X_2 = -2.3028$$

Dividing each component of **X** by its length gives the direction cosines of the eigenvector:

$$\begin{bmatrix} -0.4831 \\ -0.8031 \\ 0.3488 \end{bmatrix}$$

Example 2 Solution by means of the iterative method.

$$\mathbf{A} \cdot \mathbf{X}_{i-1} = \lambda \cdot \mathbf{X}_i$$

Set $\mathbf{X}_{i-1}$ equal to $[1 \quad -2 \quad 2]^{\mathrm{T}}$; the coefficients have been picked at random.

$$\begin{bmatrix} 2 & 3 & -1 \\ 4 & 4 & -3 \\ 3 & -4.5 & 1.5 \end{bmatrix} \begin{bmatrix} 1 \\ -2 \\ 2 \end{bmatrix} \quad \text{gives} \quad \lambda \cdot \mathbf{X}_i = \begin{bmatrix} -6 \\ -10 \\ 15 \end{bmatrix} = 15 \begin{bmatrix} -0.4 \\ -0.6667 \\ 1 \end{bmatrix}$$

$\mathbf{X}_{i-1}$ is now set to $[-0.4 \quad -0.667 \quad 1]^{\mathrm{T}}$ and the procedure continued

$$\begin{bmatrix} 2 & 3 & -1 \\ 4 & 4 & -3 \\ 3 & -4.5 & 1.5 \end{bmatrix} \begin{bmatrix} -0.4 \\ -0.6667 \\ 1 \end{bmatrix} \quad \text{gives} \quad \begin{bmatrix} -3.8 \\ -7.2667 \\ 3.3 \end{bmatrix} = 3.3 \begin{bmatrix} -1.1515 \\ -2.2020 \\ 1 \end{bmatrix}$$

$$\begin{bmatrix} 2 & 3 & -1 \\ 4 & 4 & -3 \\ 3 & -4.5 & 1.5 \end{bmatrix} \begin{bmatrix} -1.1515 \\ -2.2020 \\ 1 \end{bmatrix} \quad \text{gives} \quad \begin{bmatrix} -9.963 \\ -16.414 \\ 7.955 \end{bmatrix} = 7.955 \begin{bmatrix} -1.2456 \\ -2.0634 \\ 1 \end{bmatrix}$$

After 9 iterations the equation becomes

$$\begin{bmatrix} 2 & 3 & -1 \\ 4 & 4 & -3 \\ 3 & -4.5 & 1.5 \end{bmatrix} \begin{bmatrix} -1.3857 \\ -2.3034 \\ 1 \end{bmatrix} \quad \text{which gives} \quad \begin{bmatrix} -10.6816 \\ -17.7563 \\ 7.7084 \end{bmatrix} = 7.7084 \begin{bmatrix} -1.385 \\ -2.303 \\ 1 \end{bmatrix}$$

By comparison with the previous solution it can be seen that λ now holds the value of the largest eigenvalue and **X**, when normalized, holds the direction cosines of the corresponding eigenvector.

A SUBROUTINE to implement the iterative method for an n-dimensional vector is given in Fig. 3.18. Although the iterative procedure always converges to the largest eigenvalue, the rate of convergence can be slow when the next largest eigenvalue is of a similar magnitude. This can be appreciated by considering why the method works at all.

Any arbitrary vector $\mathbf{X}_{i-1}$ can be expressed in terms of its components in the coordinate system defined by the eigenvectors of **A**. Thus

$$\mathbf{X}_{i-1} = X_1 \cdot \mathbf{U}_1 + X_2 \cdot \mathbf{U}_2 + \cdots + X_n \cdot \mathbf{U}_n$$

where X_k is the projection of $\mathbf{X}_{i-1}$ on the eigenvector $\mathbf{U}_k$.

Multiplying both sides of the equation by **A** gives

$$\mathbf{A} \cdot \mathbf{X}_{i-1} = \mathbf{X}_i = X_1 \cdot \mathbf{A} \cdot \mathbf{U}_1 + X_2 \cdot \mathbf{A} \cdot \mathbf{U}_2 + \cdots + X_n \cdot \mathbf{A} \cdot \mathbf{U}_n$$

but since the vectors $\mathbf{U}_i$ are eigenvectors of **A**

$$\mathbf{A} \cdot \mathbf{U}_i = \lambda_i \cdot \mathbf{U}_i$$

and hence

$$\mathbf{X}_i = X_1 \cdot \lambda_1 \cdot \mathbf{U}_1 + X_2 \cdot \lambda_2 \cdot \mathbf{U}_2 + \cdots + X_n \cdot \lambda_n \cdot \mathbf{U}_n$$

Suppose the eigenvectors have been arranged so that $\mathbf{U}_n$ corresponds to the largest eigenvalue. In that case the component of **X** in the direction of $\mathbf{U}_n$ has been multiplied by the largest factor $(\lambda_n > \lambda_i)$, and the direction of $\mathbf{X}_i$ has been rotated to lie closer to the direction of $\mathbf{U}_n$ than did $\mathbf{X}_{i-1}$. Repetition of the process gives

$$\mathbf{X}_{i+1} = X_1 \cdot \lambda_1^2 \cdot \mathbf{U}_1 + X_2 \cdot \lambda_2^2 \cdot \mathbf{U}_2 + \cdots + X_n \cdot \lambda_n^2 \cdot \mathbf{U}_n$$

and each successive iteration increases the component of **X** in the direction of $\mathbf{U}_n$ relative to the sizes of its other components.

Eventually, the original arbitrary vector $\mathbf{X}_{i-1}$ will be rotated until it is in approximately the same direction as the eigenvector corresponding to the largest eigenvalue. The number of iterations necessary to complete the rotation is dependent upon the relative magnitudes of the eigenvalues.

Suppose it occurs when $i = m$:

$$\mathbf{X}_m \simeq c \cdot \mathbf{U}_n$$

where c is some constant.

Repeating the process once more gives

$$\mathbf{X}_{m+1} = \mathbf{A} \cdot \mathbf{X}_m \simeq c \cdot \mathbf{A} \cdot \mathbf{U}_n = c \cdot \lambda_n \cdot \mathbf{U}_n = \lambda_n \cdot \mathbf{X}_m$$

By comparing coefficients of $\mathbf{X}_{m+1}$ and $\mathbf{X}_m$, λ_n is determined.

```
      SUBROUTINE LEIGV(A,X,N,LIMIT,EV,EPS,X1)
      DIMENSION A(N,N),X(N),X1(N)
C LIMIT-MAXIMUM NO. OF ITERATIONS, EPS-CONVERGENCE LIMIT
C EV-LARGEST EIGENVALUE, NIT-NO. OF ITERATIONS, X-TRIAL VECTOR
      NIT=0
 1    NIT=NIT+1
C CHECK FOR MAXIMUM NO. OF ITERATIONS
      IF(NIT-LIMIT)2,2,99
 99   WRITE(6,699)(X(I),X1(I),I=1,N)
 699  FORMAT(1H^,29H***INSUFFICIENT^ITERATIONS***//
     C(1H^2E12.4/))
      STOP
C IMPROVE ESTIMATE IN X1
 2    DO 30 I=1,N
      X1(I)=0.0
      DO 30 J=1,N
 30   X1(I)=X1(I)+A(I,J)*X(J)
      XN=X1(N)
C SCALE COMPONENTS OF X1 TO GIVE X1(N)=1
      DO 31 I=1,N
 31   X1(I)=X1(I)/XN
C CHECK CONVERGENCE CRITERIA
      ER=0.0
      BIG=0.0
      DO 4 I=1,N
      ER=ER+ABS(X(I)-X1(I))
      AX1I=ABS(X1(I))
      IF(AX1I.GT.BIG)BIG=AX1I
 4    X(I)=X1(I)
C IF SUM OF DIFFERENCES BETWEEN ESTIMATED COEFFICIENTS
C DIVIDED BY THE BIGGEST COEFFICIENT IS GREATER THAN EPS CONTINUE PROCESS
      IF(ER/BIG.GT.EPS)GOTO 1
      EV=XN
C NORMALISE X
      RL=0.0
      DO 5 I=1,N
 5    RL=RL+X(I)**2
      RL=SQRT(RL)
      DO 6 I=1,N
 6    X(I)=X(I)/RL
      RETURN
      END
```

Figure 3.18 To determine largest eigenvalue

When the smallest eigenvalue is required, the iterative procedure can be used with the inverse of the matrix, since a matrix and its inverse have the same eigenvectors and their eigenvalues are reciprocals of one another.

When more than one eigenvalue of a symmetric matrix **A** is required, the orthogonality of the eigenvectors can be used to modify **A** for further processing.

If $\mathbf{A} \cdot \mathbf{X}_i = \lambda_i \cdot \mathbf{X}_i$ and λ_i, $\mathbf{X}_i$ have been determined, then if $\mathbf{X}_j$ is another eigenvector $\mathbf{X}_i^T \cdot \mathbf{X}_j = 0$. Expanding and using the form of $\mathbf{X}_i$ with $X_n = 1$ used in the iterative procedure:

$$X_{j_n} = -X_{i_1} X_{j_1} - X_{i_2} X_{j_2} - \cdots - X_{i_{n-1}} X_{j_{n-1}}$$

This expression is substituted into $\mathbf{A} \cdot \mathbf{X}_j = \lambda_j \cdot \mathbf{X}_j$ and is used to reduce **A** to an $(n-1)$-dimensional matrix $\mathbf{A}'$:

$$\mathbf{A}' = \begin{bmatrix} A_{11} & A_{12} & & A_{1,n-1} \\ A_{12} & A_{22} & \cdots & A_{2,n-1} \\ \cdots & \cdots & \cdots & \cdots \\ A_{1,n-1} & & & A_{n-1,n-1} \end{bmatrix} - \begin{bmatrix} A_{1n} \\ A_{2n} \\ \cdot \\ A_{n-1,n} \end{bmatrix} [X_{i_1} X_{i_2} \cdots X_{i_{n-1}}]$$

The iterative procedure can be used with $\mathbf{A}'$ to determine its largest eigenvalue, which is the second largest eigenvalue of **A**. The process can be continued to obtain other eigenvalues, but as each successive stage depends on the accuracy to which the direction of the eigenvector for the previous stage was determined, errors soon accumulate and accuracy is lost.

3.2 NON-LINEAR EQUATIONS

Non-linear equations are solved using iterative procedures. In essence, an approximate solution is derived and then a cyclic procedure is entered to improve that solution. The process is terminated when a specified convergence criterion has been satisfied, or if it becomes clear that instead of converging, successive solution estimates are diverging. There is no single method that unerringly converges to the correct solution and non-linear methods have to be used with great care. To minimize possible problems, a good initial estimate of a solution should be provided whenever possible.

3.2.1 Functions of one variable

Suppose a function $\phi = F(x)$ is known, and the value of x to satisfy $F(x) = 0$ is required. With a physical problem it is probable that a feasible range for x can be determined. There may be a number of values of x that satisfy the equation but only one that is consonant with the physical problem. If examination of a problem reveals a number of feasible solution ranges, then each one should be investigated separately. For engineering applications exact values of variables are rarely needed and it is sufficient to determine suitable approximations.

Before embarking on an iterative process, a number of preliminary stages should be completed:

1. Determination of the permissible range for the value of the variable to be calculated, $x_i < x < x_j$.
2. Determination of a good initial estimate of the variable. If one is not apparent the function can be sketched over the feasible range.
3. Specification of tolerances on the solution to enable convergence criteria to be derived.

3.2.1.1 Newton–Raphson procedure

Let x_n be a reasonable estimate of the root x_0. From Fig. 3.19, $\tan\theta = BC/AC$, and hence

$$\frac{dF(x_n)}{dx} = \frac{F(x_n)}{x_n - x_{n+1}}$$

Rearrangement of this equation gives an improved estimate of the root in terms of the values of the function and its first derivative at x_n. Thus

$$x_{n+1} = x_n - \frac{F(x_n)}{[dF(x_n)]/dx}$$

This formula enables progressively better estimates of x_0 to be obtained. Its major disadvantages are that it requires the first derivative to be known and it becomes unstable if the derivative approaches zero.

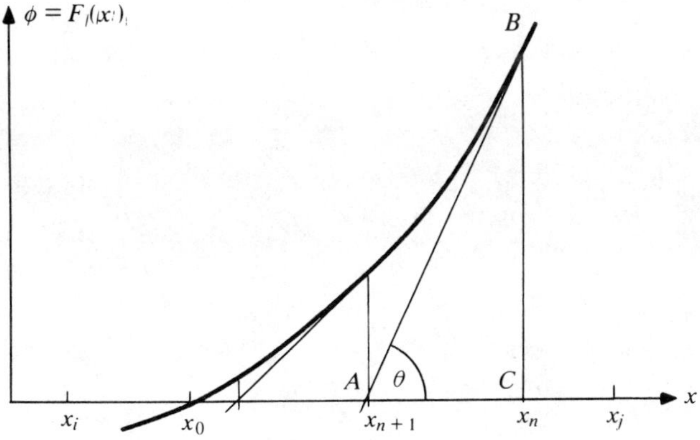

Figure 3.19 Newton–Raphson scheme

Example In 3.1.9.3, a root to the characteristic equation $F(\lambda) = 0 = \lambda^3 - 7.5\lambda^2 - 5.5\lambda + 30$ was required. Inspection shows that a root lies between 2 and 1. Since $F(2) = -3$, and $F(1) = 18$, it probably lies close to $\lambda = 2$. Writing $F'(\lambda)$ to represent $dF(\lambda)/d\lambda$,

$$F'(\lambda) = 3\lambda^2 - 15\lambda - 5.5$$

When $\lambda = 2$, $F(2) = -3$, $F'(2) = -23.5$ and a better estimate of λ is given by $\lambda = 2 - (-3)/(-23.5) = 1.872\,34$.

Repeating the process with the improved estimate gives $F(1.872\,34) = -0.026\,516$, $F'(1.872\,34) = -23.068\,13$, hence $\lambda = 1.872\,34 - (-0.026\,516)/(-23.068\,13) = 1.871\,19$.

Repeating again gives $\lambda = 1.871\,19 - (+0.000\,009\,8)/(-23.063\,79) = 1.871\,19$, and as for this particular problem λ was required to four significant digits, the process has converged to the desired degree of accuracy.

A SUBROUTINE to perform Newton–Raphson iterations is given in Fig. 3.20.

```
      SUBROUTINE NR(XN,XI,XJ,F,DF,MNIT,N1,N2,N3)
C XN-INITIAL ESTIMATE OF X,  XI,XJ-RANGE FOR X,  F,DF-FUNCTION SUBPROGRAMS
C TO EVALUATE THE FUNCTION AND ITS FIRST DERIVATIVE, THEY MUST APPEAR IN
C AN EXTERNAL STATEMENT IN THE CALLING PROGRAM,  N1,N2,N3 ARE LIMITS,
C MNIT-MAXIMUM NO. OF ITERATIONS
      REAL N1,N2,N3
      NIT=0
      FX=F(XN)
 1    DFDX=DF(XN)
      IF(ABS(DFDX).LT.N1)GOTO 91
      XN1=XN-FX/DFDX
      IF(XN1.LT.XI.OR.XN1.GT.XJ)GOTO 92
      FX=F(XN1)
      IF(ABS(FX).GT.N2)GOTO 2
      IF(ABS((XN1-XN)/XN).GT.N3)GOTO 2
      XN=XN1
      RETURN
 2    XN=XN1
      NIT=NIT+1
      IF(NIT.GT.MNIT)GOTO 93
      GOTO 1
 91   WRITE(6,691)
      STOP
 92   WRITE(6,692)
      STOP
 93   WRITE(6,693)
      STOP
 691  FORMAT(1H^,15H^DFDX^TOO^SMALL)
 692  FORMAT(1H^,22H^ESTIMATE^OUT^OF^RANGE)
 693  FORMAT(1H^,37H^NO.^OF^ALLOWABLE^ITERATIONS^EXCEEDED)
      END
```

Figure 3.20 Newton-Raphson

3.2.1.2 Method of false position

An alternative procedure which converges more slowly than the Newton–Raphson method, but which avoids the problems of using the inverse of the first derivative, is the method of false position. It is also sometimes referred to as the method of 'linear inverse interpolation' or 'regula falsi'.

To start this process, the preliminary stages described above are performed, but two starting values are required. These must lie either side of the root, so that if they are denoted by x_n and x_{n-1}, then $F(x_n)F(x_{n-1})<0$.

From Fig. 3.21, $AC/CE=AB/DE$, hence $(x_{n+1}-x_n)/(x_{n-1}-x_{n+1})=(-F(x_n)/F(x_{n-1}))$. Rearrangement of this equation gives a better estimate of the root in terms of previous estimates and the values of the function at those positions; thus

$$x_{n+1} = \frac{x_nF(x_{n-1})-x_{n-1}F(x_n)}{F(x_{n-1})-F(x_n)}$$

This formula is used to obtain a converging set of improved estimates of the root. To obtain the next approximation, the last estimate determined replaces the previous estimate on the right hand side of the equation that lies on the same side of the root as itself.

Example The characteristic equation of Sec. 3.1.9.3 which was solved by the Newton–Raphson method in the previous section will be solved for the root lying between $\lambda=1$ and $\lambda=2$. $F(\lambda)=\lambda^3-7.5\lambda^2-5.5\lambda+30$, therefore $F(2)=-3$, $F(1)=18$, and thus

$$\lambda = \frac{1(-3)-2(18)}{-3-18} = 1.857\,14$$

$F(1.857\,14)=0.323\,70$ and the improved estimate replaces $\lambda=1$ for the next iteration; thus

$$\lambda = \frac{1.857\,14(-3)-2(0.323\,70)}{-3-0.323\,70} = 1.871\,05$$

$F(1.871\,05)=0.003\,26$ and the improved estimate replaces $\lambda=1.857\,14$ for the next iteration; thus

$$\lambda = \frac{1.871\,05(-3)-2(0.003\,26)}{-3-0.003\,26} = 1.871\,60$$

$F(1.871\,60)=-0.009\,44$ and as this is negative $\lambda=1.871\,60$ replaces $\lambda=2$ for the next iteration; thus

$$\lambda = \frac{1.871\,05(-0.009\,44)-1.871\,60(0.003\,26)}{-0.009\,44-0.003\,26} = 1.871\,19$$

which is identical to the previously obtained value.

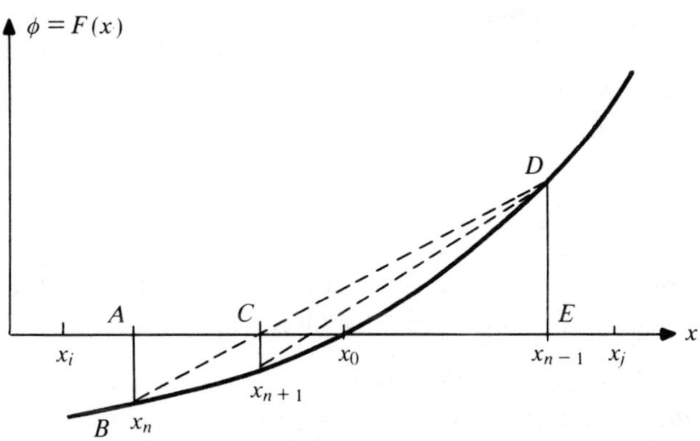

Figure 3.21 False-position scheme

A SUBROUTINE to perform the method of false position is given in Fig. 3.22.

```
      SUBROUTINE FP(XN1,XN,XI,XJ,F,N1,N2,N3,MNIT,XNP1)
C XN1,XN-ESTIMATED ROOTS EITHER SIDE OF SOUGHT ROOT X
C XI,XJ-RANGE FOR X,F-FUNCTION SUBPROGRAM
C N1,N2,N3-LIMITS,MNIT-MAXIMUM NO. OF ITERATIONS,XNP1-SOLUTION
      REAL N1,N2,N3
      FXN=F(XN)
      N35=N3*0.5
      FXN1=F(XN1)
      NIT=0
 1    IF(ABS(FXN1-FXN).LT.N1)GOTO 90
      XNP1=(XN*FXN1-XN1*FXN)/(FXN1-FXN)
      IF(XNP1.LT.XI.OR.XNP1.GT.XJ)GOTO 91
      FXNP1=F(XNP1)
      NIT=NIT+1
      IF(NIT.GT.MNIT)GOTO 92
      IF(FXN*FXNP1.GT.0.0)GOTO 2
      XN1=XNP1
      FXN1=FXNP1
      GOTO 3
 2    XN=XNP1
      FXN=FXNP1
 3    IF(ABS(FXNP1).GT.N2)GOTO 10
      IF(NIT.EQ.1)GOTO 10
      IF(ABS((XNP-XNP1)/(XNP+XNP1)).LT.N35)RETURN
 10   XNP=XNP1
      GOTO 1
 91   WRITE(6,691)
      STOP
 90   WRITE(6,690)
      STOP
 92   WRITE(6,692)
      STOP
 690  FORMAT(1H^,30H^FUNCTION^DIFFERENCE^TOO^SMALL)
 691  FORMAT(1H^,22H^ESTIMATE^OUT^OF^RANGE)
 692  FORMAT(1H^,37H^NO.^OF^ALLOWABLE^ITERATIONS^EXCEEDED)
      END
```

Figure 3.22 False position

3.2.1.3 Convergence criteria

Convergence criteria can be applied to the value of the function and to successive estimates of the root. With both Newton–Raphson and false-position methods a suitable convergence criterion for the value of the function is

$$|F(x_n)| < 1.0\text{E} - N$$

where N specifies the acceptable number of decimal places.

Suitable ways of specifying convergence to an acceptable number of decimal digits using successive estimates of a root are

1. for the Newton–Raphson procedure

$$\left|\frac{x_{n+1} - x_n}{x_n}\right| < 1.0\text{E} - N$$

and

2. for the method of false position

$$2\left|\frac{x_{n+1} - x_n}{x_{n+1} + x_n}\right| < 1.0\text{E} - N$$

where N specifies approximately the required number of significant digits.

3.2.2 Functions of more than one variable

The Newton–Raphson procedure can be deduced geometrically as described above, and also by considering a truncated approximation to Taylor's series for a function. The Taylor series for $F(x)$ in the region of x_0 is

$$F(x) = F(x_0) + \frac{(x - x_0)}{1!}\frac{\mathrm{d}F(x_0)}{\mathrm{d}x} + \frac{(x - x_0)^2}{2!}\frac{\mathrm{d}^2F(x_0)}{\mathrm{d}x^2} + \cdots$$

It can be seen that the Newton–Raphson formula is obtained by straightforward manipulation after setting $F(x) = 0$ and assuming $(x - x_0)$ to be sufficiently small for terms involving powers of $(x - x_0)$ to be ignored.

A similar truncated Taylor series for a function of two variables is:

$$F(x,y) = F(x_0,y_0) + (x - x_0)\frac{\partial F}{\partial x}(x_0,y_0) + (y - y_0)\frac{\partial F}{\partial y}(x_0,y_0)$$

Problems requiring determination of variables (x, y) that set two functions simultaneously to zero can be obtained by expanding the functions about an estimated solution (x_n, y_n). Let the functions be P and Q and let (x_{n+1}, y_{n+1}) be an improved solution. Then

$$0 = P(x_n,y_n) + (x_{n+1} - x_n)\frac{\partial P}{\partial x}(x_n,y_n) + (y_{n+1} - y_n)\frac{\partial P}{\partial y}(x_n,y_n)$$

and

$$0 = Q(x_n,y_n) + (x_{n+1} - x_n)\frac{\partial Q}{\partial x}(x_n,y_n) + (y_{n+1} - y_n)\frac{\partial Q}{\partial y}(x_n,y_n)$$

Rearrangement of these equations gives two linear simultaneous equations, from which x_{n+1} and y_{n+1} can be obtained. Thus

$$x_{n+1}\frac{\partial P_n}{\partial x} + y_{n+1}\frac{\partial P_n}{\partial y} = -P_n + x_n\frac{\partial P_n}{\partial x} + y_n\frac{\partial P_n}{\partial y}$$

$$x_{n+1}\frac{\partial Q_n}{\partial x} + y_{n+1}\frac{\partial Q_n}{\partial y} = -Q_n + x_n\frac{\partial Q_n}{\partial x} + y_n\frac{\partial Q_n}{\partial y}$$

where

$$P_n = P(x_n,y_n) \quad \text{and} \quad Q_n = Q(x_n,y_n)$$

In matrix form the equations are

$$\begin{bmatrix} \dfrac{\partial P_n}{\partial x} & \dfrac{\partial P_n}{\partial y} \\ \dfrac{\partial Q_n}{\partial x} & \dfrac{\partial Q_n}{\partial y} \end{bmatrix} \begin{bmatrix} x_{n+1} \\ y_{n+1} \end{bmatrix} = \begin{bmatrix} \dfrac{\partial P_n}{\partial x} & \dfrac{\partial P_n}{\partial y} \\ \dfrac{\partial Q_n}{\partial x} & \dfrac{\partial Q_n}{\partial y} \end{bmatrix} \begin{bmatrix} x_n \\ y_n \end{bmatrix} - \begin{bmatrix} P_n \\ Q_n \end{bmatrix}$$

hence

$$\begin{bmatrix} x_{n+1} \\ y_{n+1} \end{bmatrix} = \begin{bmatrix} x_n \\ y_n \end{bmatrix} - \begin{bmatrix} \dfrac{\partial P_n}{\partial x} & \dfrac{\partial P_n}{\partial y} \\ \dfrac{\partial Q_n}{\partial x} & \dfrac{\partial Q_n}{\partial y} \end{bmatrix}^{-1} \begin{bmatrix} P_n \\ Q_n \end{bmatrix}$$

This equation can be written in a condensed form as

$$\mathbf{X}_{n+1} = \mathbf{X}_n - \mathbf{J}^{-1} \cdot \mathbf{F}_n$$

where **X** is a vector of variables, **F** is a vector of function values and **J** is a Jacobian matrix of first derivatives. The similarity with this equation and its one-dimensional counterpart is apparent. The equation can be extended for any number of variables and functions. Solutions are, however, expensive as the Jacobian has to be inverted at each iteration. Good initial values are vital and time spent in establishing the starting point for iteration is never wasted.

Example Determine a non-zero pair of values for (x, y) that set $P = x^3 + y^2$ and $Q = x^2 + xy$ to zero. The derivatives of the functions are: $\partial P/\partial x = 3x^2$, $\partial P/\partial y = 2y$, $\partial Q/\partial x = 2x + y$, and $\partial Q/\partial y = x$. The iterative equations are

$$x_{n+1} = x_n - \frac{-P\dfrac{\partial Q}{\partial y} + Q\dfrac{\partial P}{\partial y}}{\dfrac{\partial P}{\partial y}\dfrac{\partial Q}{\partial x} - \dfrac{\partial P}{\partial x}\dfrac{\partial Q}{\partial y}} = x_n - \left(\frac{-x^4 + xy^2 + 2x^2y}{4xy + 2y^2 - 3x^3}\right)_{\substack{x=x_n \\ y=y_n}}$$

$$y_{n+1} = y_n - \frac{P\dfrac{\partial Q}{\partial x} - Q\dfrac{\partial P}{\partial x}}{\dfrac{\partial P}{\partial y}\dfrac{\partial Q}{\partial x} - \dfrac{\partial P}{\partial x}\dfrac{\partial Q}{\partial y}} = y_n - \left(\frac{-x^4 - 2x^3y + 2xy^2 + y^3}{4xy + 2y^2 - 3x^3}\right)_{\substack{x=x_n \\ y=y_n}}$$

If initial estimates of $x_n = -2$, $y_n = 1.5$ are taken, improved estimates are given by

$$x_{n+1} = -2 - \frac{-16 - 4.5 + 12}{-12 + 4.5 + 24} = -1.4848$$

$$y_{n+1} = 1.5 - \frac{-16 + 24 - 9 + 3.375}{-12 + 4.5 + 24} = 1.3561$$

Using these better estimates as initial values gives

$$x_{n+1} = -1.4848 - \frac{-1.611\,89}{5.444\,86} = -1.188\,81$$

$$y_{n+1} = 1.3561 - \frac{1.050\,63}{5.444\,86} = 1.163\,13$$

After 5 iterations the values have converged sufficiently to give $x = -1.0$, $y = 1.0$ to 5 significant digits.

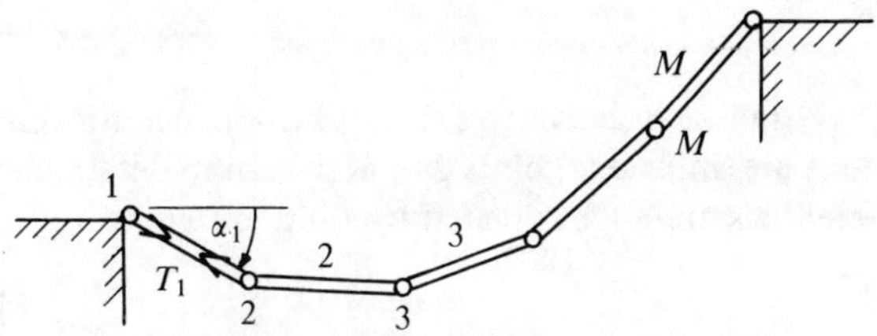

Figure 3.23 Suspension chain

Example Determine the geometry of the suspension chain shown in Fig. 3.23. The chain has M pin-ended straight, rigid members and it is assumed that all of the loading is applied at the connections. Let α_i, T_i $(i = 1, M)$ be the slope and tension in the ith member. Equations of statics are used to determine the position of the last joint. If the projections of the closing error are x and y (see Fig. 3.24), then the functions $x = P(\alpha_1, T_1)$ and $y = Q(\alpha_1, T_1)$ are only equal to zero for correct values of α_1 and T_1. If (α_n, T_n) are estimates of (α_1, T_1), then better approximations are given by

$$\alpha_{n+1} = \alpha_n - \left(-P_n \frac{\partial Q_n}{\partial T} + Q_n \frac{\partial P_n}{\partial T}\right) \Big/ \text{DETJ}$$

and

$$T_{n+1} = T_n - \left(P_n \frac{\partial Q_n}{\partial \alpha} - Q_n \frac{\partial P_n}{\partial \alpha}\right) \Big/ \text{DETJ}$$

where

$$\text{DETJ} = \frac{\partial P_n}{\partial T}\frac{\partial Q_n}{\partial \alpha} - \frac{\partial P_n}{\partial \alpha}\frac{\partial Q_n}{\partial T}$$

$$P_n = P(\alpha_n, T_n), Q_n = Q(\alpha_n, T_n)$$

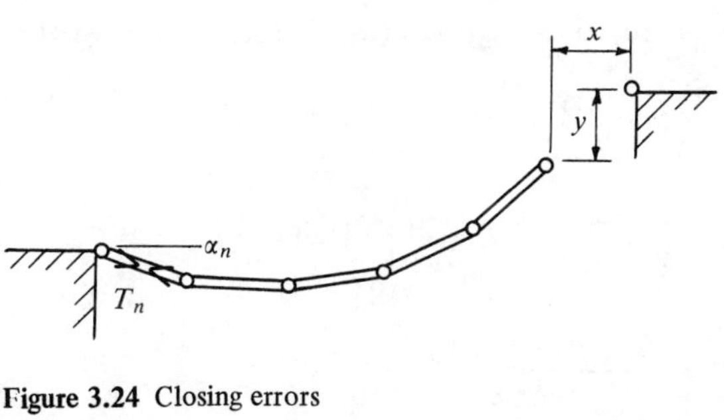

Figure 3.24 Closing errors

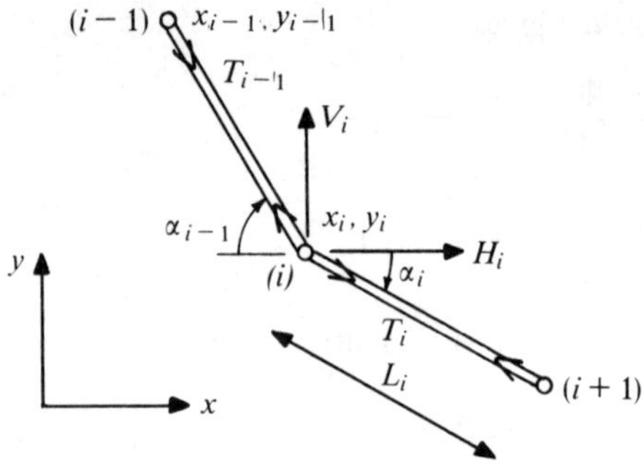

Figure 3.25 Joint forces

Explicit functions for P and Q and their derivatives cannot be obtained for this example, so equilibrium equations are applied at joints 2 to M in turn to determine the closing errors, and the differentials are approximated by finite differences; see Sec. 3.4.4.

At joint i (see Fig. 3.25),

$$H_i + T_i \cos \alpha_i - T_{i-1} \cos \alpha_{i-1} = 0$$

and

$$V_i - T_i \sin \alpha_i + T_{i-1} \sin \alpha_{i-1} = 0$$

As $(T_{i-1}, \alpha_{i-1}, H_i, V_i)$ are known, (T_i, α_i) can be calculated, and as (x_i, y_i) are known, (x_{i+1}, y_{i+1}) can be determined from the equations:

$$x_{i+1} = x_i + L_i \cos \alpha_i$$

and

$$y_{i+1} = y_i - L_i \sin \alpha_i$$

Application to joints 2 to M in turn gives the estimated position of the last joint. These operations are performed in SUBROUTINE POSLJ in the program given in Fig. 3.26.

To obtain approximations to the function derivatives, closing errors $(x + \Delta x_\alpha, y + \Delta y_\alpha)$ and $(x + \Delta x_T, y + \Delta y_T)$ are determined by using initial estimates of $(\alpha_n + \Delta\alpha_n, T_n)$ and $(\alpha_n, T_n + \Delta T_n)$, respectively. Then

$$(x + \Delta x_\alpha) - x \simeq \left(P_n + \frac{\partial P_n}{\partial \alpha} \Delta\alpha\right) - P_n$$

hence

$$\frac{\partial P_n}{\partial \alpha} \simeq \frac{\Delta x_\alpha}{\Delta \alpha} \quad \text{and similarly} \quad \frac{\partial P_n}{\partial T} \simeq \frac{\Delta x_T}{\Delta T} \quad \frac{\partial Q_n}{\partial \alpha} \simeq \frac{\Delta y_\alpha}{\Delta \alpha} \quad \frac{\partial Q_n}{\partial T} \simeq \frac{\Delta y_T}{\Delta T}$$

The equations to determine improved estimates of (α_1, T_1) can now be written in the form

$$\alpha_{n+1} = \alpha_n - \left(-P_n \frac{\Delta y_T}{\Delta T} + Q_n \frac{\Delta x_T}{\Delta T}\right) \Big/ \text{DETJ}$$

$$T_{n+1} = T_n - \left(P_n \frac{\Delta y_\alpha}{\Delta \alpha} - Q_n \frac{\Delta x_\alpha}{\Delta \alpha}\right) \Big/ \text{DETJ}$$

where

$$\text{DETJ} = \frac{\Delta x_T \, \Delta y_\alpha - \Delta x_\alpha \, \Delta y_T}{\Delta\alpha \, \Delta T}$$

These calculations are performed using the SUBROUTINE POSLJ with the parameters (α_n, T_n), $(\alpha_n + \Delta\alpha_n, T_n)$, and $(\alpha_n, T_n + \Delta T_n)$ in turn, as can be seen by studying Fig. 3.26. The finite differences ΔT_n and $\Delta\alpha_n$ are set in the statement labelled 100 to be 1 per cent of T_n and α_n, respectively. In the event of either α_n or T_n being zero the corresponding term is set equal to 0.01.

```
      DIMENSION X(20),Y(20),L(20),T(20),SA(20),CA(20),V(20),H(20)
      REAL L
C STATEMENTS TO INPUT THE NO. OF MEMBERS INTO M,
C THE JOINT CO-ORDS AND APPLIED FORCES INTO X,Y,H,V RESPECTIVELY
C THE LENGTHS OF MEMBERS INTO L
C THE CO-ORDS OF THE RIGHT HAND SUPPORT INTO XC,YC
C THE CO-ORDS OF THE LEFT HAND SUPPORT INTO X(1),Y(1)
C THE INITIAL ESTIMATES OF ALPHA 1 AND T1 INTO ALPHA AND TENS
C AND THE TOLERANCE ON THE CLOSING ERROR INTO EPS OMITTED
      COMMON/INFO/X,Y,L,T,SA,CA,V,H
 100  DA=AMAX1(ABS(ALPHA)/100.0,0.01)
      DT=AMAX1(ABS(TENS)/100.0,0.01)
C DETERMINE CLOSING ERROR AND TEST AGAINST TOLERANCE
      CALL POSLJ(M,ALPHA,TENS,X1,Y1)
      CLERR=SQRT((X1-XC)**2+(Y1-YC)**2)
      IF(CLERR.LE.EPS)GOTO 999
C DETERMINE APPROXIMATE DERIVATIVES
      CALL POSLJ(M,ALPHA+DA,TENS,X2,Y2)
      CALL POSLJ(M,ALPHA,TENS+DT,X3,Y3)
      DXDA=(X2-X1)/DA
      DXDT=(X3-X1)/DT
      DYDA=(Y2-Y1)/DA
      DYDT=(Y3-Y1)/DT
      P=X1-XC
      Q=Y1-YC
      DETJ=DXDT*DYDA-DXDA*DYDT
C IMPROVED ESTIMATES
      ALPHA=ALPHA-(-P*DYDT+Q*DXDT)/DETJ
      TENS=TENS-(P*DYDA-Q*DXDA)/DETJ
C CHECKS ON PERMISSIBLE RANGE OF ALPHA AND TENS OMITTED
      GOTO 100
 999  CONTINUE
C STATEMENTS TO PRINT SOLUTION OMITTED
      END
      SUBROUTINE POSLJ(M,A,TN,XL,YL)
      REAL L(20)
      DIMENSION X(20),Y(20),T(20),SA(20),CA(20),V(20),H(20)
      COMMON/INFO/X,Y,L,T,SA,CA,V,H
      T(1)=TN
      SA(1)=SIN(A)
      CA(1)=COS(A)
      X(2)=L(1)*CA(1)
```

Figure 3.26 Coding for chain problem

```
      Y(2)=-L(1)*SA(1)
      DO 10 I=2,M
      I1=I-1
      TICA=T(I1)*CA(I1)-H(I)
      TISA=T(I1)*SA(I1)+V(I)
      TI=SQRT(TICA**2+TISA**2)
      T(I)=TI
      SA(I)=TISA/TI
      CA(I)=TICA/TI
      X(I+1)=X(I)+L(I)*CA(I)
10    Y(I+1)=Y(I)-L(I)*SA(I)
      XL=X(M+1)
      YL=Y(M+1)
      RETURN
      END
```

Figure 3.26 (*continued*)

The above procedure produces convergence to the correct answer when good starting values are given. As with all nonlinear methods, however, the procedure can become unstable. In a complete program, limits to define acceptable ranges for 'improved' estimates of (α_1, T_1) would be provided, and to avoid needless expense computations would be halted if an estimate was outside one of the ranges.

3.3 NUMERICAL INTEGRATION

Numerical integration, or quadrature, is used to determine approximate values of definite integrals. The procedure is to calculate the exact integral of a polynomial that represents approximately the function to be integrated over the required range. A numerical integration is usually performed by summing a finite number of weighted values of the function to be integrated. It is a particularly useful method when a function is known only by its values at a discrete number of stations. In general, numerical integration is a well behaved and stable operation that presents few problems for automatic computation.

3.3.1 Functions of one variable

Numerical integration of functions of one variable between finite limits is considered in two sections. In the first, values of a function at equally spaced intervals are required. In the second section, an efficient method is considered for dealing with functions that are expensive to evaluate.

3.3.1.1 Trapezium and Simpson's rules

Let $S = \int_a^b F(x)\,dx$, where $F(x)$ is a continuous function of x in the range $a \leqslant x \leqslant b$ and let $P(x)$ be a polynomial that approximates to $F(x)$ over the desired range.

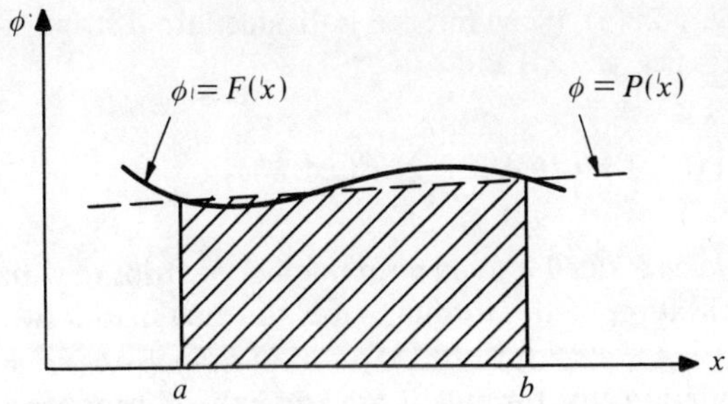

Figure 3.27 Trapezium approximation

If $P(x)$ is a linear curve passing through points $[a, F(a)]$ and $[b, F(b)]$ as shown in Fig. 3.27, then

$$S \simeq \int_a^b P(x)\,\mathrm{d}x = \frac{[F(a) + F(b)](b - a)}{2}$$

If $P(x)$ is a quadratic or cubic polynomial passing through points $[a, F(a)]$, $[(a+b)/2, F((a+b)/2)]$, $[b, F(b)]$ then

$$S \simeq \int_a^b P(x)\,\mathrm{d}x = \frac{[F(a) + 4F((a+b)/2) + F(b)](b - a)}{6}$$

The first of these two equations calculates the area of the trapezium shaded in Fig. 3.27, and is consequently called the 'trapezium rule' or 'trapezoidal rule'. It can be shown that this formulation leads to an error of order $-((b-a)^3/12)(\mathrm{d}^2F(\eta)/\mathrm{d}x^2)$. The second formulation is called Simpson's rule, and it can be shown that the error involved is of the order $-((b-a)^5/2880)(\mathrm{d}^4F(\eta)/\mathrm{d}x^4)$, where for both cases $a < \eta < b$.

These formulations can be improved by dividing the interval $(b - a)$ into n equally spaced sub-intervals as shown in Fig. 3.28. The approximate integrations are carried out over each sub-interval in turn and the results summed to give the integral over the whole range.

For the trapezium rule: $\Delta S_i = (F(x_{i+1}) + F(x_i))(x_{i+1} - x_i)/2$, where ΔS_i is

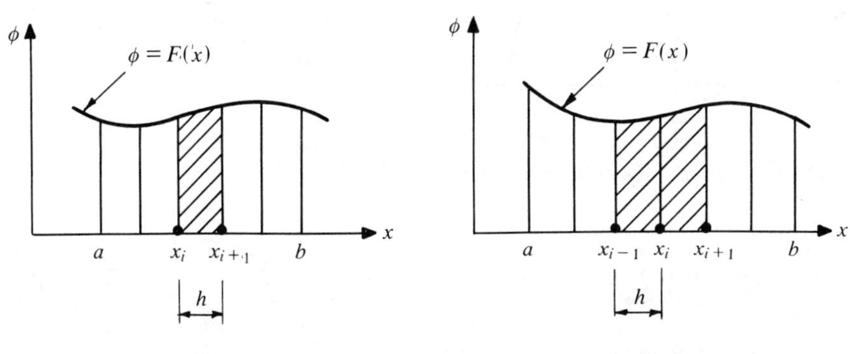

Figure 3.28 Sub-division into strips. (a) Trapezoidal strips. (b) Simpson strips

the area of the shaded strip in Fig. 3.28(a). If the interval is divided into n strips of equal width h, then $h = (b-a)/n = (x_{i+1} - x_i)$ and

$$S = \sum_{i=1}^{n} \Delta S_i = h\left((F(a)+F(b))/2 + \sum_{k=1}^{n-1} F(a+kh)\right)$$

For Simpson's rule, the interval is divided into an even number of strips n, with each of width $h = (b-a)/n$. Application of the formula gives the area of the two strips adjacent to x_i, as shown in Fig. 3.28(b), to be $\Delta S_i = h[F(x_{i-1}) + 4F(x_i) + F(x_{i+1})]/3$. For automatic computation this formula is used directly, but for hand calculations the ΔS_i are usually summed to give

$$S = \tfrac{1}{3}h\left[F(a)+F(b)+4\sum_{k=1}^{n/2} F(a+(2k-1)h) + 2\sum_{k=1}^{n/2-1} F(a+2kh)\right]$$

Simpson's rule is more efficient than the trapezium rule, since, for a given number of function evaluations, it has a smaller error term. Its only disadvantage is that it requires the variable range to be divided into an even number of strips. Numerical integration formulae for the areas under higher order polynomials can be derived, but they offer no significant advantage over the Simpson formulation.

Example Determine the area of a semicircle of radius r (see Fig. 3.29). The area is given by the integral

$$S = \int_{-r}^{r} F(x)\,dx \qquad \text{with } F(x) = \sqrt{r^2 - x^2}$$

For convenience, the integral is first non-dimensionalized by setting $x = r\xi$, thus $S = r^2 \int_{-1}^{1} \sqrt{1-\xi^2}\,d\xi$. Taking 6 strips: $a = -1, F(a) = 0$; $b = 1$, $F(b) = 0$; $h = 2/6 = 1/3$, hence

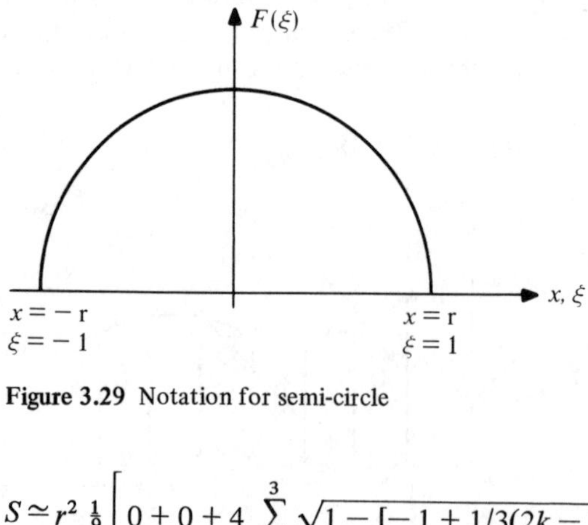

Figure 3.29 Notation for semi-circle

$$S \simeq r^2\,\tfrac{1}{9}\left[0+0+4\sum_{k=1}^{3}\sqrt{1-[-1+1/3(2k-1)]^2} + 2\sum_{k=1}^{2}\sqrt{1-(-1+2/3k)^2}\right]$$

$$S \simeq r^2/9[4(\sqrt{5/9} + \sqrt{1} + \sqrt{5/9}) + 2(\sqrt{8/9} + \sqrt{8/9})]$$

$$S \simeq 1.526r^2$$

When a function is known and can be evaluated at any point in the integration range, an automatic solution can increase the number of strips until estimated values agree to some specified tolerance. One way to do this is to continually halve the strip width. An efficient solution procedure is first illustrated with reference to the first three divisions.

Division of the range into two strips, as shown in Fig. 3.30(a), enables the following calculations to be performed:

```
H=(B–A)/2.0

SO=F(A)+F(B)

S2=0.0

S4=F(A+H)

S=(SO+2.0*S2+4.0*S4)*H/3.0
```

where H is the strip width; SO is the sum of the ordinates at the first and last stations; $S2$ is the sum of the ordinates at the odd-numbered intermediate stations; $S4$ is the sum of the ordinates at the even-numbered intermediate stations and S is the estimate of the integral.

On dividing the range into four strips, as shown in Fig. 3.30(b), it can be seen that all of the ordinates at internal stations of the previous subdivision become ordinates at odd-numbered stations in the new subdivision. Therefore:

```
H1=H/2.0

S21=S2+S4

S4=F(A+H1)+F(A+3*H1)

S=(SO+2.0*S21+4.0*S4)*H1/3.0
```

Thus, the only new function ordinates to be determined are those in the middle of the strips of the previous subdivision.

Division of the range into eight strips is shown in Fig. 3.30(c) and the calculations follow the pattern established in the previous stage:

```
H2=H1/2.0

S22=S21+S4

S41=F(A+H2)+F(A+3*H2)+F(A+5*H2)+F(A+7*H2)

S=(SO+2.0*S22+4.0*S41)*H2/3.0
```

Example The procedure is illustrated by considering the integral of the previous example

$$S/r^2 = \int_{-1}^{1} \sqrt{1-\xi^2}\, d\xi$$

$A = -1, B = 1, F(\xi) = \sqrt{1-\xi^2}$.

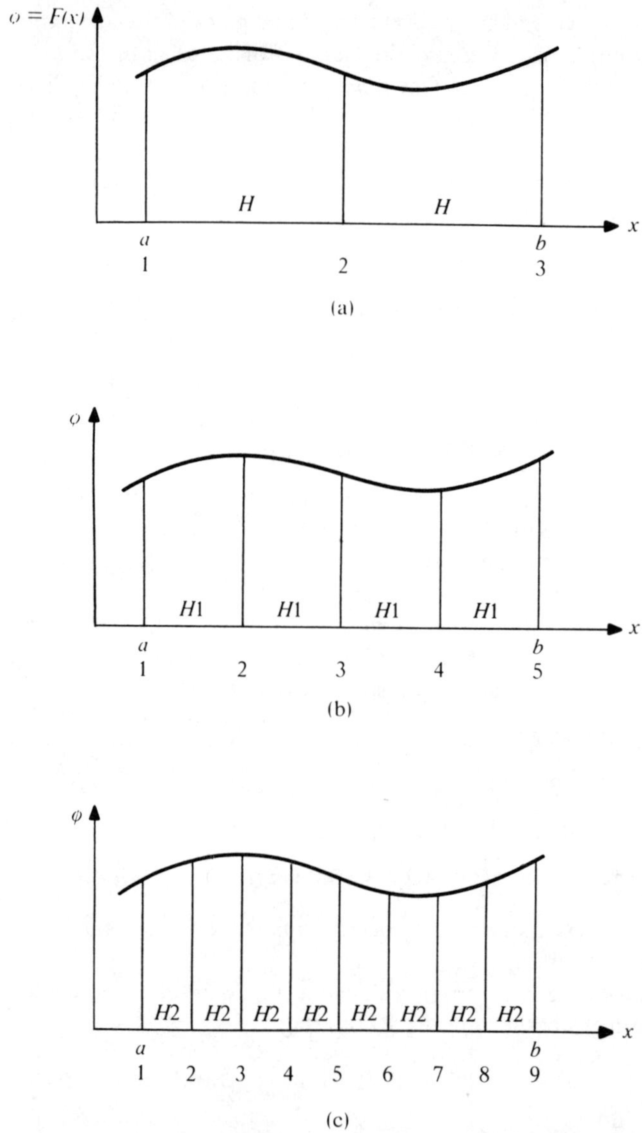

Figure 3.30 Progressive sub-division. (a) Division into two strips. (b) Division into four strips. (c) Division into eight strips

1. Taking 2 strips:

$$H = 1, \; SO = 0, \; S4 = 1$$

and hence

$$S/r^2 = (0 + 2 \times 0 + 4 \times 1) \times 1/3 = 1.333 \text{ (error 15.1 per cent)}$$

2. Taking 4 strips:

$$H1 = 0.5, \; S21 = 1, \; S4 = F(-0.5) + F(0.5) = 2\sqrt{1 - 0.5^2} = 1.732\,05$$

and hence:

$$S/r^2 = (0 + 2 \times 1 + 4 \times 1.732\,05) \times 0.5/3 = 1.488 \text{ (error 5.3 per cent)}$$

3. Taking 8 strips:

$$H2 = 0.25, \ S22 = 2.732\,05$$

$$S41 = F(-0.75) + F(-0.25) + F(0.75) = 3.259\,37$$

and hence:

$$S/r^2 = (0 + 2 \times 2.732\,05 + 4 \times 3.259\,37)/12 = 1.542 \text{ (error 1.8 per cent)}$$

4. Taking 16 strips:

$$S/r^2 = 1.5606 \text{ (error 0.6 per cent)}$$

When the trapezium rule is used, the corresponding values are:

1. taking 2 strips: $S/r^2 = 1.0$ (error 36.3 per cent)
2. taking 4 strips: $S/r^2 = 1.366$ (error 13.0 per cent)
3. taking 8 strips: $S/r^2 = 1.498$ (error 4.6 per cent)
4. taking 16 strips: $S/r^2 = 1.545$ (error 1.6 per cent)

In the SUBROUTINE SIMP2 in Fig. 3.31, the number of strips is continuously doubled until two estimates of the integral agree to a specified tolerance. Convergence is assumed to be satisfied when the difference between two estimates is less than the current estimate multiplied by a specified tolerance coefficient. It is assumed that the integral is not zero, and that an estimate will not be zero. To prevent errors, a function should be integrated in sections such that ordinates used for integration over a particular range lie on one side of the ϕ axis only. Care should be taken not to specify a tolerance that a particular computer is incapable of satisfying. Roundoff errors increase with the number of strips taken and the tolerance should take into account the number of significant digits used in calculations.

```
      SUBROUTINE SIMP2(F,A,B,TOL,LS,S)
C F-FUNCTION SUBPROGRAM, MUST APPEAR IN EXTERNAL STATEMENT
C A,B-INTEGRATION LIMITS(B.GT.A)
C TOL-ALLOWABLE RELATIVE ERROR FOR CONVERGENCE
C LS-LIMIT ON NO. OF STRIPS,  I2-NO. OF STRIPS BEING TAKEN
      IF(B.LE.A)GOTO 90
      I2=2
      H=(B-A)/2.0
      SO=F(A)+F(B)
      S2=0.0
      S4=F(A+H)
      S=(SO+4.0*S4)*H/3.0
 1    I2=I2*2
      H=H/2.0
C S1=PREVIOUS ESTIMATE OF INTEGRAL FOR CONVERGENCE CHECK
      S1=S
      S2=S2+S4
      S4=0.0
```

Figure 3.31 Simpson's rule with interval halving

```
      DO 2 J=1,I2,2
 2    S4=S4+F(A+H*FLOAT(J))
      S=(S0+2.0*S2+4.0*S4)*H/3.0
C CONVERGENCE CHECK
      IF(ABS(S-S1).LT.TOL*ABS(S))RETURN
C CHECK LIMIT ON NO. OF STRIPS
      IF(I2.LT.LS)GOTO 1
      WRITE(6,691)LS,S1,S
      STOP
 90   WRITE(6,690)B,A
      STOP
 690  FORMAT(1H‸,38H‸ERROR-LOWER‸LIMIT‸EXCEEDS‸UPPER‸LIMIT/
     C1H‸,13H‸UPPER‸LIMIT=,E13.6/1H‸,14H‸LOWER‸LIMIT‸=,E13.6)
 691  FORMAT(1H‸,24H‸ERROR-NOT‸CONVERGED‸IN‸,I5,7H‸STRIPS/
     C1H‸,20H‸PREVIOUS‸ESTIMATE‸=,E13.6/
     C1H‸,19H‸CURRENT‸ESTIMATE‸=,E13.6)
      END
```

Figure 3.31 *(continued)*

3.3.1.2 Gauss quadrature

When the effort to calculate values of the integrand represents a major part of the computation, it is desirable to minimize the number of stations at which this has to be done. The efficiency of the integration may be improved by calculating values of the function at selected stations which are no longer evenly spaced. One set of optimum positions for integration stations has been determined by Gauss, and are called the Gauss points. For functions of one variable the Gauss quadrature formula is

$$\int_{-1}^{1} F(\xi)\,d\xi \simeq \int_{-1}^{1} P(\xi)\,d\xi = \sum_{i=1}^{n+1} w_i F(\xi_i)$$

where $(n+1)$ is the number of integration stations, and w_i is the weighting coefficient associated with the Gauss point at ξ_i.

For derivation of the trapezoidal and Simpson formulations only the w_i are treated as variables, as the ξ_i are evenly spaced. If both the w_i and the ξ_i are treated as variables, then for $(n+1)$ integration stations there are $2(n+1)$ variables available to define the polynomial $P(\xi)$. As a polynomial of order $(2n+1)$ requires $2(n+1)$ conditions to uniquely specify its form, a Gauss integration formulation with $(n+1)$ integration stations provides the exact integral for polynomials of order $(2n+1)$ and below. Thus with only two integration stations a cubic is integrated exactly, and with three integration stations a quintic is integrated exactly.

Values of the ordinates ξ_i and weighting coefficients w_i for Gauss quadrature are given in Table 3.1. The Gauss formulation can be applied to any interval of x by use of a suitable coordinate transformation. Thus

$$\int_a^b G(x)\,dx \equiv \int_{-1}^{1} F(\xi)\,d\xi$$

where

$$x = \frac{(b-a)\,\xi + (a+b)}{2} \qquad \text{and} \qquad dx = \frac{b-a}{2}\,d\xi$$

Table 3.1 Gauss integration coefficients

$n+1$	$\pm\xi_i$	w_i
2	0.57735 02692	1.00000 00000
3	0.00000 00000	0.88888 88889
	0.77459 66692	0.55555 55556
4	0.33998 10436	0.65214 51549
	0.86113 63116	0.34785 48451
5	0.00000 00000	0.56888 88889
	0.53846 93101	0.47862 86705
	0.90617 98459	0.23692 68850
8	0.18343 46425	0.36268 37833
	0.52553 24099	0.31370 66459
	0.79666 64774	0.22238 10345
	0.96028 98565	0.10122 85363

Example Use of the Gauss integration formula is illustrated by considering the area of a semicircle. From the previous example, $S/r^2 = \int_{-1}^{1}\sqrt{1-\xi^2}\,d\xi$.

1. Taking 2 stations:

$$S/r^2 = 1\cdot\sqrt{1-(0.577\,35)^2} + 1\cdot\sqrt{1-(-0.577\,35)^2}$$
$$= 1.633 \text{ (error 4.0 per cent)}$$

2. Taking 3 stations:

$$S/r^2 = 0.888\,89 \times 1.0 + 0.555\,56\sqrt{1-(0.774\,60)^2}$$
$$+\ 0.555\,56\sqrt{1-(-0.774\,60)^2} = 1.5916 \text{ (error 1.3 per cent)}$$

Before extending the subject of numerical integration to two dimensions, it should be pointed out that some functions, other than algebraic polynomials, are more efficiently integrated by alternative integration schemes. In certain cases, integrals with one or more infinite limits can be handled and the interested reader should consult a more advanced text[5] for treatment of these topics.

3.3.2 Functions of two variables

3.3.2.1 Integration over a rectangular domain

The trapezoidal, Simpson, and Gauss formulations can be readily adapted for functions of two variables when their coordinate axes are orthogonal, and the domain of integration is rectangular.

Let $V = \int_{x1}^{x2}\int_{y1}^{y2} F(x, y)\,dy\,dx$, where $F(x, y)$ is a continuous function for $x_1 \leqslant x \leqslant x_2$ and for $y_1 \leqslant y \leqslant y_2$. When discussing integration schemes for double integrals, it is helpful to consider V as the volume between the surface $\phi = F(x, y)$ and its projection on the x, y plane, as shown in Fig. 3.32.

There are two basic approaches. In the first, integration is treated in two stages with each part involving integration of a function of one variable. Lines parallel to a coordinate axis are drawn through the integration stations of the orthogonal axis. In Fig. 3.32 the lines are parallel to the y axis and the cross-sectional areas $A(x_i)$, shown shaded, are determined by applying a numerical integration formula for a function of one variable. Thus

$$A(x_i) = \int_{y1}^{y2} F(x_i, y)\,\mathrm{d}x \simeq \int_{y1}^{y2} P(y)\,\mathrm{d}y$$

The required integral, V, which equals the volume under the surface, is then determined by treating the $A(x_i)$ as values of a continuous function of x, $A(x)$. Integration of this function provides an estimate of the volume under the surface. Thus:

$$V = \int_{x1}^{x2} A(x)\,\mathrm{d}x \simeq \int_{x1}^{x2} P(x)\,\mathrm{d}x$$

Treated in this manner, the problem reduces to one of repeated applications of a formula for integration of a function of one variable and suitable tolerances are set for each of the integrations.

In the alternative approach, a single-stage procedure is used and weighting coefficients are determined at a grid of integration stations. It is usual to perform the operations on a uniform grid, and a tolerance is set for the difference between successive estimates of the volume determined. Using the notation for Gauss quadrature,

$$V = \int_{x1}^{x2} \int_{y1}^{y2} G(x,y)\,\mathrm{d}y\,\mathrm{d}x = \int_{-1}^{1} \int_{-1}^{1} F(\xi,\eta)\,\mathrm{d}\eta\,\mathrm{d}\xi$$

$$V \simeq \int_{-1}^{1} \left(\sum_{j=1}^{m+1} w_j F(\xi,\eta_j) \right) \mathrm{d}\xi \simeq \sum_{i=1}^{n+1} w_i \left(\sum_{j=1}^{m+1} w_j F(\xi_i,\eta_j) \right)$$

and hence

$$V \simeq \sum_{i=1}^{n+1} \sum_{j=1}^{m+1} w_i w_j F(\xi_i,\eta_j)$$

The values of the weighting coefficients for Gauss quadrature w_i, w_j and the positions of the integration stations ξ_i, η_j are given in Table 3.1.

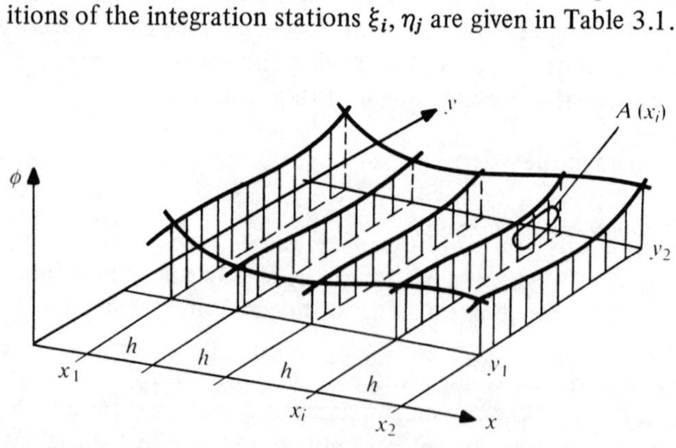

Figure 3.32 Two-stage integration

Example Using Simpson's rule, determine the volume of material above the datum level of 0.0 m of a tip, whose spot heights are given in Fig. 3.33. The Simpson weighting coefficients are shown in Fig. 3.34.

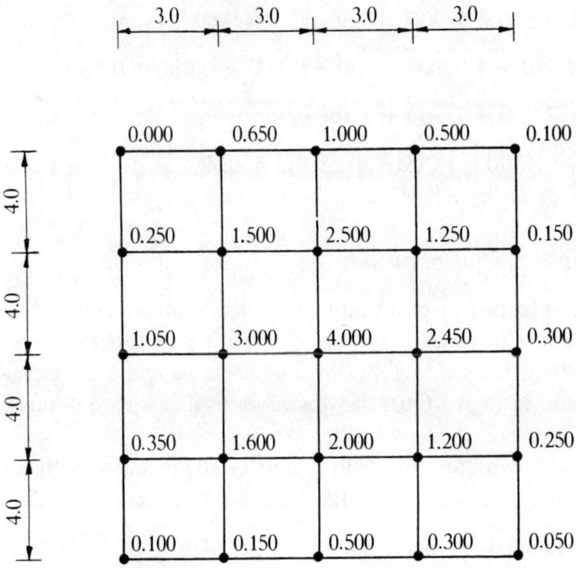

Figure 3.33 Spot heights

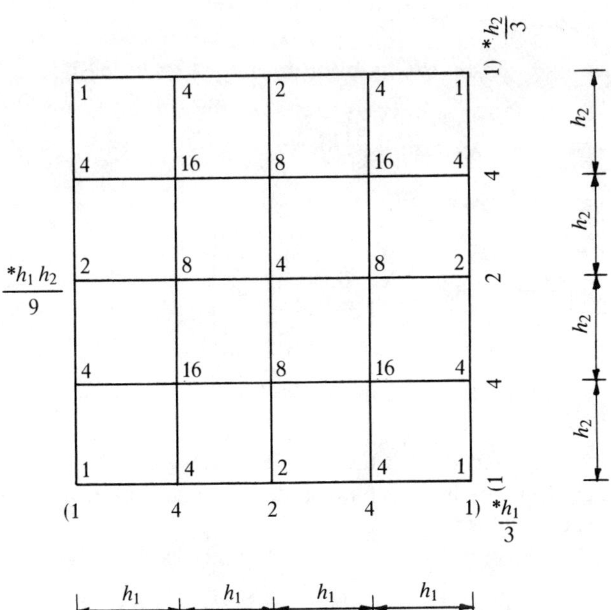

Figure 3.34 Simpson ordinate multipliers

The volume is given by

$$V \simeq \frac{3.0}{3}\frac{4.0}{3}[1(0.100 + 0.000 + 0.050 + 0.100)$$
$$+ 2(1.050 + 0.500 + 1.000 + 0.300) + 4(0.350 + 0.250$$
$$+ 0.150 + 0.650 + 4.000 + 0.300 + 0.500 + 0.250 + 0.150)$$
$$+ 8(3.000 + 2.000 + 2.500 + 2.450)$$
$$+ 16(1.600 + 1.500 + 1.200 + 1.250)] = 267.7$$

3.3.2.2 Integration over a non-rectangular domain

It is sometimes necessary to integrate over a non-rectangular domain. This is frequently the case with numerical integration of finite-element stiffness matrices; see Sec. 3.5. In such cases, transformation functions are used to relate a general curvilinear quadrilateral domain in (x, y) Cartesian coordinates to a square domain in (ξ, η) coordinates.

In Fig. 3.35 a curvilinear quadrilateral domain is illustrated, together with an expanded view of the infinitesimal shaded area $d\xi\, d\eta$. It can be seen that

$$\text{area } OAB = \Delta = \text{area } OBB' + \text{area } B'BAA' - \text{area } OAA'$$
$$\Delta = \tfrac{1}{2}BB'OB' + \tfrac{1}{2}B'A'(BB' + AA') - \tfrac{1}{2}AA'OA'$$
$$2\Delta = BB'OB' + (OA' - OB')(BB' + AA') - AA'OA'$$
$$2\Delta = OA'BB' - OB'AA'$$

But as $OA' = \partial x/\partial\xi\, d\xi$, $OB' = \partial x/\partial\eta\, d\eta$, $BB' = \partial y/\partial\eta\, d\eta$ and $AA' = \partial y/\partial\xi\, d\xi$,

$$2\Delta = \left(\frac{\partial x}{\partial\xi}\frac{\partial y}{\partial\eta} - \frac{\partial x}{\partial\eta}\frac{\partial y}{\partial\xi}\right) d\xi\, d\eta$$

In the limit the infinitesimal area is given by

$$dA = 2\Delta = \left(\frac{\partial x}{\partial\xi}\frac{\partial y}{\partial\eta} - \frac{\partial x}{\partial\eta}\frac{\partial y}{\partial\xi}\right) d\xi\, d\eta = \begin{vmatrix} \dfrac{\partial x}{\partial\xi} & \dfrac{\partial y}{\partial\xi} \\ \dfrac{\partial x}{\partial\eta} & \dfrac{\partial y}{\partial\eta} \end{vmatrix} d\xi\, d\eta$$

$$dA = |J|\, d\xi\, d\eta$$

where $|J|$ is the determinant of the Jacobian of the first derivatives.

Thus, when a function $G(x, y)$ is to be integrated over a non-rectangular domain, the integral is transformed, using

$$\iint_{\substack{\text{area}\\ \text{domain}}} G(x,y)\, dA \equiv \int_{-1}^{1}\int_{-1}^{1} [G(x(\xi,\eta), y(\xi,\eta))\, |J|]\, d\xi\, d\eta$$

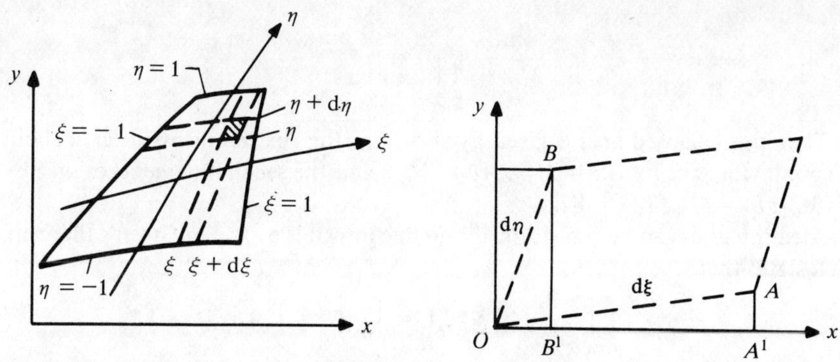

Figure 3.35 Curvilinear quadrilateral domain

In finite-element formulations, $x(\xi, \eta)$ and $y(\xi, \eta)$ are usually polynomials of second or third order. If we let $F(\xi, \eta) = G(x(\xi, \eta), y(\xi, \eta))\,|J|$, then

$$\iint_{\text{domain}} G(x, y)\,\mathrm{d}A = \int_{-1}^{1}\int_{-1}^{1} F(\xi, \eta)\,\mathrm{d}\xi\,\mathrm{d}\eta$$

and thus

$$\iint_{\text{domain}} G(x, y)\,\mathrm{d}A \simeq \sum_{i=1}^{n+1}\sum_{j=1}^{m+1} w_i w_j F(\xi_i, \eta_j)$$

The problem is thus cast in familiar terms and can be solved using the Gauss quadrature formulation described above. When $F(\xi, \eta)$ is the product of polynomials, selection of the appropriate number of Gauss points can be used to make the numerical integration result identical with the definite integral.

3.3.3 Calculation of section properties

To determine approximate values for geometric properties such as area, position of centroid, and second moments of area, use can be made of polygonal approximations to the shape boundaries.

3.3.3.1 Green's theorem

With reference to the shaded shape shown in Fig. 3.36, moments of area are given

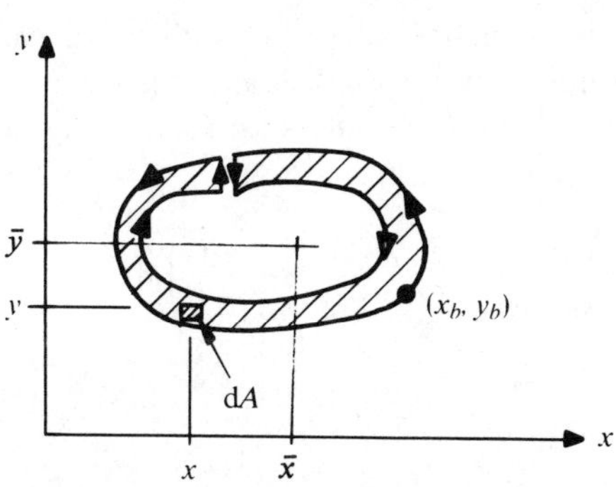

Figure 3.36 Notation for Green's theorem

by

$$M_{ij} = \iint_{\text{area}} x^i y^j \, dA$$

Thus the enclosed area is given by $A = M_{00}$; the first moments of area about the coordinate axes by $A\bar{x} = M_{10}$, $A\bar{y} = M_{01}$; and the second moments of area by $I_x = M_{02}$, $I_y = M_{20}$, $I_{xy} = M_{11}$.

Area integrals can be transformed into line integrals by use of Green's theorem, which states that

$$\iint_{\text{area}} \frac{\partial}{\partial y} f(x,y)\, dA = \int_B f(x_b, y_b)\, dx$$

and

$$\iint_{\text{area}} \frac{\partial}{\partial x} f(x,y)\, dA = \int_B f(x_b, y_b)\, dy$$

where $f(x, y)$ specifies values within the boundary B of a shape, and points (x_b, y_b) lie on its boundary, as shown in Fig. 3.36. Thus

$$M_{ij} = \iint_{\text{area}} x^i y^j \, dA \equiv \iint_{\text{area}} \frac{\partial}{\partial y}\left(\frac{x^i y^{j+1}}{j+1}\right) dA = \int_B \frac{x_b^i y_b^{j+1}}{j+1}\, dx$$

and hence

$$A = M_{00} = \int_B y_b \, dx \qquad A\bar{y} = M_{01} = \int_B \frac{y_b^2}{2}\, dx \qquad I_x = M_{02} = \int_B \frac{y_b^3}{3}\, dx$$

It is possible to develop similar expressions for $A\bar{x}$ and I_y, but for later work it is more convenient to develop expressions for them from the alternative formula. Thus

$$M_{ij} = \iint_{\text{area}} x^i y^j \, dA \equiv \iint_{\text{area}} \frac{\partial}{\partial x}\left(\frac{x^{i+1} y^j}{i+1}\right) dA = \int_B \frac{x_b^{i+1} y_b^j}{i+1}\, dy$$

and hence

$$A\bar{x} = M_{10} = \int_B \frac{x_b^2}{2}\, dy \qquad I_y = M_{20} = \int_B \frac{x_b^3}{3}\, dx$$

3.3.3.2 Polygonal boundaries

Simple expressions can be derived for the properties of shapes with polygonal boundaries. A positive direction around a boundary is specified, and it is taken to be anticlockwise, as indicated in Fig. 3.37. Vertices are numbered successively in this sense. For a polygon of n sides,

$$A = \int_B y_b \, dx = \sum_{i=1}^{n} \int_{x_i}^{x_{i+1}} \left(x \frac{y_i - y_{i+1}}{x_i - x_{i+1}} + \frac{x_i y_{i+1} - x_{i+1} y_i}{x_i - x_{i+1}} \right) dx$$

where (x_i, y_i) are the coordinates of vertex i, hence

$$A = \frac{1}{2} \sum_{i=1}^{n} (x_i - x_{i+1})(y_i + y_{i+1})$$

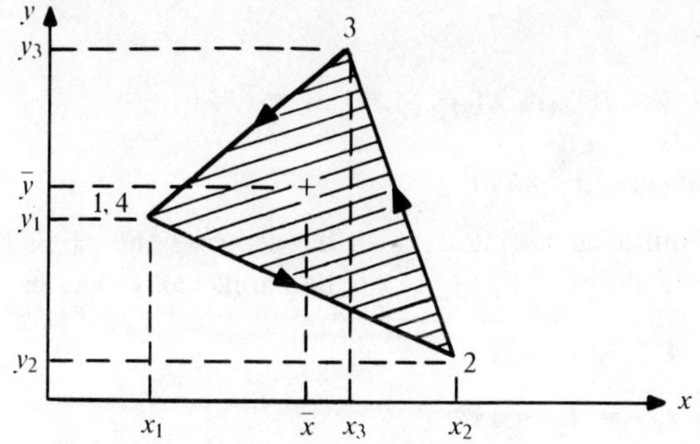

Figure 3.37 Triangular shape

It can be seen that each term of the series is the signed area of the trapezium formed by a side of the polygon and its projection on the x axis (see Fig. 3.38).

$$A\bar{y} = \int_B \frac{y_b^2}{2}\,\mathrm{d}x = \frac{1}{2}\sum_{i=1}^{n}\int_{x_i}^{x_{i+1}}\left(x\frac{y_i - y_{i+1}}{x_i - x_{i+1}} + \frac{x_i y_{i+1} - x_{i+1}y_i}{x_i - x_{i+1}}\right)^2 \mathrm{d}x$$

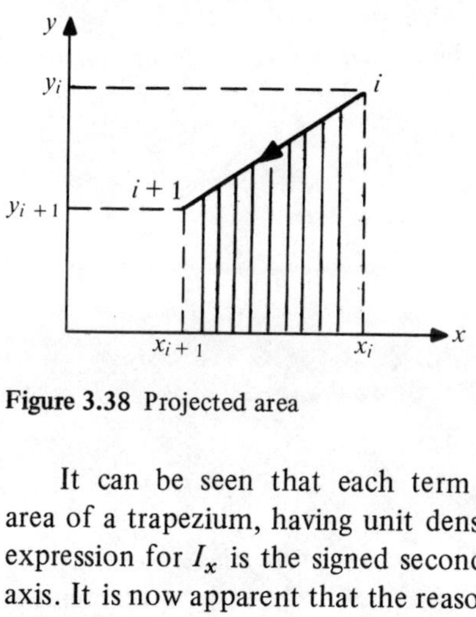

Figure 3.38 Projected area

It can be seen that each term of this series is the signed first moment of area of a trapezium, having unit density, about the x axis. Similarly, a term of the expression for I_x is the signed second moment of area of a trapezium about the x axis. It is now apparent that the reason for adopting the second formula to evaluate $A\bar{x}$ and I_y is that it gives moments of the trapezia formed by projecting sides onto the y axis. When evaluated, the algebraic expressions lead to the formulae

$$\bar{y} = \frac{1}{6A}\sum_{i=1}^{n}(x_i - x_{i+1})(y_i^2 + y_i y_{i+1} + y_{i+1}^2)$$

$$\bar{x} = \frac{1}{6A}\sum_{i=1}^{n}(y_{i+1} - y_i)(x_i^2 + x_i x_{i+1} + x_{i+1}^2)$$

$$I_x = \frac{1}{12.0}\sum_{i=1}^{n}(x_i - x_{i+1})(y_i^3 + y_i^2 y_{i+1} + y_{i+1}^2 y_i + y_{i+1}^3)$$

$$I_y = \frac{1}{12.0}\sum_{i=1}^{n}(y_{i+1} - y_i)(x_i^3 + x_i^2 x_{i+1} + x_{i+1}^2 x_i + x_{i+1}^3)$$

and

$$I_{xy} = \frac{1}{72.0} \sum_{i=1}^{n} (x_i - x_{i+1})[x_{i+1}(9y_{i+1}^2 + 6y_i y_{i+1} + 3y_i^2)$$
$$+ x_i(9y_i^2 + 6y_i y_{i+1} + 3y_{i+1}^2)]$$

Second moments of area about axes passing through the centroid and parallel to the coordinate axes are determined by making use of the parallel axis theorem. Thus

$$I_{xc} = I_x - A\bar{y}^2$$
$$I_{yc} = I_y - A\bar{x}^2$$
$$I_{xyc} = I_{xy} - A\bar{x}\bar{y}$$

Principal second moments of area and the inclination of the principal axes are given by standard formulae, thus

$$I_{1,2} = \tfrac{1}{2}\,[(I_{xc} + I_{yc}) \pm \sqrt{(I_{xc} - I_{yc})^2 + 4I_{xyc}^2}\,]$$

and

$$\alpha_1 = \tan^{-1} \frac{I_{xc} - I_1}{I_{xyc}}$$

where α_1 is the angle between the x axis and the principal axis corresponding to I_1 as shown in Fig. 3.39.

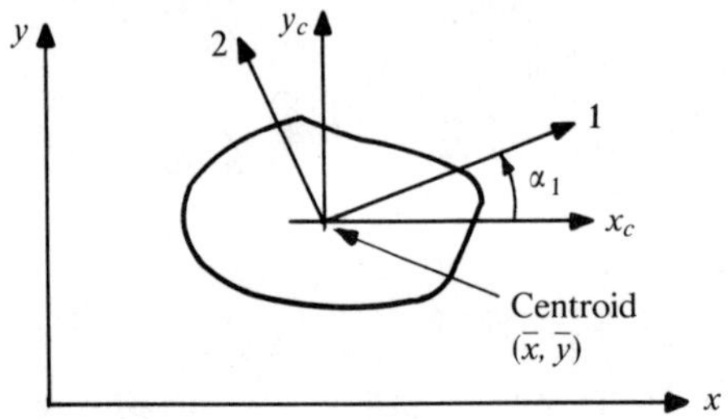

Figure 3.39 Principal axes

Example Determine approximations to the section properties of a semicircle using a four-sided polygon. With reference to Fig. 3.40, for a circle of radius r,

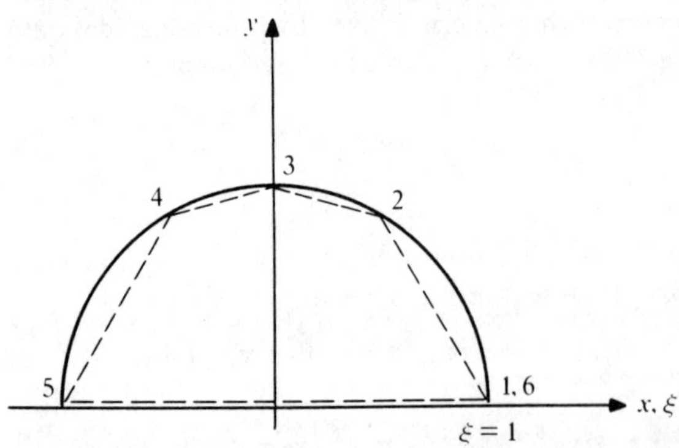

Figure 3.40 Semi-circle

$y = r\sqrt{1 - \xi^2}$, so $(x_1, y_1) = (r, 0)$; $(x_2, y_2) = (r/2, \sqrt{3}r/2)$; $(x_3, y_3) = (0, r)$; $(x_4, y_4) = (-r/2, \sqrt{3}r/2)$; $(x_5, y_5) = (-r, 0)$. Section properties of the polygonal approximation to the semicircle are given by

$$\begin{aligned}
A &= \frac{r^2}{2}\,[(1-\tfrac{1}{2})(0+\sqrt{3}/2) + (\tfrac{1}{2}-0)(\sqrt{3}/2+1) + (0+\tfrac{1}{2})(1+\sqrt{3}/2) \\
&\quad + (-\tfrac{1}{2}+1)(\sqrt{3}/2+0) + (-1-1)\,(0+0)] \\
&= 1.366r^2 \text{ (error 13 per cent)} \\
\bar{y} &= \frac{r^3}{6 \times 1.366r^2}\,\{(1-\tfrac{1}{2})(\sqrt{3}/2)^2 + (\tfrac{1}{2}-0)[(\sqrt{3}/2)^2 + \sqrt{3}/2 + 1]\} \times 2 \\
&= 0.4107r \text{ (error 3 per cent)} \\
I_x &= \frac{r^4}{12}\,\{(1-\tfrac{1}{2})[0+0+0+(\sqrt{3}/2)^3] + (\tfrac{1}{2}-0)[(\sqrt{3}/2)^3 \\
&\quad + (\sqrt{3}/2)^2 \times 1 + 1(\sqrt{3}/2) + 1]\} \times 2 \\
&= 0.3263r^4 \text{ (error 17 per cent)} \\
I_y &= \frac{r^4}{12}\,[(\sqrt{3}/2-0)(1+\tfrac{1}{2}+\tfrac{1}{4}+\tfrac{1}{8}) + (1-\sqrt{3}/2)(\tfrac{1}{8}+0+0+0)] \times 2 \\
&= 0.2734r^4 \text{ (error 30 per cent)} \\
I_{xy} &= \frac{r^4}{72}\,\{[1-\tfrac{1}{2}]\,[\tfrac{1}{2}(9 \times \tfrac{3}{4}) + 1(3 \times \tfrac{3}{4})] + (\tfrac{1}{2}-0)\{\tfrac{1}{2}\,[9 \times \tfrac{3}{4} + 6(\sqrt{3}/2) + 3]\} \\
&\quad + (0+\tfrac{1}{2})[-\tfrac{1}{2}(9 \times \tfrac{3}{4} + 6(\sqrt{3}/2) + 3)] + (-\tfrac{1}{2}+1)[-1(3 \times \tfrac{3}{4}) \\
&\quad - \tfrac{1}{2}(9 \times \tfrac{3}{4})]\} \\
&= 0
\end{aligned}$$

Although a polygon with more than four sides is needed to approximate a semicircular boundary, the simple nature of the calculations is evident.

For application to voided sections, it is possible to use a single polygon to represent the shape as illustrated in Fig. 3.41. For automatic computation, and for shapes representing cross-sections composed of a number of materials, however, it is simpler to use a set of closed polygons. The calculations are performed for the shapes enclosed by each polygon in turn, and the results weighted to reflect the relative values of the elastic moduli of the materials, before being summed to give the properties of the 'transformed' section. For a void, the weighting factor used

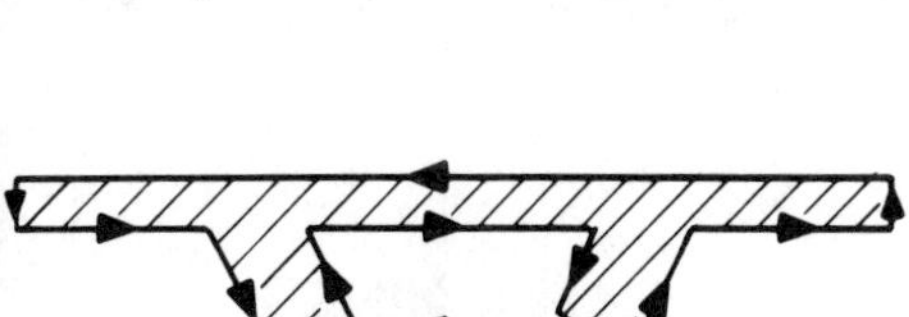

Figure 3.41 Section with a void

with the polygon defining its shape is set to minus the value used for the surrounding material.

SUBROUTINE SPR given in Fig. 3.42 provides a convenient way of determining section properties of irregular shapes. To minimize numerical errors, the origin of the Cartesian axes should be placed close to the section and, for a thin section, close to its centre of gravity. If significant roundoff errors are suspected, the coordinate origin can be shifted and the results of calculations compared. Only the values of the centroidal coordinates PROPS(2) and PROPS(3) should show a significant change.

Example The section properties of the voided section shown in Fig. 3.43 can be determined with $N = 2$, $NST(1) = 8$, $NST(2) = 4$, $WC(1) = 1.0$, $WC(2) = -1.0$; with the coordinates of the eight vertices of the outer polygon set in the first columns of X, Y; and the coordinates of the four vertices of the inner polygon set in the second columns of X and Y.

```
      SUBROUTINE SPR(N,X,Y,NST,WC,PROPS)
      REAL IX,IY,IXY,IXTOT,IYTOT,IXYTOT
      DIMENSION WC(20),NST(20),X(51,20),Y(51,20),PROPS(9)
C N-NO. OF POLYGONS IN CROSS-SECTION, 20 MAXIMUM
C X,Y-LIST CO-ORDS OF VERTICES
C NST-LISTS NO. OF VERTICES, 50 MAXIMUM EACH POLYGON
C WC-LISTS WEIGHTING COEFFS.
C PROPS-IS GIVEN THE PROPERTIES A,XBAR,YBAR,IX,IY,IXY,I1,I2,ALPHA
      IF(N.LT.1.OR.N.GT.20)GOTO 90
C ZERO TOTALS
      ATOT=0.0
      IXTOT=0.0
      IYTOT=0.0
      IXYTOT=0.0
      XBTOT=0.0
      YBTOT=0.0
      DO 10 NP=1,N
      W=WC(NP)
      NS=NST(NP)
      IF(NS.LT.3.OR.NS.GT.50)GOTO 91
C CLOSE THE POLYGON
      X(NS+1,NP)=X(1,NP)
      Y(NS+1,NP)=Y(1,NP)
      A=0.0
      IX=0.0
      IY=0.0
      IXY=0.0
      XBAR=0.0
      YBAR=0.0
C CALCULATE PROPERTIES OF POLYGONAL SHAPE
      DO 30 IST=1,NS
```

Figure 3.42 Cross-sectional properties

```
C X1,XIP1-X CO-ORDS OF VERTICES I AND I+1
      XI=X(IST,NP)
      XIPI=X(IST+1,NP)
      YI=Y(IST,NP)
      YIP1=Y(IST+1,NP)
      A=A+(XI-XIP1)*(YI+YIP1)/2.0
      YBAR=YBAR+(XI-XIP1)*(YI**2+YI*YIP1+YIP1**2)/6.0
      XBAR=XBAR+(YIP1-YI)*(XI**2+XI*XIP1+XIP1**2)/6.0
      IX=IX+(XI-XIP1)*(YI**3+YI**2*YIP1+YI*YIP1**2+YIP1**3)
     C/12.0
      IY=IY+(YIP1-YI)*(XI**3+XI**2*XIP1+XI*XIP1**2+XIP1**3)
     C/12.0
      IXY=IXY+(XI-XIP1)*(
     CXIP1*(9.0*YIP1**2+6.0*YI*YIP1+3.0*YI**2)
     C+XI*(3.0*YIP1**2+6.0*YI*YIP1+9.0*YI**2))/72.0
 30   CONTINUE
      ATOT=ATOT+A*W
      XBTOT=XBTOT+W*XBAR
      YBTOT=YBTOT+W*YBAR
      IXTOT=IXTOT+IX*W
      IYTOT=IYTOT+IY*W
      IXYTOT=IXYTOT+IXY*W
 10   CONTINUE
      XBTOT=XBTOT/ATOT
      YBTOT=YBTOT/ATOT
C USE PARALLEL AXIS THEOREM
      IXTOT=IXTOT-ATOT*YBTOT**2
      IYTOT=IYTOT-ATOT*XBTOT**2
      IXYTOT=IXYTOT-ATOT*XBTOT*YBTOT
C CALCULATE PRINCIPAL VALUES
      A=(IXTOT+IYTOT)*0.5
      B=0.5*SQRT((IXTOT-IYTOT)**2+4.0*IXYTOT**2)
      P1=A+B
      P2=A-B
      ALFA=0.0
      IF(P2.GT.P1)ALFA=1.5707963
      IF(ABS(IXYTOT).LT.1.0E-10)GOTO 40
      ALFA=ATAN((IXTOT-P1)/IXYTOT)
 40   PROPS(1)=ATOT
      PROPS(2)=XBTOT
      PROPS(3)=YBTOT
      PROPS(4)=IXTOT
      PROPS(5)=IYTOT
      PROPS(6)=IXYTOT
      PROPS(7)=P1
      PROPS(8)=P2
      PROPS(9)=ALFA
      RETURN
 90   WRITE(6,690)N
      STOP
```

Figure 3.42 (*continued*)

```
91    WRITE(6,691)NP,NS
      STOP
690   FORMAT(1H^,3H^N=,I10,27H^SHOULD^BE^BETWEEN^1^AND^20)
691   FORMAT(1H^,11H^IN^POLYGON,I3,19H^NO.^OF^VERTICES^IS,
     CI10,27H^SHOULD^BE^BETWEEN^3^AND^50)
      END
```

Figure 3.42 (*continued*)

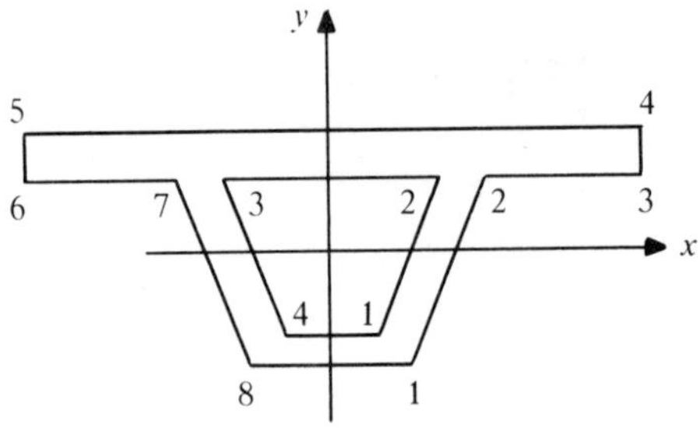

Figure 3.43 Voided section

3.4 FINITE-DIFFERENCE SOLUTION OF DIFFERENTIAL EQUATIONS

3.4.1 Introduction to Differential Equations

The development of engineering science has been founded on the formulation and solution of problems in terms of differential equations. Ordinary differential equations (o.d.e.) contain one or more derivatives with respect to a single independent variable. An example of an o.d.e. is the beam bending equation

$$M_x = EI\frac{\mathrm{d}^2 v}{\mathrm{d}x^2}.$$

Partial differential equations (p.d.e.) arise from problems involving two or more indpendent variables. An example of a p.d.e. is the Poisson equation

$$\frac{\partial^2 \phi}{\partial x^2} + \frac{\partial^2 \phi}{\partial y^2} + 2G\theta = 0$$

used to determine the distribution of torsion stresses on a cross-section.

The order of a differential equation is defined as the order of the highest derivative in the equation, while the degree of an equation refers to the exponent to which the highest derivative is raised. For example, the equation

$$\left(\frac{\mathrm{d}^3 \phi}{\mathrm{d}x^3}\right)^2 + k\phi = 0$$

is of the third order and second degree.

A differential equation of any order is linear when the dependent variable and all its derivatives are first degree, and the terms multiplying the derivatives are either constants or functions of the independent variables. For example, the equation

$$m\frac{d^2\phi}{dt^2}+c\frac{d\phi}{dt}+s\phi = 0$$

which describes the free vibration of a damped single degree of freedom system is linear, whereas the equation

$$m\frac{d^2\phi}{dt^2}+c\frac{d\phi}{dt}\left|\frac{d\phi}{dt}\right|+s\phi = 0$$

which describes the free vibration of a system with fluid drag damping, is non-linear.

An important classification of differential equations relates to the conditions imposed prior to solution. An initial value solution to an o.d.e. of order n is one in which values of the function and its derivatives, up to order $(n-1)$, are known at a given point. Initial value solutions often arise when time is the independent variable. By contrast, a boundary value problem involves specification of values of the function, or its derivatives, at more than one position. For example, solution of a beam bending equation requires support conditions to be specified in terms of known displacements. It is possible to encounter mixed initial and boundary value problems with p.d.e. Whichever type of solution is sought, however, it is assumed here that sufficient conditions are given for a unique solution to be determined.

While elegant analytical solutions are available to some differential equations, it will often be found that the equations concerned do not quite fit into the required pattern, or that mathematical manipulations become excessively difficult. An approximate numerical solution must be used in these circumstances. This section and Sec. 3.5 concentrate on numerical solutions to linear equations by finite-difference and finite-element methods respectively, while Sec. 3.7 deals with the solution of linear and non-linear o.d.e.

It is important that the reader should not totally disregard an analytical solution when one exists, for an analytical solution can reveal the properties and behaviour of a system much more fully than a single computer run of a numerical solution can ever do.

3.4.2 Finite differences

The method of finite differences converts the problem of solution of a differential equation, to one of setting up and solving a set of linear simultaneous equations. In the process approximations are made to derivatives and thus errors are introduced. It has been found, however, that for many problems, solutions with acceptably small errors can be obtained using an economical number of equations and the method can be used whenever there is difficulty in finding an explicit solution to a differential equation.

3.4.3 Functions of one variable

If $\phi = f(x)$, the first derivative of ϕ is defined by

$$\frac{d\phi}{dx} = \lim_{\Delta x \to 0}\frac{\Delta\phi}{\Delta x} = \frac{f(x+\Delta x)-f(x)}{\Delta x}$$

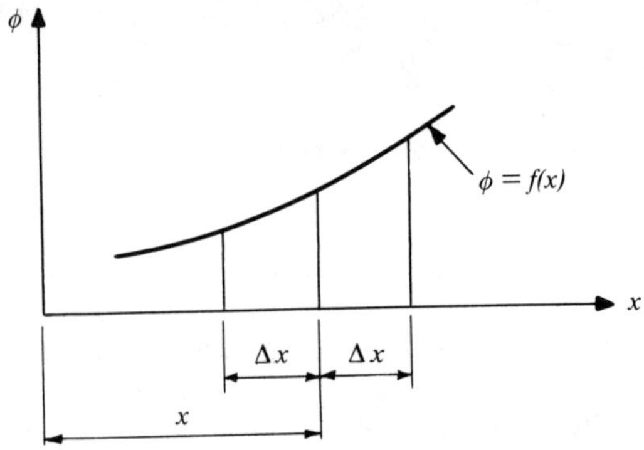

Figure 3.44 Infinitesimal differences

where symbols are defined in Fig. 3.44. The second derivative is defined by

$$\frac{d^2\phi}{dx^2} = \lim_{\Delta x \to 0} \frac{\Delta\left(\dfrac{\Delta\phi}{\Delta x}\right)}{\Delta x} = \frac{\left(\dfrac{f(x+\Delta x)-f(x)}{\Delta x}\right)-\left(\dfrac{f(x)-f(x-\Delta x)}{\Delta x}\right)}{\Delta x}$$

and higher-order derivatives are similarly defined.

3.4.3.1 Finite-difference formulae

In the method of finite differences Δx does not approach zero but is given a finite value h. The derivatives of ϕ at $x = x_i$ are approximated by formulae which use values of ϕ at stations spaced a distance h apart.

With reference to Fig. 3.45, the first derivative can be represented in one of three ways:

1. using forward differences, by

$$\left(\frac{d\phi}{dx}\right)_i \simeq \frac{\phi_{i+1}-\phi_i}{h}$$

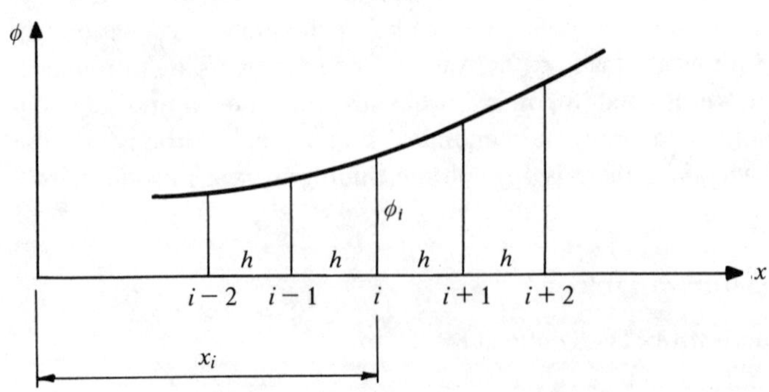

Figure 3.45 Finite differences

2. using central differences, by

$$\left(\frac{d\phi}{dx}\right)_i \simeq \frac{\phi_{i+1} - \phi_{i-1}}{2h}$$

3. using backward differences, by

$$\left(\frac{d\phi}{dx}\right)_i \simeq \frac{\phi_i - \phi_{i-1}}{h}$$

The second derivative of ϕ can also be represented in one of three ways:

1. using forward differences, by

$$\left(\frac{d^2\phi}{dx^2}\right)_i \simeq \frac{\phi_i - 2\phi_{i+1} + \phi_{i+2}}{h^2}$$

2. using central differences, by

$$\left(\frac{d^2\phi}{dx^2}\right)_i \simeq \frac{\phi_{i-1} - 2\phi_i + \phi_{i+1}}{h^2}$$

3. using backward differences, by

$$\left(\frac{d^2\phi}{dx^2}\right)_i \simeq \frac{\phi_{i-2} - 2\phi_{i-1} + \phi_i}{h^2}$$

The third derivatives are approximated similarly by:

1. using forward differences by

$$\left(\frac{d^3\phi}{dx^3}\right)_i \simeq \frac{-\phi_i + 3\phi_{i+1} - 3\phi_{i+2} + \phi_{i+3}}{h^3}$$

2. using central differences, by

$$\left(\frac{d^3\phi}{dx^3}\right)_i \simeq \frac{-\phi_{i-2} + 2\phi_{i-1} - 2\phi_{i+1} + \phi_{i+2}}{2h^3}$$

3. using backward differences, by

$$\left(\frac{d^3\phi}{dx^3}\right)_i \simeq \frac{-\phi_{i-3} + 3\phi_{i-2} - 3\phi_{i-1} + \phi_i}{h^3}$$

The fourth derivatives are given by

1. using forward differences, by

$$\left(\frac{d^4\phi}{dx^4}\right)_i \simeq \frac{\phi_i - 4\phi_{i+1} + 6\phi_{i+2} - 4\phi_{i+3} + \phi_{i+4}}{h^4}$$

2. using central differences, by

$$\left(\frac{d^4\phi}{dx^4}\right)_i \simeq \frac{\phi_{i-2} - 4\phi_{i-1} + 6\phi_i - 4\phi_{i+1} + \phi_{i+2}}{h^4}$$

3. using backward differences, by

$$\left(\frac{d^4\phi}{dx^4}\right)_i \simeq \frac{\phi_{i-4} - 4\phi_{i-3} + 6\phi_{i-2} - 4\phi_{i-1} + \phi_i}{h^4}$$

For a particular problem the selection of a finite difference formulation is to some extent dependent on boundary conditions. However, whenever a function can be evaluated at sufficient stations for the central difference expressions to be used, that formulation is generally preferred, as it results in smaller errors. Errors are discussed in Sec. 3.4.3.4.

3.4.3.2 Illustration of solution procedures

To illustrate application of the finite-difference method, the central difference formulation is applied to determine: (1) the displacements of a varying section beam subjected to a uniformly distributed normal loading of intensity w; (2) its smallest axial buckling load; and (3) its lowest natural frequency. The beam is shown in Fig. 3.46.

1. In Fig. 3.47(a) the beam is shown with normal gravity loading and associated displacements $v = f(x)$. The differential equation of flexure is

$$M_x = \frac{wLx}{2} - \frac{wx^2}{2} = EI\frac{d^2v}{dx^2}$$

and the equivalent finite-difference equation at station i is

$$\frac{wLx_i}{2} - \frac{wx_i^2}{2} = \frac{EI_i}{h^2}(v_{i-1} - 2v_i + v_{i+1})$$

The beam is shown divided into four segments with unknown displacements at stations 2, 3, and 4. Finite-difference equations are set up at these stations. At station 2, $x_i = h = L/4$, $v_{i-1} = v_1 = 0$, hence

$$\frac{3wL^2}{32} = \frac{16E \times 1.5I_0}{L^2}(-2v_2 + v_3)$$

and

$$\frac{wL^4}{256EI_0} = -2v_2 + v_3$$

At station 3, $x_i = 2h = L/2$, hence

$$\frac{wL^2}{8} = \frac{16E \times 2I_0}{L^2}(v_2 - 2v_3 + v_4)$$

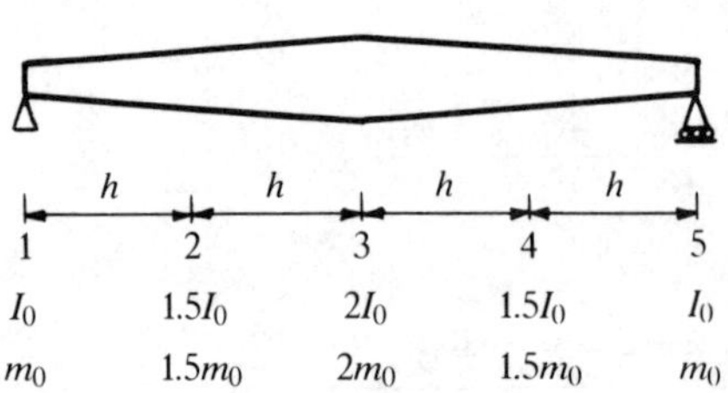

Figure 3.46 Varying section beam

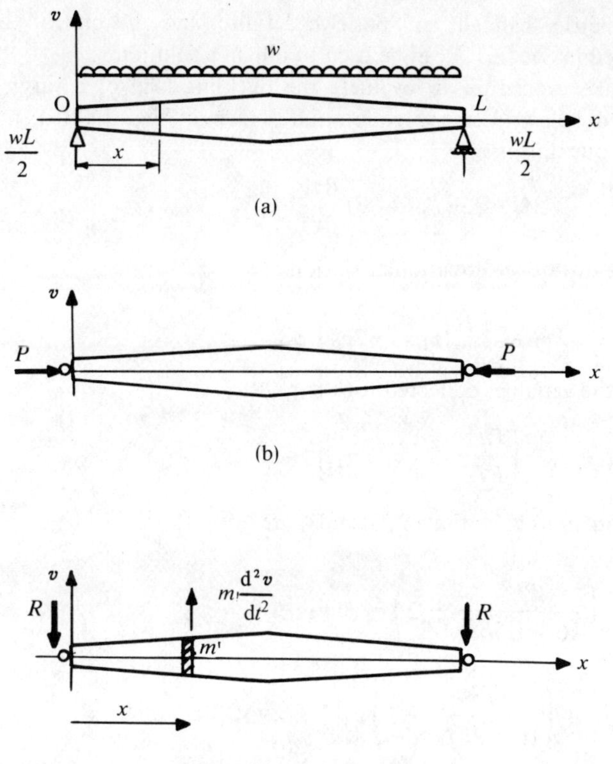

Figure 3.47 Gravity, axial, and vibration loadings. (a) Lateral loading. (b) Axial loading. (c) Vibration loading

and

$$\frac{wL^4}{256EI_0} = v_2 - 2v_3 + v_4$$

At station 4, $x_i = 3h = \frac{3}{4}L$, $v_{i+1} = v_5 = 0$, hence

$$\frac{wL^4}{256EI_0} = v_3 - 2v_4$$

writing these equations in matrix form, with positive diagonal terms,

$$\frac{wL^4}{256EI_0}\begin{bmatrix} -1 \\ -1 \\ -1 \end{bmatrix} = \begin{bmatrix} 2 & -1 & 0 \\ -1 & 2 & -1 \\ 0 & -1 & 2 \end{bmatrix}\begin{bmatrix} v_2 \\ v_3 \\ v_4 \end{bmatrix}$$

Solution of these equations gives

$$v_3 = \frac{-wL^4}{128EI_0}, \qquad v_2 = v_4 = -\frac{3wL^4}{512EI_0}$$

Although the number of stations used is too few for an accurate solution, the procedure followed is not changed for an increased number of stations. The matrix of coefficients is symmetric, banded, and positive definite, and any one of the SUBROUTINEs described in Sec. 3.1.3 can be used to obtain a solution.

2. A finite-difference procedure to evaluate the buckling load of a varying section strut is outlined below. Using the notation shown in Fig. 3.47(b), the differential equation of buckling is

$$M_x = -Pv = EI\frac{d^2v}{dx^2}$$

and the equivalent finite-difference equation at station i is

$$-Pv_i = \frac{EI_i}{h^2}(v_{i-1} - 2v_i + v_{i+1})$$

or, with coefficients of the variables collected together,

$$v_{i-1} + \left(\frac{Ph^2}{EI_i} - 2\right) v_i + v_{i+1} = 0$$

Finite-difference equations at stations 2, 3, and 4 are

at station 2,

$$\left(\frac{PL^2}{16 \times 1.5EI_0} - 2\right) v_2 + v_3 = 0,$$

at station 3,

$$v_2 + \left(\frac{PL^2}{16 \times 2EI_0} - 2\right) v_3 + v_4 = 0, \qquad \text{and}$$

at station 4,

$$v_3 + \left(\frac{PL^2}{16 \times 1.5EI_0} - 2\right) v_4 = 0$$

Setting $\lambda = PL^2/96EI_0$, and writing the equations in matrix form, gives

$$\begin{bmatrix} 0 \\ 0 \\ 0 \end{bmatrix} = \begin{bmatrix} (4\lambda - 2) & 1 & 0 \\ 1 & (3\lambda - 2) & 1 \\ 0 & 1 & (4\lambda - 2) \end{bmatrix} \begin{bmatrix} v_2 \\ v_3 \\ v_4 \end{bmatrix}$$

This is a set of homogeneous equations, and solutions can be determined using one of the methods described in Sec. 3.1.9.3.

For this simple case, the solution is obtained from the characteristic polynomial which is obtained by expanding the determinant of the matrix, thus

$$(4\lambda - 2)((3\lambda - 2)(4\lambda - 2) - 1) - (4\lambda - 2) = 0$$

$$(4\lambda - 2)(12\lambda^2 - 14\lambda + 2) = 0$$

$$(4\lambda - 2)(6\lambda - 1)(2\lambda - 2) = 0$$

and hence $\lambda_1 = 1/6, \lambda_2 = 1/2, \lambda_3 = 1$.

The estimated buckling loads are, therefore,

$$P_1 = \frac{16EI_0}{L^2} \qquad P_2 = \frac{48EI_0}{L^2} \qquad P_3 = \frac{96EI_0}{L^2}$$

and the corresponding deflected shapes of the strut are determined by back substitution.

$$\text{For } \lambda = 1/6 \qquad \begin{bmatrix} 0 \\ 0 \\ 0 \end{bmatrix} = \begin{bmatrix} -4/3 & 1 & 0 \\ 1 & -3/2 & 1 \\ 0 & 1 & -4/3 \end{bmatrix} \begin{bmatrix} v_2 \\ v_3 \\ v_4 \end{bmatrix}$$

If $v_2 = 1$, then $v_3 = 0.75$ and $v_4 = 0.75$.

The length of this displacement vector is given by $\sqrt{1 + 9/16 + 9/16} = 1.4577$; hence in normalized form

$$v_2 = 0.5145 \qquad v_3 = 0.6860 \qquad v_4 = 0.5145$$

The deflected shapes for the higher buckling loads can be determined in a similar manner and the results are illustrated in Fig. 3.48. Although the number of stations used is too few for an accurate solution, the procedure followed is unchanged for an increased number of stations and automatic solution procedures can readily be developed. Accuracy of solutions can be assessed by repeating the analysis with an increased number of stations and by comparing the two sets of results.

3. To determine the natural frequencies of free vibration of the beam, consider it to be excited into motion. The resisting inertia force, F, at x, is given by $F = -m\,\mathrm{d}^2 v/\mathrm{d}t^2$, where m is the mass at x as shown in Fig. 3.47(c).

From simple beam theory, $F = \mathrm{d}^2 M_x/\mathrm{d}x^2$, where M_x is the bending moment at x, hence $\mathrm{d}^2 M_x/\mathrm{d}x^2 = -m\,\mathrm{d}^2 v/\mathrm{d}t^2$. The bending moment is related to the beam curvature by $M_x = EI\mathrm{d}^2 v/\mathrm{d}x^2$, hence $\mathrm{d}^2 M_x/\mathrm{d}x^2 = \mathrm{d}^2/\mathrm{d}x^2\ (EI\mathrm{d}^2 v/\mathrm{d}x^2)$, and thus $-m\mathrm{d}^2 v/\mathrm{d}t^2 = \mathrm{d}^2/\mathrm{d}x^2\ (EI\mathrm{d}^2 v/\mathrm{d}x^2)$.

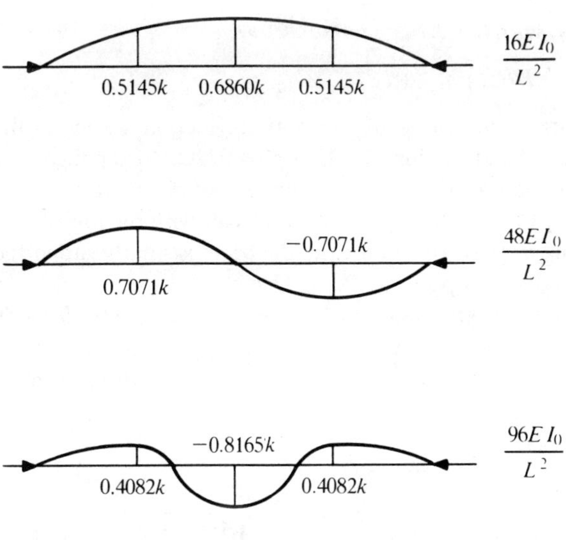

Figure 3.48 Buckling modes

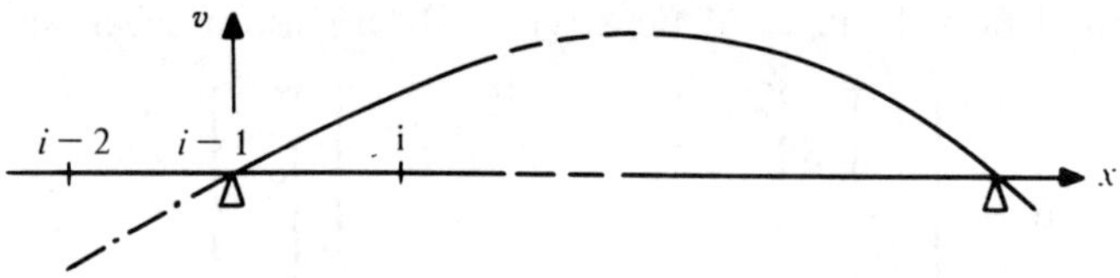

Figure 3.49 Fictitious node

For a normal mode of vibration $v = \bar{v}\sin\omega t$, where $\bar{v}$ is the maximum translation either side of the x axis and ω is the circular frequency of vibration in radians per second. If f is the frequency in cycles per second then $\omega = 2\pi f$.

As $v = \bar{v}\sin\omega t$, $\mathrm{d}^2v/\mathrm{d}t^2 = -\omega^2 v$ and thus $\omega^2 mv = \mathrm{d}^2/\mathrm{d}x^2\,(EI\mathrm{d}^2v/\mathrm{d}x^2)$. The finite-difference form of this equation is

$$\omega^2 m_i v_i = \frac{\left(EI\dfrac{\mathrm{d}^2v}{\mathrm{d}x^2}\right)_{i-1} - 2\left(EI\dfrac{\mathrm{d}^2v}{\mathrm{d}x^2}\right)_i + \left(EI\dfrac{\mathrm{d}^2v}{\mathrm{d}x^2}\right)_{i+1}}{h^2}$$

hence

$$\omega^2 m_i v_i = \frac{EI_{i-1}}{h^4}(v_{i-2} - 2v_{i-1} + v_i) - \frac{2EI_i}{h^4}(v_{i-1} - 2v_i + v_{i+1}) + \frac{EI_{i+1}}{h^4}(v_i - 2v_{i+1} + v_{i+2})$$

With coefficients of variables collected together the equation is

$$\begin{aligned}&(EI_{i-1})v_{i-2} - 2(EI_{i-1} + EI_i)v_{i-1}\\&+ (EI_{i-1} + 4EI_i + EI_{i+1} - h^4\omega^2 m_i)v_i\\&- 2(EI_i + EI_{i+1})v_{i+1} + (EI_{i+1})v_{i+2} = 0\end{aligned}$$

To determine the natural frequencies of the varying section beam of the example, this equation is applied at stations 2, 3, and 4. When it is applied to a station adjacent to a support there is a need to consider a 'fictitious' station lying outside the beam as shown in Fig. 3.49. This problem is dealt with by considering the boundary condition at the supports. For this case, the beam is simply supported and the bending moment at the support is zero. Hence, when $i = 2$, $M_{i-1} = (EI\mathrm{d}^2v/\mathrm{d}x^2)_{i-1} = 0$ and in finite difference form $EI_{i-1}(v_{i-2} - 2v_{i-1} + v_i)/h^2 = 0$. As $v_{i-1} = 0$, $v_{i-2} = -v_i$. Using this relationship, and a similar expression at the right-hand support, equations can be set up and solved in terms of the three variables v_2, v_3, v_4.

Setting $\lambda = h^4\omega^2 m_0/2EI_0$

$$\begin{bmatrix}0\\0\\0\end{bmatrix} = \begin{bmatrix}(8-3\lambda) & -7 & 2\\ -7 & (11-4\lambda) & -7\\ 2 & -7 & (8-3\lambda)\end{bmatrix}\begin{bmatrix}v_2\\v_3\\v_4\end{bmatrix}$$

Using one of the methods of Sec. 3.1.9.3, the values of λ that set the determinant of the coefficients to zero are determined. They are $\lambda_1 = 5.914$, $\lambda_2 = 2.0$, $\lambda_3 = 0.1691$, and the corresponding natural frequencies are

$$\omega_1 = 55.03\sqrt{\frac{EI_0}{L^4 m_0}} \qquad \omega_2 = 32.0\sqrt{\frac{EI_0}{L^4 m_0}} \qquad \omega_3 = 9.30\sqrt{\frac{EI_0}{L^4 m_0}}$$

The shapes of the vibration modes are given by back-substituting the values of λ into the equations, as was done to determine the buckling modes.

3.4.3.3 Boundary conditions

To determine the natural frequencies of a varying section beam it was necessary to extend the finite-difference stations beyond the domain of the displacement field. Stations outside a function's domain are referred to as 'fictitious' stations, or nodes, and are frequently encountered when higher-order derivatives are involved in a solution. It is not possible to introduce additional variable unknowns at these points, and the usual procedure is to determine the values of these variables in terms of variables within the function's domain. This can usually be achieved by consideration of the physical boundary conditions. Equations defining boundary conditions are set up using the problem variables and then converted to finite-difference form for evaluation.

The most commonly occurring boundary conditions are illustrated in Fig. 3.50, and the corresponding equations are: (1) the function ϕ has a known value on the boundary $\phi_i = \phi_b$; (2) the first derivative of the function has a known value on the boundary $d\phi/dx = C$, $(\phi_{i+1} - \phi_{i-1})/2h \simeq C$, hence $\phi_{i-1} = \phi_{i+1} - 2hC$; and (3) the second derivative of the function has a known value on the boundary $d^2\phi/dx^2 = C$, $(\phi_{i+1} - 2\phi_i + \phi_{i-1})/h^2 \simeq C$, hence $\phi_{i-1} = 2\phi_i - \phi_{i+1} + Ch^2$.

At boundaries it is not always possible to maintain a constant mesh division, h. If the spacing between a boundary station and the next station is k, as shown in Fig. 3.50(d), modified finite-difference expressions can be determined from Taylor series expansions:

$$\phi_{i-1} = f(x_i - k) = \phi_i - k\frac{d\phi_i}{dx} + \frac{k^2}{2}\frac{d^2\phi_i}{dx^2} - \cdots$$

$$\phi_{i+1} = f(x_i + h) = \phi_i + h\frac{d\phi_i}{dx} + \frac{h^2}{2}\frac{d^2\phi_i}{dx^2} + \cdots$$

The formula for the first derivative is obtained by ignoring terms involving higher-order derivatives, thus

$$\frac{d\phi_i}{dx} \simeq \frac{\phi_{i+1} - \phi_{i-1}}{h + k}$$

The expression for the second derivative is obtained by eliminating $d\phi_i/dx$ and by ignoring third- and higher-order derivatives, thus

$$\frac{d^2\phi_i}{dx^2} = \frac{h\phi_{i-1} - (h + k)\phi_i + k\phi_{i+1}}{hk(h + k)/2}$$

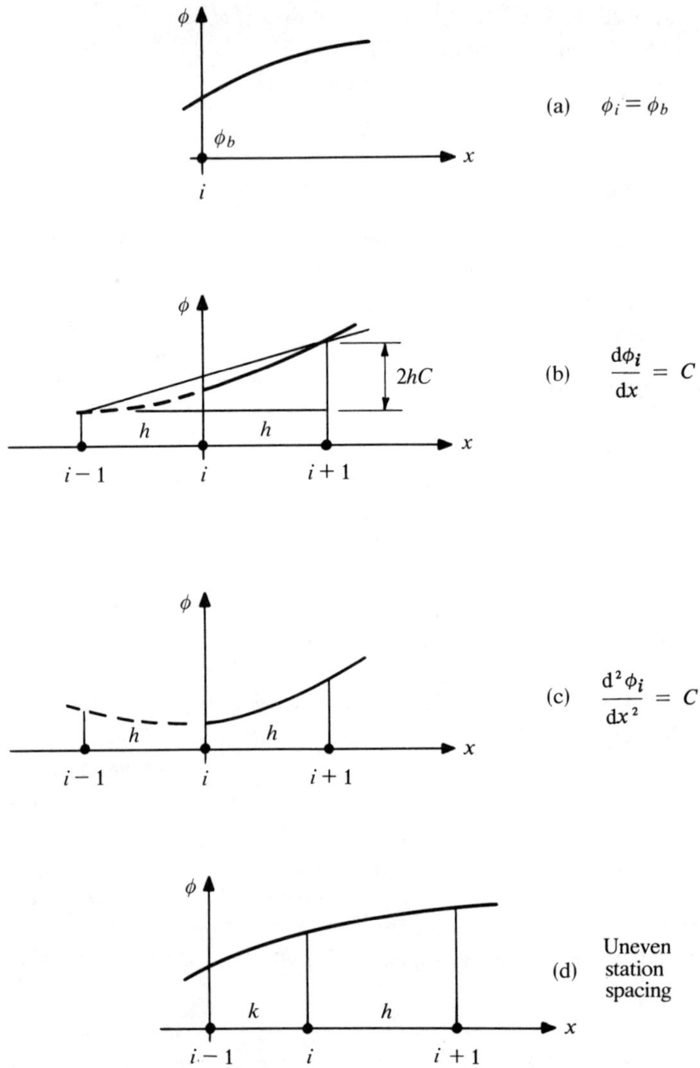

Figure 3.50 Boundary conditions

3.4.3.4 Errors in finite-difference formulae

An indication of the likely magnitude of errors involved can be determined by considering Taylor expansions of a function. The Taylor series for $\phi = f(x+h)$ about x_i is

$$f(x_i + h) = f(x_i) + \frac{h}{1!}\frac{df(x_i)}{dx} + \frac{h^2}{2!}\frac{d^2 f(x_i)}{dx^2} + \frac{h^3}{3!}\frac{d^3 f(x_i)}{dx^3} + \cdots$$

hence

$$\phi_{i+1} = \phi_i + h\frac{d\phi_i}{dx} + \frac{h^2}{2!}\frac{d^2\phi_i}{dx^2} + \cdots \frac{h^j}{j!}\frac{d^j\phi_i}{dx^j} + \cdots$$

$$\phi_{i+1} = \sum_{j=0}^{\infty} \frac{h^j}{j!} \frac{d^j \phi_i}{dx^j}$$

hence

$$\phi_{i+2} = f(x_i + 2h) = \sum_{j=0}^{\infty} \frac{(2h)^j}{j!} \frac{d^j \phi_i}{dx^j}$$

$$\phi_{i+1} = f(x_i + h) = \sum_{j=0}^{\infty} \frac{h^j}{j!} \frac{d^j \phi_i}{dx^j}$$

$$\phi_{i-1} = f(x_i - h) = \sum_{j=0}^{\infty} \frac{(-h)^j}{j!} \frac{d^j \phi_i}{dx^j}$$

$$\phi_{i-2} = f(x_i - 2h) = \sum_{j=0}^{\infty} \frac{(-2h)^j}{j!} \frac{d^j \phi_i}{dx^j}$$

Using these expressions, finite-difference formulae for the first derivative can be written as:

1. using the forward difference formula:

$$\frac{\phi_{i+1} - \phi_i}{h} = \frac{1}{h}\left(\phi_i + h\frac{d\phi_i}{dx} + \frac{h^2}{2}\frac{d^2\phi_i}{dx^2} + \frac{h^3}{6}\frac{d^3\phi_i}{dx^3} + \cdots - \phi_i\right)$$

hence

$$\frac{\phi_{i+1} - \phi_i}{h} = \frac{d\phi_i}{dx} + \left(\frac{h}{2}\frac{d^2\phi_i}{dx^2} + \frac{h^2}{6}\frac{d^3\phi_i}{dx^3} + \cdots\right)$$

The error 'e' in the forward difference formulation is given by the value of the bracketed terms.

2. using the central difference formula:

$$\frac{\phi_{i+1} - \phi_{i-1}}{2h} = \frac{1}{2h}\left(\phi_i + h\frac{d\phi_i}{dx} + \frac{h^2}{2}\frac{d^2\phi_i}{dx^2} + \frac{h^3}{6}\frac{d^3\phi_i}{dx^3} + \frac{h^4}{24}\frac{d^4\phi_i}{dx^4} \cdots \right.$$

$$\left. - \phi_i + h\frac{d\phi_i}{dx} - \frac{h^2}{2}\frac{d^2\phi_i}{dx^2} + \frac{h^3}{6}\frac{d^3\phi_i}{dx^3} - \frac{h^4}{24}\frac{d^4\phi_i}{dx^4} \cdots\right)$$

$$= \frac{d\phi_i}{dx} + \left(\frac{h^2}{6}\frac{d^3\phi_i}{dx^3} + \frac{h^4}{120}\frac{d^5\phi_i}{dx^5}\right)$$

3. using the backward difference formula:

$$\frac{\phi_i - \phi_{i-1}}{h} = \frac{1}{h}\left(\phi_i - \phi_i + h\frac{d\phi_i}{dx} - \frac{h^2}{2}\frac{d^2\phi_i}{dx^2} + \frac{h^3}{6}\frac{d^3\phi_i}{dx^3} - \cdots\right)$$

$$= \frac{d\phi_i}{dx} - \left(\frac{h}{2}\frac{d^2\phi_i}{dx^2} - \frac{h^2}{6}\frac{d^3\phi_i}{dx^3} + \cdots\right)$$

Inspection of the bracketed error terms shows that the error in the central difference formulation is proportional to third- and fifth-order derivatives and to the interval h raised to quadratic and quartic powers. If ϕ can be approximated by a quadratic polynomial over the interval $2h$ then no approximation is involved. Otherwise, if h is made sufficiently small the error is proportional to $(h^2/6)(d^3\phi_i/$

dx^3). The errors in the forward and backward difference formulations are proportional to smaller powers of h and to lower-order derivatives. They are, therefore, of greater magnitude than the error term for the central difference formulation.

Repeating the above process for the higher-order derivatives shows that the errors e in the central difference formulation are given by

(a) for the second derivative

$$e = -\frac{h^2}{12}\frac{d^4\phi_i}{dx^4} - \frac{h^4}{360}\frac{d^6\phi_i}{dx^6} \dots$$

(b) for the third derivative

$$e = -\frac{h^2}{4}\frac{d^5\phi_i}{dx^5} - \dots$$

and

(c) for the fourth derivative

$$e = -\frac{h^2}{6}\frac{d^6\phi_i}{dx^6} - \dots$$

For all cases the error terms for forward and backward difference formulations involve lower-order derivatives and smaller powers of h and they are, therefore, only used in special circumstances.

Example The errors involved in finite-difference approximations can be seen by examining the improvements in accuracy for a decreasing interval for $\phi = f(x) = \sin x$ at $x = \pi/8$.

	First derivative			Second derivative
	Central	Backward	Forward	Central
$h = \pi/10$	0.9088	0.9684	0.8491	−0.3795
$h = \pi/20$	0.9201	0.9501	0.8901	−0.3818
$h = \pi/40$	0.9229	0.9379	0.9079	−0.3824
Analytical	0.9239			−0.3827

3.4.4 Function of two variables

If $\phi = f(x, y)$ the first derivatives of ϕ are defined by

$$\frac{\partial\phi}{\partial x} = \lim_{\Delta x \to 0}\frac{\Delta\phi}{\Delta x} = \frac{f(x+\Delta x, y) - f(x, y)}{\Delta x}$$

and

$$\frac{\partial\phi}{\partial y} = \lim_{\Delta y \to 0}\frac{\Delta\phi}{\Delta y} = \frac{f(x, y+\Delta y) - f(x, y)}{\Delta y}$$

There are three second derivatives and they are defined by

$$\frac{\partial^2\phi}{\partial x^2} = \lim_{\Delta x \to 0}\frac{\Delta\left(\frac{\Delta\phi}{\Delta x}\right)}{\Delta x} = \frac{[f(x+\Delta x, y) - f(x, y)] - [f(x, y) - f(x-\Delta x, y)]}{\Delta x^2}$$

$$\frac{\partial^2 \phi}{\partial y^2} = \lim_{\Delta y \to 0} \frac{\Delta\left(\frac{\Delta\phi}{\Delta y}\right)}{\Delta y} = \frac{[f(x, y + \Delta y) - f(x, y)] - [f(x, y) - f(x, y - \Delta y)]}{\Delta y^2}$$

and

$$\frac{\partial^2 \phi}{\partial x\, \partial y} = \lim_{\Delta y \to 0} \frac{\Delta\left(\frac{\Delta\phi}{\Delta x}\right)}{\Delta y} = \lim_{\Delta x \to 0} \frac{\Delta\left(\frac{\Delta\phi}{\Delta y}\right)}{\Delta x}$$

$$= \frac{[f(x + \Delta x, y + \Delta y) - f(x, y + \Delta y)] - [f(x + \Delta x, y) - f(x, y)]}{\Delta x\, \Delta y}$$

Higher-order derivatives are defined in a similar manner.

3.4.4.1 Finite-difference formulae

The partial derivatives with respect to only one of the variables x or y have the same definitions as the corresponding derivatives of a function of one variable. The finite-difference expressions for them are, therefore, the same, but they are usually expressed with reference to a grid of stations shown in Fig. 3.51.

The formulae for the mixed derivatives are obtained by evaluating the derivatives with respect to each variable in turn. Thus

$$\left(\frac{\partial^2 \phi}{\partial x\, \partial y}\right)_{i,j} = \frac{\partial}{\partial x}\left(\frac{\partial \phi}{\partial y}\right) = \frac{\left(\frac{\partial \phi}{\partial y}\right)_{i+1,j} - \left(\frac{\partial \phi}{\partial y}\right)_{i-1,j}}{2h}$$

$$= \frac{(\phi_{i+1,j+1} - \phi_{i+1,j-1}) - (\phi_{i-1,j+1} - \phi_{i-1,j-1})}{4kh}$$

$$= \frac{(\phi_{i+1,j+1} - \phi_{i+1,j-1} - \phi_{i-1,j+1} + \phi_{i-1,j-1})}{4kh}$$

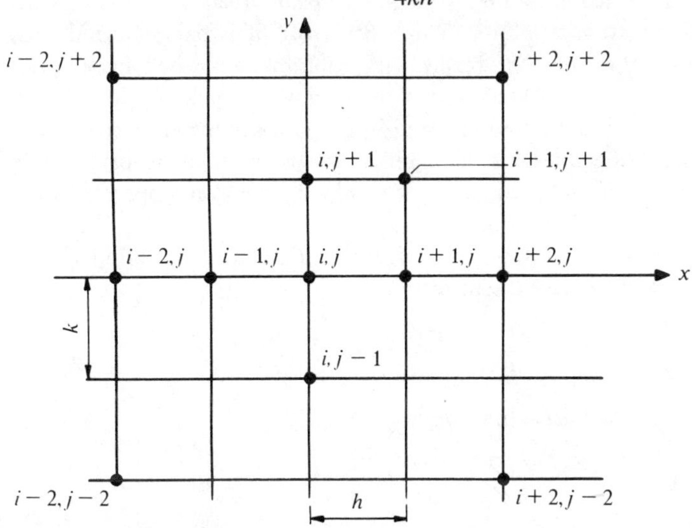

Figure 3.51 Grid of stations

$$\left(\frac{\partial^2 \phi}{\partial x\, \partial y^2}\right)_{i,j} = \frac{\partial}{\partial x}\left(\frac{\partial^2 \phi}{\partial y^2}\right)$$

$$= \frac{\phi_{i+1,j+1} - 2\phi_{i+1,j} + \phi_{i+1,j-1} - \phi_{i-1,j+1} + 2\phi_{i-1,j} + \phi_{i-1,j-1}}{2hk^2}$$

and similarly

$$\left(\frac{\partial^4 \phi}{\partial x^2\, \partial y^2}\right)_{i,j} = \frac{\partial^2}{\partial x^2}\left(\frac{\partial^2 \phi}{\partial y^2}\right)$$

$$= (\phi_{i+1,j+1} + \phi_{i+1,j-1} + \phi_{i-1,j+1} + \phi_{i-1,j-1})/(h^2k^2)$$
$$- 2(\phi_{i+1,j} + \phi_{i,j+1} + \phi_{i,j-1} + \phi_{i-1,j})/(h^2k^2) + 4\phi_{i,j}/(h^2k^2)$$

3.4.4.2 Derivatives in polar and skewed coordinates

For most problems involving a function of two variables, finite-difference formulae in Cartesian coordinates are adequate. However, polar coordinates can sometimes lead to advantages in the vicinity of curved boundaries, and use of non-orthogonal, or skewed, coordinates, can sometimes simplify a solution procedure. Finite-difference formulae for these axis systems can be derived from the formulae for a Cartesian system by means of coordinate transformations. Although the derivation is not difficult, it is not dealt with here, and the reader is referred to a more specialist text.[6]

3.4.4.3 Solution of partial differential equations

The general form of a second-order partial differential equation is

$$A(x,y)\frac{\partial^2 \phi}{\partial x^2} + B(x,y)\frac{\partial^2 \phi}{\partial x\, \partial y} + C(x,y)\frac{\partial^2 \phi}{\partial y^2} + D\left(x, y, \frac{\partial \phi}{\partial x}, \frac{\partial \phi}{\partial y}\right) = 0$$

Equations are classified according to relationships between A, B, and C. When $B^2 - 4AC < 0$ the equation is elliptic. When $B^2 = 4AC$ it is parabolic and when $B^2 - 4AC > 0$ it is hyperbolic. Problems with solutions expressed by elliptical equations have values prescribed at all points on the closed boundary to the domain of ϕ. Problems whose solutions are expressed by parabolic or hyperbolic equations do not have closed boundaries but have initial values specified on parts of the boundary, and can have open-ended regions into which a solution propagates. Here, attention is given to elliptical equations only.

Common examples of solutions to engineering problems of the elliptical type are Laplace equations which have the form:

$$\frac{\partial^2 \phi}{\partial x^2} + \frac{\partial^2 \phi}{\partial y^2} = 0$$

and Poisson equations which have the form:

$$\frac{\partial^2 \phi}{\partial x^2} + \frac{\partial^2 \phi}{\partial y^2} = E$$

where E is a constant.

Solutions to problems of lamina fluid flow and flow through an aquifer can be expressed as Laplace equations. Solutions to determine lateral displacements of a stretched membrane under uniform pressure, and to determine values of a stress function related to torsional shear stresses on a cross-section, are examples of Poisson's equation.

Finite-difference methods are also used to solve fourth-order partial differential equations for functions of two variables. Here we shall limit attention to the biharmonic equation which has the form:

$$\frac{\partial^4 \phi}{\partial x^4} + 2\frac{\partial^4 \phi}{\partial x^2\, \partial y^2} + \frac{\partial^4 \phi}{\partial y^4} = E$$

where E is a constant.

Solution to problems of plate bending and to stress analysis of planar structures can be expressed as biharmonic equations.

The finite-difference method for the solution of partial differential equations is based on the use of finite-difference approximations for derivatives. A domain is first divided into a grid of node points. A Cartesian square grid is illustrated in Fig. 3.52. Next, the finite-difference approximation to the differential equation at a typical station (i, j) of the grid is formed. Central difference expressions for Laplace, Poisson, and biharmonic equations are:

1. Poisson equation (for Laplace set $E = 0$)

$$\phi_{i,j+1} + \phi_{i,j-1} + \phi_{i+1,j} + \phi_{i-1,j} - 4\phi_{i,j} = Eh^2$$

2. Biharmonic equation

$$\begin{aligned}&(\phi_{i-2,j} + \phi_{i,j+2} + \phi_{i+2,j} + \phi_{i,j-2})\\ &+ 2(\phi_{i-1,j+1} + \phi_{i+1,j+1} + \phi_{i+1,j-1} + \phi_{i-1,j-1})\\ &- 8(\phi_{i-1,j} + \phi_{i,j+1} + \phi_{i+1,j} + \phi_{i,j-1}) + 20\phi_{i,j} = Eh^4\end{aligned}$$

A difference equation is written for each station of the grid, within the domain boundary, at which there is an unknown value of ϕ. These equations are then modified by substituting known values of ϕ at boundaries. Where necessary, fictitious nodes are introduced beyond the boundary of the domain, and subsidiary equations to relate values of ϕ at these nodes to values of ϕ at nodes within the domain boundary are set up as described in Sec. 3.4.3.3. The result is a set of

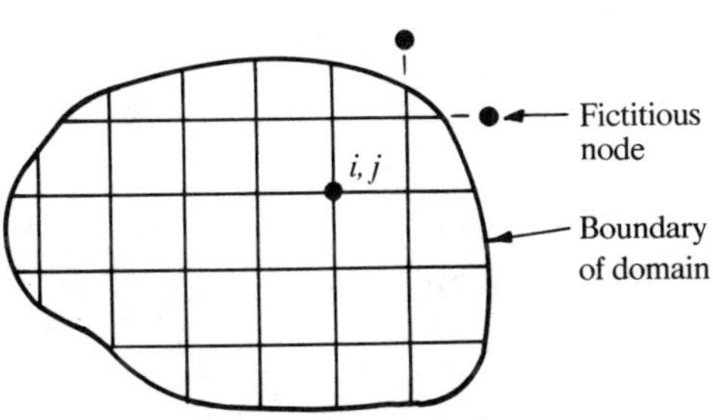

Figure 3.52 Problem of two variables

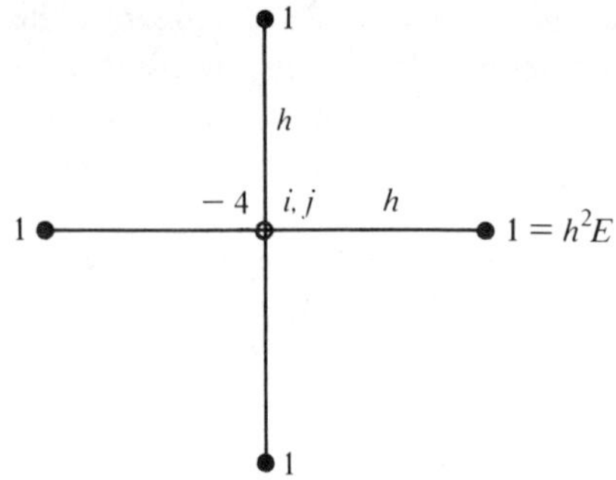

Figure 3.53 Poisson template

inhomogeneous linear simultaneous equations that can be solved using one of the techniques described in Sec. 3.1.3.

When equations are set up by hand, templates giving the coefficients of variables relevant to a particular equation are useful. In Figs. 3.53 and 3.54 templates are given for the above equations. To assemble a particular equation, the centre point of the template is imagined positioned over the pivotal station *i, j*. The stations then indicate which other variables are involved in the equation and the values of their coefficients.

3.4.4.4 Illustration of solution procedures

Solution of a simply supported square plate subjected to a uniformly distributed loading can be solved in two stages using the central difference approximation for a Poisson equation.[7] First, the equation $(\partial^2 M/\partial x^2) + (\partial^2 M/\partial y^2) = -q$ is solved. In this equation $M = (Mx + My)/(1 + \nu)$, where Mx and My are bending moments in the x and y directions, respectively, ν is the value of Poisson's ratio for the plate material, and q is the load intensity. When M has been determined, the equation: $(\partial^2 w/\partial x^2) + (\partial^2 w/\partial y^2) = -M/D$ is solved. In this equation, w is the lateral displacement of the slab and D is its flexural stiffness.

A grid of stations is drawn over the plate as shown in Fig. 3.55. Due to eight-

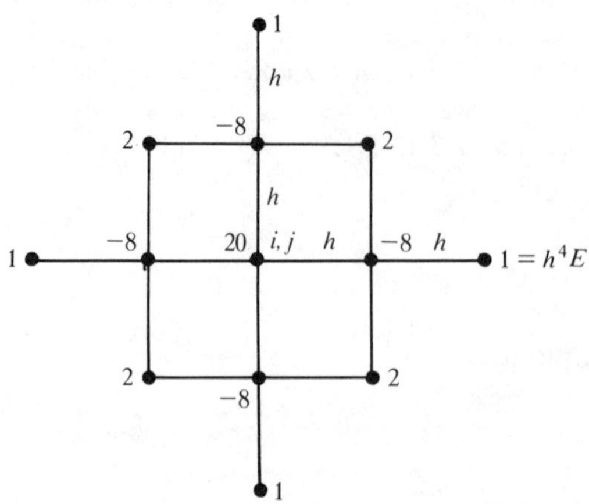

Figure 3.54 Biharmonic template

fold symmetry there are ten problem variables as shown in the figure (on the boundary $M = w = 0$). As only second-order derivatives are involved, and there are no problem variables on the boundary, no fictitious stations need be used.

The finite-difference form of the first equation is

$$M_{i-1,j} - 2M_{i,j} + M_{i+1,j} + M_{i,j-1} - 2M_{i,j} + M_{i,j+1} = \frac{-qL^2}{64}$$

and its template is shown in Fig. 3.53.

Setting the pivotal station (i, j) of the difference equation to each of the ten stations indicated in Fig. 3.55, in turn, gives

$$\frac{qL^2}{64}\begin{bmatrix} 1 \\ 1 \\ 1 \\ 1 \\ 1 \\ 1 \\ 1 \\ 1 \\ 1 \\ 1 \end{bmatrix} = \begin{bmatrix} 4 & -2 & 0 & 0 & 0 & 0 & 0 & 0 & 0 & 0 \\ -1 & 4 & -1 & 0 & -1 & 0 & 0 & 0 & 0 & 0 \\ 0 & -1 & 4 & -1 & 0 & -1 & 0 & 0 & 0 & 0 \\ 0 & 0 & -2 & 4 & 0 & 0 & -1 & 0 & 0 & 0 \\ 0 & -2 & 0 & 0 & 4 & -2 & 0 & 0 & 0 & 0 \\ 0 & 0 & -1 & 0 & -1 & 4 & -1 & -1 & 0 & 0 \\ 0 & 0 & 0 & -1 & 0 & -2 & 4 & 0 & -1 & 0 \\ 0 & 0 & 0 & 0 & 0 & -2 & 0 & 4 & -2 & 0 \\ 0 & 0 & 0 & 0 & 0 & 0 & -1 & -2 & 4 & -1 \\ 0 & 0 & 0 & 0 & 0 & 0 & 0 & 0 & -4 & 4 \end{bmatrix} \begin{bmatrix} M_1 \\ M_2 \\ M_3 \\ M_4 \\ M_5 \\ M_6 \\ M_7 \\ M_8 \\ M_9 \\ M_{10} \end{bmatrix}$$

The matrix of coefficients is banded, and if each equation is divided by a suitable factor, there is symmetry about the leading diagonal.

Solution of the equations gives

$$\begin{aligned} M_1 &= 0.017\,79qL^2 & M_2 &= 0.027\,75qL^2 & M_3 &= 0.039\,15qL^2 \\ M_4 &= 0.034\,52qL^2 & M_5 &= 0.044\,66qL^2 & M_6 &= 0.053\,76qL^2 \\ M_7 &= 0.056\,64qL^2 & M_8 &= 0.065\,22qL^2 & M_9 &= 0.068\,87qL_2 \\ M_{10} &= 0.072\,78qL^2 \end{aligned}$$

The bending moments at the centre are given by $M_y = M_x = M_{10}(1 + \nu)/2$, and for $\nu = 0.3, M_x = 0.0473\,qL^2$.

The finite-difference form of the equation relating displacements w and moments M is

$$w_{i-1,j} - 2w_{i,j} + w_{i+1,j} + w_{i,j-1} - 2w_{i,j} + w_{i,j+1} = \frac{-M_{i,j}}{D}\frac{L^2}{64}$$

This equation is set up for each of the ten pivot stations. The matrix of coefficients is the same as that for the M variables, and the left-hand side vector is proportional to the determined M vector. Solution of the equations can be performed taking advantage of the previously derived triangular decomposition of the coefficient

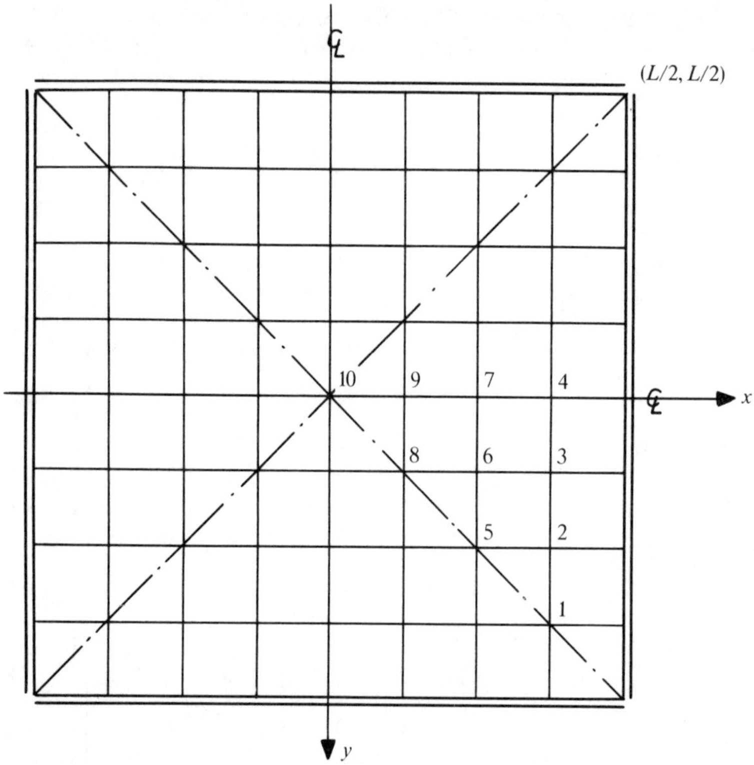

Figure 3.55 Simply supported plate

matrix. The reader should verify that the solution is

$$w_1 = 0.663k \quad w_2 = 1.186k \quad w_3 = 1.515k \quad w_4 = 1.627k$$

$$w_5 = 2.134k \quad w_6 = 2.733k \quad w_7 = 2.937k \quad w_8 = 3.507k$$

$$w_9 = 3.770k \quad w_{10} = 4.055k \quad \text{where } k = 10^{-3}qL^4/D$$

The values of central displacement and moment obtained by solving the differential equation analytically are: $w_{10} = 4.06k$ and $M_x = M_y = 0.0479qL^2$. It can be seen that sufficient accuracy has been obtained for practical purposes with this mesh.

3.4.5 Nature of errors

For functions of one variable the magnitude of errors was examined by making use of Taylor expansions. A similar study for a function of two variables would show similar trends.[6] Central difference formulations involve errors of smallest magnitude and solutions based on central differences converge most quickly with decreasing grid line spacings.

In the finite-difference method, values of a function are defined uniquely only at nodes or stations. The values of the function between nodes can vary according

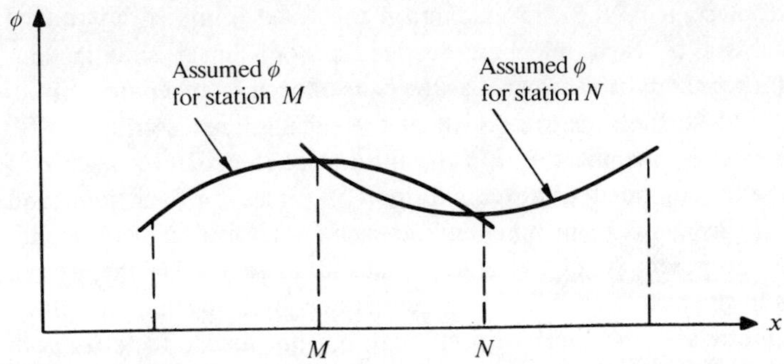

Figure 3.56 Assumed function of ϕ

to which node is being considered. In Fig. 3.56, for example, possible distributions of ϕ between nodes M and N are shown when second-order central difference formulations are being considered at nodes M and N, respectively. This is an extreme example, but it serves to illustrate a possible source of error when grid points are widely spaced.

The finite-difference expressions for derivatives are exact for low order interpolation functions. For example, second-order central differences are exact for a quadratic, nine-point, Lagrange interpolation function; see Sec. 3.6. This suggests that the error involved in a finite-difference formulation is a function of the difference between the function's actual values, and those of a polynomial approximation. It also suggests that difference formulae which give exact differentials to higher-order interpolation functions, which involve more grid points, should give greater accuracy. On the whole this is true, but there is little gain in overall computational efficiency in doing this due to the increased bandwidth of the coefficient matrix produced. Including more coefficients also leads to problems with boundary conditions, as more fictitious nodes are created. It is generally regarded as more advantageous to use the formulae given in this section at stations on a refined grid, than to use formulations for higher-order interpolation functions at stations on a coarser grid.

3.5 FINITE-ELEMENT SOLUTION OF DIFFERENTIAL EQUATIONS

The finite-element method was first introduced to civil engineering through attempts to generalize the stiffness method to deal with structural continua, such as the covering sheeting on aircraft wings. As a result, many of the concepts and much of the terminology of the stiffness method have been incorporated into the finite-element method. To understand the principles of the finite-element method, it is instructive first to consider briefly the basis of the stiffness method of structural analysis.

3.5.1 Stiffness method

The stiffness method was derived for skeletal structures. Analysis of behaviour under imposed loading is performed in stages. First, member connections are prevented from displacement and the loading on the fixed joints is determined from separate analyses of each member. Second, sets of linear simultaneous equations relating forces and displacements at the ends of each member are derived. These are called 'local stiffness matrices'. All of the calculations described so far are performed on isolated members, but in the third stage the stiffness matrix of the entire structure is compiled using equilibrium of forces on each joint and compatibility of displacements of member ends at each joint. Displacement boundary conditions are imposed at appropriate joints and these render the overall stiffness matrix non-singular. Solution of the equations gives the joint displacements and from these and the local stiffness matrices the load effects on each member are determined.

The method has a number of features that facilitate automatic handling. Local stiffness matrices of members and the joint loading from members can be determined by procedures that need take no account of the overall structural configuration. The overal stiffness matrix of a structure can be assembled automatically from the local stiffness matrices of members using only a specification of the members connected to each joint. Standard solutions to linear simultaneous equations can be used to determine joint displacements. A single computer program can be derived to solve all skeletal structures from a description of member loading, member properties, structural topology and the displacement boundary conditions. Construction of a program to solve plane framework problems is described in Chapter 4.

With such a powerful technique for automatically solving skeletal structures, it is not surprising that engineers attempted to extend the method to problems of structural continua and later to general field problems. At first, attempts were made to derive local stiffness matrices for sheet material in terms of forces and discplacements at joints and to 'connect' sheets together as though they were discrete memebers. Such attempts were not successful, because in an actual structure displacements are continuous, whereas in the analytical model the sheets, or finite elements, could have different values of displacement at points along common edges.

To improve the analytical model it is necessary to provide continuity of displacements, and in some cases of displacement derivatives along finite-element sides. Before describing how this is done, without losing the power and simplicity of the stiffness method, it is useful to consider the techniques for deriving local stiffness matrices and these will be illustrated for beam elements.

3.5.2 Thin uniform beam element

A beam element connecting nodes i and j is shown in Fig. 3.57. Its stiffness matrix relates forces exerted on the member ends to displacements of the ends. Thus

$$\begin{bmatrix} Fy_i \\ M_i \\ Fy_j \\ M_j \end{bmatrix} = \begin{bmatrix} & & & \\ & \mathbf{S}_m & & \\ & & & \end{bmatrix} \begin{bmatrix} v_i \\ \theta_i \\ v_j \\ \theta_j \end{bmatrix} \qquad \text{or} \qquad \mathbf{F}_m = \mathbf{S}_m \cdot \mathbf{a}_m$$

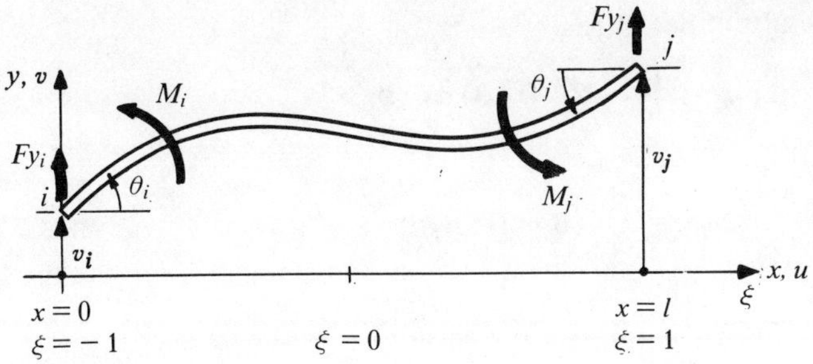

Figure 3.57 Thin beam

Structural theory shows that for a beam in flexure $d^4v/dx^4 = 0$ between loaded points and hence the lateral displacement v can be represented by a cubic polynomial. Using cubic Hermitian shape functions, the lateral displacement is given by

$$v = N_1 v_i + N_2 \theta_i + N_3 v_j + N_4 \theta_j = \mathbf{N}^T \cdot \mathbf{a}_m$$

where

$$N_1 = 1 - 3\left(\frac{x}{l}\right)^2 + 2\left(\frac{x}{l}\right)^3 \qquad N_2 = x\left(1 - \frac{x}{l}\right)^2$$

$$N_3 = 3\left(\frac{x}{l}\right)^2 - 2\left(\frac{x}{l}\right)^3 \qquad N_4 = \frac{x^2}{l}\left(\frac{x}{l} - 1\right)$$

It is assumed that shear strains are negligible and hence that $\theta = dv/dx$, and that plane sections normal to the undeflected beam axis remain plane after flexure so that $u = -\theta y$.

The strain energy stored in the beam element is given by $U_m = \frac{1}{2}\int_{vol} \boldsymbol{\sigma} \cdot \boldsymbol{\varepsilon}\, dvol$. For the assumptions made, this can be written in terms of the bending moment $M = (-\int \boldsymbol{\sigma}\, y\, dA)$ and the curvature $K \simeq d^2v/dx^2$ $(= d\theta/dx = -\epsilon/y)$; thus

$$U_m = \frac{1}{2}\int_0^l M \frac{d^2 v}{dx^2}\, dx$$

As $M = EI\,(d^2v/dx^2)$, $U_m = \frac{1}{2}\int_0^l ((d^2v/dx^2)\, EI\,(d^2v/dx^2))\, dx$.

Now $d^2v/dx^2 = \mathbf{B} \cdot \mathbf{a}_m = ((d^2N_1/dx^2), (d^2N_2/dx^2), (d^2N_3/dx^2), (d^2N_4/dx^2)) \cdot \mathbf{a}_m$ and writing a general constitutive matrix $\mathbf{D}$ for EI gives

$$U_m = \frac{1}{2}\, \mathbf{a}_m^T \cdot \int_0^l (\mathbf{B}^T \cdot \mathbf{D} \cdot \mathbf{B})\, dx \cdot \mathbf{a}_m$$

The potential energy of the end joint, or nodal, loads is given by: $V_m = -\mathbf{a}_m^T \cdot \mathbf{F}_m$, hence the total potential energy of the structural system is

$$U_m + V_m = \frac{1}{2}\, \mathbf{a}_m^T \cdot \int_0^l (\mathbf{B}^T \cdot \mathbf{D} \cdot \mathbf{B})\, dx \cdot \mathbf{a}_m - \mathbf{a}_m^T \cdot \mathbf{F}_m$$

To satisfy equilibrium conditions the total potential energy has a stationary value. Thus $\delta(U_m + V_m) = 0$, where δ indicates a change when the deflected form varies slightly from the form that gives equilibrium. As the independent parameters in the energy expression are the joint displacements

$$\delta(U_m + V_m) = \frac{\partial}{\partial \mathbf{a}_m}(U_m + V_m) = \mathbf{0}$$

Hence, using the results of Sec. 3.1.6,

$$\mathbf{F}_m = \int_0^l (\mathbf{B}^T \cdot \mathbf{D} \cdot \mathbf{B})\, dx \cdot \mathbf{a}_m$$

and by definition

$$\mathbf{S}_m = \int_0^l (\mathbf{B}^T \cdot \mathbf{D} \cdot \mathbf{B})\, dx$$

$$\mathbf{S}_m = EI \int_0^l \begin{bmatrix} \dfrac{-6}{l^2} + \dfrac{12x}{l^3} \\[2ex] \dfrac{-4}{l} + \dfrac{6x}{l^2} \\[2ex] \dfrac{6}{l^2} - \dfrac{12x}{l^3} \\[2ex] \dfrac{-2}{l} + \dfrac{6x}{l^2} \end{bmatrix} \left[\frac{-6}{l^2} + \frac{12x}{l^3},\ \frac{-4}{l} + \frac{6x}{l^2},\ \frac{6}{l^2} - \frac{12x}{l^3},\ \frac{-2}{l} + \frac{6x}{l^2} \right]$$

For this example, there are only six simple integrals and the stiffness matrix can be calculated explicitly. Thus, for example,

$$S_{11} = -S_{13} = -S_{31} = S_{33} = EI \int_0^l \left(\frac{-6}{l^2} + \frac{12x}{l^3} \right)^2 dx$$

$$= EI \left(\frac{36}{l^3} - \frac{72}{l^3} + \frac{48}{l^3} \right) = \frac{12EI}{l^3}$$

Hence

$$\begin{bmatrix} Fy_i \\ M_i \\ Fy_j \\ M_j \end{bmatrix} = \frac{EI}{l^3} \begin{bmatrix} 12 & 6l & -12 & 6l \\ 6l & 4l^2 & -6l & 2l^2 \\ -12 & -6l & 12 & -6l \\ 6l & 2l^2 & -6l & 4l^2 \end{bmatrix} \begin{bmatrix} v_i \\ \theta_i \\ v_j \\ \theta_j \end{bmatrix}$$

3.5.2.1 Numerical integration

In general, it is difficult to evaluate finite-element stiffness matrices explicitly, and the integrations are usually performed numerically within a computer program. For this example, quadratic polynomials are integrated and Simpson's rule or two-point Gauss quadrature can be used.

For example, using Gauss quadrature to evaluate S_{11} gives

$$S_{11} = EI \int_0^l \left(\frac{-6}{l^2} + \frac{12x}{l^3} \right)^2 dx \equiv \frac{EIl}{2} \int_{-1}^{1} \left(\frac{-6}{l^2} + \frac{12}{l^3} \frac{l}{2}(\xi + 1) \right)^2 d\xi$$

$$= \frac{18EI}{l^3} \left[1 \left(\frac{-1}{\sqrt{3}} \right)^2 + 1 \left(\frac{1}{\sqrt{3}} \right)^2 \right] = \frac{12EI}{l^3}$$

3.5.2.2 *Consistent nodal forces*

When loading is applied between element nodes, equivalent or consistent nodal loading is determined by a preliminary analysis. For linear behaviour, any intermediate loads can be represented by combinations of point loads and it is, therefore, only necessary to consider a single concentrated force.

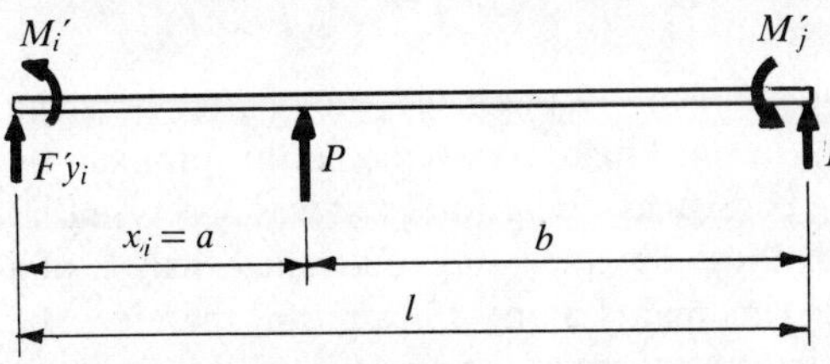

Figure 3.58 Consistent nodal forces for a point load

Using the notation of Fig. 3.58, when the point load P moves through displacement v the loss of potential energy is given by

$$-Pv = -P \cdot \mathbf{N}^T(x = x_i) \cdot \mathbf{a}_m$$

The set of nodal forces $\mathbf{F_c}$ which undergo the same loss of potential energy for compatible displacements are called the 'consistent nodal forces' and are given by

$$-\mathbf{F}_c^T \cdot \mathbf{a}_m = -P \cdot \mathbf{N}^T(x = x_i) \cdot \mathbf{a}_m$$

hence

$$\mathbf{F_c} = P \cdot \mathbf{N}(x = x_i)$$

or

$$\begin{bmatrix} F'y_i \\ M_i' \\ F'y_j \\ M_j' \end{bmatrix} = P \begin{bmatrix} 1 - 3\left(\dfrac{x_i}{l}\right)^2 + 2\left(\dfrac{x_i}{l}\right)^3 \\ x_i\left(1 - \dfrac{x_i}{l}\right)^2 \\ 3\left(\dfrac{x_i}{l}\right)^2 - 2\left(\dfrac{x_i}{l}\right)^3 \\ \dfrac{x_i^2}{l}\left(\dfrac{x_i}{l} - 1\right) \end{bmatrix} = P \begin{bmatrix} b^2(3a + b)/l^3 \\ ab^2/l^2 \\ a^2(a + 3b)/l^3 \\ -a^2b/l^2 \end{bmatrix}$$

This result is interesting, as these values agree with the fixed end values. Taking the beam element together with consistent nodal forces results in prediction of correct nodal displacements. Within the element domain, the displacements and bending moments derived from the shape functions are incorrect, but the errors do not propogate beyond the element boundaries.

3.5.2.3 *Stress resultants*

Engineers are usually more interested in values of stress resultants, such as bending moments, than in values of displacements. The results of a finite-element analysis are values of nodal displacements and these could be used to obtain stress resultants.

For example, the bending moments in a beam element are given by

$$M_x = EI\frac{d^2 v}{dx^2} = EI\frac{d^2 \mathbf{N}^T}{dx^2} \cdot \mathbf{a}_m$$

hence

$$\frac{M_x}{EI} = \left(\frac{-6}{l^2} + \frac{12x}{l^3}\right) v_i + \left(\frac{-4}{l} + \frac{6x}{l^2}\right) \theta_i + \left(\frac{6}{l^2} - \frac{12x}{l^3}\right) v_j + \left(\frac{-2}{l} + \frac{6x}{l^2}\right) \theta_j$$

A linear distribution of bending moment is predicted, no matter how the applied loading is distributed along a beam. Engineers overcome this problem by use of superposition. When discussing consistent nodal forces, it was observed that consistent joint forces are the same as those obtained from a detailed analysis of a member with fixed ends. The bending moments along a beam can, therefore, be obtained by adding the distributions from analyses of the members with fixed ends to the moments predicted by the finite-element analysis for joint loading as shown in Fig. 3.59, and Sec. 4.3.8.

Similar problems arise with determination of local effects in a continuum. In general, however, the simple physical reasoning used with discrete structural members cannot be used with analytical models of two- and three-dimensional continua, so a degree of approximation in the prediction of local effects has to be accepted.

3.5.3 Thick uniform beam elements

Behaviour of a thick beam is distinguished from that of a thin beam by the relative importance of shearing strains. In general, the rotation of a normal θ does not equal the rotation of the beam axis dv/dx, as shown in Fig. 3.60. Two approaches to the derivation of finite-element stiffness matrices for thick beams are described, as they provide relatively simple illustrations of a number of finite-element techniques.

3.5.3.1 Use of assumed stress distributions

Let the stresses acting on a rectangular beam of breadth b and depth d be given by

$$\sigma = -y(a_1 + a_2 x) \qquad \tau = (1 - 4y^2/d^2)a_3$$

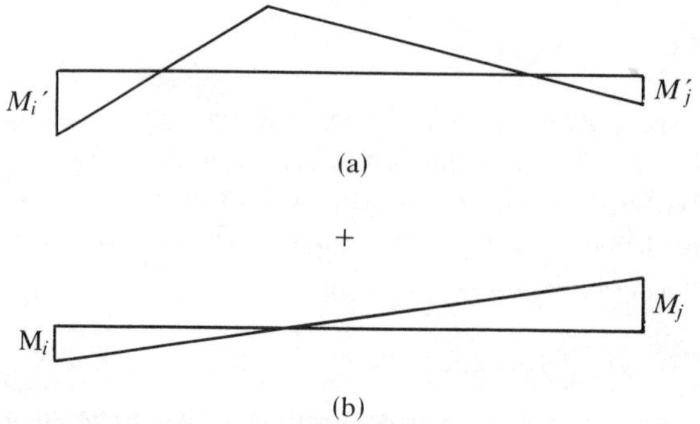

Figure 3.59 Use of superposition. (a) Bending moment from member analysis with fixed ends. (b) Bending moment due to joint displacements from fixed-end analysis

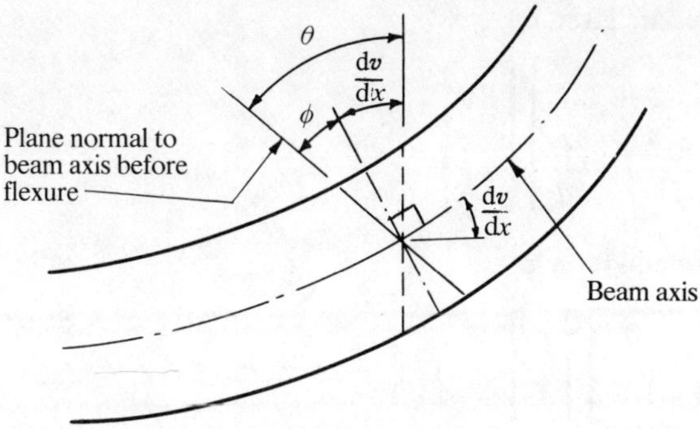

Figure 3.60 Rotation of normals in a thick beam

These stress distributions are those from simple beam theory for a member loaded only on its end faces. The equivalent stress resultants are a bending moment M and a shear Q as shown in Fig. 3.61.

$$M = -\int_{-d/2}^{d/2} \sigma y b \, dy = I(a_1 + a_2 x) \qquad \text{and} \qquad Q = \int_{-d/2}^{d/2} \tau b \, dy = \frac{2bd}{3} a_3$$

where I is the second moment of area of the cross-section about the bending axis.

At the member ends,

$$M_i = -M(x = 0) = -Ia_1 \qquad M_j = M(x = l) = I(a_1 + a_2 l)$$

$$Fy_i = -Q(x = 0) = \frac{-2bd}{3} a_3 \qquad Fy_j = Q(x = l) = \frac{2bd}{3} a_3$$

The constants are not independent, as the stress resultants must satisfy equilibrium conditions. For equilibrium of vertical forces $dQ/dx \, dx = 0$, and for moment equilibrium $Q \, dx + dM/dx \, dx = 0$, hence $2bd/3 \, a_3 + Ia_2 = 0$, or $a_3 = -(3I/2bd)a_2$.

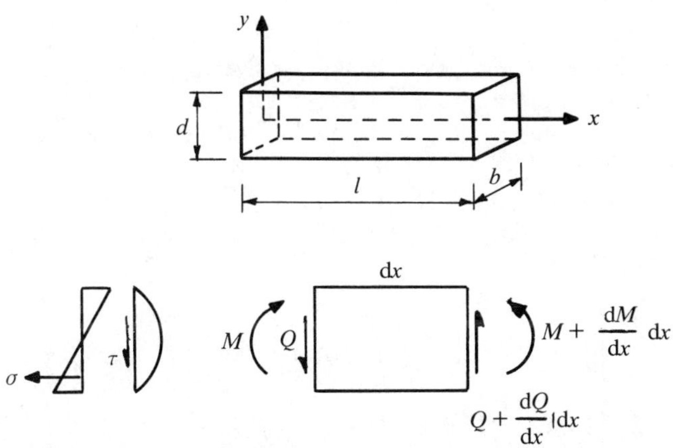

Figure 3.61 Stresses and resultants

In matrix form, the stresses are given by

$$\begin{bmatrix}\sigma\\ \tau\end{bmatrix}=\begin{bmatrix}-y & -xy\\ 0 & -\left(1-\dfrac{4y^2}{d^2}\right)\dfrac{3I}{2bd}\end{bmatrix}\begin{bmatrix}a_1\\ a_2\end{bmatrix}\qquad \text{or}\qquad \boldsymbol{\sigma}=\mathbf{G}\cdot\mathbf{C}$$

The stress–stration constitutive equation is

$$\begin{bmatrix}\epsilon\\ \gamma\end{bmatrix}=\begin{bmatrix}1/E & 0\\ 0 & 1/G\end{bmatrix}\begin{bmatrix}\sigma\\ \tau\end{bmatrix}\qquad \text{or}\qquad \boldsymbol{\varepsilon}=\bar{\mathbf{D}}\cdot\boldsymbol{\sigma}$$

The complementary strain energy stored in an element is given by

$$U_m=\tfrac{1}{2}\int_v \boldsymbol{\sigma}^{\mathrm{T}}\cdot\bar{\mathbf{D}}\cdot\boldsymbol{\sigma}\,dv=\tfrac{1}{2}\int_v \mathbf{C}^{\mathrm{T}}\cdot\mathbf{G}^{\mathrm{T}}\cdot\bar{\mathbf{D}}\cdot\mathbf{G}\cdot\mathbf{C}\,dv$$

$$U_m=\tfrac{1}{2}\mathbf{C}^{\mathrm{T}}\int_{-b/2}^{b/2}\int_{-d/2}^{d/2}\int_0^l\begin{bmatrix}y^2/E & xy^2/E\\ xy^2/E & \dfrac{x^2y^2}{E}+\dfrac{1}{G}\left[\dfrac{3I}{2bd}\left(1-\dfrac{4y^2}{d^2}\right)\right]^2\end{bmatrix}dx\,dy\,dz\,\mathbf{C}$$

$$U_m=\tfrac{1}{2}\mathbf{C}^{\mathrm{T}}\cdot\begin{bmatrix}\dfrac{Il}{E} & \dfrac{Il^2}{2E}\\ \dfrac{Il^2}{2E} & \left(\dfrac{Il^3}{3E}+\dfrac{Ild^2}{10G}\right)\end{bmatrix}\cdot\mathbf{C}=\tfrac{1}{2}\mathbf{C}^{\mathrm{T}}\cdot\mathbf{H}\cdot\mathbf{C}$$

Let the displacements of the end faces be $\mathbf{a}_m$, where $\mathbf{a}_m^{\mathrm{T}}=[v_i,\theta_i,v_j,\theta_j]$ and the nodal forces be $\mathbf{F}_m$, where $\mathbf{F}_m^{\mathrm{T}}=[Fy_i,M_i,Fy_j,M_j]$. From the end conditions,

$$\mathbf{F}_m=\begin{bmatrix}0 & I\\ -I & 0\\ 0 & -I\\ I & Il\end{bmatrix}\begin{bmatrix}a_1\\ a_2\end{bmatrix}=\mathbf{R}\cdot\mathbf{C}\qquad \text{hence}\qquad \mathbf{C}=\mathbf{R}^{-1}\cdot\mathbf{F}_m$$

The potential energy of the end joint, or nodal loads is given by:

$$V_m=-\mathbf{F}_m^{\mathrm{T}}\cdot\mathbf{a}_m=-\mathbf{C}^{\mathrm{T}}\cdot\mathbf{R}^{\mathrm{T}}\cdot\mathbf{a}_m.$$

Thus the total complementary energy $(U_m+V_m)=\tfrac{1}{2}\mathbf{C}^{\mathrm{T}}\cdot\mathbf{H}\cdot\mathbf{C}-\mathbf{C}^{\mathrm{T}}\cdot\mathbf{R}^{\mathrm{T}}\cdot\mathbf{a}_m$.

For a stationary value $\partial/\partial\mathbf{C}\,(U_m+V_m)=\mathbf{0}$

Therefore, $\quad \mathbf{0}=\mathbf{H}\cdot\mathbf{C}-\mathbf{R}^{\mathrm{T}}\cdot\mathbf{a}_m=\mathbf{H}\cdot\mathbf{R}^{-1}\cdot\mathbf{F}_m-\mathbf{R}^{\mathrm{T}}\cdot\mathbf{a}_m$.

Hence $\mathbf{F}_m=(\mathbf{H}\cdot\mathbf{R}^{-1})^{-1}\cdot\mathbf{R}^{\mathrm{T}}\cdot\mathbf{a}_m=\mathbf{R}\cdot\mathbf{H}^{-1}\cdot\mathbf{R}^{\mathrm{T}}\cdot\mathbf{a}_m$, and by definition the stiffness matrix $\mathbf{S}_m=\mathbf{R}\cdot\mathbf{H}^{-1}\cdot\mathbf{R}^{\mathrm{T}}$.

$$\mathbf{S}_m=\frac{E}{Il}\begin{bmatrix}0 & I\\ -I & 0\\ 0 & -I\\ I & Il\end{bmatrix}\begin{bmatrix}1 & l/2\\ l/2 & l^2/3+Ed^2/10G\end{bmatrix}^{-1}\begin{bmatrix}0 & -I & 0 & I\\ I & 0 & -I & Il\end{bmatrix}$$

hence

$$\mathbf{S}_m = \frac{12EI}{l(l^2+12g)} \begin{bmatrix} 1 & l/2 & -1 & l/2 \\ l/2 & (l^2/3+g) & -l/2 & (l^2/6-g) \\ -1 & -l/2 & 1 & -l/2 \\ l/2 & (l^2/6-g) & -l/2 & (l^2/3+g) \end{bmatrix}$$

where $g = Ed^2/10G$

3.5.3.2 Assumed displacement distributions with reduced integration

This formulation of a stiffness matrix for a thick beam illustrates use of quadratic shape functions, and reduced integration. A typical beam element is shown in Fig. 3.62. There are two independent displacement functions: $\theta(x)$ for rotation of cross-sections; and $v(x)$ for lateral displacement of the beam axis. There are three nodal points with coordinates (x_1, x_2, x_3), at which there are independent nodal parameters $(v_1, \theta_1, v_2, \theta_2, v_3, \theta_3)$.

$$v = N_1 v_1 + N_2 v_2 + N_3 v_3 = \mathbf{N}^\mathrm{T} \cdot \mathbf{V}_m$$

$$\theta = N_1 \theta_1 + N_2 \theta_2 + N_3 \theta_3 = \mathbf{N}^\mathrm{T} \cdot \boldsymbol{\theta}_m$$

$$x = N_1 x_1 + N_2 x_2 + N_3 x_3 = \mathbf{N}^\mathrm{T} \cdot \mathbf{X}_m$$

where $N_1 = \xi(\xi-1)/2$, $\quad N_2 = (1-\xi)(1+\xi)$, $\quad N_3 = \xi(1+\xi)/2$.

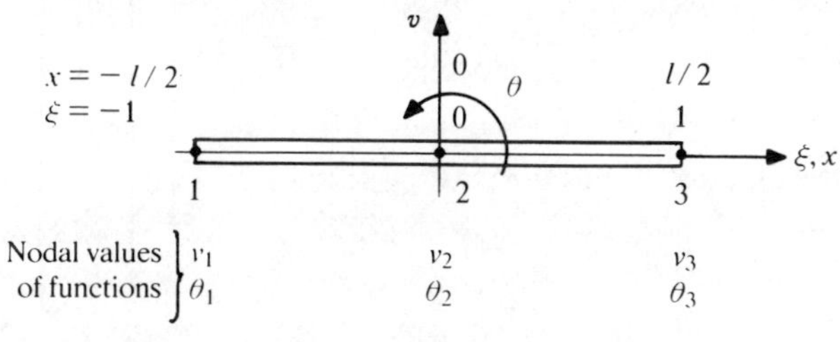

Figure 3.62 Quadratic beam element

The same shape functions are used to describe the beam geometry and displacements, so the formulation is called 'isoparametric'. The shape functions are illustrated in Fig. 3.63, and for a straight beam element with a midpoint node

$$x = \xi(\xi-1)/2x_1 + (1-\xi)(1+\xi)x_2 + \xi(1+\xi)/2x_3$$

hence

$$\frac{\mathrm{d}x}{\mathrm{d}\xi} = (\xi - \tfrac{1}{2})x_1 - 2\xi x_2 + (\xi + \tfrac{1}{2})x_3 = l/2$$

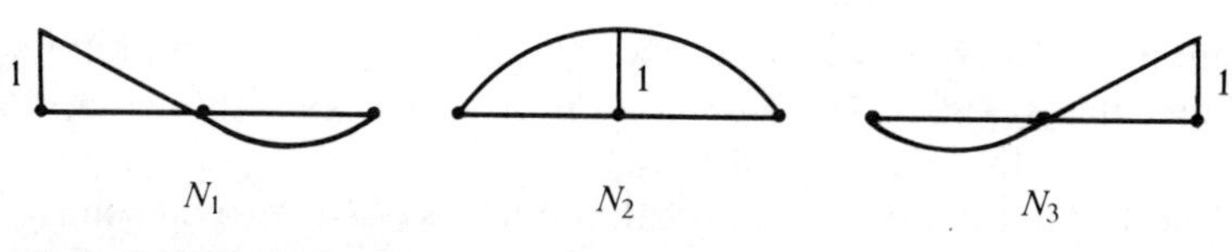

Figure 3.63 Shape functions

The strain energy stored in an element is given by

$$U_m = \tfrac{1}{2}\int_l M\frac{d\theta}{dx}\,dx + \tfrac{1}{2}\int_l Q\phi\,dx$$

where M and Q are the bending moment and shear at x respectively, and θ and ϕ are as defined in Fig. 3.60.

The constitutive equations are $M = EI\,d\theta/dx$ and $Q = GA\phi$.

Hence

$$\begin{bmatrix} M \\ Q \end{bmatrix} = \begin{bmatrix} EI & 0 \\ 0 & GA \end{bmatrix}\begin{bmatrix} \dfrac{d\theta}{dx} \\ \phi \end{bmatrix} \qquad \text{or} \qquad \boldsymbol{\sigma} = \mathbf{D}\cdot\boldsymbol{\varepsilon}$$

and the strain energy is given by $U_m = \frac{1}{2}\int_l \boldsymbol{\varepsilon}^T\cdot\mathbf{D}\cdot\boldsymbol{\varepsilon}\,dx$.

$$\boldsymbol{\varepsilon} = \begin{bmatrix} \dfrac{d\theta}{dx} \\ \phi \end{bmatrix} = \begin{bmatrix} \dfrac{d\theta}{dx} \\ \theta - \dfrac{dv}{dx} \end{bmatrix} = \begin{bmatrix} \dfrac{d\theta}{d\xi}\dfrac{d\xi}{dx} \\ \theta - \dfrac{dv}{d\xi}\dfrac{d\xi}{dx} \end{bmatrix} = \begin{bmatrix} \dfrac{2}{l}\dfrac{d\theta}{d\xi} \\ \theta - \dfrac{2}{l}\dfrac{dv}{d\xi} \end{bmatrix}$$

Now, $d\theta/d\xi = \partial\mathbf{N}^T/\partial\xi\ \boldsymbol{\theta}_m = (\xi - \frac{1}{2})\theta_1 - 2\xi\theta_2 + (\xi + \frac{1}{2})\theta_3$,
and $dv/d\xi = \partial\mathbf{N}^T/\partial\xi\ \mathbf{V}_m$;
hence

$$\boldsymbol{\varepsilon} = \begin{bmatrix} 0 & \dfrac{2}{l}(\xi - \frac{1}{2}) & 0 & \dfrac{-4\xi}{l} & 0 & \dfrac{2}{l}(\xi + \frac{1}{2}) \\ \dfrac{2}{l}(\frac{1}{2} - \xi) & \dfrac{\xi}{2}(\xi - 1) & \dfrac{4\xi}{l} & (1 - \xi^2) & \dfrac{-2}{l}(\xi + \frac{1}{2}) & \dfrac{\xi}{2}(\xi + 1) \end{bmatrix}\begin{bmatrix} v_1 \\ \theta_1 \\ v_2 \\ \theta_2 \\ v_3 \\ \theta_3 \end{bmatrix}$$

or

$$\boldsymbol{\varepsilon} = \mathbf{B}\cdot\mathbf{a}_m \qquad \text{and} \qquad U_m = \tfrac{1}{2}\mathbf{a}_m^T \int_l \mathbf{B}^T\cdot\mathbf{D}\cdot\mathbf{B}\,dx\cdot\mathbf{a}_m$$

The potential energy of the end joint, or nodal loads, is given by

$$\begin{aligned} V_m &= -Fy_1v_1 - M_1\theta_1 - Fy_2v_2 - M_2\theta_2 - Fy_3v_3 - M_3\theta_3 \\ &= -\mathbf{a}_m^T\cdot\mathbf{F}_m \end{aligned}$$

For a stationary value of the total potential energy,

$$\frac{\partial}{\partial\mathbf{a}_m}(U_m + V_m) = 0 = \int_l \mathbf{B}^T\cdot\mathbf{D}\cdot\mathbf{B}\cdot dx\cdot\mathbf{a}_m - \mathbf{F}_m$$

hence the stiffness matrix $\mathbf{S}_m = \int_{-l/2}^{l/2}\mathbf{B}^T\cdot\mathbf{D}\cdot\mathbf{B}\cdot dx = \int_{-1}^{1}\mathbf{B}^T\cdot\mathbf{D}\cdot\mathbf{B}\cdot l/2\,d\xi$.

The integration could be performed explicitly, or by using Gauss quadrature as part of a computer program. The latter course of action is usually adopted. Inspection of the terms to be integrated shows that multipliers of EI are polynomials of ξ of up to the third power, and that multipliers of GA are polynomials of ξ up to the fourth power. Exact integration of the former terms is, therefore, given by 2-station Gauss quadrature and of the latter terms by 3-station Gauss quadrature (see Sec. 3.3.1.2). However, experience has shown that analyses using the element in this form are uneconomic and results with few elements can be very inaccurate.

To overcome the problem, all terms are integrated using 2-station Gauss quadrature, and the stiffness matrix obtained is as follows:

$$\mathbf{S}_m = \frac{EI}{3l}\begin{bmatrix} 0 & 0 & 0 & 0 & 0 & 0 \\ 0 & 7 & 0 & -8 & 0 & 1 \\ 0 & 0 & 0 & 0 & 0 & 0 \\ 0 & -8 & 0 & 16 & 0 & -8 \\ 0 & 0 & 0 & 0 & 0 & 0 \\ 0 & 1 & 0 & -8 & 0 & 7 \end{bmatrix}$$

$$+\frac{GA}{6}\begin{bmatrix} 14/l & 3 & -16/l & 4 & 2/l & -1 \\ 3 & 2l/3 & -4 & 2l/3 & 1 & -l/3 \\ -16/l & -4 & 32/l & 0 & -16/l & 4 \\ 4 & 2l/3 & 0 & 8l/3 & -4 & 2l/3 \\ 2/l & 1 & -16/l & -4 & 14/l & -3 \\ -1 & -l/3 & 4 & 2l/3 & -3 & 2l/3 \end{bmatrix}$$

Reduced integration is a commonly used technique with finite-element derivation. In general, its justification is that it works, and as progressively smaller elements are used, results converge to the correct values. For beam bending, a physical argument can also be used to support the procedure.

When a beam is subjected to a linear variation of bending moment, equilibrium requires a constant shear along its length. Because of the undifferentiated shape function coefficients in the expression for shearing strain, ϕ, the formulation predicts a quadratic variation of shear. Clearly, this is nonsense and the problem is overcome by using reduced integration.

To see why, consider deformation of a beam element consistent with it being subjected to end couples; see Fig. 3.64. Displacements for the first component of loading can be represented by quadratic shape functions for v and θ and need not be considered further. The displaced shape for the second loading component, with rigid body deformations removed, is shown in Fig. 3.64(b). The rotations of cross-sections, θ, are composed of a flexural component θ_b and a shear 'strain' θ_s.

The assumed shape functions imply a linear variation of curvature, which ensures that the flexural strain energy is represented correctly. However, the shearing strain ϕ is equal to θ, since v is predicted to be zero. With respect to rigid body motion, $v_1 = v_2 = v_3 = 0$ and since v is a quadratic function, it will be zero everywhere along the beam. The predicted value of $\phi (= \theta_s)$ gives the correct value at

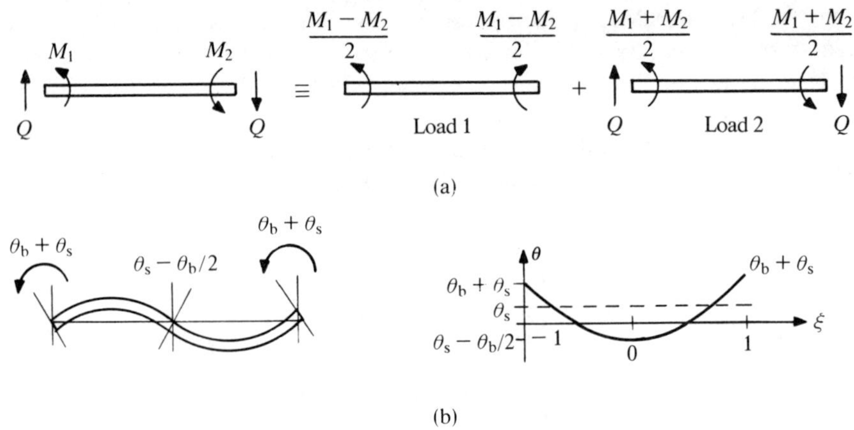

Figure 3.64 Shear mode. (a) Loading. (b) Displacements

two points. Their positions are given by

$$\theta_s = \theta = \xi(\xi - 1)/2\theta_1 + (1 - \xi^2)\,\theta_2 + \xi(1 + \xi)/2\theta_3$$

substituting nodal values of θ gives

$$\theta_s = [\xi(\xi - 1)/2 + \xi(1 + \xi)/2](\theta_b + \theta_s) + (1 - \xi^2)(\theta_s - \theta_b/2)$$

Hence:

$$\theta_s = \theta_s + \theta_b(3\xi^2/2 - 1/2)$$

so

$$\xi = \pm \quad 1/\sqrt{3}$$

Thus, using two-station Gauss quadrature results in the correct values of shear 'strain' being sampled and the correct contribution to the strain energy being determined.

To obtain consistent nodal loads, $\mathbf{F}_c$, for a vertical force P, at $\xi = \xi_i$, the loss of potential energies for a small displacement are equated. Thus:

$$\mathbf{F}_c^T \cdot \mathbf{a}_m = P \cdot \mathbf{N}^T(\xi = \xi_i) \cdot \mathbf{V}_m$$

and hence

$$F_{y1} = P\xi_i(\xi_i - 1)/2, \qquad F_{y2} = P(1 - \xi_i^2), \qquad F_{y3} = P\xi_i(1 + \xi_i)/2$$

For this element, the consistent load vector for a force has no couple components!

A further interesting feature of this formulation is that if the stiffness matrix is reduced to a 4×4 matrix by condensing the equations to remove v_2 and θ_2 as independent variables, the resulting matrix is identical to the one obtained in Sec. 3.5.3.1, using assumed stress-resultant fields.

3.5.4 Finite-element solution of field problems

Many solutions to physical problems that can be expressed as a differential equation can also be expressed as the minimization of a functional, such as the total potential energy of a system. The finite-element method provides a means of obtaining approximate solutions which minimize a functional, and which utilize the pro-

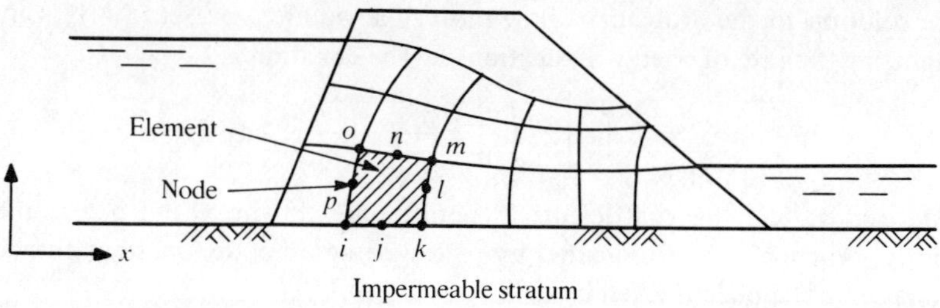

Figure 3.65 Flow through an aquifer

cedures of the stiffness method to facilitate automatic solutions. When the method is applied to essentially planar problems, such as flow of a liquid through an aquifer (see Fig. 3.65), or bending of a bifurcated bridge deck (see Fig. 3.66), the domain of the problem is first divided into a number of sub-domains or finite elements as shown in the figures and 'stiffness' matrices are determined for each element.

3.5.4.1 Flow through an aquifer

To determine flow through an aquifer it is necessary to determine a continuous function to describe the hydraulic head, $h(x, y)$, causing flow. Over each element, the function is approximated by an interpolation polynomial of the form $h = \mathbf{N}^T \cdot \mathbf{a}_e$, where $\mathbf{N}$ is a vector of shape functions and $\mathbf{a}_e$ is a vector of nodal values of h. Nodal points are assigned to each element (they correspond to joints in the stiffness method) and they are listed in a fixed sequence. Nodal points are usually positioned on element boundaries to enable the interpolation polynomials to give unique values to the function on element sides. When this is done, the interpolation polynomials, taken together, give what is called a 'piecewise continuous approximation' to a function. Values of the approximated function are continuous over the entire domain of a problem, but function derivatives can be discontinuous on element boundaries.

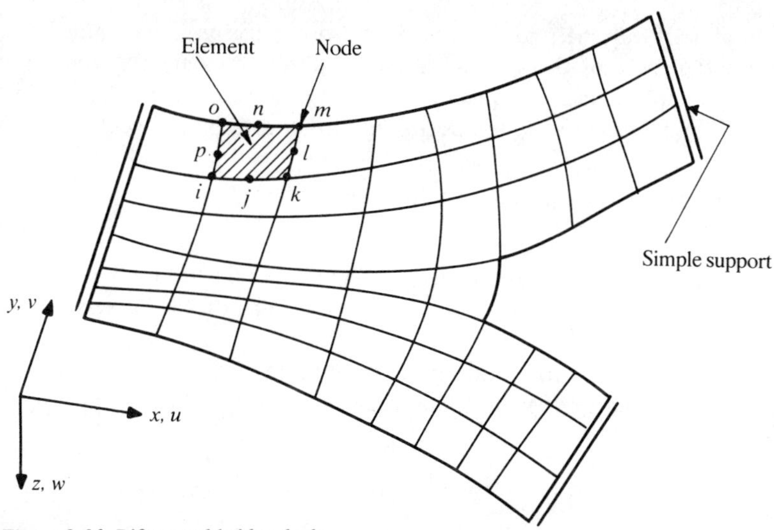

Figure 3.66 Bifurcated bridge deck

The solution to the problem of flow through an aquifer, see Sec. 5.4.1, is given by minimizing the rate of energy dissipation, $\dot{E}$. The equation is

$$\delta \dot{E} = 0 = \iint \left[k_x \left(\frac{\partial h}{\partial x} \right)^2 + k_y \left(\frac{\partial h}{\partial y} \right)^2 \right] \mathrm{d}x\, \mathrm{d}y$$

where k_x and k_y are the coefficients of permeability in the x and y directions respectively. When h is approximated by piecewise continuous functions the best approximation obtainable is given by

$$\delta \dot{E} = \sum_{e=1}^{m} \frac{\partial \dot{E}}{\partial \mathbf{a}_e} = 0$$

where m is the number of elements in the domain.

If

$$\boldsymbol{\varepsilon} = \begin{bmatrix} \dfrac{\partial h}{\partial x} \\[2ex] \dfrac{\partial h}{\partial y} \end{bmatrix} = \begin{bmatrix} \dfrac{\partial \mathbf{N}^{\mathrm{T}}}{\partial x} \\[2ex] \dfrac{\partial \mathbf{N}^{\mathrm{T}}}{\partial y} \end{bmatrix} \cdot \mathbf{a}_e = \mathbf{B} \cdot \mathbf{a}_e$$

and

$$\mathbf{D} = \begin{bmatrix} k_x & 0 \\ 0 & k_y \end{bmatrix}$$

then the rate of energy dissipation in an element is

$$\dot{E}_e = \int_{A_e} \left[k_x \left(\frac{\partial h}{\partial x} \right)^2 + k_y \left(\frac{\partial h}{\partial y} \right)^2 \right] \mathrm{d}A = \mathbf{a}_e^{\mathrm{T}} \int_{A_e} (\mathbf{B}^{\mathrm{T}} \cdot \mathbf{D} \cdot \mathbf{B})\, \mathrm{d}A \cdot \mathbf{a}_e$$

and

$$\frac{\partial \dot{E}_e}{\partial \mathbf{a}_e} = 0 = \left(\int_{A_e} \mathbf{B}^{\mathrm{T}} \cdot \mathbf{D} \cdot \mathbf{B}\, \mathrm{d}A \right) \cdot \mathbf{a}_e$$

By analogy with the stiffness method, the expression in the round brackets is called the local 'stiffness' matrix of the element. Once it has been determined, the overall 'stiffness' matrix of the system can be compiled, boundary conditions for nodal values of h applied, and the equations solved in the usual manner. The solution to problems of flow through an aquifer is treated further in Chapter Five.

3.5.4.2 *Two dimensional elasticity*

The stresses in a structure loaded in its own plane can be determined using two-dimensional elasticity, provided the material of the structure behaves in a linear elastic manner. In Fig. 3.67, a concrete dam is shown with a possible discretion into finite elements.

The displacements of a structure are represented by orthogonal components $u(x, y)$ and $v(x, y)$ in the x and y directions, respectively. If u and v are represented by the vector $\mathbf{a}$, then

$$\mathbf{a} = \begin{bmatrix} u \\ v \end{bmatrix}$$

and within each element $\mathbf{a} = \mathbf{N}^T \cdot \mathbf{a}_e$, where $\mathbf{a}_e$ is a vector of values of u and v at nodes and $\mathbf{N}$ is a shape function matrix containing interpolation polynomials.

The strain displacement matrix $\mathbf{B}$ is defined by

$$\boldsymbol{\varepsilon} = \begin{bmatrix} \epsilon_x \\ \epsilon_y \\ \gamma_{xy} \end{bmatrix} = \begin{bmatrix} \frac{\partial}{\partial x} & 0 \\ 0 & \frac{\partial}{\partial y} \\ \frac{\partial}{\partial y} & \frac{\partial}{\partial x} \end{bmatrix} \mathbf{a} = \mathbf{B} \cdot \mathbf{a}_e$$

The constitutive matrix for plane stress conditions in an isotropic material is given by

$$\begin{bmatrix} \sigma_x \\ \sigma_y \\ \tau_{xy} \end{bmatrix} = \frac{E}{1-\nu^2} \begin{bmatrix} 1 & \nu & 0 \\ \nu & 1 & 0 \\ 0 & 0 & (1-\nu)/2 \end{bmatrix} \begin{bmatrix} \epsilon_x \\ \epsilon_y \\ \gamma_{xy} \end{bmatrix} \quad \text{or} \quad \boldsymbol{\sigma} = \mathbf{D} \cdot \boldsymbol{\varepsilon}$$

The strain energy stored in an element of thickness t is given by

$$U_e = \tfrac{1}{2} \int_{\mathrm{Vol}_e} \boldsymbol{\varepsilon}^T \cdot \boldsymbol{\sigma} \cdot \mathrm{d}v = t/2 \int_{A_e} \boldsymbol{\varepsilon}^T \cdot \boldsymbol{\sigma}\, \mathrm{d}A$$

hence $U_e = t/2 \cdot \mathbf{a}_e^T \int_{A_e} \mathbf{B}^T \cdot \mathbf{D} \cdot \mathbf{B}\, \mathrm{d}A \cdot \mathbf{a}_e$.

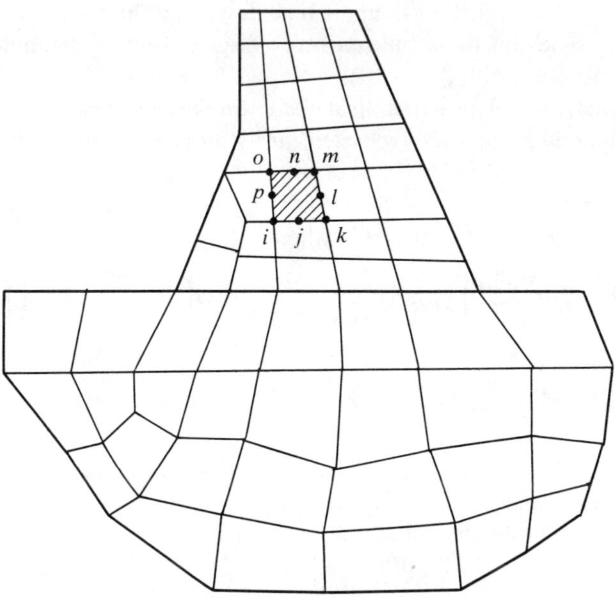

Figure 3.67 Plane stress problem

If the loading is represented by its components, F_x and F_y in the x and y directions, respectively, and $\mathbf{F}^\mathrm{T} = [F_x, F_y]$, then the potential energy of the loading is given by

$$V_e = -\int_{A_e} \mathbf{a}^\mathrm{T} \cdot \mathbf{F} \cdot \mathrm{d}A = -\mathbf{a}_e^\mathrm{T} \int_{A_e} \mathbf{N} \cdot \mathbf{F}\, \mathrm{d}A$$

The total potential energy of the structural system is given by $\Sigma_{e=1}^{m} (U_e + V_e)$ where m is the number of elements, and for a stationary value

$$\sum_{e=1}^{m} \left(\frac{\partial U_e}{\partial \mathbf{a}_e} + \frac{\partial V_e}{\partial \mathbf{a}_e} \right) = \mathbf{0}$$

hence

$$\sum_{e=1}^{m} \int_{A_e} \mathbf{N} \cdot \mathbf{F} \cdot \mathrm{d}A = \sum_{e=1}^{m} \left(t \int_{A_e} \mathbf{B}^\mathrm{T} \cdot \mathbf{D} \cdot \mathbf{B}\, \mathrm{d}A \right) \cdot \mathbf{a}_e$$

This equation is identical in form to the stiffness method equation and can be solved in a similar manner. The element 'stiffness' matrix $\mathbf{S}_e$ is given by $\mathbf{S}_e = t \int_{A_e} \mathbf{B}^\mathrm{T} \cdot \mathbf{D} \cdot \mathbf{B} \cdot \mathrm{d}A$ and the consistent nodal loading from an element is given by $\mathbf{F}_e = \int_{A_e} \mathbf{N} \cdot \mathbf{F}\, \mathrm{d}A$.

3.5.5 Plate bending

Derivation of finite-element stiffness matrices to analyse plates in bending has taxed research workers for many years. To date there is no universally accepted best solution and efforts to improve techniques are continuing. There are, however, a number of formulations that give satisfactory performances when used with care.

3.5.5.1 Kirchhoff bending theory

When shear strains are negligible and the Kirchhoff boundary conditions are used, bending of a plate may be described by the transverse displacement of the mid-surface of the plate, $w(x, y)$.[7]

For finite-element analysis, a plate is first divided into finite elements as shown in Fig. 3.66 and w is approximated over each element by an interpolation polynomial of the form $w = \mathbf{N}^\mathrm{T} \cdot \mathbf{a}_e$ where $\mathbf{N}$ is a vector of shape functions and $\mathbf{a}_e$ is a vector of nodal displacements. Solution of the problem is given by minimizing the total potential energy of the structural system, PE, where

$$PE = \tfrac{1}{2} \int_{A_e} \left[DX \left(\frac{\partial^2 w}{\partial x^2} \right)^2 + DY \left(\frac{\partial^2 w}{\partial y^2} \right)^2 + 2D1 \left(\frac{\partial^2 w}{\partial x^2} \frac{\partial^2 w}{\partial y^2} \right) + 4DXY \left(\frac{\partial^2 w}{\partial x\, \partial y} \right)^2 \right] \mathrm{d}A$$

$$- \int_{A_e} q(x, y) w(x, y)\, \mathrm{d}A - \sum_{i=1}^{k} P_i w(x_i, y_i)$$

given that DX, DY, $D1$, DXY are flexural stiffnesses, $q(x, y)$ is the distributed loading, and P_i are the k point loads.

For a stationary value of total potential energy

$$\delta PE \simeq \sum_{e=1}^{m} \frac{\partial PE}{\partial \mathbf{a}_e} = 0$$

where m is the number of elements into which the domain has been divided.

If:

$$\boldsymbol{\varepsilon} = \begin{bmatrix} -\dfrac{\partial^2 w}{\partial x^2} \\ -\dfrac{\partial^2 w}{\partial y^2} \\ \dfrac{2\partial^2 w}{\partial x\, \partial y} \end{bmatrix} = \begin{bmatrix} -\dfrac{\partial^2 \mathbf{N}^{\mathrm{T}}}{\partial x^2} \\ -\dfrac{\partial^2 \mathbf{N}^{\mathrm{T}}}{\partial y^2} \\ \dfrac{2\partial^2 \mathbf{N}^{\mathrm{T}}}{\partial x\, \partial y} \end{bmatrix} \mathbf{a}_e = \mathbf{B} \cdot \mathbf{a}_e$$

and

$$\mathbf{D} = \begin{bmatrix} DX & D1 & 0 \\ D1 & DY & 0 \\ 0 & 0 & DXY \end{bmatrix}$$

then the strain energy stored in an element is given by

$$U_e = \tfrac{1}{2}\, \mathbf{a}_e^{\mathrm{T}} \int_{A_e} (\mathbf{B}^{\mathrm{T}} \cdot \mathbf{D} \cdot \mathbf{B})\, \mathrm{d}A \cdot \mathbf{a}_e$$

The potential energy of the loading is given by

$$V_e = -\mathbf{a}_e^{\mathrm{T}} \cdot \int_{A_e} \mathbf{N} \cdot q(x,y)\, \mathrm{d}A - \mathbf{a}_e^{\mathrm{T}} \cdot \sum_{i=1}^{k} \mathbf{N}(x_i, y_i) \cdot P_i$$

For a stationary value of the total potential energy of the structural system,

$$\sum_{e=1}^{m} \frac{\partial PE_e}{\partial \mathbf{a}_e} = \sum_{e=1}^{m} \frac{\partial (U_e + V_e)}{\partial \mathbf{a}_e} = \mathbf{0}$$

hence

$$\sum_{e=1}^{m} \left(\int_{A_e} \mathbf{N} \cdot q(x,y)\, \mathrm{d}A + \sum_{i=1}^{k} \mathbf{N}(x_i, y_i) \cdot P_i \right) = \sum_{e=1}^{m} \left(\int_{A_e} (\mathbf{B}^{\mathrm{T}} \cdot \mathbf{D} \cdot \mathbf{B})\, \mathrm{d}A \cdot \mathbf{a}_e \right)$$

The terms in parenthesis on the left hand side of the equation give the equivalent or consistent nodal 'forces' and the term to be integrated on the right hand side of the equation is equivalent to the 'stiffness' matrix of a plate element.

In this formulation of the plate bending problem, second-order derivatives of the function w appear in the functional to be minimized. This means that not only must w be continuous over the domain, but, strictly speaking, so also must the first derivatives of w. For this reason, w is usually specified in terms of w, $\mathrm{d}w/\mathrm{d}x$ and $\mathrm{d}w/\mathrm{d}y$ at nodal points. It is thus possible to ensure that w, $\mathrm{d}w/\mathrm{d}x$ and $\mathrm{d}w/\mathrm{d}y$ have unique values at the nodal points. To date it has not been possible to derive suitable shape functions that give unique values of first derivatives on element boundaries between nodes and that also result in an efficient formulation. Solutions to plate bending problems by this method, therefore, lie somewhere between a physical approximation to the plate 'stiffness' matrix and a true finite-element solution. Functions of w that violate continuity of first derivatives lead to 'non-conforming' solutions and many of them give results with adequate accuracy for design purposes.

3.5.5.2 Mindlin bending theory

In this formulation shear strains are permitted, and independent functions are specified for the lateral displacement w and the rotation of normals θ_x, θ_y: see Fig. 3.60. The total potential energy of the structural system PE is given by

$$PE = \tfrac{1}{2}\int_{A_E}\left[DX\left(\frac{\partial\theta_x}{\partial x}\right)^2 + DY\left(\frac{\partial\theta_y}{\partial y}\right)^2 + 2D1\left(\frac{\partial\theta_x}{\partial x}\frac{\partial\theta_y}{\partial y}\right) + DXY\left(\frac{\partial\theta_x}{\partial y} + \frac{\partial\theta_y}{\partial x}\right)^2 \right.$$
$$\left. + SX\left(\theta_x - \frac{\partial w}{\partial x}\right)^2 + SY\left(\theta_y - \frac{\partial w}{\partial y}\right)^2\right]\mathrm{d}A$$
$$- \int_{A_e} q(x,y)w(x,y)\,\mathrm{d}A - \sum_{i=1}^{k} P_i w(x_i, y_i) - \sum_{i=1}^{c} C_i\theta(x_i, y_i)$$

where SX, SY are shear stiffnesses and C_i is a concentrated couple. For a stationary value,

$$\delta PE \simeq \sum_{e=1}^{m}\frac{\partial PE}{\partial \mathbf{a}_e} = 0$$

The shape functions specify independent functions for θ_x, θ_y, and w and the $\mathbf{a}_e$ vector contains nodal values of θ_x, θ_y, and w for each node in sequence.

For an isoparametric formulation, the same shape functions are used for x, y, θ_x, θ_y, and w. The flexural 'strains' $\boldsymbol{\varepsilon}_\mathrm{f}$ are given by

$$\boldsymbol{\varepsilon}_\mathrm{f} = \begin{bmatrix} \frac{\partial}{\partial x} & 0 & 0 \\ 0 & \frac{\partial}{\partial y} & 0 \\ \frac{\partial}{\partial y} & \frac{\partial}{\partial x} & 0 \end{bmatrix}\begin{bmatrix}\theta_x \\ \theta_y \\ w\end{bmatrix} = \begin{bmatrix} \frac{\partial \mathbf{N}^\mathrm{T}}{\partial x} & 0 & 0 \\ 0 & \frac{\partial \mathbf{N}^\mathrm{T}}{\partial y} & 0 \\ \frac{\partial \mathbf{N}^\mathrm{T}}{\partial y} & \frac{\partial \mathbf{N}^\mathrm{T}}{\partial x} & 0 \end{bmatrix}\mathbf{a}_e = \mathbf{B}_\mathrm{f}\cdot\mathbf{a}_e$$

The shear 'strains' $\boldsymbol{\varepsilon}_\mathrm{s}$ are given by

$$\boldsymbol{\varepsilon}_\mathrm{s} = \begin{bmatrix} 1 & 0 & -\frac{\partial}{\partial x} \\ 0 & 1 & -\frac{\partial}{\partial y} \end{bmatrix}\begin{bmatrix}\theta_x \\ \theta_y \\ w\end{bmatrix} = \begin{bmatrix} \mathbf{N}^\mathrm{T} & 0 & -\frac{\partial \mathbf{N}^\mathrm{T}}{\partial x} \\ 0 & \mathbf{N}^\mathrm{T} & -\frac{\partial \mathbf{N}^\mathrm{T}}{\partial y} \end{bmatrix}\mathbf{a}_e = \mathbf{B}_\mathrm{s}\cdot\mathbf{a}_e$$

The constitutive matrices for a slab with orthotropic properties are

$$\mathbf{D}_\mathrm{f} = \begin{bmatrix} DX & D1 & 0 \\ D1 & DY & 0 \\ 0 & 0 & DXY \end{bmatrix} \quad \text{and} \quad \mathbf{D}_\mathrm{s} = \begin{bmatrix} SX & 0 \\ 0 & SY \end{bmatrix}$$

In matrix form, the strain energy stored in an element is, therefore, given by

$$U_e = \tfrac{1}{2}\,\mathbf{a}_e^\mathrm{T}\left(\int_{A_e}\mathbf{B}_\mathrm{f}^\mathrm{T}\cdot\mathbf{D}_\mathrm{f}\cdot\mathbf{B}_\mathrm{f}\cdot\mathrm{d}A + \int_{A_e}\mathbf{B}_\mathrm{s}^\mathrm{T}\cdot\mathbf{D}_\mathrm{s}\cdot\mathbf{B}_\mathrm{s}\,\mathrm{d}A\right)\cdot\mathbf{a}_e$$

The potential energy of the loading is expressed using consistent nodal load vectors $\mathbf{F}_{ce}$ and is given by $V_e = -\mathbf{a}_e^{\mathrm{T}} \cdot \mathbf{F}_{ce}$. As with the equivalent beam element formulation described in Sec. 3.5.3.2, lateral loads produce only vertical nodal forces, and no couples.

The total potential energy of the structural system is given by $PE = \Sigma_{e=1}^{m} PE_e = \Sigma_{e=1}^{m} (U_e + V_e)$, and for a stationary value $\Sigma_{e=1}^{m} \partial PE_e/\partial \mathbf{a}_e = \mathbf{0}$.

Thus, for each element,

$$\left(\int_{A_e} \mathbf{B}_{\mathrm{f}}^{\mathrm{T}} \cdot \mathbf{D}_{\mathrm{f}} \cdot \mathbf{B}_{\mathrm{f}}\, \mathrm{d}A + \int_{A_e} \mathbf{B}_{\mathrm{s}}^{\mathrm{T}} \cdot \mathbf{D}_{\mathrm{s}} \cdot \mathbf{B}_{\mathrm{s}}\, \mathrm{d}A\right) \cdot \mathbf{a}_e - \mathbf{F}_{ce} = 0$$

The expression in the brackets is the element 'stiffness' matrix. The element 'stiffness' matrices for all elements are compiled automatically and the resulting equations are solved using a standard linear simultaneous equation solver.

In the Mindlin formulation of plate bending theory the total potential energy functional contains first derivatives of the functions w, θ_x, θ_y only. The required order of continuity of these functions is C_0 (values only) and for this reason Mindlin plate theory has become very popular. Quadratic isoparametric elements, with reduced integration, are widely used for plate bending, as well as for plane stress and field problems. However, recent research[8] indicates that use of Lagrange shape function for θ_x and θ_y, and serendipity shape functions for w (see Sec. 3.6.1.1), with 3×3 integration for flexural energy and 2×2 integration for the shear energy component, gives the best formulation for plate bending problems.

3.5.6 Linear quadrilateral element

At first a triangular element with corner nodes appears attractive for field problems, as its formulation is computationally efficient, and it peımits a domain to be divided into elements with great flexibility. Experience has, however, shown that this element behaves erratically and it is not recommended.

The next obvious choice is a quadrilateral element with corner nodes and its formulation is described in some detail for the problems of two-dimensional elasticity (see Sec. 3.5.4.2).

A typical element is shown in Fig. 3.68, with local axes (ξ, η) and global axes

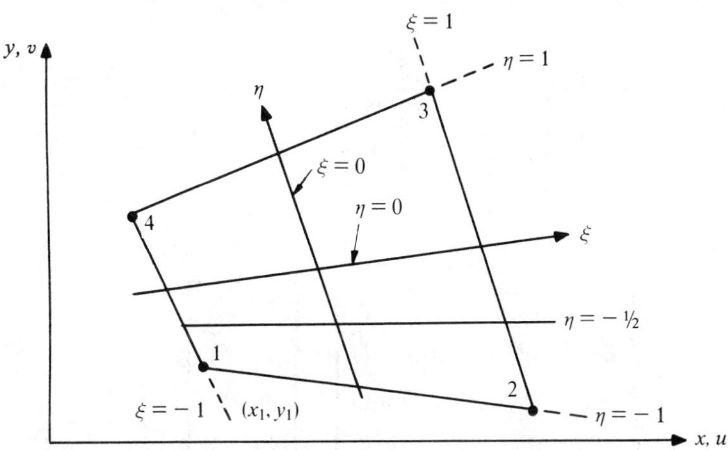

Figure 3.68 Linear quadrilateral element

(x, y). For isoparametric formulation, the same shape functions are used for geometry and displacements u, v.

Thus

$$
\begin{aligned}
x &= N_1x_1 + N_2x_2 + N_3x_3 + N_4x_4 \\
y &= N_1y_1 + N_2y_2 + N_3y_3 + N_4y_4 \\
u &= N_1u_1 + N_2u_2 + N_3u_3 + N_4u_4 \\
v &= N_1v_1 + N_2v_2 + N_3v_3 + N_4v_4
\end{aligned}
$$

where x_i, y_i are the coordinates of node i and u_i, v_i are its displacement components. The shape functions are given by

$$
\begin{aligned}
N_1 &= \tfrac{1}{4}(1-\xi)(1-\eta) \qquad & N_2 &= \tfrac{1}{4}(1+\xi)(1-\eta) \\
N_3 &= \tfrac{1}{4}(1+\xi)(1+\eta) \qquad & N_4 &= \tfrac{1}{4}(1-\xi)(1+\eta)
\end{aligned}
$$

They each have the value 1 at the appropriate node, zero at all other nodes, and give a linear variation over the domain of the element. Their derivatives are given by

$$
\begin{bmatrix} \dfrac{\partial}{\partial \xi} \\[2ex] \dfrac{\partial}{\partial \eta} \end{bmatrix} \mathbf{N}^{\mathrm{T}} = \frac{1}{4} \begin{bmatrix} -(1-\eta), & (1-\eta), & (1+\eta), & -(1+\eta) \\ -(1-\xi), & -(1+\xi), & (1+\xi), & (1-\xi) \end{bmatrix}
$$

To obtain the 'strain' matrix $\boldsymbol{\varepsilon}$, the derivatives of $\mathbf{N}$ with respect to x and y are required. The chain rule of differentiation is used to obtain them. In matrix notation:

$$
\begin{bmatrix} \dfrac{\partial}{\partial \xi} \\[2ex] \dfrac{\partial}{\partial \eta} \end{bmatrix} = \begin{bmatrix} \dfrac{\partial x}{\partial \xi} & \dfrac{\partial y}{\partial \xi} \\[2ex] \dfrac{\partial x}{\partial \eta} & \dfrac{\partial y}{\partial \eta} \end{bmatrix} \begin{bmatrix} \dfrac{\partial}{\partial x} \\[2ex] \dfrac{\partial}{\partial y} \end{bmatrix} = \mathbf{J} \begin{bmatrix} \dfrac{\partial}{\partial x} \\[2ex] \dfrac{\partial}{\partial y} \end{bmatrix}
$$

hence

$$
\begin{bmatrix} \dfrac{\partial}{\partial x} \\[2ex] \dfrac{\partial}{\partial y} \end{bmatrix} = \mathbf{J}^{-1} \begin{bmatrix} \dfrac{\partial}{\partial \xi} \\[2ex] \dfrac{\partial}{\partial \eta} \end{bmatrix}
$$

The Jacobian $\mathbf{J}$ is given by

$$
\mathbf{J} = \begin{bmatrix} \dfrac{\partial N_1}{\partial \xi} & \dfrac{\partial N_2}{\partial \xi} & \dfrac{\partial N_3}{\partial \xi} & \dfrac{\partial N_4}{\partial \xi} \\[2ex] \dfrac{\partial N_1}{\partial \eta} & \dfrac{\partial N_2}{\partial \eta} & \dfrac{\partial N_3}{\partial \eta} & \dfrac{\partial N_4}{\partial \eta} \end{bmatrix} \begin{bmatrix} x_1 & y_1 \\ x_2 & y_2 \\ x_3 & y_3 \\ x_4 & y_4 \end{bmatrix}
$$

The inverse of **J** can be expressed in terms of its determinant and coefficients by

$$\mathbf{J}^{-1} = \frac{1}{|\mathbf{J}|}\begin{bmatrix} \mathbf{J}_{22} & -\mathbf{J}_{12} \\ -\mathbf{J}_{21} & \mathbf{J}_{11} \end{bmatrix}$$

It is a straightforward matter to evaluate **J** at any point (ξ, η), and the inversion is usually performed numerically.

If the nodal variables are listed in the order

$$\mathbf{a}_e^{\mathrm{T}} = (u_1, v_1, u_2, v_2, u_3, v_3, u_4, v_4)$$

then the **B** matrix is

$$\begin{bmatrix} \frac{\partial N_1}{\partial x} & 0 & \frac{\partial N_2}{\partial x} & 0 & \frac{\partial N_3}{\partial x} & 0 & \frac{\partial N_4}{\partial x} & 0 \\ 0 & \frac{\partial N_1}{\partial y} & 0 & \frac{\partial N_2}{\partial y} & 0 & \frac{\partial N_3}{\partial y} & 0 & \frac{\partial N_4}{\partial y} \\ \frac{\partial N_1}{\partial y} & \frac{\partial N_1}{\partial x} & \frac{\partial N_2}{\partial y} & \frac{\partial N_2}{\partial x} & \frac{\partial N_3}{\partial y} & \frac{\partial N_3}{\partial x} & \frac{\partial N_4}{\partial y} & \frac{\partial N_4}{\partial x} \end{bmatrix}$$

and each of its coefficients can be evaluated numerically for a point (ξ, η).

Using the transformation described in Sec. 3.3.2.2, the 'stiffness' matrix

$$\mathbf{S}_e = t\int_{A_e} \mathbf{B}^{\mathrm{T}}\cdot\mathbf{D}\cdot\mathbf{B}\,dA \equiv t\int_{-1}^{1}\int_{-1}^{1} \mathbf{B}^{\mathrm{T}}\cdot\mathbf{D}\cdot\mathbf{B}\,|\mathbf{J}|\,d\xi\,d\eta$$

is evaluated using Gauss quadrature. For exact integration, a 2 x 2 grid of Gauss stations is required. In practice this formulation has tended to result in 'over-stiff' solutions and to overcome the problem selective reduced integration is advocated by some. The 2 x 2 integration grid is retained for the strain energy associated with normal strains ϵ_x, ϵ_y and a single central integration station is used for the shear strain energy component. This scheme is advocated for similar reasons to those used to justify reduced integration of shear terms in the formulation of the quadratic isoparametric beam element. The possible straining modes permitted by the shape functions are illustrated in Fig. 3.69(a–e). When the shear strain energy is only sampled at the centre of an element, the energy associated with mode (c) gives the correct contribution, while no contribution is obtained from modes (d) and (e) since the shear strain at the centre is zero for those modes. Effectively, for the purposes of energy calculation, modes (d) and (e) are replaced by those of (f) and (g). Since these modes are often closer to actual strain conditions, solutions obtained using selective reduced integration tend to converge more quickly, with reduction in element size, to theoretical values.

3.5.7 Quadratic isoparametric element

One of the most popular elements for the solution of field equations that govern such problems as flow through an aquifer and plane stress analysis, is an isoparametric quadrilateral with quadratic shape functions. Formulation of this element follows the same stages as those illustrated for a linear quadrilateral element, but

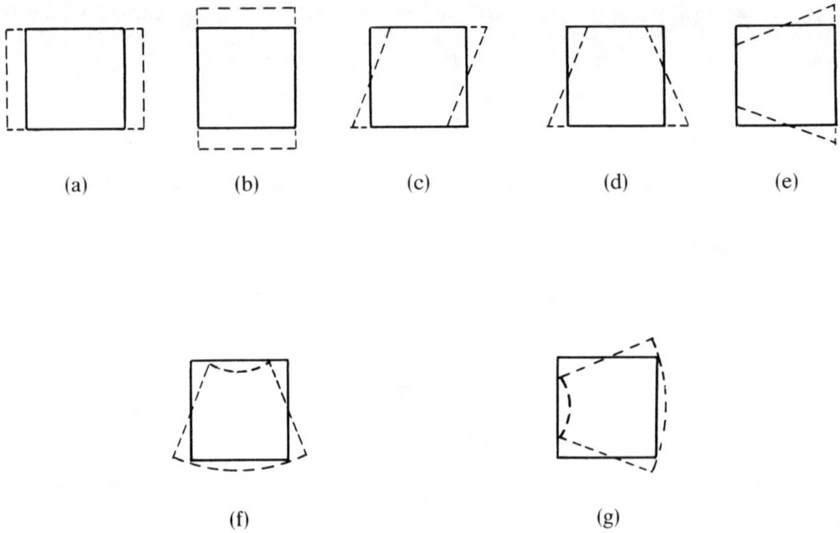

Figure 3.69 Straining modes. (a–e) Straining modes. (f, g) Effective straining modes

the interested reader is referred to a more advanced text for details.[9] The main advantages of this element are that it can follow curved boundaries and that it predicts linear 'stress' distributions over each element.

3.5.8 Classification of finite elements

Finite elements are classified by their geometry, by the type and order of interpolation functions used, and by the suitability of their interpolation functions.

Elements for functions of one variable can be either straight or curved. A linear element has end nodes only, and the interpolation function gives a linear distribution of the function between nodal values. A quadratic interpolation function requires a third node, which is usually positioned in the middle of the element. With three nodes it is possible to specify a quadratic shape to an element. When the shape functions used to describe the shape are the same as those used for the function, the formulation is said to be 'isoparametric'.

Elements for functions of two variables are usually either three- or four-sided, as shown in Fig. 3.70. The sides are straight when a linear interpolation function is used, but can be curved when higher-order interpolation functions are used in conjunction with additional nodes. Details of linear and quadratic interpolation functions are given in Sec. 3.6. Higher-order interpolation functions can be used with additional nodes, but this is not usually economic.

For some problems, for example beam and plate bending using the Kirchhoff hypotheses, second-order derivatives appear in the functional to be minimized. In such cases, first-order derivatives should be continuous over the problem domain

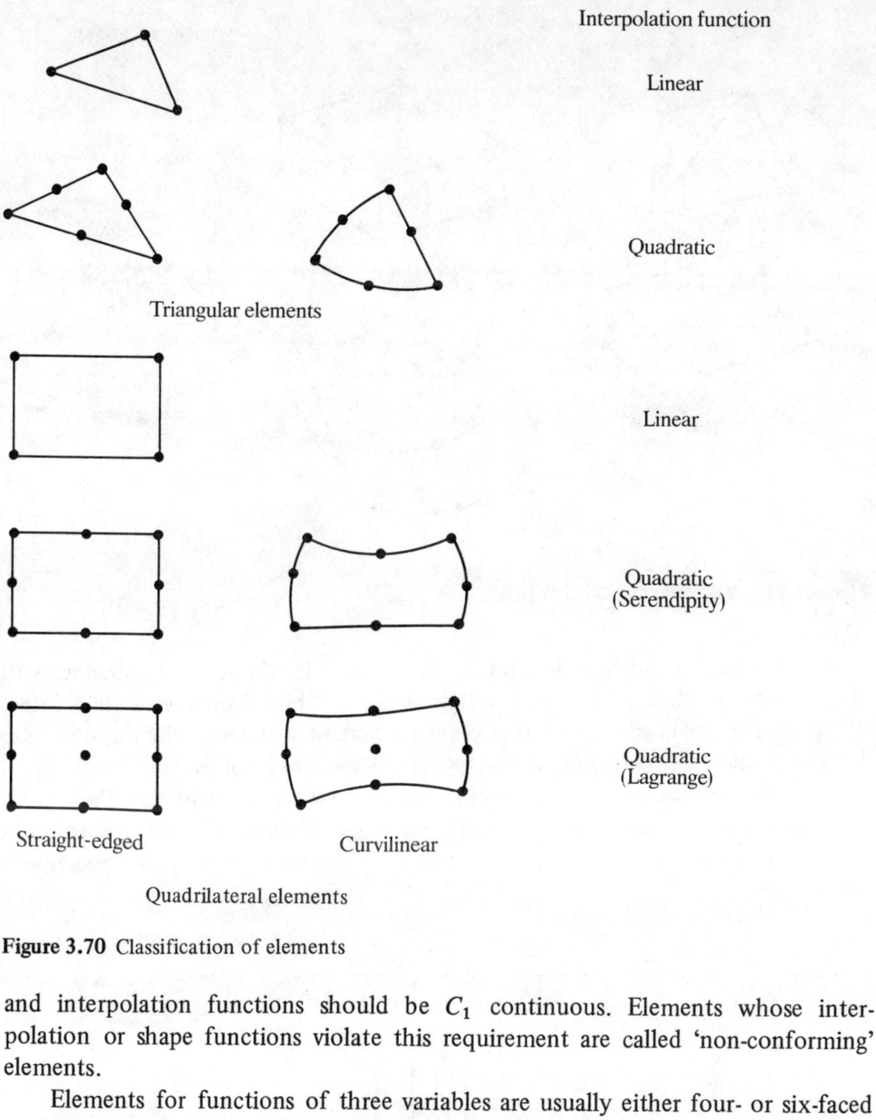

Figure 3.70 Classification of elements

and interpolation functions should be C_1 continuous. Elements whose interpolation or shape functions violate this requirement are called 'non-conforming' elements.

Elements for functions of three variables are usually either four- or six-faced as shown in Fig. 3.71. Although solid elements are treated in a similar manner to one and two-dimensional elements they will not be discussed in detail in this text. In practice, hexagonal bricks are easier to use than tetrahedrons, since it is easier to visualize how they fit together in a mesh.

3.5.9 Discretization, or division of a domain into elements

Division of a domain into elements is called discretization. In most computer programs the 'stiffness' matrix of each element type is set up and economy is gained by having as many identical elements as possible. It is, however, an advantage of the finite-element method that more elements can be used in areas where the function to be determined is known to vary rapidly.

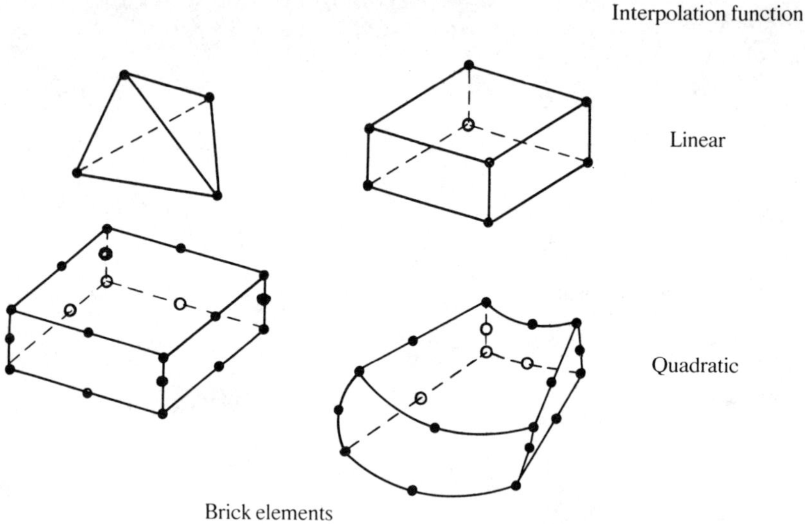

Figure 3.71 Three-dimensional elements

It is generally felt that best results with triangular elements are obtained with shapes close to that of an equilateral triangle, and best results with quadrilateral elements are obtained with shapes close to that of a square. When curved sides have to be used the distortion should be kept as small as possible.

Graded meshes are easily achieved. A method for rapidly increasing the number of quadrilateral elements is shown in Fig. 3.72. When using such a device care should be taken not to produce shapes that deviate far from a parallelogram with equal sides.

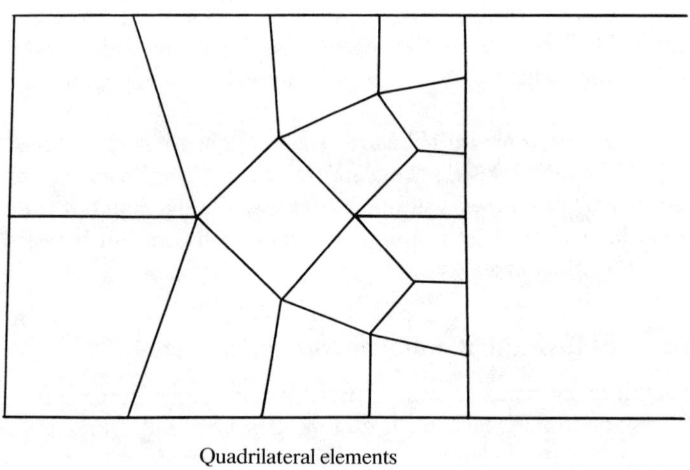

Figure 3.72 Grading of meshes

3.5.10 Convergence

A sequence of solutions can be obtained by using successively finer meshes of elements, and it is desirable that such solutions should converge to the correct solution. It is advantageous that solutions should approach the true solution in a uniform or monotonic manner as shown in Fig. 3.73, for then a qualitative idea of convergence can be obtained by extrapolation.

Convergence to the correct solution can be expected when:

1. the displacement field given by the interpolation functions is continuous within each element; and
2. the 'strains' predicted by derivatives of the interpolation functions are constant when nodal values of the functions are given values that correspond to a constant 'strain' state.

For a given element formulation, the first requirement is easy to check. It is also easy to comply with and is rarely a problem. The second requirement is not so easy to check when elements are distorted into curved shapes. A procedure known as the 'patch-test' is used to obtain a numerical check on this criterion, and a more advanced text[9] should be consulted for details.

Convergence to the correct solution is achieved by non-conforming elements that satisfy the above criteria. This is because derivatives on boundaries of such elements become continuous when elements are very small. Although non-conforming elements cannot be guaranteed to converge in a monotonic manner, they possess a compensating advantage. Solutions based on conforming elements predict a total potential energy greater than that for the problem they are modelling. This is because the assumed shape functions do not possess the infinite number of degrees of freedom possessed by a continuum. Solutions are thus 'stiff', i.e. taken overall, nodal variables tend to be underestimated. With a non-conforming solution, additional flexibility is introduced by the violation of first-derivative continuity on boundaries and for a given mesh size, most non-conforming elements give better results than those with continuous first derivatives. As a result, a considerable amount of research effort has been expended in attempts to produce reliable non-

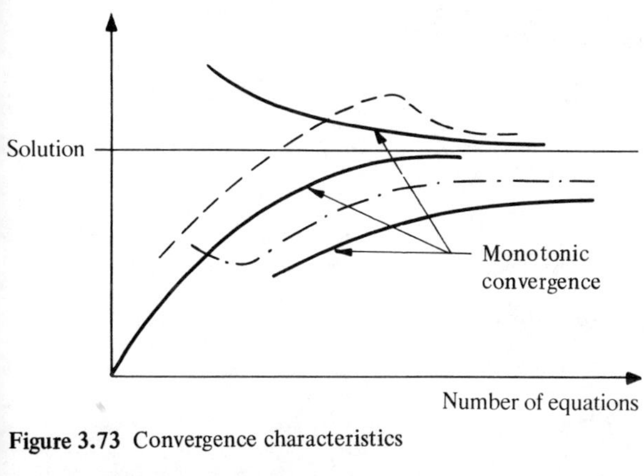

Figure 3.73 Convergence characteristics

conforming elements, but the reader must consult more advanced texts for details of this topic.[10]

3.5.11 Computer programming

Development of a computer program for solution of problems by the finite-element method is a major task. It is likely that the major stages in the solution process will be similar to those used for the stiffness method. Because the task is complex, and specialist monographs are available, only brief comments on desirable characteristics of programs are given here.

3.5.11.1 Data

Specification of data is the first contact a user has with a program. It is likely that some users will have no knowledge of the intricacies of finite element formulation, so data specification should be in a format natural to the particular problem in hand. Errors in data are common and needless expense is avoided by the inclusion of algorithms to check the validity of data and to terminate operations when an error is detected. To enable a user to check whether his intentions have been satisified, data should be listed at the head of results. For regular meshes, automatic mesh generating routines save time and help to reduce errors.

Calculation of consistent nodal 'loads' is tedious and the process will not be meaningful to many users. Facilities to compute consistent nodal 'loads' from data describing the distribution of loading are useful.

3.5.11.2 Element stiffness matrices

At the centre of most stiffness matrix routines is a shape function routine. This computes the values of the shape functions, or interpolation function components, and their derivatives at the integration points. For the purpose of illustration, SUBROUTINE SHF4Q, given in Fig. 3.74, determines values for the four-node quadrilateral element described in Sec. 3.5.6.

```
      SUBROUTINE SHF4Q(XI,ETA,NN,XYN,DJAC,SHF)
C SHAPE FUNCTION ROUTINE FOR 4 NODE QUADRILATERAL
C XI,ETA CO-ORDINATES WHERE SHAPE FUNCTION EVALUATED
C SHF(1,I)VALUE OF SHAPE FUNCTIONS N1,N2,N3,N4
C SHF(2,I)THEIR FIRST DERIVATIVES WRT X
C SHF(3,I)THEIR FIRST DERIVATIVES WRT Y
C NN NO. OF NODES - XYN NODAL CO-ORDS, X IN ROW1, Y IN ROW2
C JAC JACOBIAN,DJAC ITS DETERMINANT
      REAL JAC(2,2)
      DIMENSION SHF(3,4), C1(4),C2(4),XYN(2,NN)
      DATA C1(1),C1(2),C1(3),C1(4)/-1.0,1.0,1.0,-1.0/
      DATA C2(1),C2(2),C2(3),C2(4)/-1.0,-1.0,1.0,1.0/
C SHAPE FUNCTION AND DERIVATIVES WRT XI AND ETA
      DO 1 I=1,4
```

Figure 3.74 Shape-function routine

```
      SHF(1,I)=0.25*(1.0+C1(I)*XI)*(1.0+C2(I)*ETA)
      SHF(2,I)=C1(I)*0.25*(1.0+C2(I)*ETA)
 1    SHF(3,I)=C2(I)*0.25*(1.0+C1(I)*XI)
      DO 2 I=1,2
      I1=I+1
      DO 2 J=1,2
      JAC(I,J)=0.0
      DO 2 K=1,4
 2    JAC(I,J)=JAC(I,J)+SHF(I1,K)*XYN(J,K)
C DETERMINANT OF JACOBIAN
      DJAC=JAC(1,1)*JAC(2,2)-JAC(1,2)*JAC(2,1)
C SHAPE FUNCTION DERIVATIVES WRT X AND Y
      DO 3 I=1,4
      TEMP=(JAC(2,2)*SHF(2,I)-JAC(1,2)*SHF(3,I))/DJAC
      SHF(3,I)=(JAC(1,1)*SHF(3,I)-JAC(2,1)*SHF(2,I))/DJAC
 3    SHF(2,I)=TEMP
      RETURN
      END
```

Figure 3.74 *(continued)*

Integration of $\mathbf{B}^T \cdot \mathbf{D} \cdot \mathbf{B} \cdot |\mathbf{J}|$ is determined numerically. It is rarely efficient for a computer to perform the matrix multiplications directly as many of the coefficients of **B** and **D** are likely to be zero. As the resulting stiffness matrix is symmetrical, only slightly over half of the terms need be calculated. To illustrate the procedure usually adopted, SUBROUTINE PS4Q, which calculates the stiffness matrix for plane stress problems, is listed in Fig. 3.75 and should be studied by the interested reader.

```
      SUBROUTINE PS4Q(NG,XG,YG,WG,NN,XYN,D,S)
      DIMENSION XG(NG),YG(NG),WG(NG),D(3),S(16,16),SHF(3,8),XYN(2,NN)
C NG-NO. OF INTEGRATION STATIONS, NN-NO. OF NODES
C XYN X,Y CO-ORDS OF NODES
C XG,YG CO-ORDS OF INTEGRATION STATIONS, WG WEIGHTING VALUES
C D(1)=E/(1-NU*NU) D(2)=NU*D(1) D(3)=E/(2+2*NU)
C S-ELEMENT STIFFNESS MATRIX, SET TO ZERO BEFORE ENTRY, 8X8 FOR
C 4 NODE FORMULATION, 16X16 FOR QUADRATIC SHAPE FUNCTIONS WITH 8 NODES
      DO 1 IN=1,NG
C CALL APPROPRIATE SHAPE FUNCTION ROUTINE
      CALL SHF4Q(XG(IN),YG(IN),NN,XYN,DJAC,SHF)
      C=DJAC*WG(IN)
      D11=D(1)*C
      D12=D(2)*C
      D33=D(3)*C
C DB=D*B*DETJ
      DO 1 J=1,NN
      SHF2J=SHF(2,J)
      SHF3J=SHF(3,J)
      DB11=D11*SHF2J
```

Figure 3.75 Element stiffness matrix

```
      DB12=D12*SHF3J
      DB21=D12*SHF2J
      DB22=D11*SHF3J
      DB31=D33*SHF3J
      DB32=D33*SHF2J
      J2=J*2
C S=BT*DB
      DO 1 I=1,J
      SHF2I=SHF(2,I)
      SHF3I=SHF(3,I)
      I2=I*2
      S(I2-1,J2-1)=S(I2-1,J2-1)+SHF2I*DB11+SHF3I*DB31
      S(I2-1,J2)=S(I2-1,J2)+SHF2I*DB12+SHF3I+DB32
      S(I2,J2-1)=S(I2,J2-1)+SHF2I*DB31+SHF3I*DB21
 1    S(I2,J2)=S(I2,J2)+SHF2I*DB32+SHF3I*DB22

C LOWER PART OF S FROM SYMMETRY
      NN2=NN*2
      DO 2 I=2,NN2
      DO 2 J=1,I
 2    S(I,J)=S(J,I)
      RETURN
      END
```

Figure 3.75 *(continued)*

3.5.11.3 Assembly of system stiffness matrix and solution of equations

The stiffness matrix can be assembled from its component element stiffness matrices in the manner described for skeletal structures in Sec. 4.3.2, and the equations solved by use of SUBROUTINE BSOLV, see Sec. 3.1.3.3. For very large systems of equations, it may be necessary to use a more sophisticated technique. A simple refinement, for sets of equations with widely differing band widths, is to keep a record of the band width profile in place of using the largest non zero offset to control operations. A totally different and popular approach is the 'frontal solution' devised by Irons, but for this the reader is referred to a more advanced text.[10]

3.5.11.4 Stress resultants

A user is most interested in the results of an analysis, so values should be presented in a form needed for subsequent processing. Values of nodal parameters are useful, but many users will require values of stress or pressure head, etc., within a problem domain. The consistent nodal forces which were analogous to the forces on member ends are often not directly useful, as it can be difficult to give them a physical interpretation. As was demonstrated in Sec. 3.5.2.3, values of 'stress resultants' derived from material properties and derivatives of shape functions can be inaccurate.

It can be shown that 'stress resultants' are most accurately predicted at the Gauss integration points.[9] Values at these points should be given, whenever possible. If a user requires values at nodal points, they should be obtained, by extrapolation, from values at the Gauss points. For elements using quadratic shape functions, a bi-linear extrapolation, in (ξ, η) coordinates, is recommended.

3.5.12 Use of the finite-element method

The finite-element method can be used to obtain approximate solutions to a wide variety of physical problems whose governing equations are known. Unlike the finite-difference method, meshes can be graded with ease, boundary conditions can be satisified without specifying nodes outside the domain of a problem, and values of functions are specified uniquely.

The method can only be used with the aid of computer processing and many commercial programs are available. In this text an attempt has been made to give a sketch of the background theory to the technique. 'Stiffness' matrices are still being developed, and there is no general formulation that is best for all problems. At present, isoparametric formulations using serendipity shape functions are most widely used for problems requiring C_0 continuity. Mindlin plate theory is preferred to Kirchhoff plate theory, and the 'heterosis' plate bending element[8] offers advantages over other elements. This element is a nine-node quadrilateral which employs serendipity shape function for the transverse displacement w, and Lagrange shape functions for rotations of normals θ_x and θ_y.

This text has concentrated on finite-element solutions based on the minimization of the total potential energy of a system. There are other approaches. In particular, the total complementary energy can be minimized with the distribution of stress resultants specified by interpolation functions. An example of this technique was given in Sec. 3.5.3.1 and it has been successfully used in other areas. There are hybrid approaches in which stress resultants are specified over an element and displacement functions are specified on element boundaries. For details of this, and other techniques, the reader is referred to more advanced texts.[9,10]

The finite-element method is the most recent of those described in this chapter and it draws on techniques of interpolation functions, matrix algebra, numerical integration, and network analysis. It is still the subject of much research and should be used with care. Results of a finite-element analysis should always be checked to ensure that they comply with the physical laws of the problem being studied.

3.6 FUNCTION APPROXIMATION AND CURVE FITTING

The need to approximate a complex function by one or more simpler functions arises in many engineering applications. For example, in Simpson's rule for numerical integration (see Sec. 3.3), a quadratic function is fitted to three adjacent values of the function to be integrated. In using digital terrain models for highway alignment design, ground levels at arbitrary positions are found by fitting interpolation functions through positions with known elevations. Finally, interpolation or shape functions are key components in finite-element analysis (see Sec. 3.5).

A different situation is met in dealing with experimental data which is to be used to derive the relationship between the dependent and independent variables of a problem. The presence of unknown measurement errors in the data may make it quite unreasonable to expect the curve being fitted to pass through every data point. The least-square error method of approximation is found to be useful in many of these applications.

3.6.1 Interpolation functions

3.6.1.1 Lagrange interpolation

Consider the problem of approximating a continuous function $\psi(x)$ by a function $\phi(x)$ given that the interpolation function ϕ must match ψ at m points i.e. $\phi(x_i) \equiv \psi(x_i)$, $i = 1, m$. Now, with reference to Fig. 3.76, a polynomial $(N_i(x))$ of order m-1 can be established to pass through the points $x_i, i = 1, m$ such that

$$N_i(x_j) = 1 \qquad \text{for } j = i$$

and

$$N_i(x_j) = 0 \qquad \text{for } j \neq i$$

where $N_i(x)$ take the form

$$N_i(x) = \frac{(x - x_1)(x - x_2)\cdots(x - x_{i-1})(x - x_{i+1})\cdots(x - x_m)}{(x_i - x_1)(x_i - x_2)\cdots(x_i - x_{i-1})(x_i - x_{i+1})\cdots(x_i - x_m)}$$

$$= \prod_{\substack{j=1 \\ j \neq i}}^{m} [(x - x_j)/(x_i - x_j)]$$

Now $\phi(x)$ can be expressed as

$$\phi(x) = \sum_{i=1}^{m} N_i(x)\psi(x_i)$$

$$= \sum_{i=1}^{m} N_i(x)\phi_i$$

$$= [N_1, N_2 \cdots N_m] \begin{bmatrix} \phi_1 \\ \phi_2 \\ \vdots \\ \phi_m \end{bmatrix}$$

or, in matrix form,

$$\phi(x) = \mathbf{N}^{\mathrm{T}} \cdot \mathbf{\Phi}$$

where, by definition, $\phi_i \equiv \phi(x_i) \equiv \psi(x_i)$. In this form $\phi(x)$ is called the Lagrange

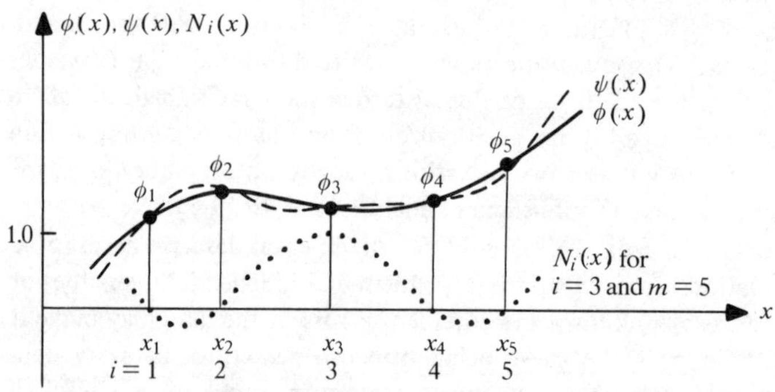

Figure 3.76 Lagrange interpolation in one dimension

interpolation function. It may be shown[11] that the error (e) in approximating $\psi(x)$ at $x = \zeta$ by $\phi(\zeta)$ is given by

$$e = \frac{1}{m!}\left(\prod_{i=1}^{m} (\zeta - x_i)\right)\left[\frac{d^m \psi}{dx^m}\right]_{x=\eta}$$

where $x_1 \leqslant \zeta \leqslant x_m$ and η is some unknown position within the same interval of x. The main value of such an expression is that although η may not be defined, it is often possible to calculate an upper bound value of $[d^m\psi/dx^m]$ over the interval for use in estimating likely errors.

Example Consider the problem of calculating a table of values of a function $\psi(x)$ over the interval $0.5 \leqslant x \leqslant 2.0$. The function has been evaluated at three stations, i.e.

$$\psi(x = 0.5) = 0.19146 \qquad \psi(1.0) = 0.34134 \qquad \psi(2.0) = 0.47726$$

Using $x_1 = 0.5$, $x_2 = 1.0$ and $x_3 = 2.0$ the shape functions N_1, N_2, and N_3 are found to be

$$N_1(x) = 4(x^2 - 3x + 2)/3$$

$$N_2(x) = -2x^2 + 5x - 2$$

$$N_3(x) = (2x^2 - 3x + 1)/3$$

and hence

$$\phi(x) = 0.19146N_1(x) + 0.34134N_2(x) + 0.47726N_3(x)$$

The quadratic shape functions and the interpolation function $\phi(x)$ are shown in Fig. 3.77. In fact, the function $\psi(x)$ in this example is known and its values at the interpolation stations can be compared with $\phi(x)$, given that

$$\psi(x) = \frac{1}{\sqrt{2\pi}}\int_0^x \exp\left(\frac{-y^2}{2}\right) dy$$

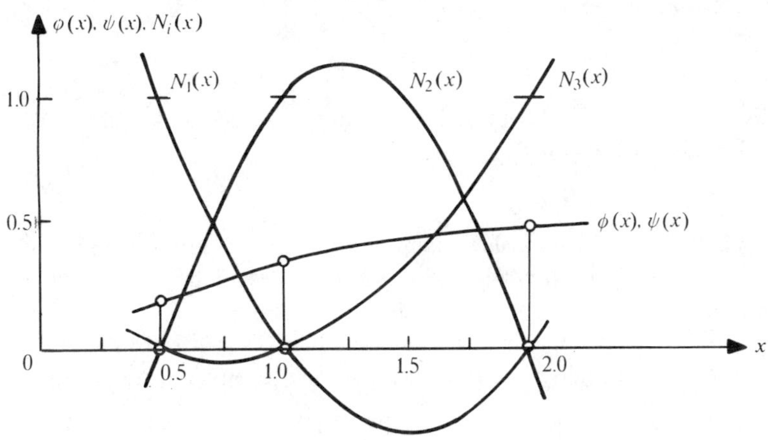

Figure 3.77 Example of Lagrange interpolation

Table 3.2 Example of Lagrange interpolation

x	$\phi(x)$	$\psi(x)$	$\phi_1(x)$
0.50†	0.19146	0.19146	0.19146
0.75	0.27323	0.27337	0.26640
1.00†	0.34134	0.34134	0.34134
1.25	0.39580	0.39435	0.37532
1.50	0.43661	0.43319	0.40930
1.75	0.46376	0.45994	0.44328
2.00†	0.47726	0.47726	0.47726

† Denotes given data points.

The values of $\phi(x)$ given in Table 3.2 approximate $\psi(x)$ to within 1 per cent. For comparison, the results of using linear interpolation in two steps, i.e. between $x = 0.5$ and 1.0 and between $x = 1.0$ and 2.0, are given in the column $\phi_1(x)$.

Although Lagrange functions can be written for interpolation over a set of points at unequal intervals i.e. $(x_i - x_{i-1}) \neq (x_{i+1} - x_i)$, it is good practice not to introduce very large variations in the sample point spacings. Furthermore, the use of several low-order polynomials over sub-sets of the sample points may be more efficient in terms of computation and may lead to lower interpolation errors than fitting a single high-order polynomial over the whole interval $x_1 \leqslant x \leqslant x_m$. However, it must be remembered that such piecewise interpolation will not, in general, ensure continuity of the gradient and curvature of $\phi(x)$ at the common stations between sub-sets of points; see Sec. 3.6.1.3.

Lagrange polynomials may be generated for interpolation in two or more dimensions. For example, $\phi(x, y)$ may be fitted over a rectangular mesh of $(m \times n)$ points to the target function $\psi(x, y)$ such that

$$\phi(x_i, y_j) \equiv \psi(x_i, y_j) \qquad \text{for } i = 1, m \text{ and } j = 1, n$$

i.e.

$$\begin{aligned}\phi(x, y) = {} & N_{11}\phi_1 + N_{12}\phi_{m+1} + \cdots N_{1n}\phi_{(n-1)m+1} \\ & + N_{21}\phi_2 + N_{22}\phi_{m+2} + \cdots N_{2n}\phi_{(n-1)m+2} \\ & + \cdots \\ & + N_{m1}\phi_m + N_{m2}\phi_{2m} + \cdots N_{mn}\phi_{mn}\end{aligned}$$

The suffices of the shape functions relate to the row and column numbers of the mesh (see Fig. 3.78(a)) such that

$$N_{ij} = N_i^{(m)}(x) N_j^{(n)}(y)$$

where $N_i^{(m)}(x)$ is the one-dimensional, m point formula written in the x direction for the ith column of stations or nodes. $N_j^{(n)}(y)$ is the corresponding expression in the y direction for the nodes lying on the jth row of the mesh.

To particularize the two-dimensional Lagrange scheme, Fig. 3.78(b) shows the quadratic mesh with step lengths a and b in the x and y directions. The interpolation function $\phi(x, y)$ is given by

$$\begin{aligned}\phi(x, y) = {} & N_{11}\phi_1 + N_{12}\phi_4 + N_{13}\phi_7 + N_{21}\phi_2 + N_{22}\phi_5 \\ & + N_{23}\phi_8 + N_{31}\phi_3 + N_{32}\phi_6 + N_{33}\phi_9\end{aligned}$$

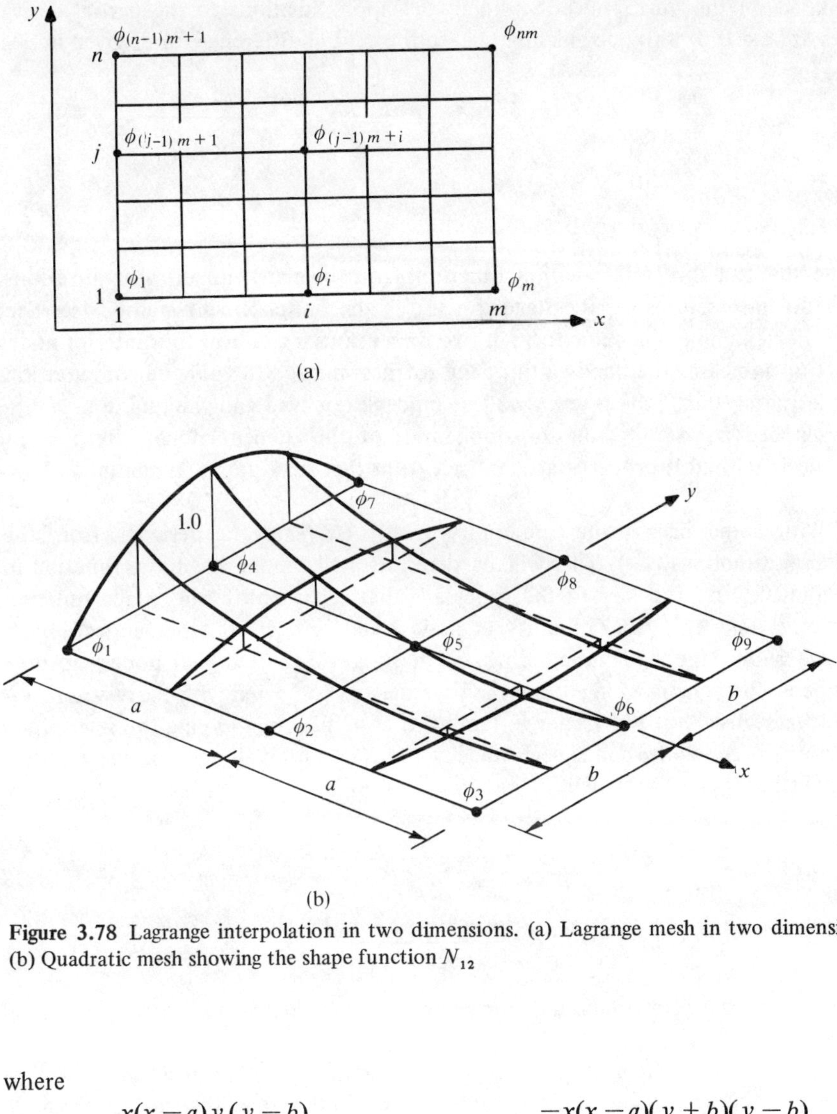

Figure 3.78 Lagrange interpolation in two dimensions. (a) Lagrange mesh in two dimensions. (b) Quadratic mesh showing the shape function N_{12}

where

$$N_{11} = \frac{x(x-a)y(y-b)}{4a^2b^2} \qquad N_{12} = \frac{-x(x-a)(y+b)(y-b)}{2a^2b^2}$$

$$N_{13} = \frac{x(x-a)(y+b)y}{4a^2b^2} \qquad N_{21} = \frac{-(x+a)(x-a)y(y-b)}{2a^2b^2}$$

$$N_{22} = \frac{(x+a)(x-a)(y+b)(y-b)}{a^2b^2} \qquad N_{23} = \frac{-(x+a)(x-a)(y+b)y}{2a^2b^2}$$

$$N_{31} = \frac{(x+a)xy(y-b)}{4a^2b^2} \qquad N_{32} = \frac{-(x+a)x(y+b)(y-b)}{2a^2b^2}$$

$$N_{33} = \frac{(x+a)x(y+b)y}{4a^2b^2}$$

Based on the quadratic polynomial, the approximations to the partial derivatives at $(x = 0, y = 0)$ become identical to the central difference forms given in Sec. 3.4, e.g.

$$\frac{\partial \phi}{\partial x} = \frac{\phi_6 - \phi_4}{2a} \quad \text{and} \quad \frac{\partial^2 \phi}{\partial y^2} = \frac{\phi_8 - 2\phi_5 + \phi_2}{b^2}$$

3.6.1.2 Serendipity interpolation functions

While the Lagrange interpolation functions arise in many numerical applications, they do have serious disadvantages for use in the finite-element method (see Sec. 3.5). For example, the cubic form in two dimensions introduces four interior nodes and thus increases the bandwidth of the stiffness matrix. It would be computationally advantageous if the interior nodes could be removed and the function $\psi(x, y)$ be matched by $\phi(x, y)$ on the boundaries of the element alone. Interpolation functions with this property are referred to in the literature as 'serendipity' functions.

With some insight the serendipity family $(\bar{N}_i)$ may be derived[9] from the Lagrange functions (N_i). This will be demonstrated for the quadratic function in two dimensions. The key to the process is that each contributing shape function $(\bar{N}_i)$ must take the value of unity at node i and zero at all other nodes. Figure 3.79(a) shows the node numbering and it should be noted that nodes are now numbered in cyclic fashion around the boundary as compared with the row numbering scheme used for the Lagrange family. It is helpful in applying the serendipity functions if the derivation is performed in terms of a normalized coordinate system (ξ, η) rather than (x, y) where

$$\xi = \frac{2x - (x_2 + x_1)}{x_2 - x_1}$$

and

$$\eta = \frac{2y - (y_2 + y_1)}{y_2 - y_1}$$

In this way the element boundaries represent lines at ± 1 relative to the system (ξ, η).

Now the mid-side shapes are generated from the product of a quadratic Lagrange term along the side and a linear term perpendicular to the side e.g. for node 2 (see Fig. 3.79(a)).

$$\begin{aligned} \bar{N}_2 &= N_2^{(3)}(\xi) N_1^{(2)}(\eta) \\ &= \frac{(\xi + 1)(\xi - 1)}{(0 + 1)(0 - 1)} \frac{(\eta - 1)}{(-1 - 1)} \\ &= (1 - \xi^2)(1 - \eta)/2 \end{aligned}$$

For the corner nodes, it is noted that a linear Lagrange function, written in terms of the corner nodes only, would take non-zero values at the midside nodes adjacent to the corner in question. However, this can be corrected by subtracting half the adjacent mid-side functions from the linear corner node function; e.g. see Fig. 3.79(b) for node 1.

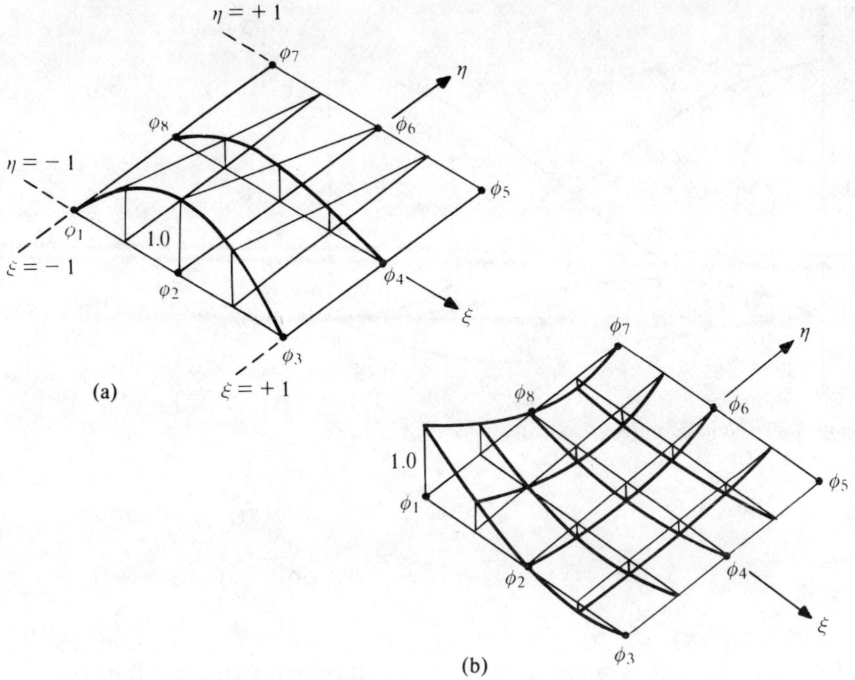

Figure 3.79 Serendipity interpolation functions. (a) Midside shape function $\bar{N}_2$ (b) Corner node shape function $\bar{N}_1$

$$\begin{aligned}\bar{N}_1 &= N_1 - (\bar{N}_2 + \bar{N}_8)/2 \\ &= (1-\xi)(1-\eta)/4 - (\bar{N}_2 + \bar{N}_8)/2 \\ &= -(1-\xi)(1-\eta)(1+\xi+\eta)/4\end{aligned}$$

where

$$\bar{N}_8 = (1-\xi)(1-\eta^2)/2$$

Similar expressions may be developed for the remaining nodes then

$$\phi(\xi, \eta) = \sum_{i=1}^{8} \bar{N}_i \phi_i$$

In general, the element geometry as well as the target function may be described by the serendipity function. The use of curvilinear coordinates provides a flexible method for interpolation over irregular meshes.

3.6.1.3 Hermitian interpolation and cubic splines

The Lagrange and serendipity polynomials discussed in the previous sections primarily ensure a match between the target function ψ and the interpolation function ϕ at the sample or node points and along the boundaries. This level of matching may be extended to the derivatives of both functions by use of Hermitian or osculatory polynomials, with obvious advantages when, say, establishing a highway alignment. Limiting the degree of continuity to the function values and their

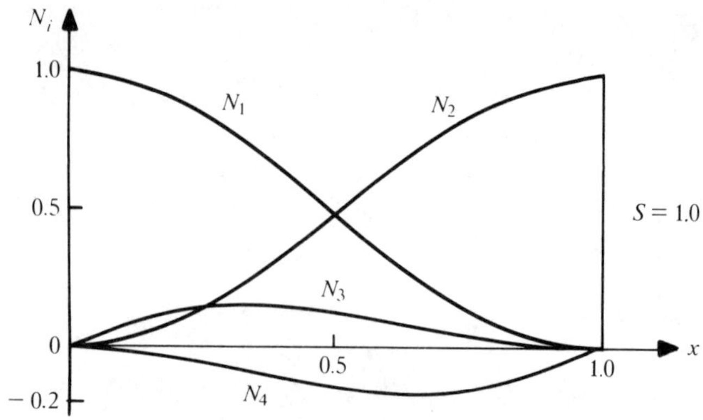

Figure 3.80 Cubic Hermitian shape functions

first derivatives only, the m point Hermitian polynomial $\phi(x)$ may be written as

$$\phi(x) = \sum_{i=1}^{m} N_i\phi_i + \sum_{i=1}^{m} N_{m+i}\phi_i'$$

where ϕ_i' is $\{d\phi/dx\}_{x=x_i}$, $\psi(x_i) = \phi(x_i)$, and $\psi'(x_i) = \phi'(x_i)$ for $i = 1, m$, and the shape functions N_i, N_{m+i} are in most cases distinct from the Lagrange forms etc.

Interpolation functions which produce a match up to the kth-order derivative are termed C_k continuous e.g. the Lagrange family in general are C_0 continuous while $\phi(x)$ above is C_1 continuous.

A commonly used example of Hermitian interpolation is the two-point beam function (see Fig. 3.80); let $x_1 = 0$ and $x_2 = s$, then

$$N_1 = 1 - 3x^2/s^2 + 2x^3/s^3 \qquad N_2 = 3x^2/s^2 - 2x^3/s^3$$

and

$$N_3 = x(1 - 2x/s + x^2/s^2) \qquad N_4 = x(x^2/s^2 - x/s)$$

Note that the above N_i satisfy the requirement for a valid interpolation shape function, being unity at their associated sample point and zero at the other nodes, i.e.:

$$\phi(x = 0) = \phi_1 \qquad \therefore N_1 = 1,\ N_2 = N_3 = N_4 = 0$$

$$\phi'(x = 0) = \phi_1' \qquad \therefore N_3 = 1,\ N_1 = N_2 = N_4 = 0$$

$$\phi(x = s) = \phi_2 \qquad \therefore N_2 = 1,\ N_1 = N_3 = N_4 = 0$$

$$\phi'(x = s) = \phi_2' \qquad \therefore N_4 = 1,\ N_1 = N_2 = N_3 = 0$$

The concept of piecewise interpolation was introduced in the discussion of Lagrange polynomials. A useful family of piecewise, cubic interpolation functions arise from the basic Hermitian polynomial given above.

Let $\psi(x)$ be the target function defined over some interval (a, b) such that a piecewise cubic polynomial $\phi(x)$ interpolates $\psi(x)$ at the m points, so that

$$a = x_1 < x_2 < x_3, \cdots, < x_m = b$$

then it is possible to construct a series of cubic polynomials $\phi_i(x)$, for $i = 1, m - 1$, which take the form

$$\phi_i(x) = C_{i1} + C_{i2}(x - x_i) + C_{i3}(x - x_i)^2 + C_{i4}(x - x_i)^3$$

where

$$\phi(x) = \phi_i(x), \qquad x_i \leqslant x \leqslant x_{i+1}$$

and the coefficients (C_{ij}, $j = 1, 4$) vary from one interval to the next. The coefficients may be chosen such that $\phi(x)$ is continuous over (a, b), i.e.

$$\phi_{i-1}(x_i) = \phi_i(x_i), \qquad i = 2, m-1$$

But the cubic polynomial given above may be written in a form suitable for $\phi_i(x)$ as

$$\phi_i(x) = \phi_i + \phi_i'(x - x_i) + \left(\frac{3(\phi_{i+1} - \phi_i)}{s_i^2} - \frac{(2\phi_i' + \phi_{i+1}')}{s_i}\right)(x - x_i)^2$$
$$+ \left(\frac{\phi_{i+1}' + \phi_i'}{s_i^2} - \frac{2(\phi_{i+1} - \phi_i)}{s_i^3}\right)(x - x_i)^3$$

where s_i is $x_{i+1} - x_i$ and care must be exercised to distinguish between $\phi_i(x)$, the ith function and $\phi_i = \psi(x_i)$, i.e. the value of the function at $x = x_i$. Now it can be seen that the coefficients C_{ij} depend on the nodal values of the function together with their first derivatives or slopes and the interval length s_i.

$$C_{i1} = \phi_i \qquad C_{i2} = \phi_i'$$
$$C_{i3} = 3(\phi_{i+1} - \phi_i)/s_i^2 - (2\phi_i' + \phi_{i+1}')/s_i$$
$$C_{i4} = (\phi_{i+1}' + \phi_i')/s_i^2 - 2(\phi_{i+1} - \phi_i)/s_i^3$$

Furthermore, it may be shown that the function $\phi(x)$ and its first derivative are continuous from one interval to the next, i.e.

$$\frac{d\phi_i(x_i)}{dx} = \frac{d\phi_{i+1}(x_i)}{dx} = \phi_i' = \psi'(x_i) \qquad i = 2, m-1$$

Use of the piecewise polynomial requires a knowledge of the slopes at the sample points ϕ_i' etc., which may not be known explicitly. However, these derivatives could be estimated from the values ϕ_i, using the finite-difference approximation discussed in Sec. 3.4, subject to the comments regarding errors in numerical differentiation.

A further adaptation of piecewise cubic interpolation is the so-called 'cubic spline' interpolation. The term arises from a draughtsman's spline, a thin flexible strip used to produce a smooth curve between a series of points. The relationship between this spline and a continuous beam, and hence the cubic deflected form, is obvious. Cubic spline interpolation produces a function $\phi(x)$ which matches the target function $\psi(x)$ at x_i, $i = 1$, m in a piecewise fashion such that both the first and second derivatives of $\phi(x)$ are continuous from one interval to the next i.e.

$$\phi_i'(x_i) = \phi_{i-1}'(x_i) \qquad i = 2, m-1$$

and

$$\phi_i''(x_i) = \phi_{i-1}''(x_i) \qquad i = 2, m-1$$

but

$$\phi_i(x) = C_{i1} + C_{i2}(x - x_i) + C_{i3}(x - x_i)^2 + C_{i4}(x - x_i)^3$$

and therefore

$$C_{i-1,3} + 3C_{i-1,4}s_{i-1} = C_{i3} \qquad i = 2, m-1$$

Substituting for C_{ij} in terms of ϕ and ϕ' gives, after some manipulation, a set of $m-2$ simultaneous equations in the form

$$s_i\phi'_{i-1} + 2(s_{i-1} + s_i)\phi'_i + s_{i-1}\phi'_{i+1}$$
$$= 3s_i(\phi_i - \phi_{i-1})/s_{i-1} + 3s_{i-1}(\phi_{i+1} - \phi_i)/s_i \qquad i = 2,\ m-1$$

Thus, given the two additional equations specifying the slopes at $x_1 = a$ and $x_m = b$, i.e. ϕ'_1 and ϕ'_m, the system of equations above may be solved by Gaussian elimination for the interval slopes ϕ'_i, $i = 2, m-1$ (see Sec. 3.1.3.1). The coefficients C_{ij}, $i = 1, m-1$, $j = 1, 4$ may be calculated in order to define $\phi_i(x)$, $i = 1, m-1$, which interpolates $\psi(x)$ over (a, b) and is moreover twice continuously differentiable.

The method can be applied to target functions which possess known slope discontinuities by terminating the first spline run at one side of the discontinuity and commencing a second spline fit with the other known slope at the discontinuity as the initial condition (ϕ'_1) etc.

Example A cubic spline is fitted to the data shown in Fig. 3.81. A total of

i	1	2	3	4	5	6	7	8
x_i	1.00	3.00	4.50	6.00	8.00	10.00	11.00	12.00
ϕ_i	1.00	2.25	2.50	2.31	1.82	1.60	1.41	1.00
ϕ_i'	1.00	–	–	–	–	–	–	−0.50
S_i	2.00	1.50	1.50	2.00	2.00	1.00	1.00	–

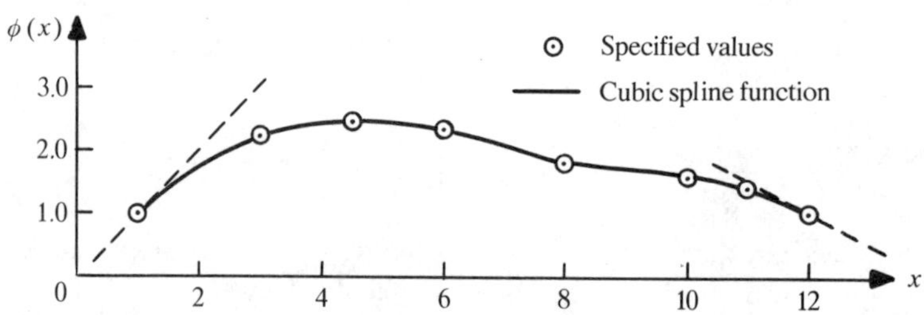

Figure 3.81 Example of cubic spline interpolation

eight positions are specified together with the first and last value of ϕ'. Six equations, derived as above, may be written in matrix form for the interval data points $i = 2, 7$ as

$$\begin{bmatrix} 7.0 & 2.0 & 0 & 0 & 0 & 0 \\ 1.5 & 6.0 & 1.5 & 0 & 0 & 0 \\ 0 & 2.0 & 7.0 & 1.5 & 0 & 0 \\ 0 & 0 & 2.0 & 8.0 & 2.0 & 0 \\ 0 & 0 & 0 & 1.0 & 6.0 & 2.0 \\ 0 & 0 & 0 & 0 & 1.0 & 4.0 \end{bmatrix} \begin{bmatrix} \phi'_2 \\ \phi'_3 \\ \phi'_4 \\ \phi'_5 \\ \phi'_6 \\ \phi'_7 \end{bmatrix} = \begin{bmatrix} 2.3125 \\ 0.1800 \\ -1.8625 \\ -2.1300 \\ -1.4700 \\ -1.300 \end{bmatrix}$$

where the known values of end slope ϕ'_1 and ϕ'_8 have been introduced and then eliminated from the above equations. Such a system of equations is termed 'tri-diagonal' and the solution coding can be optimized since only one term below the diagonal must be eliminated in each column. The coefficients for each cubic segment are given in Table 3.3 and the spline is plotted in Fig. 3.81.

Table 3.3 Example of cubic spline analysis

Segment i	$C(1, i)$	$C(2, i)$	$C(3, i)$	$C(4, i)$
1	1.00	$1.000_{10^{-1}}$	$-2.270_{10^{-1}}$	$1.973_{10^{-2}}$
2	2.25	$3.289_{10^{-1}}$	$-1.086_{10^{-1}}$	$2.661_{10^{-4}}$
3	2.50	$5.005_{10^{-3}}$	$-1.074_{10^{-1}}$	$1.306_{10^{-2}}$
4	2.31	$-2.289_{10^{-1}}$	$-4.859_{10^{-2}}$	$2.028_{10^{-2}}$
5	1.82	$-1.799_{10^{-1}}$	$7.311_{10^{-2}}$	$-1.907_{10^{-2}}$
6	1.60	$-1.164_{10^{-1}}$	$-4.134_{10^{-2}}$	$-3.228_{10^{-2}}$
7	1.41	$-2.959_{10^{-1}}$	$-1.382_{10^{-1}}$	$2.409_{10^{-2}}$

3.6.2 Least-square error procedures

3.6.2.1 Function approximation

The previous section discussed various types of interpolation function (ϕ) which approximated the target function (ψ) by producing an exact match of values at a finite set of points. There are several other criteria by which ψ may be approximated. For example, let $\psi(x)$ be defined on the interval $a \leqslant x \leqslant b$ and let $\phi(x, c_1, c_2, \cdots, c_n)$ be the function which, in some sense, is to approximate ψ over the interval, given the selection of values for the parameters (c_i, $i = 1, n$) in ϕ. At a given point, the error (ϵ) between ψ and ϕ is

$$\epsilon = \psi(x) - \phi(x, c_1, \cdots, c_n)$$

and the total error (Γ_1) over the interval is a function of the parameters c_i, i.e.

$$\Gamma_1(c_1, \cdots, c_n) = \int_a^b \psi(x) - \phi(x, c_1, \cdots, c_n)\,\mathrm{d}x$$

The values of c_i could be chosen to minimize Γ_1 but this would be unsatisfactory since unacceptably large positive and negative values of error (ϵ) could occur within the interval which, nevertheless, partially cancelled each other in the total error expression (Γ_1). A more satisfactory procedure would be to calculate the squared value of error over the interval, i.e.

$$\Gamma_2(c_1, \cdots, c_n) = \int_a^b \{\psi(x) - \phi(x, c_1, \cdots, c_n)\}^2\,\mathrm{d}x$$

The above expression reflects the magnitude but not the sign of the error.

The least-square method for selecting the parameters (c_i) is based on solving the system of equations

$$\frac{\partial \Gamma_2}{\partial c_i} = 0 \qquad i = 1, n$$

in order to find the c_i which minimize Γ_2.

If the error between ψ and ϕ is judged to be of more significance over one part of the interval than another, then the selection of c_i may be biased to reflect this by weighting the error with a non-negative function ($w(x) \geqslant 0$), e.g.

$$\Gamma_2(c_1, \cdots, c_n) = \int_a^b w(x)\, \{\psi(x) - \phi(x, c_1, \cdots, c_n)\}^2\, dx$$

The target function (ψ) may be available only in terms of discrete values ($\psi(x_k), k = 1, m$). The least-square error procedure may then be used in the form

$$\Gamma_2(c_1, \cdots, c_n) = \sum_{k=1}^{m} w(x_k)[\psi(x_k) - \phi(x_k, c_1, \cdots, c_n)]^2$$

where Γ_2 is minimized by solution of

$$\frac{\partial \Gamma_2}{\partial c_i} = 0 \qquad i = 1, n$$

as before.

It is important to stress that the above procedure does not necessarily lead to an exact matching of ψ and ϕ at any particular point in the interval.

The choice of ϕ is left to the analyst, though the nature of some problems may indicate that one form is to be preferred to another. For example, it may be shown that a series of sinusoidal functions ($c_i \sin(2\pi i x/T)$ and $c_j \cos(2\pi j x/T)$) are particularly suited to approximating a periodic function ψ, where $\psi(x) = \psi(x + kT)$, $k = \pm 1, \pm 2, \cdots$, and T is the period of repetition. This will be recognized as no more than the well-known Fourier series analysis[12] which, nevertheless, is linked to the general least-square error method. In another case, the parameters (c_i) may appear in a non-linear form, e.g.

$$\phi(x, c_1, c_2) = c_1 \exp c_2 x$$

However, only least-square approximation with linear parameters and simple polynomial forms for ϕ will be considered here.

Let $\psi(x_k)$, ($k = 1, m$), be the known values of ψ and let ϕ be written as a linear combination of simple component functions ϕ_j such that

$$\phi(x, c_1, \cdots, c_n) = c_1\phi_1(x) \cdots + c_j\phi_j(x) \cdots + c_n\phi_n(x)$$

where $n < m$, then the total error is given by

$$\Gamma(c_1, \cdots, c_n) = \sum_{k=1}^{m} \{w(x_k)[\psi(x_k) - \sum_{j=1}^{n} c_j\phi_j(x_k)]^2\}$$

Minimizing Γ with respect to c_i requires that

$$\frac{\partial \Gamma}{\partial c_i} = 0 \qquad i = 1, n$$

or

$$\frac{\partial \Gamma}{\partial c_i} = -2 \sum_{k=1}^{m} \{w(x_k)[\psi(x_k) - \sum_{j=1}^{n} c_j\phi_j(x_k)]\, \phi_i(x_k)\}$$

$$= 0 \qquad i = 1, n$$

In general, the n equations above may be rewritten as

$$c_1 \sum_{k=1}^{m} w(x_k)\phi_i(x_k)\phi_1(x_k), \cdots, + c_i \sum_{k=1}^{m} w(x_k)\phi_i^2(x_k), \cdots,$$

$$+ c_n \sum_{k=1}^{m} w(x_k)\phi_i(x_k)\phi_n(x_k) = \sum_{k=1}^{m} w(x_k)\phi_i(x_k)\psi(x_k)$$

Defining the elements of the matrices **S** and **T** as

$$S_{ij} = \sum_{k=1}^{m} w(x_k)\phi_i(x_k)\phi_j(x_k)$$

and

$$T_i = \sum_{k=1}^{m} w(x_k)\phi_i(x_k)\psi(x_k)$$

enables the equation to be written as

$$\mathbf{S} \cdot \mathbf{C} = \mathbf{T}$$

where **C** is the column matrix of the, as yet, unknown parameters (c_i). However, solving the matrix equation for **C**, by any appropriate method described in Sec. 3.1.3, enables the values of parameters to be found which minimize the squared error between ϕ and ψ over the given data points. If required, the sum of the squared errors may now be found by substitution of c_i into the expression for Γ.

Example Consider the measured values of $\psi(x)$ given in Table 3.4 and shown in Fig. 3.82. The data is known to contain measurement errors and, from the nature of the problem, it is believed that a quadratic form is appropriate. Therefore, $\phi(x)$ is taken as

$$\phi(x) = c_1 + c_2 x + c_3 x^2$$

i.e., $\phi_1(x) = 1$, $\phi_2(x) = x$, $\phi_3(x) = x^2$ and $n = 3$. The measurement errors, referred to earlier, are considered to be larger in the higher values of the independent variable x and this is reflected in the choice of weighting factors.

Using the expressions for S_{ij} and T_i gives

$$\mathbf{S} = \begin{bmatrix} 11.0 & 30.65 & 109.957 \\ 30.65 & 109.975 & 447.538 \\ 109.975 & 447.538 & 1958.669 \end{bmatrix} \quad \mathbf{T} = \begin{bmatrix} 15.261 \\ 57.626 \\ 243.786 \end{bmatrix}$$

and solution of $\mathbf{S} \cdot \mathbf{C} = \mathbf{T}$ gives

$$\mathbf{C} = \begin{bmatrix} 2.251_{10}{}^{-1} \\ 8.815_{10}{}^{-2} \\ 9.168_{10}{}^{-2} \end{bmatrix} \quad \text{i.e.} \quad \phi(x) = 0.2251 + 0.088\,15x + 0.091\,68x^2$$

The function $\phi(x)$ is plotted on Fig. 3.82 for comparison with the given data points.

In the numerical example, the low-order polynomial fitted to the measured data produced a smooth function, in contrast to the Lagrange interpolation which

Table 3.4 Data for least-square analysis

x_k	0.5	1.0	1.5	2.0	2.5	3.0	3.5	4.0	4.5	5.0	5.5
$\psi(x_k)$	0.35	0.35	0.46	0.91	0.93	1.35	1.80	1.87	2.40	3.25	3.34
$w(x_k)$	1.1	1.1	1.1	1.1	1.1	1.1	1.1	1.1	0.9	0.7	0.6

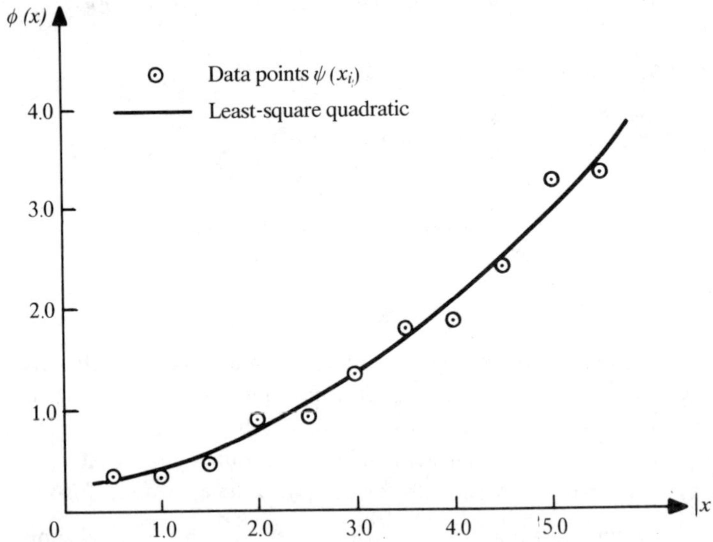

Figure 3.82 Example of least-square error curve fitting

would have been forced to pass through each data point involving perhaps several maxima, minima, or points of contraflexure totally unrelated to the real behaviour of the function under study. This suggests that the least-square method may be used to smooth data and thereby control the effects of random error or noise in the measurements. For example, if data points are available at equally spaced points, ie., $\psi(x_k)$ is known, then smoothed data may be obtained by fitting, say, a quadratic function over five successive points in turn, e.g.

$$\phi(x_{k+2}) = \tfrac{1}{35}[-3\psi(x_k) + 12\psi(x_{k+1}) + 17\psi(x_{k+2}) + 12\psi(x_{k+3}) - 3\psi(x_{k+4})]$$

for $k = 1, m-4$. Obviously two data points at each end of the series cannot be smoothed by the formula above, but it may be reasonable to obtain these missing points with quadratic forms that are not symmetrical about the point to be smoothed.

The smoothing property of such functions can be particularly useful if an estimate of the gradient must be made. The Lagrange interpolation functions may be unduly affected by noise, whereas a reasonable stable estimate of $d\phi/dx = \phi'(x)$ may be derived from the least-square error approximation. Again, using the quadratic polynomial over five points, equally spaced at intervals of s, gives

$$\phi'(x_{k+2}) = \frac{1}{10s}\{-2\psi(x_k) - \psi(x_{k+1}) + \psi(x_{k+3}) + 2\psi(x_{k+4})\}$$

Consider estimating the first derivative of the function at $x = 3.0$ for the data given in the example. The gradient at $x = 3.0$ is estimated to be 0.64, by differentiating the quadratic polynomial fitted over the whole range $0.5 \leqslant x \leqslant 5.5$, while the formula above gives 0.56 and the use of the basic finite-difference approximation gives 0.87. The derivation of the five-point formulae for $\phi(x_{k+2})$ and $\phi'(x_{k+2})$ is left as an exercise for the reader.

From the foregoing discussion it might appear that an automatic procedure for function approximation could be adopted in which monomials would be chosen for ϕ_i, i.e., $\phi_1(x) = 1, \phi_i = x^{i-1}$, and the corresponding system of equations $\mathbf{S} \cdot \mathbf{C} = \mathbf{T}$ set up and solved for increasing values of n until a minimum value of Γ, the total error, is detected. There are several objections to such a course of action. First, physical understanding of this problem may indicate a more suitable choice for the form of ϕ_i, e.g., $\phi_i = \cos(2\pi i x/T)$. Second, the procedure is computationally inefficient since the matrices **S** and **T** established for $n = j - 1$ are of little use in the next stage when $n = j$; i.e., the parameters (c_i) may be completely different for one solution to the next. Finally, the matrix **S** will be ill conditioned for large n and the resulting values of c_i may become numerically unstable. Some of these difficulties may be reduced or completely avoided by selecting families of orthogonal functions[11] for ϕ_i. This topic is beyond the scope of the present discussion. Notwithstanding the objection above, the use of the least-square error procedure demonstrated herein will normally be successful when $n \leqslant 5$; provided always that a sensible use is made of any physical properties of the problem. For example, if the curve is known to pass through the origin then ϕ should be chosen to exclude a non-zero constant term.

3.6.2.2 The solution of over-constrained equations

A somewhat different application of the least-square method arises in the solution of over-constrained linear equations. Let there be m linear equations in n variables x_j where $n < m$ and the values of a_{ij} and y_i are known in the typical equation

$$a_{i1}x_1 + a_{i2}x_2 \cdots + a_{ij}x_j \cdots + a_{in}x_n = y_i \qquad i = 1, m$$

As they stand, the set of equations have no unique solution since $m \neq n$. However, if an error term e_i is associated with each equation then a solution may be obtained which minimizes the total square error. Thus the original equations may be modified to give:

$$a_{i1}x_1 \cdots + a_{ij}x_j \cdots + a_{in}x_n - y_i = e_i$$

or in matrix notation

$$\mathbf{A} \cdot \mathbf{X} - \mathbf{Y} = \mathbf{E}$$

where **A** is the $m \times n$ matrix formed from a_{ij}, etc.

The total squared error may be given as:

$$\Gamma(\mathbf{X}) = (\mathbf{A} \cdot \mathbf{X} - \mathbf{Y})^{\mathrm{T}}\mathbf{W}(\mathbf{A} \cdot \mathbf{X} - \mathbf{Y})$$

where, for generality, a $m \times m$ diagonal matrix of weight factors **W** is introduced. The least-square error solution for **X** is obtained by setting $\partial\Gamma(\mathbf{X})/\partial\mathbf{X}$ to zero. With reference to Sec. 3.1.6, it may be shown that:

$$\frac{\partial \Gamma}{\partial \mathbf{X}} = -2\mathbf{A}^{\mathrm{T}} \cdot \mathbf{W}(\mathbf{A} \cdot \mathbf{X} - \mathbf{Y})$$
$$= 0$$

from which it follows that

$$\mathbf{A}^{\mathrm{T}} \cdot \mathbf{W} \cdot \mathbf{A} \cdot \mathbf{X} = \mathbf{A}^{\mathrm{T}} \cdot \mathbf{W} \cdot \mathbf{Y}$$

Now $\mathbf{A}^{\mathrm{T}} \cdot \mathbf{W} \cdot \mathbf{A}$ is a $n \times n$ symmetric matrix and the above equation may be solved, by any of the procedures discussed in Sec. 3.1, to yield the roots **X**.

This technique is used in surveying where station coordinates or elevations are often determined by several independent measurements, each with an inherent random error.

3.6.3 Regression analysis – curve fitting for random data

Many of the variables met in engineering are inherently random. It may be necessary to estimate a probability of occurrence in terms of a function or distribution which is calibrated by fitting it to some observed data. Another situation is encountered when a statistical property, say the mean value, of one variable is required to be expressed as a function of another variable. This technique is termed 'regression analysis'. As a preliminary to this discussion, it is necessary to revise certain definitions relating to probability theory and random data.

3.6.3.1 Probability theory

The probability or chance that some event A_i will occur is denoted by Prob $\{A_i\}$, where A_i is drawn from a sample space of possible outcomes $\{A_1, A_2, \cdots, A_i, \cdots\}$. A probability is numerical and axiomatically taken in the range 0 to 1, which represent an impossible and a certain event respectively. A random variable x is a variable which can take all the numerical values of the outcomes in a sample space and hence individual values of the variable are associated with levels of probability. A random variable may be discrete, i.e. take exact values, or it may be continuous, taking any of the infinite number of values within its specified range.

The probability distribution of a random variable is defined as

$$P(x_i) = \text{Prob } \{x \leqslant x_i\}$$

and, for a continuous random variable, the probability density function of x is denoted by $p(x)$ where

$$p(x) = \frac{\mathrm{d}P(x)}{\mathrm{d}x}$$

Table 3.5 summarizes useful properties and relationships for continuous random variables. Where appropriate, the corresponding expressions for discrete variables are obtained by replacing integrals by summations, etc.

3.6.3.2 Linear regression

With reference to Fig. 3.83, data consisting of n pairs of values (x_i, y_i) indicate that y tends to increase with increasing x, i.e., the mean value of y increases with x. If this relationship is linear then the conditional mean or expected value of y can be expressed as

$$E[y|x = x_i] = c_1 + c_2 x_i$$

Table 3.5 Basic properties of random variable

1. Probability distribution $P(x)$ (cumulative distribution function or c.d.f.)	$P(x_1) = \text{Prob}\{x \leqslant x_1\}; P(x_1 = -\infty) = 0.0; P(x_1 = \infty) = 1.0;$ $P(x_2) - P(x_1) = \text{Prob}\{x_1 < x \leqslant x_2\}$
	$p(x) = \lim_{\Delta x \to 0} \dfrac{P(x + \Delta x/2) - P(x - \Delta x/2)}{\Delta x} = \dfrac{dP(x)}{dx};$
2. Probability density function or p.d.f. $p(x)$ for a continuous variable	$p(x_1)\,\Delta x \simeq \text{Prob}\{x_1 - \Delta x/2 < x < x_1 + \Delta x/2\};$ $\int_{-\infty}^{x_1} p(x)\,dx = P(x_1); \int_{-\infty}^{\infty} p(x)\,dx = 1.0$
3. Expected value of a function $\phi(x)$ i.e., $E\{\phi(x)\}$	$E\{\phi(x)\} = \int_{-\infty}^{\infty} \phi(x)\,p(x)\,dx$
4. Absolute statistical moments (ν_j) of x, about the origin	$\nu_j = E\{x^j\} = \int_{-\infty}^{\infty} x^j\,p(x)\,dx$
5. Central statistical moments (μ_j) of x, about the mean (ν_1)	$\mu_j = E\{(x - \nu_1)^j\} = \int_{-\infty}^{\infty} (x - \nu_1)^j\,p(x)\,dx$
6. Particular moments and related properties (a) Mean (ν_1) (b) Standard deviation (σ_x) and variance (σ_x^2)	$\nu_1 = E\{x\} = \int_{-\infty}^{\infty} x\,p(x)\,dx = \bar{x};$ $\sigma_x^2 = \mu_2 = \nu_2 - \nu_1^2;$ $\sigma_x = \sqrt{\mu_2}$
7. Joint c.d.f. and p.d.f. of random variables x and y	$P(x_1, y_1) = \text{Prob}\{x \leqslant x_1 \text{ and } y \leqslant y_1\}; p(x, y) = \dfrac{\partial^2 P(x, y)}{\partial x\,\partial y}$ $p(x) = \int_{-\infty}^{\infty} p(x, y)\,dy$
8. Conditional p.d.f. of x given $y = y_1, p(x \mid y_1)$	$p(x \mid y) = p(x, y)/(p(y))$ x and y are statistically independent only if $p(x, y) = p(x)p(y)$

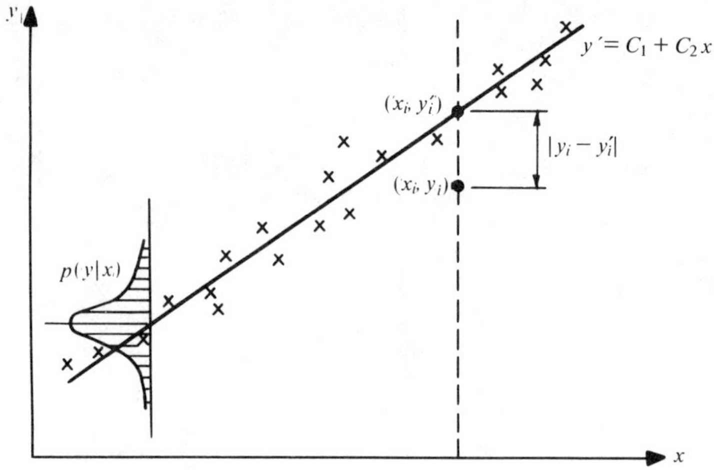

Figure 3.83 Linear regression of y on x

The equation for the line $y' = c_1 + c_2x$ may be found by minimizing the sum of the squares of the differences between y'_i and the observed values y_i at each x_i. Assume initially that the variance of y conditional on x is a constant, i.e., the 'width' of the conditional probability density function (p.d.f.) $[p(y|x)]$ is constant and forming the sum

$$\Gamma = \sum_{i=1}^{n} (y_i - y'_i)^2$$

$$= \sum_{i=1}^{n} (y_i - c_1 - c_2x_i)^2$$

the coefficients c_1 and c_2 which minimize the sum of the squares are given by the solution of

$$\frac{\partial \Gamma}{\partial c_1} = 0$$

$$= -2\left(\sum_{i=1}^{n} (y_i - c_1 - c_2x_i)\right)$$

$$\frac{\partial \Gamma}{\partial c_2} = -2\left(\sum_{i=1}^{n} x_i(y_i - c_1 - c_2x_i)\right)$$

Expanding the brackets and taking the individual sums gives the least-squares estimates of c_1 and c_2 as

$$\hat{c}_1 = \frac{1}{n}\left(\sum_{i=1}^{n} y_i - \hat{c}_2 \sum_{i=1}^{n} x_i\right)$$

$$= \bar{y} - \hat{c}_2\bar{x}$$

and

$$\hat{c}_2 = \frac{\sum_{i=1}^{n} x_iy_i - n\bar{x}\bar{y}}{\sum_{i=1}^{n} x_i^2 - n\bar{x}^2} = \frac{\sum_{i=1}^{n} (x_i - \bar{x})(y_i - \bar{y})}{\sum_{i=1}^{n} (x_i - \bar{x})^2}$$

It should be emphasized that $\hat{c}_1$ and $\hat{c}_2$ are estimates of the true c_1 and c_2 since the n data points (x_i, y_i) are only a finite sample drawn from the whole population of x and y. Furthermore, the line is strictly valid only between the minimum and maximum values of x observed in the sample. Finally, it should be noted that the regression of x on y (to yield $E[x|y=y_i] = c_1' + c_2'y$) will not in general be the same straight line, though both regression lines will pass through the point $(\bar{x}, \bar{y})$ where $\bar{x}$ and $\bar{y}$ are the respective mean values.

When the conditional variance of $y(\sigma^2_{y|x})$ is assumed constant for all x, then

$$\begin{aligned}\hat{\sigma}^2_{y|x} &= \frac{1}{n-2}\sum_{i=1}^{n}(y_i - y_i')^2 \\ &= \frac{\Gamma}{n-2} \\ &= \frac{1}{n-2}\left(\sum_{i=1}^{n}(y_i-\bar{y})^2 - \hat{c}_2^2\sum_{i=1}^{n}(x_i-\bar{x})^2\right)\end{aligned}$$

Now the variance of y regardless of the value of x is estimated from

$$\hat{\sigma}^2_y = \frac{1}{n-1}\sum_{i=1}^{n}(y_i-\bar{y})^2$$

but comparison of the expressions for the two variances will show that

$$\sigma^2_{y|x} \leqslant \sigma^2_y$$

and the reduction in variance can be expressed in terms of r where

$$r^2 = 1 - \frac{\sigma^2_{y|x}}{\sigma^2_y}$$

and r is an estimate of the linear correlation coefficient. Note that r lies in the range $-1 \leqslant r \leqslant 1$.

The positive and negative linear correlations between x and y can be clearly appreciated in the data shown in Fig. 3.84(a) and 3.84(c), while there is little correlation ($r \to 0$) for the data shown in Fig. 3.84(b). However, the dangers of inferring too much from the value of r are demonstrated in Fig. 3.84(d), where there is a clear relationship between values of x and y despite the low value of the linear correlation coefficient. While correlation coefficients may suggest causal relationships, the proof of such links must always be argued from the basic properties of the variables concerned.

Example One method of quickly estimating the strength of concrete without testing samples to destruction is by means of a rebound hammer. As part of the calibration procedure tests are carried out in which concrete cubes of different water/cement ratio, and hence different cube strength, are tested with a hammer and then crushed. A linear regression analysis of typical results is shown below.

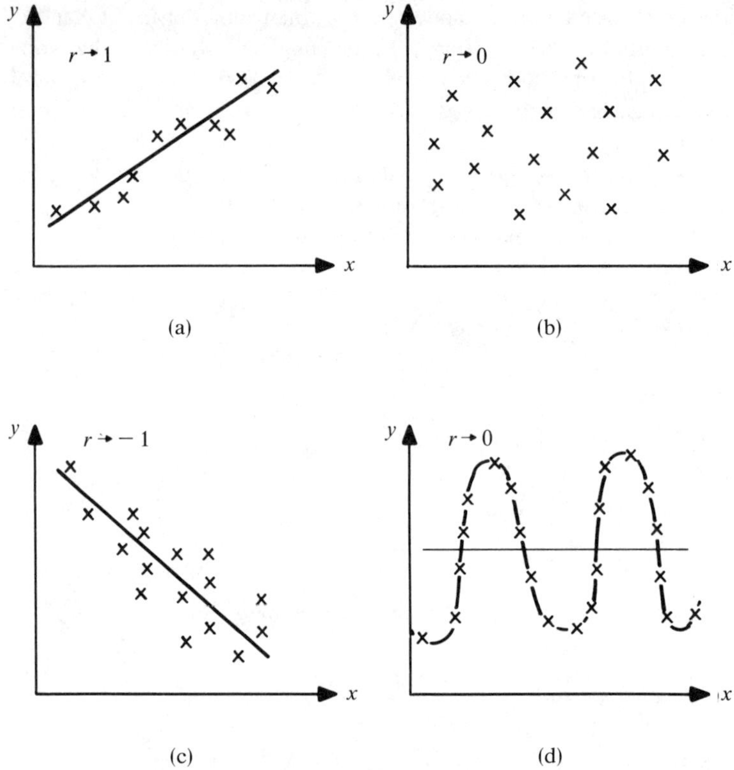

Figure 3.84 Examples of data with varying degrees of correlation

Rebound number x	Cube strength $y/\text{N mm}^{-2}$	xy	x^2	$(y-y')^2$
23.6	17.2	405.9	557.0	1.99
28.0	21.5	602.0	784.0	11.84
26.2	22.6	592.1	686.4	1.97
28.2	26.1	736.0	795.2	0.55
29.5	28.0	826.0	870.3	0.0
33.3	31.1	1035.6	1108.9	23.66
31.3	34.8	1089.2	979.7	8.98
34.3	37.8	1296.5	1176.5	0.06
38.3	49.1	1880.5	1466.9	7.49
Σ 272.7	Σ 268.2	Σ 8463.8	Σ 8424.9	Σ 56.54

$$\bar{x} = \frac{272.7}{9} = 30.3; \qquad \bar{y} = \frac{268.2}{9} = 29.8$$

$$\hat{c}_2 = \frac{\Sigma x_i y_i - n\bar{x}\bar{y}}{\Sigma x_i^2 - n\bar{x}^2} = \frac{8463.8 - 9*30.3*29.8}{8424.9 - 9*(30.3)^2} = 2.08$$

$$\hat{c}_1 = \bar{y} - \hat{c}_2\bar{x} = -33.3 \text{ N mm}^{-2}$$

The standard deviation of rebound number and cube strength are

$$\sigma_x = 4.5 \qquad \text{and} \qquad \sigma_y = 9.7\ \text{N mm}^{-2}$$

$$\Gamma = \Sigma(y_i - y_i')^2 = 56.5$$

Assuming a constant conditional variance,

$$\sigma_{y|x}^2 = \frac{\Gamma}{n-2} = \frac{56.5}{7} = 8.1 \qquad \text{and} \qquad r = 0.96$$

Thus, the mean value of cube strength deduced from a rebound number of x is given by

$$E[y|x] = 2.08x - 33.3$$

for this mix of concrete *and* for a range of x given by $23.6 \leqslant x \leqslant 38.3$.

Now, if it were assumed that the conditional probability density function $p(y|x)$ were Gaussian then the probability that a sample of concrete had a strength y less than 25 N mm^{-2}, given that the rebound number on test was 30.1, can be calculated as follows:

$$E[y|x = 30.1] = 2.08*30.1 - 33.3$$
$$= 29.3\ \text{N mm}^{-2}$$

The standardized variable is

$$y^* = (y - E[y|x])/\sigma_{y|x}$$
$$= (25.0 - 29.3)/\sqrt{8.1} = -1.5$$

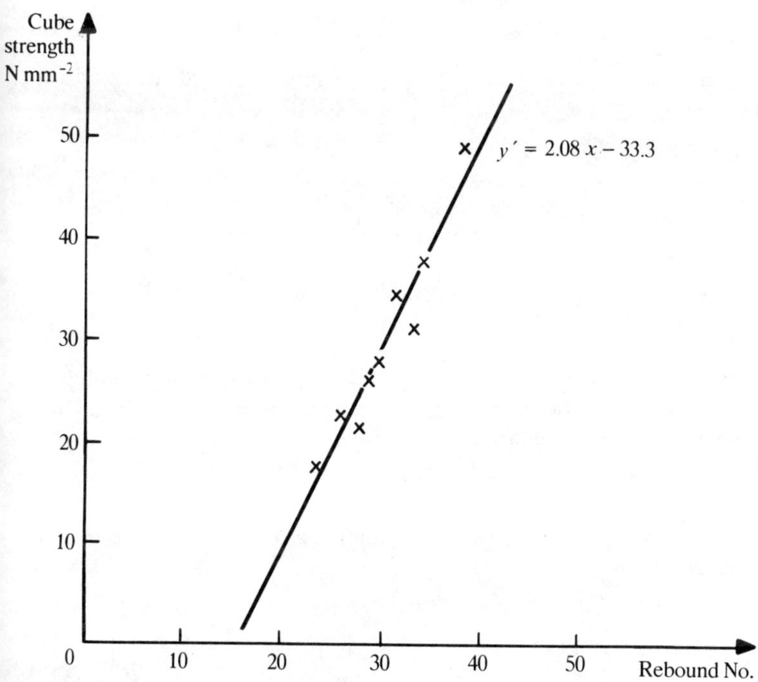

Figure 3.85 Calibration of rebound hammer

From standard Gaussian probability tables,

$$\text{Prob}\{y \leqslant 25\ \text{N mm}^{-2} \mid x = 30.1\} = \text{Prob}\{y^* \leqslant -1.5\} = 0.067$$

The data points and the regression line are plotted in Fig. 3.85.

3.7 SOLUTION OF ORDINARY DIFFERENTIAL EQUATIONS

The classification of differential equations was discussed in Sec. 3.4, where finite-difference procedures were established for the solution of linear partial differential equations. Techniques are presented herein for the solution of ordinary differential equations which may be linear or nonlinear. Only the initial value problem is considered and the reader is referred to other sources[11] for the development of solutions to boundary value problems. For convenience and clarity y' denotes dy/dx and y'' denotes d^2y/dx^2 etc.

3.7.1 Single-step techniques for initial-value problems

Consider the solution of the first-order equation:

$$y' = \psi(x, y)$$

subject to the initial condition that $y = y_0$ at $x = x_0$. The function ψ may be of any linear or non-linear form. The numerical solution of $y' = \psi(x, y)$ consists of a set of values $y_1, y_2, \ldots, y_j \ldots$, at the positions $x_j = x_0 + js$, where s is the step length. Now the function could be expanded into a Taylor series about $x = x_0$ in the form

$$y_1 = y_0 + s\,y'(x_0) + \frac{s^2}{2}\,y''(x_0) + \ldots$$

where the derivatives are

$$\begin{aligned} y' &= \psi(x, y) \\ y'' &= \frac{\partial \psi}{\partial x} + \frac{\partial \psi}{\partial y}\frac{dy}{dx} \\ &= \frac{\partial \psi}{\partial x} + \frac{\partial \psi}{\partial y}\,\psi \end{aligned}$$

and so on. Calculation of the higher derivatives of y could rapidly become prohibitive unless the form of ψ were particularly simple. Nevertheless, in principle the Taylor series could be used to find the solution y_1 (at $x = x_1$) to the differential equation. The function would then be expanded as the Taylor series about $x = x_1$ and the solution y_2 found, etc.

Following the above procedure, while retaining only the first-order term in the series expansion, gives

$$\begin{aligned} y_1 &= y_0 + s\,y'(x_0) \\ &= y_0 + s\,\psi(x_0, y_0) \\ y_2 &= y_1 + s\,\psi(x_1, y_1) \end{aligned}$$

and, in general,

$$y_{j+1} = y_j + s\,\psi(x_j, y_j)$$

This extremely simple procedure is called Euler's method for the solution of the equation. Unfortunately, it is rarely used as it is necessary to calculate with a very small step length if an acceptable accuracy is to be achieved. This can be demonstrated by considering the solution of

$$y' = y + 1$$

given $y_0 = 0$ at $x_0 = 0$. Table 3.6 shows the results of using the Euler solution with different step lengths, e.g., for $s = 0.2$:

$$\begin{aligned} y_1 &= y_0 + s\,\psi(x_0, y_0) \\ &= y_0 + s(y_0 + 1) \\ &= 0.2 \\ y_2 &= y_1 + s(y_1 + 1) \\ &= 0.44 \end{aligned}$$

In this case the analytical solution of $y' = y + 1$ is known to be

$$y = e^x - 1$$

and the exact values are given in column 4 for comparison with the Euler results given in columns 2 and 3. The fifth column contains results of another method of solution which will be discussed below. The poor performance of Euler's method can be understood when it is realized that in fact it represents a straight-line extrapolation from the point (x_j, y_j), using the gradient at that point, in order to find y_{j+1}. Any error introduced in the extrapolation is carried forward and accumulates through the solution; see Fig. 3.86. It is possible to estimate the error committed in one step since the Taylor series should be given as

$$y_{j+1} = y_j + s\,\psi(x_j, y_j) + \frac{s^2}{2}\,y''(\eta)$$

where η is some value in the range $x_j \leqslant \eta \leqslant x_{j+1}$.

Table 3.6 Numerical results for the solution of $y' = y + 1$

1 x_j	2 y_j, $s = 0.2$	3 y_j, $s = 0.1$	4 y_j, exact	5 y_j, R–K solution
0.0	0.0	0.0	0.0	0.0
0.1	–	0.1	0.10517	–
0.2	0.2	0.21	0.22140	0.22140
0.3	–	0.331	0.34986	–
0.4	0.44	0.4641	0.49182	0.49182
0.5	–	0.61051	0.64872	–
0.6	0.728	0.77156	0.82212	0.82211
0.7	–	0.94872	1.01375	–
0.8	1.0736	1.14359	1.22554	1.22552
0.9	–	1.35795	1.45960	–
1.0	1.48832	1.59374	1.71828	1.71825

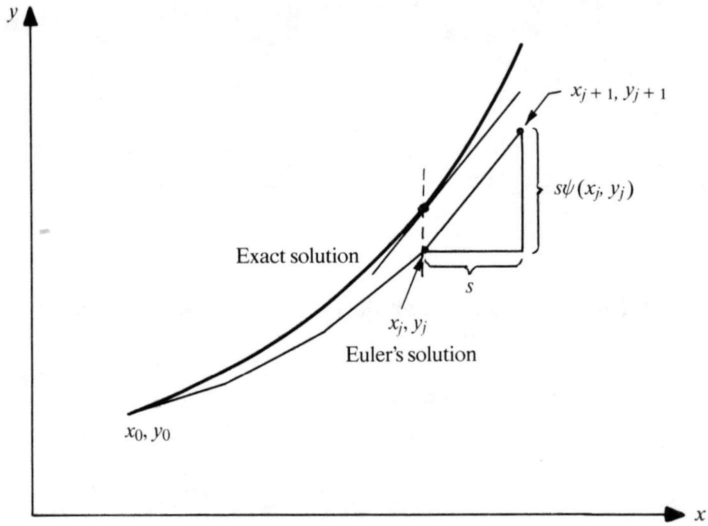

Figure 3.86 Euler's solution to $y' = \Psi(x, y)$.

The form of the Euler solution suggests that more accurate solution procedures could be developed provided the analyst was prepared to evaluate ψ at additional points within the interval x_j to x_{j+1}. One particularly successful scheme of this nature is the Runge–Kutta solution, which takes the general form

$$y_{j+1} = y_j + a_1 k_1 + a_2 k_2 + a_3 k_3 + \ldots a_i k_i + \ldots$$

where

$$k_1 = s\,\psi(x_j, y_j)$$

$$k_2 = s\,\psi(x_j + \alpha_2 s, y_j + \beta_2 k_1)$$

$$k_3 = s\,\psi(x_j + \alpha_3 s, y_j + \beta_3 k_2)$$

etc. The Euler scheme is equivalent to the Runge–Kutta of order $i = 1$, where a_1 is set to unity. The second order scheme $i = 2$ is given by

$$y_{j+1} = y_j + \tfrac{1}{2}(k_1 + k_2)$$

where

$$k_1 = s\psi(x_j, y_j)$$

$$k_2 = s\psi(x_j + s, y_j + k_1)$$

The fourth-order Runge–Kutta scheme is particularly popular, i.e.

$$y_{j+1} = y_j + \tfrac{1}{6}(k_1 + 2k_2 + 2k_3 + k_4)$$

with

$$k_1 = s\,\psi(x_j, y_j)$$

$$k_2 = s\,\psi\left(x_j + \frac{s}{2}, y_j + \frac{k_1}{2}\right)$$

$$k_3 = s\,\psi\left(x_j + \frac{s}{2}, y_j + \frac{k_2}{2}\right)$$

and

$$k_4 = s\,\psi(x_j + s, y_j + k_3)$$

The optimum choice of a_i, α_i, and β_i can be made by indirect use of Taylor series,[11] but the details are not pursued here. Nevertheless a geometric interpretation of the method can be made. With reference to the second-order scheme, the first step is to calculate the gradient k_1/s at (x_j, y_j) and this value is used to step to the point $(x_j + s, y_j + k_1)$ where a second gradient is calculated (k_2/s). Finally, the Runge–Kutta equation is used to step from (x_j, y_j) to (x_{j+1}, y_{j+1}) using the average value of the two gradients.

The program RK4 given in Fig. 3.87 is based on the fourth-order Runge–Kutta

```
C     RK4-A RUNGE-KUTTA 4TH ORDER SOLUTION OF
C     ORDINARY DIFFERENTIAL EQUATIONS.  INPUT DATA
C     IS AS FOLLOWS  XO, YO - INITIAL VALUE.
C                       S - STEP LENGTH.
C                       N - NO. OF STEPS.
C     OUTPUT IS AS FOLLOWS  XJ, YJ - SOLUTION
C                           YJD - DERIVATIVE AT XJ, YJ
C     FUNCTION PSI(X,Y) TO BE SUPPLIED BY USER
C     TO SUIT EQUATION YJD=PSI(X,Y)
      REAL K1,K2,K3,K4
      READ(5,50)XO,YO,S,N
 50   FORMAT(3E14.5,I4)
      WRITE(6,60)
 60   FORMAT(1H1,2HXJ,12X,2HYJ,12X,3HYJD)
      YJD=PSI(XO,YO)
      WRITE(6,61)XO,YO,YJD
 61   FORMAT(1H ,1P3E14.5)
      X=XO
      Y=YO
      DO 100 J=1,N
      K1=S*YJD
      K2 =S*PSI(X+S/2.0,Y+K1/2.0)
      K3=S*PSI(X+S/2.0,Y+K2/2.0)
      K4=S*PSI(X+S,Y+K3)
      Y=Y+(K1+2.0*(K2+K3)+K4)/6.0
      X=X+S
      YJD=PSI(X,Y)
      WRITE(6,61)X,Y,YJD
 100  CONTINUE
      WRITE(6,62)
 62   FORMAT(1H ,13H RK4 FINISHED,////)
      STOP
      END
```

Figure 3.87 Fourth order Runge–Kutta program

scheme. The user must provide a FUNCTION called PSI which will evaluate the particular form of ψ, which is the equation being solved.

The program RK4 may be used to solve the example discussed earlier. The FUNCTION required is particularly simple:

```
FUNCTION PSI(X, Y)
PSI=Y+1.0
RETURN
END
```

The result of running RK4 with a step length of $s = 0.2$ is shown in column 5 of Table 3.6. The dramatic improvement in accuracy compared with the Euler scheme only warrants the observation that RK4 evaluates $\psi(x, y)$ four times in each step. Thus accuracy is paid for by increased computation, especially when the function ψ is lengthy. In fact the error in one step of the fourth-level Runge–Kutta solution is of order s^5 compared with order s^2 for the Euler scheme. But, although it is easily shown that RK4 is more accurate than Euler's scheme, it is difficult to derive the absolute value of the error at any stage. This is a disadvantage of the Runge–Kutta procedures and it may be necessary, when dealing with a new problem, to carry out the solution with different step lengths, e.g., s, $s/2, \ldots$, to assess the accuracy of the solution. However, it should be remembered that in halving the step length, the analyst has doubled the number of steps and hence increased the possibility of errors from numerical roundoff. This point should be given particular consideration when using single-precision arithmetic on minicomputers with, typically, sixteen-bit word length.

Many other techniques are available for the solution of differential equations such as the multiple-step or predictor–corrector schemes.[11] Although it is possible with such schemes to calculate errors, they are not self-starting and in some cases they are unstable, regardless of the reduction of step length.

3.7.2 Solution of high-order, initial-value problems

The previous section considered schemes for the solution of a single, first-order equation:

$$y' = \psi(x, y)$$

subject to some initial condition (x_0, y_0). These techniques can also be used to solve the nth order equation:

$$y^{(n)} = \psi\,[x, y, y', y'', \ldots, y^{(n-1)}]$$

by replacing the differentials with new variables. This procedure is illustrated for the second-order equation:

$$y'' = \psi(x, y, y')$$

Let $z = y'$; then the above equation becomes the pair of simultaneous first-order equations:

$$y' = z$$

$$z' = \psi(x, y, z)$$

and now the initial conditions required to ensure a unique solution are (x_0, y_0, z_0), i.e., the initial slope of y at x_0 must be specified.

The pair of first-order equations can be written in the general form

$$y' = \psi_1(x, y, z)$$
$$z' = \psi_2(x, y, z)$$

showing that the solution of a single high-order equation is equivalent to the problem of the simultaneous solution of a general set of first-order equations.

Using the fourth-order Runge–Kutta scheme the general solution at x_{j+1} is given by the following system of equations:

$$k_1 = s\,\psi_1(x_j, y_j, z_j)$$
$$l_1 = s\,\psi_2(x_j, y_j, z_j)$$
$$k_2 = s\,\psi_1\left(x_j + \frac{s}{2}, y_j + \frac{k_1}{2}, z_j + \frac{l_1}{2}\right)$$
$$l_2 = s\,\psi_2\left(x_j + \frac{s}{2}, y_j + \frac{k_1}{2}, z_j + \frac{l_1}{2}\right)$$
$$k_3 = s\,\psi_1\left(x_j + \frac{s}{2}, y_j + \frac{k_2}{2}, z_j + \frac{l_2}{2}\right)$$
$$l_3 = s\,\psi_2\left(x_j + \frac{s}{2}, y_j + \frac{k_2}{2}, z_j + \frac{l_2}{2}\right)$$
$$k_4 = s\,\psi_1(x_j + s, y_j + k_3, z_j + l_3)$$
$$l_4 = s\,\psi_2(x_j + s, y_j + k_3, z_j + l_3)$$

and, finally,

$$y_{j+1} = y_j + \tfrac{1}{6}(k_1 + 2k_2 + 2k_3 + k_4)$$
$$z_{j+1} = z_j + \tfrac{1}{6}(l_1 + 2l_2 + 2l_3 + l_4)$$

3.7.3 Special techniques for dynamic problems

Certain differential equations occur so frequently that special purpose schemes have been developed for them. The dynamic response of linear systems to external excitation is of particular interest to civil engineers. Dynamic response of a single degree of freedom system can, by definition, be described by the single variable $y(t)$, where

$$m\frac{d^2y}{dt^2} + c\frac{dy}{dt} + sy = f(t)$$

represents the dynamic equilibrium of the system with mass m, damping represented by c, and stiffness by s, subject to external excitation $f(t)$. A detailed

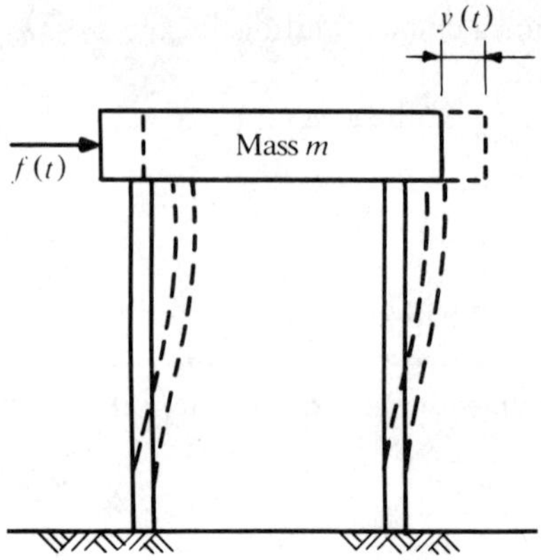

Figure 3.88 Example of a single degree of freedom system

discussion of the above equation is presented in Chapter 4 but, for the present, it could be taken as applying to the portal structure shown in Fig. 3.88, subject to a horizontal force $f(t)$.

It will be assumed that at the initial point ($t = t_0$), the velocity and displacement y'_0, y_0 are known. The initial acceleration (y''_0) is found directly from

$$my''_0 + cy'_0 + sy_0 = f(t_0)$$

Thus

$$y''_0 = \frac{1}{m}\,[f(t_0) - cy'_0 - sy_0]$$

With reference to Fig. 3.89, if it is assumed that acceleration varies linearly between $t = t_0$ and $t = t_1$, then

$$y''(t) = y''_0 + \left(\frac{t - t_0}{\Delta t}\right)(y''_1 - y''_0)$$

where Δt is the step length. Integrating once with respect to t gives

$$y'(t) = y'_0 + y''_0(t - t_0) + \frac{(t - t_0)^2}{2\Delta t}(y''_1 - y''_0)$$

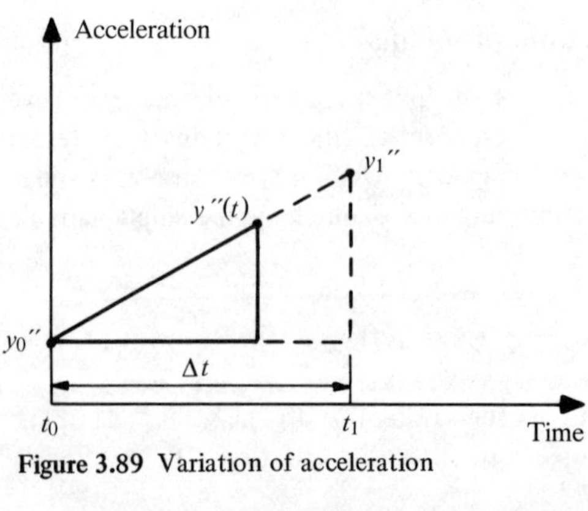

Figure 3.89 Variation of acceleration

and integrating again gives

$$y(t) = y_0 + y_0'(t - t_0) + y_0'' \frac{(t-t_0)^2}{2} + \frac{(t-t_0)^3}{6\Delta t}(y_1'' - y_0'')$$

Thus, on the assumption of linear acceleration, the displacement and velocity of the system at $t = t_1$ may be expressed in terms of the acceleration y_1'' and the known response at $t = t_0$, i.e.

$$y_1 = y_0 + y_0' \Delta t + \frac{\Delta t^2}{6}(2y_0'' + y_1'')$$

and

$$y_1' = y_0' + \frac{\Delta t}{2}(y_0'' + y_1'')$$

These recurrence equations may be generalized to give

$$y_{j+1} = y_j + y_j' \Delta t + \frac{\Delta t^2}{6}(2y_j'' + y_{j+1}'')$$

and

$$y_{j+1}' = y_j' + \frac{\Delta t}{2}(y_j'' + y_{j+1}'')$$

Writing the equation for dynamic equilibrium at time $t_{j+1} = (j+1)\,\Delta t$ gives

$$m\,y_{j+1}'' + c\,y_{j+1}' + s\,y_{j+1} = f(t_{j+1})$$

and substituting for y_{j+1}' and y_{j+1} enables the above equation to be recast as

$$\left(m + c\frac{\Delta t}{2} + s\frac{\Delta t^2}{6}\right) y_{j+1}'' = f(t_{j+1}) - \left(c\frac{\Delta t}{2} + s\frac{\Delta t^2}{3}\right) y_j''$$

$$- (c + s\Delta t)\,y_j' - s\,y_j$$

from which the value of y_{j+1}'' may be found. This value is substituted in the recurrence equations to give the displacement and velocity, at which point the whole procedure may be repeated in stepping from $t = t_{j+1}$ to $t = t_{j+2}$, etc.

If the system parameters (m, c, and s) are constants, then the acceleration at $t = (j+1)\,\Delta t$ is easily written in the form

$$y_{j+1}'' = a_1 f(t_{j+1}) + a_2 y_j'' + a_3 y_j' + a_4 y_j$$

where

$$a_1 = 1\Big/\left(m + c\frac{\Delta t}{2} + s\frac{\Delta t^2}{6}\right)$$

etc. However, it is possible to deal with variable parameters (e.g., s as a function of y) and situations in which the excitation may be a function of the response, i.e., $f(t, y, y', y'')$. The normal procedure in these cases is to make initial estimates of the parameters and to iterate at each time step until the estimates converge within

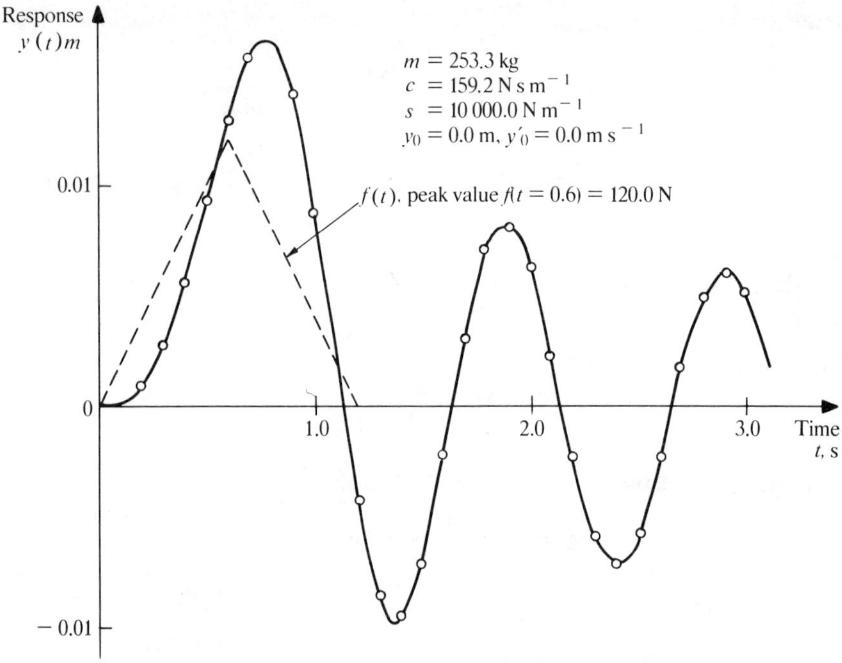

Figure 3.90 Displacement time history for a SDOF

a given limit. In order to obtain a stable solution, the step length Δt should be a fraction of the natural period of vibration of the system, i.e., $\Delta t < \pi/5\omega_1$ where $\omega_1 = (s/m)^{1/2}$.

Example A simple program can be written based on the linear acceleration procedure. Such a program was used to compute the response of the idealized portal frame, shown in Fig. 3.88, to a triangular force time history shown in Fig. 3.90. In this example, the properties of the system were taken as $m = 253.3$ kg, $c = 159.2$ N s m^{-1} and $S = 10\,000$ N m^{-1}. The step length was chosen as $\Delta t = 0.1$ s. on the basis of the calculated natural frequency. The initial displacement and velocity, at $t = 0$, were assumed to be zero. The sidesway response has been calculated until $t = 3.0$ s and this displacement time history is shown in Fig. 3.90.

3.8 NETWORK ANALYSIS

3.8.1 Introduction

In general terms a network is composed of links interconnected at nodes. The nodes may represent positions in space or events. The links may be distances or activities relating to the nodes. In civil engineering terms the former interpretation of a network arises in transportation problems in which a set of origin and destination nodes are linked by roads or in some other way. It is of some interest to find the shortest path between any two nodes (*I*, *J*), where the path may be measured in distance, travel time or cost. Another example of network analysis arises in the critical path method (CPM) used widely in industry for the scheduling and subsequent control of projects involving interdependent activities.

This section deals with shortest path and CPM techniques which are related to the more general field of dynamic programming, i.e., techniques for the solution of multistage decision problems in which the options available at any one stage are conditioned by previous decisions taken.

3.8.2 The shortest-path problem

Consider the network shown in Fig. 3.91 involving eight nodes connected by links with the given distances. The majority of links are two-way with identical distances when traversed in either direction. However, the links between nodes (3, 6) and (5, 7) have different values depending on the sense of travel and the link between (3, 2) is uni-directional. In this problem the order of node numbering is immaterial.

The network can be described by a matrix **L**, with each row I referring to an origin node and each column J referring to a destination node, e.g.

	1	2	3	4	5	6	7	8
1	0	∞	1	2	∞	∞	∞	∞
2	∞	0	∞	∞	1	∞	1	∞
3	1	4	0	1	∞	3	∞	1
4	2	∞	1	0	1	∞	∞	∞
5	∞	1	∞	1	0	∞	3	∞
6	∞	∞	5	∞	∞	0	3	∞
7	∞	1	∞	∞	4	3	0	∞
8	∞	∞	1	∞	∞	∞	∞	0

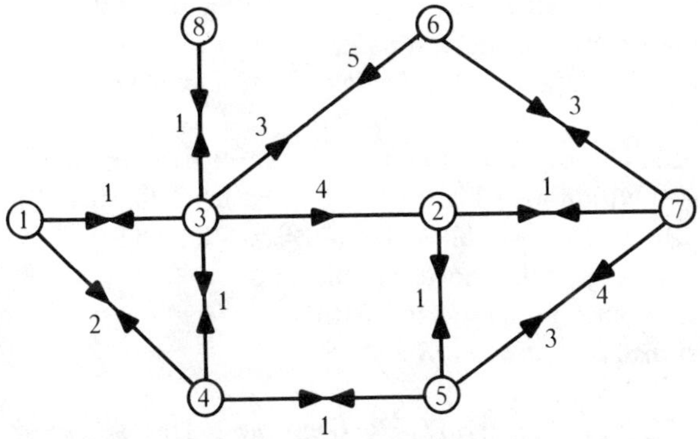

Figure 3.91 Example of minimum-path analysis

When nodes I and J are not linked the value ∞ or, in practice, some very large number, is associated with the link.

It is apparent that the minimum path between I and J must be formed from a series of interconnected sub-paths which are themselves the shortest paths between their respective start and finish nodes. If this were not so, then a non-optimal path ($I1$ to $J1$ via $K1$) could be substituted by a shorter path ($I1$ to $J1$ via $K2$) involving an overall reduction in distance. This property of the minimum path network is used to find the distance involved and the nodes through which the path lies.

To find the shortest path between the start node *IS* and the finish node *JF*, the following procedure is used:

1. Label node *IS* with distance 0.
2. From all the links starting at *IS* select the one with the minimum value and label the node (J) at which it terminates with the distance $0 + \mathbf{L}(IS, J)$.
3. Consider all the links which have a labelled origin and an unlabelled destination node. Form the sum of the origin label and the link value for each such link, selecting the minimum value.
4. Label the destination node with the minimum value found in (3). Check whether the finish node (*JF*) has been reached and, if not, return to (3). If *JF* has been reached then its label value is the shortest path from *IS* to *JF*.
5. The nodes lying on the shortest path are found by a backward pass through the network starting at *JF*. One of the links terminating at *JF* will originate from a node, say K, such that the distance from *IS* to K (i.e., the label value for K) plus the link $\mathbf{L}(K, JF)$ exactly equals the label for *JF*. All other nodes will give a larger sum. Thus node K must lie on the shortest path. The process is repeated by considering links terminating at K and so on until the start node (*IS*) is reached.

The SUBROUTINE MPATH given in Fig. 3.92 executes the five steps described above with the following parameters:

NMX	Maximum number of nodes allowable.
LMX	Maximum number of links allowable.
N	Actual number of nodes.
INF	The large INTEGER value to be used in indicating no link exists.
IS, *JF*	Start and finish nodes for shortest path.
L(*NMX*, *NMX*)	A matrix in which **L**(I, J) holds the distance from node I to node J.
LINK (*LMX*, 3)	A matrix used as workspace for holding link information.
NODE (*NMX*)	A matrix used within MPATH for holding the label distances for each node. On return from MPATH, **NODE** will hold a list of the $NL + 1$ nodes lying on the shortest path.
NL	The number of links on the shortest path.
MIJ	The shortest distance between *JS* and *JF*.

Note that distances in MPATH are INTEGER quantities. This is not as restrictive as it might appear, since suitable units can normally be adopted to

```
      SUBROUTINE MPATH(NMX,LMX,N,INF,IS,JF,L,LINK,NODE,NL,MIJ)
      DIMENSION L(NMX,NMX),LINK(LMX,3),NODE(NMX)
C     INITIALISE FORWARD SEARCH
      DO 100 I=1,N
  100 NODE(I)=-1
      NODE(IS)=0
      K=0
      DO 105 J=1,N
      IF(L(IS,J).EQ.INF) GOTO 105
      IF(J.EQ.IS) GOTO 105
      K=K+1
      LINK(K,1)=IS
      LINK(K,2)=J
      LINK(K,3)=L(IS,J)
  105 CONTINUE
C     SEARCH FOR NEXT NODE (NN) TO LABEL
  200 KIJ=INF
      DO 205 I=1,K
      IF(LINK(I,1).EQ.0) GOTO 205
      IF(LINK(I,3).GE.KIJ) GOTO 205
      NN=LINK(I,2)
      KIJ=LINK(I,3)
  205 CONTINUE
      NODE(NN)=KIJ
      IF(JF.EQ.NN) GOTO 300
C     CANCEL ALL LINKS ENDING AT NODE NN
      DO 210 I=1,K
      IF(LINK(I,1).EQ.0) GOTO 210
      IF(LINK(I,2).EQ.NN) LINK(I,1)=0
  210 CONTINUE
C     ADD NEW LINKS STARTING AT NN
      DO 215 J=1,N
      IF(NODE(J).GT.-1) GOTO 215
      IF(L(NN,J).EQ.INF) GOTO 215
      K=K+1
      LINK(K,1)=NN
      LINK(K,2)=J
      LINK(K,3)=KIJ+L(NN,J)
  215 CONTINUE
      GOTO 200
C     MIN PATH FOUND DO BACKWARD SEARCH USING LINK(I,1)
  300 MIJ=KIJ
      J=JF
      K=1
      LINK(1,1)=JF
  305 DO 310 I=1,N
      LIJ=L(I,J)
      IF(LIJ.EQ.0) GOTO 310
```

Figure 3.92 Minimum path SUBROUTINE, MPATH

```
      IF(LIJ.EQ.INF) GOTO 310
      IF((LIJ+NODE(I)).EQ.KIJ)NN=I
310   CONTINUE
      K=K+1
      LINK(K,1)=NN
      J=NN
      KIJ=NODE(NN)
      IF(J.NE.IS) GOTO 305
C     LOAD NODE(I) WITH NODE NOS. ON MIN PATH
      DO 315 I=1,K
      J=K-I+1
315   NODE(I)=LINK(J,1)
      NL=K-1
      RETURN
      END
```

Figure 3.92 (*continued*)

describe links in INTEGER form. The use of integer link distances enables more streamlined programming and, in general, faster execution time.

MPATH begins by setting all node labels to −1 with the exception of **NODE** (*IS*) which is initialized as zero. The links starting from *IS* are entered into **LINK** then the standard search routine scans **LINK** to find the next node for labelling (say *NN*). Once found, all links ending at *NN* are barred from further consideration during scans of **LINK** and new links starting at *NN* are introduced at the end of the stack. The minimum distance from *IS* to *NN* is stored in **NODE**(*NN*).

Referring to the network in Fig. 3.91, calling MPATH with **L** as given earlier, will yield the following shortest paths:

IS	JS	Distance	Nodes on path					
1	7	5	1	3	4	5	2	7
6	4	6	6	7	2	5	4	
7	8	5	7	2	5	4	3	8
7	1	5	7	2	5	4	1	

It will be seen that the first and last example paths indicate the existance of alternative shortest paths. MPATH will find one, but which one will depend on the ordering of the nodes.

A little thought will show that MPATH can be simply modified to yield the minimum distance from *IS* to all nodes in the network by continuing to search for nodes to label until all nodes are labelled. Furthermore, MPATH will fail if it attempts to find a path where none exists. The reader may like to carry out the edits necessary to cover these considerations.

3.8.3 The critical path method

An essential element in good construction management is the scheduling of the labour, materials, plant, and money involved in a project. A project may be described in terms of a series of interlinked activities. The execution of a particular activity generally, though not necessarily, implies the use of resources (e.g., labour or plant) for a certain duration. The start of the activity may be dependent upon the completion of certain other stages and in turn the completion of the activity then enables succeeding activities to be started. Thus a project may be expressed in terms of activities (links) and events (nodes) in a similar manner to the networks described in the previous section. However, in this application, the links are only in one direction, i.e., with increasing time.

Consider the following problem. The Livcivil Construction Company must carry out a construction project involving eight distinct activities:

Activity	Duration months	Inter-relationships
A	3	Independent of all other activities
B	5	Independent of all other activities
C	2	Dependent on completion of A
D	7	Dependent on completion of A and B
E	8	Dependent on completion of B
F	4	Dependent on completion of C
G	6	Dependent on completion of D, E, and F
H	1	Dependent on completion of E

Figure 3.93 shows the activities as links in a network. Apart from the original activities, A to H inclusive, additional or dummy links are introduced in order to satisfy the necessary interrelationships between activities. The dummy activities are shown as dotted links and they have a zero duration assigned to them.

The nodes at the heads and tails of the activities are numbered in order to provide the means of referring to activities. A fairly strict rule is observed in numbering the nodes, i.e., the node at the start of the project is node 1. The remaining nodes are given consecutive integers in ascending order. A node can only be assigned a number once all the activities terminating at that node have originated from previously numbered nodes. Two activities which start and finish

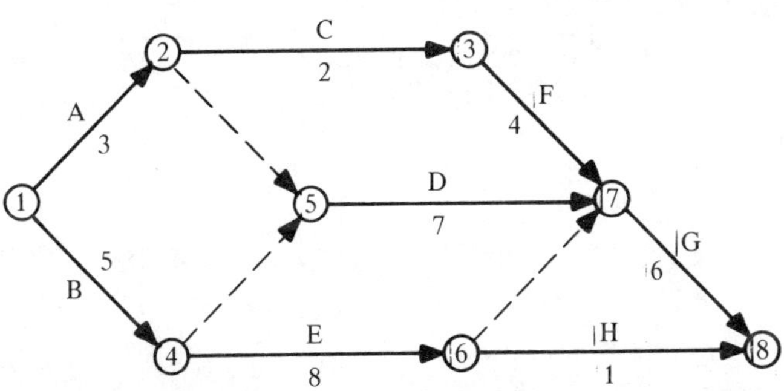

Figure 3.93 Critical path example (Livcivil Construction Co.)

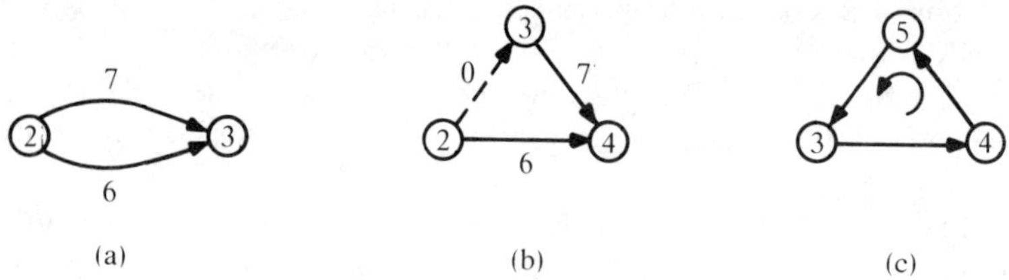

Figure 3.94 Dummy links and loops in CPM

at the same nodes must be split up by introducing a dummy activity (see Fig. 3.94 (a, b)). These rules ensure that each activity may be referred to by a unique pair of node numbers and that the tail number is lower than the head number. Thus it is impossible to commit the logical error of incorporating a closed loop (see Fig. 3.94).

The network in the Livcivil example may now be described in the numerical terms:

Tail node	1	1	2	2	3	4	4	5	6	6	7
Head node	2	4	3	5	7	5	6	7	7	8	8
Duration	3	5	2	0	4	0	8	7	0	1	6

The problem is to find the project duration, which is the sum of the individual activity durations along the LONGEST path through the network. This path is called the critical path since an increase in the durations of the activities on the path will directly affect the overall project duration to the same extent. The solution to this example may be found by completing Table 3.7.

No activity may be started until all activities upon which it depends have been completed. Thus the earliest start time (*EST*) of an activity is derived by considering the total times taken up by prior activities on paths leading to it. An activity's earliest finish time (*EFT*) is its *EST* plus its duration. In Table 3.7 *EST* for activity 7–8 is 13 months since the largest *EFT* for an activity terminating at node 7 is 13 months (*EFT* for activity 6–7). Consequently, *EFT* for 7–8 is 13 + 6 = 19 months. Node 8 happens to be the last in the network and since *EFT* for activity 6–8 is only 14 months it follows that, for example, the project duration is 19 months.

Table 3.7 Critical path example

Tail node	Head node	Duration	EST	EFT	LFT	LST	F
1	2	3	0	3	6	3	3
1	4	5	0	5	5	0	0
2	3	2	3	5	9	7	4
2	5	0	3	3	6	6	3
3	7	4	5	9	13	9	4
4	5	0	5	5	6	6	1
4	6	8	5	13	13	5	0
5	7	7	5	12	13	6	1
6	7	0	13	13	13	13	0
6	8	1	13	14	19	18	5
7	8	6	13	19	19	13	0

The above forward working (or forward pass) through the network is initialized by setting to zero the *EST*s of the activities emanating from node 1. The next stage in the analysis of the network calls for the calculation of the latest start and finish times for the activities. This is achieved by working backwards (carrying out a backwards pass) through the network. The process is initialized by setting the latest finish time (*LFT*) for each activity, terminating at the final node equal to the project duration. Thus, in the present example, *LFT* for activities 6–8 and 7–8 is 19 months. It follows that the latest start time (*LST*) for activity 6–8 is 18 months (its *LFT* minus its duration). *LST* for 7–8 is 19–6 = 13 months.

Just as *EST* for any particular activity was derived by considering the times taken up by prior activities leading to it, so its *LFT* must be determined by considering the times taken up by activities on paths leading from it. Thus, in general, *LFT* of any particular activity is set equal to the smallest *LST* of the activities originating from its head node. In this way the table may be completed as shown.

Those activities for which *LST–EST* is zero must be critical activities, i.e., any increase in their durations will produce a corresponding change in the overall project time. Other activities will possess a positive (total) float $F = LST-EST$, indicating that they do not lie on the critical path. In the present example, the following activities are critical: 1–4, 4–6, 6–7, 7–8.

This basic analysis provides the manager with information to prepare summaries of the labour, materials, and plant requirements on a time basis. Changes to the mode of construction can then be evaluated in terms of differences in the resource requirements. The resources may also be converted into monetary terms enabling cash flows to be predicted. This area is discussed further in Chapter 7.

SUBROUTINE CPM is given in Fig. 3.95, based on the procedure given above. CPM is called with the following parameters:

```
CALL      CPM(NA,NH,N,A,PDURN,MK,NAX)
```

where *NA* is the number of activities, including dummies;

NAX is the maximum number of activities permitted;

NH is the highest node number;

N is the matrix **N**(*NAX*, 2), where **N**(*I*, 1) holds the tail node number (*NS*) and **N**(*I*, 2) holds the head node number (*NF*) for the *I*-th activity;

A is the matrix **A**(*NAX*, 6) which on call to CPM holds the duration of the *I*-th activity in **A**(*I*, 1). On return from CPM the elements **A**(*I*, *J*), $J = 2, 5$ contain the values of *EST, EFT, LFT, LST* and float *F* appropriate to the *I*-th activity;

PDURN is the project duration; and

MK will be + 1 if the SUBROUTINE has been executed in a normal manner. A logical error will be indicated by $MK = -1$.

```
      SUBROUTINE CPM(NA,NH,N,A,PDURN,MK,NAX)
      DIMENSION N(NAX,2),A(NAX,6)
      REAL LSTM
C     FORWARD PASS
      PDURN=1.0
      I=1
```

Figure 3.95 Critical path method SUBROUTINE, CPM

```
  200   NS=N(I,1)
        NF=N(I,2)
        IF(NS-1) 999,205,210
C       ACTIVITY LINKED TO START OF NETWORK
  205   A(I,2)=0.0
        A(I,3)=A(I,1)
        GOTO 215
  210   IF(NS-N(I-1)) 999,220,225
C       START NODE FOR THIS ACTIVITY PREVIOUSLY DETECTED
  220   A(I,2)=EFTM
        A(I,3)=EFTM+A(I,1)
        IF(NF-NH) 215,240,999
  240   IF(A(I,3).GT.PDURN) PDURN=A(I,3)
        GOTO 215
C       FIND EST. FOR THIS START NODE FROM EFT.MAX.PREV. ACTIVITY
  225   EFTM=-1.0
        I1=I-1
        DO 230 J=1,I1
        IF(N(J,2)-NS) 230,235,230
  235   IF(A(J,3).GT.EFTM) EFTM=A(J,3)
  230   CONTINUE
        IF(EFTM.LT.0.0) GOTO 999
        GOTO 220
C       INCREMENT ACTIVITY COUNT
  215   I=I+1
        IF(NA-I) 300,200,200
C       BACKWARD PASS
  300   I=NA
  305   NF=N(I,2)
        LSTM=PDURN
        IF(NF-NH) 310,315,999
C       SEARCH FOR MIN OF ALL LST FOR NODE NF
  310   I1=I+1
        DO 320 J=I1,NA
        IF(N(J,1)-NF) 320,325,315
  325   IF(A(J,5).LT.LSTM) LSTM=A(J,5)
  320   CONTINUE
C       ENTER LFT AND LST FOR ACTIVITY I
  315   A(I,4)=LSTM
        A(I,5)=LSTM-A(I,1)
C       CALCULATE TOTAL FLOAT AND DECREMENT ACTIVITY COUNT
        A(I,6)=A(I,4)-A(I,3)
        I=I-1
        IF(I) 400,400,305
  400   MK=+1
        RETURN
C       LOGICAL ERROR DETECTED IN NETWORK
  999   MK=-1
        RETURN
        END
```

Figure 3.95 *(continued)*

The reader should check the punching of CPM by testing it with the example given herein. Another simple network should then be constructed and a table computed manually in order to appreciate the logic of the analysis. This table can be checked by calling CPM.

It will be apparent that, for a given network, more than one path may be critical to the project. This condition will be detected by careful consideration of the total float for each activity.

The programs available commercially are naturally more sophisticated than the simple SUBROUTINE given herein. For instance, it may not be necessary to start with node 1 and the node numbers need not follow consecutively nor need the tail and head nodes for an activity be in ascending order. However, the simple node numbering rule given earlier is a useful discipline and enables the logic of the network to be checked whereas the detection of loops in an arbitrarily numbered network can be difficult. A further development of the CPM approach enables the user to introduce variability into the estimations of likely activity durations. These programmes are given the general title PERT (program evaluation and review technique).

3.9 SIMULATION TECHNIQUES

3.9.1 Introduction

In the present context, 'simulation' refers to the use of a numerical model which in some sense reproduces the behaviour of the physical system under study. Time is normally the principal independent variable in the problem and the output from a simulation is in terms of the changes, with time, in certain properties of the system resulting from specified changes in the input to the system. Simulation is commonly used when the behaviour of the input or the system is complex and thereby prevents the formulation of an analytical, closed-form solution to the problem.

Simulation techniques fall under the two broad classifications of discrete event simulation (DES) and continuous time simulation (CTS). For example, the operation of a container terminal in a port involves the arrivals and departures of containers by road or rail links, the arrival or departure of container ships, and the movements of the individual containers within the marshalling area of the terminal. Simplified analyses using queueing theory[13] can provide some guidance in planning the number of ship berths and the mechanical handling plant to be provided, etc. However, for complex systems it may be necessary to use DES in order to study the performance of the proposed terminal in terms of freight throughput or other measures of efficiency. A numerical analog of the terminal would be programmed to include an internal clock so that, at specified increments in time, the state of each element of the system would be considered and the appropriate changes effected, e.g., berth No. 1 vacant – commence docking container vessel waiting in the approach channel.

In the above example it is necessary to establish lists (arrays) describing the state or properties of the various users and service channels. The processing of such lists may be performed using FORTRAN programs or, since many aspects of DES are repetitious, special high-level languages have been developed which ease the preparation of the program. Presentation of the specialized simulation languages, such as GPSS and SIMSCRIPT, is beyond the scope of the present text. The reader should refer to the literature[14,15] covering these developments, having first established whether they are available on the computer system to be used.

The example given above of DES involves discrete changes in the properties of some element of the simulation, e.g., ship arrival. In many engineering problems the need arises to simulate input and system behaviour which is continuously varying in time (CTS). For example, the response of a major building to foundation motion as a result of earthquake action involves the specification of the ground accelerations as input to the dynamic structural analysis of the building which, in turn, may involve the nonlinear elasto-plastic behaviour of the structure. Although a solution of the differential equations governing the dynamic equilibrium of a structure may be carried out in small steps of time, the problem is essentially one of CTS, where the timestep is chosen to be sufficiently small that a reasonable approximation to the continuous behaviour of the system can be established. Other examples of CTS arise in considering wind and wave action on structures.

A common element to both DES and CTS problems is the randomness of some input variables. For example, the handling time for a container from the marshalling area to the ship hold will have a mean or average value about which there is some variation. The variability of handling time may be described by an appropriate probability distribution. Again, the pressure on the side of a building at a particular point will be related to the mean wind speed but, superimposed on the mean pressure, there will be a random component of pressure due to the turbulent wind gusting. The object of this section is to discuss the means of generating random processes within the simulation program. The first step is to generate a list of random numbers that possess the required probability distribution regardless of the order of occurrences (i.e., an uncorrelated random process). The final discussion indicates some ways of introducing correlation between successive values of the random process. The application of these techniques is illustrated in more detail in Chapter 7.

3.9.2 Random number generators

A completely random sequence of numbers would contain no element of predictability or pattern in the order in which the numbers occur. In practice it is very difficult to design a system which will generate truly random sequences. However, for most engineering purposes, it is sufficient to generate sequences that apparently possess the target or required statistical properties although they may repeat themselves after a suitably long period. These are termed 'pseudo-random' sequences.

Tables of random digits are often reproduced in statistics texts but to use these in a program would involve writing a large file on the backing store (disk or magnetic tape unit) and then transferring the numbers when required. It is generally considered better to generate pseudo-random numbers as required.

Most computer systems provide a random number generator which will produce statistically independent numbers with a uniform probability distribution between zero and unity; see Fig. 3.96. The majority of generators are based on the following congruence relationship:

$$X_{i+1} = [A * X_i] \bmod [B]$$

The random number X_{i+1} is the remainder from the product of the constant A and the previous number X_i when divided by the constant B, for example.

Let $A = 5, B = 19$, and $X_0 = 11$; then

$$X_1 = 17 \qquad \text{since } 5 \times 11 = 2 \times 19 + 17$$

$$X_2 = 9 \qquad \text{since } 5 \times 17 = 4 \times 19 + 9$$

etc. In this simple example, the whole sequence repeats after nine steps:

$$11, 17, 9, 7, 16, 4, 1, 5, 6, 11, 17$$

A sequence of REAL numbers in the range $0 < Y_i < 1$ could be produced from the above by setting $Y_i = X_i/B$.

The choice of A and B above was purely arbitrary. However, a great deal of theoretical study has been undertaken on which combinations of A and B yield long sequences with the desired statistical properties.[15,16] The choice of A and B is governed by the computer word length. For example, if A, B, and X_0 are INTEGERS and calculations are programmed in FORTRAN then the product $A*B$ must not exceed the maximum INTEGER available (normally $\pm 2^{b-1} - 1$, where b is the word length).

If certain conditions are met by A, B, and X_0 then number theory may be used to prove the sequence length. If the conditions are not met then the sequence may repeat in a very short period (C) where $C \ll B$. In general, it is dangerous to use a routine developed for one computer on another, with a different word length, unless it is fully tested. The statistical tests include the chi-square test for a uniform distribution, run tests, and the calculation of auto-correlation functions. These tests are described in the references given but it is worth introducing the concept of auto-correlation at this stage as it appears in subsequent discussions.

In a sequence containing N values of X, the average correlation between pairs of X taken k intervals apart is given by the auto-correlation function $R_{xx}(k)$, where

$$R_{xx}(k) = \frac{1}{N-k} \sum_{i=0}^{N-k-1} X_i * X_{i+k}$$

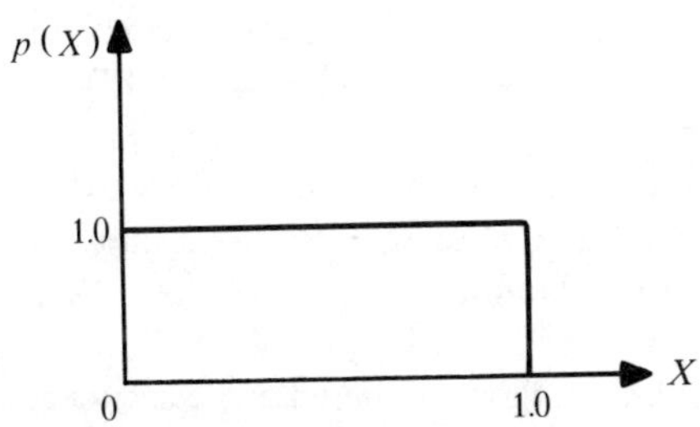

Figure 3.96 Uniform probability density function

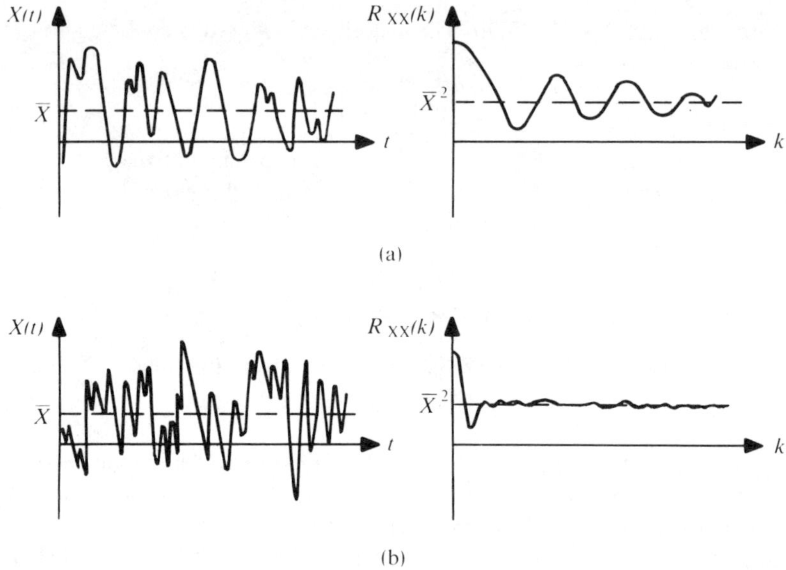

Figure 3.97 Typical correlated time series. (a) High correlation. (b) Low correlation.

If X_i are drawn from a random process then $R_{xx}(k = 0)$ will be recognized as an estimate of the mean square value of X while, for large N and a stationary random process, $R_{xx}(k \to N) \to (\bar{X})^2$, i.e., the square of the mean value of X. Figure 3.97(a, b) shows $R_{xx}(k)$ for sequences with a high and low correlation between successive values. Sequences of independent random numbers should possess low correlations, close to the square of the mean, except at $k = 0$.

The FUNCTION RND1 given in Fig. 3.98 will produce a pseudo-random

```
FUNCTION RND1(IS)
IS=MOD(193*IS,37447)
RND1=FLOAT(IS)/37447.0
RETURN
END
```

Figure 3.98 Basic uniform random number generator, RND1

sequence of 37 446 REAL numbers between 0 and 1 based on the simple congruence relationship given earlier. In this case $A(= 193)$ and $B(= 37\,447)$ are chosen to be prime INTEGERS such that A is near to $\sqrt{B}$ and the product $A*B$ will not produce INTEGER overflow on a typical computer with 24 bits to a word. For a 16-bit word machine, A should be set to 29 and B to 997. Before calling the function RND1 (IS) for the first time, IS should be initialized by any INTEGER between 0 and 37 447 exclusively, i.e., $0 < IS < 37\,447$. The variable IS must not be used for any other purpose within the calling program, otherwise the sequence will be interrupted. Figures 3.99(a, b) show the histogram and the auto-correlation function derived from RND1 compared with the theoretical uniform distribution, etc.

Before completing discussion of the uniform pseudo-random number generators, it should be mentioned that the basic congruence relationships can be efficiently implemented if programmed in machine code, enabling INTEGER multiplication and the automatic discarding of the most significant bits. This is loosely analogous to the MOD FUNCTION in FORTRAN.

Pseudo-random sequences (Y) with a uniform independent distribution between the general limits $X1$ and $X2$ ($X1 < X2$) are simply derived by rescaling the basic sequence, e.g.

$$Y = X1 + (X2 - X1)*\text{RND1}(IS)$$

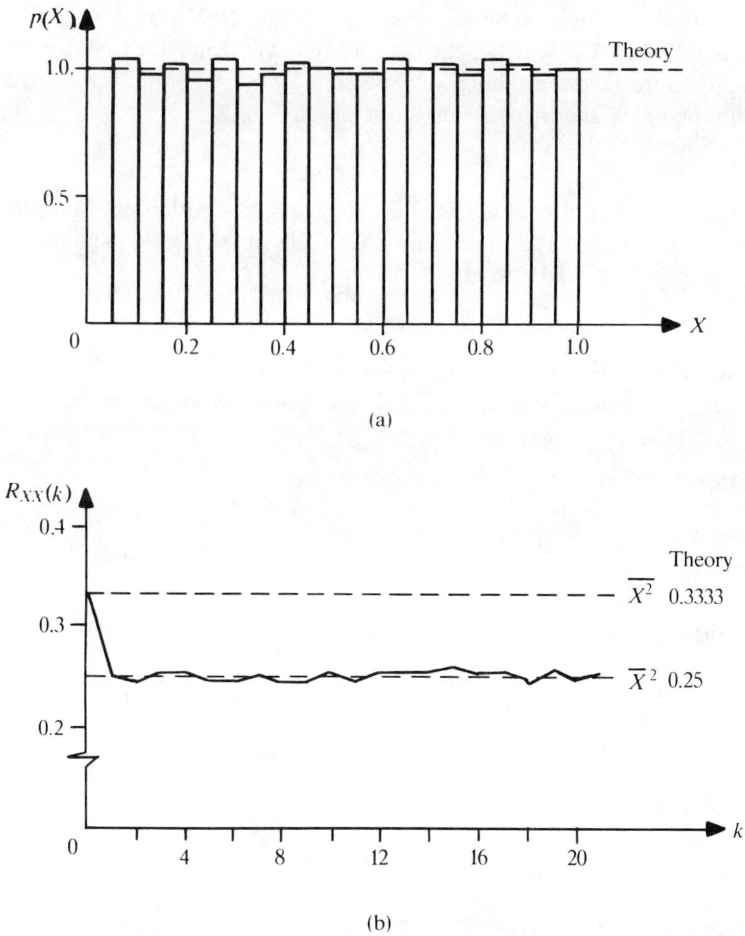

Figure 3.99 PDF and auto-correlation from the basic pseudo-random number generator, RND1. (a) Histogram for RND1 sequence. (b) Auto-correlation for RND1 sequence.

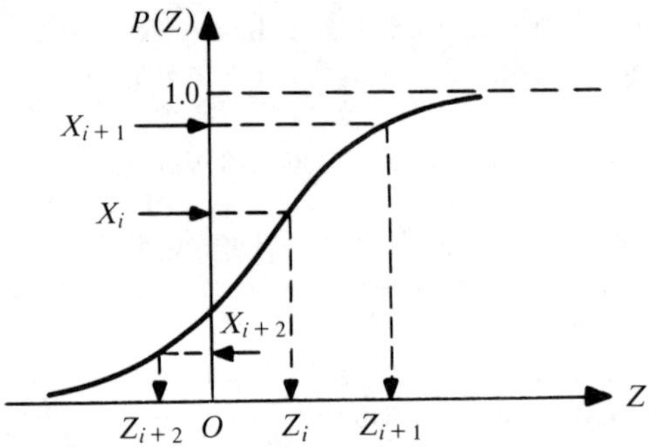

Figure 3.100 Procedure for generating a time series with arbitrary distribution. $P(Z)$

A sequence for some other independent distribution of numbers (Z) may be found from the inverse of the cumulative distribution function ($P(Z)$) by noting that $P(-\infty) = 0.0$ and $P(\infty) = 1.0$, which is the range of the basic generator RND1 given earlier. The procedure involves calling, say, RND1 to obtain a sample from the uniform distribution of X and then solving the equation

$$X = P(Z)$$

for the corresponding value of Z which will have the required distribution. This procedure is indicated in Fig. 3.100. The coding (RNDE) for the basic exponential distribution is given in Fig. 3.101, where

$$P(Z) = 1.0 - \exp(-Z)$$

The coding (RNDN) for the basic normal or Gaussian distribution, with zero mean and unit standard deviation, is given in Fig. 3.102 where the inverse of $P(Z)$ has

```
      FUNCTION RNDE(IS)
      RNDE=-ALOG(RND1(IS))
      RETURN
      END
```

Figure 3.101 Basic exponential random number generator, RNDE

```
      FUNCTION RNDN(IS)
      AK=1.0
      X=RND1(IS)
      IF(X.LE.0.5) GOTO 100
      AK=-1.0
      X=1.0-X
100   T=SQRT(ALOG(1.0/(X*X)))
      RNDN=AK*(T-(2.30753+0.27061*T)/(1.0+T*(0.99229+0.04481*T)))
      RETURN
      END
```

Figure 3.102 Basic normal random number generator, RNDN

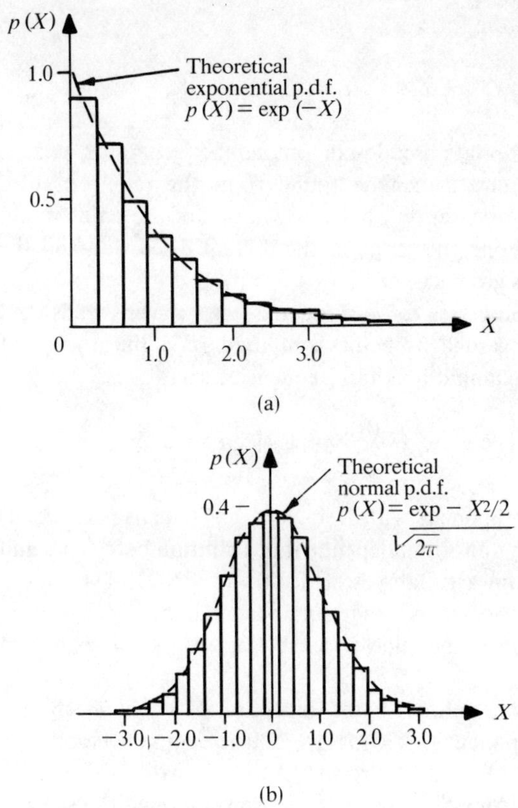

Figure 3.103 P.D.F.s from the exponential and normal random number generators. (a) Histogram for RNDE sequence. (b) Histogram for RNDN sequence

been fitted by an algebraic approximation.[17] Figure 3.103(a, b) show the histograms of the exponential and the Gaussian sequences compared with the theoretical forms. The reader may wish to carry out the modifications to rescale RNDE and RNDN for more general forms of the distribution, e.g., by introducing a non-zero mean and general standard deviation for the Gaussian sequence from RNDN.

3.9.3 Correlated time series

The pseudo-random sequences given in the previous section are approximating an independent distribution and, therefore, possess almost zero correlation between adjacent values. Many simulation problems model real physical processes in which successive values of the sequence are correlated. Statisticians have made wide use of two linear models for such correlated sequences,[18, 19] i.e., the moving-average (MA) and auto-regressive (AR) processes. The moving-average model takes the form

$$X_i = \sum_{j=0}^{M} \alpha_j Z_{i-j} \qquad i = 1, N$$

and the auto-regressive model is in the form

$$X_i = \sum_{j=1}^{M} \beta_j X_{i-j} + Z_i \qquad i = 1, N$$

where Z_i are drawn from an appropriate pseudo-random number generator, such as RND1, and the coefficients α_j and β_j can be found from the required auto-correlation function. A detailed presentation of the calculation of the order M and coefficients for the models is beyond the scope of the present discussion and the reader is directed to the references given earlier.

Many of the environmental processes to be simulated (e.g., waves, winds, and ground accelerations) may be regarded as being composed of a linear sum of harmonic components with certain amplitudes and frequencies, e.g.

$$X(i\,\Delta t) = A_0 + \sum_{j=1}^{M} A_j \cos\left[\omega_j\,(i\,\Delta t) + \theta_j\right] \qquad i = 0, N$$

where the amplitude A_j of the component with frequency ω_j (radians per second) has a phase angle θ_j drawn from a uniform independent distribution between 0 and 2π. The phase angles may be from a suitably scaled form of RND1. The central limit theorem of probability theory shows that for independent θ_j and a large number of components M, the resulting time series $X(i\,\Delta t)$ will tend to have a Gaussian probability distribution.

Each component in the summation, with the exception of A_0, is mean zero and the variance of the j-th component ($j \neq 0$) is $A_j^2/2$. It is common practice to describe the total variance (σ_x^2) of random process (X) in terms of the relative distribution of variance with frequency.[20,21] This distribution is termed the spectral density function of X, i.e., $G_x(\omega)$, where

$$\sigma_x^2 = \int_0^\infty G_x(\omega)\,d\omega$$

If the spectrum of X is available then it may be divided into a finite number M of discrete components, such that

$$A_j^2/2 \simeq G_x(\omega_j)\,\Delta\omega$$

from which it follows that

$$\sigma_x^2 \simeq \sum_{j=1}^{M} A_j^2/2$$

and

$$A_j = \left[2G_x(\omega_j)\,\Delta\omega\right]^{1/2}$$

Figure 3.104 shows the spectrum of a process $X(t)$ divided into M discrete components between the lower and upper cutoff frequencies. The choice of the timestep (Δt) is dictated by the need to represent the highest frequency component (ω_M) adequately. This problem is related to the aliasing phenomenon in Fourier series analysis[20] (i.e., $\Delta t < \pi/\omega_M$).

The coding given in Fig. 3.105 covers part of a program to simulate a mean-zero Gaussian distributed time series using the following variables:

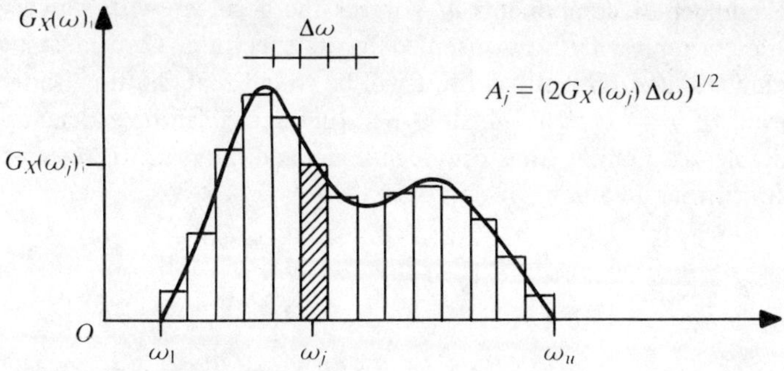

Figure 3.104 Discrete representation of a spectrum

M	Number of components.
N	Number of timesteps.
DT	Timestep.
*PI*2	2 * π.
WL, WU	Lower and upper frequency limits of the spectrum $G_x(\omega)$.
DW	Frequency step.
A	An array containing the *M* values of the components amplitudes set equal to SQRT(2.0**GX*(*WJ*)**DW*) elsewhere in the program.
W	An array containing *M* uniform and independent phase angles between 0.0 and 2π.
T, TS	General time variable and start time of simulation.
X	An array containing the *N* values of the time series.
RND1	The function, previously discussed in Sec. 3.9.2, for the generation of uniform and independent random numbers, arbitrarily initialized with the seed integer *IS* = 531.
Label 999	Statement to cover the error in choosing too large a value of *DT*.

```
C     SIMULATION OF A MEAN-ZERO GAUSSIAN TIME SERIES
      PI2=8.0*ATAN(1.0)
      DW=(WU-WL)/FLOAT(M)
      DO 100 J=1,M
 100  W(J)=WL+DW*(FLOAT(J)-0.5)
      IF(DT.GT.(PI2/(2.0*W(M)))) GOTO 999
C     CALCULATE UNIFORM PHASE ANGLES
      IS=531
      DO 105 J=1,M
 105  P(I)=PI2*RND1(IS)
C     SIMULATE X(I*DT) STARTING AT T=TS
      T=TS
      DO 110 I=1,N
      S=0.0
      DO 115 J=1,M
 115  S=S+A(J)*COS(W(J)*T+P(J))
      X(I)=S
 110  T=T+DT
```

Figure 3.105 Gaussian time series simulation

Obviously the number of components M governs the accuracy with which a particular time series is represented, as specified by its spectrum. Care must be exercised in choosing DW and WL, otherwise it will be found that the time series repeats after a period of $T = 2\pi/DW$. Finally, such time series can be efficiently simulated using suitable fast Fourier transform techniques and the reader is referred to specialist texts for further details.

REFERENCES

1. Livesley, R. K., *Matrix Methods of Structural Analysis*, 2nd edn, Pergamon, Oxford, 1975.
2. Meek, J. L., *Matrix Structural Analysis*, McGraw-Hill, New York, 1971.
3. Wilkinson, J. H. *The Algebraic Eigenvalue Problem*, Clarendon Press, Oxford, 1965.
4. Harrison, H. B. *Computer Methods in Structural Analysis*, Prentice-Hall, Englewood Cliffs, N.J., 1973.
5. Krylov, V. I. *Approximate Calculations of Integrals*, trans. A. H. Stroud, Macmillan, New York, 1962 (ACM Monograph Series).
6. Wong, P. C. *Numerical and Matrix Methods in Structural Mechanics*, Wiley, New York, 1966.
7. Timoshenko, S. P. and S. Woinowsky-Krieger, *Theory of Plates and Shells*, McGraw-Hill, New York, 1959.
8. Hughes, T. J. R. and M. Cohen, 'The heterosis finite element for plate bending', *Computers & Structures* 9, 445–450, Pergamon, Oxford, 1978.
9. Zienkiewicz, O. C., *The Finite Element Method*, McGraw-Hill, London, 1977.
10. Irons, B. and S. Ahmad, *Techniques of Finite Elements*, Wiley, Chichester, 1980.
11. Conte, S. D. and C. de Boor, *Elementary numerical analysis*, 2nd edn, McGraw-Hill Kogakusha, Tokyo, 1972.
12. Hamming, R. W., *Numerical Methods for Scientists and Engineers*, 2nd edn, McGraw-Hill, New York, 1973.
13. Stark, R. M., and R. L. Nicholls, *Mathematical Foundations for Design*, McGraw-Hill, New York, 1972.
14. Mitchell, G. H. *Operational Research: Techniques and Examples*, English University Press, London, 1972.
15. Naylor, Balintfy, Burdick and Chu, *Computer Simulation Techniques*, Wiley, New York, 1966.
16. Thesen, A. *Computer Methods in Operational Research*, Academic Press, New York, 1978.
17. Zelen, M., Severo, N. C. 'Probability functions', Ch. 26 in M. Abramowitz and I. A. Stegun (eds), *Handbook of Mathematical Functions*, Dover, New York, 1972.
18. Chatfield, C. *The Analysis of Time-series: Theory and Practice*, Chapman & Hall, London, 1975.
19. Box, G. E. P., and G. M. Jenkins, *Time-series Analysis – Forecasting and Control*, Holden-Day, San-Francisco, 1976.
20. Newland, D. E., *An Introduction to Random Vibration and Spectral Analysis*, Longman, London, 1975.
21. Bendat, J. S., and A. G. Piersol, *Random Data: Analysis and Measurement Procedures*, 2nd edn, Wiley–Interscience, New York, 1971.

CHAPTER
FOUR

STRUCTURAL ANALYSIS AND DESIGN

4.1 INTRODUCTION

The aim of structural design is safety, fulfilment of functional requirements and economy. An engineer first gathers information on the task in hand. From this data, potential solutions are created and assessed. Those schemes that are acceptable are then subjected to a detailing procedure when member sizes are fixed.

A computer can assist this process by providing a designer with immense calculating power, ready access to information, and the experience of many specialists. A computer program to analyse bridge decks, for example, contains the products of years of research into methods of structural idealization, numerical analysis, and material mechanics, while a program to detail structural members contains the recommendations of teams of experts, who formulate codes of practice after many years of study.

Use of computers leads to a number of advantages:

1. A design can be completed more quickly. This enables more schemes to be investigated in a given time and encourages designers to experiment with novel forms of solution.
2. It can enable changes to a client's requirements to be incorporated in a design more easily.
3. It should reduce the occurrence of errors due to arithmetic mistakes, over-simplification of structural behaviour, and by minimizing the amount of data to be handled manually.

When a structural engineer considers using a computer he has to assess the relative merits of computer-aided design on the one hand and fully automatic design on the other. The best approach depends on the nature of the work in hand. With a computer-aided design process, operations are under control of the engineer, who goes through the process of evolving concepts and developing trial designs in the traditional manner. However, with the aid of a computer, secondary tasks, such as analysis and member detailing, can be accomplished more quickly and with less effort. With fully automatic design, on the other hand, a designer specifies the nature of a problem and the computer does the rest.

Ideally, the design process should be automatic when the intuition, skill and experience of an engineer are not required. Such occasions are few in structural engineering, although it can be useful to automate secondary tasks, such as dimensioning a member for minimum cost. To devise a fully automatic design program requires all criteria for decisions to be formalized and related to cost. This is an expensive procedure and usually can be justified only when many similar items are to be produced. For such cases, the accumulative cost savings on each item pay for the development of the computer program.

Because of its limited applicability, and the complexity of many of its procedures, fully automatic design, or structural optimization, is not considered further in this text. In this chapter some procedures to assist a designer in computer-aided design are described, and methods to predict the response of skeletal structures are explained in some detail.

4.2 ANALYSIS

Structural analysis in its broadest sense includes defining the actions on a structure (load, temperature change, subsidence, etc.), and predicting response to those actions (including those incurred during construction). It requires structural idealization, or, the creation of a simplified mathematical model of the structure to be analysed. Structural idealization is a process in which a substantial amount of engineering judgement is needed, and is, therefore, beyond the scope of this text. Here, we shall be concerned with computer-based methods to predict the response of mathematical models of real structures. In particular we shall consider analysis of structures that can be represented by a skeleton of straight-line members with stiffnesses to bending, axial force, and shear.

A computer is most effective for analysing highly redundant structures and structures with members of unusual shape. Reinforced concrete building frames and grillages of beams are typical applications. The method most commonly used is known as the 'equilibrium' or 'stiffness' method. This is a very versatile approach and can include the effects of axial loading on a member's flexural stiffness, large changes in geometry, dynamic loads, and material nonlinearity.

4.3 STIFFNESS METHOD

The stiffness method for analysis of linear elastic structures has four basic stages. In the first, equations relating end forces and displacements of each member are set up. The coefficients relating forces and displacements of a member form its local stiffness matrix.

In the second stage of an analysis, the stiffness matrix for the whole structure is compiled from the member stiffness matrices. This is accomplished by forming equations of equilibrium at each member connection and by stipulating that the members meeting at a connection, or joint, have the same displacement components as the joint. When the global stiffness matrix has been assembled, displacement boundary conditions are imposed. This is done by setting displacements at rigid supports to zero, or by adding stiffness coefficients to simulate the action of the connecting structural system.

Loading causes a structure to deflect, and an equilibrium position is reached when the internal end forces produced by deflected members balance the external, applied load at each joint. In the third stage of an analysis, a set of linear simultaneous equations is obtained relating applied joint forces to displacements, and the solution of these equations gives displacements of all joints.

In the fourth stage, the end forces acting on individual members are determined by multiplying the local stiffness matrices by the determined joint displacements. The effects of these end loads are added to those obtained by analysing members with fixed ends, to determine the total effects of loading imposed on members.

4.3.1 Local or member stiffness matrices

A local stiffness matrix expresses the relationships between joint forces and displacements in terms of a member's geometric and material properties. For straight members, of constant cross-section, their derivation is straightforward and is described in standard texts on structural analysis.[1] For illustration, the stiffness matrix for a member of a rigid-jointed plane framework is derived.

Plane framework equations are used when all of the members meeting at a joint experience the same rotation as well as the same translation. The notation for a typical straight member of constant cross-section is shown in Fig. 4.1. Starting with the well-known slope deflection equations (see Sec. 3.5.2), the equation of axial stiffness, and using the notation of Fig. 3.5;

$$\begin{bmatrix} Fp_i \\ Fq_i \\ M_i \\ \hline Fp_j \\ Fq_j \\ M_j \end{bmatrix} = \left[\begin{array}{ccc|ccc} \frac{EA}{L} & 0 & 0 & -\frac{EA}{L} & 0 & 0 \\ 0 & \frac{12EI}{L^3} & \frac{6EI}{L^2} & 0 & -\frac{12EI}{L^3} & \frac{6EI}{L^2} \\ 0 & \frac{6EI}{L^2} & \frac{4EI}{L} & 0 & -\frac{6EI}{L^2} & \frac{2EI}{L} \\ \hline -\frac{EA}{L} & 0 & 0 & \frac{EA}{L} & 0 & 0 \\ 0 & -\frac{12EI}{L^3} & -\frac{6EI}{L^2} & 0 & \frac{12EI}{L^3} & -\frac{6EI}{L^2} \\ 0 & \frac{6EI}{L^2} & \frac{2EI}{L} & 0 & -\frac{6EI}{L^2} & \frac{4EI}{L} \end{array}\right] \begin{bmatrix} Dp_i \\ Dq_i \\ \theta_i \\ \hline Dp_j \\ Dq_j \\ \theta_j \end{bmatrix}$$

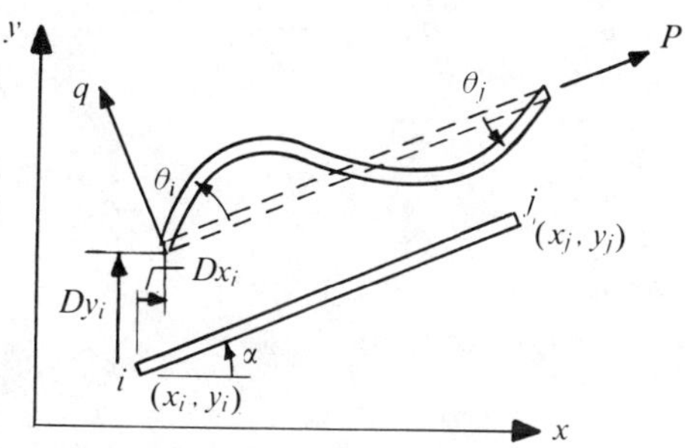

Figure 4.1 Plane framework member

In shorthand notation, the equations are

$$\begin{bmatrix} \mathbf{F}_{pq_i} \\ \mathbf{F}_{pq_j} \end{bmatrix} = \begin{bmatrix} \bar{\mathbf{S}}_{ii} & \bar{\mathbf{S}}_{ij} \\ \bar{\mathbf{S}}_{ji} & \bar{\mathbf{S}}_{jj} \end{bmatrix} \begin{bmatrix} \mathbf{D}_{pq_i} \\ \mathbf{D}_{pq_j} \end{bmatrix}$$

At each joint the transformation matrix (see Sec. 3.1.8.1) is given by

$$\begin{bmatrix} Dp \\ Dq \\ \theta \end{bmatrix} = \begin{bmatrix} \cos\alpha & \sin\alpha & 0 \\ -\sin\alpha & \cos\alpha & 0 \\ 0 & 0 & 1 \end{bmatrix} \begin{bmatrix} Dx \\ Dy \\ \theta \end{bmatrix} \quad \text{or} \quad \mathbf{D}_{pq} = \mathbf{T}\cdot\mathbf{D}_{xy}$$

and

$$\begin{bmatrix} Fx \\ Fy \\ M \end{bmatrix} = \begin{bmatrix} \cos\alpha & -\sin\alpha & 0 \\ \sin\alpha & \cos\alpha & 0 \\ 0 & 0 & 1 \end{bmatrix} \begin{bmatrix} Fp \\ Fq \\ M \end{bmatrix} \quad \text{or} \quad \mathbf{F}_{xy} = \mathbf{T}^{\mathrm{T}}\cdot\mathbf{F}_{pq}$$

Hence the member stiffness matrix referred to the global axis system is

$$\begin{bmatrix} \mathbf{F}_{xy_i} \\ \mathbf{F}_{xy_j} \end{bmatrix} = \begin{bmatrix} \mathbf{T}^{\mathrm{T}}\cdot\bar{\mathbf{S}}_{ii}\cdot\mathbf{T} & \mathbf{T}^{\mathrm{T}}\cdot\bar{\mathbf{S}}_{ij}\cdot\mathbf{T} \\ \mathbf{T}^{\mathrm{T}}\cdot\bar{\mathbf{S}}_{ij}^{\mathrm{T}}\cdot\mathbf{T} & \mathbf{T}^{\mathrm{T}}\cdot\bar{\mathbf{S}}_{jj}\cdot\mathbf{T} \end{bmatrix} \begin{bmatrix} \mathbf{D}_{xy_i} \\ \mathbf{D}_{xy_j} \end{bmatrix}$$

or

$$\begin{bmatrix} \mathbf{F}_{xy_i} \\ \mathbf{F}_{xy_j} \end{bmatrix} = \begin{bmatrix} \mathbf{S}_{ii} & \mathbf{S}_{ij} \\ \mathbf{S}_{ij}^{\mathrm{T}} & \mathbf{S}_{jj} \end{bmatrix} \begin{bmatrix} \mathbf{D}_{xy_i} \\ \mathbf{D}_{xy_j} \end{bmatrix}$$

Writing s for $\sin\alpha$ and c for $\cos\alpha$,

$$S_{ii} = \begin{bmatrix} c^2\dfrac{EA}{L} + s^2\dfrac{12EI}{L^3} & sc\left(\dfrac{EA}{L} - \dfrac{12EI}{L^3}\right) & -s\dfrac{6EI}{L^2} \\ sc\left(\dfrac{EA}{L} - \dfrac{12EI}{L^3}\right) & s^2\dfrac{EA}{L} + c^2\dfrac{12EI}{L^3} & c\dfrac{6EI}{L^2} \\ -s\dfrac{6EI}{L^2} & c\dfrac{6EI}{L^2} & \dfrac{4EI}{L} \end{bmatrix}$$

Coefficients of $\mathbf{S}_{jj}$ are similar to those of $\mathbf{S}_{ii}$, but with opposite signs for the $6EI/L^2$ terms.

$$\mathbf{S}_{ij} = -\begin{bmatrix} c^2\dfrac{EA}{L}+s^2\dfrac{12EI}{L^3} & sc\left(\dfrac{EA}{L}-\dfrac{12EI}{L^3}\right) & s\dfrac{6EI}{L^2} \\ sc\left(\dfrac{EA}{L}-\dfrac{12EI}{L^3}\right) & s^2\dfrac{EA}{L}+c^2\dfrac{12EI}{L^3} & -c\dfrac{6EI}{L^2} \\ -s\dfrac{6EI}{L^2} & c\dfrac{6EI}{L^2} & -\dfrac{2EI}{L} \end{bmatrix}$$

A similar approach is used for pin-ended plane and space frameworks and for grillages of beams.

4.3.1.1 Computer coding

To determine member stiffness matrices it is first necessary to specify their geometric and material properties. In the computer progam of Fig. 4.2, this is done by SUBROUTINE INPUT. Variable *NDF* is set to the number of degrees of freedom at a joint. For a plane framework, each joint has three degrees of freedom, two components of translation, and a rotation. Values specifying the numbers of members and joints for a particular problem are set to variables *NM* and *NJ*, respectively. The number of member types (numbers of members with a different stiffness matrix with respect to the x, y coordinate system) is set to variable *NMT*.

Geometric properties for each member type are held in subscripted variable *P*. For each member of type I, $P(I, 1)$ = member length, $P(I, 2) = \cos\alpha$, $P(I, 3) = \sin\alpha$, $P(I, 4) = EA$, $P(I, 5) = EI$ and $P(I, 6)$ stores the number of members of this type. The data cards to be input to enable these values to be determined are specified in Fig. 4.3 on page 242. Here, 'card' refers to card images, or records.

Member, or local, stiffness matrices with respect to (x, y) coordinates are determined in SUBROUTINE LSM, and stored in subscripted variables *SD* and *SOFD*. Advantage is taken of symmetry about the leading diagonal, and of the repetition of coefficients, to reduce the amounts of calculation and storage. Because it is more efficient to operate with singly subscripted variables, *SD* and *SOFD* are one-dimensional. The order in which the stiffness matrix coefficients of a member with three degrees of freedom at each joint are stored is

$$SD = [S_{11}, S_{12}, S_{13}, S_{22}, S_{23}, S_{33}, S_{44}, S_{45}, S_{46}, S_{55}, S_{56}, S_{66}]$$

$$SOFD = [S_{14}, S_{15}, S_{16}, S_{24}, S_{25}, S_{26}, S_{34}, S_{35}, S_{36}]$$

```
      DIMENSIØN P(30,6),PRØPS(5),S(100,50),R(100),SØFD(9),SD(12)
      INTEGER BWNLC,M(50,2)
C     SET PRØBLEM FRØM DATA
      CALL INPUT(P,M,NM,NJ,NMT,NDF,IBW,NLC,S,R,NZERØ)
      NEQ=NJ*NDF
      KEY=0
100   MC=0
      DØ 3 I=1,NMT
      DØ 2 J=1,5
    2 PRØPS(J)=P(I,J)
C     ASSEMBLE LØCAL STIFFNESS MATRIX
      IF(KEY.EQ.0)CALL LSM(SD,SØFD,PRØPS)
      J=P(I,6)+0.5
      DØ 3 JJ=1,J
      MC=MC+1
C     ASSEMBLE GLØBAL STIFFNESS MATRIX
      IF(KEY.EQ.0)CALL ASSMBL(S,SD,SØFD,M(MC,1),M(MC,2),NDF)
      IF(KEY.EQ.1)CALL MEF(S,PRØPS,M(MC,1),M(MC,2),NDF,IBW,BWNLC)
    3 CØNTINUE
      IF(KEY.EQ.1)STØP
      BWNLC=IBW+NLC
C     APPLY RESTRAINTS
      CALL APREST(S,R,NEQ,BWNLC)
C     SØLVE EQUATIØNS
      CALL BSØLV(S,  NEQ,IBW,BWNLC,1E-20)
C     PRINT JØINT DISPLACEMENTS
      DØ 4 LC=1,NLC
      LCW=LC+IBW
      J2=0
      WRITE(6,6000)LC
      WRITE(6,6002)
      DØ 30 JNT=1,NJ
      J1=J2+1
      J2=J2+NDF
   30 WRITE(6,6001)JNT,(S(J,LCW),J=J1,J2)
    4 CØNTINUE
      WRITE(6,6003)
C     MEMBER END FØRCES
      KEY=1
      GØTØ 100
6000  FØRMAT(1H1,14HLØAD CASE NØ  ,I3/1H ,17(1H-)//)
6001  FØRMAT(1H ,I3,3(3X,E12.5))
6002  FØRMAT(1H ,5HJØINT,6X,2HDX,13X,2HDY,11X,5HTHETA/)
6003  FØRMAT(///)
      END

      SUBRØUTINE INPUT(P,M,NM,NJ,NMT,NDF,IW,NLC,S,R,NZ)
      DIMENSIØN P(30,6),M(50,2),S(100,50),R(100)
      DIMENSIØN TITLE(20)
C     NDF - NØ. ØF DEGREES ØF FREEDØM AT A JØINT
C     P - MEMBER PRØPERTIES , M - MEMBER JØINT NUMBERS
      WRITE(6,662)
      NDF=3
      READ(5,500)TITLE
      WRITE(6,600)TITLE
      READ(5,501)NM,NJ,NMT
      WRITE(6,601)NM,NJ,NMT
      MC=1
      DØ 10 I=1,NMT
      READ(5,502)P(I,6)
      WRITE(6,602)P(I,6)
C     X,Y PRØJECTIØNS
      READ(5,503)X,Y
      WRITE(6,603)X,Y
      XYL=SQRT(X**2+Y**2)
      P(I,1)=XYL
      P(I,2)=X/XYL
      P(I,3)=Y/XYL
      READ(5,503)P(I,4),P(I,5)
      WRITE(6,604)(P(I,J),J=1,5)
      MCP=MC+IFIX(P(I,6)+0.5)-1
      READ(5,506)(M(J,1),M(J,2),J=MC,MCP)
      WRITE(6,606)(M(J,1),M(J,2),J=MC,MCP)
   10 MC=MCP+1
      IF(MC-1.EQ.NM)GØTØ 11
```

Figure 4.2 Plane framework program

```
      MC=MC-1
      WRITE(6,901)NM,MC
      STØP
   11 IW=0
C   NE - NØ. ØF EQUATIØNS
      NE=NJ*NDF
      DØ 12 I=1,NM
      J=IABS(M(I,1)-M(I,2))
      IW=MAX0(IW,J)
   12 CØNTINUE
C   IW - BANDWIDTH
      IW=(IW+1)*NDF
C   NLC - NØ. ØF LØADING CASES (R.H.S)
      READ(5,504)NLC
      WRITE(6,614)NLC
C   IWNLC - NØ. ØF CØLUMNS ØF S TØ BE PRØCESSED
      IWNLC=IW+NLC
      DØ 13 I=1,IWNLC
      DØ 13 J=1,NE
   13 S(J,I)=0.0
C   LØADING
      DØ 14 I=1,NLC
      WRITE(6,607)I
      JS=IW+I
      READ(5,501)J1
C   J1 - NØ. ØF LØADED JØINTS
      WRITE(6,612)J1
      DØ 14 J=1,J1
C   JN - LØADED JØINT NUMBER
      READ(5,501)JN
      J2=JN*NDF
      J3=J2-NDF+1
C   LØAD FØR EACH DEGREE ØF FREEDØM
      READ(5,505)(S(K,JS),K=J3,J2)
      WRITE(6,613)JN,(S(K,JS),K=J3,J2)
   14 CØNTINUE
      K1=1
      K2=NLC
      J1=NLC/6
      IF(J1.GT.0)K2=6
   18 WRITE(6,608)K1,K2
      K1W=K1+IW
      K2W=K2+IW
      DØ 16 I=1,NE
      WRITE(6,609) I,(S(I,K),K=K1W,K2W)
   16 CØNTINUE
      K1=K1+6
      K2=K2+6
      IF(K1.GT.NLC)GØTØ 17
      IF(K2.GT.NLC)K2=NLC
      GØTØ 18
C   JØINT RESTRAINTS
   17 DØ 19 I=1,NE
   19 R(I)=0.0
C   NZ - NØ. ØF JØINTS HAVING AT LEAST 1 DEGREE ØF FREEDØM RESTRAINED
      READ(5,504)NZ
      WRITE(6,611)NZ
      DØ 20 I=1,NZ
C   J - JØINT NØ. WITH RESTRAINTS
      READ(5,504)J
      J1=J*NDF
      J2=J1-NDF+1
C   KEY STIFFNESS FØR EACH DEGREE ØF FREEDØM
      READ(5,505)(R(K),K=J2,J1)
   20 CØNTINUE
      WRITE(6,610)(I,R(I),I=1,NE)
      RETURN
C   FØRMAT STATEMENTS
  500 FØRMAT(20A4)
501   FØRMAT(3I5)
502   FØRMAT(F5.0)
503   FØRMAT(2E15.6)
504   FØRMAT(I2)
505   FØRMAT(6E13.6)
```

Figure 4.2 (*continued*)

```
506   FØRMAT(2I5)
600   FØRMAT(1H ,20A4)
601   FØRMAT(1H ,17HNUMBER ØF MEMBERS,I5/
     * 1H ,16HNUMBER ØF JØINTS,I5/
     * 1H ,22HNUMBER ØF MEMBER TYPES,I5/)
602   FØRMAT(1H ,F5.0,24H MEMBERS WITH PRØPERTIES/)
603   FØRMAT(1H ,9HX PRØJ = ,E12.5,13H     Y PRØJ = ,E12.5)
604   FØRMAT(1H ,2HL=,E12.5,4H CA=,E12.5,4H SA=,E12.5/
     * 1H ,3HEA=,E12.5,4H EI=,E12.5)
606   FØRMAT(1H ,8H MEMBERS/1H ,10H    I    J/(1H ,2I5))
607   FØRMAT(1H ,10H LØAD-CASE,I4)
608   FØRMAT(1H ,13H LØAD VECTØRS,I4,4H TØ ,I4)
609   FØRMAT(1H ,I3,6E13.6)
610   FØRMAT(1H ,10HRESTRAINTS//(1H ,I2,E13.6))
611   FØRMAT(1H ,24HNØ ØF RESTRAINED JØINTS ,I5)
612   FØRMAT(1H ,21HNØ ØF LØADED JØINTS =,I5)
613   FØRMAT(1H ,5HJØINT,10X,5HLØADS/1H ,I3,7E15.4)
614   FØRMAT(1H ,19HNØ ØF LØAD CASES = ,I5)
662   FØRMAT(1H ,11HPLANE FRAME/)
901   FØRMAT(1H ,22HERRØR IN NØ ØF MEMBERS/
     * 1H ,13HSTATED NØ IS ,I4/
     * 1H ,30HSUMMATIØN ØF MEMBERS ØF TYPES ,I4/)
      END

      SUBRØUTINE APREST(S,RESTS,NEQ,BWNLC)
      INTEGER BWNLC
      DIMENSIØN S(100,50),RESTS(100)
C
C   APPLY RESTRAINTS TØ STIFFNESS MATRIX
C
      DØ 1 I=1,NEQ
      IF(RESTS(I))2,1,2
    2 S(I,1)=1.0E30
      DØ 3 J=2,BWNLC
      S(I,J)=0.0
    3 CØNTINUE
    1 CØNTINUE
      RETURN
      END
      SUBRØUTINE LSM(SD,SØFD,PRØPS)
      DIMENSIØN SD(12),SØFD(9),PRØPS(5),S1(6)
C   SD - STIFFNESS CØEFFICIENTS , SØFD - RESTRAINT CØEFFICIENTS
      EA=PRØPS(4)
      EI=PRØPS(5)
      C=PRØPS(2)
      S=PRØPS(3)
      RL=1.0/PRØPS(1)
      C2=C**2
      S2=S**2
      SC=S*C
      EIL6=6.0*EI*RL**2
      EIL4=4.0*EI*RL
      EIL12=2.0*EIL6*RL
      EAL=EA*RL
      S1(1)=C2*EAL+S2*EIL12
      S1(2)=SC*(EAL-EIL12)
      S1(3)=-S*EIL6
      S1(4)=S2*EAL+C2*EIL12
      S1(5)=C*EIL6
      S1(6)=EIL4
      SØFD(1)=-S1(1)
      SØFD(2)=-S1(2)
      SØFD(3)=S1(3)
      SØFD(4)=-S1(2)
      SØFD(5)=-S1(4)
      SØFD(6)=S1(5)
      SØFD(7)=-S1(3)
      SØFD(8)=-S1(5)
      SØFD(9)=0.5*S1(6)
      DØ 30 I=1,6
      SD(I)=S1(I)
   30 SD(I+6)=S1(I)
      SD(9)=-SD(9)
```

Figure 4.2 (*continued*)

```
      SD(11)=-SD(11)
      RETURN
      END
      SUBRØUTINE ASSMBL(S,SD,SØFD,I,J,NDF)
      DIMENSIØN S(100,50),SD(12),SØFD(9)
      I1=NDF*(I-1)
      J1=NDF*(J-1)
C   ØFFSET FØR ØFF-DIAGØNAL TERMS
      IJ=IABS(I1-J1)
      IJD=IJ+1
      IP=0
      ID=NDF+1
C   ND - NØ. ØF CØEFFICIENTS FØR A JØINT
      ND=(NDF*(NDF+1))/2
      DØ 10 IC=1,NDF
C   I1IC , J1IC - RØW CØUNTS FØR JØINTS I,J RESP.
      I1IC=I1+IC
      J1IC=J1+IC
      ID=ID-1
C  DIAGØNAL TERMS
      DØ 11 IDC=1,ID
      IP=IP+1
      NDIP=ND+IP
      S(I1IC,IDC)=S(I1IC,IDC)+SD(IP)
      S(J1IC,IDC)=S(J1IC,IDC)+SD(NDIP)
   11 CØNTINUE
C  ØFF DIAGØNAL TERMS
      ICNDF=(IC-1)*NDF
      IJDC=IJD-IC
      IF(I1.LT.J1)GØTØ 12
      DØ 13 K=1,NDF
      IJDCK=IJDC+K
      ICNK=IC+NDF*(K-1)
      S(J1IC,IJDCK)=SØFD(ICNK)
   13 CØNTINUE
      GØTØ 10
   12 DØ 14 K=1,NDF
      IJDCK=IJDC+K
      ICNK=ICNDF+K
      S(I1IC,IJDCK)=SØFD(ICNK)
   14 CØNTINUE
   10 CØNTINUE
      RETURN
      END

      SUBRØUTINE MEF(SS,PRØPS,JI,JJ,NDF,IBW,BWNLC)
      DIMENSIØN SS(100,50),PRØPS(5)
      INTEGER BWNLC
      WRITE(6,6000)
      IR=JI*NDF
      JR=JJ*NDF
      EI=PRØPS(5)
      EA=PRØPS(4)
      S=PRØPS(3)
      C=PRØPS(2)
      RL=PRØPS(1)
      IBW1=IBW+1
      DØ 1 I=IBW1,BWNLC
      L=I-IBW
      DX=SS(JR-2,I)-SS(IR-2,I)
      DY=SS(IR-1,I)-SS(JR-1,I)
      THI=SS(IR,I)
      THJ=SS(JR,I)
      AF=EA/RL*(C*DX-S*DY)
      SF=12.0*EI/RL**3*((S*DX+C*DY)+(THI+THJ)*RL/2.0)
      BMI=6.0*EI/RL**2*((S*DX+C*DY)+(2.0*THI+THJ)*RL/3.0)
      BMJ=SF*RL-BMI
    1 WRITE(6,6001)L,JI,JJ,BMI,BMJ,SF,AF
6000  FØRMAT(1H ,24HLC    I    J         MØMENT I,
     * 42H        MØMENT J           SHEAR    AXIAL FØRCE)
6001  FØRMAT(1H ,I2,2X,I2,2X,I2,4(E14.6))
      RETURN
      END
```

Figure 4.2 (*continued*)

4.3.2 Compilation of overall stiffness matrix

Once a member stiffness matrix has been determined, its contributions to the stiffness matrix of the whole structure can be assembled using the joint numbers at its ends. Rows of the overall stiffness matrix are formed by writing equilibrium equations at joints of the structure.

The process is illustrated by first considering the terms for joint 6 of a structure having three degrees of freedom at each joint. Assume that three members meet at joint 6, and that the joint numbers at their other ends are as shown in Fig. 4.4. The arrows on the members indicate the positive directions of the local p axes. Thus, for member M_1, $i = 3$ and $j = 6$; for member M_2, $i = 6$ and $j = 7$; and for member M_3, $i = 10$ and $j = 6$.

Let $\mathbf{F}_6^{m1}$, $\mathbf{F}_6^{m2}$, $\mathbf{F}_6^{m3}$ be the forces exerted on the ends of members M_1, M_2, M_3 at joint 6, and $\mathbf{F}_6^{a}$ be the externally applied force to joint 6. For a joint with three degrees of freedom, each **F** vector has three components and it is assumed that they are referred to the global axis system, so that corresponding components are in the

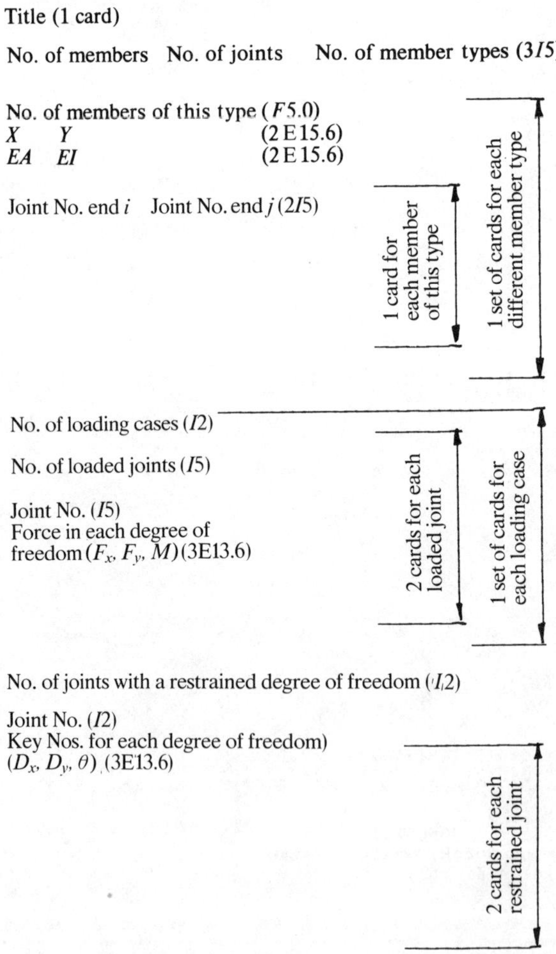

Figure 4.3 Layout of data

same directions. Equilibrium of forces acting at joint 6 gives

$$\mathbf{F}_6^a = \mathbf{F}_6^{m1} + \mathbf{F}_6^{m2} + \mathbf{F}_6^{m3}$$

If $\mathbf{D}_6, \mathbf{D}_3, \mathbf{D}_7, \mathbf{D}_{10}$, are the vectors of displacements, with components referred to the global axis system, of joints, 6, 3, 7, 10, respectively; $\mathbf{S}_{ii}^{m1}, \mathbf{S}_{ii}^{m2}, \mathbf{S}_{ii}^{m3}, \mathbf{S}_{jj}^{m1}$, $\mathbf{S}_{jj}^{m2}, \mathbf{S}_{jj}^{m3}$, are 3 × 3 sub-matrices of stiffness coefficients of members connecting joints i and j; and $\mathbf{S}_{ij}^{m1}, \mathbf{S}_{ij}^{m2}, \mathbf{S}_{ij}^{m3}, \mathbf{S}_{ji}^{m1}, \mathbf{S}_{ji}^{m2}, \mathbf{S}_{ji}^{m3}$, are 3 × 3 sub-matrices of restraint coefficients; then

$$\mathbf{F}_6^a = \mathbf{S}_{jj}^{m1}\mathbf{D}_6 + \mathbf{S}_{ji}^{m1}\mathbf{D}_3 + \mathbf{S}_{ii}^{m2}\mathbf{D}_6 + \mathbf{S}_{ij}^{m2}\mathbf{D}_7 + \mathbf{S}_{jj}^{m3}\mathbf{D}_6 + \mathbf{S}_{ji}^{m3}\mathbf{D}_{10}$$

or

$$\mathbf{F}_6^a = (\mathbf{S}_{jj}^{m1} + \mathbf{S}_{ii}^{m2} + \mathbf{S}_{jj}^{m3})\mathbf{D}_6 + \mathbf{S}_{ji}^{m1}\mathbf{D}_3 + \mathbf{S}_{ij}^{m2}\mathbf{D}_7 + \mathbf{S}_{ji}^{m3}\mathbf{D}_{10}$$

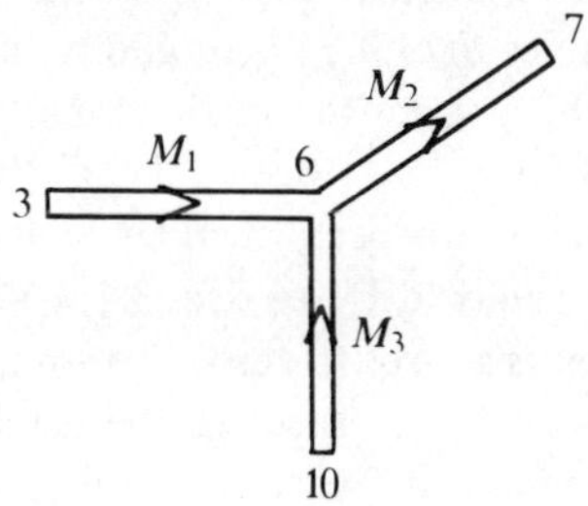

Figure 4.4 Member connectivity

This equation contains all of the non-zero terms of equations 16, 17, 18 of the overall stiffness matrix equation. If **SS** represents the overall stiffness matrix, then the non-zero coefficients corresponding to joint 6 are given by

$$\mathbf{SS}_{6,6} = (\mathbf{S}_{jj}^{m1} + \mathbf{S}_{ii}^{m2} + \mathbf{S}_{jj}^{m3}) \qquad \mathbf{SS}_{6,3} = \mathbf{S}_{ji}^{m1} \qquad \mathbf{SS}_{6,7} = \mathbf{S}_{ij}^{m2}$$

$$\mathbf{SS}_{6,10} = \mathbf{S}_{ji}^{m3}$$

Procedures to automatically compile an overall stiffness matrix can be constructed from member stiffness matrices and end joint numbers. If the joint numbers of ends i, j of member K are held in $M(K, 1)$ and $M(K, 2)$, respectively, the following FORTRAN coding illustrates the computational procedure.

```
      DO 1 I=1, 2
C     NDF—NO. OF DEGREES OF FREEDOM AT A JOINT
      IR=(M(K, I)–1)*NDF
      DO 1 J=1, 2
      JC=(M(K, J)–1)*NDF
      DO 1 I1=1, NDF
      ISS=IR+I1
      IS=I1+(I–1)*NDF
```

```
      DO 1 J1=1, NDF
      JSS=JC+J1
      JS=J1+(J-1)*NDF
1     SS(ISS, JSS)=SS(ISS, JSS)+S(IS, JS)
```

4.3.2.1 Computer coding

Although this coding illustrates the simple nature of operations to compile a stiffness matrix, the need for computational efficiency does not allow it to be used directly. Operations are complicated, as only the upper triangular part of member stiffness matrices are held in singly subscripted variables *SD, SOFD.* In addition, only part of the overall stiffness matrix is held, and this is arranged in the doubly subscripted variable *S*, using the layout shown in Fig. 3.10.

In the program in Fig. 4.2, preliminary operations are performed in SUBROUTINE INPUT. Between statements 11 and 13 the bandwidth (see Sec. 3.1.3.3) *IW* is calculated and all overall stiffness matrix coefficients are set to zero. The total number of equilibrium equations to be set up and solved, *NE*, is set to the total number of joints *NJ,* multiplied by the number of degrees of freedom at a joint, *NDF*. The bandwidth is calculated from the maximum difference between joint numbers at the ends of any member +1, multiplied by *NDF*. This indicates that joints should be numbered in such a manner that the maximum difference between joint numbers is made as small as possible. Variable *S* is augmented by increasing the number of columns to hold the applied load vectors. The number of applied load vectors (or, number of loading cases) is held by variable *NLC.*

The overall stiffness matrix is assembled during execution of the DO statement with terminating statement labelled '3' in the main program segment. The loop is executed for each member type. First, the member stiffness matrix coefficients are calculated and stored in *SD* and *SOFD* by SUBROUTINE LSM. SUBROUTINE ASSMBL is then executed for each member having that local stiffness matrix. The joint numbers at the ends of members are held in subscripted variable *M*, and variable *MC* is used to pick the joints of each member in turn.

Study of ASSMBL will show that it performs the basic operations outlined in Sec. 4.3.2, but with additional positional counters, because of the storage arrangements used. This form of storage is adequate for most purposes, but for structures with an exceptionally large number of joints, the coefficients of the overall stiffness matrix would be held in a singly subscripted variable using a variable bandwidth.

4.3.3 Loading

Loading is applied to the joints of the mathematical model of the structure. This is done by specifying the number of joints subjected to an applied load, and, for each, the joint number and the components of load corresponding to each degree of freedom.

Critical conditions at different parts of a structure can be caused by different arrangements of loading. It is, therefore, usual to analyse a structure for a number of loading cases. As the solution of any number of loading cases can be obtained from a single processing of the stiffness matrix coefficients, the loading vectors are inserted into the columns of the augmented S matrix and processed in turn (see Sec. 3.1.3).

4.3.3.1 Computer coding

Loading data is set by SUBROUTINE INPUT. After the statement labelled 12, the number of load vectors is read and set to variable *NLC*. The DO statements, with terminating label 13, set the columns of *S* used to hold coefficients of the load vectors to zero. Non-zero coefficients are read and set in the statements controlled by the DO statement with terminating label 14. The layout of corresponding data is given in Fig. 4.3.

4.3.4 Displacement boundary conditions

The actions of the supporting structural system are simulated by modifying diagonal coefficients of the stiffness matrix. If it is known that a joint is supported, so that movement in any, or all, of its potential degrees of freedom is prevented, then very large numbers are added to the corresponding diagonal coefficients. This has the effect of imposing zero displacements in the directions associated with those degrees of freedom. It is essential that sufficient restraints to prevent displacement of the structure as a whole (rigid-body displacement) in any direction are specified, as otherwise the set of equations would be homogeneous and would not have a unique solution.

4.3.4.1 Computer coding

Boundary condition data is set by SUBROUTINE INPUT. A singly subscripted variable *R* is set to zero by the DO statement with terminating label 19. The number of joints with at least one zero displacement component is read and set to variable *NZ*. For each of these joints, the joint number, and key values for each degree of freedom are input. The key is non-zero for a restrained degree of freedom. In the part of the program controlled by the DO statement with terminating label 20, coefficients of *R* are given a non-zero value for each equation corresponding to a restrained degree of freedom.

When SUBROUTINE INPUT has been executed, the main program transfers control to SUBROUTINE APREST. This applies the restraints by adding 1.0E30 to each diagonal term of the stiffness matrix, for which the value of the corresponding row of **R** is non-zero. It also sets the other coefficients of *S* on these rows to zero.

4.3.5 Solution of equations

The equations are solved using the SUBROUTINE BSOLV described in Sec. 3.1.3.3. Because of the way that supports are represented, the statement:

```
IF(RESTR(I))200,206,200
```

can be added immediately before the statement labelled 206 in Fig. 3.9. The coefficients of *RESTR* correspond to those of *R*. The effect of incorporating this statement is to prevent further unnecessary processing of equations corresponding to restrained degrees of freedom.

4.3.6 Displacements and end forces

Solution of the equilibrium equations results in values of joint displacements. Although they are of limited value in design, all joint displacement components are usually printed by a computer program.

End forces on each member are determined by back-substituting the determined joint deflections into the stiffness equations. For a typical member,

$$\begin{bmatrix} Fpq_i \\ Fpq_j \end{bmatrix} = \begin{bmatrix} \bar{S}_{ii} \cdot T & \bar{S}_{ij} \cdot T \\ \bar{S}_{ji} \cdot T & \bar{S}_{jj} \cdot T \end{bmatrix} \begin{bmatrix} Dxy_i \\ Dxy_j \end{bmatrix}$$

4.3.6.1 Computer coding

In the program of Fig. 4.2, the displacement values are printed by the DO statement with terminating label 30.

The end forces on members are calculated by transferring control back to the statement labelled 100 in the main program segment with KEY=1. This causes SUBROUTINE MEF to calculate and print the member end forces for each loading case. The results are given for each member, in the order in which the members are listed in the data.

4.3.7 Member loading

Loading applied to members of a structure is treated in three stages. First, each member is analysed with its ends restrained against displacement. Effectively, the analyst adds a set of joint forces, which, together with the member loadings, results in no joint displacements. The contributions of each member to these additional joint forces are the reactions necessary to prevent end displacements. For a prismatic beam member, they are the familiar fixed end forces.

In the second stage, the structure is analysed for the effects of the applied joint loads, minus the member reactive forces calculated in the first stage. The procedure is completed by summing the results of the first two stages. It should be appreciated that the additional joint forces, introduced for the first stage, are removed by the second-stage analysis.

4.3.8 Example

To illustrate the solution procedure, consider analysis of the simple plane framework shown in Fig. 4.5. The joint numbering, restraints, and loading used in the analysis are shown in Fig. 4.6. Results of the analysis form Fig. 4.7 and Fig. 4.8. As an exercise the interested reader should construct the data submitted to the computer program. The information in Fig. 4.7 is expressed in kN and mm units.

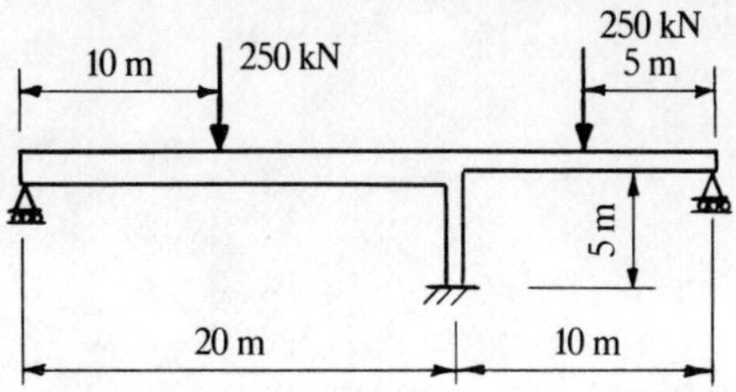

Figure 4.5 Example framework

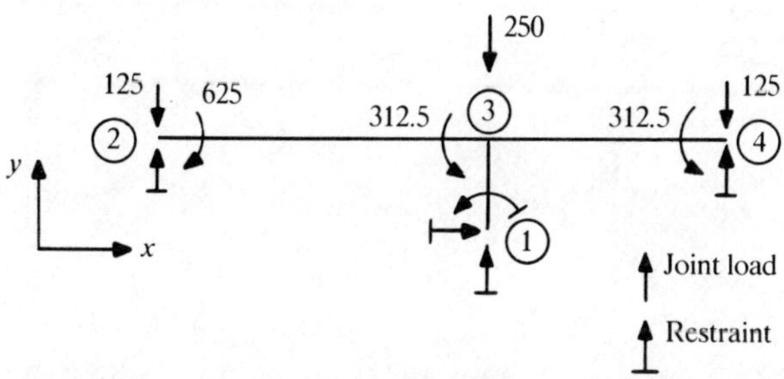

Figure 4.6 Skeletal structure analysed by program

```
PLANE FRAME

EXAMPLE
NUMBER ØF MEMBERS     3
NUMBER ØF JØINTS     4
NUMBER ØF MEMBER TYPES     3

   1. MEMBERS WITH PRØPERTIES

X PRØJ =  0.20000E 05     Y PRØJ =  0.00000E 00
L= 0.20000E 05 CA= 0.10000E 01 SA= 0.00000E 00
EA= 0.10000E 08 EI= 0.41700E 12
 MEMBERS
    I     J
    2     3
   1. MEMBERS WITH PRØPERTIES

X PRØJ =  0.10000E 05     Y PRØJ =  0.00000E 00
L= 0.10000E 05 CA= 0.10000E 01 SA= 0.00000E 00
EA= 0.80000E 07 EI= 0.20800E 12
 MEMBERS
    I     J
    3     4
   1. MEMBERS WITH PRØPERTIES

X PRØJ =  0.00000E 00     Y PRØJ =  0.50000E 04
L= 0.50000E 04 CA= 0.00000E 00 SA= 0.10000E 01
EA= 0.50000E 07 EI= 0.10400E 12
 MEMBERS
    I     J
    1     3
NØ ØF LØAD CASES =      1
 LØAD-CASE    1
NØ ØF LØADED JØINTS =      3
JØINT          LØADS
  2      0.0000E 00    -0.1250E 03     -0.6250E 06
JØINT          LØADS
  3      0.0000E 00    -0.2500E 03      0.3125E 06
JØINT          LØADS
  4      0.0000E 00    -0.1250E 03      0.3125E 06
```

Figure 4.7

```
LØAD VECTØRS    1 TØ    1
  1 0.000000E 00
  2 0.000000E 00
  3 0.000000E 00
  4 0.000000E 00
  5-0.125000E 03
  6-0.625000E 06
  7 0.000000E 00
  8-0.250000E 03
  9 0.312500E 06
 10 0.000000E 00
 11-0.125000E 03
 12 0.312500E 06
NØ ØF RESTRAINED JØINTS     3
RESTRAINTS

  1 0.100000E 01
  2 0.100000E 01
  3 0.100000E 01
  4 0.000000E 00
  5 0.100000E 01
  6 0.000000E 00
  7 0.000000E 00
  8 0.000000E 00
  9 0.000000E 00
 10 0.000000E 00
 11 0.100000E 01
 12 0.000000E 00

LØAD CASE NØ     1
-----------------


JØINT        DX                DY                THETA

   1      0.00000E 00      0.00000E 00      0.00000E 00
   2     -0.80592E 01      0.00000E 00     -0.91324E-02
   3     -0.80592E 01     -0.35351E 00      0.32237E-02
   4     -0.80592E 01      0.00000E 00      0.21972E-02


LC   I   J       MØMENT I        MØMENT J          SHEAR     AXIAL FØRCE
 1   2   3 -0.625000E 06 -0.109754E 06 -0.367377E 02  0.000000E 00
LC   I   J       MØMENT I        MØMENT J          SHEAR     AXIAL FØRCE
 1   3   4  0.355201E 06  0.312500E 06  0.667701E 02  0.000000E 00
LC   I   J       MØMENT I        MØMENT J          SHEAR     AXIAL FØRCE
 1   1   3 -0.670524E 05  0.670524E 05  0.581145E-07 -0.353508E 03
```

Figure 4.7 (*continued*)

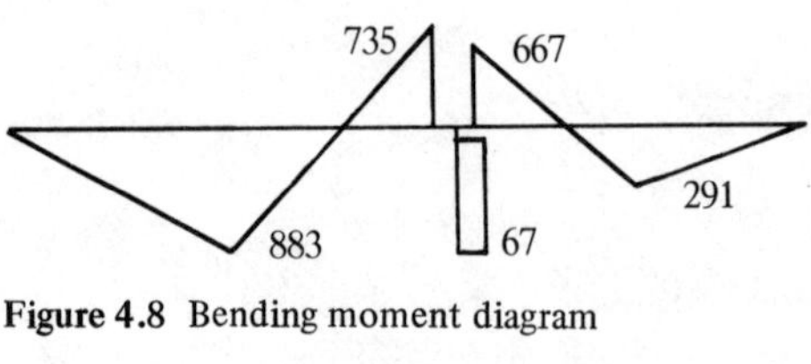

Figure 4.8 Bending moment diagram

4.3.9 Applied displacements

In the program of Fig. 4.2. there is a facility to impose zero displacement in the directions of selected degrees of freedom. This facility can be used to represent rigid supports, and also to reduce the number of equations that need to be assembled when there is a plane of symmetry.

Engineers sometimes have to determine the effects of specified non-zero displacements at joints of a structure. For such analyses the stiffness matrix and load vector have to be modified before solution. The technique is illustrated using the equations $\mathbf{F} = \mathbf{S} \cdot \mathbf{D}$, where $\mathbf{F}$ is the load vector, $\mathbf{S}$ the assembled stiffness matrix for a complete structure, and $\mathbf{D}$ the displacement vector. Suppose that the equations are given by

$$\begin{bmatrix} F_1 \\ F_2 \\ F_3 \\ F_4 \\ F_5 \end{bmatrix} = \begin{bmatrix} S_{11} & S_{12} & S_{13} & S_{14} & S_{15} \\ S_{12} & S_{22} & S_{23} & S_{24} & S_{25} \\ S_{13} & S_{23} & S_{33} & S_{34} & S_{35} \\ S_{14} & S_{24} & S_{34} & S_{44} & S_{45} \\ S_{15} & S_{25} & S_{35} & S_{45} & S_{55} \end{bmatrix} \begin{bmatrix} D_1 \\ D_2 \\ D_3 \\ D_4 \\ D_5 \end{bmatrix}$$

and that D_4 equals the specified value d. Instead of five unknowns, there are now only four, and any one of the equations can be removed from the set. To maintain symmetry of the stiffness matrix coefficients, the equation corresponding to the degree of freedom of the known displacement is removed. In a computer program it is usually more efficient to retain the layout of the stiffness matrix, and to insert zeros to eliminate any effect from the redundant equation. The processed equations for solution are

$$\begin{bmatrix} F_1 - S_{14}d \\ F_2 - S_{24}d \\ F_3 - S_{34}d \\ d \\ F_5 - S_{45}d \end{bmatrix} = \begin{bmatrix} S_{11} & S_{12} & S_{13} & 0 & S_{15} \\ S_{12} & S_{22} & S_{23} & 0 & S_{25} \\ S_{13} & S_{23} & S_{33} & 0 & S_{35} \\ 0 & 0 & 0 & 1 & 0 \\ S_{15} & S_{25} & S_{35} & 0 & S_{55} \end{bmatrix} \begin{bmatrix} D_1 \\ D_2 \\ D_3 \\ d \\ D_5 \end{bmatrix}$$

Once the load vector has been modified, the processing is similar to that for a restrained degree of freedom.

4.3.10 Instability

When the columns of a framework are subjected to high compressive axial forces P $(= Fp)$, the structural response becomes non-linear; see Fig. 4.9. Standard texts on

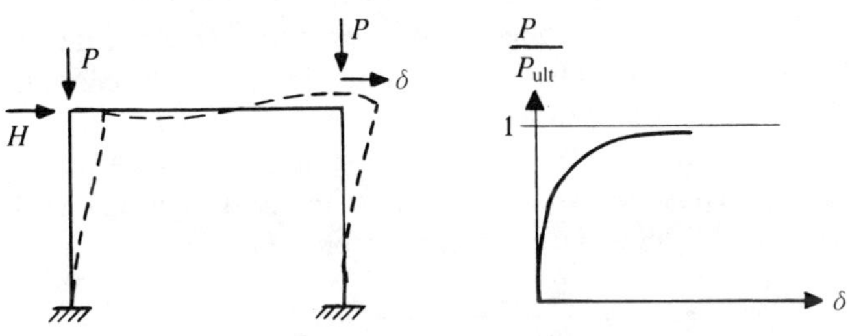

Figure 4.9 Instability effect

structural analysis[1] show that if

$$k = \frac{EI}{L} \qquad \bar{\alpha} = \frac{L}{2}\sqrt{\frac{P}{EI}} \qquad \bar{s} = \frac{(1 - 2\bar{\alpha} \cot 2\bar{\alpha})\,\bar{\alpha}}{\tan \bar{\alpha} - \bar{\alpha}}$$

and

$$\bar{c} = \frac{2\bar{\alpha} - \sin 2\bar{\alpha}}{\sin 2\bar{\alpha} - 2\bar{\alpha} \cos 2\bar{\alpha}}$$

then the member stiffness matrix with respect to local coordinate axes (p, q) is

$$\left[\begin{array}{ccc|ccc}
\frac{EA}{L} & 0 & 0 & -\frac{EA}{L} & 0 & 0 \\
0 & \beta_1 \frac{k}{L} & \beta_2 \frac{k}{L} & 0 & -\beta_1 \frac{k}{L} & \beta_2 \frac{k}{L} \\
0 & \beta_2 \frac{k}{L} & \bar{s}\,k & 0 & -\beta_2 \frac{k}{L} & \bar{s}\,\bar{c}\,k \\
\hline
-\frac{EA}{L} & 0 & 0 & \frac{EA}{L} & 0 & 0 \\
0 & -\beta_1 \frac{k}{L} & -\beta_2 \frac{k}{L} & 0 & \beta_1 \frac{k}{L} & -\beta_2 \frac{k}{L} \\
0 & \beta_2 \frac{k}{L} & \bar{s}\,\bar{c}\,k & 0 & -\beta_2 \frac{k}{L} & \bar{s}\,k
\end{array}\right]$$

where $\beta_1 = 2(\bar{s}(1 + \bar{c}) - 2\bar{\alpha}^2)/L$ and $\beta_2 = \bar{s}(1 + \bar{c})$

For $P = 0$, the matrix is the same as that given in Sec. 4.3.1. As P increases, $\bar{s}$ decreases, and becomes negative when P is greater than 2.05 times the Euler buckling load. The parameter $\bar{c}$ increases with P, at first slowly and then rapidly until, at the same value of P, it too changes sign. Loads higher than the Euler buckling load can be supported because of the restraining action of the members connected to the column ends.

For many structures, the effects of axial force on flexural stiffness coefficients are negligible. When an engineer decides it is necessary to assess them, an iterative procedure can be used to circumvent the problems of nonlinear analysis. First, the structure is analysed assuming no interaction effects, or with stiffnesses modified for estimated values of axial loading. The values of axial forces obtained are then used to obtain improved values of stiffnesses for a further analysis. The process is repeated, until an acceptable degree of accuracy has been obtained. Since the process is straightforward, and can proceed without human intervention, the computer program can be modified to perform all of the operations automatically.

A tensile axial force in a member also effects the flexural stiffness coefficients. In particular, $\bar{s}$ increases progressively with P, as can be observed by watching the rotor blades of a helicopter straighten under centrifugal force. For this case,

$$\bar{s} = \frac{(1 - 2\bar{\alpha} \coth 2\bar{\alpha})\,\bar{\alpha}}{\tanh \bar{\alpha} - \bar{\alpha}} \qquad \bar{c} = \frac{2\bar{\alpha} - \sinh 2\bar{\alpha}}{\sinh 2\bar{\alpha} - 2\bar{\alpha} \cosh 2\bar{\alpha}}$$

and $\bar{\alpha}$ is determined using the absolute value of P.

4.3.11 Shear strains

For members whose flexural behaviour is likely to be influenced by shear strains, the stiffness coefficients should be amended. The modifications can be achieved by simply multiplying the coefficients by parameters related to the section properties. The terms $6EI/L^2$ and $12EI/L^3$ are multiplied by $n/(n+12)$, $4EI/L$ terms are multiplied by $(n+3)/(n+12)$, and $2EI/L$ terms are multiplied by $(n-6)/(n+12)$, where $n = \beta AGL^2/EI$. A is the cross-sectional area, I the second moment of area about the bending axis, E and G are the elastic moduli for axial and shear stresses, and β is a fraction whose value depends upon the cross-section shape. For a rectangular beam, $\beta = \frac{5}{6}$, for an I-beam or box beam $\beta \simeq$ area of web/A. In the formula for n, L is the distance between applied forces which cause shearing strains.

For most members, the value of n will be so large that the multipliers will be close to unity. When this is not the case, a specialist text on structural analysis[2] should be consulted to obtain values of β. It should be noted that the expressions for a rectangular cross-section are in agreement with those obtained using finite-element methods in Sec. 3.5.3.1.

4.3.12 Pinned member

For a pinned member in a plane framework, it is convenient to retain 3 degrees of freedom at each joint. Since the rotation at the end of a pinned member is not the same as that of the joint, there is actually an extra degree of freedom for each pinned end at the joint.

For example, at joint 4 of the structure shown in Fig. 4.10, the method of construction ensures that moments cannot be transmitted between the beam and

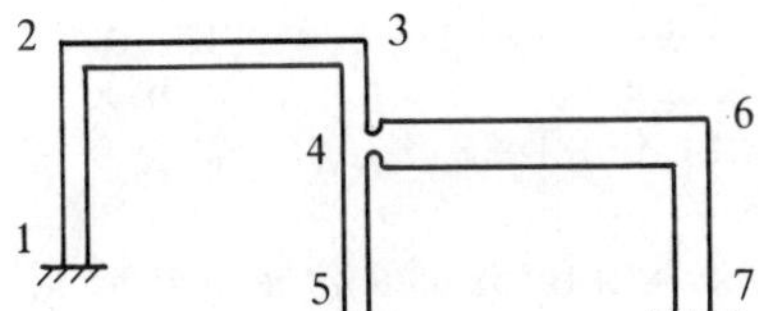

Figure 4.10 Member with 'pinned' end

column. The stiffness matrix for member 4–6 is given by

$$\begin{bmatrix} M_4 \\ F_4 \\ M_6 \\ F_6 \end{bmatrix} = \frac{EI}{L} \begin{bmatrix} 4 & 6/L & 2 & -6/L \\ 6/L & 12/L^2 & 6/L & -12/L^2 \\ 2 & 6/L & 4 & -6/L \\ -6/L & -12/L^2 & -6/L & 12/L^2 \end{bmatrix} \begin{bmatrix} \theta_4 \\ Dq_4 \\ \theta_6 \\ Dq_6 \end{bmatrix}$$

Since $M_4 = 0$, $\theta_4 = -1.5/L\ Dq_4 - 0.5\theta_6 + 1.5/L\ Dq_6$, and hence the stiffness equation can be written in the form

$$\begin{bmatrix} M_4 \\ F_4 \\ M_6 \\ F_6 \end{bmatrix} = \frac{3EI}{L^2} \begin{bmatrix} 0 & 0 & 0 & 0 \\ 0 & 1/L & 1 & -1/L \\ 0 & 1 & L & -1 \\ 0 & -1/L & -1 & 1/L \end{bmatrix} \begin{bmatrix} \theta_4 \\ Dq_4 \\ \theta_6 \\ Dq_6 \end{bmatrix}$$

In a computer program which caters for members with pinned ends, it is necessary to have statements to set up such matrices and for conditional statements to select which matrix to use. One of the popular methods for identifying a member with a pinned end is to give the relevant joint number a negative sign when the member joint numbers are specified as data.

If the pinned connection is formed in concrete, a designer may be interested in the rotation at the hinge, in order to assess the rotational capacity of the section. This can be readily obtained from the information to hand, as will be demonstrated for joint 4 of the example. The rotation of the column θ_{4c} is given by the stiffness analysis of the framework, and the rotation of the beam is shown above to be given by $\theta_{4b} = -1.5/L\ Dq_4 - 0.5\theta_6 + 1.5/L\ Dq_6$. The rotational discontinuity at the hinge is given by $\theta_{4c} - \theta_{4b}$.

4.3.13 Plastic hinges

In elastic–plastic theory, a member is assumed to behave in a linear elastic manner under increasing load, until all of the material on a cross-section has yielded. When this happens, a plastic hinge is assumed to have formed at the section and this has zero stiffness to any further loading. Effectively, the end moment is constant, and its value can be determined from the geometric and material properties of the cross-section. An estimate of the collapse load for a framework can be obtained by following the successive formation of hinges with increasing load intensity until a mechanism forms. A computer program for analysis of skeletal structures can be amended to automatically follow the behaviour of a framework as it is loaded progressively to failure. In addition to the data described in Fig. 4.3, it is necessary to specify the full plastic moment capacity at the ends of each member. Since plastic moments can form only under concentrated loading, a joint is specified at each point of load application, and distributed loading is replaced by a series of concentrated loads.

Loading is applied to a frame and the member section at which the next hinge will form is determined. This calculation involves the ratios of applied moment to the plastic moment of each section and the rate of change of moment as loading is increased. The loading is then factored, so that at the critical section the applied moment becomes equal to its fully plastic moment. A record is taken of all joint displacements, and the stiffness matrix is recomputed with member stiffness matrices for members with pinned ends used for those members with a plastic hinge. The loading is then increased until the next plastic hinge forms. By repeating this process, the load-displacement history of a structure can be traced. The analysis is terminated when a limiting displacement is reached or when a mechanism forms.

The rotational discontinuities at hinges can be assessed by the method described for a pinned member, but in this case the end moments are equal to the full plastic moments and not to zero.

4.3.14 Varying section members

When geometric properties, such as overall depth, web width, or flange thickness, vary along a member's length, explicit stiffness matrices are not used. There is an infinite number of possible cross-sectional variations for a member, and the only feasible approach for automatic analysis is to have a SUBROUTINE to determine the stiffness matrix coefficients for any member from its geometric and material properties. The procedure is illustrated for a beam member. The local (p, q) axis system has its origin located at the centroid of end i, with the p axis passing through the centroids of all sections. Its deviation from a straight line is assumed not to affect the analysis. In general terms, the stiffness matrix for a beam element can be expressed as

$$\begin{bmatrix} M_i \\ F_i \\ M_j \\ F_j \end{bmatrix} = \begin{bmatrix} S_{11} & S_{12} & S_{13} & S_{14} \\ S_{12} & S_{22} & S_{23} & S_{24} \\ S_{13} & S_{23} & S_{33} & S_{34} \\ S_{14} & S_{24} & S_{34} & S_{44} \end{bmatrix} \begin{bmatrix} \theta_i \\ Dq_i \\ \theta_j \\ Dq_j \end{bmatrix}$$

Equilibrium equations enable the number of coefficients to be reduced, so that:

$$\begin{bmatrix} M_i \\ F_i \\ M_j \\ F_j \end{bmatrix} = \begin{bmatrix} S_{11} & S_{12} & LS_{12}-S_{11} & -S_{12} \\ S_{12} & S_{22} & LS_{22}-S_{12} & -S_{22} \\ LS_{12}-S_{11} & LS_{22}-S_{12} & (L^2S_{22}-2LS_{12}+S_{11}) & S_{12}-LS_{22} \\ -S_{12} & -S_{22} & S_{12}-LS_{22} & S_{22} \end{bmatrix} \begin{bmatrix} \theta_i \\ Dq_i \\ \theta_j \\ Dq_j \end{bmatrix}$$

The three independent coefficients remaining are determined with the aid of Castigliano's theorem. If U is the strain energy stored in a member when end loads are applied, then

$$\frac{\partial U}{\partial M_i} = \theta_i \qquad \frac{\partial U}{\partial F_i} = Dq_i \qquad \frac{\partial U}{\partial M_j} = \theta_j \qquad \frac{\partial U}{\partial F_j} = Dq_j$$

When flexural energy is the major part of the strain energy, $U = \int_0^L M^2 \, dp/2EI$, where M is the bending moment at p, I is the second moment of area about the bending axis at p, and E is Young's modulus. Therefore, as $M = F_i p - M_i$,

$$\theta_i = \frac{\partial}{\partial M_i}\left(\int_0^L \frac{(F_i p - M_i)^2}{2EI} \, dp\right) = \int_0^L \frac{M_i - F_i p}{EI} \, dp$$

and

$$Dq_i = \frac{\partial}{\partial F_i}\left(\int_0^L \frac{(F_i p - M_i)^2}{2EI} \, dp\right) = \int_0^L \frac{F_i p^2 - M_i p}{EI} \, dp$$

These expressions are valid for all values of joint displacements, and if we consider the case $Dq_i = \theta_j = Dq_j = 0$,

$$F_i \int_0^L \frac{p^2 \, dp}{EI} = M_i \int_0^L \frac{p \, dp}{EI} \qquad \text{and hence} \qquad \theta_i = M_i\left(\int_0^L \frac{dp}{EI} - \frac{\left(\int_0^L \frac{p\,dp}{EI}\right)^2}{\int_0^L \frac{p^2\,dp}{EI}}\right)$$

For the displacements taken $M_i = S_{11}\theta_i$, and hence:

$$S_{11} = \frac{I_2}{I_0 I_2 - I_1^2}$$

where

$$I_0 = \int_0^L \frac{dp}{EI} \qquad I_1 = \int_0^L \frac{p\,dp}{EI} \qquad I_2 = \int_0^L \frac{p^2\,dp}{EI}$$

As $F_i I_2 = M_i I_1$,

$$F_i = \frac{I_1}{I_0 I_2 - I_1^2}\theta_i \qquad \text{and hence} \qquad S_{12} = \frac{I_1}{I_0 I_2 - I_1^2}$$

S_{22} is determined by analysing the beam with $\theta_i = \theta_j = Dq_j = 0$. As $\theta_i = \int_0^L (M_i - F_i p)/EI\,dp = 0$,

$$M_i I_0 = F_i I_1 \qquad \text{and hence} \qquad M_i = \frac{I_1}{I_0} F_i$$

As $Dq_i = \int_0^L (F_i p^2 - M_i p)/EI\,dp$,

$$Dq_i = F_i I_2 - F_i \frac{I_1^2}{I_0} \quad \text{thus} \quad F_i = \frac{I_0}{I_0 I_2 - I_1^2} Dq_i \quad \text{and hence} \quad S_{22} = \frac{I_0}{I_0 I_2 - I_1^2}$$

In a computer program, values of the second moment of area I are input at a number of stations along the span. If necessary, the method described in Sec. 3.3.3 can be used to determine values of I for complicated cross-sectional shapes. The integrals I_0, I_1, I_2 are determined using a numerical integration procedure. When evenly spaced stations are used, Simpson's method is used as described in Sec. 3.3.1.1, but for maximum computational efficiency, a Gauss integration scheme would be used; see Sec. 3.3.1.2.

4.3.15 Influence lines

Influence lines can be used as a guide to the positioning of mobile loads to produce the worst effects at a section of interest. The ordinates of an influence line (or surface) diagram give the values of a particular stress resultant (moment, axial force, shear) due to loading at the points where the ordinates are located.

An influence line can be determined by analysing a structure for unit loads placed at each ordinate position in turn. Values of the stress resultant at the section of interest are plotted to give the influence line. This can be done automatically by a computer program, but the process is inefficient, unless a relatively large number of influence lines are required.

When few influence lines are needed, each one can be produced from a single analysis of a structure by use of specially devised load vectors. The procedure is illustrated by considering the influence line for the end couple on a beam. The end couple at the left-hand end is given by

$$M_i = \frac{6EI}{L^2} Dq_i + \frac{4EI}{L}\theta_i - \frac{6EI}{L^2} Dq_j + \frac{2EI}{L}\theta_j + MF_i$$

where MF_i is the couple at end i caused by loading incident on the member with ends of the member restrained against displacement (fixed end moment). The influence line for M_i can, therefore, be thought of as the influence line for Dq_i multiplied by $6EI/L^2$ + the influence line for θ_i scaled by $4EI/L$, etc., plus the effects of MF_i on the member i–j itself. Standard texts on structural analysis[1] show that the influence line for a displacement is given by the ordinates of the deflected shape of a structure when a unit load, acting in the same direction as the displacement, is applied at the point for which the influence line is required. The influence line for M_i is, therefore, given by the deflected shape of the structure due to the load vector:

$$Fq_i = \frac{6EI}{L^2} \qquad M_i = \frac{4EI}{L} \qquad Fq_j = -\frac{6EI}{L^2} \qquad M_j = \frac{2EI}{L}$$

with modification to the ordinates for member i–j due to MF_i. For a unit vertical load distance p from i, $MF_i = -p(L-p)^2/L^2$, and this expression, therefore, gives the additional ordinates over member i–j.

The procedure is illustrated for a three-span beam in Fig. 4.11.

4.3.16 Finite-element analysis

The finite-element procedure enables a structural continuum such as a slab, or a

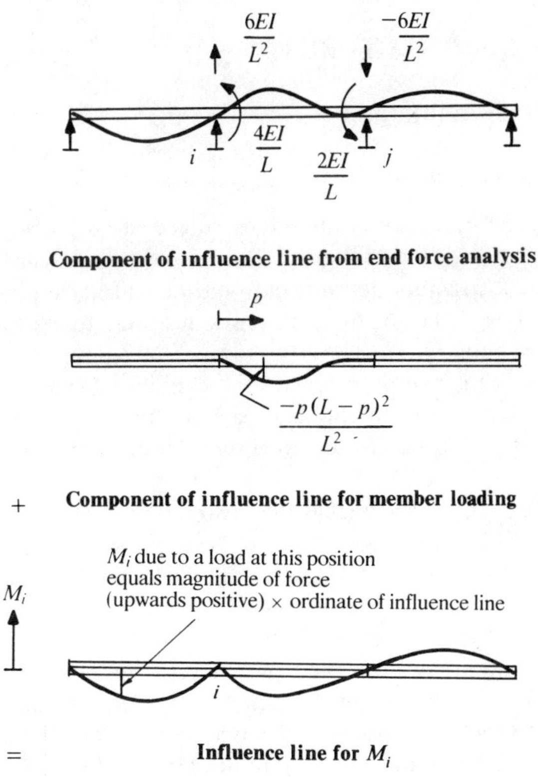

Figure 4.11 Illustration of influence line determination

shell, to be analysed by the stiffness method. In Sec. 3.5, techniques for deriving 'member' stiffness matrices were discussed. For a few simple cases, it was shown that matrices identical in form to member stiffness matrices could be derived and assembled automatically to form the 'stiffness' matrix for a continuum. Specialists texts[3] give many alternative finite-element stiffness matrices, which now cover most practical problems.

The computational procedure to solve finite-element formulations is similar to that used for skeletal structures, and it is a simple matter to amend a computer program for the solution of skeletal structures to solve finite-element problems. Connectivity is specified by giving the node (joint) numbers of each element in a prescribed order, as was done for linear members. The number of 'equilibrium' equations for each node is set by specifying the number of degrees of freedom, as was done for skeletal structures. The same solution-of-equations procedure can be used to obtain the nodal 'displacements'. An engineer is not usually interested in values of nodal 'forces', unless they are reactions. Once nodal displacements have been obtained, derivatives of the shape functions and material properties are used to give estimates of the distribution of 'stress-resultants' over each element. This is too advanced a topic to deal with in detail here, and the interested reader is referred to monographs on the finite-element method.[3]

4.4 DYNAMIC RESPONSE OF STRUCTURES

4.4.1 Equations of Dynamic Equilibrium

4.4.1.1 Basic properties of a dynamic structure

The previous section discussed the response of structures subjected to loading which is constant or slowly varying with the passage of time. Under these circumstances the static equilibrium of a structure depends only on the equality established between the external loading $\mathbf{F}$ and the internal, elastic restoring forces $\mathbf{F}_s$ generated as a result of its deformation.

When loading varies quickly with time, it is found that additional forces are generated within a structure and that these inertial and damping forces must be considered, together with the elastic restoring forces, to ensure a state of dynamic equilibrium exists.

The time-varying nature of external loads implies that a structure's pattern of deformations is changing with time and therefore there will be a pattern of structural accelerations which act on the structure's mass to generate the internal inertial forces $\mathbf{F}_i$.

All physical structures dissipate energy as they deform. The non-conservative nature of structural systems has no effect on static load analysis. However, the energy loss (damping) property of structures is important in predicting their response to dynamic loads. The exact description of damping is complex. For a wide range of problems, it is possible to represent the internal damping forces $\mathbf{F}_d$ as linear functions of the velocity distributions. This form of damping is termed 'linear viscous' damping and it is the only type of damping to be considered here.

If the physical structure is idealized mathematically by a series of elements interconnected at nodes, as described in Secs. 3.5 and 4.3, then behaviour of the structure is described by a vector **D** composed of the nodal displacements or degrees of freedom. In a dynamic analysis, it is necessary to include the derived vectors:

$$\dot{\mathbf{D}} = \mathrm{d}\mathbf{D}/\mathrm{d}t$$

and

$$\ddot{\mathbf{D}} = \mathrm{d}^2\mathbf{D}/\mathrm{d}t^2$$

i.e., the velocity and acceleration vectors corresponding to the chosen degrees of freedom of the mathematical model of the structure.

It is then possible to express the state of dynamic equilibrium for a structure in the form

$$\mathbf{F}_\mathrm{i} + \mathbf{F}_\mathrm{d} + \mathbf{F}_s = \mathbf{F}$$

As will be shown below, for a linear elastic structure idealized with a finite number n of degrees of freedom, the dynamic equilibrium equation may be written in the form

$$\mathbf{MS}\cdot\ddot{\mathbf{D}}_{xy} + \mathbf{CS}\cdot\dot{\mathbf{D}}_{xy} + \mathbf{SS}\cdot\mathbf{D}_{xy} = \mathbf{F}_{xy}$$

where **MS** is the mass matrix describing the distribution of the mass of the structure

CS is the matrix of damping coefficients appropriate to the assumed equivalent linear viscous damping

SS is the stiffness matrix for the structure, which is assembled in exactly the same way as described in Sec. 4.3

$\mathbf{D}_{xy}$ is the vector of nodal degrees of freedom, referred to the global system of coordinates, having applied the necessary boundary or support conditions.

For the sake of clarity, subscripts xy will be omitted from the global vector $\mathbf{D}_{xy}$ where no confusion can occur between the global displacements and $\mathbf{D}_{pq}$, i.e., those nodal degrees of freedom referred to in the coordinate system local to an element.

The motion of a structure, when subject to some initial set of displacement ($\mathbf{D}(t=0) = \mathbf{D}_0$) and velocities ($\dot{\mathbf{D}}(t=0) = \dot{\mathbf{D}}_0$), is termed 'free vibration', provided the external forces **F** are zero at all times (t).

4.4.1.2 The free vibration of a single degree of freedom system

To take a simple case of free vibration, it may be shown[4] that the free vibration of a single degree of freedom system can be described by the scalar equation

$$M\ddot{D} + C\dot{D} + SD = 0$$

and, subject to the initial conditions $D(t = 0) = D_0$ and $\dot{D}(t = 0) = \dot{D}_0$, the solution is

$$D(t) = \exp(-\beta\omega_1 t)\left[\left(\frac{\dot{D}_0 + \beta\omega_1 D_0}{\omega_\mathrm{d}}\right)\sin\omega_\mathrm{d}t + D_0\cos\omega_\mathrm{d}t\right]$$

where ω_1 is $\sqrt{S/M}$, the frequency of free vibration (natural frequency) of the undamped system with $C = 0$

ω_d is the damped natural frequency where $\omega_d = \omega_1\sqrt{1-\beta^2}$

β is $C/2\omega_1 M$. If $C = 2\omega_1 M$, i.e. $\beta = 1$, the system would be critically damped and, when released from its initial position, would not execute vibrational motion, but rather move to its position of neutral equilibrium in a monotonic manner. Thus β reflects the proportion of the critical damping which the system possesses.

The simple single degree of freedom system is shown in idealized form in Fig. 4.12(a) and the free vibration due to $D(t = 0) = D_0$ and $\dot{D}_0 = 0$ is shown in Fig. 4.12(b). The rate at which the displacement decays depends on the value of β. Civil engineering structures are normally found to be lightly damped ($0.01 < \beta < 0.1$), hence the damped and undamped natural frequencies tend to be similar (i.e., $\omega_d \simeq \omega_1$).

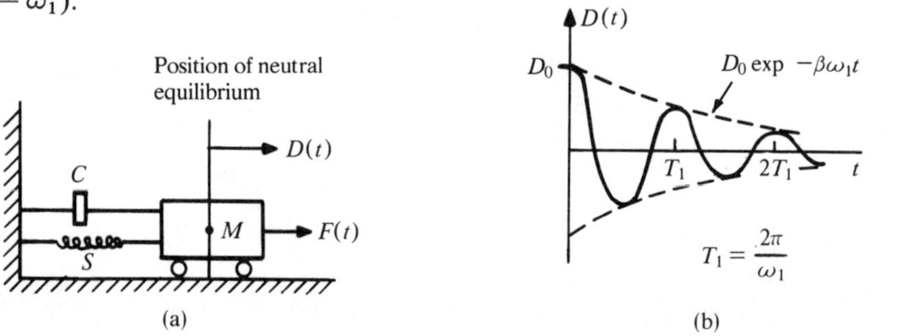

Figure 4.12 Single degree of freedom system. (a) Idealized system. (b) Free vibration ($\dot{D}_0 = 0$)

When the external force is not zero, a system will execute forced vibration. An example of forced response of a single degree of freedom has been given in Sec. 3.7. This motion will, in general, contain a free vibration component due to the initial conditions (D_0 and $\dot{D}_0$) and a component resulting from the response to F. It is apparent that, at some stage, the free vibration component will have decayed to zero and subsequent motion will depend only on the variations of F.

4.4.1.3 The mass matrix

For a multi-degree of freedom system (m.d.o.f.), it is necessary to discuss the formulation of the mass matrix **MS**. In some analyses a simple representation of mass is used in which inertial terms are calculated for each degree of freedom (translational and rotational) as though the mass of a structure was concentrated at nodes alone, and individual elements or members are treated as being without mass. This approach is termed a 'lumped mass idealization' and it results in a diagonal mass matrix (i.e., only the leading diagonal terms of **MS** are non-zero). A more sophisticated approach is to consider the distribution of mass over each element. With reference to the plane frame element shown in Fig. 4.1, the transverse translation D^* in the local coordinate system at a distance p from end i of the element can be expressed in terms of the nodal values of transverse translation and rotation $\mathbf{D}_{pq}$ and the cubic Hermitian polynomials **N** introduced in Sec. 3.5.2 (and Sec. 3.6.1.3):

$$D^* = \mathbf{N}\cdot\mathbf{D}_{pq}$$

and hence the transverse acceleration at p is

$$\ddot{D}^* = \mathbf{N}\cdot\ddot{\mathbf{D}}_{pq}$$

The inertial force per unit length of the element is $m\ddot{D}^*$ and the work done under a virtual displacement (δD^*) is $\delta D^* m\ddot{D}^*$, where m is the mass per unit length. The equivalent set of nodal inertial forces $\mathbf{F}_i$ acting through the corresponding vector of virtual nodal displacements $(\delta\mathbf{D}_{pq})$ must do the same work as the distributed inertial forces over the length L of the element, i.e.

$$\delta\mathbf{D}_{pq}^{\mathrm{T}}\cdot\mathbf{F}_i = \int_0^L \delta D^* m\ddot{D}^*\,dp$$

$$= \delta\mathbf{D}_{pq}^{\mathrm{T}}\int_0^L \mathbf{N}^{\mathrm{T}}\cdot m\cdot\mathbf{N}\,dp\cdot\ddot{\mathbf{D}}_{pq}$$

$$= \delta\mathbf{D}_{pq}^{\mathrm{T}}\cdot\mathbf{M}_{pq}\cdot\ddot{\mathbf{D}}_{pq}$$

As the virtual displacements are arbitrary, the work-consistent mass matrix of an element, in terms of local coordinates, is defined by

$$\mathbf{M}_{pq} = \int_0^L m\cdot\mathbf{N}^{\mathrm{T}}\cdot\mathbf{N}\,dp$$

The element mass matrix for a plane frame element may be developed as above, with the addition of terms for axial inertia based on a linear shape function for axial displacements. Thus

$$\mathbf{M}_{pq} = \frac{\rho AL}{420}\begin{bmatrix} 140 & 0 & 0 & 70 & 0 & 0 \\ 0 & 156 & 22L & 0 & 54 & -13L \\ 0 & 22L & 4L^2 & 0 & 13L & -3L^2 \\ 70 & 0 & 0 & 140 & 0 & 0 \\ 0 & 54 & 13L & 0 & 156 & -22L \\ 0 & -13L & -3L^2 & 0 & -22L & 4L^2 \end{bmatrix}$$

where a constant mass per unit length has been assumed (i.e., $m = \rho A$, where ρ is the mass density and A the cross-sectional area). The order of the nodal displacements in $\mathbf{D}_{pq}$ follows the same pattern as for the static analysis, i.e., $\mathbf{D}_{pq}^{\mathrm{T}} = [D_{p_i}, D_{q_i}, \theta_i, D_{p_j}, D_{q_j}, \theta_j]$.

$\mathbf{M}_{pq}$ is written in local coordinates and it must be transformed to the global form $\mathbf{M}_{xy}$ using exactly the same transformation matrix $\mathbf{T}$ as for the stiffness matrices discussed in Sec. 4.3. The assembly of element mass matrices $\mathbf{M}_{xy}$ into the mass matrix for the whole structure **MS** also follows the same rules as set out for assembly of stiffness matrices **SS**.

Discussion of the damping matrix **CS** is deferred to the next section.

4.4.2 Natural frequencies and modes of a structure

4.4.2.1 The eigenvalue problem in the dynamics of structures

The equations of motion for the free vibration of an undamped m.d.o.f. system are given by

$$\mathbf{MS}\cdot\ddot{\mathbf{D}} + \mathbf{SS}\cdot\mathbf{D} = 0$$

and, in a similar manner to the analysis of the single degree of freedom system, it may be assumed that the motion is simple harmonic (i.e., a cosine or sine function) in the form

$$\mathbf{D}(t) = \mathbf{X}\cos(\omega t + \theta)$$

where $\mathbf{X}$ is the vector giving the deformation shape of the structure, ω is the frequency of vibration and θ is an arbitrary phase angle. Substitution of $\mathbf{D}$ and $\ddot{\mathbf{D}}$ into the equations of motion gives

$$[-\omega^2\cdot\mathbf{MS} + \mathbf{SS}]\cdot\mathbf{X}\cos(\omega t + \theta) = 0$$

For a non-trivial solution (i.e., $\mathbf{X}\cos(\omega t + \theta) \neq 0$) it follows that

$$[\mathbf{SS} - \omega^2\cdot\mathbf{MS}]\cdot\mathbf{X} = 0$$

The above equation will be recognized as the eigenvalue problem discussed in Sec. 3.1.9, since multiplying throughout by the inverse of $\mathbf{SS}$ and dividing throughout by ω^2 gives

$$[\mathbf{A} - \lambda\mathbf{I}]\cdot\mathbf{X} = 0$$

where $\lambda = 1/\omega^2$, $\mathbf{I}$ is an identity matrix, and $\mathbf{A}$ is $\mathbf{SS}^{-1}\cdot\mathbf{MS}$.

If there are n unrestrained degrees of freedom then there will be n distinct eigenvalues λ_i, $i = 1, n$ with corresponding eigenvectors $\mathbf{X}_i$, $i = 1, n$, which satisfy the homogeneous equation. The n natural frequencies of vibration ω_i which are given by $1/\sqrt{\lambda_i}$ and $\mathbf{X}_i$, $i = 1, n$, correspond to the natural modes or deformation patterns for each frequency. Note that the modal shapes do not give the absolute magnitude of the deformations but only the relative sizes of each displacement. It is common practice to scale the terms in $\mathbf{X}$ so that either the largest term is unity, or so that the vector has unit length.

The lowest natural frequency ω_1 corresponds to the largest eigenvalue λ_1 and, therefore, the direct iteration procedure described in Sec. 3.1.9 could be used to find ω_1 and $\mathbf{X}_1$, the modal shape. The literature concerning solution of eigenvalue problems is extensive[4,5] and many other methods are available for the identification of all the frequencies and modes. Figure 4.13 shows the first three modal shapes and natural frequencies for the simple case of a cantilever and a fixed-ended beam.

A general property of eigenvectors is their mutual orthogonality (see Sec. 3.1.9). In the present case it can be shown that

$$\begin{aligned} \mathbf{X}_j^{\mathrm{T}}\cdot\mathbf{MS}\cdot\mathbf{X}_i &= 0 \qquad i \neq j \\ &= \hat{M}_i \qquad i = j \end{aligned}$$

and

$$\mathbf{X}_j^{\mathrm{T}} \cdot \mathbf{SS} \cdot \mathbf{X}_i \; = 0 \qquad i \neq j$$
$$= \hat{S}_i \qquad i = j$$

where $\hat{M}_i$ and $\hat{S}_i$ are scalar terms, usually referred to as the 'diagonalized mass and stiffness' in the i-th mode.

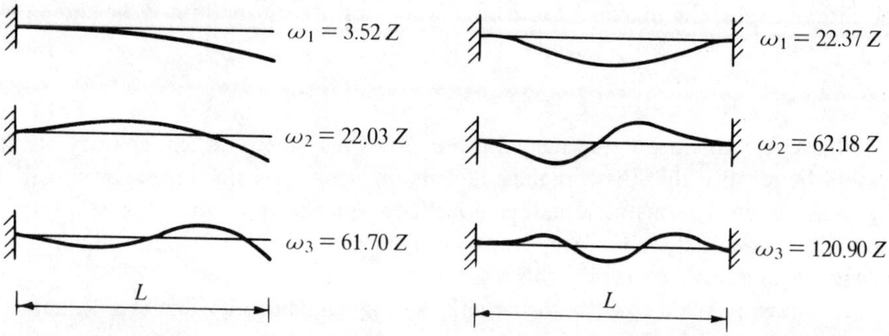

$$Z = \left(\frac{EI}{\rho A L^4}\right)^{1/2}$$

Figure 4.13 Natural frequencies and modes for a cantilever and fixed-end beam

4.4.2.2 Decoupling the equations of motion

The orthogonal property of the modal vectors $\mathbf{X}_i$ may be used to transform the coupled equations of dynamic equilibrium for the m.d.o.f. structure into a set of independent or decoupled equations, as follows. For many civil engineering problems, it is reasonable to represent the real deflection pattern $\mathbf{D}(t)$ as the linear sum of only m of the n modal shapes (e.g., $\mathbf{X}_i$, $i = 1, m; m < n$) factored by time varying modal participation factors $R_i(t)$. At each instant $R_i(t)$, $i = 1, m$ represents the amount of the displacement pattern $\mathbf{X}_i$ required to make up the actual displacement vector $D(t)$, i.e.

$$\mathbf{D}(t) = \sum_{i=1}^{m} \mathbf{X}_i \cdot R_i(t)$$
$$= \mathbf{Q} \cdot \mathbf{R}(t)$$

where $\mathbf{Q}$ is an $n \times m$ matrix formed from columns of $\mathbf{X}_i$ and $\mathbf{R}$ is the $m \times 1$ vector of modal participation factors. It follows that

$$\ddot{\mathbf{D}} = \mathbf{Q} \cdot \ddot{\mathbf{R}}$$

and

$$\dot{\mathbf{D}} = \mathbf{Q} \cdot \dot{\mathbf{R}}$$

Substituting for $\mathbf{D}$, $\dot{\mathbf{D}}$, $\ddot{\mathbf{D}}$ in the equations of motion and then pre-multiplying by $\mathbf{Q}^{\mathrm{T}}$ gives

$$\mathbf{Q}^{\mathrm{T}} \cdot \mathbf{MS} \cdot \mathbf{Q}\, \ddot{\mathbf{R}} + \mathbf{Q}^{\mathrm{T}} \cdot \mathbf{CS} \cdot \mathbf{Q} \cdot \dot{\mathbf{R}} + \mathbf{Q}^{\mathrm{T}} \cdot \mathbf{SS} \cdot \mathbf{Q} \cdot \mathbf{R} = \mathbf{Q}^{\mathrm{T}} \cdot \mathbf{F}_{xy}$$

The matrix products $\mathbf{Q}^T \cdot \mathbf{MS} \cdot \mathbf{Q}$ and $\mathbf{Q}^T \cdot \mathbf{SS} \cdot \mathbf{Q}$ become diagonal matrices with the only non-zero terms being $\hat{M}_i$ and $\hat{S}_i$, $i = 1, m$, on the leading diagonals. This follows from the orthogonality properties referred to previously. The damping matrix product will also diagonalize if **CS** can be expressed as a linear combination of **MS** and **SS**, i.e.

$$\mathbf{CS} = c_1 \cdot \mathbf{MS} + c_2 \cdot \mathbf{SS}$$

or, alternatively, the diagonalized damping terms for each mode may be chosen in terms of an assumed critical damping factor, i.e.

$$\hat{C}_i = 2\beta_i \omega_i \hat{M}_i \qquad i = 1, m$$

These treatments of the damping properties may seem rather arbitrary but it should be recalled that the complicated damping properties are being approximated by linear viscous terms as a mathematical convenience and, with experience, it is normally possible to choose appropriate values with which to approximate the behaviour of a real structure in this respect.

It is now possible to write the equations of dynamic equilibrium as a decoupled set of second-order differential equations in terms of $R_i(t)$ and the appropriate derivatives

$$\hat{M}_i \ddot{R}_i + \hat{C}_i \dot{R}_i + \hat{S}_i R_i = \mathbf{X}_i^T \cdot \mathbf{F}_{xy} = \hat{F}_i \qquad i = 1, m$$

Each equation can be treated as a single degree of freedom system and, once the modal participation vector **R** is found at some instant of time, it is possible to recover the real deflections from

$$\mathbf{D} = \mathbf{Q} \cdot \mathbf{R}$$

One procedure for the solution of the equations of motion is developed in the next section. But, before closing the present section, it is worth noting the following. The selection of the modes to be included in **Q** partly depends on the nature of the excitation $\mathbf{F}_{xy}$. For example, forces with frequencies at or near to any of the natural frequencies of the structure will lead to an increase in response compared with that which would occur if the same amplitude force were applied as a static load, i.e., there will be a dynamic magnification of displacements. Secondly, the internal stresses are found from the elastic properties of the structure and the displacements in the usual manner.[4,6] However, it is normally necessary to include more modes in **Q** in order to achieve accurate predictions of dynamic stresses than is required to represent the displacements above. Finally, the choice of the highest mode to be included in the analysis affects the choice of timestep Δt to be used in any time domain solution of the equations of motion. This topic is developed further in the next section.

4.4.3 Forced vibration of multi-degree of freedom structures

4.4.3.1 Solutions in the time domain

In the previous section it was shown that the full matrix equation for dynamic equilibrium could be transformed into a set of scalar differential equations in the form

$$\hat{M}_i\ddot{R}_i + \hat{C}_i\dot{R}_i + \hat{S}_iR_i = \hat{F}_i \qquad i = 1, m$$

Now, each equation can be solved in steps of time Δt starting at $t = 0$ using the same recurrence equations, based on an assumed linear variation of acceleration over each step, as demonstrated in Sec. 3.7.3, i.e.

$$\left(\hat{M}_i + \hat{C}_i\frac{\Delta t}{2} + \hat{S}_i\frac{\Delta t^2}{6}\right)\ddot{R}_i[(j+1)\Delta t] = \hat{F}_i[(j+1)\Delta t]$$

$$-\left(\hat{C}_i\frac{\Delta t}{2} + \hat{S}_i\frac{\Delta t^2}{3}\right)\ddot{R}_i(j\Delta t) - (\hat{C}_i + \hat{S}_i\,\Delta t)\dot{R}_i(j\Delta t) - \hat{S}_iR_i(j\Delta t)$$

from which $\ddot{R}_i\,((j+1)\,\Delta t)$ may be found, given that the acceleration, velocity and displacement are known for the j-th timestep. The values of $\dot{R}_i\,[(j+1)\,\Delta t]$ and $R_i\,[(j+1)\,\Delta t]$ are then found from

$$\dot{R}_i[(j+1)\Delta t] = \dot{R}_i[j\,\Delta t] + \frac{\Delta t}{2}\{\ddot{R}_i(j\,\Delta t) + \ddot{R}_i[(j+1)\,\Delta t]\}$$

and

$$R_i[(j+1)\Delta t] = R_i(j\,\Delta t) + \dot{R}_i(j\,\Delta t)\,\Delta t + \frac{\Delta t^2}{6}\{2\ddot{R}_i(j\,\Delta t) + \ddot{R}_i\,[(j+1)\Delta t]\}$$

As before, $R_i(t = 0)$ is found from the special step:

$$\ddot{R}_i(t=0) = \frac{1}{\hat{M}_i}\,[\hat{F}_i(t=0) - \hat{C}_i\dot{R}_i(t=0) - \hat{S}_iR_i(t=0)]$$

where $\dot{R}_i(t=0)$ and $R_i(t=0)$ are deduced from the specification of the initial conditions, $\mathbf{D}(t=0)$ and $\dot{\mathbf{D}}(t=0)$.

For stability of the numerical scheme it is necessary to choose Δt from the relationship $\Delta t < \pi/5\omega_m$, where ω_m is the natural frequency of the highest mode included in $\mathbf{Q}$. The value of solving the equations in terms of $\mathbf{R}$ is seen when it is realized that had the equations been solved in terms of the real nodal degrees of freedom $\mathbf{D}$, it would be necessary to use $\Delta t < \pi/5\omega_n$, where ω_n may be much higher than ω_m. This restriction can be removed by use of a modified procedure known as Wilson's θ method,[4] which introduces very high artificial damping for the higher modes. The details of this procedure are beyond the scope of the present discussion.

Example The reader should now investigate the dynamic properties of the propped cantilever shown in Fig. 4.14. The geometrical and material properties are:

Young's modulus E	2.0E + 11 N m^{-2}
density ρ	7980 kg m^{-3}
cross-sectional area A	1.4E–03 m^2
cross-sectional inertia I	5.0E–06 m^4

The structure is idealized by three plane frame elements of equal length (L = 2.0 m), for which only the transverse deflection and rotational degree of freedom

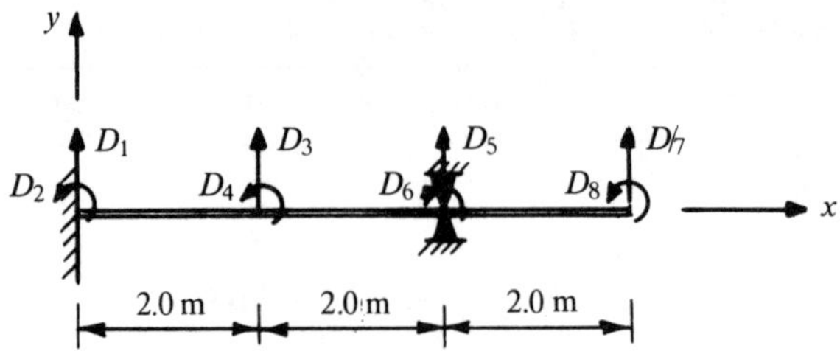

Figure 4.14 Dynamic response example propped cantilever

are considered (i.e., axial terms are omitted). The element stiffness and mass matrices are assembled in the usual manner to give the stiffness and mass matrices for the structure. Before applying the support conditions, these matrices are 8 x 8, referring to **D** (i.e., $\mathbf{D}^T = (D_1, D_2, D_3, \ldots, D_8)$). However, due to the fixed support at the left-hand end of the beam and the prop, $D_1 = D_2 = D_5 = 0$. The corresponding rows and columns may be removed, leaving the stiffness and mass matrices for the structure as shown below:

$$\begin{array}{c} \\ \mathbf{SS} = 5.0\text{E}{+}05* \end{array}\begin{array}{c} \begin{array}{ccccc} 3 & 4 & 6 & 7 & 8 \end{array} \\ \begin{bmatrix} 6 & 0 & 3 & 0 & 0 \\ 0 & 8 & 2 & 0 & 0 \\ 3 & 2 & 8 & -3 & 2 \\ 0 & 0 & -3 & 3 & -3 \\ 0 & 0 & 2 & -3 & 4 \end{bmatrix} \end{array}$$

$$\begin{array}{c} \\ \mathbf{MS} = 5.32\text{E}{-}02* \end{array}\begin{array}{c} \begin{array}{ccccc} 3 & 4 & 6 & 7 & 8 \end{array} \\ \begin{bmatrix} 312 & 0 & -26 & 0 & 0 \\ 0 & 32 & -12 & 0 & 0 \\ -26 & -12 & 32 & 26 & -12 \\ 0 & 0 & 26 & 156 & -44 \\ 0 & 0 & -12 & -44 & 16 \end{bmatrix} \end{array}$$

where the column headings indicated the free degrees of freedom.

Now, inverting **SS** and forming the matrix product $\mathbf{SS}^{-1} \cdot \mathbf{MS}$ gives **A** as below:

$$\mathbf{A} = 1.108333\text{E}{-}09* \begin{bmatrix} 9\,360 & 480 & -2\,528 & -7\,056 & 2\,016 \\ 2\,184 & 624 & -1\,200 & -3\,528 & 1\,008 \\ -8\,736 & -960 & 4\,224 & 14\,112 & -4\,032 \\ -17\,472 & -1\,920 & 10\,624 & 43\,968 & -12\,160 \\ -8\,736 & -960 & 5\,568 & 24\,864 & -6\,720 \end{bmatrix}$$

Solving the eigenvalue problem for the first and second natural modes gives

$$\omega_1 = 142.61 \text{ r/s}$$

$$\omega_2 = 383.83 \text{ r/s}$$

$$\mathbf{X}_1 = \begin{bmatrix} 0.0 \\ 0.0 \\ -0.195\,153 \\ -0.086\,858 \\ 0.0 \\ 0.340\,008 \\ 1.0 \\ 0.558\,822 \end{bmatrix} \quad \text{and} \quad \mathbf{X}_2 = \begin{bmatrix} 0.0 \\ 0.0 \\ 1.0 \\ 0.095\,031 \\ 0.0 \\ -0.325\,666 \\ 0.771\,843 \\ 0.665\,686 \end{bmatrix}$$

where the restrained degrees of freedom have been introduced into $\mathbf{X}_1$ and $\mathbf{X}_2$. The modal shapes are plotted in Fig. 4.15.

Using the orthogonal properties of the modes and assuming 5 per cent and 10 per cent of critical damping in the first and second modes, respectively (i.e., $\beta_1 = 0.05$ and $\beta_2 = 0.10$), the diagonalized masses, damping coefficients and stiffnesses are given by

$$\hat{M}_1 = 7.71 \text{ kg} \qquad \hat{C}_2 = 109.95 \text{ N s m}^{-1} \qquad \hat{K}_1 = 1.5861\text{E}{+}05 \text{ N m}^{-1}$$

and

$$\hat{M}_2 = 20.23 \text{ kg} \qquad \hat{C}_2 = 1553.06 \text{ N s m}^{-1} \qquad \hat{K}_2 = 2.9804\text{E}{+}06 \text{ N m}^{-1}$$

The linear acceleration technique for the solution of forced vibration in the time domain may now be applied to calculate the dynamic response of the structure to various types of loading. For example, consider a single sinusoidal force F_k

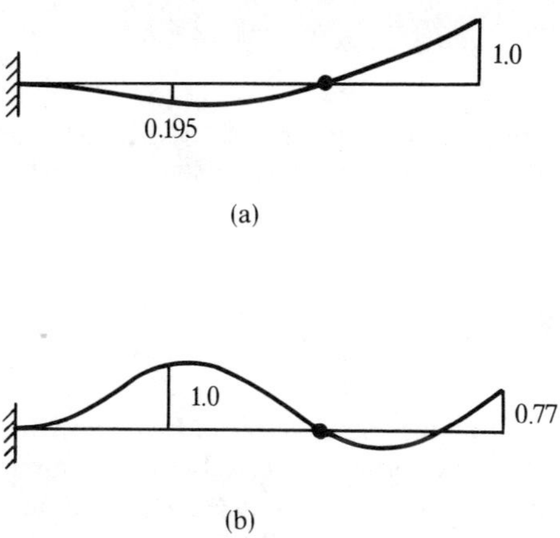

Figure 4.15 Natural frequencies and nodes of propped cantilever. (a) First mode ($\omega_1 = 142.6$ r/s). (b) Second mode ($\omega_2 = 383.8$ r/s)

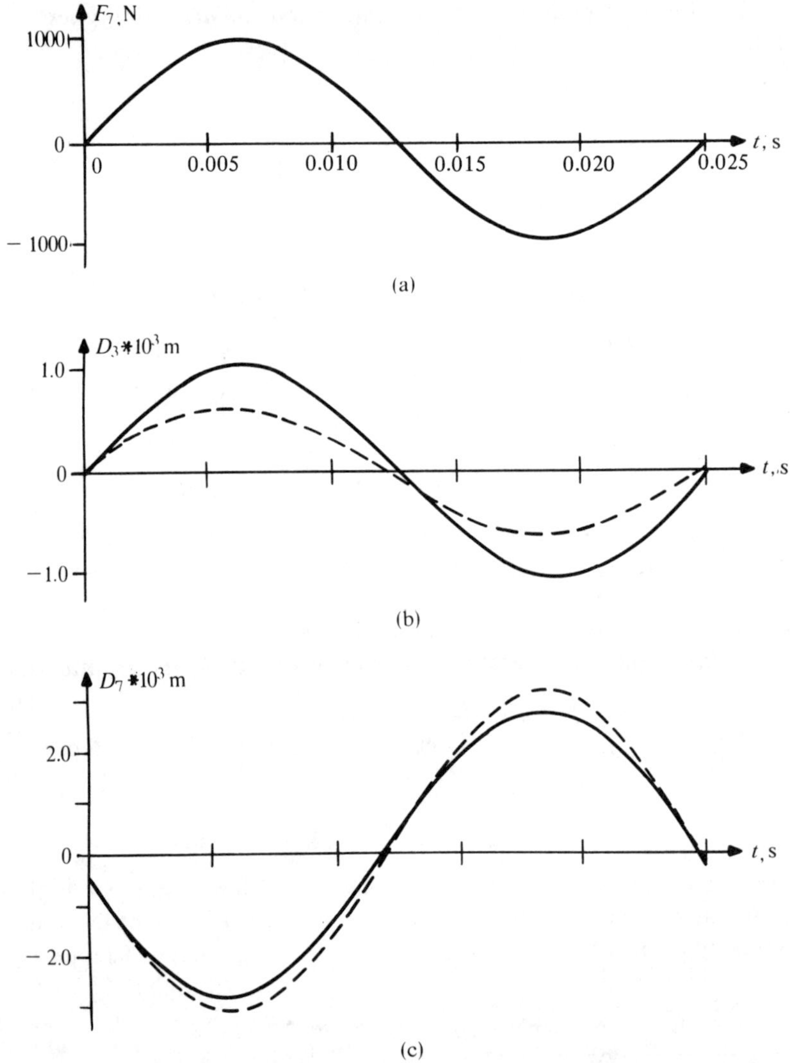

Figure 4.16 Forced response of propped cantilever. (a) Excitation. (b) Midspan deflection (broken line: first mode; solid line: first and second modes) (c) Cantilever deflection (broken line: first mode; solid line: first and second modes)

applied vertically in the direction of the k-th degree of freedom of the form

$$F_k = 1000.0 \sin \Omega t \text{ N}$$

where Ω is the frequency of excitation. Figure 4.16 shows a typical cycle of response to such a force, applied at the tip of the cantilever (i.e., $k = 7$), with a a frequency of 250 r/s. The analysis has been performed using only the first mode and then repeated using both modes. For this excitation, the calculated maximum cantilever deflections D_7 are not very different for the two analyses, though there is a more noticeable difference in the maximum values of midspan deflection for the beam section D_3. In this case, the first mode is a reasonable approximation to the deflected shape of a propped cantilever subject to a point load on the cantilever tip.

The reader should repeat the analysis for the point load at the midspan of the beam ($k = 3$) and compare the results from considering both modes or only the first mode. It is also instructive to repeat the analysis for the force applied at the tip of the cantilever ($k = 7$) but with the frequency $\Omega = \omega_1, \omega_1/2$, and $\omega_1/10$, noting the changes in phase between the force and tip deflection as well as the increasing dynamic magnification of the deflection as $\Omega \rightarrow \omega_1$, i.e., resonance in the first mode.

4.4.3.2 Additional aspects of forced vibration

Although a sinusoidal force has been considered in the above example, the time domain solution is of general applicability and it is particularly useful when dealing with transient loads or nonlinear material properties. Indeed, there are more efficient methods for the dynamic analysis of the special case of sinusoidal excitation, based on the fast Fourier transform, which involve solution of the response in the frequency domain.[4] These techniques are widely used for the calculation of response to random excitation, e.g., wind, wave, and earthquake loading.

In some cases it is necessary to consider the effects of high axial forces on the bending stiffness of beam elements and other forms of the stiffness and mass matrices are available in the literature[7] which include such aspects as shear stiffness and rotational inertia, etc.

It should be apparent that, although this discussion has centred on the problem of plane frames, the dynamic response of space frames, plates, and shells, and elastic continua may be analysed using the same basic techniques.

Finally, the computation of the natural frequencies and modes for complex structures is a lengthy process and advanced techniques are required to compute, with reasonable accuracy and efficiency, their deflections and stresses.

4.5 COMPUTER-AIDED DESIGN

Computer programs are frequently used to assist with engineering calculations. Programs on desk top computers can be used to predict bending moment diagrams, to detail reinforcement, or to select a standard steel section for a structural member. Minicomputers can be used to predict the moment envelopes for building frames and grillages, and to produce documents and sketches to enable them to be constructed. Before the advent of office-based computers, these operations could be performed using a link to a remote time-shared computer, and some work is still done in this way.

4.5.1 Program packages

The first major program suite for Civil Engineers, ICES (Integrated Civil Engineering System), was developed in the USA. In Britain, the most popular program suite is GENESYS (General Engineering System).[8] It was developed using resources provided by government, but is now operated by a commercial organization. It first became available on large time-shared computers in 1972, and is now also available to be operated on office-based minicomputers.

GENESYS comprises: a centre, to provide technical support; the GENTRAN programming language, which is an extension of FORTRAN; GENTRAN 'pre-compilers', to translate programs to suit a wide range of computers (it is this facility that gives rise to its claim to be independent of a particular type of computer); an operating system, which includes the precompilers, and which automatically handles all problems of transferring data between primary and secondary storage facilities; and a library of subsystems to solve engineering problems. Of particular interest to the structural engineer are subsystems for analysis of frameworks, reinforced concrete building design and detailing, and slab bridge design.

The reinforced concrete building subsystem provides a good example of the use of computers for problems where the design process can be codified. From input of the proposed basic geometry of a structure and its components, the programs can produce a 'design', and detail the structural elements. The information provided by the computer includes bar bending, fixing, and weight schedules, together with detail and general arrangement drawings that can be used on site.

4.5.2 Interactive design

In general, there are no unique solutions to design problems, and results are dependent on the decisions of a designer. Interactive design processes are devised to utilize the decision-making capabilities of a design engineer, with the calculating and data handling power of computers. The basis of interactive programs is continuous communication between designer and computer during the evolution of a scheme. The role of the engineer is to direct operations by taking decisions based on information supplied by the computer.

To enable smooth flow of operations, the computer-produced results have to be presented on demand, and in a form suitable for rapid assimilation by the designer. Visual display of information is essential, and as fast response is required, office-based computers are preferred to remote time-shared systems. Rapid methods of analysis are necessary to minimize disruptive delays. Savings in time are achieved by use of specialized analytical techniques designed to give approximate results with minimum computational effort.

A typical computer system for interactive design is shown in Fig. 4.17. To operate an interactive program, an engineer sits by a keyboard and visual display screen and manipulates the keys and cursors. Programs for interactive design can be written in FORTRAN, provided graphics programs are available that can be referenced as SUBROUTINEs. Most computer systems have facilities that enable this to be done easily.

In general, before an engineer commences work at the computer, a conceptual solution to a problem is produced with trial member sizes and layouts at various construction states. From this position, he proceeds through a design, with the aid of computer programs. All of the instructions given, and information received, are in a form normally used so that concentration can be given to the design and is not wasted with programming considerations. In exceptional cases, an engineer may complete a trial solution at one computer sitting, but it is more likely that he will need to break from time to time to assess progress.

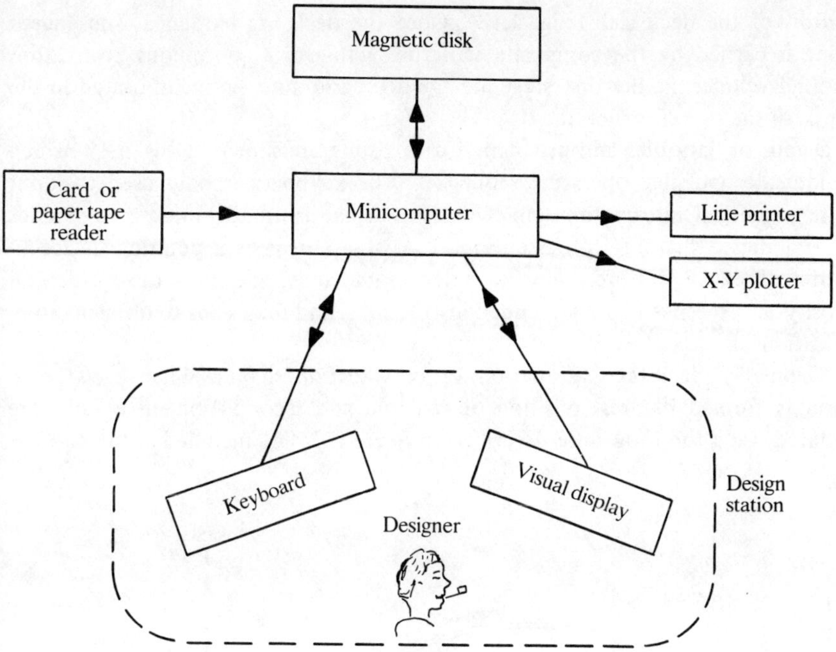

Figure 4.17 Computer system for interactive design

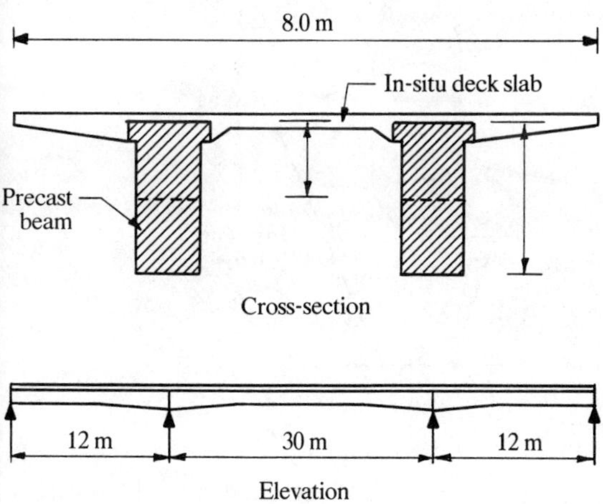

Figure 4.18 Three-span bridge

4.3.2.1 Example procedure

Typical of the type of problem that can be dealt with by such an approach is design of a varying-section prestressed concrete bridge. To demonstrate the application to construction sequence, the case considered is where precast prestressed members act initially as simply supported beams.[9] These carry, in addition to their self weight, the loads from wet concrete, shuttering, and plant during the in-situ construction of the deck slab (Fig. 4.18). Once the deck has hardened, subsequent loading is carried by the composite structure acting as a continuous beam, thus stresses developed in the first stage are 'built in' and must be incorporated in the analysis of the overall structure.

Details of data files and programs for this suite are shown in Fig. 4.19, which also indicates possible operating sequences. The keyboard is only used to input precise numerical information and the visual display is used to initiate commands and to indicate features for attention. Use of a cursor as a pointing device to identify displayed features, and to select commands, alleviates the burden of verbosity and the need to learn coded instructions, and thus leads to efficient communication.

'Geometry' facilitates formation of cross-section shapes. When each cross-section is formed its area, position of centroid and second moment of area are calculated using the procedure described in Sec. 3.3.3, and included in the disk file

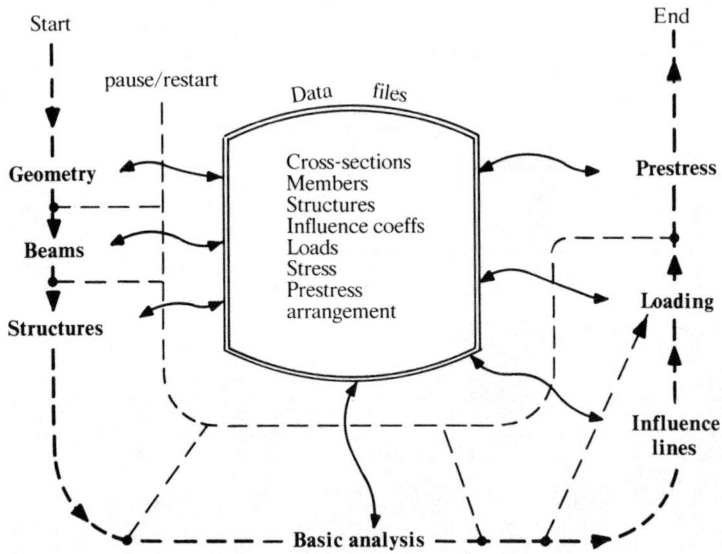

Figure 4.19 Prestressed beam design suite

storing details of the section shape. This program can be recalled later in the design process to permit sections to be added or amended.

'Beams' is used when all of the cross-sectional shapes have been formed and stored. Each member is defined by assigning cross-sections to stations along its length. Since this procedure is straightforward and requires only a small exchange of data, it is undertaken at the keyboard using a computer prompt and user reply scheme. Elevations of completed beams are drawn on the screen to act as a check. There is a restart facility to permit sections to be changed, if later work shows this to be desirable.

'Structures' is used to assemble members for analysis. To provide a check on layout, a line drawing is displayed with joint and member numbers annotated.

'Basic analysis' is called for each substructure. Member stiffness matrices are computed using the procedure described in Sec. 4.3.14 and compiled to form the global stiffness matrix, which is then inverted. 'Loading' is used to produce moment envelopes. Self weight is calculated automatically, and imposed forces are specified as uniformly distributed over a member, and as concentrated loads on member stations. 'Prestress' enables interactive graphical detailing of prestressing tendons.

For the example described, the first stage is the detailing of precast simply supported members for loadings ranging from transfer conditions, to those from the in-situ deck slab with associated shuttering and construction operations. At this stage, there is no composite action, and the initial calculation of minimum prestress force is based on satisfying specified permissible stress levels at extreme fibres, allowing for constructional tolerances. Such details are demanded and supplied via the terminal and used in conjunction with member specification and loading details called from the appropriate disk file.

Details of prestressing forces, cable profiles, and stress levels are transferred to disk files at the end of this design stage for later interrogation by subsequent programs. To enable a model of a subsequent structure to be created, the appropriate previously designed members must be identified by the engineer. This enables existing section details and stress levels to be incorporated with the live load moment envelopes and section properties of the composite continuous structure. Prestressing details may then be developed throughout the structure. Screen size limits the display to one member at a time, but a guide to cables in adjacent members is provided. Approximate positions of points of zero slope and points of contraflexure are indicated by cursor. These are automatically rounded off to practical

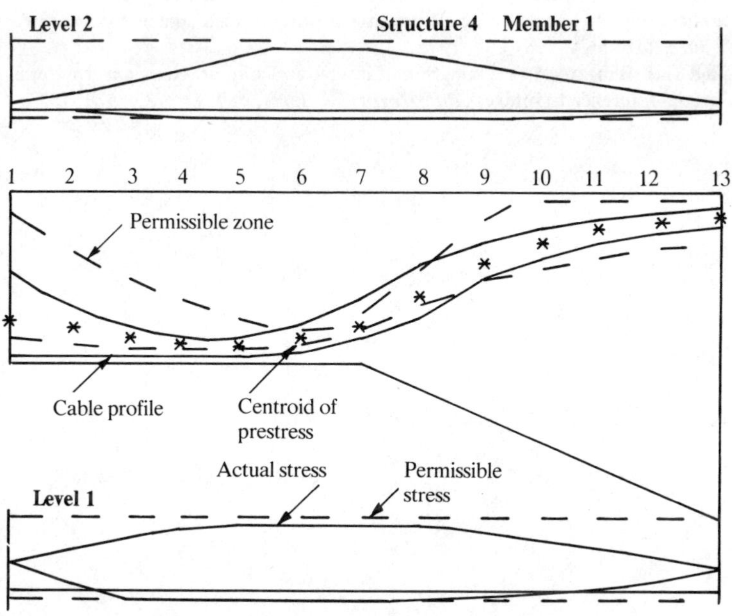

Figure 4.20 Graphical display used to specify prestressing details.

limits and curved profiles are generated and stored for output at the completion of the design.

Displayed design aids (see Fig. 4.20) consist of a permissible zone, based on stress levels at extreme fibres of the composite section as an initial guide, and graphs of stress levels relative to allowable limiting values. These are computed from initial values in precast sections, live loading on composite section and prestressing, and are calculated at soffit and top of precast member and top of composite member. The engineer may call either of the latter two cases as alternatives, while the former is displayed permanently.

Secondary effects due to prestressing are not calculated until the initial cable arrangement has been completed throughout the structure. Amended stress levels and cable zones are then displayed, but if proper use has been made of the design guides, the effects will be small and few modifications if any will be necessary.

REFERENCES

1. Coates, R. C., M. G. Coutie, and F. K. Kong, *Structural Analysis*, Nelson, Sunbury-on-Thames, 1980.
2. Allen, H. G., *Analysis and Design of Structural Sandwich Panels,* Pergamon, Oxford, 1969.
3. Zienkiewicz, O. C. *The Finite Element Method*, McGraw-Hill, London, 1977.
4. Clough, R. W., and J. Penzien, *Dynamics of Structures*, McGraw-Hill, New York, 1975.
5. Bathe, K. G., and E. L. Wilson, *Numerical Methods in Finite Element Analysis*, Prentice-Hall, Englewood Cliffs, N.J. 1976.
6. Hurty. W. C., and M. F. Rubenstein, *Dynamics of Structures*, Prentice-Hall, Englewood Cliffs, N.J. 1964.
7. Przemieniecki, J. S. *Theory of Matrix Structural Analysis*, McGraw-Hill, New York, 1968.
8. 'Computer applications for detailed design calculations of reinforced concrete structures'. *Structural Engineer* (10) **56A**, 275–288, 1978.
9. Cope, R. J., and J. H. Bungey, 'An examination of interactive computer usage in structural design, with special reference to bridges', *Proc. Instn Civ. Engrs*, Pt 2, **61**, 525–538, 1976.

CHAPTER

FIVE

APPLICATIONS IN SOIL MECHANICS

5.1 INTRODUCTION

Many problems in soil mechanics are particularly suited to solution by computer. The vast majority of methods of solution fall into two broad categories: limit analyses and stress deformation analyses. Limit analyses are used for ensuring adequate factors of safety against the shear failure of earth masses behind retaining walls, under foundations, in slopes, etc., and a number of trial calculations are usually required before a critical failure mechanism can be identified. Stress deformation analyses are used to estimate movements of earth masses and earth-retaining structures which are of importance with respect to settlement of embankments, settlement and differential settlement of buildings, yielding of retaining walls, etc. These movements and the stresses in the associated structures are dependent on construction and loading sequences, all of which can be taken into account using the finite-element method. This method can also be used to determine pore pressures in earth masses and for studying flows through earth dams, and under impervious dams.

In the first part of this chapter, the method of limit analysis is applied to the design of slopes and sheetpile walls and computer program documentation is included. In the second part the finite-element method is applied to steady-state seepage problems.

5.2 ANCHORED SHEETPILE WALL DESIGN

5.2.1 The free earth support method for a wall in a homogeneous stratum

Sheetpile walls are widely used for a variety of waterfront structures and for slope stability and erosion protection. The simplest design approach is the free earth support method. The assumed pressure distribution and identification of terms for an anchored sheetpile wall in a homogeneous granular soil are illustrated in Fig. 5.1. A satisfactory design requires sufficient depth of penetration of the sheeting below dredge level to provide an adequate safety margin against failure by rotation of the piling about the anchor level. This is determined by dividing the passive resistance by an appropriate safety factor F and considering moment equilibrium about O.

Thus

$$P_A \times \tfrac{2}{3}(h + d - a) = \frac{P_P}{F}(h + \tfrac{2}{3}d - a) \tag{5.1}$$

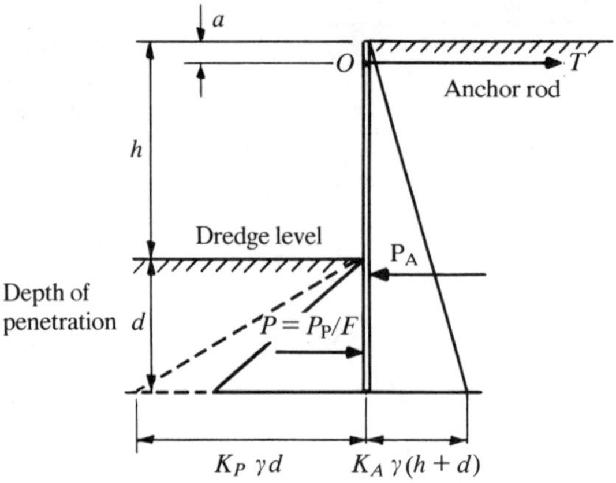

Figure 5.1 Anchored sheetpile wall in homogeneous granular soil

where the active force $P_A = \frac{1}{2} K_A \gamma\ (h + d - a)^2$ and the factored passive force $P_P/F = \frac{1}{2}\,(K_P/F)\gamma d^2$. Wall friction will be developed on the active side due to flexure of the piling and hence the Coulomb K_A value is generally recommended where $K_A = [\cos\phi/(1 + \sqrt{\sin(\phi + \delta)\sin\phi/\cos\delta})]^2$ and wall friction angle $\delta = 2\phi/3$. However, in deriving the passive resistance wall friction is often neglected, hence $K_P = \tan^2(45 + \phi/2)$. Insertion of the above expressions for P_A and P_P in Eq. (5.1) yields a cubic polynomial in d which may be solved by the Newton–Raphson technique described in Sec. 3.2.1.

5.2.2 Elemental layer analysis for a wall in stratified soil

An alternative approach which is particularly suited to more complex geometries involving several strata, groundwater, and surcharges is to subdivide each stratum into a series of elemental layers. The effective stress at each depth is calculated and factored by the appropriate earth pressure coefficient. The forces on each incremental length of piling are then computed, together with their moments about the anchor level. Forces and moments due to water pressures on the structure are considered separately in a similar manner. Values of factor of safety F are derived at successive depth increments below dredge level where

$$F = \sum \text{Passive/moments} \left(\sum \text{Active moments} + \sum \text{`Active' water moments} - \sum \text{`Passive' water moments} \right)$$

The procedure is terminated immediately a specified factor of safety is exceeded. The anchor rod tension is then calculated by considering horizontal equilibrium and the maximum bending moment in the sheeting selected from values calculated at all elemental levels. Flexure of the sheeting can cause considerable redistribution of pressures on the piling and the free earth support design values must be modified; see Rowe[1] for example.

5.2.3 The Computer Program SHEETPILE

The program SHEETPILE shown in Fig. 5.2 uses the elemental procedure described.

Up to fifteen strata may be specified in any order, a sorting routine rearranging them into ascending order of base level. Calculations are made at 0.5 m depths down the structure.

```
      MASTER SHEET
      INTEGER FIN
      REAL MPAT,MPPT,MTB,MT
      DIMENSIØN BY(20),ADENS(20),PDENS(20),ASWT(20),PSWT(20),
     1          AKC(20),PKC(20)
C
C     INPUT BASIC GEØMETRY AND SØIL DATA
C
      READ(5,500)YTB,YDL,AHWT,PHWT
      WRITE(6,600)YTB,YDL,AHWT,PHWT
      READ(5,500)AQ,PQ,FØS
      WRITE(6,601)AQ,PQ,FØS
      READ(5,501)NSTRAT
      WRITE(6,602)NSTRAT
      DØ 10 I=1,NSTRAT
      READ(5,500)BY(I),ADENS(I),AKC(I),PKC(I)
      WRITE(6,603)BY(I),ADENS(I),AKC(I),PKC(I)
   10 CØNTINUE
C
C     SØRT STRATA INTØ ASCENDING ØRDER ØF BY
C
      IF(NSTRAT.EQ.1)GØTØ 40
   20 I=0
      DØ 30 J=2,NSTRAT
      IF(BY(J).GE.BY(J-1))GØTØ 30
      I=1
      T=BY(J)
      BY(J)=BY(J-1)
      BY(J-1)=T
      T=ADENS(J)
      ADENS(J)=ADENS(J-1)
      ADENS(J-1)=T
      T=AKC(J)
      AKC(J)=AKC(J-1)
      AKC(J-1)=T
      T=PKC(J)
      PKC(J)=PKC(J-1)
      PKC(J-1)=T
   30 CØNTINUE
      IF(I.NE.0)GØTØ 20
   40 CØNTINUE
      IF(YTB.GT.BY(NSTRAT))GØTØ 190
      IF(YDL.GT.BY(NSTRAT))GØTØ 200
C
C     SPLIT STRATA AT BØTH WATER TABLES , TIE-BAR AND DREDGE LEVEL
C
      CALL SPLIT(AHWT,BY,ADENS,AKC,PKC,NSTRAT)
      CALL SPLIT(PHWT,BY,ADENS,AKC,PKC,NSTRAT)
      CALL SPLIT(YTB,BY,ADENS,AKC,PKC,NSTRAT)
      CALL SPLIT(YDL,BY,ADENS,AKC,PKC,NSTRAT)
C
C     SET DENSITIES EQUAL TØ START WITH
C
      DØ 50 I=1,NSTRAT


   50 PDENS(I)=ADENS(I)
C
C     ADJUST DENSITIES FØR WATER TABLES
C
      DØ 60 I=1,NSTRAT
      IF(BY(I).GT.AHWT)ADENS(I)=ADENS(I)-9.81
      IF(BY(I).GT.PHWT)PDENS(I)=PDENS(I)-9.81
   60 CØNTINUE
C
C     SET PDENS TØ 0.0 ABØVE DREDGE LEVEL
C
```

Figure 5.2 Program SHEETPILE

```
      DØ 70 I=1,NSTRAT
      IF(BY(I).LE.YDL)PDENS(I)=0.0
   70 CØNTINUE
C
C     CALCULATE ØVERBURDEN AT EACH STRATUM BØUNDARY
C
      ASWT(1)=AQ
      PSWT(1)=0.0
      YTØP=0.0
      DØ 100 I=2,NSTRAT
      ASWT(I)=ASWT(I-1)+(BY(I-1)-YTØP)*ADENS(I-1)
      PSWT(I)=0.0
      IF(BY(I)-YDL)100,80,90
   80 PSWT(I)=PQ
      GØTØ 100
   90 PSWT(I)=PSWT(I-1)+(BY(I-1)-YTØP)*PDENS(I-1)
  100 YTØP=BY(I-1)
C
C     ANALYSE WØRKING IN NØMINAL 0.5 MTR STEPS FRØM TØP
C
      T=0.0
      K=1
  110 YTØP=0.0
      BMMIN=0.0
      BMMAX=0.0
      PA=0.0
      PP=0.0
      PAMT=0.0
      PPMT=0.0
      WAMT=0.0
      WPMT=0.0
      MPAT=0.0
      MPPT=0.0
      MTB=0.0
      WA=0.0
      WP=0.0
      DWA=0.0
      DWP=0.0
      DMTB=0.0
      APA=0.0
      APP=0.0
      AWA=0.0
      AWP=0.0
      FIN=0
      DØ 150 I=1,NSTRAT
      H=YTØP
      NSTEP=IFIX(2.0*(BY(I)-YTØP))
      IF(NSTEP.LT.1)NSTEP=1
      DH=(BY(I)-YTØP)/FLØAT(NSTEP)
      IF(H.GE.YTB)DMTB=T*DH
      IF(H.GE.AHWT)DWA=9.81*DH
      IF(H.GE.PHWT)DWP=9.81*DH
      DPA=DH*ADENS(I)*AKC(I)
      DPP=DH*PDENS(I)*PKC(I)
      PA=ASWT(I)*AKC(I)
      PP=PSWT(I)*PKC(I)
      DØ 140 J=1,NSTEP
  120 H=H+DH
      DPAMT=PA*DH*(H-DH/2.0-YTB)+DPA*DH*(H-DH/3.0-YTB)/2.0
      DPPMT=PP*DH*(H-DH/2.0-YTB)+DPP*DH*(H-DH/3.0-YTB)/2.0
      DWAMT=WA*DH*(H-DH/2.0-YTB)+DWA*DH*(H-DH/3.0-YTB)/2.0
      DWPMT=WP*DH*(H-DH/2.0-YTB)+DWP*DH*(H-DH/3.0-YTB)/2.0
      PAMT=PAMT+DPAMT
      PPMT=PPMT+DPPMT
      WAMT=WAMT+DWAMT
      WPMT=WPMT+DWPMT
      IF(H.LT.YDL)GØTØ 130
      FS=PPMT/(PAMT+WAMT-WPMT)
      IF(FIN.EQ.1.ØR.FS.LT.FØS)GØTØ 130
      PAMT=PAMT-DPAMT
      PPMT=PPMT-DPPMT
      WAMT=WAMT-DWAMT
      WPMT=WPMT-DWPMT
C
```

Figure 5.2 (*continued*)

```
C    PREDICT FINAL DEPTH ØF PENETRATIØN BY INTERPØLATIØN
C
      ØLDFØS=PPMT/(PAMT+WAMT-WPMT)
      D=DH*(FØS-ØLDFØS)/(FS-ØLDFØS)
      DMTB=DMTB*D/DH
      DPA=DPA*D/DH
      DPP=DPP*D/DH
      DWA=DWA*D/DH
      DWP=DWP*D/DH
      H=H-DH
      DH=D
      FIN=1
      GØTØ 120
  130 Y=H-YDL
      MTB=MTB+DMTB
      MPAT=MPAT+(APA+AWA)*DH+(PA+WA)*DH**2/2.0+(DPA+DWA)*DH**2/6.0
      MPPT=MPPT+(APP/FØS+AWP)*DH+(PP/FØS+WP)*DH**2/2.0
     1    +(DPP/FØS+DWP)*DH**2/6.0
      MT=MTB-MPAT+MPPT
      APA=APA+(PA+DPA/2.0)*DH
      APP=APP+(PP+DPP/2.0)*DH
      AWA=AWA+(WA+DWA/2.0)*DH
      AWP=AWP+(WP+DWP/2.0)*DH
      PA=PA+DPA
      PP=PP+DPP
      WA=WA+DWA
      WP=WP+DWP
      IF(MT.GT.BMMAX)BMMAX=MT
      IF(MT.LT.BMMIN)BMMIN=MT
      IF(K.EQ.2.AND.H.GT.YDL)WRITE(6,607)Y,PA,PP,MT,FS
      IF(FIN.EQ.1)GØTØ (160,170),K
  140 CØNTINUE
      YTØP=BY(I)
  150 CØNTINUE
      WRITE(6,608)
      STØP
  160 T=(APA+AWA-APP/FØS-AWP)
      Y=H-YDL
      WRITE(6,609)Y,FS,T
      K=2
      GØTØ 110
  170 IF(BMMAX.LT.ABS(BMMIN))BMMAX=ABS(BMMIN)
      WRITE(6,610)BMMAX
      STØP
  190 WRITE(6,604)
      STØP
  200 WRITE(6,605)
      STØP
  500 FØRMAT(8F10.3)
  501 FØRMAT(I5)
  600 FØRMAT(19H SHEETPILE ANALYSIS/1X,19(1H=)
     1     //27H DEPTH  ØF  TIE  BAR   =    ,F10.3
     2      /27H DREDGE   LEVEL   =         ,F10.3
     3      /27H ACTIVE SIDE WATER LEVEL =  ,F10.3
     4      /27H PASSIVE  WATER  DEPTH  =   ,F10.3//)
  601 FØRMAT(30H SURCHARGE ( ACTIVE SIDE )  = ,F10.3
     1      /30H SURCHARGE ( PASSIVE SIDE ) = ,F10.3
     2      /30H REQUIRED FACTØR ØF SAFETY  = ,F10.3//)
  602 FØRMAT(20H NUMBER ØF STRATA = ,I5//
     1  52H          BASE-Y       DENSITY            KA            KP/)
  603 FØRMAT(1H ,4(3X,F10.3))
  604 FØRMAT(/37H ERRØR : TIE BAR BELØW BØTTØM STRATUM//)
  605 FØRMAT(/34H ERRØR : DREDGE LEVEL BELØW STRATA//)
  607 FØRMAT(1H ,5(2X,F10.3))
  608 FØRMAT(32H ERRØR : NØT ENØUGH DEPTH FØR FØS//)
  609 FØRMAT(/24H DEPTH ØF PENETRATIØN = ,F6.2,5H MTRS
     1        /24H FACTØR  ØF  SAFETY  =  ,F10.3
     2        /24H TIE  BAR  TENSIØN    =  ,F10.1,12H KN/MTR. RUN///
     3 59H    PEN DEPTH            PA            PP        BMØM           FØS/
  610 FØRMAT(///23H MAX. BENDING MØMENT = ,E10.3,10H KN - MTRS/)
      END

      SUBRØUTINE SPLIT(Y,YS,DENS,AK,PK,N)
```

Figure 5.2 (*continued*)

```
      DIMENSIØN YS(20),DENS(20),AK(20),PK(20)
      I=1
10    IF(YS(I)-Y)20,50,30
20    I=I+1
      IF(I-N)10,10,50
30    DØ 40 J=I,N
      K=N-J+I
      YS(K+1)=YS(K)
      DENS(K+1)=DENS(K)
      AK(K+1)=AK(K)
      PK(K+1)=PK(K)
40    CØNTINUE
      YS(I)=Y
      N=N+1
50    RETURN
      END
      FINISH
```

Figure 5.2 (*continued*)

The program requires the following data:

1. Profile details (1 card): anchor level – *YTB,* dredge level – *YDL*, water level (active side) – *AHWT*, water level (passive side) – *PHWT*.
2. Surcharge details and factor of safety (1 card): surcharge (active side) – *AQ* (kN m^{-2}), surcharge (passive side) – *PQ* (kN m^{-2}), *FOS.*
3. Number of Strata (1 card): *NSTRAT.*
4. Strata Details (1 card for each stratum): base level – *BY*, bulk specific weight – *ADENS* (kN m^{-3}), active and passive earth pressure coefficients – *AKC, PKC*.

Note. All levels in metres are expressed relative to the top of the piling, downwards positive.

5.3 SLOPE STABILITY ANALYSIS

5.3.1 Slip circle analysis by the Swedish method of slices

An analysis of slope stability is a prerequisite for the safe but economic design of any engineering project involving the formation of embankments and cuttings, typical examples being in the design of dams, highways, and railways. The stability of natural slopes in hilly or mountainous areas can also be a serious problem in geotechnical engineering. In a slope failure the outer portion of the mass slides downwards and outwards in relation to the remainder, often along a fairly well defined slip surface. A stability analysis involves identification of the forces causing and resisting instability and determination of the relevant soil properties. Although in certain circumstances a slip surface may be assumed to consist of a series of linear sections or have the shape of a logarithmic spiral, the most commonly adopted geometry is circular. This has the advantage of simplicity and is based on the essentially rotational sliding mechanism observed in most slope failures.

Due to its flexibility for analysing the stability of slopes consisting of a number of soil strata or where soil properties vary with depth, the Swedish method of slices is most commonly adopted. A typical geometry associated with this analysis is shown in Fig. 5.3(a). A trial slip circle with centre of rotation *O* and radius *R* is selected and the failure mass subdivided into several main sections, defined either by changes in profile geometry or by intersections between strata and the slip circle. The geometry is modified to allow for the formation of tension cracks to depth h_c given by

$$h_c = \frac{2c'}{\gamma} \tan\left(45 + \frac{\phi'}{2}\right)$$

where c' and ϕ' are the shear strength parameters in terms of effective stress. Each main section is further subdivided into vertical elemental slices sufficiently small in width to enable each element to be considered trapezoidal. The forces acting on such an element are shown in Fig. 5.3(b). The analysis is complicated by the inclusion of the interslice forces P_n, P_{n+1}, V_n, V_{n+1} and various authors, for example, Bishop,[2] Spencer[3] and Whitman and Bailey,[4] have attempted to assess the potential errors involved in the omission of such forces from the analysis. Fortuitously it was shown that very little error is introduced by the most common simplification, which is to assume that interslice forces approximately balance. Interslice forces are therefore neglected in the analysis which follows. The vertical force W acting on the base of each slice comprises the self-weight of all soils in the slice, the weight of water directly above the slice, and any vertical loads acting on the ground surface at that section. The average effective normal force on the base of the slice is then

$$N' = W \cos\alpha - \frac{ub}{\cos\alpha}$$

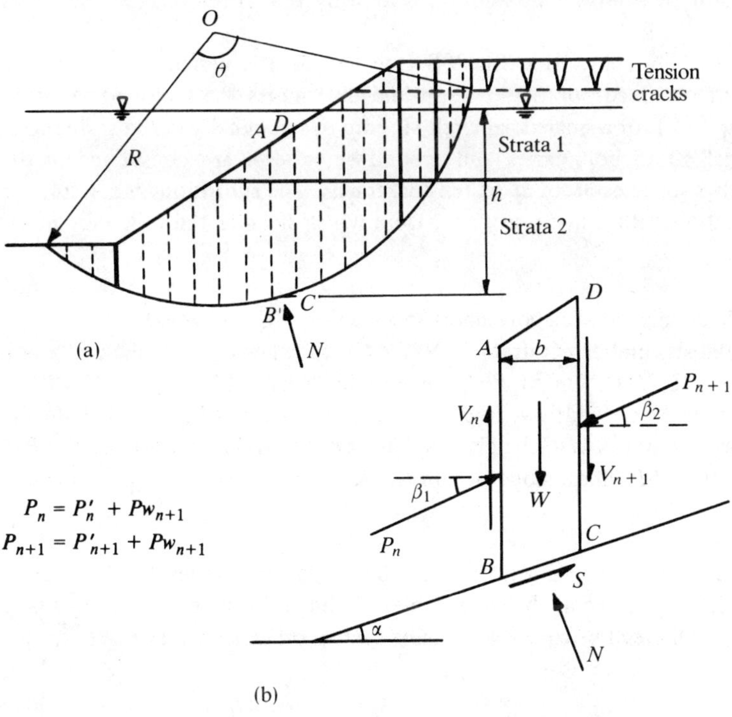

$P_n = P'_n + Pw_{n+1}$
$P_{n+1} = P'_{n+1} + Pw_{n+1}$

Figure 5.3 Swedish method of slices. (a) Typical geometry in method of slices. (b) Forces acting on an element

where $u(=\gamma_\omega h$ in the case of static ground water) is the pore pressure in the soil at the centre of the slice base. The shear strength is given by

$$s = c' + \sigma' \tan \phi'$$

where c' and ϕ' are shear strength parameters for the soil at the base of the slice.

Hence the resisting force is

$$S = \frac{c'b}{\cos \alpha} + \left(W \cos \alpha - \frac{ub}{\cos \alpha}\right) \tan \phi'$$

while the overturning force is $W \sin \alpha$.

Moment equilibrium for all slices about the centre of rotation O is considered and a factor of safety simply defined as

$$F = \frac{\Sigma \text{ resisting moments}}{\Sigma \text{ overturning moments}}$$

Hence

$$F = \frac{\Sigma\, c'b/\cos \alpha + (W \cos \alpha - ub/\cos \alpha) \tan \phi'}{\Sigma\, W \sin \alpha} \tag{5.2}$$

It is necessary to determine the critical circle which yields a minimum value of F.

Bishop[2] derived a more rigorous solution by allowing for the fact that only a fraction of the shear strength is mobilized on the slip plane for a slope with a reasonable factor of safety. This solution is used by the GENESYS (see Sec. 1.2) program SLIPCIRCLE/1.[5]

The FUNCTION subroutine SLIPFS (see Fig. 5.4) is designed to analyse a simple slope or one incorporating a berm and determines the factor of safety as defined by Eq. (5.2) for a single trial circle. It employs nominally 0.5 m wide slices; only horizontal strata boundaries and ground-water level are considered in the analysis, which also takes account of tension cracks. The subroutine is suitable for use in conjunction with a main program, from which it takes the following information.

1. Trial circle details: centre coordinates and radius – *XC, YC, RAD*
2. Strata details: number of strata – *NSTRAT*, base level – *BY*, shear strength parameters – *COH* (kN m^{-2}), *PHI*, bulk specific weight (kN m^{-3}) – *DENS.*
3. Profile details: base width – *BWIDTH*, total embankment height – *EMBHT*, side slope – 1 in *GRADC*, height of water table – *HWT*, berm height – *HB*, berm length – *BL*, berm slope – 1 in *GRADB*, base level of tension cracks – *YTC*.

Note. Strata must be arranged in descending order of base level and a stratum boundary must be specified at the water table. All dimensions are metres and where applicable should be relative to the coordinate system origin shown in Fig. 5.5.

```
      FUNCTION SLIPFS(XC,YC,RAD,NSTRAT,BY,COH,PHI,DENS,
     1  BWIDTH,EMBHT,GRADC,HWT,HB,BL,GRADB,YTC)
      DIMENSION BY(NSTRAT),COH(NSTRAT),PHI(NSTRAT),DENS(NSTRAT),X(100)
C
C     CALCULATE INTERSECTIONS OF CIRCLE WITH PROFILE
C
      IF(YC.GE.RAD)GOTO 20
      XL=XC-SQRT(RAD**2-YC**2)
      XR=2.0*XC-XL
      IF(XR.LE.0.0.OR.XL.GE.0.0)GOTO 20
      IF(XL.LT.-BWIDTH)GOTO 10
      GOTO 40
   10 XL=XC-SQRT(RAD**2-(YC-YTC)**2)
      IF(XL.LE.(-BWIDTH-YTC*GRADC))GOTO 40
      XL=(XC-(YC+BWIDTH/GRADC)/GRADC-SQRT((XC-(YC+BWIDTH/GRADC)/GRADC)
     & **2-(1.0+(1.0/GRADC)**2)*(XC**2+(YC+BWIDTH/GRADC)**2-RAD**2)))
     &/(1.0+(1.0/GRADC)**2)
      GOTO 40
   20 E=(XC+YC/GRADC)**2-(1.0+(1.0/GRADC)**2)*(XC**2+YC**2-RAD**2)
      IF(E.GT.0.0)GOTO 30
      WRITE(6,600)
      GOTO 140
   30 XL=(XC+YC/GRADC-SQRT(E))/(1.0+(1.0/GRADC)**2)
   40 XTC=XC+SQRT(RAD**2-(YC-YTC)**2)
      IF(XTC.GE.YTC*GRADC)GOTO 50
      WRITE(6,601)
      GOTO 140
C
C   CALCULATE INTERSECTIONS WITH STRATA BASES
C
   50 X(1)=XL
      J=1
      DO 70 I=1,NSTRAT
      IF((YC-BY(I)-0.01).GT.RAD)GOTO 80
      IF(BY(I).GE.YTC)GOTO 70
      IF(ABS(BY(I)-YC+RAD).LE.0.01)GOTO 70
      X1=XC-SQRT(RAD**2-(YC-BY(I))**2)
      X2=2.0*XC-X1
      IF(X1.LT.XL)GOTO 60
      J=J+1
      X(J)=X1
   60 IF(X2.LT.XL.OR.X2.GT.XTC)GOTO 70
      J=J+1
      X(J)=X2
   70 CONTINUE
   80 NSECT=J+1
      X(NSECT)=XTC
C
C    ARRANGE IN ASCENDING ORDER OF 'X'
C
   90 K=0
      DO 100 I=2,NSECT
      IF(X(I-1).LT.X(I))GOTO 100
      K=1
      T=X(I-1)
      X(I-1)=X(I)
      X(I)=T
  100 CONTINUE
      IF(K.NE.0)GOTO 90
      SUM1=0.0
      SUM2=0.0
      Y1=EMBHT
      Y2=EMBHT-HB
      X3=Y2*GRADC
      X2=X3+BL
      X1=X2+HB*GRADB
      X4=-BWIDTH
      X5=X4-Y2*GRADC
      X6=X5-BL
      X7=X6-HB*GRADB
      DO 130 I=2,NSECT
      W=X(I)-X(I-1)
      IW=IFIX(2.0*W)
      IF(IW.LE.0)IW=1
```

Figure 5.4 Function SLIPFS

```
C
C     USE AT LEAST ØNE STEP ØF NØMINAL 0.5 MTRS WIDTH
C
      DELTX=W/FLØAT(IW)
      XR=X(I-1)
      DØ 130 K=1,IW
      XL=XR
      XR=XL+DELTX
      XMID=(XL+XR)/2.0
      YMIDB=YC-SQRT(RAD**2-(XC-XMID)**2)
      WEIGHT=0.0
      IF(XMID.GE.X1.ØR.XMID.LE.X7)YT=Y1
      IF(XMID.GE.X2.AND.XMID.LE.X1)YT=Y2+(XMID-X2)/GRADB
      IF((XMID.GE.X3.AND.XMID.LE.X2) .ØR.
     1   (XMID.GE.X6.AND.XMID.LE.X5)    )YT=Y2
      IF(XMID.GE.0.0.AND.XMID.LE.X3)YT=XMID/GRADC
      IF(XMID.GE.X4.AND.XMID.LE.0.0)YT=0.0
      IF(XMID.GE.X5.AND.XMID.LE.X4)YT=(X4-XMID)/GRADC
      IF(XMID.GE.X7.AND.XMID.LE.X6)YT=Y2+(X6-XMID)/GRADB
      DØ 110 J=1,NSTRAT
      JJ=J
      YB=BY(J)
      IF(YT.LE.YB)GØTØ 110
      IF(YB.LT.YMIDB)YB=YMIDB
      D=DENS(J)
      IF(YB.LT.HWT)D=D-9.81
      WEIGHT=WEIGHT+(YT-YB)*D
      IF(YB.EQ.YMIDB)GØTØ 120
      YT=YB
  110 CØNTINUE
  120 SUM2=SUM2+DELTX*WEIGHT*(XMID-XC)/RAD
      SUM1=SUM1+CØH(JJ)*DELTX*RAD/(YC-YMIDB)+
     1  TAN(0.0174533*PHI(JJ))*DELTX*WEIGHT*(YC-YMIDB)/RAD
  130 CØNTINUE
      SLIPFS=SUM1/SUM2
      RETURN
C
C     ERRØR CØNDITIØN
C
  140 STØP
  600 FØRMAT(28H CIRCLE DØES NØT CUT PRØFILE)
  601 FØRMAT(33H CIRCLE MEETS YTC ØUTSIDE PRØFILE)
      END
```

Figure 5.4 *(continued)*

5.3.2 Automatic search for critical circle

Although for simple slopes in homogeneous material, geometric constructions are available to enable the critical circle giving the minimum factor of safety to be located, in most situations which involve a complex geometry and stratified soil conditions, a large number of trial computations are usually necessary before the critical circle can be determined.

For example, a series of circles passing through a specific point in the soil profile and whose centres form a regular grid may be analysed, the results enabling the critical centre to be interpolated from contours of equal factors of safety. Not surprisingly, considerable savings in computation can be achieved by including an automatic search routine in the computer analysis.

In principle the subroutine SEARCH, see Fig. 5.6, directs selection of successive centres down the steepest slope of the three-dimensional elliptic valley-shaped surface defined by the circle centre coordinates and associated factors of safety. The safety factor F_0, for the trial centre initially specified to have centre coordinates (X_0, Y_0), is first determined, followed by further factors F_1 and F_2 for centres $(X_0 + 0.1 \times DELTA, Y_0)$ and $(X_0, Y_0 + 0.1 \times DELTA)$ respectively. The

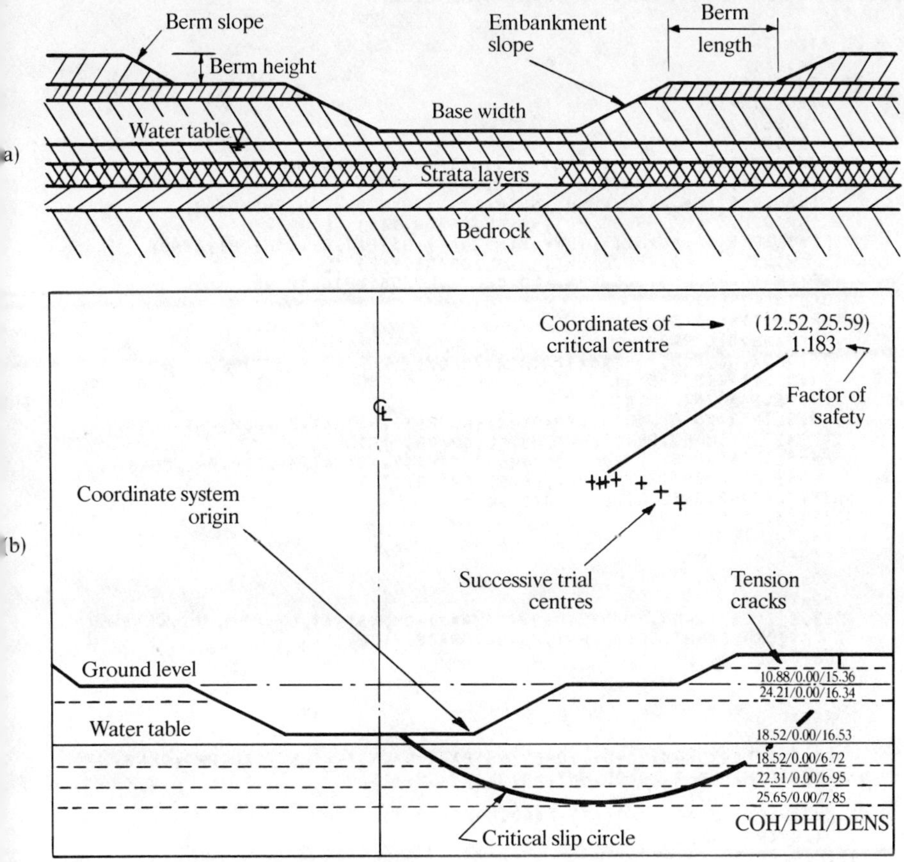

Figure 5.5 Slope stability analysis of highway embankment. (a) Definition of design parameters. (b) Typical screen display

```
      SUBRØUTINE SEARCH(XO,YO,FO,BY,CØH,PHI,DENS,NSTRAT,EGL,EMBHT,BWIDTH,
     1    GRADC,HB,BL,GB,HWT)
      DIMENSIØN BY(NSTRAT),CØH(NSTRAT),PHI(NSTRAT),DENS(NSTRAT)
      GRADB=GB
      IF(GB.EQ.0.0)GRADB=1.0
      DELTA=1.0
      DSTØP=0.1
      RELF=0.5
      EPS=0.001
      YTØP=EMBHT
C
C     CALCULATE YTC WITHØUT BERM WØRKING FRØM TØP ØF PRØFILE
C
      N=0
      WEIGHT=0.0
      YT=EMBHT
   10 N=N+1
      ALPH=(45.0+PHI(N)/2.0)*0.0174533
      YTCN=(2.0*CØH(N)*TAN(ALPH)-WEIGHT)/DENS(N)
C
C     YTCN IS VALUE ØF YTC IN THIS STRATUM
C     CHECK IF CRACKS GØ TØ NEXT STRATUM
C
      IF(YTCN.LE.YT-BY(N))GØTØ 20
      WEIGHT=WEIGHT+(YT-BY(N))*DENS(N)
      YT=BY(N)
      GØTØ 10
```

Figure 5.6 Subroutine SEARCH

```
   20 YTC=YT-YTCN
      FO=1.E10
   30 CONTINUE
      DX=DELTA/10.0
      DY=DELTA/10.0
      OLDFS=FO
      FO=SLIPFS(XO,YO,YO-BY(NSTRAT),NSTRAT,BY,COH,PHI,DENS,
     1  BWIDTH,EMBHT,GRADC,HWT,HB,BL,GRADB,YTC)
      F1=SLIPFS(XO+DX,YO,YO-BY(NSTRAT),NSTRAT,BY,COH,PHI,DENS,
     1  BWIDTH,EMBHT,GRADC,HWT,HB,BL,GRADB,YTC)
      F2=SLIPFS(XO,YO+DY,YO+DY-BY(NSTRAT),NSTRAT,BY,COH,PHI,DENS,
     1  BWIDTH,EMBHT,GRADC,HWT,HB,BL,GRADB,YTC)
      IF(ABS(FO-OLDFS).LE.EPS.AND.DELTA.LT.DSTOP)GOTO 90
      DFDY=(F2-FO)/DY
      DFDX=(F1-FO)/DX
      THETA=1.5707963
      IF(DFDX.NE.0.0)THETA=ATAN(DFDY/DFDX)
      DX=DELTA*COS(THETA)
      DY=DELTA*SIN(THETA)
      F3=SLIPFS(XO+DX,YO+DY,YO+DY-BY(NSTRAT),NSTRAT,BY,COH,PHI,DENS,
     1  BWIDTH,EMBHT,GRADC,HWT,HB,BL,GRADB,YTC)
      F4=SLIPFS(XO-DX,YO-DY,YO-DY-BY(NSTRAT),NSTRAT,BY,COH,PHI,DENS,
     1  BWIDTH,EMBHT,GRADC,HWT,HB,BL,GRADB,YTC)
   40 IF(F3+F4-2.0*FO.GT.0.0)GOTO 60
      IF(F4.LT.F3)GOTO 50
      F4=FO
      FO=F3
      XO=XO+DX
      YO=YO+DY
      F3=SLIPFS(XO+DX,YO+DY,YO-BY(NSTRAT)+DY,NSTRAT,BY,COH,PHI,DENS,
     1  BWIDTH,EMBHT,GRADC,HWT,HB,BL,GRADB,YTC)
      GOTO 40
   50 F3=FO
      FO=F4
      XO=XO-DX
      YO=YO-DY
      F4=SLIPFS(XO-DX,YO-DY,YO-BY(NSTRAT)-DY,NSTRAT,BY,COH,PHI,DENS,
     1  BWIDTH,EMBHT,GRADC,HWT,HB,BL,GRADB,YTC)
      GOTO 40
   60 RMIN=(F4-F3)*DELTA/((F3+F4-2.0*FO)*2.0)
      D=ABS(RMIN*RELF)
   70 IF(D.GT.DELTA)GOTO 80
      DELTA=DELTA/1.5
      GOTO 70
   80 XO=XO+RMIN*RELF*COS(THETA)
      YO=YO+RMIN*RELF*SIN(THETA)
      GOTO 30
C
C   POSITION HAS BEEN FOUND TO GIVEN ACCURACY
C
   90 RETURN
      END
```

Figure 5.6 *(continued)*

direction of maximum gradient, the r-axis in Fig. 5.7, is estimated from the ratio of slopes $(F_1 - F_0)/(0.1 \times DELTA)$ and $(F_2 - F_0)/(0.1 \times DELTA)$. Analyses at centres $(X_0 + DELTA \cos\theta, Y_0 + DELTA \sin\theta)$ and $(X_0 - DELTA \cos\theta, Y_0 - DELTA \sin\theta)$, giving factors F_3 and F_4 respectively along the r-axis, enable a quadratic fit to be made to the surface profile using F_0, F_3, and F_4.

Thus

$$f(r) = ar^2 + br + c \tag{5.3}$$

and

$$f'(r) = 2ar + b \tag{5.4}$$

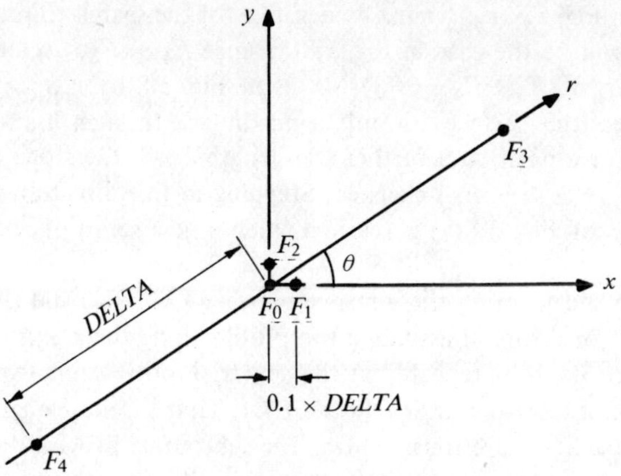

Figure 5.7 Positions of trial centres in search routine

By substituting in Eq. (5.3),

$$f(0) = F_0 = c \tag{5.5}$$

$$f(+DELTA) = F_3 = a(DELTA)^2 + b(DELTA) + c \tag{5.6}$$

$$f(-DELTA) = F_4 = a(-DELTA)^2 + b(-DELTA) + c \tag{5.7}$$

Combining Eqs (5.5), (5.6), and (5.7),

$$F_3 + F_4 = 2a(DELTA)^2 + 2F_0$$

Therefore

$$a = \frac{F_3 + F_4 - 2F_0}{2(DELTA)^2} \tag{5.8}$$

If the minimum of the quadratic occurs at a point $r = r_{min}$, Eq. (5.4) gives

$$f'(r_{min}) = 2a(r_{min}) + b = 0$$

Therefore

$$r_{min} = -b/2a$$

Now $f'(0) = b$ and is also given approximately by

$$f'(0) = \left(\frac{F_3 - F_0}{DELTA} + \frac{F_0 - F_4}{DELTA}\right) /2$$

$$= \left(\frac{F_3 - F_4}{2 \times DELTA}\right) \tag{5.9}$$

From Eqs (5.8) and (5.9),

$$r_{min} = \left(\frac{F_4 - F_3}{F_3 + F_4 - 2F_0}\right) \times \frac{DELTA}{2}$$

For the situation given in Fig. 5.8, r_{min} must be negative for the search to proceed down the surface. This will be the case in Fig. 5.8(a) since $F_4 - F_3 < 0$ and $(F_3 + F_4 - 2F_0) > 0$. However, if $(F_3 + F_4 - 2F_0) \leqslant 0$, as in Fig. 5.8(b), $r_{min} > 0$ and the search is directed up the surface towards a maximum. In such a situation a factor of safety F'_4 for a position a further step length down the slope is determined and the term $(F_0 + F'_4 - 2F_4)$ checked. Stepping in this direction is continued until the geometry of Fig. 5.8(a) is reached when a new series of trial calculations is initiated.

A relaxation factor is applied to r_{min}, the distance between (X_0, Y_0) and the predicted minimum, to allow for errors in assuming the profile along the r axis to be quadratic in shape. The procedure is repeated at the new trial centre using two-thirds the previous step length if $|RMIN \times RELF| \leqslant DELTA$. Thus the step length is reduced as the search approaches the critical centre. The subroutine SEARCH is terminated when *DELTA* is less than 0.1 m and when the difference between successive factors of safety is less than 0.001. Suitable values of *RELF* = 0.5 and *DELTA* = 1.0 m have been established after continued usage. The subroutine is designed for use with a main program from which it takes the centre coordinates (*XO*, *YO*) of an initial trial circle in addition to the data required by SLIPFS (see Sec. 5.3.1). Computations of factor of safety for a succession of trial centres are carried out using function SLIPFS; the base level of tension cracks and radii of trial circles required by SLIPFS are calculated in SEARCH. Base circles to the lowest specified stratum are automatically considered but the program could be extended to analyse other circles. The subroutine finally hands back the value of the minimum factor of safety and centre coordinates of the associated critical circle to the main program.

5.3.3 Advantage of computer graphics

Automatic search routines may give misleading and possibly unsafe solutions if used indiscriminately, in particular when complex profiles or more than one minimum exist and when the computed minimum is unrealistic or geometrically impossible. However, such dangers can be largely overcome by the use of computer graphics, which provide the designer with an immediate visual check of the circles under consideration.

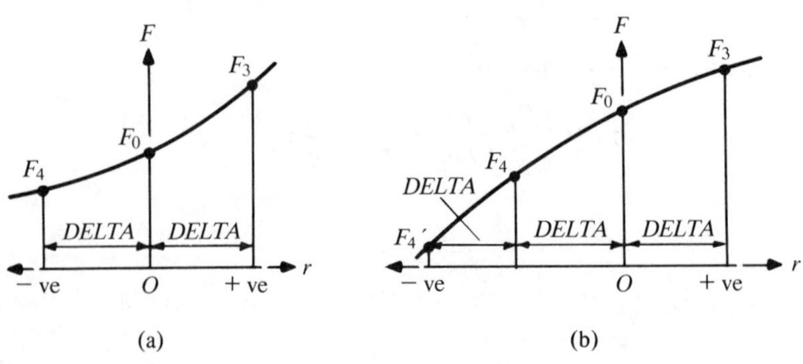

Figure 5.8 Alternative procedures during search routine

The programs described have associated graphic routines which have been omitted for brevity. A typical screen display showing successive trial centres during an immediate stability analysis ($\phi = 0$) for a highway embankment incorporating a berm is illustrated in Fig. 5.5.

5.3.4 Slope stability analysis of embankment dam undergoing seepage

With some modification the program may be used to examine the stability of the slopes of an embankment dam undergoing seepage. In this case, the pore pressure values used in Eq. (5.2) are interpolated from a data file created by a finite element analysis similar to that described later in this chapter.

The FUNCTION subprogram PFIND given in Fig. 5.9 uses the coordinate

```
      FUNCTIØN PFIND(XCL,YCL)
      CØMMØN XXX(300),YYY(300),PPP(300),NN
      I1=0
      I2=0
      I3=0
      D1=1.0E50
      D2=1.0E50
      D3=1.0E50
      DØ 1 I=1,NN
      D=SQRT((XCL-XXX(I))**2+(YCL-YYY(I))**2)
      IF(D.GT.D3)GØTØ 1
      D3=D
      I3=I
      IF(D.GT.D2)GØTØ 1
      D3=D2
      D2=D
      I3=I2
      I2=I
      IF(D.GT.D1)GØTØ 1
      D2=D1
      D1=D
      I2=I1
      I1=I
    1 CØNTINUE
      PFIND=(D2*D3*PPP(I1)+D1*D3*PPP(I2)+D1*D2*PPP(I3))/(D2*D3
     *   +D1*D3+D1*D2)
      RETURN
      END
```

Figure 5.9 Function PFIND

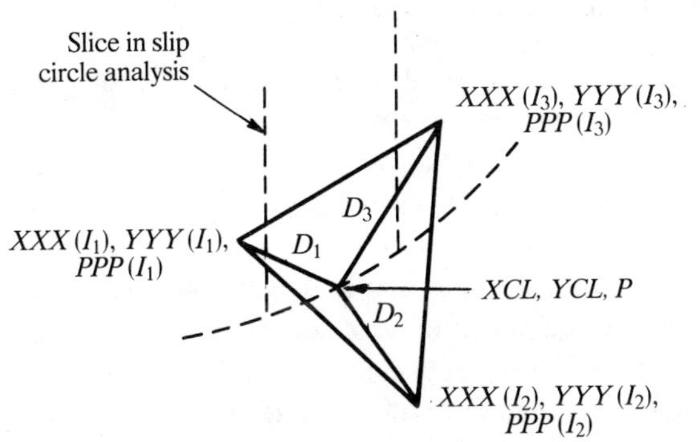

Figure 5.10 Interpolation of pore pressures from data file

positions and pore pressure values from the seepage data file, selects the three closest points to the centre base of the slice under consideration as shown in Fig. 5.10, and calculates the appropriate pore pressure value using the linear interpolation formula

$$P(XCL,\ YCL) = \frac{D_2 \times D_3 \times PPP(I_1) + D_1 \times D_3 \times PPP(I_2) + D_1 \times D_2 \times PPP(I_3)}{D_2 \times D_3 + D_1 \times D_3 + D_1 \times D_2}$$

5.4 SOLUTION OF SEEPAGE PROBLEMS BY THE FINITE-ELEMENT METHOD

Typical problems involving two-dimensional confined and unconfined flow are shown in Fig. 5.11. Flow through the soil regions is assumed to be continuous and irrotational and to obey Darcy's law. While the permeable foundation in Fig. 5.11(a) can be considered as having infinite horizontal extent it is necessary, when using any physical or numerical modelling techniques, to introduce artificial boundaries and consider finite length of foundation. It has been shown by King[6] that solutions will not be affected unduly, providing $B/L > 1$ and $B/b > 6$. The location of the free surface in Fig. 5.11(b) is not known a priori. The boundary conditions to both problems can be expressed in terms of the total head function h and the stream function ψ as indicated.

The finite element method was first applied to confined flow problems by Zienkiewicz, Meyer, and Cheung.[7] They considered flow through zoned anisotropic flow regions and obtained solutions in terms of the distribution of total head, $h(x, y)$. An iterative technique for applying this basic procedure to unconfined flow problems was illustrated by Finn[8] and King and Chowdhury[9] added a routine for discharge computation. Ponter[10] showed that solutions to confined flow problems can also be obtained in terms of the stream function $\psi(x, y)$ which inherently include an evaluation of discharge. He demonstrated that the alternative procedures of minimizing energy, with respect to total head or to stream function, are analogous to those of minimizing total potential energy or complementary energy in elasticity problems and thereby that they would yield upper and lower bounds respectively on the discharge.

5.4.1 General formulation of finite-element models

The total potential energy (strictly rate of energy dissipation or power) for steady flow of water through a bounded region can be expressed as

$$\dot{E} = \frac{\gamma_w}{2} \int\int_R [i_x v_x + i_y v_y]\, dx\, dy - \gamma_w H q \qquad (5.10)$$

in which i_x, i_y, v_x, and v_y are hydraulic gradients and velocities in x and y directions respectively, γ_w is the specific weight of water and H the hydraulic head responsible for the discharge q. The first term represents the rate of energy dissipation within the region and the second the potential energy of the hydraulic head. They are analogous to the stored energy of an elastic body and the potential energy of the loads applied to it in a structural problem (see Sec. 3.5.4.2).

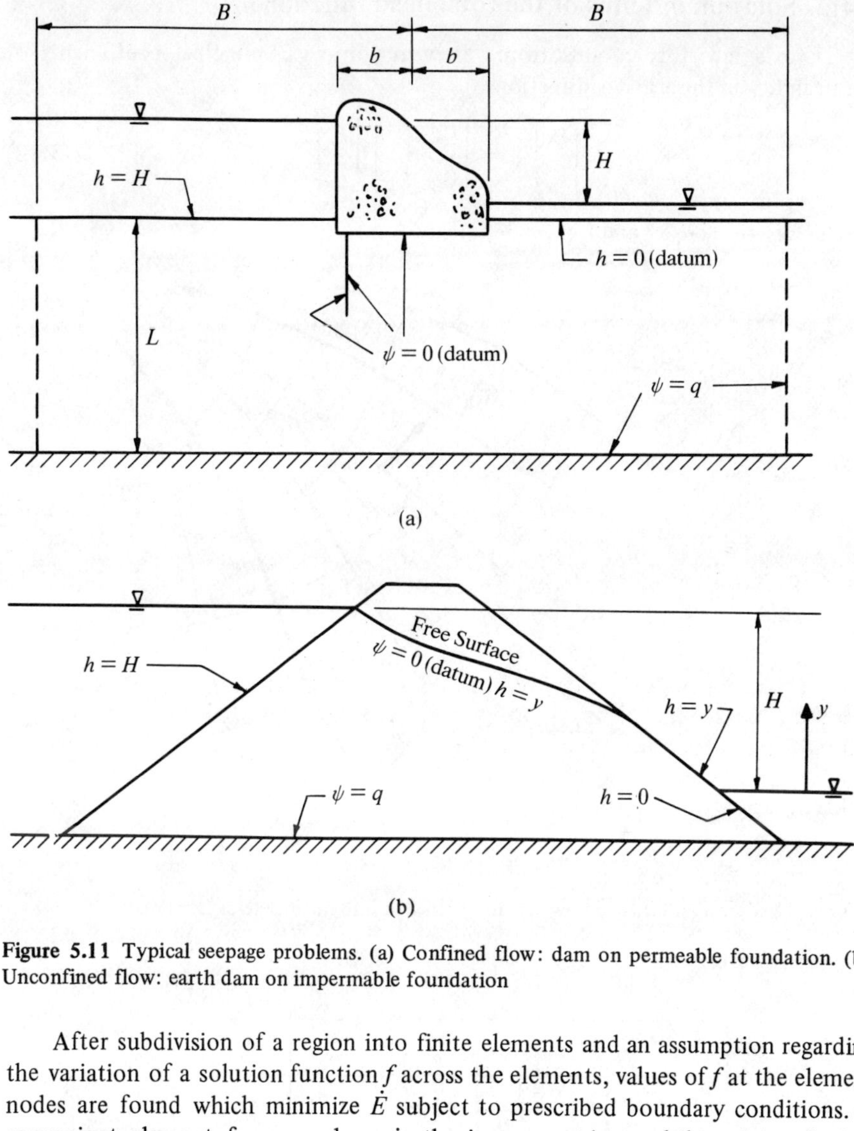

Figure 5.11 Typical seepage problems. (a) Confined flow: dam on permeable foundation. (b) Unconfined flow: earth dam on impermable foundation

After subdivision of a region into finite elements and an assumption regarding the variation of a solution function f across the elements, values of f at the element nodes are found which minimize $\dot{E}$ subject to prescribed boundary conditions. A convenient element for general use is the isoparametric quadrilateral in which f varies as

$$f = \alpha_1 + \alpha_2 \xi + \alpha_3 \eta + \alpha_4 \xi\eta \tag{5.11}$$

where ξ and η are linear interpolation parameters. This function provides linear variation of f along element sides. Irregular boundary shapes, variation in permeability from zone to zone through a region and anisotropy within each zone are readily accounted for.

When boundaries are rectilinear and aligned in the directions of the principal coefficients of permeability, the quadrilaterals can also be rectilinear with the advantage that automatic mesh generation procedures can be used.

5.4.2 Solution in terms of the total head function h

By Darcy's law for an anisotropic flow region with principal coefficients of permeability in the x and y directions,

$$\begin{bmatrix} v_x \\ v_y \end{bmatrix} = \begin{bmatrix} k_x & 0 \\ 0 & k_y \end{bmatrix} \begin{bmatrix} i_x \\ i_y \end{bmatrix} \tag{5.12}$$

in which $i_x = -\partial h/\partial x$ and $i_y = -\partial h/\partial y$.

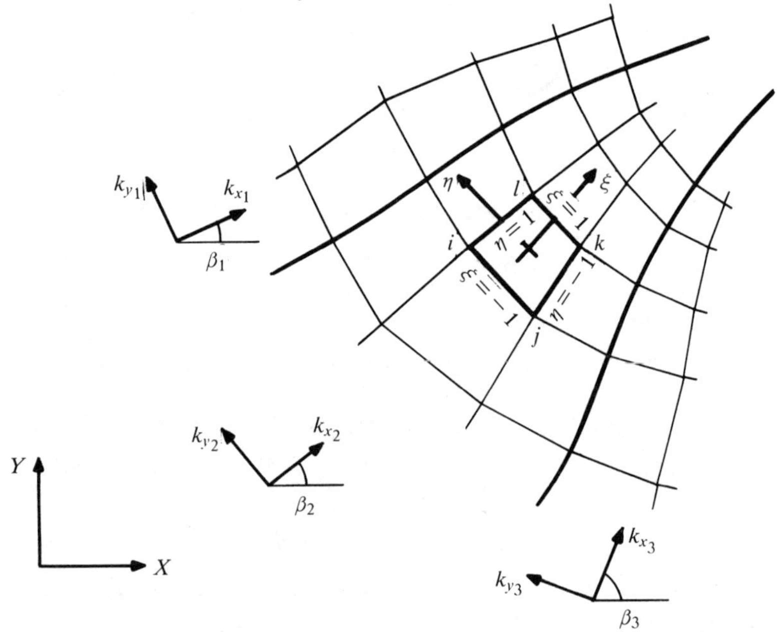

Figure 5.12 Zoned anisotropic flow region subdivided into quadrilateral elements

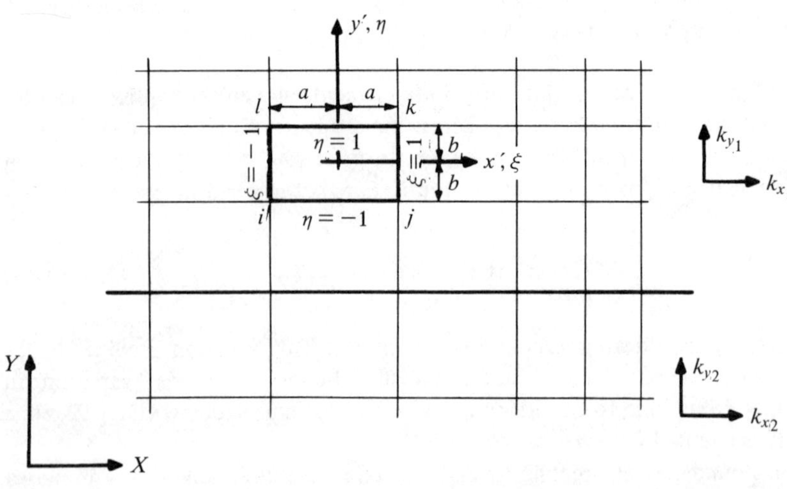

Figure 5.13 Layered anisotropic flow region subdivided into rectilinear elements

Substitution in Eq. (5.10) yields

$$\dot{E}_h = \frac{\gamma_w}{2} \iint_R \left[k_x \left(\frac{\partial h}{\partial x}\right)^2 + k_y \left(\frac{\partial h}{\partial y}\right)^2 \right] dx\, dy - \gamma_w H q \tag{5.13}$$

and it is required to minimize $\dot{E}_h$ with respect to nodal values of h. Noting that the second term yields no contributions to derivatives $\partial \dot{E}_h/\partial h$, the first term alone is acceptable as the functional to be minimized subject to prescribed boundary values. The region is divided into small elements as indicated in Figs. 5.12 and 5.13 and their nodal coordinates specified in a global (X, Y) coordinate system. (Boundaries between zones form element sides and smaller elements are used in regions where rapid variation in total head is anticipated.) For quadrilateral elements such as those in Fig. 5.12 these coordinates are transformed into the local (x, y) coordinate system, defined by the directions of principal coefficients of permeability in the element, using the equations:

$$\begin{bmatrix} x \\ y \end{bmatrix} = \begin{bmatrix} \cos\beta & \sin\beta \\ -\sin\beta & \cos\beta \end{bmatrix} \begin{bmatrix} X \\ Y \end{bmatrix}$$

in which β is the inclination of the x axis to the X axis.

For a rectilinear element the interpolation parameters of Eq. (5.11) are simply $\xi = x'/a$ and $\eta = y'/b$, where $2a$ and $2b$ are the dimensions in the x and y directions respectively and x' and y' are coordinates with respect to the centroid of the element. Since the equations must be satisfied by nodal head values the total head at any point within the element is given by

$$h = \frac{1}{4ab} \begin{bmatrix} (ab - bx' - ay' + x'y'), (ab + bx' - ay' - x'y') \\ (ab + bx' + ay' + x'y'), (ab - bx' + ay' - x'y') \end{bmatrix} \begin{bmatrix} h_i \\ h_j \\ h_k \\ h_l \end{bmatrix} \tag{5.14}$$

Differentiation of Eq. (5.14) yields

$$\begin{bmatrix} \partial h/\partial x \\ \partial h/\partial y \end{bmatrix} = \frac{1}{4ab} \begin{bmatrix} (-b+y'), (b-y'), (b+y'), (-b-y') \\ (-a+x'), (-a-x'), (a+x'), (a-x') \end{bmatrix} \begin{bmatrix} h_i \\ h_j \\ h_k \\ h_l \end{bmatrix} \tag{5.15}$$

After substitution of these gradients into Eq. (5.13), and performing the required integration, differentiation with respect to the nodal values (see Sec. 3.5.4.1) yields the following contributions to the nodal derivatives from this element

$$\left[\frac{\partial \dot{E}_h}{\partial h_e}\right] = [S]\,[h_e] \tag{5.15}$$

in which $[h_e]$ is the total head vector $[h_i, h_j, h_k, h_l]^{\mathrm{T}}$ and

$$[S] = \begin{bmatrix} P+Q, & -P+Q/2, & -P/2-Q/2, & P/2-Q \\ & P+Q, & P/2-Q, & -P/2-Q/2 \\ \text{Symmetric} & & P+Q, & -P+Q/2 \\ & & & P+Q \end{bmatrix}$$

with $P = bk_x/3a$ and $Q = ak_y/3b$.

The corresponding matrix for the general quadrilateral cannot be expressed explicitly but is evaluated numerically as indicated in Secs. 3.5.4.1 and 3.5.6, following essentially the same procedure as that described above.

The sum of the contributions to the differential with respect to a node from all elements adjacent to that node is equated to zero; i.e., for m elements connected at node r

$$\sum_{e=1}^{m} \left(\frac{\partial \dot{E}_h}{\partial h_r}\right)_e = 0 \tag{5.16}$$

Similar summations for all nodes results in a set of simultaneous linear equations. Assembly of the equations is most conveniently carried out element by element and the equations can be expressed as

$$\left[\frac{\partial \dot{E}_h}{\partial h}\right] = \sum_{e=1}^{m} \left[\frac{\partial \dot{E}_h}{\partial h}\right]_e = 0 \tag{5.17}$$

in which m is the number of elements in the region.

Equation (5.17) can be simply expressed as

$$[SM]\ [h] = 0 \tag{5.18}$$

in which $[SM]$ is the seepage matrix for the whole region and $[h]$ the total head vector for all nodes. After modification for prescribed boundary values the numerical solution of Eq. (5.18) yields the required nodal head values.

Now consider the subsequent evaluation of the energy derivatives defined by Eq. (5.15). For a rectilinear element two of these values are:

$$\frac{\partial \dot{E}_h}{\partial h_i} = P(h_i - h_j - h_k/2 - h_l/2) + Q(h_i + h_j/2 + h_k/2 + h_l)$$

and

$$\frac{\partial \dot{E}_h}{\partial h_l} = P(h_i/2 - h_j/2 - h_k + h_l) + Q(-h_i - h_j/2 + h_k/2 + h_l)$$

Adding these yields

$$\frac{\partial \dot{E}_h}{\partial h_i} + \frac{\partial \dot{E}_h}{\partial h_l} = 2bk_x \frac{\dfrac{h_i + h_l}{2} - \dfrac{h_i + h_k}{2}}{2a}$$

which can be recognized as a finite-difference approximation (see Sec. 3.4.3) to Darcy's law for the discharge across side il of the element. The discharge across a side of an element is thus given approximately by the sum of the energy derivatives at adjacent nodes. The terms $\partial\dot{E}/\partial h_i$ etc. are in fact equivalent nodal flows analogous to the equivalent nodal forces in a structural problem and Eqs. (5.16) and (5.17) can be interpreted as providing equilibrium of nodal flows.

The overall discharge through a region can therefore be evaluated simply by summing the equivalent nodal flows from the elements on one side of any section which connects the extreme flow boundaries. For n nodes,

$$q = \sum_{r=1}^{n} \frac{\partial \dot{E}_h}{\partial h_r} \tag{5.19}$$

Equations (5.15) and (5.19) also apply for regions divided into quadrilateral elements.

5.4.3 Solution of terms of the stream function ψ

The stream function ψ is defined such that:

$$\begin{bmatrix} v_x \\ v_y \end{bmatrix} = \begin{bmatrix} \partial\psi/\partial y \\ -\partial\psi/\partial x \end{bmatrix}$$

The value of ψ is constant on any stream line and the difference between the ψ values on any two stream lines represents the flow between them.

Using Eq. (5.12) and substituting in Eq. (5.10) yields:

$$\dot{E}_\psi = \frac{\gamma_w}{2} \iint_R \left[\frac{1}{k_y} \left(\frac{\partial\psi}{\partial x} \right)^2 + \frac{1}{k_x} \left(\frac{\partial\psi}{\partial y} \right)^2 \right] dx\, dy - \gamma_w H q \tag{5.20}$$

Here, since the total flow or discharge q is directly related to the boundary ψ values, the second term contributes to changes in $\dot{E}_\psi$ consequent on changes in the boundary values and must be included. Indeed it is only through this term that the appropriate value of hydraulic head is introduced into the solution routine in the absence of prescribed boundary values.

Substitution of $1/k_y$ for k_x and $1/k_x$ for k_y in Eq. (5.15) readily yields seepage matrices which appertain to the first term only and enables a system of equations:

$$[SM]\ [\psi] = 0$$

to be formed. The arbitrary values $\psi = 0$ are then introduced on one flow boundary. On the other, the condition that all ψ values should be equal, i.e. $\psi = q$, is accounted for by modifying the equations at the nodes adjacent to this boundary, by adding the coefficients which relate to the common ψ value, and by combining all coefficients in the equations at nodes on this boundary into a new equation. The derivative $\partial\dot{E}_\psi/\partial q = -\gamma_w H$ from the second term in Eq. (5.20) is included in this equation. (It should be noted that the new equation will involve the nodal head values of all the elements adjacent to boundary $\psi = q$. Special provision for this equation may be required in the solution routine.)

Now consider again the subsequent evaluation and summation of two adjacent energy derivatives for a rectilinear element.

For example

$$\frac{\partial \dot{E}_\psi}{\partial \psi_i} + \frac{\partial \dot{E}_\psi}{\partial \psi_l} = \frac{2b}{k_y} \frac{\dfrac{\psi_i + \psi_l}{2} - \dfrac{\psi_j - \psi_k}{2}}{2a}$$

In finite-difference form, the right hand side can be written as $\Delta y(-v_y/k_y) = -i_y \Delta y = \Delta h$ and therefore

$$\frac{\partial \dot{E}_\psi}{\partial \psi_i} + \frac{\partial \dot{E}_\psi}{\partial \psi_l} = \Delta h_{i-l}$$

is an approximation to the head drop along side *il* of the element.

The terms $\partial \dot{E}_\psi / \partial \psi_i$ etc. are in fact equivalent nodal head drops and it follows that head values can be determined by progressive summation of terms $\partial \dot{E}_\psi / \partial \psi_r$ at the nodes along any section line joining equipotential boundaries. The most useful line of course is that along the underside of an impermeable structure.

5.4.4 Comparative solutions of a typical confined flow problem

Consider flow beneath the impervious dam shown in Fig. 5.14 due to a hydraulic head H. The dam is symmetrical with end cutoff walls and is founded on a homogeneous isotropic stratum with coefficient of permeability k. Solutions were obtained in terms of total head and in terms of stream function using the element subdivision shown.

The values obtained for discharge and either nodal heads or nodal head drops around the structure are shown in Fig. 5.15. The difference between the upper and lower bound estimates of the discharge is suitably small and the agreement between the resulting distributions of total head is most satisfactory.

5.4.5 Solution of unconfined flow problems

When flow is unconfined the positions of free surfaces have to be determined using an iterative procedure until the boundary condition

$$\text{Total head } h = \text{position head } Y$$

is satisfied along them.

Consider flow through the earth dam shown in Fig. 5.16. A free surface AD is assumed and the enclosed region divided into quadrilateral elements. For this kind of discharge face with $B\hat{C}D < 90°$, the assumed exit point D must be placed below the true position E. For the prescribed boundary conditions, $h = H$ on the upstream equipotential boundary AB and $h = Y$ on the surface of seepage CD, the distribution of total head through this region is determined and the values of total head h' at the nodes on the assumed free surface compared with their position heads Y'. These nodes are then assigned new ordinates $Y = (Y' + h')/2$ provided that this does not bring them above the downstream face of the dam. When this happens the node is only elevated onto the face where it assumes the fixed value $h = Y$ appropriate to a point on the surface of seepage.

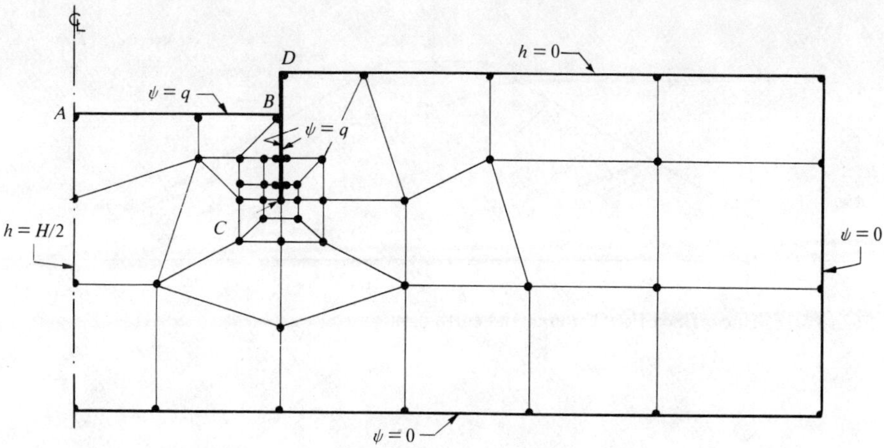

Figure 5.14 Confined flow example: geometry and finite-element idealization

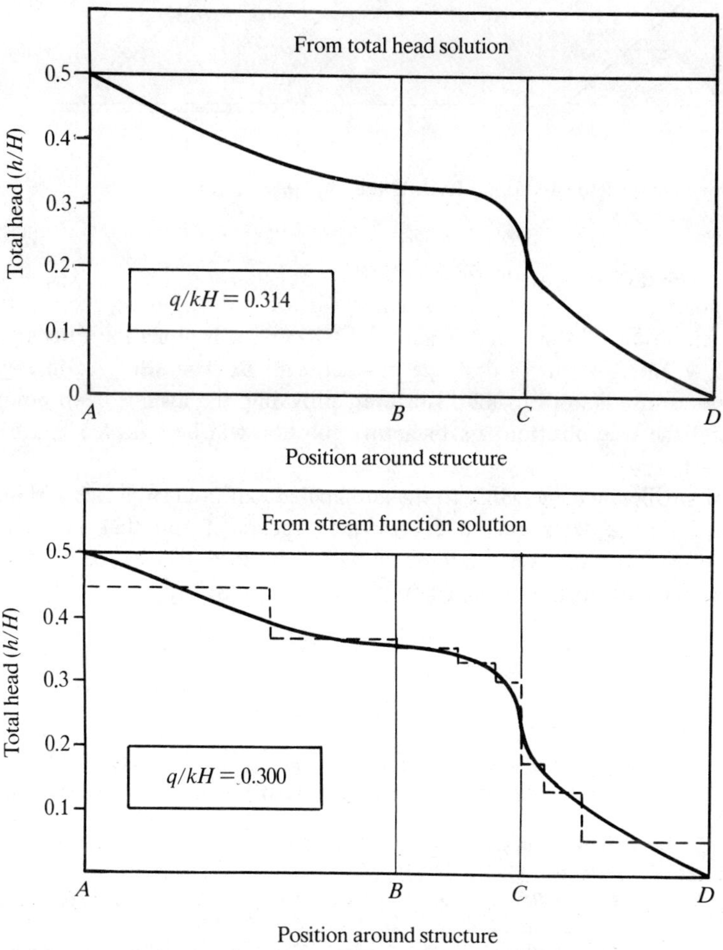

Figure 5.15 Upper and lower bound estimates of discharge and calculated distributions of total head around underside of structure

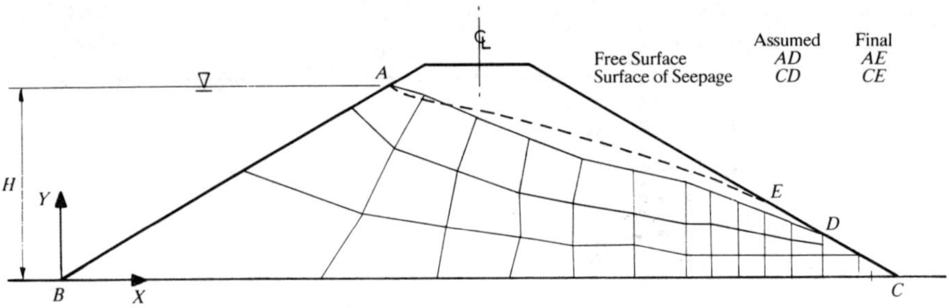

Figure 5.16 Unconfined flow through and earth dam

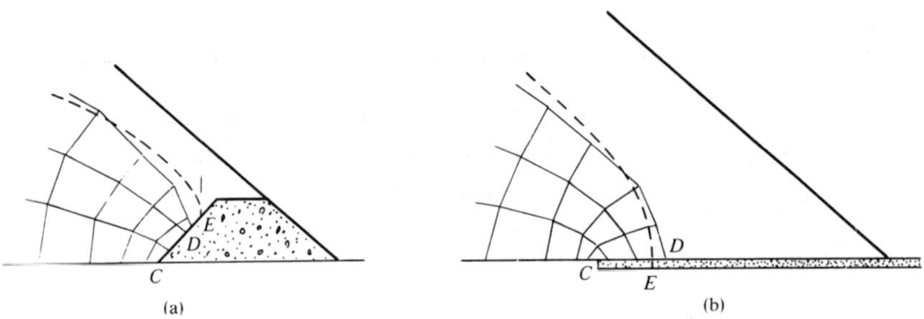

Figure 5.17 Earth dams with toe drains. (a) Rockfill toe. (b) Underdrain

When flow emerges into a toe filter with $B\hat{C}D \geqslant 90^\circ$, as in Fig. 5.17(a), the assumed exit point D must be treated as a free surface point. During successive iterations the elevation of this point is adjusted by moving it along the discharge face. When flow emerges into a drainage blanket with $B\hat{C}D = 180^\circ$, as in Fig. 5.17(b), this procedure is not possible. However, providing the assumed exit point is taken beyond the true position, a satisfactory solution will be achieved as indicated.

The use of smaller elements close to the anticipated exit point of a free surface enables its position to be determined with reasonable accuracy. Note that the nodes connected to those on a free surface must lie below the true position of the free surface to avoid the overlapping of elements.

REFERENCES

1. Rowe, P. W. 'Anchored sheetpile walls', *Proc. Instn Civ. Engrs,* **1**, 27–71, 1952.
2. Bishop, A. W. 'The use of the slip circle in the stability analysis of slopes', *Geotechnique,* **5**, 7–17, 1955.
3. Spencer, E. 'A method of analysis of the stability of embankments assuming parallel inter-slice forces', *Geotechnique* **17**, (1), 11–26, 1967.
4. Whitman, T. V., and W. A. Bailey, 'Use of computers for slope stability analysis', *J. Soil Mech. and Foundn. Div. Am. Soc. Civ. Engrs.*, **93** (SM4), 475–98, 1967.
5. The Genesysis Centre, *'User's Manual for 'Slip-Circle/1'*, University of Technology, Loughborough, 1974.

6. King, G. J. W., 'The effect of foundation length on the solution to confined flow seepage problems', *2nd South East Asian Reg. Conf. on Soil Engg.*, Inst. of Engrs., Singapore, 497–509, 1970.
7. Zienkiewicz, O. C., P. Meyer, and Y. K. Cheung, 'Solutions of anisotropic seepage by finite elements', *J. Eng. Mech. Div., Am. Soc. Civ. Engrs.*, **92** (EM1), 111–20, 1966.
8. Finn, W. D. Liam, 'Finite element analysis of seepage through dams', *J. Soil Mech. and Foundn. Div. Am. Soc. Civ. Engrs.*, **93** (SM6), 41–53, 1967.
9. King, G. J. W. and R. N. Chowdhury, 'Finite element solution for quantity of steady seepage', *Civ. Eng. and P. W. Rev.*, **66,** 1317–21, 1971.
10. Ponter, A. R. S. 'The application of dual minimum theorems to the finite element solution of potential problems with special reference to seepage', *Int. J. Num. Meth. in Engg.*, **4,** 85–93, 1972.

CHAPTER

SIX

APPLICATIONS IN FLUID MECHANICS

6.1 INTRODUCTION

Problems tackled by computer involving civil engineering fluid mechanics, which covers the fields of water resources engineering, hydrology, water supply, sewage disposal, river engineering, and coastal and offshore engineering, will, for convenience, be loosely categorized here into three groups: relatively simple problems which cannot be solved by direct substitution; problems involving matrix algebra unsuitable for hand calculation; and geometrically complex problems requiring repetitive computations. Some typical applications within these categories are illustrated in the following sections of this chapter.

6.2 SIMPLE PROBLEMS

Problems for which solution by hand computation is laborious to perform fall into this category, often because of the need for either iteration or numerical integration procedures. In this section, some applications relating to steady free surface (or open channel) flow are introduced and illustrated by means of an example of their solution in the case of circular conduits.

6.2.1 Flow in Open Channels of Arbitrary Shape

6.2.1.1 Critical depth

Flow at critical depth represents a condition producing maximum discharge, Q, for a given value of specific energy (fluid energy per unit weight above the local channel floor).

Referring to Fig. 6.1, the critical depth, y_c, is obtained as the solution to

$$F_1(y) = 0 = 1 - \frac{Q^2 T(y)}{g\{A(y)\}^3} \tag{6.1}$$

where g is the gravitational acceleration.

This equation cannot be solved directly for y, except in the case of rectangular channel sections, so solution by trial must, therefore, be employed. Use of convergence formulae in the iteration process optimises the computation (see Sec. 3.2.1.1). The Newton–Raphson formula might be employed for situations where $F(y)$ is differentiable, for example in the case of channels of trapezoidal section. Where this is not the case, the 'bisection' method or method of 'false position' could be used.

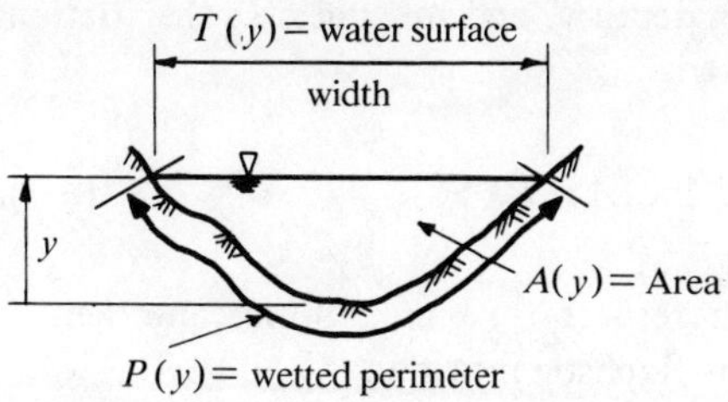

Figure 6.1 Flow section parameters for channel of arbitrary shape

6.2.1.2 Normal depth

The normal depth of flow represents the equilibrium depth attained in a long channel of constant slope when the gravitational force on the fluid, acting in the downstream direction, is balanced by the frictional resistance forces imposed by the channel surface in contact with the fluid. Under these conditions the flow is said to be uniform. Examples of formulae describing uniform flow are

1. *Chezy*

$$Q = cA(y)\sqrt{m(y)S_0} \tag{6.2}$$

2. *Manning*

$$Q = \frac{A(y)}{n}\{m(y)\}^{2/3}S_0^{1/2} \tag{6.3}$$

3. *Colebrook-White*

$$Q = -4A(y)\sqrt{2gm(y)S_0}\log\left(\frac{k}{14.8m(y)} + \frac{1.255\nu}{4m(y)\sqrt{2gm(y)S_0}}\right)$$

$$= f(y, S_0, k, \nu) \tag{6.4}$$

where c, n, and k are constants which reflect the roughness of the channel surface
S_0 is the channel slope
ν is the kinematic viscosity of the fluid
$m(y) = A(y)/P(y)$ is the hydraulic mean depth

Solution for the normal depth, y_n, associated with a given flow rate, Q, must again be determined by trial using, for Colebrook-White,

$$F_2(y) = 0 = 1 - \frac{f(y, S_0, k, \nu)}{Q} \tag{6.5}$$

6.2.1.3 Friction factor

The friction factor λ is the dimensionless coefficient used to describe the frictional resistance to flow. Using the Colebrook-White equation this may be expressed as

$$\frac{1}{\sqrt{\lambda}} = -2\log\left(\frac{k}{14.8m(y)} + \frac{0.627}{R(y)\sqrt{\lambda}}\right) \tag{6.6}$$

where $R(y) = [(V(y)m(y)/\nu)]$ is the Reynolds number
$V(y) = Q/A(y)$ is the flow velocity

For known conditions of flow rate Q, depth y, and roughness k, the friction factor for the channel must be obtained by trial.

Rearranging Eq. (6.6) yields

$$F(\lambda) = 0 = \lambda^{-1/2} + 2\log(A + B\lambda^{-1/2}) \quad (6.7)$$

where A and B are constants.

This expression is differentiable with respect to λ as follows, and hence solution may be achieved using the Newton–Raphson method:

$$\frac{dF(\lambda)}{d\lambda} = -\frac{1}{2}\lambda^{-3/2}\left(1 + \frac{2B}{A + B\lambda^{-1/2}}\right) \quad (6.8)$$

6.2.1.4 Surface profile evaluation

This section of hydraulics deals with the computation of the water surface profile by the solution of the general equation of gradually varied steady flow. The problem is to compute the change in water depth y, with distance x from some point of control in the channel, such as at a sluice or weir, where the depth is known.

The general equation can be written as

$$\frac{dy}{dx} = [S_0 - S_f(y)] \Big/ \left[1 - \frac{Q^2 T(y)}{g\{A(y)\}^3}\right] = f(y) \quad (6.9)$$

where $S_f(y)$ is the friction slope, obtained as the solution for S_0 in the uniform flow formulae, Eqs (6.2)–(6.4).

The solution required is the distance x for a given change in depth, working upstream from the control, at $x = 0$, when flow is subcritical (i.e. when normal depth in the channel is greater than critical depth), or working downstream when flow is supercritical. Integrating Eq. (6.9) yields

$$X = \int_{y_1}^{y_2} \frac{dy}{f(y)} \quad (6.10)$$

The form of $f(y)$ is such that, for other than wide rectangular channels, it cannot be integrated analytically and hence numerical techniques must be employed (see Sec. 3.3 for 'trapezoidal' and 'Simpson's rule' algorithms).

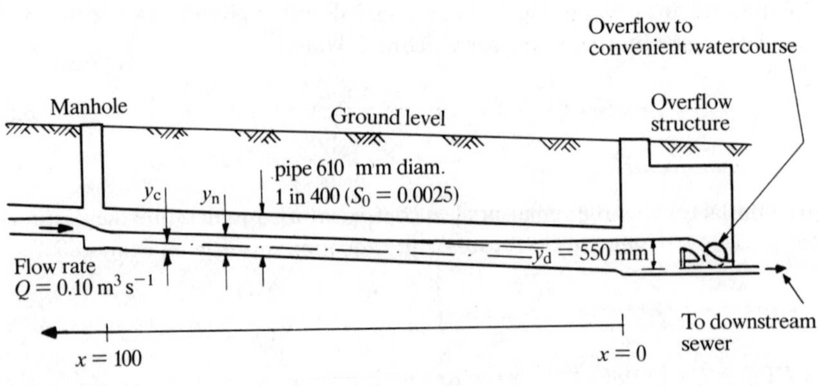

Figure 6.2

6.2.2 Example: flow conditions in a circular conduit

Consider the flow situation sketched in Fig. 6.2, where a single pipe length of sewer upstream of an overflow device, which controls the downstream water level, is subjected to a discharge less than the 'open channel' pipe capacity. It is required to compute the critical depth y_c; the normal depth y_n, the water surface profile behind the weir; and the friction factor for the uniform, normal-depth flow, assuming flow to be described by the Colebrook-White formula, Eq. (6.4), with $k = 0.15$ mm and $\nu = 1.14 \times 10^{-6}$ m^2 s^{-1}.

The steps required in the solution, presented in the form of a computer programme (see Fig. 6.3), may be summarized as follows:

1. Check whether the subcritical flow condition sketched is appropriate by comparing computed values of y_c and y_n, obtained using the iterative solutions of Eqs (6.1) and (6.4) respectively, based on the method of false position. (If this is not the case, the surface profile will be complicated by the presence of an hydraulic jump.)
2. Solve Eq. (6.10) for X corresponding to various values of depth, y, between control value y_d = 550 mm, at x = 0, and normal depth, y_n, using the 'Simpson rule' method of numerical integration. Note that solution for the friction slope $\hat{Sf}(y)$ in Eq. (6.9) also requires iterative solution, being the solution for S_0 in Eq. (6.5).
3. Solve Eq. (6.6) for the uniform, normal depth, flow conditions to yield the friction factor λ, using the 'Newton–Raphson' method.

```
      MASTER CONDF
C             ******************************
C     PROFILE EVALUATION IN CIRCULAR CONDUITS FROM DOWNSTREAM CONTROL
C     (SUBCRITICAL FLOW)
C             ******************************
      EXTERNAL FUNCC,FUNCN,FUNCS,FUNCF,FUNCFD,ARCCOS
      DIMENSION FYINV(51)
      REAL L
      COMMON Q,D,L,S0,RK,YD,VK,PI,G,TYS,AYS,YMS,YN
      REAL NC1,NC2,NC3,NN1,NN2,NN3,NS1,NS2,NS3,NF1,NF2,NF3
C             ******************************
C     READ DATA
      READ(5,900) Q,D,L,S0,RK,YD,VK,N
      WRITE(6,910) Q,D,L,S0,RK,YD,VK,N
C     Q=FLOW RATE
C     D=PIPE DIAMETER
C     L=PIPE LENGTH
C     S0=PIPE SLOPE
C     RK=PIPE ROUGHNESS
C     YD= DOWNSTREAM CONTROL DEPTH
C     VK=KINEMATIC VISCOSITY
C     N=NO. CALCULATION POINTS FOR SURFACE PROFILE
C             ******************************
      MNIT=1000
C     MNIT=LIMIT ON ITERATIONS
      G=9.81
      PI=3.14159
C             ******************************
C     CALCULATE PIPE CAPACITY USING COLEBROOK-WHITE
      AY=PI*D**2/4.0
      YM=D/4.0
      CALL DISCH(AY,YM,S0,QC)
C     QC=PIPE CAPACITY
      WRITE(6,940) QC
C             ******************************
```

Figure 6.3

```
C     CALCULATE CRITICAL DEPTH USING METHØD ØF FALSE PØSITIØN
C     (FIRSTLY ØBTAIN ESTIMATES BØUNDING RØØT)
      YCL=0.001*D
      YCU=0.999*D
      DYC=(YCU-YCL)/20.0
      CALL RANGE(YCL,YCU,FUNCC,DYC)
C     RØØT LIES BETWEEN YCL AND YCU
      YCI=0.0
      YCJ=D
C     RANGE ØF PØSSIBLE YC
      NC1=1.0E-03
      NC2=1.0E-03
      NC3=1.0E-03
C     CØNVERGENCE LIMITS
      CALL FP(YCL,YCU,YCI,YCJ,FUNCC,NC1,NC2,NC3,MNIT)
      YC=YCU
C             *****************************
C     CALCULATE NØRMAL DEPTH USING METHØD ØF FALSE PØSITIØN
C     (FIRSTLY ØBTAIN ESTIMATES BØUNDING RØØT)
      YNL=0.001*D
      YNU=0.999*D
      DYN=(YNU-YNL)/20.0
      CALL RANGE(YNL,YNU,FUNCN,DYN)
C     RØØT LIES BETWEEN YNL AND YNU
      YNI=0.0
      YNJ=D
C     RANGE ØF PØSSIBLE YN
      NN1=1.0E-03
      NN2=1.0E-03
      NN3=1.0E-03
C     CØNVERGENCE LIMITS
      CALL FP(YNL,YNU,YNI,YNJ,FUNCN,NN1,NN2,NN3,MNIT)
      YN=YNU
C             *****************************
      WRITE(6,920) YC,YN
      IF(YC.LE.YN) GØ TØ 40
      WRITE(6,950)
C     FLØW SUPERCRITICAL !
   40 CØNTINUE
C             *****************************
C     CØMPUTATIØN ØF SURFACE PRØFILE
C     CALCULATE DISTANCE X FRØM CØNTRØL TØ DEPTH Y
C     CØNSIDER N VALUES ØF Y BETWEEN YD AND 1.001YN
C     IF FLØW SUPERCRITICAL TRUNCATE SURFACE PRØFILE AT DEPTH YC
C     SINCE HYDRAULIC JUMP WILL BE PRESENT DØWNSTREAM ØF TRUNCATIØN PØINT
      DY=(YD-1.001*YN)/N
      IF(YN.LT.YC) DY=(YD-YC)/N
      Y=YD
      X=0.0
      WRITE(6,930) Y,X
      NS=21
      DYS=DY/(NS-1)
      Y=Y+DYS
      DØ 10 I=1,N
C     NUMERICAL INTEGRATIØN USING SIMPSØNS RULE WITH NS ØRDINATES
      DØ 20 J=1,NS
      IF(J.EQ.1.AND.I.NE.1) GØ TØ 50
      Y=Y-DYS
      CALL SECPRP(Y,TYS,AYS,YMS)
C     CALCULATE FRICTIØN SLØPE SFY USING METHØD ØF FALSE PØSITIØN
C     (FIRSTLY ØBTAIN ESTIMATES BØUNDING RØØT)
      SFL=1.0E-08
      SFU=SØ
      DSF=(SFU-SFL)/20.0
      CALL RANGE(SFL,SFU,FUNCS,DSF)
C     RØØT LIES BETWEEN SFL AND SFU
      SFI=0.0
      SFJ=SØ
C     RANGE ØF PØSSIBLE SFY
      NS1=1.0E-06
      NS2=1.0E-03
      NS3=1.0E-03
C     CØNVERGENCE LIMITS
```

Figure 6.3 *(continued)*

```
      CALL FP(SFL,SFU,SFI,SFJ,FUNCS,NS1,NS2,NS3,MNIT)
      SFY=SFU
      FY=(S0-SFY)/FUNCC(Y)
      FYINV(J)=1.0/FY
      GO TO 20
   50 FYINV(J)=FYINV(NS)
   20 CONTINUE
      CALL SIMP1(FYINV,NS,DYS,DX)
      X=X+DX
      WRITE(6,930) Y,X
      IF(X.GT.L) GO TO 30
   10 CONTINUE
   30 CONTINUE
C           *****************************
C     CALCULATE CHANNEL FRICTIØN FACTØR FF UNDER UNIFØRM
C     NØRMAL DEPTH FLØW USING NEWTØN-RAPHSØN
C     (FIRSTLY ØBTAIN ESTIMATES BØUNDING RØØT)
      FFL=3.0E-03
      FFU=1.0E-01
C     RANGE ØF PØSSIBLE FF
      DFF=(FFU-FFL)/20.0
      CALL RANGE(FFL,FFU,FUNCF,DFF)
      FF=(FFL+FFU)/2.0
C     INITIAL ESTIMATE ØF FF
      NF1=1.0E-03
      NF2=1.0E-03
      NF3=1.0E-03
C     CØNVERGENCE LIMITS
      CALL NR(FF,FFL,FFU,FUNCF,FUNCFD,MNIT,NF1,NF2,NF3)
      WRITE(6,940) FF
C           *****************************
  900 FØRMAT(1P5E10.3,/,1P2E10.3,I5)
  910 FØRMAT(1P5E10.3,/,1P2E10.3,I5)
  920 FØRMAT(5X,1PE10.3,5X,1PE10.3)
  930 FØRMAT(5X,1PE10.3,5X,1PE10.3)
  940 FØRMAT(5X,1PE10.3)
  950 FØRMAT(5X,23H FLØW SUPERCRITICAL !!!)
C           *****************************
      STØP
      END

      SUBRØUTINE SECPRP(Y,TY,AY,YM)
C     CALCULATES SECTIØN PRØPERTIES AT DEPTH Y
      CØMMØN Q,D,L,S0,RK,YD,VK,PI,G,TYS,AYS,YMS,YN
      YY=Y
      IF(Y.LT.(D/2.0)) YY=D-Y
      X=(2.0*YY/D)-1.0
      PSI=2.0*ARCCØS(X)
      IF(Y.LT.(D/2.0)) PSI=2.0*PI-PSI
      TY=D*SIN(PSI/2.0)
C     WATER SURFACE WIDTH
      AY=D**2*(PI-(PSI-SIN(PSI))/2.0)/4.0
C     FLØW SECTIØN AREA
      PY=D*(PI-PSI/2.0)
      YM=AY/PY
C     YM=HYDRAULIC MEAN DEPTH
      RETURN
      END

      SUBRØUTINE DISCH(AY,YM,S,QQ)
C     CALCULATES FLØW RATE USING CØLEBRØØK-WHITE
      CØMMØN Q,D,L,S0,RK,YD,VK,PI,G,TYS,AYS,YMS,YN
      C1=SQRT(2.0*G*YM*S)
      C2=1.255*VK/(4.0*YM*C1)
      C3=RK/(14.8*YM)
      C4=ALØG10(C3+C2)
      QQ=-4.0*AY*C1*C4
      RETURN
      END

      SUBRØUTINE RANGE(RL,RU,FR,DR)
C     STEPWISE REDUCTIØN IN RANGE ØF RE CØNTAINING RØØT ØF FR(RE)
      FRL=FR(RL)
      RE=RL
```

Figure 6.3 (*continued*)

```
    1 RE=RE+DR
      IF(RE.GT.RU) GØ TØ 91
      FRE=FR(RE)
      IF((FRL*FRE).LT.0.0) GØ TØ 2
      RL=RE
      FRL=FRE
      GØ TØ 1
    2 RMAG=ABS(FRL/FRE)
      IF(RMAG.LT.10.0.AND.RMAG.GT.0.10) GØ TØ 3
      DR=DR/10.0
      RE=RL
      GØ TØ 1
    3 RU=RE
      RETURN
   91 WRITE(6,910)
      STØP
  910 FØRMAT(1H ,22H ESTIMATE ØUT ØF RANGE)
      END
```

```
      SUBRØUTINE FP(XN1,XN,XI,XJ,F,N1,N2,N3,MNIT)
C     ITERATIØN USING METHØD ØF FALSE PØSITIØN
      REAL N1,N2,N3
      FXN=F(XN)
      N3=0.5*N3
      FXN1=F(XN1)
      NIT=0
    1 IF(ABS(FXN1-FXN).LT.N1) GØ TØ 90
      XNP1=(XN*FXN1-XN1*FXN)/(FXN1-FXN)
      FXNP1=F(XNP1)
      IF(XNP1.LT.XI.ØR.XNP1.GT.XJ) GØ TØ 91
      NIT=NIT+1
      IF(NIT.GT.MNIT) GØ TØ 92
      IF(FXN*FXNP1.GT.0.0) GØ TØ 2
      XN1=XNP1
      FXN1=FXNP1
      GØ TØ 3
    2 XN=XNP1
      FXN=FXNP1
    3 IF(ABS(FXNP1).GT.N2) GØ TØ 1
      IF(NIT.EQ.1) GØ TØ 10
      IF(ABS((XNP-XNP1)/(XNP+XNP1)).LT.N3) GØ TØ 20
   10 XNP=XNP1
      GØ TØ 1
   20 XN=XNP1
      RETURN
   91 WRITE(6,910)
      STØP
   90 WRITE(6,900)
      STØP
   92 WRITE(6,920)
      STØP
  900 FØRMAT(1H ,30H FUNCTIØN DIFFERENCE TØØ SMALL)
  910 FØRMAT(1H ,22H ESTIMATE ØUT ØF RANGE)
  920 FØRMAT(1H ,36HNØ. ØF ALLØWABLE ITERATIØNS EXCEEDED)
      END
```

```
      SUBRØUTINE SIMP1(F,NS,H,S)
C     SIMPSØNS RULE NUMERICAL INTEGRATIØN
      DIMENSIØN F(NS)
C     F=FUNCTIØN ØRDINATES AT NS STATIØNS,H=STRIP WIDTH
C     CHECK WHETHER AN EVEN NØ. ØF STRIPS
      IF ((NS/2)*2.EQ.NS) GØ TØ 90
      N=NS-1
      S=0.0
      DØ 1 I=2,N,2
    1 S=S+F(I-1)+4.0*F(I)+F(I+1)
      S=S*H/3.0
      RETURN
   90 WRITE(6,900)
  900 FØRMAT(1H ,38H ERRØR IN SIMP1 ØDD NUMBER ØF STATIØNS)
      STØP
      END
```

Figure 6.3 (*continued*)

```
      SUBROUTINE NR(XN,XI,XJ,F,DF,MNIT,N1,N2,N3)
C     ITERATION USING NEWTON-RAPHSON
      REAL N1,N2,N3
      NIT=0
      FX=F(XN)
    1 DFDX=DF(XN)
      IF(ABS(DFDX).LT.N1) GO TO 91
      XN1=XN-FX/DFDX
      IF(XN1.LT.XI.OR.XN1.GT.XJ)GO TO 92
      FX=F(XN1)
      IF(ABS(FX).GT.N2) GO TO 2
      IF(ABS((XN1-XN)/XN).GT.N3) GO TO 2
      XN=XN1
      RETURN
    2 XN=XN1
      NIT=NIT+1
      IF(NIT.GT.MNIT) GO TO 93
      GO TO 1
   91 WRITE(6,910)
      STOP
   92 WRITE(6,920)
      STOP
   93 WRITE(6,930)
      STOP
  910 FORMAT(1H ,15H DFDX TOO SMALL)
  920 FORMAT(1H ,22H ESTIMATE OUT OF RANGE)
  930 FORMAT(1H ,36HNO. OF ALLOWABLE ITERATIONS EXCEEDED)
      END


      FUNCTION FUNCC(Y)
C     EQN (6.1)
      COMMON Q,D,L,S0,RK,YD,VK,PI,G,TYS,AYS,YMS,YN
      CALL SECPRP(Y,TY,AY,YM)
      FUNCC=1.0-Q**2*TY/(G*AY**3)
      RETURN
      END


      FUNCTION FUNCN(Y)
C     EQN (6.5)
      COMMON Q,D,L,S0,RK,YD,VK,PI,G,TYS,AYS,YMS,YN
      CALL SECPRP(Y,TY,AY,YM)
      CALL DISCH(AY,YM,S0,QCWN)
      FUNCN=1.0-(QCWN/Q)
      RETURN
      END


      FUNCTION FUNCS(S)
C     EQN (6.5)
      COMMON Q,D,L,S0,RK,YD,VK,PI,G,TYS,AYS,YMS,YN
      CALL DISCH(AYS,YMS,S,QCWS)
      FUNCS=1.0-(QCWS/Q)
      RETURN
      END


      FUNCTION FUNCF(F)
C     EQN (6.7)
      COMMON Q,D,L,S0,RK,YD,VK,PI,G,TYS,AYS,YMS,YN
      CALL SECPRP(YN,TY,AY,YM)
      VELY=Q/AY
      REY=VELY*YM/VK
      A=RK/(14.8*YM)
      B=0.627/REY
      FUNCF=1.0/SQRT(F)+2.0*ALOG10(A+B/SQRT(F))
      RETURN
      END
```

Figure 6.3 (*continued*)

```
      FUNCTIØN FUNCFD(F)
C     EQN (6.8)
      CØMMØN Q,D,L,SØ,RK,YD,VK,PI,G,TYS,AYS,YMS,YN
      CALL SECPRP(YN,TY,AY,YM)
      VELY=Q/AY
      REY=VELY*YM/VK
      A=RK/(14.8*YM)
      B=0.627/REY
      FUNCFD=-1.0*(1.0+2.0*B/(A+B/SQRT(F)))/(2.0*F*SQRT(F))
      RETURN
      END

      FUNCTIØN ARCCØS(X)
C     INVERSE CØSINE; PRINCIPLE VALUES BETWEEN 0 AND PI
      CØMMØN Q,D,L,SØ,RK,YD,VK,PI,G,TYS,AYS,YMS,YN
      IF(X.EQ.0.0) GØ TØ 10
      ARCCØS=ATAN(SQRT(1.0-X*X)/X)
      GØ TØ 20
   10 CØNTINUE
      ARCCØS=PI/2.0
   20 CØNTINUE
      RETURN
      END

      FINISH
```

Figure 6.3 (*continued*)

6.3 PROBLEMS UNSUITABLE FOR HAND COMPUTATION

Problems are placed in this category which require the simultaneous solution of multidimensional sets of equations generally resulting from some form of matrix analysis. Such problems are too complex for hand computation and must, therefore, be tackled by computer. They often arise from the application of either finite-element or implicit finite-difference analyses of differential equations. Since these methods have been introduced previously in this text (see Secs. 3.5 and 3.4) it is considered sufficient here to identify some problem areas often dealt with using the techniques, as follows:

1. Diffusion, dispersion, and circulation analyses of estuaries and reservoirs with applications to water quality or pollution studies.
2. Non-steady flow analysis with application to river channels and estuaries for the study of flood wave and tidal motions, including problems of harbour resonance and sediment transport.
3. Steady and non-steady seepage flow through soil media; see Chapter 5.
4. Potential flow analyses with applications to the studies of wave motion and flow around and over obstructions, for example cylinders and weirs.

6.4 COMPLEX PROBLEMS

Many of the computer program 'packages' offered by commerical computer bureaux in the field of hydraulic engineering fall into this category. The problems tackled are too complicated to be practicable for hand computation, due to the repetitive nature of the calculations, even though the computations may involve only simple mathematical manipulations. In many of these problems, it is often the geometric complexity of the system to be analysed which leads to the repetition, although this is sometimes enhanced by the necessity for inclusion of iteration and numerical integration algorithms.

The applications outlined above in Sec. 6.3 should strictly be included in this category; however, the intention of this section is to identify problems for which the computations may be solved by hand, and often were before the introduction of computers, but which are then only practicable for simple systems. Some examples in this category are:

1. determination of surface profiles in real river channels
2. refraction of waves in coastal regions
3. storm water drainage design

The further examples of pipe network analysis and hydraulic river flow routing are considered appropriate for detailed treatment in the following sections.

6.5 THE HYDRAULIC DESIGN AND ANALYSIS OF PIPE NETWORKS

Accurate methods of analysing flow in pipe networks are of vital importance in the provision of an adequate water supply to all consumers within the area covered by a particular distribution system. The adequacy of supply is measured primarily in terms of the flow rate and pressure provided at the points of drawoff. It is therefore essential that water engineers have at their disposal a modelling technique which can evaluate the pressure and flow rate at all points within a pipe network. Such a model enables assessment of current hydraulic performance of the system under the most severe conditions to check that certain minimum requirements are being satisfied. The model is also useful as a design tool for the provision of additional facilities to meet future increases in demand.

The first step in the analysis is to reduce the actual distribution system to a simplified network, illustrated in Fig. 6.4, which usually excludes the smallest mains serving individual household connections. On completion of the mathematical model derived from this idealization, field trials must be undertaken, to measure the actual distributions of pressure and flow rate through the system, as a check on the model and adjustments to model parameters must then be made if deviations are found excessive.

Although analysis of the network problem by hand computation is possible and, indeed, is probably covered in most degree courses in Civil Engineering, it is laborious and becomes impractical for large systems. Solution by digital computer, following essentially the same procedure as by hand, is usually employed today for large complex networks as described by Adams[1] and Williams and Pestkowski.[2] The method is one of successive approximation as outlined briefly below.

From the idealized network (see Fig. 6.4), where all pipes and nodes (pipe junctions or changes in diameter) are numbered, the following data must be compiled for input to the computer:

1. the numbers assigned to the nodes at the ends of each pipe length;
2. the length, diameter, and resistance of each pipe length;
3. the water levels in service reservoirs and water towers;
4. the setting of any pressure reducing valves;
5. the characteristics of any pumps; and
6. the rates of drawoff at each node.

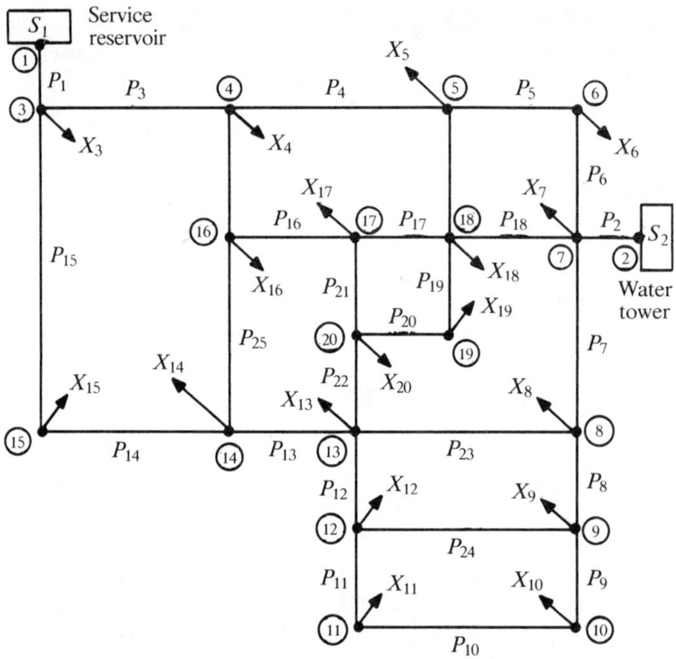

Figure 6.4 Simple, 'idealized' water distribution network with no pumping or pressure-reducing facilities. X_i: rate of drawoff at each node; P_i: pipe data for length i (including length, diameter, and resistance); S_i: water levels in service reservoirs or water towers

The hydraulic conditions which must be satisfied by the flow through the pipe network may be summarized as follows:

1. Friction head loss in any pipe length may be expressed as

$$h_f = rQ^m \tag{6.11}$$

where m is a constant dependent upon the pipe friction formula used
r is a constant dependent upon the pipe friction formula and the pipe length and diameter
Q is the flow rate

2. In any closed circuit within the network, the algebraic sum of friction head losses must be zero.
3. At each node of the network, the sum of the inflows must equal the sum of the outflows.

There are various methods of solution of the network problem posed above which usually require an initial guess to be made of either the flow rates in each pipe length ('head balance' method) or the total 'energy' head at each node ('quantity balance' method). Considering the latter, with initial estimates of the total head at all nodes, a typical procedure would be to consider each node where a pressure estimate was required and to evaluate the head loss in each pipe length joining this node. From this head loss, the flow rate in each of these pipes could be computed using condition (1) and then the total head estimate at the node would be adjusted until condition (3) is satisfied, a necessarily iterative procedure as illustrated in the example below.

Having then balanced the flows at this node and updated the total head estimate, the same procedure would be performed at the remaining nodes. This process is also iterative, since any adjustment to the total head at one node will upset the flow balances at adjacent nodes, so that, in general, a number of cycles through the system will be required before an acceptable flow balance for the whole network is attained.

In practice, the speed of convergence achieved in the iteration procedure may be improved by the incorporation of convergence formulae into the process of head adjustment. In the case of solution as above, by 'quantity balance', an expression proposed by Cornish is often employed, while for 'head balance' methods, flow adjustments are often made using the expression devised by Hardy Cross, both of which are described by Webber.[3]

To illustrate the 'quantity balance' procedure, consider an intermediate stage of computation at a particular pipe node involving n pipes, for which the current total head estimates at the remote ends are $h_1, h_2, \ldots, h_n$ and the required unknown 'balancing' head at the node is h.

The 'Cornish' algorithm for determination of h is as follows:

1. make a reasonable assumption for h;
2. compute the head loss for each pipe, $h_{fi} = (h_i - h)$ (note that the sign of h_f defines the direction of flow);
3. compute the corresponding discharges Q_i from Eq. (6.11) using the known values of r and m, the latter being the same for all pipes;
4. unless the head estimates are correct the algebraic sum of the flows at the nodes will not be zero. Compute the excess or deficiency of inflow ΣQ_i;
5. compute $\Sigma(Q_i/h_{fi})$ for all pipes without regard to sign:
6. determine the correction $\Delta h = m\Sigma(Q_i)/\Sigma(Q_i/h_{fi})$;
7. corrected head at node is $h^1 = h + \Delta h$;
8. repeat (1)–(7) until Δh is within the chosen tolerance on the head estimate.

A computer program for the solution of the problem is given in Fig. 6.5.

```
      MASTER FLØW
C     CØRNISH METHØD FØR HEAD ESTIMATIØN AT PIPE JUNCTIØN (NØDE)
C     N=NUMBER ØF PIPES JØINING AT NØDE
C     CM=PIPE FRICTIØN FØRMULA CØEFF
C     H(I)=KNØWN TØTAL HEAD VALUES AT REMØTE ENDS ØF EACH PIPE
C     R(I)=PIPE CØNSTANTS FUNCTIØNS ØF LENGTH,DIAMETER AND FRICTIØN FØRMULA
C     HNØDE=TØTAL HEAD ESTIMATE AT NØDE
C     QI=FLØW RATE FRØM HFI=(H(I)-H)=R(I)*QI**CM
C     DHMAX=ACCEPTED TØLERANCE ØN HEAD ESTIMATE
      DIMENSIØN H(20),R(20)
      READ(5,900) N
      READ(5,905) CM,DHMAX
      READ(5,905) ((H(I),R(I)),I=1,N)
      WRITE(6,910)
      WRITE(6,915) N,CM,DHMAX
      WRITE(6,920) ((H(I),R(I)),I=1,N)
      WRITE(6,925)
C     INITIAL ESTIMATE ØF H
      HT=0.0
      DØ 10 I=1,N
      HT=HT+H(I)
   10 CØNTINUE
      HNØDE=HT/N
      DH=0.0
      WRITE(6,920) HNØDE,DH
   15 CØNTINUE
```

Figure 6.5

```
C     CØMPUTE PIPE FLØWS
      SUM1=0.0
      SUM2=0.0
      DØ 20 I=1,N
      SIGN=1.0
      HFI=H(I)-HNØDE
      IF(HFI.LT.0.0) SIGN=-1.0
      HFI=ABS(HFI)
      QI=(HFI/R(I))**(1.0/CM)
      QHFI=0.0
      IF(HFI.NE.0.0) QHFI=QI/HFI
      QI=QI*SIGN
      SUM1=SUM1+QI
      SUM2=SUM2+QHFI
   20 CONTINUE
C     NODAL HEAD CØRRECTIØN
      DH=CM*SUM1/SUM2
C     NEW HEAD ESTIMATE
      HNØDE=HNØDE+DH
      WRITE(6,920) HNØDE,DH
      IF(ABS(DH).LT.DHMAX) GØ TØ 25
      GØ TØ 15
   25 CONTINUE
      WRITE(6,930) HNØDE
      STOP
  900 FØRMAT(I5)
  905 FØRMAT(1P2E10.3)
  910 FØRMAT(//,5X,26HCØRNISH NØDAL FLØW BALANCE,//5X,4HDATA,/)
  915 FØRMAT(5X,2HN=,I5,/,5X,3HCM=,1PE10.3,/,5X,6HDHMAX=,1PE10.3)
  920 FØRMAT(5X,1P2E10.3)
  925 FØRMAT(/,5X,6HØUTPUT,/,2X,5HHNØDE,3X,2HDH)
  930 FØRMAT(/,5X,15HSØLUTIØN:HNØDE=,1PE10.3)
      END

      FINISH
```

Figure 6.5 *(continued)*

6.6 HYDRAULIC FLOW ROUTING ALONG RIVER CHANNELS

The general object of flow, or 'flood', routing procedures is to evaluate the attenuation and peak-time-lag of a flood wave as it travels along the reach of a river channel for flood forecasting purposes. The aim is, therefore, to evaluate the outflow hydrograph, or the hydrograph at station *B* in Fig. 6.6 from knowledge of the inflow hydrograph to the reach or hydrograph at station *A* and the initial flow conditions in the river channel prior to the flood.

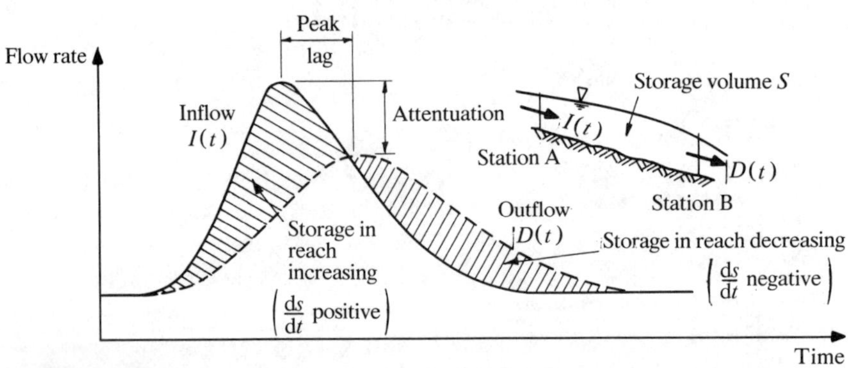

Figure 6.6 Inflow and outflow hydrographs for the reach of a river channel

Solution of the problem is achieved by splitting the reach between stations A and B into a number of subreaches and applying expressions derived from the continuity and momentum equations to the stations forming the subreach boundaries.

6.6.1 Application of the Continuity and Momentum Equations to an Infinitely Short Reach

For simplicity, consider a stretch of river of rectangular section and of constant width b. Furthermore, assume that: the flow is unidirectional and velocities are uniform over the entire cross-section; the variation of pressure with depth is hydrostatic; and the slope of the river bed is small. A more general model would include a variable cross-sectional geometry and lateral inflow of runoff from the contributing catchment.

A sketch of an elemental reach of such a channel, of length δx, is included in Fig. 6.7, which shows the section parameters and the force components acting on the element along the line of flow.

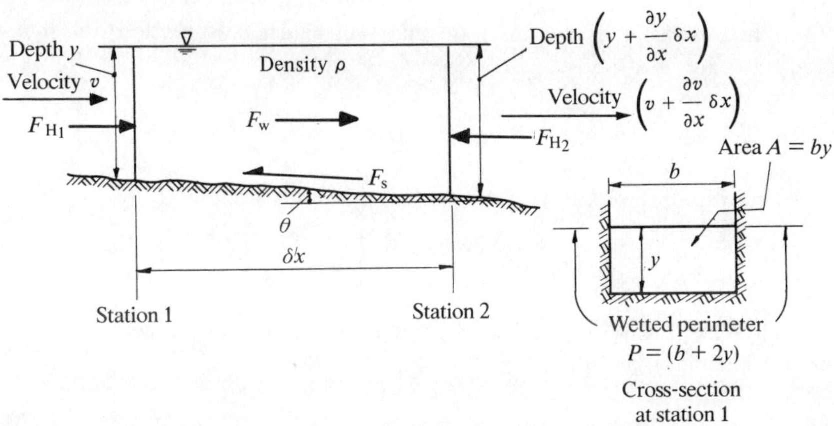

Figure 6.7 Elemental reach of rectangular river channel showing section parameters and force components acting along the line of flow. Forces: F_{H_1}, F_{H_2}, hydrostatic thrusts. F_W component of self weight. F_S shear force on boundary

The continuity equation, applied to this element, states that the inflow minus the outflow must equal the rate of change of storage within the reach.

$$I(t) - D(t) = \frac{dS}{dt} \tag{6.12}$$

Considering a finite (small) timestep δt,

$I(t)\,\delta t - D(t)\,\delta t = \delta S =$ change in storage during the time interval δt

Using the parameters of Fig. 6.7 this becomes

$$by\,v\,\delta t - b\left(y + \frac{\partial y}{\partial x}\delta x\right)\left(v + \frac{\partial v}{\partial x}\delta x\right)\delta t$$

$$= b\left[\frac{\partial}{\partial t}\left(y + \frac{\partial y}{\partial x}\frac{\delta x}{2}\right)\delta t\right]\delta x$$

Simplifying,

$$-b\,\delta t\,\delta x\left(y\frac{\partial v}{\partial x}+v\frac{\partial y}{\partial x}+\frac{\partial y}{\partial x}\frac{\partial v}{\partial x}\,\delta x\right)=b\,\delta t\,\delta x\left(\frac{\partial y}{\partial t}+\frac{\partial^2 y}{\partial x \partial t}\frac{\partial x}{2}\right)$$

The last terms in each of the brackets will be small compared with the other terms and can therefore be neglected to give

$$y\frac{\partial v}{\partial x}+v\frac{\partial y}{\partial x}+\frac{\partial y}{\partial t}=0 \tag{6.13}$$

The momentum equation, applied to the element, states that the rate of change of momentum of the fluid between stations 1 and 2 is equal to the resultant force on the fluid element in the direction of the momentum change.

With reference to Fig. 6.7, the change in momentum takes place in a direction parallel to the channel bed, and the resultant force in this direction is

$$F = F_{\mathrm{H1}}+F_{\mathrm{w}}-F_{\mathrm{s}}-F_{\mathrm{H2}} \tag{6.14}$$

For hydrostatic pressure variation and rectangular cross-section, the hydrostatic thrusts are

$$F_{\mathrm{H1}} = by\left(\rho g\frac{y}{2}\right)=\frac{\rho g b y^2}{2} \qquad F_{\mathrm{H2}}=\frac{\rho g b}{2}\left(y+\frac{\partial y}{\partial x}\,\delta x\right)^2$$

The gravitational, or self weight, force component is given by

$$F_{\mathrm{w}} = \rho g\left[b\left(y+\frac{\partial y}{\partial x}\frac{\delta x}{2}\right)\delta x\right]\theta \qquad \text{for small } \theta$$

Finally, the shear, or friction, force component can be obtained using the Chezy (or Manning) formula,

$$\text{Shear stress at station 1}\quad \tau_1=\frac{\rho g}{c^2}\,v^2$$

where c is the Chezy coefficient

$$\text{Shear stress at station 2}\quad \tau_2=\frac{\rho g}{c^2}\left(v+\frac{\partial v}{\partial x}\,\delta x\right)^2$$

Assuming a linear variation in shear stress between stations 1 and 2, the shear force, as the product of stress and wetted area, is

$$F_{\mathrm{s}}=\frac{\tau_1+\tau_2}{2}\,\frac{P_1+P_2}{2}\,\delta x$$

where P_1 and P_2 are the wetted perimeters at stations 1 and 2.

Hence,

$$F_{\mathrm{s}}=\frac{\rho g}{c^2}\left[v^2+v\frac{\partial v}{\partial x}\,\delta x+\frac{1}{2}\left(\frac{\partial v}{\partial x}\,\delta x\right)^2\right]\left[b+2y+\frac{\partial y}{\partial x}\,\delta x\right]\delta x$$

Substituting the above into Eq. (6.14) and neglecting the second order of small quantities,

$$F = \rho g b\, \delta x \left(y\theta - \frac{v^2}{c^2 b} \left(b + 2y \right) - y \frac{\partial y}{\partial x} \right) \tag{6.15}$$

The rate of change of momentum of the fluid mass is given by

$$\frac{\mathrm{d}}{\mathrm{d}t}(mv) = m \frac{\mathrm{d}v}{\mathrm{d}t} \tag{6.16}$$

where m is the mass of fluid contained between stations 1 and 2 and neglecting the second order of small quantities, $m = \rho\, \delta x\, by$. Equating Eqs (6.15) and (6.16) and expressing $\mathrm{d}v/\mathrm{d}t$ in terms of partial derivatives yields

$$\frac{\partial v}{\partial t} + v \frac{\partial v}{\partial x} + g \frac{\partial y}{\partial x} + g \frac{b + 2y}{c^2 yb} v^2 - g\theta = 0 \tag{6.17}$$

Equations (6.13) and (6.17) representing respectively the continuity and momentum expressions, may now be solved simultaneously for unknowns v and y at each of the subreach boundaries between stations A and B of Fig. 6.6, subject to a particular set of boundary conditions.

6.6.2 Explicit method of solution of the routing problem using finite-difference technique (see Sec. 3.4)

With reference to Fig. 6.8 for a particular sub-reach boundary, location X and time T, the following finite-difference approximations will be used for substitution into Eqs (6.13) and (6.17):

$$\left. \begin{aligned} \left(\frac{\partial v}{\partial x}\right)_{X,T} &= \frac{v(X + \Delta x, T) - v(X - \Delta x, T)}{2\Delta x} \\ \left(\frac{\partial y}{\partial x}\right)_{X,T} &= \frac{y(X + \Delta x, T) - y(X - \Delta x, T)}{2\Delta x} \end{aligned} \right\} \text{central differences}$$

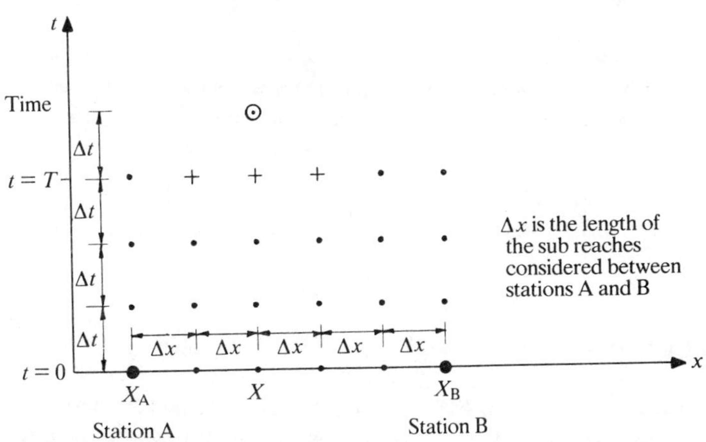

Figure 6.8 Finite-difference grid for the reach of river channel between stations A and B

$$\left.\begin{aligned}\left(\frac{\partial y}{\partial t}\right)_{X,\,T} &= \frac{y(X,\,T+\Delta t)-y(X,\,T)}{\Delta t}\\[2ex] \left(\frac{\partial v}{\partial t}\right)_{X,\,T} &= \frac{v(X,\,T+\Delta t)-v(X,\,T)}{\Delta t}\end{aligned}\right\}\ \text{forward differences}$$

Substituting these expressions into Eq. (6.13) for location X at time T we obtain

$$\begin{aligned}y(X,\,T+\Delta t) &= y(X,\,T)-\frac{\Delta t}{2\Delta x}\,\{y(X,\,T)\,[v(X+\Delta x,\,T)-v(X-\Delta x,\,T)]\\ &\qquad + v(X,\,T)[y(X+\Delta x,\,T)-y(X-\Delta x,\,T]\}\end{aligned}\tag{6.18}$$

Thus, using this equation, the depths of flow along the forward time line ($t = T + \Delta t$) (see Fig. 6.8), may be evaluated from knowledge of the velocities and depths of flow at all finite difference points on the previous time line ($t = T$).

In a similar manner, substituting the finite-difference approximations into the momentum expression, Eq. (6.17) at location X and time T,

$$\begin{aligned}v(X,\,T+\Delta t) &= v(X,\,T)+g\theta(X)\,\Delta t-\frac{g\,[b+2y(X,\,T)]\,v^2\,(X,\,T)\,\Delta t}{c^2y(X,\,T)b}\\ &\qquad -\frac{\Delta t}{2\Delta x}\,\{v(X,\,T)\,[v(X+\Delta x,\,T)-v(X-\Delta x,\,T)]\\ &\qquad + g[y(X+\Delta x,\,T)-y(X-\Delta x,\,T)]\}\end{aligned}\tag{6.19}$$

Hence evaluation of the velocities of flow in the forward time line ($t = T + \Delta t$) follows from knowledge of velocities and depths of flow at all points in the previous time line.

Solution for all internal points in the finite-difference grid can now proceed upon specification of the initial flow conditions in the channel prior to the flood and the boundary conditions at stations A and B.

The initial conditions to be specified are the values of y and v at all points when $t = 0$ and are usually evaluated assuming the flow to be steady between the two stations. Thus, assuming uniform flow at each grid point and applying the Chezy equation,

$$I(t=0) = D(t=0) = cby(X,\,0)\sqrt{\frac{by(X,\,0)\theta(X)}{b+2y(X,\,0)}} = v(X,\,0)by(X,\,0)\tag{6.20}$$

for which knowledge of the initial flow rate, $I(t = 0)$, is sufficient to define the initial conditions.

In most flood routing problems, the upstream boundary conditions, at station A, may be determined from the inflow hydrograph, given as input data to the problem, usually in the form of flow rates recorded at fixed time intervals at station A.

Since the depth of flow and velocity are unknowns at sections upstream of station A, it is necessary to amend the finite-difference approximation used at station A as follows:

$$\left(\frac{\partial v}{\partial x}\right)_{XA,\,T} = \frac{v(X_A + \Delta x, T) - v(X_A, T)}{\Delta x}$$

and

$$\left(\frac{\partial y}{\partial x}\right)_{XA,\,T} = \frac{y(X_A + \Delta x, T) - y(X_A, T)}{\Delta x}$$

Thus Eq. (6.18) must be amended accordingly:

$$y(X_A, T + \Delta t) = y(X_A, T) - \frac{\Delta t}{\Delta x,} \{y(X_A, T)[v(X_A + \Delta x\ T) - v(X_A, T)]$$

$$+ v(X_A, T)[y(X_A + \Delta x, T) - y(X_A, T)]\} \qquad (6.18a)$$

Also:

$$v(X_A, T + \Delta t) = \frac{I(T + \Delta T)}{by(X_A, T + \Delta t)}$$

Similarly, for the downstream boundary, at station B, an adjustment to finite-difference equations, of the form indicated above, is required, for which Eq. (6.18) must be amended to

$$y(X_B, T + \Delta t) = y(X_B, T) - \frac{\Delta t}{\Delta x} \{y(X_B, T)[v(X_B, T) - v(X_B - \Delta x, T)]$$

$$+ v(X_B, T)[y(X_B, T) - y(X_B - \Delta x, T)]\} \qquad (6.18b)$$

Assuming that the flow is uniform at station B, the Chezy equation can be applied to give the velocity at the boundary:

$$v(X_B, T + \Delta t) = c\sqrt{\frac{by(X_B, T + \Delta t)\theta(X_B)}{b + 2y(X_B, T + \Delta t)}} \qquad (6.19a)$$

Starting from the initial conditions at $t = 0$ it is now possible to work through the time domain solving for the unknowns y and v at all the grid points in Fig. 6.8 by the application of Eqs (6.18) and (6.19).

One of the disadvantages of this explicit method of solution is the tendency for solutions to become unstable if Δt is chosen to be too large relative to Δx and checks on the stability should be made on any application of the method.

Although the procedure developed above can be solved by hand computation, it would be extremely tedious and time-consuming to perform. On the other hand, repetitive calculations of this form are ideally suited to solution by digital computer, which requires the construction of only a relatively simple computer program, as demonstrated in Fig. 6.9.

```
      MASTER FLØØD
C     HYDRAULIC FLØØD RØUTING : EXPLICIT FINITE DIFFERENCE METHØD
C     REACH ØF RECTANGULAR CHANNEL (LENGTH XT,WIDTH B,SLØPE SO AND CHEZY
C     CØEFF CH) INITIALLY PASSING STEADY FLØW Q0 AT NØRMAL DEPTH YØ IS
C     SUBJECTED TØ FLØØD WAVE AT UPSTREAM STATIØN CHARACTERISED BY
C     INFLØW HYDRØGRAPH QIN (DEFINED BY NIH FLØW RATES MEASURED AT DTIH
C     SEC TIME INTERVALS)
C     PRØGRAM ØUTPUTS DISCHARGE HYDRØGRAPH AT DØWNSTREAM STATIØN QØUT
C     (AT TIME INTERVALS DTW MINS) USING CALCULATIØNS BASED ØN TIME
C     STEPS DT SECS AND N INCREMENTAL CHANNEL REACHES ØF EQUAL LENGTH
C     CØMPUTATIØNS CEASE AT TIME TMAX SECS
C     NØTE: DT MUST BE FACTØR ØF DTIH
C           G=GRAVITATIØNAL ACCELERATIØN
C           Y=FLØW DEPTH
C           V=FLØW VELØCITY
      DIMENSIØN Y(2,101),V(2,101),QQ(2,101),QIN(101)
      READ(5,900) XT,B,SO,CH,G
      READ(5,905) DTW,TMAX,DT,N
      WRITE(6,910) XT,B,SO,CH,G
      WRITE(6,915) DTW,TMAX,DT,N
      DX=XT/N
      DTX=DT/DX
      DTX2=DTX/2.0
      NT=TMAX/DT
      N1=N+1
C     READ INFLØW HYDRØGRAPH
      READ(5,920) YØ,DTIH,NIH
      READ(5,925) (QIN(J),J=1,NIH)
      WRITE(6,930) YØ,DTIH,NIH
      WRITE(6,935) (QIN(J),J=1,NIH)
      TIH=DTIH*(NIH-1)
C     INITIAL CØNDITIØNS
      HR=B*YØ/(B+2.0*YØ)
      QØ=CH*B*YØ*SQRT(SO*HR)
      VØ=QØ/(B*YØ)
      T=0.0
      WRITE(6,940)
      WRITE(6,945)
      WRITE(6,950) T,YØ,VØ,QØ,YØ,VØ,QØ
      DØ 10 J=1,N1
      Y(1,J)=YØ
      V(1,J)=VØ
   10 CØNTINUE
      TWRITE=DTW
      KK=1
      Q=QIN(1)
C     VARIATIØN IN INFLØW CØNDITIØNS
      DØ 15 K=1,NT
      T=T+DT
      K1=KK+1
      IF(T.GT.TIH) GØ TØ 20
      Q=Q+((QIN(K1)-QIN(KK))*DT/DTIH)
      GØ TØ 21
   20 Q=QØ
   21 CØNTINUE
C     UPSTREAM BØUNDARY
      Y(2,1)=Y(1,1)-DTX*(Y(1,1)*(V(1,2)-V(1,1))+V(1,1)*(Y(1,2)-Y(1,1)))
      V(2,1)=Q/(B*Y(2,1))
C     INTERNAL STATIØNS
      DØ 25 J=2,N
      J1=J-1
      J2=J+1
      YD=Y(1,J2)-Y(1,J1)
      VD=V(1,J2)-V(1,J1)
      Y(2,J)=Y(1,J)-DTX2*(Y(1,J)*VD+V(1,J)*YD)
      C2=CH**2
      V2=V(1,J)**2
      B2Y=(B+(2.0*Y(1,J)))/(B*Y(1,J))
      GVBC=G*V2*B2Y*DT/C2
      V(2,J)=V(1,J)+(G*SO*DT)-GVBC-(DTX2*((V(1,J)*VD)+(G*YD)))
      QQ(2,J)=V(2,J)*Y(2,J)*B
   25 CØNTINUE
C     DØWNSTREAM BØUNDARY
      M=N1
      Y(2,M)=Y(1,M)-DTX*(Y(1,M)*(V(1,M)-V(1,N))+V(1,M)*(Y(1,M)-Y(1,N)))
```

Figure 6.9

```
      HRB=B*Y(2,M)/(B+2.0*Y(2,M))
      V(2,M)=CH*SQRT(HRB*S0)
      QØUT=V(2,M)*Y(2,M)*B
      DØ 30 J=1,M
      Y(1,J)=Y(2,J)
   30 V(1,J)=V(2,J)
      TE=DTIH*KK
      IF(T.GE.TE) KK=KK+1
      TT=T+DT/10.0
      IF(TT.LT.TWRITE) GØ TØ 15
      TWRITE=TWRITE+DTW
      TMINS=T/60.0
      WRITE(6,950) TMINS,Y(2,1),V(2,1),Q,Y(2,M),V(2,M),QØUT
   15 CØNTINUE
      STØP
  900 FØRMAT(1P5E10.3)
  905 FØRMAT(1P3E10.3,I5)
  910 FØRMAT(//,5X,23HHYDRAULIC FLØØD RØUTING,//,5X,12HCHANNEL DATA,/,
     1 5X,7HLENGTH=,1PE10.3,5X,6HWIDTH=,1PE10.3,5X,6HSLØPE=,1PE10.3,
     2 5X,12HCHEZY CØEFF=,1PE10.3,/,5X,2HG=,1PE10.3,/)
  915 FØRMAT(5X,18HCØMPUTATIØNAL DATA,/,5X,19HTIME STEP (ØUTPUT)=,
     1 1PE10.3,5X,11HTIME LIMIT=,1PE10.3,5X,17HTIME STEP (CALC)=,
     2 1PE10.3,/,5X,13HNØ. STATIØNS=,I3,/)
  920 FØRMAT(1P2E10.3,I5)
  925 FØRMAT(1P5E10.3)
  930 FØRMAT(5X,9HFLØW DATA,/,5X,14HINITIAL DEPTH=,1PE10.3,/,5X,
     1 19HINFLØW HYDRØGRAPH  ,5X,10HTIME STEP=,1PE10.3,5X,
     2 14HNØ. ØRDINATES=,I5,/)
  935 FØRMAT(5X,1P5E10.3)
  940 FØRMAT(//,5X,6HØUTPUT,/,13X,16HUPSTREAM STATIØN,
     1   32X,18HDØWNSTREAM STATIØN,/)
  945 FØRMAT(8X,10HTIME(MINS),5X,5HDEPTH,10X,8HVELØCITY,7X,9HDISCHARGE,
     1   6X,5HDEPTH,10X,8HVELØCITY,7X,9HDISCHARGE,/)
  950 FØRMAT(2X,1P7E15.3)
      END


      FINISH
```

Figure 6.9 (*continued*)

REFERENCES

1. Adams, R. W., 'Distribution analysis by electronic computer', *J. Inst. Water Engrs,* 15, 415–428, 1961.
2. Williams, J. D. and Pestkowski, T., 'Distribution system analysis by digital computer', *J. Inst. Water Engrs*, 27, 381–391, 1973.
3. Webber, N. B., *Fluid Mechanics for Civil Engineers*', Chapman & Hall, London, 1971.

CHAPTER

SEVEN

APPLICATIONS IN MANAGEMENT

7.1 INTRODUCTION

Successful management is the creation of conditions which bring about the effective use of manpower, materials, finance, and the other resources available to an enterprise, in the attainment of a particular goal. In civil engineering, the efforts of the promoter who initiates the project and provides the funds, of the engineer who designs the project, and of the contractor who builds it are all generally directed towards the same end: the construction of the works to the required specification and within a budgeted amount and specified time.

Successful engineering management is a balanced combination of art and science. The art is in the skill used to achieve the desired end through the motivation, organization, and control of the various groups of people who contribute to the project. This art is complimented by a very large number of scientific techniques and methods which assist in the decision-making aspects of management. Many of these methods were first developed and applied in industries other than building and civil engineering, mostly in the manufacturing and processing industries. They include investment appraisal methods, work study, critical path analysis, linear programming, queueing theory, bidding strategy, and so on. This chapter considers just three of the many topics: investment appraisal, critical path analysis, and simulation, and indicates how the computer may be used to carry out the routine mathematics associated with each of them.

7.2 INVESTMENT APPRAISAL

All civil engineering projects cost money. Some reduce existing costs or generate profits and it is necessary to be able to decide whether investments in such projects will produce sufficient savings or generate sufficiently large profits to make the schemes worthwhile. Some civil engineering projects result in neither savings nor profit but improve services of one kind or another. While these improvements may not be easily quantified in terms of money the fact will remain that, generally, there will be a number of alternative means of effecting these improvements and the engineer will need to judge the relative economic merits of the alternatives if he is to ensure that he obtains the best value from the resources available to him. Investment appraisal methods provide the engineer with the means for making these judgements.

7.2.1 Discounting

Given the choice between receiving £100 now or £100 in a year's time, most people would opt to have £100 now. One of the reasons for this choice is that money received now could be invested to earn interest. It would then amount to more than £100 in a year's time. For example, £100 invested at 10 per cent per annum would have grown to £110 after one year. While these two sums of money are not equal they may be regarded as equivalent. The concept of equivalence is important in evaluating alternative engineering proposals since costs and benefits associated with different schemes may arise at different times and it is essential to be able to compare them on a common basis.

If a sum of money P is invested now at an interest rate of R per period (e.g. per month or per year) then in n periods time it will yield a total, S_n, given by the compound interest formula

$$S_n = P(1+R)^n \tag{7.1}$$

Looked at in another way, the present value or present worth P of the sum S_n associated with the end of period n is given by:

$$P = (1+R)^{-n} S_n \tag{7.2}$$

Using Eq. (7.2) to calculate the present value of a future sum is called 'discounting' and the factor $(1 + R)^{-n}$ is called the 'discount factor' or 'present worth factor'. Methods of investment appraisal which make use of discounting are known as discounted cash flow (or DCF) methods.

7.2.2 Discounted cash flows

During the lifetime of a project, capital will be flowing out of the project account at some stages, usually in the expectation that at later stages rather more cash will flow back into it. These movements into and out of the project account are known as cash flows. A receipt represents a positive cash flow while a payment represents a negative cash flow. The net cash flow for any period of a project's life will be the difference between payments and receipts during that period.

Using Eq. (7.2), the present value of all future payments or receipts may be written as

$$PV = \sum_{n=1}^{n=L} (1+R)^{-n} S_n \tag{7.3}$$

in which S_n is now the net cash flow associated with the end of period n. L is the lifetime of the project. The *net* present value of the project is found by subtracting from PV the investment or capital cost C necessary to initiate the project:

$$NPV = -C + \sum_{n=1}^{n=L} (1+R)^{-n} S_n \tag{7.4}$$

The value given by Eq. (7.4) represents the difference, expressed in terms of present worth, between the outlays and receipts associated with the project. Thus if the NPV is negative the receipts are insufficient to cover the sum of the capital cost and possible future costs (e.g. for maintenance). In this case investment in the project would normally be rejected. On the other hand, if the NPV is positive then investment may be worthwhile. However, in providing money for any project the investor is foregoing the opportunity to invest that money elsewhere. Consequently, for a project to be acceptable not only must it provide a positive *NPV* but the value must also be greater than that for any alternative investment, of equal risk, which it displaces because finance is limited.

7.2.3 Discount rate and *DCF* yield

In order to determine the net present value of a project it is necessary to adopt a figure for the discount rate R. This value will be the minimum rate of return which is regarded as acceptable by the investor and it may be determined by considering the rates of return available on competing investments of equal risk.

As an alternative (or in addition) to determining the net present value of a project, some investors like to determine the rate of interest they will earn on their capital outlay C by determining the value of R which makes the future net cash flows exactly balance this initial outlay. In this case

$$C = \sum_{n=1}^{n=L} (1+R)^{-n} S_n \tag{7.5}$$

or, from Eq. (7.4),

$$NPV = -C + \sum_{n=1}^{n=L} (1+R)^{-n} S_n = 0 \tag{7.6}$$

The solution to this equation, which is the discount rate producing a net present value of zero, is known as the internal rate of return or the *DCF* yield. If the yield on the initial investment is greater than the minimum acceptable rate of return required by the investor then the project might be regarded as worthwhile. Unfortunately, under certain conditions Eq. (7.6) may have no positive solution for R or may have more than one (see Sec. 7.2.4 and Pilcher[1]). Furthermore, in assessing competing investments, comparing their internal rates of return may suggest conclusions which are different from those reached by comparing net present values (see also Pilcher[1]). Consequently, particular care is required in the interpretation of the results of yield calculations.

7.2.4 A Simple *DCF* program

Figure 7.1 gives a simple program to determine the net present value *NPV* of a project given the discount rate *RATE* expressed as a percentage, the life of the project

```
      MASTER DCF1
      REAL NPV
      DIMENSION S(100)
C
C     PROGRAM READS AND WRITES DISCOUNT RATE (RATE) EXPRESSED AS A
C     PERCENTAGE, LIFE OF PROJECT (L) AND CAPITAL COST (C)
C
      READ(5,501)RATE,L,C
  501 FORMAT(F10.2,I5,F15.2)
      WRITE(6,601)RATE,L,C
  601 FORMAT(17H DISCOUNT RATE IS,F10.2,15H PERCENT/PERIOD//
     1       16H PROJECT LIFE IS,I5,30H PERIODS (MONTHS, YEARS, ETC.)//
     2       16H CAPITAL COST IS,F15.2)
C
```

Figure 7.1 Simple *DCF* program

```
C     PRØGRAM READS AND WRITES FUTURE NET CASH FLØWS
C
      READ(5,502)(S(N),N=1,L)
  502 FØRMAT(8F10.2)
      WRITE(6,602)
  602 FØRMAT(1H0,7H PERIØD,11X,14H NET CASH FLØW)
      DØ 10 N=1,L
      WRITE(6,603)N,S(N)
  603 FØRMAT(1H ,I5,15X,F10.2)
   10 CØNTINUE
C
C     PRØGRAM DETERMINES UNDISCØUNTED PRØFIT (UP) AND NET PRESENT
C     VALUE (NPV) ØF PRØJECT
C
      R=RATE/100.0
      SIGMA1=0.0
      SIGMA2=0.0
      DØ 20 N=1,L
      SIGMA1=SIGMA1+S(N)
      SIGMA2=SIGMA2+S(N)/(1.0+R)**N
   20 CØNTINUE
      UP=SIGMA1-C
      NPV=SIGMA2-C
      WRITE(6,604)UP,NPV
  604 FØRMAT(1H0,23H UNDISCØUNTED PRØFIT IS,F15.2//
     1           22H  NET PRESENT VALUE IS,F15.2)
C
C     PRØGRAM CHECKS WHETHER DCF YIELD IS REQUIRED. TØ ØBTAIN
C     YIELD IRR IS ASSIGNED AN INTEGER VALUE ØTHER THAN ZERØ
C
      READ(5,503)IRR
  503 FØRMAT(I5)
      IF(IRR.EQ.0)GØTØ 9999
C
C     PRØGRAM DETERMINES DCF YIELD BY ITERATIØN USING
C     NEWTØN-RAPHSØN PRØCEDURE
C
      NIT=0
      R=0.0
   30 DNPVDR=0.0
      SIGMA2=0.0
      DØ 40 N=1,L
      DNPVDR=DNPVDR-FLØAT(N)*S(N)/(1.0+R)**(N+1)
      SIGMA2=SIGMA2+S(N)/(1.0+R)**N
   40 CØNTINUE
      NPV=SIGMA2-C
      IF(ABS(NPV).LT.1.0E-2)GØTØ 50
      IF(R.EQ.0.0.AND.DNPVDR.GE.0.0)GØTØ 60
      IF(ABS(DNPVDR).LT.1.0E-10)GØTØ 70
      R=R-NPV/DNPVDR
      NIT=NIT+1
      IF(NIT.GT.1000)GØTØ 80
      GØTØ 30
   50 RATE=100.0*R
      WRITE(6,605)RATE
  605 FØRMAT(1H0,13H DCF YIELD IS,F10.2,15H PERCENT/PERIØD)
      GØTØ 9999
   60 WRITE(6,606)
  606 FØRMAT(1H0,45H D(NPV)/DR IS NØT NEGATIVE WHEN R EQUALS ZERØ)
      GØTØ 9999
   70 WRITE(6,607)
  607 FØRMAT(1H0,49H ABSØLUTE VALUE ØF D(NPV)/DR IS LESS THAN 1.0E-10)
      GØTØ 9999
   80 WRITE(6,608)
  608 FØRMAT(1H0,40H ALLØWABLE NUMBER ØF ITERATIØNS EXCEEDED)
C
 9999 STØP
      END

     FINISH
```

Figure 7.1 (*continued*)

L and its capital cost C. The future net cash flows are also specified and are held within the array $S(100)$.

Besides calculating the *NPV*, the program also determines the undiscounted profit *UP* which is given when $R(= RATE/100)$ is zero. Furthermore, if the engineer wishes to know the *DCF* yield then he may assign, as data input, any integer value other than zero to *IRR*. Provided the slope of the curve relating the net present value to the discount rate is negative at $R = 0$ (see Fig. 7.2(a)) then the *DCF* yield is determined in the program using the Newton–Raphson iteration procedure (see Sec. 3.2.1.1) starting from the initial estimate $R = 0$. Note that from Eq. (7.4) the slope of the curve is given by

$$D(NPV)/DR = \sum_{n=1}^{n=L} -n(1+R)^{-n-1} S_n \tag{7.7}$$

The variation of *NPV* with R shown in Fig. 7.2(a) is typical of what is usually found; as the discount rate is increased the net present value of the project falls. Note that if the undiscounted profit is negative (i.e. a loss is made on the project rather than a profit) then a negative yield should be expected.

One possible problem with calculations of the *DCF* yield occurs when there is more than one value of R providing a solution to Eq. (7.6). Figure 7.2(b) shows two possible examples, one in which the undiscounted profit is positive and the other in which it is negative. In general, such situations may arise when there is more than one change in the arithmetic sign of the net cash flows during the project life. An example of such a case in civil engineering might be in the net cash flows of an open-cast coalmining project for which there would be an initial outlay for plant, followed by income from the sale of the coal, followed by further expenditure in restoring the site.

The interpretation of multiple yields is not simple and for a project for which they may occur it is recommended that the curve corresponding to those shown in Fig. 7.2(b) should be established. This could be done, for example, by including a DO loop to vary the value of *RATE* in the first part of the program given in Fig. 7.1.

7.2.5 An example

A promoter is considering investing £250 000 in a particular project. Following the investment he expects a net income at the end of each of the following five years of £90 000, £110 000, £70 000, £60 000 and £80 000, respectively, after which there will be no further receipts (or payments). Determine

1. the net present value of the project to the promoter if the minimum acceptable rate of return on the promoter's capital is 14 per cent; and
2. the *DCF* yield on the promoter's initial investment.

This problem may be solved very easily using the program given in Fig. 7.1; the program output is shown in Fig. 7.3. It may be seen that with a discount rate of 14 per cent the *NPV* of the project is nearly £38 000. The yield on the initial investment is found to be 20.58 per cent.

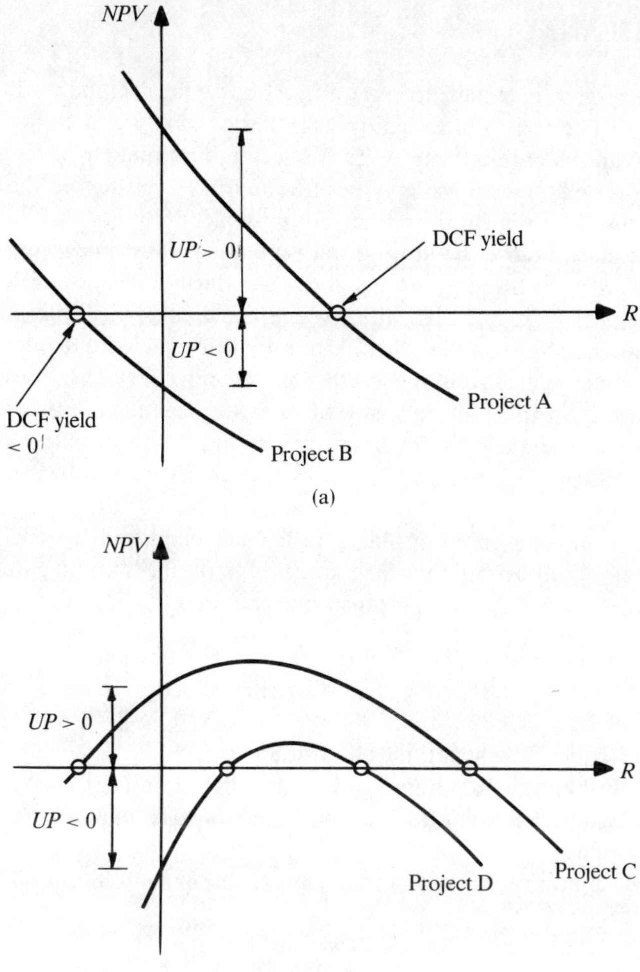

Figure 7.2 Variation of *NPV* with *R*

```
DISCØUNT RATE IS        14.00 PERCENT/PERIØD

PRØJECT LIFE IS     5 PERIØDS (MØNTHS, YEARS, ETC.)

CAPITAL CØST IS        250000.00

 PERIØD                NET CASH FLØW
    1                     90000.00
    2                    110000.00
    3                     70000.00
    4                     60000.00
    5                     80000.00

UNDISCØUNTED PRØFIT IS          160000.00

NET PRESENT VALUE IS          37911.11

DCF YIELD IS      20.58 PERCENT/PERIØD
```

Figure 7.3 Output from *DCF* program

7.3 CRITICAL PATH ANALYSIS

Every civil engineering project is certain to have at least a few details (and most have many) which are unique to it. Consequently, it is unwise to rely entirely on experience to organize and coordinate site work. While the construction of the foundations of a building will almost invariably need to be carried out before the roof is put on, it may not be so obvious whether, for example, the prefabricated wall panels should be erected before the heating and ventilating plant is delivered to site. Allowing the plant to be lifted in through the spaces finally to be occupied by the walls might avoid considerable difficulties which could otherwise arise in getting the plant into the building. On the other hand, early delivery would require that the plant be properly protected from the weather and other hazards. Decisions on matters such as these have to be made many times throughout the course of each civil engineering project and it is preferable if they are made at the planning stage so that there is sufficient time to consider the various possible consequences of the decisions.

One of the most commonly used planning techniques employed by civil engineers is critical path analysis (CPA) which makes use of the critical path method introduced in Sec. 3.8.3. CPA helps planners in many ways:

1. it allows the required time for completion of the project to be forecast;
2. it provides start and finish times for the various activities which go to make up the project;
3. it identifies those activities for which timing is critical;
4. it allows decisions to be made in advance of exactly what resources (money, men, materials, or plant) are going to be needed and, equally importantly, when they will be needed;
5. it allows the various alternative ways of overcoming timing and resource problems to be assessed; and
6. it allows progress on the project to be monitored in such a way that the consequences of any delays or difficulties may be rapidly forecast.

7.3.1 Network construction

In order to plan and run a project using the critical path method it is necessary to go through the following stages:

1. The project is broken down into a list of separate activities. An activity is an operation consuming time and resources (such as 'pour concrete') or time only (such as 'allow concrete to harden').
2. Next the sequence in which the activities must logically take place is established and the dependencies listed. These define the interrelationships between the activities (see, for example, the Livcivil problem in Sec. 3.8.3).
3. The network is drawn showing the dependencies (e.g. Fig. 3.93). Care must be taken to ensure that no artificial restraints are placed on activities. For example, if activity Z is dependent on the completion of activities W and Y and activity X is dependent only upon completion of W then the correct network is shown in Fig. 7.4(a). If the network were drawn as shown in Fig. 7.4(b) then

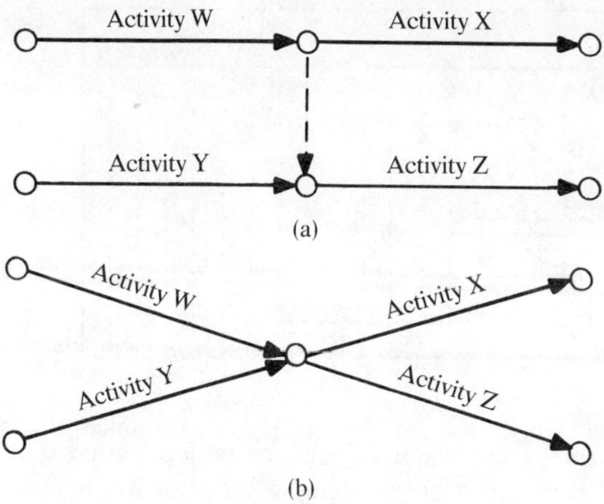

Figure 7.4 Use of dummy activity to preserve logic

an artificial restraint would be placed on activity X by making it follow activity Y as well as activity W.

4. Apart from dummy activities, which are used to preserve logic and to avoid ambiguity in referring to activities by their head and tail node numbers, each activity will take some time to complete. The activity durations must now be estimated. They may be refined later (see Sec. 7.3.2).
5. Analysis of the network may then begin in order to determine the project duration, the critical path (or paths) and the earliest and latest start and finish times of each activity. For this purpose the subroutine CPM, given in Fig. 3.95, might be used. If the project duration turns out to be longer than desired then some replanning will be necessary, with particular attention being paid to those activities on the critical path.
6. A detailed timetable of work may now be derived from the analysed network. Frequently this will be expressed in the form of a bar chart. A bar chart with each of the activities from Fig. 3.93 starting as early as possible (i.e. starting at its *EST* and finishing at its *EFT*) is shown in Fig. 7.5.
7. The bar chart may also be used to help in determining the total requirements for various resources throughout each period of the life of the project. This process, known as resource aggregation, is dealt with in Sec. 7.3.2 which also deals with the problem of smoothing resource requirements.
8. Finally, the analysed network, the associated bar chart, and any related schedule of resources may be used in the monitoring and control of the project as it is running. Any departure from the plan will call for revision of the network. If the changes prove undesirable the network may then be used in helping to decide what corrective action should be taken.

7.3.2 Resource allocation

In arriving at the initial estimates of the activity durations it is usual to assume that all the resources to do the work will be available as and when required. However, a review of the network may show, for example, that the same plant is required for different activities falling on parallel paths of the network. Similarly, there may be

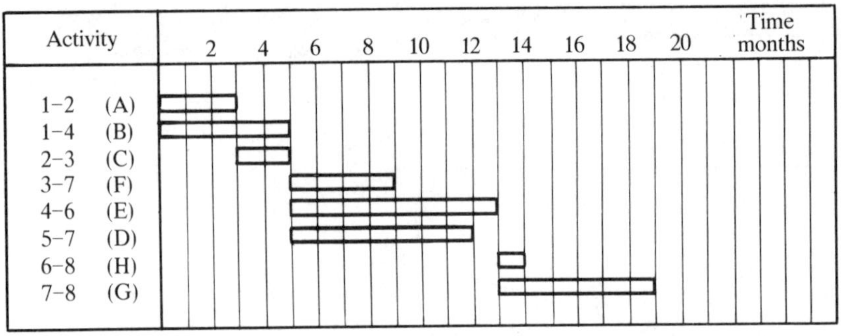

Figure 7.5 Bar chart for Livcivil example

widely fluctuating demands for labour and materials over the project period. The aim of resource allocation is to overcome such problems. First, activities may be moved within their floats. However, if demand for resources still exceeds availability after this operation then either the project duration will have to be increased or other possibilities explored such as employing different construction methods or different plant.

Consider the following problem. A network diagram has been prepared for a small construction project for which the activity durations and manpower requirements are as follows:

Activity		Duration,	
Tail node	Head node	weeks	Men
1	2	2	5
1	3	4	6
1	4	6	4
2	5	8	3
3	5	10	2
4	5	12	6

It is assumed that the men employed are capable of performing any of the activities.

Figure 7.6(a) is a bar chart showing each activity starting at its earliest start time. The manpower requirements for each activity have been inserted and the total requirements for each week of the project determined; this process is known as 'resource aggregation'. It may be seen that there is considerable variation in demand for labour. Assuming that the maximum number of men available to undertake the project was 11, then during the first few weeks demand would exceed availability. If, in spite of this, a decision were made to start all the activities in accordance with the bar chart then clearly the early activities would take longer than planned and there would be an associated increase in the project duration. However, from the end of week 4 to the end of week 6 and from the end of week 10 to the end of week 18, the resource aggregation suggests that the availability of labour would exceed demand and men would be idle. Clearly, then, it is sensible to move the non-critical activities away from the period of high demand for manpower to those

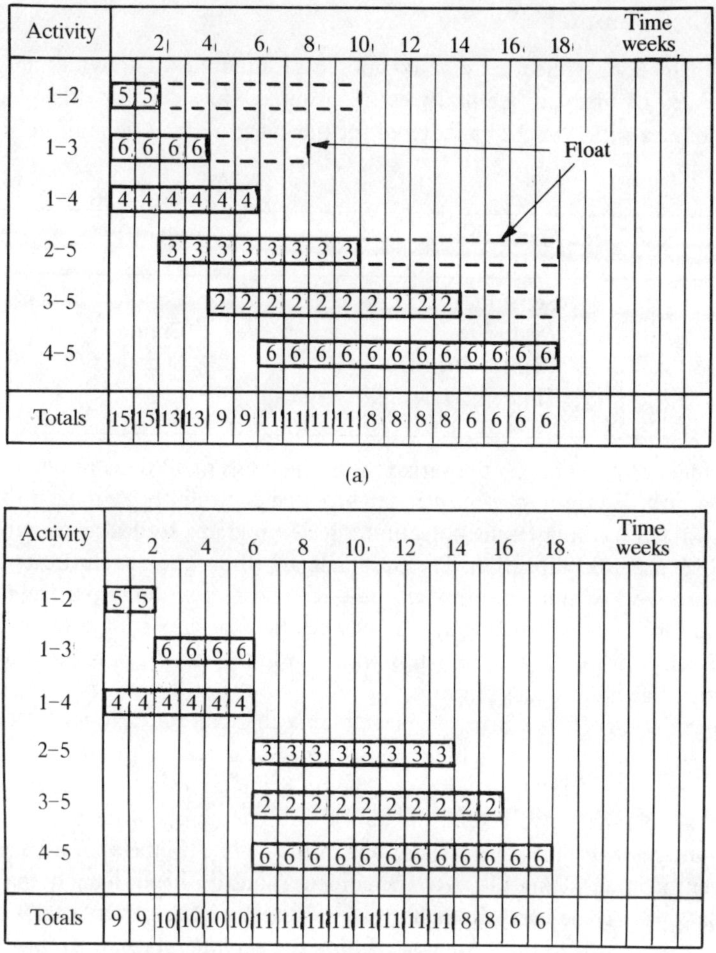

Figure 7.6 Resource aggregation and smoothing

periods when demand is low. Figure 7.6(b) is a revised version of Fig. 7.6(a). The start of activity 1–3 has been delayed by 2 weeks which means that 3–5 must also be delayed by at least 2 weeks. Activity 2–5 has been delayed by 4 weeks. In carrying out an exercise such as this to level resource requirements the original network diagram is effectively being modified by the addition of activities such as 'wait for men to become available'. Activities of this type are called 'restraints'. Their incorporation in the network will reduce the floats available to the original activities.

In the above example the activities were treated as being continuous; i.e., once started, work on them continued until they were completed. Note, however, that it is sometimes possible to split an activity into two or more periods of time to reduce peak demands for resources. Furthermore, when the float of an activity is very large, consideration should also be given to the possibility of reducing the resources allocated to that activity and allowing its duration to increase.

7.3.3 Use of the computer

Any real civil engineering project may be composed of hundreds of activities and will involve the use of many different types of resource. Consider, for example, some of the resources which might be required for the construction of a reinforced concrete structure:

Men	Materials	Plant
Carpenters	Cement	Concrete mixers
Steelfixers	Aggregate	Cranes
Concretors	Reinforcing bars	Dumpers
Scaffolders	Timber shuttering	

Clearly, the problem of checking on the variations in the levels of all these resources is a considerable task. However, the burden can be eased enormously by the use of a computer. Most large computer manufacturers have programs to deal with network analysis and resource allocation. The programs are often quite sophisticated and may be set to work within specified resource restraints or within a particular project duration. Different priorities may also be specified for allocating resources to activities. Usually, however, the activities with the lowest total floats (i.e. the most critical) would be given highest priority.

There is often a lot of work involved in preparing the data for CPA computer programs, particularly if the project is broken down into a very large number of activities. However, once the data is ready and the program has been run once then it is a relatively simple matter to amend the data for selected parts of the network and to run the program again. This illustrates one of the main advantages of using a computer instead of undertaking the network computations by hand, namely that repeated calculations may be carried out not only accurately but also very rapidly. It is often necessary to utilize this advantage during the planning stage of a project in order to compare alternative proposals for overcoming timing and/or resource problems. The facility for rapid recalculation of activity times and resource requirements is also useful in the monitoring and control of a project once work has started. Then the data for the network may be updated by assigning actual durations and resource requirements to completed activities. Data for forthcoming activities may also be modified in the light of experience of the project. In this way, potential major departures from the project plan may be detected in advance and, if necessary, further computer runs may be carried out to help in deciding what corrective action should be taken.

Another advantage of using a computer for network calculations is that the same output may readily be displayed in a variety of different ways for different purposes. For example, activities may be listed in sequence with the earliest printed first and the latest printed last. Alternatively, attention may be focussed on the most critical activities by listing them in order of increasing total float. It is possible also with some programs to produce separate printouts of activities involving different trades. This latter facility can be particularly useful for providing network plans for the subcontractors involved in a project.

7.4 SIMULATION TECHNIQUES

The concept of building a numerical model of some physical system, in order to study its behaviour with the passage of time, was introduced in Sec. 3.9. A distinction was drawn between discrete event simulation (DES) and continuous time simulation (CTS). It is the former type of model which is of primary concern in management situations. Such models may be used to advantage in the initial planning and specification of a facility and in the development of an optimum strategy for its operation. In certain cases simulation may also be used to plan the construction of a facility.

The potential applications of DES are many and diverse, e.g.

1. for the study of complex signalized road intersections and the layout of toll plazas,
2. for the study of ports, airports, and transportation interchanges,
3. for the study of production lines, maintenance facilities, and stock control.

The problems listed above may normally be broken down into a set of common elements, namely the arrival of units or customers at the facility, the development of a queue of units awaiting service, and finally the service facility itself, which may consist of one or more service channels; see Fig. 7.7. The rate of arrivals and the service times will often be random variables and study of the system behaviour will require information covering the following points:

1. the probability distribution of arrival times,
2. the size or nature of the customers, since this may effect the service required.
3. the limitations, if any, on the queue size and the strategy for selecting customers to be serviced, e.g. first come, first served, or some priority scale,
4. the probability distribution of the service times and the number of service channels.

Where the probability distributions of arrivals and service times follow the Poisson-exponential laws or certain other classical distributions, it may be possible

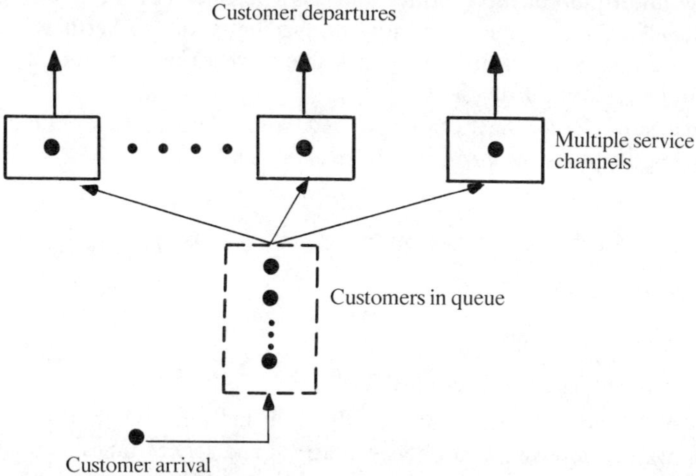

Figure 7.7 The basic queue system

to investigate the behaviour of the system by the use of queueing theory.[2,3] However, many practical problems can only be tackled by numerical techniques and these can best be illustrated with a simple example of DES.

Consider the design of an exporting crude oil terminal which is located on the coast. It is supplied by a pipeline from the oilfields. Tankers of varying size will arrive in some random way to load the crude oil. The engineer must decide on the number of berths required and he must specify the loading capacities of each berth. If the site is exposed, then wind or wave conditions may limit the availability of the berths. He must establish the storage capacity of the tank farm necessary to cover the absence of tankers or the periods of downtime due to the wind or wave conditions. In the final analysis, the cost of providing many berths with low loading rates or fewer berths with higher throughputs, the cost of storage on land, the costs incurred in tankers lying idle in the anchorage and the capital costs of providing protection against wave action, etc., must be weighed against each other in arriving at the optimum system.

The simulation model for this problem is complicated and the approach will be illustrated through a simplified situation. Let the time between tankers' arrivals A be described by the exponential distribution

$$\begin{aligned} P_A(A) &= 1 - \exp(-\lambda A) \qquad & A \geqslant 0 \\ &= 0 & A < 0 \end{aligned}$$

where λ is the average arrival rate, measured in tankers per unit time. For a single berth with a given configuration of loading hoses, etc., it is proposed that the total service time S, i.e. the time taken to dock, load, and undock a tanker, is described by the probability distribution

$$\begin{aligned} P_S(S) &= 1.0 - \exp\left[-\left(\frac{S - S_{\min}}{C}\right)^2\right] \qquad & S \geqslant S_{\min} \\ &= 0 & S < S_{\min} \end{aligned}$$

where $S_{\min}$ is the lower limit on service times and C is a parameter of the problem. In this case S could include an allowance for the possibility of the berth being vacant when the waiting tanker is unable to dock due to weather conditions, but this aspect will not be pursued further here.

The performance of the terminal can be studied, with reference to a notional clock, by identifying the following key times for the ith tanker;

T_{ai} the time of arrival

T_{bi} the time at which docking commences

T_{ci} the time at which the tanker departs

T_{qi} the time spent in the queue

T_{ti} the total time spent at the terminal

Assuming that A and S are both jointly and individually statistically independent, listings of successive times between arrival and service times may be generated from the appropriate psuedo-random number generators described in Sec. 3.9. If the clock is started at $T = 0$ when the first tanker arrives then

$$T_{a1} = 0 \quad \text{and} \quad T_{b1} = 0,$$

$$T_{c1} = T_{b1} + S_1$$

$$T_{q1} = 0 \quad \text{and} \quad T_{t1} = S_1$$

The next step refers to the second tanker, where

$$T_{a2} = T_{a1} + A_2 \quad \text{and} \quad T_{b2} = T_{c1} \text{ or } T_{a2}$$

whichever is the greater;
i.e.

$$T_{b2} = \max(T_{c1}, T_{a2})$$

$$T_{c2} = T_{b2} + S_2$$

$$T_{q2} = T_{b2} - T_{a2} \quad \text{and} \quad T_{t2} = T_{c2} - T_{a2}$$

The equations for the ith tanker follow by induction:

$$T_{ai} = T_{a(i-1)} + A_i \quad \text{and} \quad T_{bi} = \max(T_{c(i-1)}, T_{ai})$$

$$T_{ci} = T_{bi} + S_i$$

$$T_{qi} = T_{bi} - T_{ai} \quad \text{and} \quad T_{ti} = T_{ci} - T_{ai}$$

Now let λ be 0.041 667 tankers per hour, S_{min} be 10.0 hours, and C be 5.0 hours; see Fig. 7.8. The uniform random number generator (RND1) may be called, say, $2m$ times to generate a list of independent random numbers X with a uniform distribution between 0 and 1. The first, third, fifth, etc. values of X are used to generate the m values of A from

$$A_i = P_A^{-1}(X_j)$$

or

$$A_i = -\log_e(X_j)/\lambda$$

$$j = 2i - 1 \quad \text{for } i = 1, m$$

and the second, fourth, etc. values of X provide the service times from

$$S_i = P_S^{-1}(X_j)$$

or

$$S_i = C[-\log_e(X_j)]^{1/2} + S_{min}$$

where

$$j = 2i \quad \text{for } i = 1, m$$

These relationships follow directly from the inversion of the respective probability distributions.

Table 7.1 shows an extract of the output from the simulation. It is possible to calculate such properties of the system as the average queue time and total time at the terminal. Furthermore, if the tanker capacities were stated explicitly, it would be possible to calculate the cumulative throughput and knowing the rate of supply

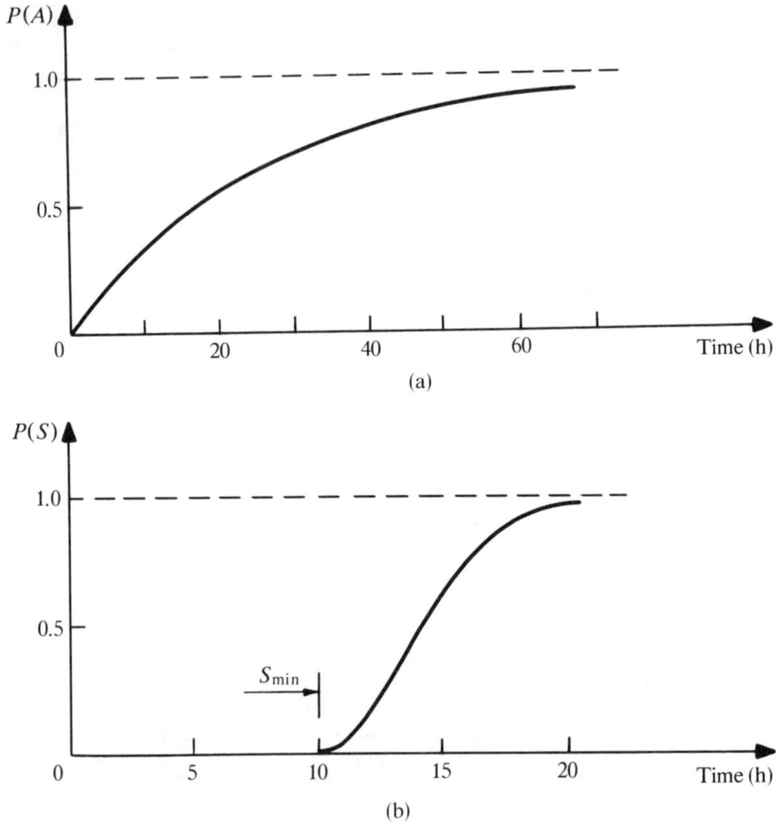

Figure 7.8 Probability distributions for oil terminal simulation. (a) Cumulative distribution of arrival gaps, $P(A)$. (b) Cumulative distribution of service times, $P(S)$

from the oilfields it would be possible to compute the storage requirement. It is likely that the performance of the oil terminal will stabilize, in a statistical sense, after a number of tankers have arrived for service. The user must decide whether he wants to gather information about the transient, initial behaviour or simulate long enough for the averaged parameters, such as queue length, etc., to reach a steady-state condition. The need to simulate a reasonable number of tanker arrivals is obvious. If the simulation run is too short, the statistics derived will be subject to unacceptable sampling errors.

The model could be rerun with different values of S_{min} and C, reflecting different loading plant, in order to see the changes in the terminal performance. One advantage of the psuedo-random number generators is that the second and subsequent runs can be performed with the same set of tanker arrival data in order to compare performances of the alternative systems.

Of course, the distributions chosen for A and S in the present example could be much more complicated in practice. For example, the probability of arrivals could be modified if the tanker owners know that a queue of vessels has developed at the terminal. Similarly, the service times can be dependent on the number of vessels waiting to load.

Table 7.1 Extract from the output of simulation example

Tanker No.	Arrival gap A	Time at arrival T_a	Time at berthing T_b	Service time S	Depart time T_c	Queue time T_q	Total time T_t
.	.	.	.	.	.	.	.
.	.	.	.	.	.	.	.
.	.	.	.	.	.	.	.
20	–	459.7	–	–	473.7	–	–
21	6.8	466.5	473.7	11.9	485.6	7.2	19.1
22	17.0	483.5	485.6	12.1	497.7	2.1	14.2
23	26.6	510.1	510.1	15.9	526.0	0.0	15.9
24	15.6	525.7	526.0	13.8	539.8	0.3	14.1
25	10.9	536.6	539.8	17.2	557.0	3.2	20.4
26	5.4	542.0	557.0	14.5	571.5	15.0	29.5
27	19.1	561.1	571.5	16.8	588.3	10.4	27.2
28	7.0	568.1	588.3	18.4	606.7	20.2	38.2
29	7.1	575.2	606.7	13.5	620.2	31.5	45.0
30	69.1	644.3	644.3	13.9	658.2	0.0	13.9
31	34.5	678.8	678.8	13.4	692.2	0.0	13.4
32	2.1	680.9	692.2	11.7	703.9	11.3	23.0
33	0.3	681.2	703.9	13.7	717.6	22.7	36.4
34	81.1	762.3	762.3	13.3	775.6	0.0	13.3
35	9.3	771.6	775.6	10.5	786.1	4.0	14.5
.	.	.	.	.	.	.	.
.	.	.	.	.	.	.	.
.	.	.	.	.	.	.	.

Mean arrival gap = 24.0
Mean service time = 14.4
Mean queue time = 10.2
Mean total time = 24.6

Note: All times are in hours.

Finally, the model could be extended to consider two or more berths and to consider the occurrence of downtime due to weather. The basic performance statistics would be converted into monetary terms for the purpose of economic appraisal.

REFERENCES

1. Pilcher, R. *Appraisal and Control of Project Costs,* McGraw-Hill, London, 1973.
2. Stark, R. M. and Nicholls, R. L. *Mathematical Foundations for Design,* McGraw-Hill, New York, 1972.
3. Mitchell, G. H. *Operational Research: Techniques and Examples,* English University Press, London, 1972.

CHAPTER

EIGHT

COMPUTERS IN HIGHWAY AND TRAFFIC ENGINEERING

8.1 HIGHWAY ENGINEERING

A road is part of the basic economic infrastructure of a country and the location and design of new roads has become a complex exercise where costs, traffic service, environmental impact, and other socio-economic factors must be taken into account. In recent years the necessity of allowing proposed improvements to the highway network to be debated at public enquiry has required a far greater number of route variations to be considered than was hitherto deemed necessary. The quantity of design work to establish the costs for these alternatives was thereby greatly increased, and since the traditional design of highway works was time-consuming and repetitive, highway engineers were quick to realize the potential of the computer to assist in the laborious tasks involved.

Highway design requires the three-dimensional location of a large number of points on the alignment so that the existing ground levels can be compared with the design levels to give the quantities of earthworks involved in the particular location. This relationship also determines the drainage requirements, and additional ancillary structures (retaining walls, culverts, bridges, etc.) associated with the design. The first stage in the traditional design process was the horizontal alignment where the constraints of topography and land use gave a possible route which could then be approximated by relatively simple geometric elements – straight, circular arc, and transition spiral as described in standard highway or surveying texts[1,2] [see Fig. 8.1(a)]. It should be noted, however, that there was no intrinsic merit in these traditional elements of alignment. They were simply those most readily adaptable to the existing means of calculation so that the exact location of any point could readily be determined, as could the measurements necessary to set out the elements in the field. The horizontal alignment had to conform to certain design constraints associated with operational safety of vehicles such as minimum curve radius and minimum transition curve length.

The horizontal design was then compared with the contoured plans so that a plot could be made of the groundlevel variation along the chosen alignment. On this plot the vertical alignment of the highway could be designed as a series of straights or gradients connected by parabolic vertical curves to form a smooth transition between them (see Fig. 8.2). The vertical alignment had to obey certain constraints of maximum and minimum gradients and the connecting curves had to be of sufficient length to allow adequate sight distance for safety. Further constraints might be introduced where the road crossed a river, railway, or other road where a minimum clearance must be provided. Within these constraints the object of the vertical design was to effect the most economic earthworks construction by

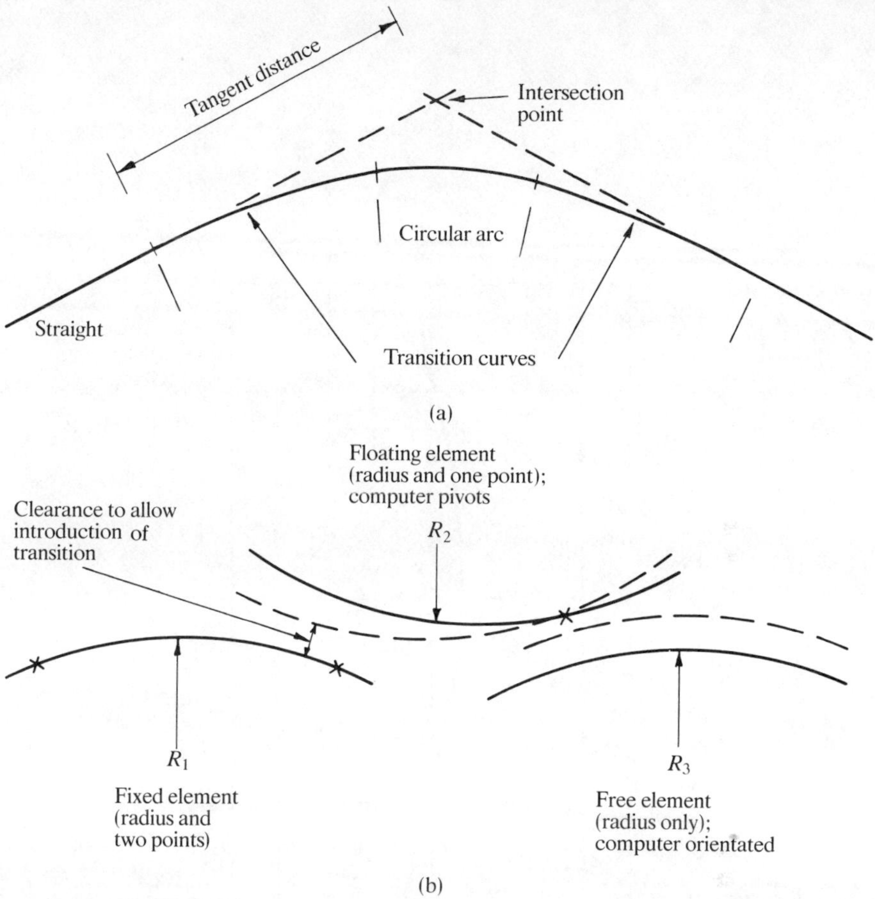

Figure 8.1 (a) Elements of traditional horizontal alignment. (b) Horizontal alignment by method of elements

balancing excavation and embankment works ('cut' and 'fill'). The earthwork costs, which might equal 40 per cent of the total construction costs, were the most variable of the costs and were mainly dependent on the engineer's chosen alignment. In order to arrive at the quantities of earthworks a further time-consuming exercise was the drawing of ground and new highway cross-sections at specified chainage intervals along the alignment. The areas of cut and fill on each cross-section were then determined, often by planimeter, and a suitable calculation used to determine the cumulative volumes along the alignment. It can readily be appreciated that on a major design scheme the volume of work involved did not allow a number of alternative vertical alignments to be compared for earthwork economy.

As a variety of computers became available in the late fifties, each with its own specific machine code, highway engineers developed programs to serve their particular needs. Since these needs were similar in most design offices a large number of programs were developed for identical problems but differing in execution since they were specifically related to individual computers and, therefore, not directly interchangeable. It was obvious that some form of coordination

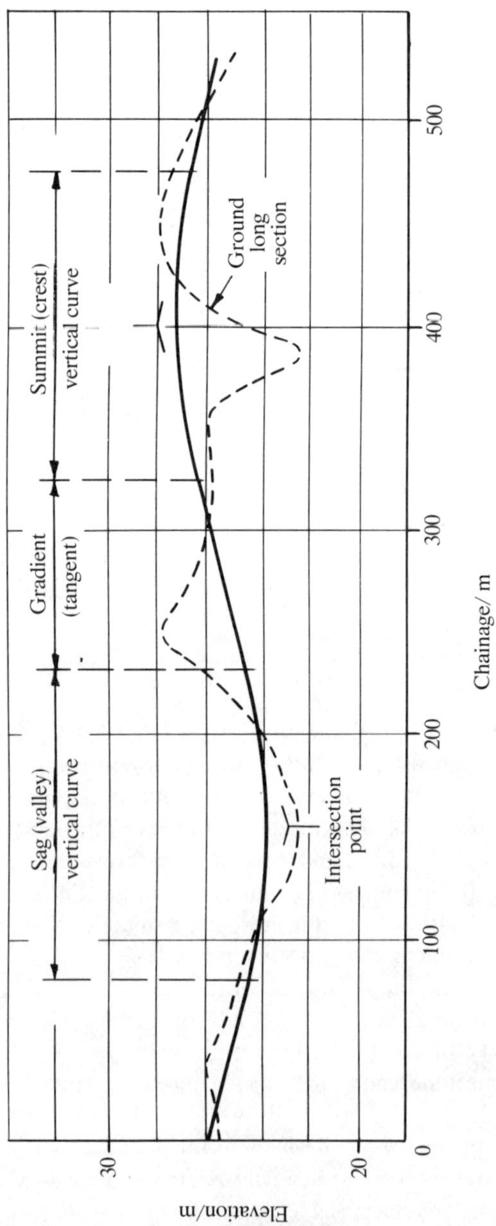

Figure 8.2 Vertical alignment elements (not to scale)

was necessary and in 1964 the County Surveyors Society and the then Ministry of Transport set up a Joint Computer Panel and, later, a Joint Computer Programming Committee to carry out the development of a suite of programs for highway design which could be used for the separate stages of design or integrated for the design of a complete scheme. This was done by amalgamating the most suitable of the programs then existing and standardizing the input/output formats to produce the British Integrated Program System for Highway Design (BIPS1).[3] The following year an improved version, BIPS2, was issued which included programs for use with plotting machines to draw alignments and cross-sections.

Other countries were producing their own design suites but within Britain BIPS remained preeminent until 1975 when the GENESYS organization produced a subsystem HIGHWAYS/1[4] as part of their comprehensive approach to computer-aided design and MOSS[5,6] was developed by a consortium of British county authorities, based upon a more complex model of the terrain. More recently, BIPS3[7] has further added to the sophistication of the general computer-aided design packages now available to the highway engineer. The widespread use of these packages for the design of highways makes the description of individual programs unnecessary but as well as reproducing, for far more rapid calculation, the design procedures originally used, the computer has enabled the engineer to develop new techniques to improve the quality and accuracy of his design. The more important of the techniques will, therefore, be described below.

8.2 COMPUTER-AIDED HIGHWAY DESIGN

8.2.1 Ground model

Highway engineers readily interpret the information carried on a contoured plan by visual inspection but for the computer to carry out design work the representation of the topography must be in a different form (Fig. 8.3). Survey information is sampled to give an acceptable minimum number of points uniquely described by two horizontal coordinates and a height. This data is stored in digital form as a digital ground model (DGM) or digital terrain model (DTM). The information may be obtained from:

1. digitized plans (when contoured or spot height drawings already exist)
2. photogrammetry
3. ground surveying

The form of sampling is usually as a regular grid or as a 'string' of significant levels.

8.2.1.1 Regular grid

The levels stored are at the intersection points of a grid of known spacing. This reduces storage requirement in the computer since rectangular blocks of ground can be stored as arrays and if the horizontal coordinates of one fixed point are known then the array subscripts, together with the spacing of the grid points, can be used to determine the exact location of the required level point. The ground model may be rectangular or square, and, as the sampling may have to be varied according to

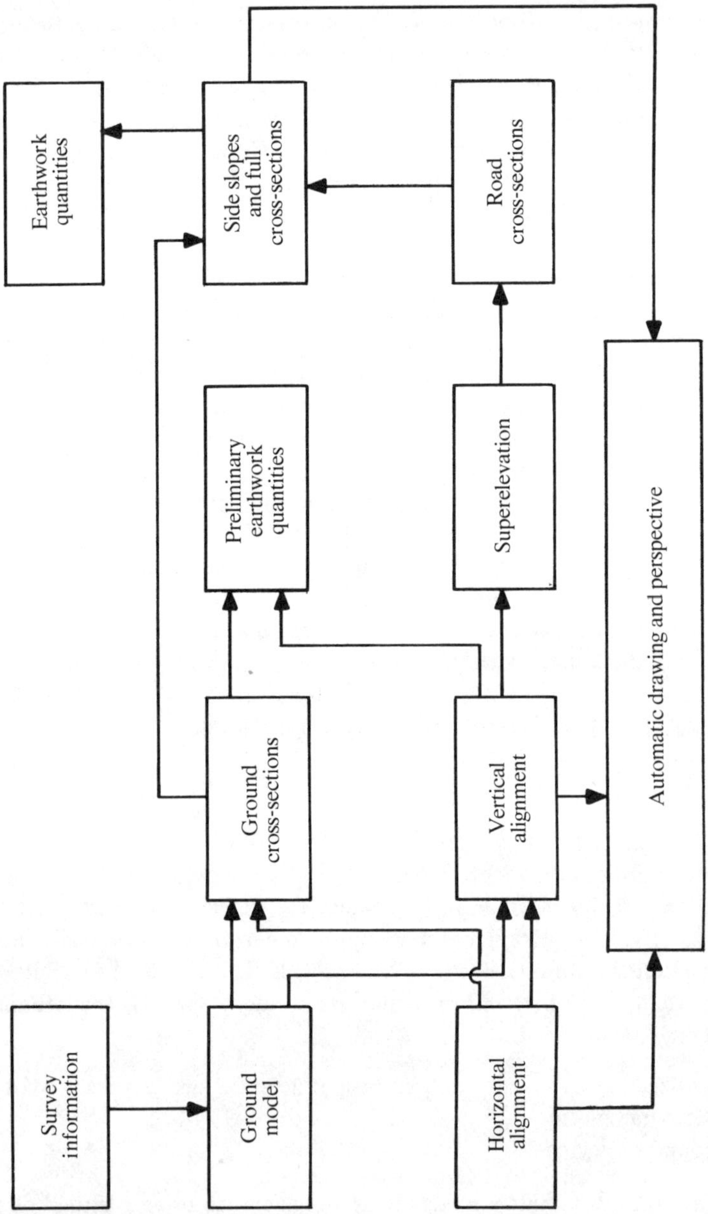

Figure 8.3 Simplified flow diagram for computer-aided highway design

the irregularity of the terrain, provision is made for the area of interest to be covered by blocks, each block having a mesh size specified by the engineer to give a suitable representation of the ground.

8.2.1.2 String DGM

Intermediate levels between the sampled points are obtained by interpolation from the nearest stored data and in certain situations (e.g., urban areas, complex industrial areas) this could give rise to problems where sudden level changes occur within the grid element. In these circumstances a suitable storage method is to use lines or 'strings' of significant levels defining specific features. These could be contours (a two-dimensional string) but more usually are salient topographical features, e.g., the tops and bottoms of railway embankments and the centre lines and channels of existing roads. The concept of the MOSS system is based on physical surfaces being represented by strings of three-dimensional spatial coordinates. In the same way that the terrain features are described by 'strings', the designed road surfaces can also be so represented.

8.2.1.3 Triangular models

The improved speed of modern ground surveying methods can provide rapid data acquisition. Tacheometry or electronic distance measurement enables the engineer closely to control the sampling of points at the apices of random plane triangles.

8.2.1.4 Interpolation

The basic calculation required from the DGM is the determination of the heights of points on the ground, corresponding with specific points on the given highway alignment. For this some form of interpolation is required; see Sec. 3.6.

For the regular grid the required height is interpolated from the heights of the nodes of the mesh unit surrounding. Greater sophistication may be introduced by treating the surface joining the nodes not as a plane but rather as a more complex surface such as an hyperbolic paraboloid, but this obviously leads to an increase in computation time.

Interpolation from terrain strings requires identification of points on the strings which run closest to the unknown point.

8.2.2 Horizontal alignment

The standard traditional format of the horizontal alignment – straight, transition curve, circular arc – was easily adapted to the computer with the additional accuracy of rapid calculation of coordinates for any required point on the alignment. This has brought an improvement in the methods of setting out of curves in the field, since the location of the alignment can be related to a coordinate system (National Grid or local) and the accumulation of inaccuracies which may occur from deflection angle and length measurements is therefore avoided.

Even with the traditional elements of the alignment, however, the computer has brought about simplified methods of design. In the traditional approach a framework of straights meeting at intersection points was specified together with circular arcs displaced from the tangential straights by an amount equal to the 'shift' necessary to insert the required transitions. The alternative method, available with BIPS and HIGHWAYS/1, requires only the specification of sections actually on the required alignment as arcs (a straight being an arc of radius infinity). These are defined as 'primary elements', with transition curves as 'secondary elements'. Since the design speed for the road and the parameter which determines the rate of change of curvature over the length of the transitions are constants, the length of transition varies inversely with the radius of the arc it is joining. Accordingly, allowance may be made for inserting transitions of the correct length simply by ensuring that the adjacent primary elements are separated by a clearance which is unique for the given pair of radii and respective directions of curvature or 'hand' of the arcs.

A primary element is classified according to the number of points on it which are fixed in location, its degree of fixity. The coordinates of two points uniquely locate an arc as a 'fixed' element, while only one fixed point allows the arc to pivot about that point and classifies it as a 'floating' element. It can, therefore, be manoeuvred about the fixed point to achieve the standard clearance from an adjacent element. The third type of primary element, the 'free' element, has only its radius and 'hand' specified so that it can readily be moved to the correct clearances with the elements bounding it; see Fig. 8.1(b).

Using this approach a draft alignment can quickly be specified using railway curves (plastic templates of given radius used for drawing highway curves), the degree of fixity of the element being dependent on the constraints on that section of the alignment. The program analyses the initial geometry of the alignment, assigns the required transition curves and adjusts the positions of the adjacent elements in order to accommodate these transitions, thus producing a complete centre line.

8.2.3 Advanced alignment techniques

The location of a highway involves determining areas or features to be avoided along the desired route which give rise to constraints on the alignment. Specific points of passage may be delineated with a maximum displacement giving 'gates' through which the line must pass. Between such gates the location process may be less rigidly controlled and the methods outlined above involve fitting a line of standard elements which does not offend against the stipulated restrictions yet achieves the required standards. Modern methods of design utilize unconventional curves well suited to the analytical capabilities of the computer in which the radius of curvature may be constantly changing to give great flexibility of alignment.

Higher-order curves such as polynomials and cubic splines (see Sec. 3.6.1.2), have been used for roads constructed in the United Kingdom but it is the cubic spline which has won the greater acceptance and is incorporated in BIPS3. The major feature of the cubic spline design which recommends it to highway engineers is that the alignment can be visually displayed by a physical element forming the curve. A geometric definition of the line can then be determined by a curve type which approximates the physical curve and obeys satisfactory design criteria. The method uses piano wire, which is positioned on a plan of the route corridor by fixing start and finish positions and bearings and locating the wire through various 'points of passage' chosen by the engineer to suit the economic and aesthetic criteria influencing his choice of route. Because of the flexible properties of the wire it takes up a shape that is curving throughout its length and if there is continuity of curvature with the minimum radius and other built-in safety criteria obeyed it forms an acceptable line. The spline fit is accomplished by the computer connecting each adjacent pair of points defined by their coordinates with a section of a third-degree polynomial and matching up these sections so that the first and second derivatives (gradient and rate of change of gradient) are continuous at each point.

8.2.4 Vertical alignment

The conventional alignment of gradients connected by vertical parabolas will be designed by the engineer on a long section or profile of the existing ground along the chosen horizontal alignment with the heights of points at specified intervals interpolated from the ground model. The integrated nature of design suites such as BIPS ensures storage of the output from any individual program which can be called up as input to some other manipulative program. Thus the ground model output and the horizontal alignment output, as coordinates of points, together become input for the ground section program. Similarly this data is output for the vertical alignment design but stored for future use by the preliminary earthworks program. As a further example of the labour-saving abilities of the computer BIPS incorporates an additional program which will produce further longitudinal ground sections parallel to the centre line and at specified distances on both sides of it. These 'triple' ground long sections are of use in assessing the effect of sidelong ground on a trial vertical alignment.

The design of a suitable vertical alignment is intended to minimize earthwork construction costs while observing the constraints of maximum and minimum gradients and the provision of vertical curves giving the requisite sight distances for safe stopping or overtaking at summits. In traditional manual design, a considerable amount of work was necessary after the design of the vertical alignment in the drawing of cross-sections relating the road level to the existing ground so that the areas of successive sections could be used to obtain earthwork volumes. For a significant length of road it was rarely possible to compare a number of alternative vertical alignments and much depended on the expertise of the engineer in achieving a satisfactory earthworks balance and thus minimum costs of construction. Accordingly, the rapid analysis of alternative alignments is an important benefit brought by computer-aided design.

The sophistication of more advanced curve designs described above for horizontal alignment can be similarly applied to the vertical alignment. BIPS provides for the 'element' method or the cubic spline approach to be used as alternatives to the traditional design. HIGHWAYS/1 uses the method of elements.

8.2.5 Additional design aids

Once the basic alignments have been decided upon, the available suites have a variety of additional programs to complete the design requirements.

8.2.5.1 Superelevation

Before the full road cross-section can be determined, the required sideways slope of the pavement surface must be calculated. This is the superelevation, the canting up of the road surface to reduce the effects of centrifugal force acting on vehicles travelling in curved paths. The amount of inclination towards the centre of curvature is inversely proportional to the curvature at that point, and directly proportional to the design speed for the particular road. There are a number of constraints which must be observed; maximum and minimum crossfalls, allowable rate of change of gradient along a curve where the radius and, therefore, the complementary superelevation is changing. The designer must decide to which highway edge (or channel) he will design the calculated vertical alignment, with the other channel levels being calculated according to the required superelevation.

8.2.5.2 Road cross-sections

The ground cross-sections are obtained from the ground model and horizontal alignment with heights being calculated at specified points on either side of the centre line. The road cross-section widths and superelevation relationship are combined to give the levels at the outer edges of the highway so that the required side slopes can be calculated. Programs allow for variations in slope in different materials, and for the removal of the topsoil and unsuitable materials from beneath embankments. In certain materials, when the embankments exceed a certain height it is good practice to step the side slope by means of a berm to ensure greater stability and this is also allowed for in the side slope program.

8.2.5.3 Earthworks

With the information from the cross-section group now available the areas of 'cut' and 'fill' on the sections can be calculated and hence the quantities of earthwork requirements along the chosen alignment, with allowances for bulking or shrinkage of materials. The BIPS program uses end area methods with prismoidal and curvature corrections for greater accuracy in determining the quantities between successive cross-sections. HIGHWAYS/1 has a more complex approach to volume calculations, whereby the shape defined between adjacent cross-sections is divided into a number of quadrilateral prisms. The volume of each prism is calculated by a finite-element method which fits a hyperbolic paraboloid surface to the top and bottom face of each prism. Although involving greater computer time this gives a more accurate calculation than a simple end area approach where the surfaces can only be considered as planes.

8.2.5.4 Automatic drawing

Programs have been developed to draw accurately the output from the standard suites. The BIPS group includes programs to instruct graph plotters to draw horizontal and vertical alignment. road plans, ground and road longitudinal sections, road cross-sections, and mass haul diagrams for earthworks. Similar facilities exist for MOSS and HIGHWAYS/1, though in the latter case plotting is carried out by a further GENESYS subsystem called HIGHPLOT using the HIGHWAYS/1 data. BIPS also makes provision for a perspective drawing giving a view along the road showing curvature, side slopes, etc., which enables an assessment of the quality of the design to be made.

8.3 OPTIMIZATION OF HIGHWAY DESIGNS

The major developments in recent years in the application of the computer to highway design have been in the field of optimization of designs to minimize the values of certain objective functions. Simultaneously methods are being devised whereby the computer will carry out automatic alignment generation to produce suitable designs within the limits of the constraints provided by the engineer, these designs providing the preliminary trial alignment on which the optimization programs will operate. The general optimization approach may be described in four stages:

1. Represent the problem in mathematical form.
2. Determine suitable objective functions to be maximized or minimized (e.g., construction cost).
3. Set out the constraints within which a solution may be found (e.g., the use of maximum and minimum gradients in designing a vertical alignment).
4. Devise a suitable optimization technique or approach by which the objective function may be maximized or minimized.

8.3.1 Vertical optimization

The optimization techniques are most easily described for the vertical alignment, since the major effect of variation in the design is on the cost of the earthworks and a design to minimize these costs is readily envisaged. In Britain the major suite for this is the Highway Optimizations Program System (HOPS) which adapts for the computer the process the engineer would follow in manual design, but using a variety of numerical techniques to compensate for and refine the judgement inherent in the traditional approach.

The necessary starting point is the ground logitudinal section, obtained as described above (Sec. 8.2.4). This is operated on by program VENUS[8,9] to generate a quasi-vertical alignment by smoothing out undulations. A smooth alignment is produced, closely following the existing ground and approximately balancing cut and fill as it intersects the profile irregularities. Any specific level control points such as clearances which must be provided at crossing points of roads, railways, rivers, etc., are obeyed by adjusting the line to pass through the required level. The smoothed alignment must now be approximated by a conventional alignment of gradients and parabolic curves. The points where the smoothed alignment changes from summit curve to sag curve (points of inflection) are located and straight lines are fitted tangentially to these points, meeting at the vertical intersection points. Maximum possible curve lengths are then fitted to this framework of tangent gradients using least-squares techniques to approximate the parabolas to the quasi-vertical alignment.

The alignment must now be checked to ensure that the design constraints are not violated and modified by program FEASBL where required. A further program JANUS[10] coordinates or 'phases' the horizontal and vertical curvature to avoid these combinations which give rise to visual defects, for both aesthetic and safety reasons.

With this basic alignment as a starting point, the process of modifying the design to minimize earthwork costs is carried out by program MINERVA.[11] The variables controlling the alignment at each intersection point (chainage and level of intersection point, curve length) are adjusted in turn, with the other variables being held constant. The process continues until a lowest earthwork cost has been arrived at for a specific setting of a particular variable and the next variable is then incrementally adjusted in a similar fashion. This procedure continues through all variables at all intersection points and is repeated until no further reduction in the objective function can be obtained.

Vertical alignment optimization typically can save 15–20 per cent of earthwork costs by comparison with a typical manual design alignment and in the UK this can amount to 3–4 per cent of the total works cost.

8.3.2 Horizontal alignment optimization

A relatively recent extension of the principles outlined above has been to include the horizontal alignment in the optimization process. The program NOAH operates on a conventional alignment of curves, straights, and transitions, with variables taken as the positions of the horizontal curves and their radii. The objective function may be the total construction cost alone, the traffic operating costs alone, or the sum of the two. A similar approach to the vertical alignment optimization is applied, with the variables in turn being incrementally altered to achicvc a minimum of the objective function. The optimization of the vertical alignment can then be carried out on the horizontal alignment so obtained.

8.4 OTHER DESIGN PROGRAMS

Major highway schemes are evaluated by means of a cost-benefit analysis whereby a relationship is derived between the construction cost of a scheme and the operating costs of traffic along it together with the costs of anticipated accidents. This may be compared with the 'do-nothing' case to show the viability of any scheme at all, or may be used to determine the best alternative. This appraisal is carried out by a suite COBA which accomplishes the complex assessment of traffic operating costs for forecast traffic over a thirty year period.

DAPHNE is a program for the design of highway drainage systems but which can be adapted for urban systems. A recent addition optimizes the layout with respect to construction costs.

8.5 TRAFFIC ENGINEERING AND TRANSPORTATION PLANNING

Traffic engineering studies the complex interplay between traveller, vehicle and track, although the major emphasis has necessarily been on the relationship between the road and its vehicles to provide 'the safe, rapid, comfortable, convenient and economic movement of people and goods'. The need to forecast future traffic movements and to make proposals for the area-wide provision of transport facilities led to the development of transportation planning as a specialist discipline linked with the overall planning of urban areas. The importance of the transport network as part of the basic infrastructure of an area requires all forms of transport to be considered in any study with a combination of social, economic, and political objectives to be achieved.

This division of emphasis has led to the traffic engineer in local and national government being concerned mainly with aspects of traffic management: the design of measures for the control of vehicle and pedestrian traffic on the existing street network together with those features affecting traffic operation on new facilities. In consulting engineers' organizations the dividing line may be less rigid, with the transportation section considering all relevant work within the overall discipline.

Transport studies in general grew with the development of the computer, and it may be said that this growth was entirely dependent on the expansion of computing facilities. Traffic problems frequently require the collection and analysis of a large amount of data which shows great variability of any measured parameter (i.e. traffic speeds, parking duration, etc.). The handling, storage, and analysis of such data is ideally dealt with by a computer where special techniques can be used for sorting, classifying, and abstracting. Variable data also requires statistical analysis so that the representative parameter values can be determined, and, as the data gathered is frequently a sample, standard statistical methods are necessary to estimate the reliance that may be placed on the values. Consequently there is no section of this diverse subject in which the computer is not an essential tool, and the software developed by the computer firms, government agencies, and consultancies has proliferated to such an extent that it is possible to describe only representative areas of application.

8.6 EXAMPLE OF TRAFFIC ANALYSIS–JUNCTIONS

To design road traffic facilities a knowledge of the behaviour of vehicles and their drivers is necessary but there is such great variability in the manoeuvres of individual vehicles in specific situations that observation alone can rarely do more than indicate that a particular mix of vehicles is behaving in a particular way when a number of variables have the values appropriate to the period of study. For example, the simplest traffic operation of travel along a section of highway can be influenced in quantity and quality by the amount and type of traffic, the opportunities for overtaking, the road layout in cross-section and alignment, the weather, the condition of the road surface, and a number of other factors. Even where the influence of variables can be accounted for by long-term observation it can be difficult to extrapolate to future conditions, a necessary procedure in design. Accordingly, in traffic analysis it is usual to translate the real situation into a model comprising a set of representative mathematical symbols in which a required traffic event is described in terms of a number of variables which have a quantified interrelationship. The greater the number of influencing variables the more complex the analysis, and it has taken the power of the computer to expand this aspect of traffic engineering. The problems of junction design are a good example of the use of the computer to arrive at design standards from the manipulation of such models.

Junctions on road networks may have a great variety of layout and dimensions but may briefly be categorized as:

1. At-grade (surface level)

   (a) Major–minor priority where traffic on the major road has priority with traffic on the minor road being constrained to wait until a suitable gap appears in the main flow.

(b) Roundabout with priority being given to vehicles already circulating on the roundabout.

(c) Traffic signal. Right of way is shared between a number of approaches in turn.

2. Grade separated (flyover type)
Cross traffic is not impeded but problems similar to 1(a) are experienced by traffic joining any major road from slip roads.

The important measure at junctions is the capacity, the number of vehicles which can pass through them without undue delay or hazard, and for types 1(a) and 1(b) the main variable is the occurrence of gaps between vehicles on the major road of a length of time suitable for particular manoeuvres such as merging with or crossing the stream. Different manoeuvres require different size gaps and the analysis is complicated by the fact that different drivers require different acceptable gaps for the same manoeuvre. The physical dimensions of the junction influence the ability of the driver to judge the available gap or determine how a manoeuvre may be carried out (acceleration lane for emerging vehicles, central reservation so that crossing may be accomplished in two movements, etc.) With this number of variables empirical models based on observation would be difficult to calibrate to obtain a general relationship.

Over a long time period such as an hour the arrival of vehicles may be totalled but for shorter time periods such as those which must be studied for the delay characteristics of junctions, the number of arrivals will vary considerably so that we must consider the probability of a number of vehicles arriving. It has been shown that when traffic flow is light traffic arrivals at a point may be described in probabilistic terms by the Poisson distribution.

This states that for random events (the arrival of a number of vehicles in a particular time interval is independent of the number arriving in any previous time interval) the probability of exactly n vehicles arriving in any time interval t is given by

$$P(n) = \frac{m^n \mathrm{e}^{-m}}{n!} \tag{8.1}$$

where $n! = 1 \times 2 \times 3 \times \ldots \times (n-1) \times n$

m = average number of vehicle arrivals in time t

e = base of Napierian logarithms (natural logarithms)

A gap of time t means that no vehicles arrive in this time so that the probability of a gap, h, being equal to or greater than t is

$$P(h > t) = \mathrm{e}^{-m} \tag{8.2}$$

Equation (8.2) is a continuous function and can be developed to give the probable distribution of gap sizes within a particular traffic stream. Such analyses are fully described in standard traffic engineering texts[12,13] and their development leads to sophisticated junction models. J. C. Tanner[14] derived the following model for the maximum number of vehicles that emerge from a minor road

$$q_2\,(\max) = \frac{q_1(1-\beta_1 q_1)}{\mathrm{e}^{q_1(\alpha-\beta_1)}(1-\mathrm{e}^{-\beta_2 q_1})} \tag{8.3}$$

where q_1 = major road volume

q_2 = minor road volume
β_1 = minimum gap between major road vehicles
β_2 = minimum gap between vehicles emerging from the minor road
α = minimum acceptable gap in major road stream for emerging minor road vehicles

If the values for α are estimated for particular junction layouts a simple computer program will calculate minor road capacity for differing values of major road flow and these can be shown graphically as a design aid.[20] Average delays in minor road vehicles which are used in evaluating alternative junction layouts can also be derived from such analysis.

Even with stochastic techniques simplifications must be made and the complex variables influencing flow must be reduced to simple values. For instance, the gap acceptance value is assumed to be a step function where 100 per cent of drivers are assumed to accept a gap equal to or greater than a given value, while all will reject a gap of less than it. More sophisticated models of gap distribution than that derived from wholly random flow assumptions add to the complexity of the analysis.

8.6.1 Simulation

The techniques of simulation (see Sec. 3.9) have had a special value in the analysis of junction operation. Simulation models can be developed to cover a wide range of variables which can be specified as any relevant distribution. The use of pseudo-random numbers (see Sec. 3.9.2) as input can generate within the computer a simulated flow of vehicles arriving with the probable frequency forecast by the distribution. Using the previous example of a major–minor priority junction, this sequence of gaps can then be examined by arrivals at the junction on the minor road (or roads), simulated by the same method. The manoeuvre required by each arrival can be randomly allocated from the overall pattern of possible manoeuvres, as can the gap acceptable to the vehicle from a distribution of gap acceptance. In this way the behaviour of each vehicle can be modelled and design parameters such as delay and vehicle flow obtained. For a fuller description of the basic techniques the reader should consult standard texts.[12,15]

8.6.2. Traffic Signals

A major design procedure derived from simulation studies is that used for the design of traffic signal settings in Britain. F. V. Webster[16] combined simulation studies with theoretical analysis to determine the most suitable settings for the light change sequence of vehicle actuated traffic signals to give the least overall delay. The controlling times are the overall cycle time (the time for a complete sequence of colours for an individual signal) and the way in which the total available green time is allocated to the different directions of travel. Other important design criteria were also derived, such as delay expected for particular settings. This work has been amplified in a later design publication.[17]

8.6.3 Urban Traffic Control

A development of the individual signal settings was the progressive system which would provide a linked sequence of signals along a major route where priority could be given to the predominant direction of travel. A platoon of traffic travelling at the design speed for the progression would meet a green aspect at the successive signals. As traffic on the cross routes built up, usually nearer the urban centre, this design could lead to increased delay for the opposing traffic so methods were evolved to coordinate signals over an area with the object of minimizing delay to all traffic within the coordinated area. A series of experiments was set up to test different systems of coordinated control. Essential to them all was the computer to determine the sequences of settings for the signals for any given traffic pattern within the area and also to give instructions when necessary to change the settings to respond to changes in traffic. Most major cities in Britain now have their central area signals controlled in this way.

Although it is possible for the computer to receive information on actual traffic flow from detectors in the roads and adjust the required settings accordingly, in practice the increased efficiency has not yet been shown to compensate for the increased cost and complexity of the systems. The preferred approach is to calculate the optimum settings for a number of anticipated traffic patterns calculated from observed flow variations. The standard computer program used is TRANSYT (Traffic Network Study Tool).[18] This creates a model of the way traffic movement within the area is affected by the traffic signal settings, and by using an optimizing approach similar to that for highway optimization (Sec. 8.3.2), incrementally varying the offset between successive signal greens achieves a minimum value of delay and stops, weighted according to the engineer's assessment of the relative importance of these criteria. Successive versions of TRANSYT have incorporated variations of greater flexibility, such as BUS TRANSYT[19] which allows priority to be given to flows which include a significant number of buses by weighting the effects of delay on such vehicles.

8.7 TRANSPORTATION PLANNING AND THE COMPUTER

Transportation planning is concerned with forecasting the demand for travel in a specified area at some future design date and determining the best total transport system, balanced between public and private transport facilities, to provide the required access to all parts of the developed area. This must be achieved while preserving an acceptable environment in those areas through which the major sections of the system pass, and ensuring that the expenditure of funds gives the best value to the community by maximizing those benefits considered most desirable.

The process is carried out in four principal stages (see Fig. 8.4).

8.7.1 Survey and analysis

Data is collected on the travel habits of a sample of people living and working in the designated plan area. This area is divided into sub-areas or zones of a suitable size which serve as the origins and destinations of the trips associated with the development within them. Travel patterns are derived from the matrix of aggregated trips between these zones. The greater part of the travel data is collected at the home end of the trips by home interview surveys. As well as travel information, details are obtained of a number of socio-economic factors considered important in influencing the amount and type of this travel.

Inventories are also made of the road and public transport systems together with the traffic operation on them to build up a complete description of travel facilities in the study area. Traffic counts and origin–destination surveys are carried out at selected locations to serve as a check on the accuracy of the grossing-up of the sample home survey and to collect details of trips passing through the area or entering it from outside.

Developments in planning techniques have sought to reduce the dependance on this expensive and time-consuming survey phase by the use of generalized relationships which can be applied to similar areas when certain parameters have been calibrated with smaller scale surveys. Nevertheless, there is normally a large amount of data to be stored and processed on the computer.

8.7.2 Model formulation

In this phase a set of linked models is developed to describe the sequence of travel decisions which must be examined. Four sub-models are used, the output from one forming the input for the next, and the basic techniques must be calibrated from the collected data so that they relate to the actual patterns determined in the survey stage. Using the zone, for example, as the unit, the model first determines the total number of trips leaving and entering each individual zone (the generation model). The next step is to determine how these trips are spread between the various destination options available (the distribution model). This model links trips with zones but does not describe specific routes taken. This is the purpose of the assignment model which determines how the traffic makes particular route choices. The fourth model which may appear either before or after the distribution stage is the modal split, which concerns the division of trips between the competing private and public modes of travel. The calibration of these models involves a number of mathematical or statistical analysis techniques involving handling large volumes of data so that without the computer the transportation planning process could not be carried out.

A brief description of the individual models will refer to the more common of the techniques used though for a fuller analysis reference can be made to the many texts available.[21,22]

8.7.2.1 Trip generation models

These predict the number of trips entering and leaving each zone. Many variables influence trip making and the aim of the analysis is to identify those variables which have a significant effect on the number of trips. A technique frequently used to determine the numerical relationship between the dependent variable, trips, and the independent influencing variables is that of multiple linear regression. This is an extension of the least-squares approach of simple linear regression (see Sec. 3.6.2) where variation in the dependent variable may be explained by variations in several independent variables such as income, family size, etc. Estimates are made of the parameters of the model (regression coefficients) which give the best fit to the survey data to produce a relationship of the form:

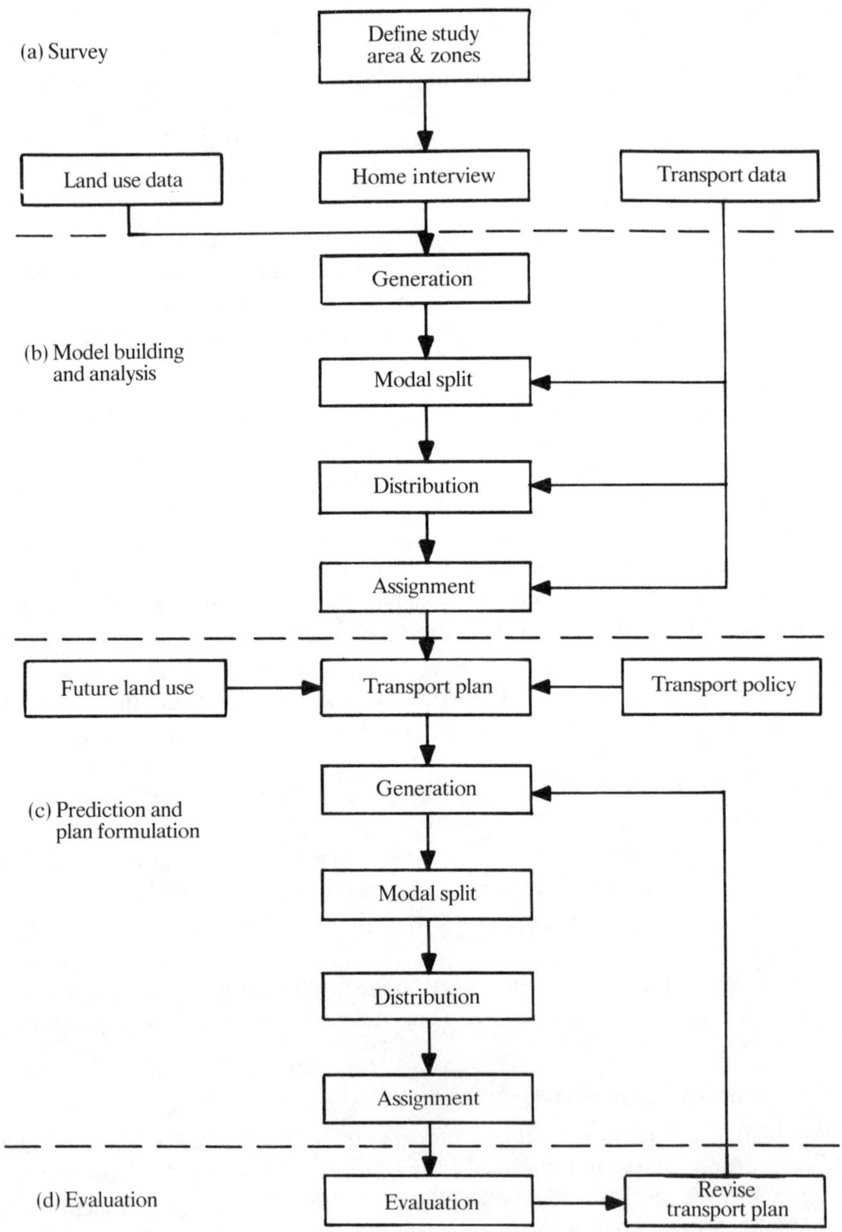

Figure 8.4 Simplified flow diagram of the transportation planning process

$$y = k + b_1x_1 + b_2x_2 \ldots b_\eta x_\eta$$

where y is the dependent variable, $x_1 \ldots x_\eta$ are the independent variables, k is a constant, and b_1 b_η are the regression coefficients. Statistical tests are necessary to determine the significance of each variable, and the overall fit of the model.

Another approach is that of category analysis, which is a technique for estimating the trip production from households which have been sorted into a number of separate groups or categories according to a set of properties that characterize the households. The independent variables (usually car ownership, income, and employment structure) are divided into a number of broad classes to give a number of categories by cross-classification. Each category has a trip rate associated with it, either obtained from home interview techniques or estimated from other studies. The households in a zone are sorted into appropriate categories by the computer from the home interview socio-economic data or by applying standard statistical distributions to estimated zonal means. Multiplication of the numbers in each category by the appropriate trip rate gives the total trips.

8.7.2.2 Distribution models

Distribution models are concerned with establishing the links between a number of zones for which trip generation calculations have previously been made. These links are best described in the form of an $\eta \times \eta$ matrix for η zones where the sums of individual rows are the total number of trips originating from the specific zones and the column totals are the number of trips having the zones as their destination.

The most widely used method of trip distribution is the gravity model, so called because of its basic similarity to the concept of gravitational attraction between two masses, with the number of trips between two zones i and j being directly proportional to the number of trips originating in zone i and the number of trips attracted to zone j and inversely proportional to some function of the distance or travel cost between them. In its simplest form it may be written:

$$T_{i\text{-}j} = k0_iD_j \frac{1}{f(d_{ij})}$$

where T_{i-j} is the number of trips between zones i and j

0_i is the total number of trips produced in zone i

D_j is the total number of trips attracted to zone j

$f(d_{ij})$ is a function of the separation of i and j

The computer is used to calibrate the model by determining the constant of proportionality, and the nature of the travel deterrence function $f(d_{ij})$. An iterative technique is used to adjust successively the values of the parameters until the totals in the rows and columns of the interzonal distribution matrix equal the known values for each zone derived from the generation model. For large urban areas the complex analysis is extremely demanding of computer time.

8.7.2.3 Assignment models

The final trip distribution matrix must now be assigned to the network of routes linking zones. The network must be described for the computer as a sequence of links meeting at nodes together with detailed information on the operational parameters of each link such as capacity, length, existing flow, etc. In the simplest assignment method the minimum path between zones through the network is obtained using methods similar to that described in Sec. 3.8.2 and all traffic from the interzonal matrix is loaded on to this path using an 'all-or-nothing' approach. When this is carried out for all pairs of zones the assignment is complete.

With this technique links may be loaded beyond their capacity so that deterrence to travel along an overloaded link will be increased. This might cause a change of route for the shortest path and more advanced techniques known as 'capacity restraint' will incrementally load proportions of the traffic in turn on to the network. At the end of each loading the link deterrence is recalculated from a speed–volume relationship and the minimum-path 'tree' is again determined with the next increment and a proportion of the previous loading being loaded on the derived minimum routes.

8.7.2.4 Modal split

The most complex section of the planning process is the model describing the division of travel between competing modes, and the types of model vary according to the position of modal split in the overall process. Regression techniques and stochastic analysis have been used as well as simpler models where relative travel cost on time of alternatives is related to observed modal split.

8.7.3 Prediction and plan formulation

Once the models have been derived and calibrated from the present travel pattern they are used to predict future travel. The correlation coefficients derived from a regression analysis generation model are considered to remain constant over the planning period so that forecasts of the relevant values of the independent variables for the plan year will be used in the equation to give the generated trips for each zone. Similar forecasts are required for the category analysis approach.

The distribution will depend on the relative attractions between zones and the deterrence function as described above with O_i, D_j (See Sec. 8.7.2.2) being obtained from the predicted generation. The deterrence function will vary according to the particular plan put forward so that at this stage a further input in the network is to be considered.

The assignment is also a function of the network, while modal split requires input of forecast values of the controlling variables.

8.7.4 Evaluation

A number of transport plans will be analysed by the models, each alternative model mix giving rise to different costs and different benefits, some measurable in financial terms, some not. These alternative systems must then be evaluated in terms of those social, economic, operational, and environmental goals considered desirable.

8.8 CONCLUSION

This chapter has endeavoured to show the student the importance of the computer in a major area of civil engineering – highway and traffic engineering. The range of both these topics is vast so that only representative uses could be described and it has been assumed that the student's knowledge of the subjects is rudimentary. It has therefore been necessary to place the subjects in a more general descriptive context, though the pressures of space have decreed that the description must, of necessity, be brief. There is no section of design, planning, or construction management to which the computer has not made a significant contribution, and in cases such as transportation planning an essential one.

REFERENCES

1. Bannister, A., and S. Raymond, *Surveying*, Pitman, London, 1972.
2. Ashworth, R., *Highway Engineering*, Heinemann, London, 1966.
3. BIPS1, *User Manual,* Highway Engineering Computer Branch, Department of Transport, London, 1969.
4. *GENESYS, HIGHWAYS/1 User Manual*, Genesys Ltd, Loughborough, 1975.
5. *MOSS MANUAL*, Moss Consortium, Northamptonshire County Council, Northampton, 1975.
6. Craine, G. S., J. M. Houlton, and E. Malcolmson, 'MOSS-modelling systems', *Highway Engr*, **24** (4), 26–33, 1977.
7. BIPS3, *User Manual,* Highway Engineering Computer Branch, Department of Transport, London, 1975.
8. Robinson, R., 'A computer method for designing the vertical alignment of a road: Program Venus 1', *TRRL Report LR 457*, Transport and Road Research Laboratory, Crowthorne, Berkshire, 1972.
9. Robinson, R. 'A further computer method for designing the vertical alignment of a road: Program Venus II', *TRRL Report LR458*, Transport and Road Research Laboratory, Crowthorne, Berkshire, 1972.
10. Baker, A. B., 'The design and phasing of horizontal and vertical alignments: Program JANUS', *TRRL Report LR 469*, Transport and Road Research Laboratory, Crowthorne, Berkshire, 1972.
11. Davies, H. E. H., 'Optimizing highway vertical alignments to minimize construction costs: program Minerva', *TRRL Report LR463*, Transport and Road Research Laboratory, Crowthorne, Berkshire, 1972.
12. Wohl, M., and B. V. Martin, *Traffic System Analysis for Engineers and Planners,* McGraw-Hill, New York, 1967.
13. Salter, R. J., *Highway Traffic Analysis and Design*, Macmillan, London, 1976.
14. Tanner, J. C., 'A theoretical analysis of delays at an uncontrolled intersection', *Biometrika*, **49**, 163–170, 1962.
15. Drew, D. R., *Traffic Flow Theory and Control*, McGraw-Hill, New York, 1968.
16. Webster, F. V., 'Traffic signal selling', *Road Research Technical Paper No. 39*, HSMO, London, 1958.
17. Webster, F. V., and B. M. Cobbe, 'Traffic signals', *Road Research Technical Paper No. 56*, HMSO, London, 1966.
18. Robertson, D. I., 'Transyt', *RRL Report LR253*, Road Research Laboratory, Crowthorne, Berkshire, 1969.
19. Pierce, J. R., and K. Wood, '*Bus Transyt – a user guide*', *TRRL Report SR266*, Transport and Road Research Laboratory, Crowthorne, 1977.
20. 'The design of major/minor priority junctions', *Technical Memorandum H11/76*, Department of the Environment, London, 1976.
21. Bruton, M. J., *Introduction to Transportation Planning*, Hutchinson, London, 1970.
22. Hutchinson, B. G., *Principles of Urban Transport System Planning*, McGraw-Hill, New York, 1974.

APPENDIX

AN INTRODUCTION TO BASIC

After FORTRAN, BASIC is probably the most popular language with engineers. As some desk top computers do not yet have a FORTRAN compiler, this appendix gives a brief guide to enable the reader, who has become familiar with FORTRAN, to use such machines.

BASIC is an acronym for Beginner's All Purpose Symbolic Instruction Code and it has been widely available since the middle sixties. The language does not have all the facilities found in FORTRAN since it was developed to enable non-professional users to have access to a computer with the minimum of effort and preparation.

Unlike FORTRAN, BASIC is not defined by a universally recognized standard. The principal features of BASIC are discussed below, but most compilers will provide an extended range of facilities. The reader should refer to a particular computer documentation for details of these and for instructions on how to run programs or manipulate files of data or program listings.

The example given below is of a BASIC program, using Simpson's rule with automatic interval halving, to evaluate probability for the normal or Gaussian distribution:

$$\text{Prob}\,(A < X < B) = S$$

$$= \int_A^B \frac{1}{\sqrt{2\pi}\,X2} \exp\left\{-0.5 * \left(\frac{X - X1}{X2}\right)^2\right\} \, dX$$

where $X1$ is the mean value of X and $X2$ is the standard deviation of X.

```
10 REM SIMPSON'S RULE EVALUATION OF NORMAL PROBABILITY
15 READ T1, L1, X1, X2
20 PRINT "NORMAL DISTRIBUTION MEAN"; X1; "STD DEV"; X2
25 PRINT "TOLERANCE"; T1; "MAX NO OF STRIPS"; L1
30 PRINT "GIVE LOWER AND UPPER LIMITS"
35 INPUT A, B
40 IF B > A THEN 50
45 STOP
50 LET I2 = 2
55 LET H = (B - A)/2
60 LET X = A
65 GOSUB 300
70 LET S0 = F
75 LET X = B
80 GOSUB 300
```

```
85  LET SØ = SØ + F
9Ø  LET S2 = Ø.Ø
95  LET X = A + H
1ØØ GOSUB 3ØØ
1Ø5 LET S4 = F
11Ø LET S = (SØ + 4.Ø*S4)*H/3.Ø
115 LET I2 = I2*2
12Ø LET H = H/2
125 REM S1 IS PREVIOUS ESTIMATE OF INTEGRAL
13Ø LET S1 = S
135 LET S2 = S2 + S4
14Ø LET S4 = Ø.Ø
145 FOR J = 1 TO I2 STEP 2
15Ø LET X = A + H*J
155 GOSUB 3ØØ
16Ø LET S4 = S4 + F
165 NEXT J
17Ø LET S = (SØ + 2.Ø*S2 + 4.Ø*S4)*H/3.Ø
175 REM CONVERGENCE CHECK
18Ø IF ABS(S – S1) < T1*ABS(S) THEN 21Ø
185 REM CHECK LIMIT ON NO OF STRIPS
19Ø IF I2 < L1 THEN 115
195 PRINT "ERROR – NOT CONVERGED IN"; L1; "STRIPS"
2ØØ PRINT "PREVIOUS ESTIMATE"; S1; "CURRENT ESTIMATE"; S
2Ø5 STOP
21Ø PRINT "PROBABILITY (A < X < B)"; S
22Ø GOTO 3Ø
225 REM SUBROUTINE TO EVALUATE F FROM X
3ØØ LET Y = (X – X1)/X2
3Ø5 LET F = 3.989423E-1*EXP(–Ø.5*Y↑2)/X2
31Ø RETURN
4ØØ DATA 1.ØE-3, 2ØØ, 1.Ø, 1.5
999 END
```

The program is based on the FORTRAN SUBROUTINE SIMP2, which is described in Sec. 3.3. The following discussion covers the features of BASIC by reference to the sample program.

PROGRAM STATEMENTS

Every statement in BASIC must be preceded by a line number (label), which can be any integer between 1 and 9999. The line numbers determine the order in which the statements are executed. In the writing of a program, line numbers should be incremented in steps of 5 or 1Ø to enable additional statements to be added, in the appropriate position, during development. Errors in any particular statement can be removed by typing the correct version of the statement and this is automatically inserted and executed in running the program. A statement may be deleted by typing the line number, leaving the rest of the line blank.

NUMBERS

Numbers may be written in any of three forms (e.g. 987, 987.Ø, or 9.87E+2). No distinction is made between integer and real or floating-point numbers. BASIC does not possess a form of manipulation corresponding to INTEGER arithmetic in FORTRAN.

VARIABLES

BASIC does not differentiate between INTEGER and REAL variables. Scalar variable names may be a single letter from A to Z or one letter followed by a single digit between Ø and 9, e.g. H, I2, S4. One- or two-dimensional array elements are represented as single-letter subscripted variables, e.g. $A(13)$, $B(K)$, or $C(K, G)$. In this case the subscripts are treated as integers and any decimal part is truncated. All arrays should be 'dimensioned' by use of a DIM statement, e.g.,

```
1Ø DIM A(2Ø,25), B(2ØØ)
```

GENERAL STATEMENTS

Remark (comment) statements are labelled and begin with REM. They are not executed when the program is run.

The highest numbered line in any BASIC program should be an END statement and only one END should be used. However, several STOP statements may appear and their effect is to stop execution of the program and return control to the system.

ASSIGNMENT STATEMENTS

Variables are assigned values by LET statements, e.g.

```
5Ø    LET I2  = 2
11Ø   LET S   = (SØ + 4.Ø*S4)*H/3.Ø
```

Some forms of BASIC permit multiple assignments, e.g.

```
3ØØØ    LET X = Y = A + B
```

ARITHMETIC EXPRESSIONS

The same priority rules for the order in which the operations + − / * ↑ are executed apply in BASIC as were established in FORTRAN and brackets may be necessary to ensure the correct evaluation of an expression.

INPUT AND OUTPUT STATEMENTS

READ, DATA, and INPUT statements are used to feed data to a program. READ statements give a list of variables to which numerical values are to be assigned and the corresponding DATA lines give the numerical values; see lines 15 and 4ØØ in the example. Commas separate the elements in the READ and DATA lists. The first element in the first READ statement to be executed is associated with the first element in the lowest numbered DATA line, and so on. DATA lines should follow the READ statements which are to access them, but they do not have to be adjacent. New data values may be introduced by retyping the DATA lines, including their line numbers, at the end of the program listing.

In interactive mode, the statement INPUT followed by a list of variables causes execution to pause until the appropriate number of numerical values are typed on the keyboard; see line 35 in the example.

Output is achieved with PRINT statements. The list following PRINT may be formed from numerical values, variable identifiers, expressions or alphanumeric strings, e.g.,

```
15ØØ      PRINT "ANS", A1, Ø.Ø5, 2*A + B
```

Use of commas as separators between the elements in a PRINT list causes the printed line to be divided into zones, usually 1Ø or 15 spaces wide; with each element printed in a separate zone. Use of semicolon separators causes the list to be packed more densely; see lines 2Ø, 25, etc. in the example. In the case of semicolon separators, the spaces assigned to each element of the list depends on the particular BASIC compiler in use.

BRANCHING STATEMENTS

Program execution may be transferred using unconditional or conditional branching statements. For example an unconditional branching statement is in the form

line number GOTO line number

where the second line number refers to the next statement to be executed; see line 22Ø in the example. A conditional branching statement is the form

line number IF [Variable or expression] [Relational operator] [Numerical value, or expression] THEN line number

The symbols for the relational operators are different from those of FORTRAN:

BASIC	=	<	>	<>	<=	>=
FORTRAN	.EQ.	.LT.	.GT.	.NE.	.LE.	.GE.

See lines 18Ø and 19Ø in the example.

LOOP STATEMENTS

Repeated calculations may be performed in BASIC by using FOR and NEXT statements. The FOR statement is in the form

line number FOR [variable] = [Numerical value, variable, or expression] TO [Numerical value, variable expression] STEP [Numerical value, variable or expression]

Each FOR statement must be contained on one line. The STEP modifier is optional. If it is omitted then a step length of 1 is assumed. In the sample program, line 145 is an example of a FOR statement. Other FOR statement constructions take the forms

```
1ØØØ      FOR I  = N TO 1ØØ
15ØØ      FOR A  = X+Y TO A/B STEP X1
```

A NEXT statement dictates the scope of the loop and has the form

line number   NEXT   [variable]

where the variable is the same as that given on the left of the equality sign in the FOR statement; see line 165 in the example.

Loops may be nested, just as in FORTRAN, and it is permissible to jump out of a loop but it is not permissible to jump into a loop. BASIC provides greater flexibility than FORTRAN in relation to loops, e.g. real numbers and expressions may be used as elements of BASIC FOR statements.

SUB-PROGRAMS

Sub-program facilities in BASIC are available through the use of GOSUB and RETURN statements. A statement in the form

line number   GOSUB   line number

transfers execution to the second line number given and computation proceeds from that point until a statement in the form

line number   RETURN

is encountered. Execution then returns to the statement immediately following the GOSUB which initiated the call; see lines 65 and 310 in the example. BASIC is less flexible than FORTRAN in regard to sub-program facilities. Arguments may not be passed across with changes in names, as can be done in FORTRAN. For example, it is not possible to develop the BASIC coding to solve the matrix equation $AX = Y$ and then to call it directly for the solution of $CR = S$.

FUNCTIONS

BASIC provides a limited set of standard functions, e.g.

```
1ØØØ      LET Y = SIN(X)
15ØØ      LET Z = SQR(X)
```

It is also possible to include user-defined functions provided that the coding, necessary for the calculation of the value of the function, can be accommodated on one statement line. This is done using a DEF statement, e.g.,

```
2ØØØ      DEF FNK(X) = A↑2 + B↑2 − 2*A*B*COS(X)
```

The parameters of FNK, i.e. *A*, *B*, and *X*, must be known before FNK is used. The name of the function must be in the form FN followed by any single letter from A to Z. Statement 2ØØØ could be used with statement 35ØØ below to print the values of the square of the sides of triangles with opposite angle X and other sides A and B, e.g.

```
35ØØ     PRINT FNK(Ø.25), FNK(Ø.5), FNK(Ø.75)
```

EXTENDED BASIC

Other than those statement types discussed earlier, most systems offer extensions to BASIC such as computed GOTO, advanced manipulation of alphanumeric strings, and the use of special commands for matrix operations.

CLOSURE

From the above brief description, it will be apparent that the techniques of computer programming are similar in both FORTRAN and BASIC. When a user has a choice, BASIC, because of its easy data transfer facilities etc., is preferable for short one-off jobs. FORTRAN, on the other hand, with its greater flexibility for data transfers within a program, use of arguments lists and COMMON blocks for example, is to be preferred for major programming exercises.

INDEX